T0327598

RESEARCH IN MARITIME HISTORY
NO. 50

THE BATTLE FOR THE MIGRANTS: THE INTRODUCTION OF STEAMSHIPPING ON THE NORTH ATLANTIC AND ITS IMPACT ON THE EUROPEAN EXODUS

Torsten Feys

International Maritime Economic History Association

St. John's, Newfoundland
2013

ISSN 1188-3928
ISBN 978-1-927869-00-0

Research in Maritime History is available free of charge to members of the International Maritime Economic History Association. The price to others is US $25 per copy, plus US $5 postage and handling.

Back issues of *Research in Maritime History* are available:

No. 1 (1991) David M. Williams and Andrew P. White (comps.), *A Select Bibliography of British and Irish University Theses about Maritime History, 1792-1990*

No. 2 (1992) Lewis R. Fischer (ed.), *From Wheel House to Counting House: Essays in Maritime Business History in Honour of Professor Peter Neville Davies*

No. 3 (1992) Lewis R. Fischer and Walter Minchinton (eds.), *People of the Northern Seas*

No. 4 (1993) Simon Ville (ed.), *Shipbuilding in the United Kingdom in the Nineteenth Century: A Regional Approach*

No. 5 (1993) Peter N. Davies (ed.), *The Diary of John Holt*

No. 6 (1994) Simon P. Ville and David M. Williams (eds.), *Management, Finance and Industrial Relations in Maritime Industries: Essays in International Maritime and Business History*

No. 7 (1994) Lewis R. Fischer (ed.), *The Market for Seamen in the Age of Sail*

No. 8 (1995) Gordon Read and Michael Stammers (comps.), *Guide to the Records of Merseyside Maritime Museum, Volume 1*

No. 9 (1995) Frank Broeze (ed.), *Maritime History at the Crossroads: A Critical Review of Recent Historiography*

No. 10 (1996) Nancy Redmayne Ross (ed.), *The Diary of a Maritimer, 1816-1901: The Life and Times of Joseph Salter*

No. 11 (1997) Faye Margaret Kert, *Prize and Prejudice: Privateering and Naval Prize in Atlantic Canada in the War of 1812*

No. 12 (1997) Malcolm Tull, *A Community Enterprise: The History of the Port of Fremantle, 1897 to 1997*

No. 13 (1997) Paul C. van Royen, Jaap R. Bruijn and Jan Lucassen (eds.), *"Those Emblems of Hell"? European Sailors and the Maritime Labour Market, 1570-1870*

No. 14 (1998) David J. Starkey and Gelina Harlaftis (eds.), *Global Markets: The Internationalization of The Sea Transport Industries Since 1850*

No. 15 (1998) Olaf Uwe Janzen (ed.), *Merchant Organization and Maritime Trade in the North Atlantic, 1660-1815*

No. 16 (1999) Lewis R. Fischer and Adrian Jarvis (eds.), *Harbours and Havens: Essays in Port History in Honour of Gordon Jackson*

No. 17 (1999) Dawn Littler, *Guide to the Records of Merseyside Maritime Museum, Volume 2*

No. 18 (2000) Lars U. Scholl (comp.), *Merchants and Mariners: Selected Maritime Writings of David M. Williams*

No. 19 (2000) Peter N. Davies, *The Trade Makers: Elder Dempster in West Africa, 1852-1972, 1973-1989*

No. 20 (2001) Anthony B. Dickinson and Chesley W. Sanger, *Norwegian Whaling in Newfoundland: The Aquaforte Station and the Ellefsen Family, 1902-1908*

No. 21 (2001) Poul Holm, Tim D. Smith and David J. Starkey (eds.), *The Exploited Seas: New Directions for Marine Environmental History*

No. 22 (2002) Gordon Boyce and Richard Gorski (eds.), *Resources and Infrastructures in the Maritime Economy, 1500-2000*

No. 23 (2002) Frank Broeze, *The Globalisation of the Oceans: Containerisation from the 1950s to the Present*

No. 24 (2003) Robin Craig, *British Tramp Shipping, 1750-1914*

No. 25 (2003) James Reveley, *Registering Interest: Waterfront Labour Relations in New Zealand, 1953 to 2000*

No. 26 (2003) Adrian Jarvis, *In Troubled Times: The Port of Liverpool, 1905-1938*

No. 27 (2004) Lars U. Scholl and Merja-Liisa Hinkkanen (comps.), *Sail and Steam: Selected Maritime Writings of Yrjö Kaukiainen*

No. 28 (2004) Gelina Harlaftis and Carmel Vassallo (eds.), *New Directions in Mediterranean Maritime History*

No. 29 (2005) Gordon Jackson, *The British Whaling Trade*

No. 30 (2005) Lewis Johnman and Hugh Murphy, *Scott Lithgow: Déjà vu All Over Again! The Rise and Fall of a Shipbuilding Company*

No. 31 (2006) David Gleicher, *The Rescue of the Third Class on the Titanic: A Revisionist History*

No. 32 (2006) Stig Tenold, *Tankers in Trouble: Norwegian Shipping and the Crisis of the 1970s and 1980s*

No. 33 (2007) Torsten Feys, Lewis R. Fischer, Stéphane Hoste and Stephan Vanfraechem (eds.), *Maritime Transport and Migration: The Connections between Maritime and Migration Networks*

No. 34 (2007) A.B. Dickinson, *Seal Fisheries of the Falkland Islands and Dependencies: An Historical Review*

No. 35 (2007) Tapio Bergholm, Lewis R. Fischer and M. Elisabetta Tonizzi (eds.), *Making Global and Local Connections: Historical Perspectives on Ports*

No. 36 (2008) Mark C. Hunter, *Policing the Seas: Anglo-American Relations and the Equatorial Atlantic, 1819-1865*

No. 37 (2008) Lewis R. Fischer and Even Lange (eds.), *International Merchant Shipping in the Nineteenth and Twentieth Centuries: The Comparative Dimension*

No. 38 (2008) Adrian Jarvis and Robert Lee (eds.), *Trade, Migration and Urban Networks in Port Cities, c.1640-1940*

No. 39 (2009) Henry T. Chen, *Taiwanese Distant-Water Fisheries in Southeast Asia, 1936-1977*

No. 40 (2009) John Armstrong, *The Vital Spark: The British Coastal Trade, 1700-1930*

No. 41 (2009) Carina E. Ray and Jeremy Rich (eds.), *Navigating African Maritime History*

No. 42 (2010) S.G. Sturmey, *British Shipping and World Competition*

No. 43 (2010) Maria Fusaro and Amélia Polónia (eds.), *Maritime History as Global History*

No. 44 (2010) Silvia Marzagalli, James R. Sofka and John J. McCusker (eds.), *Rough Waters: American Involvement with the Mediterranean in the Eighteenth and Nineteenth Centures*

No. 45 (2011) Jaap R. Bruijn, *The Dutch Navy of the Seventeenth and Eighteenth Centuries*

No. 46 (2011) Lewis R. Fischer and Even Lange (eds.), *New Directions in Norwegian Maritime History*

No. 47 (2011) John Armstrong and David M. Williams, *The Impact of Technological Change: The Early Steamship in Britain*

No. 48 (2012) Ralph Davis, *The Rise of the English Shipping Industry in the Seventeenth and Eighteenth Centuries*

No. 49 (2012) Gordon Boyce, *The Growth and Dissolution of a Large-Scale Business Enterprise: The Furness Interest 1892-1919*

Research in Maritime History would like to thank Memorial University of Newfoundland for its generous financial assistance in support of this volume.

Table of Contents

About the Author

TORSTEN FEYS <Torsten.Feys@UGent.be> obtained his PhD in history at the European University Institute (Florence). He is currently working as a postdoctoral researcher in the Research Foundation Flanders (FWO) at the Department of History of Ghent University on a project titled "The Global Rise of Modern Borders and Irregular Maritime Migration Networks (1875-1930): A Comparative Research Project on Atlantic and Pacific Migration Systems." His research centres on the commercialization of migrant transport, illegal migration, and maritime and migration polices and their implementation at state borders. Besides publications in scholarly journals and books, the results of the research have been translated to a broader public through a long-standing collaboration with the Red Star Line Museum in Antwerp, resulting in contributions to museum presentations, television documentaries and popular books. This interest in popularizing history also resulted in a book and digital exhibition on the history of the Flemish institution charged with managing soil and waste management (OVAM) under the auspices of the Public History Institute at Ghent University.

Acknowledgements

Growing up my career aspirations shifted quite often. As it became clear that my childhood dream of becoming a professional football player would not materialize, I started to contemplate a variety of alternatives. One that never really crossed my mind, however, was to become an academic. That I eventually wrote a doctoral dissertation is something I owe in the first place to Prof. dr. Eric Vanhaute who supervised my MA thesis at Ghent University and motivated me to apply for a number of grants. This book is a revision of my PhD thesis written under the supervision of Prof. dr. Heinz-Gerhard Haupt at the European University Institute (EUI) in Florence and submitted in 2008.

I rewrote the thesis for publication in 2009 after doing freelance work at the Red Star Line Museum in Antwerp, where I provide information on some additional American archival sources. The reworked version is based on the valuable recommendations of the members of my thesis examination committee comprising Lewis R. Fischer, Bartolomé Yun-Casalilla and Eric Vanhaute. I am grateful also to Michael Miller, Donna Gabaccia, Patrick Weil and Frank Caestecker for taking time to read parts or the dissertation and sharing insights and recommendations for this book.

While preparing the book for publication, two of my close colleagues, Dr. Drew Keeling and Dr. Per-Kristian Sebak, have either published a reworked version of their dissertation (Keeling) or successfully defended a PhD thesis (Sebak). Although I was unable to integrate these materials into this book, it was inspiring to exchange ideas and to share insights over the past few years. In the end, our works complement each other to a great extent and are all parts of a process to re-evaluate and highlight the importance of transatlantic passenger transport companies in business, maritime and migration history.

Researching and writing *The Battle for the Migrants* has brought me into contact with a plethora of people and organizations. It is impossible to adequately acknowledge all of them, and I apologize to anyone I may unintentionally omit. I have been very positively surprised by the readiness of scholars to assist and advise a young researcher. Listing all the colleagues who helped me by name would require an additional (and lengthy) appendix. For this reason, I trust that this nameless wink reaches all of you that have given of your time and expertise. More specifically, though, I want to express my gratitude to the staff, professors and researchers at the EUI for making the Institute a stimulating place for research. In particular, the staff of the library and the Department of History and Civilization greatly facilitated the literature and archival research. I am grateful to Giovanni Federico and Bartolomé Yun-Casalilla for their insights and guidance in structuring the work. I owe a special debt to Heinz-Gerhard Haupt, for his guidance in exploring this broad topic and his continuous encouragement in all the ventures that contributed to writing the doctoral dissertation and the subsequent book.

The research would not have been possible without the valuable help of the staff of the following archives, libraries and research institutions; General State Archives, Brussels; Archives of the Belgian Ministry of Foreign Affaires, Brussels; Albertina Library, Brussels; Center for American Studies, Brussels; Provincial State Archives, Antwerp; Centre d'Archives du Monde du Travail, Roubaix; French Line Archives, Le Havre; French Diplomatic Archives, Nantes; Hamburg; Bremen State Archives; Cunard Line Archives, Liverpool; Dutch National Archives, The Hague; US National Archives, Washington, DC; and the YIVO and Ellis Island archives in New York. In particular, I want to acknowledge the staff of the Rotterdam Community Archives for their and helpfulness. If it were not for their long opening hours, liberal policies on using digital cameras and promptness in retrieving innumerable files this research would have taken much longer. I also want to acknowledge the Roosevelt Study Center for awarding me a research grant, as well as for their hospitality during my stay in Middelburg. I want to thank Hans Krabbendam for getting the research under way. Finally, a special thanks to all the people of the Red Star Line Museum, particularly Mandy Nauwelaerts, for providing a forum to translate some of this research into museum exhibits. It was an inspirational and enriching experience.

I also have to extend my gratitude to the International Maritime Economic History Association and its members for its important role in developing this work. I will remain deeply indebted to Lewis R. Fischer for his support with grant applications, in getting some of my first publications out, his priceless suggestions and ideas over the years, and not least for the meticulous editing of this volume. I also need to acknowledge the editing work of Miriam Nyhan and Vaughan Curd on earlier works and drafts. I am grateful to Robert Swierenga, Annick Foucrier and Jochen Oltmer for acting as referees. This brings me back to where it all began – the History Department at Ghent University. I want to thank the Department for providing working space during and after the completion of the PhD, but more importantly for the comradeship and support of its members, in particular Stephane Hoste, Frank Caestecker and Stephan Vanfraechem.

I was extremely fortunate that in all the places where I conducted research or wrote various parts of this work, whether in Belgium, Italy, Spain or the United States, I was able to rely on good friends to make sure that I did not get absorbed solely in this project. I cannot name you all here, but I thank you for the good times and look forward to many more in the future. The greatest and most important influence which sustained me through this process has been my family. Thanks a million Yvan and Marie-Henriette, Yvonne and Valère, Marc and Françoise, Niels, Bjorn and Nele for your unconditional support in all the endeavours into which I have launched myself.

Figures and Tables

FIGURES

TABLES

Introduction

Why do we need another study on European mass migration to the United States during the long nineteenth century at a time when many historians are encouraging a shift away from an Atlantic and modern focus that has long dominated the sub-discipline?[1] The answer is that we need such a study because one recurring question remains unanswered: how did the migrant trade evolve with the introduction of steamships and influence the relocation of approximately thirty-five million people across the North Atlantic during the long nineteenth century? More than half a century ago, Maldwyn Jones, Frank Thistlewaite and Rolf Engelsing drew attention to the fact that transatlantic migration was determined by trade routes.[2] On the North Atlantic, migrants became a very valuable cargo because previously ships sailing from Europe to the United States had travelled westbound in ballast. Rolf Engelsing documented how the maritime business community responded to this opportunity by erecting inland networks, directing a continuous flow of human cargo to the port of Bremen during the sailing ship era.[3] Marianne Wokeck later stressed the Atlantic dimensions of these networks by dating the origins of non-colonial mass migrations to the eighteenth century.[4] Yet a comprehensive analysis of the further development of the trade during the steamship era is still lacking. This explains why migration historians, such as Dudley Baines, or maritime historians, as Michael Miller, have observed that: "we know very little about the activities of shipping companies and shipping agents" and that "oddly

---

[1]Jan Lucassen and Leo Lucassen (eds.), *Migration, Migration; History, History: Old Paradigms and New Perspectives* (Bern, 1997; 3rd rev. ed., Bern, 2005), 28-30; and Dirk Hoerder, *Cultures in Contact: World Migrations in the Second Millennium* (Durham, NC, 2002), 10-18.

[2]Maldwyn Allen Jones, *American Immigration* (Chicago, 1960; 2nd ed., Chicago, 1992); Frank Thistlewaite, "Migration from Europe Overseas in the Nineteenth and Twentieth Century," in XI International Congress of Historical Sciences, *Rapport V: Histoire contemporaine* (Stockholm, 1960), 32-61; reprinted in Rudolph J. Vecoli and Suzanne M. Sinke (eds.), *A Century of European Migrations, 1830-1930* (Urbana, IL, 1991), 17-49; and Rolf Engelsing, *Bremen als Auswandererhafen, 1683-1880* (Bremen, 1961).

[3]Engelsing, *Bremen*.

[4]Marianne S. Wokeck, *Trade in Strangers: The Beginnings of Mass Migration to North America* (University Park, PA, 1998; reprint, University Park, PA, 2003).

enough, migration historians and maritime historians have often written about transoceanic crossings like two ships passing in the night."[5] As Miller has pointed out, maritime historians have also failed to pick up on the early observations of Robert Albion and Engelsing regarding the influence of human cargoes on port activities.[6] Despite the pioneering role of the North Atlantic passenger business in introducing both technological and organizational innovations to the shipping industry, few maritime historians have broached the topic. Indeed, even the exceptions to this generalization, including Robin Bastin, Francis Hyde and Birgit Ottmüller-Wetzel, have limited their analysis to a single port or company.[7]

Frank Broeze argued that the restricted scope of most maritime studies have failed to address the overall dynamics of port competition which propagated the expansion of international maritime networks. He encouraged scholars to adopt transnational, comparative, multi-disciplinary and multi-thematic approaches.[8] This study aims to answer this call by integrating the work of migration historians with that of maritime historians, neither of whom have found a common ground despite the interrelationship between maritime and migration networks that converged in ports. The analysis is centred on the evolution of Rotterdam as a transatlantic migration gateway within the Hamburg-Le Havre range in competition with British ports. The Holland-America Line (HAL), played a crucial role in this as a member of various shipping conferences regulating the North Atlantic passenger trade. The competition greatly influenced the delimitation of both hinterland and foreland that these ports connected and from where they tapped the pool of migrants. In order to emphasize the Atlantic dimension of these networks, this study focuses on the foreland –

[5]Dudley Baines, *Emigration from Europe, 1815-1930* (Cambridge, 1991), 48; and Michael B. Miller, "Conclusion," in Torsten Feys, *et al.* (eds.), *Maritime Transport and Migration: The Connections between Maritime and Migration Networks* (St. John's, 2007), 175.

[6]Robert Greenhalgh Albion, *The Rise of New York Port, 1815-1860* (New York, 1939; reprint, Boston, 1984); and Engelsing, *Bremen*.

[7]Robin Bastin, "Cunard and the Liverpool Emigrant Traffic, 1860-1900" (Unpublished MA thesis, University of Liverpool, 1971); Francis E. Hyde, *Cunard and the North Atlantic, 1840-1973: A History of Shipping and Financial Management* (London, 1975); and Birgit Ottmüller-Wetzel, "Auswanderung über Hamburg: Die HAPAG und die Auswanderung nach Nordamerika, 1870-1914" (Unpublished MA thesis, Freie Universität Berlin, 1986).

[8]Frank Broeze (ed.), *Maritime History at the Crossroads: A Critical Review of Recent Historiography* (St. John's, 1995); and Broeze, "At Sea and Ashore: A Review of the Historiography of Modern Shipping since the 1970s," *NEHA Bulletin*, XII, No. 1 (1998), 3-37.

the American market for prepaid and return tickets – and on how it helped shape the expansion of the hinterland in southern and eastern Europe.

This focus is also influenced by the sources used. Alfred Chandler encouraged the treatment of business history as institutional history by promoting the use of non-quantifiable sources such as letters, periodicals, memoranda and general accounts which often provide data for analyzing economic change in greater depth than the mere compilation and manipulation of numbers. Chandler supported John Higham's endorsement of a history that is less concerned with motives than with structure and process, leading to "a better understanding of how groups and agencies such as political parties, corporations and communities have moulded behaviour and regulated distribution of power."[9] By using qualitative rather than quantitative evidence, this study will try to improve our understanding of how people moved – rather than why they moved – by reconstructing the "visible hand" of steamship companies in the transatlantic migration process.

Diplomatic correspondence from countries with an economic interest in transatlantic migrant transport is used to analyze the attempts of ports to lure migrants and to open steamship connections with US ports in the period 1830-1870. Consuls constituted an important source of information about trade opportunities and established contacts with local authorities and businesses to promote trade relations with domestic shipping enterprises. Especially in developing markets, consuls played a vital "pre-conditioning" role in locales far from home.[10] Research into the correspondence of representatives in New York and Washington about the opening of migrant routes in the French Diplomatic Archives in Nantes, the Dutch National Archives in The Hague, the Belgian Ministry of Foreign Affairs in Brussels and the State Archives in Hamburg and Bremen produced mixed results. Practical problems, such as whether the correspondence has been preserved or whether permission to use a digital camera was granted, influenced the findings. So did the interests of the government on the issue and the quality of information sent by the consul. The

---

[9]Alfred D. Chandler, Jr., "Business History as Institutional History," in George Rogers Taylor and Lucius F. Ellsworth (eds.), *Approaches to American Economic History* (Charlottesville, VA, 1971), reprinted in Thomas K. McGraw (ed.), *The Essential Alfred Chandler: Essays Towards A Historical Theory of Big Business* (Boston, 1988), 301-302.

[10]Leos Müller, "Swedish-American Trade and the Swedish Consular Service, 1780-1840," *International Journal of Maritime History*, XIV, No. 1 (2002), 173-188; and Müller and Jari Ojala, "Consular Services of the Nordic Countries during the Eighteenth and Nineteenth Century: Did They Really Work?" in Gordon Boyce and Richard Gorski (eds.), *Resources and Infrastructures in the Maritime Economy, 1500-2000* (St. John's, 2002), 23-41.

Belgian archives, for example, revealed the most information on views from local and national authorities on the migrant trade.

The search for archives of shipping companies operating from ports within the Hamburg-Le Havre range in the pre-World War I period also produced mixed results. Documents of the Compagnie Générale Transatlantique can be found at the Centre d'Archives du Monde du Travail in Roubaix and the French Line Archives in Le Havre. Both contain mainly official reports on various meetings with shareholders, boards of administration and boards of directors, revealing little about the organization of the traffic. The fate of the archives of the Antwerp-based Red Star Line remains a mystery, but it seems unlikely that they have been preserved. The North German Lloyd (NDL) archives were destroyed, and access to the Hamburg-America Line (HAPAG) archives was denied. Based on the inventory and research of other scholars, the majority of the documents held, especially the annual reports which were available to the public, would have revealed little inside information on the organization of the traffic.

Conversely, the HAL collection at the Community Archives of Rotterdam stands out for its accessibility and for the wealth of materials preserved. For the first decade of HAL's operations, the information is scarce, but from the mid-1880s the complete letter books of directors and agents on all sorts of operating issues can be found. Furthermore, the collection contains agreements, minutes of meetings and correspondence among members of shipping conferences in the North Atlantic migrant trade in which all companies within the Hamburg-Le Havre range participated. This research is based predominantly on letters from the New York head-agent to the directors. As all North Atlantic passenger lines had their most important foreign offices in New York, the correspondence not only reveals inside information on the company's operations but also on its competitors. It is divided into two series, one labelled as general correspondence which dates from 1884, and the other as passage correspondence, running from 1889 onwards. The general correspondence is comprised of daily or weekly reports on the pressing issues of HAL's operations ranging from freight to passengers, infrastructure, fleet, personnel and the like. The even more regular passage correspondence deals exclusively with all aspects of first-, second- and third-class passenger transport. Both sets of records also include attachments, such as newspaper articles, pamphlets or even replies and coded telegrams of directors or letters of third parties. In the last category, reports on congressional activities relevant to migration and maritime issues by the shipping lobbyist Claude Bennett provide extra information on the industry's lobbying strategies in Washington and beyond. To complement the information in the letters, various other files were consulted for information pertaining to earlier years.

Moreover, the various conference agreements and minutes of the meetings were analyzed, in particular those of the New York Continental Conference that regulated the migrant-agent network and set the ocean passage rates for lines operating within the Hamburg-Le Havre range. A brief comparison with the Cunard Line Archives in Liverpool, also used for this research, underlines the value and completeness of the HAL archives. Some electronic resources facilitated access to valuable contemporary documents. The Harvard University Online Open Collections Program provided easy access to government documents and correspondence of the Immigration Restriction League. The e-library program of Stanford University gave access to all the volumes of the Dillingham Commission. The *New York Times* Online Archive represents a unique tool to reconstruct contemporary debates. Finally, research in the National Archives in Washington produced additional information on American immigration policies.

The initial intention of the research was to compare two ports and companies. But the disproportionate amount of archival material and the way the migration business was organized imposed the more appropriate "transnational entangled histories" approach. As Jürgen Kocka and David Thelen pointed out, entanglements are inherent in studies of migration and transnational commerce, and people studying both topics pioneered the development of this methodology. This study confirms the far-reaching mutual interaction which pertained in the migrant trade. The major advantage of this method is that a multi-dimensional and dynamic approach allows for a binding of the micro- and macro-levels of analysis, the need for which has been emphasized by both maritime and migration historians.[11]

Over the last fifty years the analytic models of transatlantic migration movements have both expanded and contracted. The studies focusing on the impact of the movement on the donor country at one end, and on the receiving country at the other, led to the "push-pull" model that attempted to establish the point on the continuum that determined the flows. Subsequent researchers suggested amplifying the scope from the national to the international level, focusing on the interactions between both ends of the trajectory and the formation of an "Atlantic World" in which both parts converged. Globalization studies and the neglect of other long-distance migration movements moved scholars to broaden the scope to "world-systems." In the meantime, other models developed which criticized the broad top-down perspectives for failing to consider the individual migrant and the non-quantifiable social, cultural and politi-

[11]Heinz-Gerhard Haupt and Jürgen Kocka, "Comparative History: Methods, Aims, Problems," in Deborah Cohen and Maura O'Connor (eds.), *Comparison and History: Europe in Cross-National Perspective* (New York, 2004), 33; Kocka, "Comparison and Beyond," *History and Theory*, XLII, No. 1 (2003), 42-43; David Thelen, "Transnational History Perspectives on the United States," *Journal of American History*, LXXXVI, No. 3 (1999), 970-973; and Michael Werner and Bénédicte Zimmerman, "Penser l'histoire croisée: entre empire et réflexivité," *Annales: Histoire, Sciences Sociales*, LVIII, No. 1 (2003), 11-16.

cal aspects of the movement. Many of the migrants made their decision to leave within the context of the family economy and relied on personal networks to make the move. These bottom-up studies allowed for the reconstruction of chain-migration patterns based on "interpersonal ties connecting migrants to former migrants, and non-migrants in origin and destination areas through ties of kinship, friendship and shared community of origin." These constitute a form of social capital which stimulated the movement by reducing the costs, fears and risks of migration. Around these migration networks institutions, organizations and entrepreneurs with particular interests tried to profit from and influence the moves.[12] The discipline's biggest challenge remains in developing a system-based approach, connecting micro- and macro-levels of analysis.[13] To bridge the gap, Dirk Hoerder and Alejandro Portes advocated social and human capital approaches on a meso-level of "mediating networks and interacting segments, including mental maps of the world systems, offering a more comprehensive perspective on [the] migration process."[14]

David Gerber later suggested a higher level of analysis by linking the meso with the macro level, taking up Nina Glick Schiller's concept of "transnational social fields" that connected the individual networks that do the planning and make the resources available to the institutions, businesses and agencies, in the process facilitating the movement and encompassing the influence

---

[12]Douglas Massey, "Why Does Immigration Occur? A Theoretical Synthesis," in Charles Hirschman, Philip Kasinitz and Josh DeWind (eds.), *The Handbook of International Migration: The American Experience* (Chicago, 1999), 43-47.

[13]Monica Boyd, "Family and Personal Networks in International Migration: Recent Developments and New Agendas," *International Migration Review*, XXIII, No. 3 (1989), 641; James T. Fawcett and Fred Arnold, "Explaining Diversity: Asian and Pacific Immigration Systems," in Fawcett and Benjamin V. Cariño (eds.), *Pacific Bridges: The New Immigration from Asia and the Pacific Islands* (New York, 1987), 456; Fawcett, "Networks, Linkages and Migration Systems," *International Migration Review*, XXIII, No. 3 (1989), 672-675; James H. Jackson, Jr. and Leslie Page Moch, "Migration and the Social History of Modern Europe," *Historical Methods*, XXII, No. 1 (1989), 27-36; reprinted in Dirk Hoerder and Moch (eds.), *European Migrants: Global and Local Perspectives* (Boston, 1996), 60-68; and Ewa Morawska, "Labour Migrations of Poles in the Atlantic World Economy, 1880-1914," *Comparative Studies in Society and History*, XXXI, No. 2 (1989), 237-272; reprinted in Hoerder and Moch (eds.), *European Migrants*, 186-187.

[14]Dirk Hoerder, "Segmented Microsystems and Networking Individuals: The Balancing Functions of Migration Processes," in Lucassen and Lucassen (eds.), *Migration, Migration*, 84; Hoerder, *Cultures in Contact*, 10-18; and Alejandro Portes, "Immigration Theory for a New Century: Some Problems and Opportunities," *International Migration Review*, XXXI, No. 4 (1997), 799-825; reprinted in Hirschman, Kasinitz and DeWind (eds.), *Handbook of International Migration*, 21-33.

of governments, businesses and public agencies on how networks take shape and evolve. This underlines the need for comprehensive studies that include the social, economic and political processes that shape transnational migrations.[15] This study sets itself on this level by projecting John Salt and Jeremy Stein's suggestion to view international migration as a business. In so doing, the pivotal role of shipping companies as mediators between individual networks and governments, businesses and public agencies becomes explicit.[16] By analyzing this transnational process in which nations and nation-states continue to be important constituents we can link the macro with the micro.[17]

The first part of this book analyzes the simultaneous rise of transatlantic mass migration and the introduction of long-distance steamshipping in the period 1830-1870. Although the commercialization of migrant transport by steamships only fully broke through after the end of the American Civil War in 1865, this period influenced the migrant routes and the growth of shipping companies during the subsequent period. This sailing ship era also was when the business networks which sustained the mass migration movement throughout the nineteenth century began to emerge. Their impact will be analyzed through the measures adopted by various authorities to regulate migrant transport and to open transatlantic steamship connections. It allows us to highlight the connections between trade and migrant routes and to examine the influence of governmental migration and trade policies on the ensuing trajectories. Only recently have migration researchers brought the state back into the debate. Even so, the perception of control so far has been too myopic in focussing on the abilities (or inabilities) of nations to regulate the emigration of its citizens and immigration of aliens. This section of the book draws our attention to the fact that between the emigration and immigration countries, other nations positioned themselves because of the economic interests involved in transporting migrants. The number of laws regulating the migrant trade exceeded the laws regulating the movements of citizens and aliens. As will be argued, understanding that migration was first a trade issue helps to amplify Cheryl Shanks'

---

[15] Nina Glick Schiller, "Transmigrants and Nation States: Something Old and Something New in the US Immigrant Experience," in Hirschman, Kasinitz and DeWind (eds.). *Handbook of International Migration*, 97-98; and David Gerber, "Internationalization and Transnationalization," in Reed Ueda (ed.), *A Companion to American Immigration* (Oxford, 2006), 231-238.

[16] John Salt and Jeremy Stein, "Migration as a Business: The Case of Trafficking," *International Migration*, XXXV, No. 4 (1997), 467-468.

[17] Donna R. Gabaccia, "Is Everywhere Nowhere? Nomads, Nations and the Immigration Paradigm of United States History," *Journal of American History*, LXXXVI, No. 3 (1999), 1117-1118.

observation that debates first centred on whether nations had the right to exclude migrants, and only later moved to how many and who to exclude.[18]

This first part of the book thus provides the essential context for understanding how transatlantic migrant transport became a big business. The organization of the trade in the period between 1870 and the outbreak of World War I – the temporal focus of the second part of the volume – is reconstructed on three different levels by placing the steamship companies at the heart of the story. The first level analyzes how these firms headed the business networks that developed around the burgeoning movement and comprised migrant brokers, agents, labour recruiters, charity organizations, railroad companies and banks. These networks, as Michael Miller has so presciently noted, "provided the organization, means and often initiatives by which the great transoceanic migration flows of humanity occurred."[19] The study tries to uncover the maritime origins on which the migrant agent-networks and the migrant business were structured. These were networks that extended to both sides of the Atlantic and provided the shipping companies with a direct link to the purchasers of the tickets, whether they were the actual migrants or family, friends, charities, landowners or employers. How they managed these relationships sheds more light on the profile of migrant agents, brokers and banks, as well as on the marketing strategies they used to promote ocean passage sales and the variety of services made available to the migrants. It gives a new perspective on these middlemen that too often have been considered as mere ticket agents. Finally this chapter clarifies how a passenger service like the Holland-America Line structured the business through these networks on both sides of the ocean.

The organization of these networks connecting the shipping companies to individual migrants can only be fully understood by analyzing how shipping lines competed for the migrants. This leads us to the second level which looks at how the HAL interacted with other shipping companies. The keen competition for this lucrative market pushed lines to collude and form cartels, although these colloquially were called "shipping conferences." In these conferences the shipping companies tried to ameliorate some of the fierce competitive pressures, both internal and external. The theoretical framework supplied by maritime historians on shipping cartels regulated cargo traffic will be applied to carriage of human cargoes, especially the migrant steerage market. How these horizontal combinations affected vertical integration, and hence the structure of these companies, will be discussed The analysis of how these conferences worked sheds more light on the formation of migrant routes and the subdivision of the North Atlantic market. It also allows us tc discuss the various fac-

[18]Cheryl Shanks, *Immigration and the Politics of American Sovereignty, 1890-1990* (Ann Arbor, 2001).

[19]Michael B. Miller, "Pilgrims' Progress: The Business of the Hajj," *Past and Present,* No. 191 (2006), 190.

tors influencing these routes. Because price agreements were at the heart of the way conferences operated, an original price series for the ocean crossing from Rotterdam to New York for the period 1885-1914 will be a used as a surrogate for success. It also enables us to analyze how price competition affected railroad prices to and from the migration ports, the rates for berths on the ship and the quality of service offered. Besides fixing prices, the agreements sought to regulate the agent networks; by examining them we can gain additional insights on how they managed their sales and the impact they had on the market.

Finally, the third level reassesses the way shipping companies positioned themselves between the migrant and the state as the latter tried to increase its control on the movements of the former. This part discusses the gradual shift from considering immigration as a trade issue to seeing it as a matter affecting national sovereignty. Accordingly, attempts to regulate migration through international agreements gave way to unilateral decisions. The US Supreme Court decision in the 1870s to transfer control over all issues relating to migration from the states to the federal government, which was based on the argument that this was indeed an issue of foreign commerce, underlines the entanglement between migration and trade. It also allowed American authorities to standardize legislation and inspections which it tried to export outside its borders. To do so, authorities increasingly made the responsibility for the enforcement of the laws and inspections a job for the shipping firms. By seeing how the companies handled this we can get a firsthand account of how the laws were enforced and the consequences thereof. This part of the volume responds to Erika Lee's call to refine the way research into US immigration policies has traditionally been conducted by focussing myopically on congressional debates and the laws which ensued.[20] While many scholars have noted the gap rhetoric and reality and have stressed the unintended consequences that often followed, in this study we will look not so much at what the laws said but rather at how they were enforced.[21] How the shipping companies used their privileged position to protect their interests, i.e., to land as many passengers as possible, will also be analyzed.

The visible hand of the shipping companies not only acted as the enforcers of the laws but also played a role in their enactment. Just as a business approach to transatlantic migration highlights the close connections between migration and trade, so too does it offer insights about the relationship between migration and maritime policies. In Europe, this relationship induced many

[20]Erika Lee, "A Nation of Immigrants and a Gatekeeping Nation: American Immigration Law and Policy," in Ueda (ed.), *Companion to American Immigration*, 7-12.

[21]Kitty Calavita, "US Immigration Policymaking: Contradictions, Myths and Backlash," in Anita Böcker, *et al.* (eds.), *Regulation of Migration: International Experiences* (Amsterdam, 1998), 147.

countries to pass measures directing citizens or trans-migrants to travel on national lines and hence to stimulate the national flag carriers. As a receiving country, the US was in an ideal position to adopt this approach and in the process to revive its merchant marine which during the sailing ship era had dominated the migrant trade. In spite of the growing nationalist and jingoist tendencies, though, it did not do so. By examining the shipping lobby in the United States, we will try to generate new insights into this behaviour. We will also reassess the role of this lobby as part of a broader interest group which opposed barriers to immigration. This study therefore aims to fill a lacuna by uncovering the industry's lobbying strategies and assessing their alertness to institutional changes. How did shipping companies prevent, obstruct, delay or amend immigration laws aimed at restricting their main source of revenue? The answers shed new light on Claudia Goldin's observation that the perplexing part of the history of US immigration restriction is that it took so long for the country to close its doors to the international migrant stream.[22]

In short, this study demonstrates one point above all others: that the connections between maritime and migration history are embedded in social and economic interests and political decisions. Only an analysis of all aspects of this equation can come close to providing a fuller picture of the impact of steamshipping companies on transatlantic migration.

[22]Claudia Goldin, "The Political Economy of Immigration Restriction in the United States, 1890-1921," in Goldin and Gary D. Libecap (eds.), *The Regulated Economy: A Historical Approach to Political Economy* (Chicago, 1994), 223.

Part I
State Policies and Their Influence on the Connections between Maritime and Migration Networks, 1830-1870

Transatlantic migrants have relied strongly on existing trade routes. The paths they used were embedded in pre-existing commercial networks which, as restrictions to migrate decreased, embraced this new trade. Merchants quickly observed the profitability of transporting human cargoes during the first non-colonial mass migration movement of Germans to the United States in the eighteenth century and used their commercial networks to set up the so-called "Redemptioner System" to facilitate this pioneer migration. These transatlantic networks connecting donor with recipient regions converged in ports where competition for the carriage of migrants was concentrated. This contest among carriers intensified during the nineteenth century as migrant flows increased. Ships on the North Atlantic bringing grain, sugar, tobacco timber and cotton to Europe often sailed westbound in ballast. Migrants therefore constituted an especially valuable commodity that drew ships to emigration gateways. As the business of human relocation business attracted other trades, hence contributing to a port's general development, some authorities began to develop policies to direct migrants to travel via certain routes. Migration policies in turn became integrated with maritime policies, especially with the opening of transatlantic steamship lines from the 1840s onwards.

In this study we will pay special attention to the failures and successes in establishing these connections and in attracting migrants. By contrasting Antwerp with Rotterdam within the broader context of the Hamburg-Le Havre range of Western European ports we will be able to study the impact of commercial networks on the path dependency of migrants. Moreover, we will be able to examine the organization of the transport mode and the influence of government policies during both the age of sail and the steamship period that followed. The use of the correspondence of French, Bremen, Dutch and Belgian diplomats in the United States sheds new light on how the trade in migrants affected ports' competitive positions during the steamship era.

Origins

As Nicholas Canny has argued, the demand for labour demand by itself is not enough to trigger in-migration. Instead, no major migration movement takes place until it becomes profitable for the owners of the carriers of human cargo to make the connection between supply and demand.[1] The eighteenth-century carriers of German and Irish migrants used the improvements in shipping technology and management strategies developed for the slave trade. The route those migrants took depended on the accessibility of the port, the trade connections emanating from it and the maritime policies of the governments involved. Marianne Wokeck discovered that the pioneering, non-colonial, transatlantic migrations were organized around commercial networks and trade routes. The majority of the migrants from southwestern Germany used the Rhine to gain access to seaports. Moreover, pre-existing business contacts between Rotterdam, London and Philadelphia provided a comparative advantage which allowed Rotterdam merchants to dominate the trade, keeping Amsterdam a distant second. As the movement spread to northern and eastern Germany, Hamburg became more important due to its close trade relations with England. The English Navigation Acts restricted trade with its colonies to vessels flying the national flag and obliged ships to call at English ports on their transatlantic runs. This turned London into a key node for migrant traffic.

Initially, the flow of migrants was irregular and organized in groups. English shipowners obtained information on when and how many migrants were preparing to move through Dutch shipping agents. Accordingly, they chartered vessels to call at Rotterdam where the agent fitted-out and provisioned the ship. The agent also contracted the passengers and coordinated their arrival at the port according to the planned departure of the ship to limit the transit costs and avoid trouble with the Dutch authorities. To prevent destitute migrants from getting stuck at the port and becoming public charges, authorities only allowed passengers with passports and contracts for ocean passage to enter the country. Groups required military escorts.

As the migrant flow reached its apex midway through the eighteenth century, competition for the trade intensified. Shipping agents specialized to become migrant brokers, diversifying their strategies to attract migrants. The contacts that informed them about the supply of migrants in the hinterland consisted primarily of boatmen working on the Rhine waterway system who served as go-betweens on a commission basis. They were joined by an expanding network of inland agents who solicited migrants. Contacts elsewhere in Europe informed the broker of "newlanders" bound for Germany. These return migrants often travelled home for American land speculators and employers who were aware of their ability to influence chain-migration patterns. Therefore, migrant brokers soon incorporated them into their sales network. Finally, border agents were recruited to ensure a smooth transition. The in-

[1]Nicholas Canny as quoted in Magnus Mörner, "Divergent Perspectives," in P.C. Emmer and Magnus Mörner (eds.), *European Expansion and Migration: Essays on the Intercontinental Migration from Africa, Asia, and Europe* (New York, 1992), 277.

crease in the number of re-locaters during the peak years allowed new merchants into the market despite the growing specialization. Some new brokers used Hamburg to avoid both transit obligations and competition from members of the well-established Rotterdam networks.[2]

The increasing competition was a factor in the dominance of the Redemptioner System. Migrant brokers helped settlers to assist friends and relatives to join them by agreeing to delay accepting payment until arrival in Philadelphia. The price of the crossing fluctuated between £5 and £8, yet the services included varied according to the nature of the contract. If money for the ocean passage could not be recovered from relatives, there were employers willing to pay the newcomer's outstanding debt in exchange for an indenture of servitude. This system, in which brokers provided credit for the crossing to migrants who were willing to work it off by tying themselves to an employer, reflected the growing influence of the foreland. Initially, Charleston, New York and Halifax tried to lure German settlers to populate the surrounding lands. Rhinelanders were drawn to Philadelphia, however, because of what they perceived to be better employment opportunities and excellent commercial networks. More of the new arrivals disembarked from vessels owned by Philadelphians in the second half of the eighteenth century. At the same time, London began to lose its importance as a node. The peak years led to a degree of concentration, as illustrated by the Stedman agency, the leading migrant brokers. The English brothers advanced from being captains, to becoming agents in Rotterdam and Philadelphia, to eventually owning seven ships.

The Redemptioner System gave more importance to Philadelphia merchants who gauged the demand for servitude labour and were responsible for cashing in the deferred passage payment. Philadelphia's control of the market can be seen in the legislation that regulated the traffic. Pennsylvania authorities imposed stricter regulations over space allotment and provisions, improving the travelling conditions for the migrants. In the Redemptioner System, healthy migrants were worth more, so the increasing cost of transport could be regained through longer periods of servitude. The laws made it harder for those who participated only during peak periods to penetrate the market, further enhancing the level of concentration.[3]

The Seven Years' War (1756-1763) marked a turning point for the German migrant trade, which never recovered from the conflict's dislocations.

---

[2]Marianne S. Wokeck, *Trade in Strangers: The Beginnings of Mass Migration to North America* (University Park, PA, 1998; reprint, University Park, PA, 2003), 58-115.

[3]*Ibid.*; and George Fertig, "Eighteenth-Century Transatlantic Migration and Early German Anti-Migration Ideology," in Jan Lucassen and Leo Lucassen (eds.), *Migration, Migration; History, History: Old Paradigms and New Perspectives* (Bern, 1997; 3rd rev. ed., Bern, 2005), 271-290.

Transatlantic migrant flows ebbed as Germans began to look eastward rather than toward America. As the number of migrants decreased, the commercial networks that served them deteriorated. The subsequent American and French revolutions completely disrupted the existing maritime and migration networks. Rotterdam's close ties with England had a negative impact on its trade with Philadelphia during the American War of Independence. Instead, Amsterdam became the port of choice for the reduced traffic, which came to a standstill during the Continental Blockade.[4] The relocation of more than 100,000 Germans pioneered the networks through which the nineteenth-century exodus took place. Indeed, when the movement resumed there were many similarities, such as expanding migrant-agent networks embedded in maritime networks, competition for the trade from ports on both sides of the Atlantic, increasing concentration and specialization and a trend toward drafting legislation to regulate the transit and ocean transport of migrants.

Threat to Welfare Systems or a Lucrative Commodity?

The end of the Napoleonic wars ushered in an era in which the bonds that tied many people to the land were severed. This process made the subsequent transatlantic exodus possible. This new mobility in turn undermined the organization of poor relief based on place of birth. The congregation of large numbers of destitute people in the cities - especially in port cities - was increasingly apparent. Passengers who lacked the means to complete their emigration were often stranded and became public charges. Authorities faced a classic dilemma: to facilitate the business of shipping companies that could transport migrants to new homes or to block the migrants from entering the ports and thereby prevent them from becoming charges on the public purse. As the migrant trade grew in importance, some authorities actively collaborated with shipping interests to allow certain ports to have a competitive edge over rivals which lacked this support.

Amsterdam

The end of the Napoleonic wars, combined with a persistent agricultural crisis, triggered a new surge in migration from the Rhinelands. This created congestion at Amsterdam, especially since the number of direct sailings to the US had decreased. Some migrants spent their passage money while awaiting a ship at the port while many others arrived with insufficient means, relying instead on the Redemptioner System through which approximately half of the eighteenth-century settlers had made the crossing. Yet the collapse of the market over

[4]Leo A. van der Valk, "Landverhuizers via Rotterdam in de negentiende eeuw," *Economisch en Sociaal historisch jaarboek* (Amsterdam, 1976), 150-152.

time had eviscerated the networks that supported the system. A limited supply of ships and an excessive demand for berths inflated the cost of transport and hence the periods of servitude. Shippers exploited the situation by overcrowding their ships.[5]

These conditions increased mortality rates and led to the arrival of a growing number of so-called "coffin ships" at American ports.[6] Combined with rumours of lengthening servitude contracts and Dutch authorities deporting destitute aliens, authorities in some German states tried to halt emigration, while the French tried to prevent the departure of nationals without sufficient means of support. The experience temporarily ended the use of Dutch ports by German migrants. Moreover, the Redemptioner System was never re-established on the same scale because of the introduction of new methods to finance the move. As chain-migration patterns strengthened, the poorest migrants began to rely on remittances from abroad rather than signing indentures. The events also generated indignation in the US and led in 1819 to the first federal migration law which regulated space allotments and provisions on any vessel intending to land migrants on America's shores.[7]

The experience with stranded migrants pushed Dutch politicians to pass a law in 1828 to avoid a recurrence. This legislation prohibited the entrance of migrants who did not have tickets for their passage already in hand. They also needed a passport and a special migrant certificate from the Dutch consul in their homeland. Moreover, all responsibility for their maintenance on Dutch soil fell upon the merchant who arranged the crossing. These measures

---

[5]Farley Grubb, "The End of European Immigrant Servitude in the United States: An Economic Analysis of Market Collapse, 1772-1835," *Journal of Economic History*, LIV, No. 4 (1994), 803-804; Nicole Fouché, *Émigration Alsacienne aux États-Unis, 1815-1870* (Paris, 1992), 143-156; van der Valk, "Landverhuizers," 151; and Klaus J. Bade, *Europa in Bewegung: Migration von späten 18. Jahrhudert bis Gegenwart* (Munich, 2000), 16.

[6]While ships used to make transatlantic crossings in the eighteenth century averaged about 150 tons and had room for around 300 migrants, the ship *April* left Amsterdam with more than 1000 migrants, nearly half of whom died before reaching Philadelphia. On 6 March 1818, three ships sailed into New Orleans with only 597 of the 1100 souls who had embarked in Holland. On the passages in the period, see Grubb, "End of European Immigrant Servitude," 794-824; Bade, *Europa in Bewegung*, 128; Oscar Handlin, *The Uprooted: The Epic Story of the Great Migration that Made the American People* (Boston, 1973; 2nd ed., Philadelphia, 2002), 50; and Wokeck, *Trade in Strangers*, 78.

[7] Grubb, "End of European Immigrant Servitude," 794-824; Fouché, *Émigration Alsacienne*, 19-30; Bade, *Europa in Bewegung*, 130-134; and van der Valk, "Landverhuizers," 151; and Aristide R. Zolberg, *A Nation by Design: Immigration Policy in the Fashioning of America* (New York, 2006), 99-122.

illustrate the main concern of officials around the Atlantic rim throughout the nineteenth century: the fear of destitute aliens.[8] Little is known about the implementation or impact of these laws at the borders. Wokeck found that even in the eighteenth century, migrants were blocked if they could not produce passage contracts when entering the Netherlands. Yet at the same time, border agents became an integral part of the network through which migrant brokers contracted their passengers. The increased formalities hardly forced migrants to find alternative routes but instead contributed to the spread of inland agents who could consolidate the networks through which migrants travelled. But when these commercial networks deteriorated, the Dutch laws did become a force driving migrants to rival ports. Dutch authorities, interested primarily in the development of colonial trades, remained indifferent to this evolution.[9] As a result, Amsterdam and Rotterdam fell out of the developing cotton triangle which shaped nineteenth-century migrant routes to the United States.

Le Havre and the Cotton Triangle

Besides the transatlantic movement of Germans, there was a parallel migrant stream emanating from the British Isles. Many Irish had moved through similar networks directly from Irish ports. In the nineteenth century, this movement was diverted through English ports, mainly Liverpool. On the other side of the Atlantic, the potential of this human freight did not go unnoticed by merchants in Boston, New York, Philadelphia and Baltimore who managed to attract an increasing share of the primary goods grown in the southern states to ship to European ports from which they pick up cargoes of dry goods and migrants for the return leg.[10] Liverpool, Bremen and La Havre became the principal European nodes for this particular trade route.

---

[8]Frank Caestecker, "The Changing Modalities of Regulation in International Migration within Continental Europe, 1870-1940," in Anita Böcker, *et al.* (eds.), *Regulation of Migration: International Experiences* (Amsterdam, 1998), 74-76; Caestecker, "The Transformation of 19th Century Expulsion Policy, 1880-1914," in Andreas Fahrmeir, Olivier Faron and Patrick Weil (eds.). *Migration Control in the North Atlantic World: The Evolution of State Practices in Europe and the United States from the French Revolution to the Inter-war Period* (New York, 2003), 122; Leo Lucassen, "Eternal Vagrants? State Formation, Migration and Travelling Groups in Western Europe, 1350-1914," in Lucassen and Lucassen (eds.), *Migration, Migration*, 241-250; and Gérard Noiriel, *Le Creuset Français: Histoire de l'immigration (XIX et XX siècle)* (Paris, 1988), 74.

[9]Edwin Horlings, *The Economic Development of the Dutch Service Sector, 1800-1850* (Amsterdam, 1995), 132-150.

[10]Wokeck, *Trade in Strangers*, 168-219; and Robert Greenhalgh Albion, *The Rise of New York Port, 1815-1860* (New York, 1939; reprint, Boston, 1984), 94-122.

The liberalization of trade resulted in a new French-American agreement in 1822 which allowed Le Havre to become the European node for the cotton trade. Coaches transporting American cotton to regions with large numbers of potential out-migrants, such as Alsace and even Switzerland, picked up migrants on their way back to Le Havre, a port which had various advantages compared to its rivals. For starters, the crossing was shorter and more direct, and ships did not have to wait for favourable winds to gain access to the sea. Moreover, passport regulations were seldom observed, and frequent departures limited wait times at the port. The innovation of liner shipping further decreased transit times. The first experiments with ships leaving on fixed schedules, as opposed to tramps that waited for a certain amount of cargo, began to sail between Liverpool and New York in 1818. The success of this endeavour soon attracted competition from other routes with trade volumes that could sustain liner shipping. American merchants and shipowners dominated the New-York Le Havre route, and migrant brokers such as Washington Finlay supplied them with human cargoes for the westward passage through inland agents using aggressive advertising, pricing and recruiting methods.[11]

Despite this apparent success, the problem of destitute migrants being stranded on French territory worried the Minister of the Interior. In 1830, he sent circulars to consuls in regions of out-migration outside France stipulating that US-bound migrants needed to obtain a visa from a French consul. Moreover, the visa could only be obtained if the applicant possessed 200 *florins*, a sum that was soon doubled. In 1836, entry into France was restricted to passengers with a contract for ocean passage or the cash equivalent. Once again, however, there was a gap between rhetoric and reality. The lack of border control stations hindered the implementation of these laws, and the network of migrant agents provided means to circumvent the regulations by smuggling passengers across borders or providing false passports.[12] On the other hand, the lack of legislation regulating ocean transport or preventing migrants from abuse reflected the meagre interest in France in stimulating the migrant trade.

Bremen, "the" Migrant Gateway

Officials in Bremen were the first on the European continent to realize the importance of the migrant trade, and they pushed for laws which could aid its development. The appointment in 1796 of Frederich Wichelhausen as US consul in Bremen reflected the importance to the US of the growing trade with the

---

[11]Fouché, *Émigration Alsacienne*, 150-151; Anne Horan, *et al.*, *De Grote Oversteek* (Amsterdam, 1982), 80-106; Agnes Bretting and Hartmut Bickelmann, *Auswanderungagenturen und Auswanderungsvereine im 19. und 20. Jahrhundert* (Stuttgart, 1991), 51 and 65; and van der Valk, "Landverhuizers," 152.

[12]Fouché, *Émigration Alsacienne*, 68-72.

Hanseatic city. Indeed, the consul tried to establish a passenger shipping line to Baltimore. Despite this interest, several factors mitigated against Bremen in its competition with rival ports. Bremen lacked good access to out-migration regions, and during the 1820s, the Bremen merchant marine declined dramatically because of a lack of exports (two-third of all ships left the port in ballast). Although American vessels carried rice, sugar, coffee and tobacco to the Hanseatic city, they called elsewhere for a return cargo. Contemporaries noted that bilateral trades the country with the larger volume of exports had a natural advantage.[13]

Nonetheless, restrictive measures in other countries and the unstable political situation in France and the Low Countries drove 3500 migrants to Bremen in 1830.[14] This movement would have a far-reaching impact on the further development of Bremen's commerce. The migrant became *the* commodity around which the shipping industry developed. Aware of the geographic disadvantages, the merchant community made a great effort to establish networks of migrant agents to divert the flow to Bremen. Agencies were opened in Frankfurt, Darmstadt and Giessen, and further south in Mannheim, Stuttgart, Karlsruhe and Nürnberg to promote Bremen as a migrant gateway, as well as selling passages and helping the migrants in other ways.

The migrant business was strictly regulated due to a situation peculiar to Bremen. The lack of a prosperous hinterland forced merchants to establish shipowning firms managing both trade and transport. The city's corporate structure mandated the appointment of official brokers to assist and supervise the freighting and outfitting of ships for which they received small fees regulated by law. They were not allowed to act on their own initiative or to receive commissions; this led to the formation of an external network of private entrepreneurs to recruit migrants and negotiate transport rates. Efforts to block these entrepreneurs were in vain and pushed brokers to engage in extra-legal recruiting. The fear of losing control of the trade led the authorities to legalize the activities of the entrepreneurs who then increased their grip on the business to the detriment of the official brokers.[15]

---

[13]Rolf Engelsing, *Bremen als Auswandererhafen, 1683-1880* (Bremen, 1961), 49-79.

[14]Arno Armgort, *Bremen-Bremerhaven-New York, 1683-1960* (Bremen, 1992), 15-42; and Birgit Gelberg, *Auswanderung nach Übersee: Soziale Probleme der Auswanderungbeförderung in Hamburg und Bremen von der Mitte der 19. Jahrhunderts bis zum Ersten Weltkrieg* (Hamburg, 1973), 10.

[15]Dirk Hoerder, "The Traffic of Emigration via Bremen/Bremerhaven: Merchants' Interests, Protective Legislation, and Migrants' Experiences," *Journal of American Ethnic History*, XIII, No. 1 (1993), 74-75; and F. Prüser, "Hamburg-Bremer

The close ties between the authorities and the merchant community resulted in the passage in 1832 of progressive migrant transport laws which were designed not only to safeguard the city from destitute migrants but also to protect migrants from abuse. The law encouraged migrants to book their trip in advance to reduce waiting periods at the port. Passengers unable to pay for the crossing were expelled from the city. The American Passenger Act of 1819 served a model to regulate the ocean leg of the passage. City officials controlled the seaworthiness of ships and provisions. It placed the responsibility of provisioning on shipowners, putting an end to the practice of self-provisioning. Finally, shipowners were required to carry insurance to refund the passengers in case of accidents.[16]

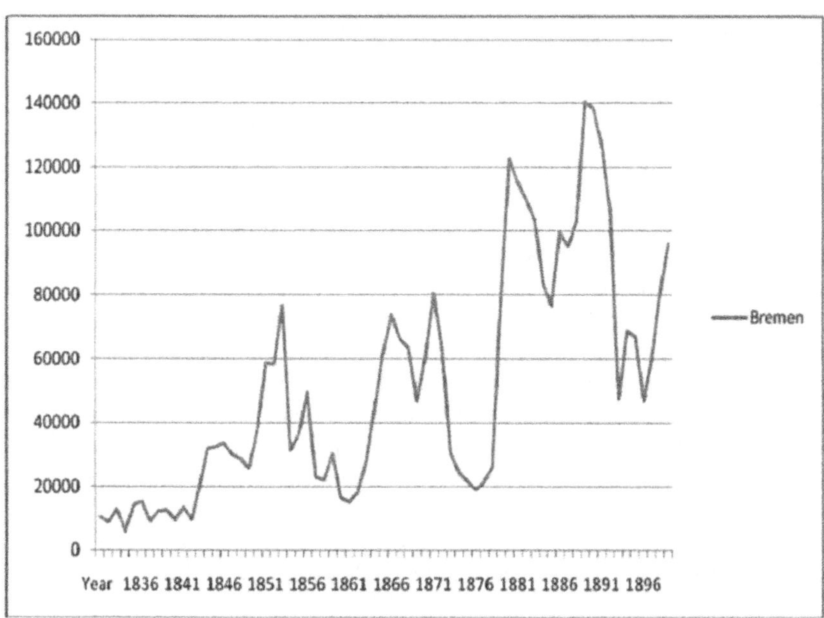

Figure 1: Emigration through Bremen, 1832-1900

Source: Arno Armgort, *Bremen-Bremerhaven-New York, 1683-1960* (Bremen, 1992), 125.

Schiffahrtwettbewerb in der Zeit der grossen Segelschiffahrt und Dampfer," *Zeitschrift des Vereins fur Hamburgische Geschichte*, XLIX (1964), 156.

[16]Armgort, *Bremen-Bremerhaven-New York*, 42-44; and Hoerder, "Traffic," 74.

Despite making travel more expensive compared to rival ports, the law actually helped Bremen merchants to increase the flow of migrants through the port (see figure 1). The visionary merchant community realized the importance of the quality of service and the reputation of the port. From a collective fund raised by a tax levied on each passenger they set up advertising campaigns with broadsheets, posters and newspaper ads pointing out the advantages of Bremen as a migrant gateway. Word-of-mouth publicity was ensured by satisfied migrants and an expanding network of agents. Letters from satisfied customers in America urged friends and relatives to travel as they had done. The migrant flow swelled to 10,000 in 1832 and surpassed 15,000 five years later. This migrant business enabled Bremen shipowners to quote lower rates for freight, mainly tobacco, allowing them to take control of the inbound trades. This turned Bremen into the European capital for the tobacco business which remained the city's most important industry up to the end of the century. By 1840, the trade to the US was controlled by Bremen shipowners, driving American ships to Le Havre and Antwerp.[17]

The metamorphosis in Bremen's trading environment illustrates the importance of migrant transport to a number of trade routes. Whereas until that point migrants for the most part had followed established trade routes, now trade began to follow migrant routes. Despite the geographical disadvantages and the higher cost of ocean transport, the Hanseatic city quickly rivalled Le Havre as the main transatlantic gateway for migrants. Bremen demonstrated that the choice of route was not based solely on rational economic factors such as cost and time. The dynamic merchant community compensated for the poor accessibility with progressive legislation and advertising campaigns. The merchants understood the importance of gaining the confidence of those who considered taking the plunge to a new continent and went out of their way to familiarize them with how to do so. While authorities in many rival ports feared migrants, Bremen's officials embraced them. The early engagement of Bremen merchants gave the port an edge it would not lose. But this is not to say that Bremen's success story was unnoticed in neighbouring ports.

Revival of Antwerp

Antwerp was the first continental port to challenge Bremen and Le Havre. Belgian authorities tried to back up their political independence with an active economic policy. By establishing commercial relations with other countries, the young nation hoped to create goodwill and consolidate its independence.

---

[17]Armgort, *Bremen-Bremerhaven-New York*, 43; Walter D. Kamphoefner, Wolfgang Helbich and Ulrike Sommer (eds.), *News from the Land of Freedom: German Immigrants Write Home* (Ithaca, NY, 1991), *passim*; Engelsing, *Bremen*, 49-76; and Prüser, *Hamburg-Bremer*, 156.

Antwerp, which after two and half centuries had managed to break the Dutch stranglehold over the Scheldt, was the nodal point for this purpose.[18] Positioning the port on the booming North Atlantic trade routes was a priority. Merchants and officials, both local and national, were aware of the importance of the migrant trade and set out to capture as much of it as they could.

Turning Antwerp into a Migrant Gateway

A Belgian official named Désiré Behr, reported the following on the migrant transport via Bremen:

> We know that Germany sends out thousands of emigrants to America every year. The city of Bremen has passed such perfect regulations for the transport of emigrants that only this port organizes these transports. Once arrived in Bremen this cargo moves itself without extra costs and it allows the Bremen merchants on their way back to ship a variety of goods such as tobacco and cotton at half the regular price. As most of the German emigrants come from Westphalia, Thuringia and Switzerland it is very likely that they would prefer to travel through Antwerp if they would find the same conditions as in Bremen.[19]

Belgian authorities used the Bremen and American laws to regulate migrant transport, abrogating those that dated back to Dutch rule. The requirement of five tons of space for every two passengers was borrowed from the American law, while the provision requirement for ninety days was copied from Bremen. A commission of city officials controlled the seaworthiness of ships, provisions, amounts of medicine aboard, accommodations and space allotments between decks. The authorities also launched a broad advertising campaign in

---

[18]The rebellion in the Low Countries against Spain and the subsequent formation of the Republic of the Seven United Netherlands led to the closure of the port of Antwerp. Many tradesmen moved to Amsterdam and contributed to its economic development. Only under French rule two centuries later did Antwerp regain its access to the sea. During the subsequent Dutch rule, Antwerp's interests were subordinated to Dutch ports. The Netherlands refused to recognize Belgium after the revolution of 1830 and hindered sailings on the Westerscheldt, the port's access to the North Sea. When signing the XXIV articles, recognizing Belgium's independence, the Dutch preserved the right to levy toll on the Westerscheldt. See Hans Blom and Emiel Lamberts (eds.). *Geschiedenis van de Nederlanden* (Baarn, 1995), 120 and 256.

[19]Archives of the Belgian Ministry of Foreign Affairs (ABMFA), 2020, Emigration I: 1834-1848, report, 5 April 1838.

Germany and Switzerland to promote Antwerp's advantages. The consular corps distributed advertisements to local newspapers and migrant agents. Consuls also assisted Antwerp shipowners to establish agencies in the area.[20]

The main advantage Antwerp had in securing passengers from the southwestern German states was the opening of the Iron Rhine connecting Cologne with Antwerp in 1843. The policy of turning Belgium into an important transit country resulted in a dense rail network that was unequalled on the European continent. Prior to the opening of the railroad connection, migrants used the cheap Rhine waterways to Rotterdam from where they were shipped to Antwerp. Getting the often voluminous luggage of migrants to the port of embarkation was one of the main logistical problems for the inland leg of the journey. The fact that transport was easier by water than by coach influenced the choice of migrant routes. The Belgian authorities obtained free transport of luggage from the railroad company and used it to start a new advertising campaign promoting Antwerp as a migrant gateway. It was the first port to be directly connected to the hinterland by rail. Yet despite these efforts, the flow through Antwerp actually declined.[21]

In the meantime, Hamburg and Rotterdam entered the competition. The Belgian authorities appointed a special commission to investigate the decline and to propose measures to counter the increased competition. The report reflected the various factors which influenced migrant flows. It found that strong winds had hindered access to Antwerp in April and May, diverting American vessels to Rotterdam and Le Havre. Second, a proposal to increase tariffs drove away a number of American ships bringing in tobacco and hoping to carry migrants on their return passage. A third factor was the high death rates in the Belgian colony of Santo Thomas de Guatemala. Many colonists came from Germany, where the event received wide press coverage, and rival migrant agents used the incident to advise against migrating through Belgium. Fourth, Bremen had built up an impressive fleet dedicated to transport migrants, while Rotterdam's connection to the Rhine provided a cheap connection to the hinterland. To compete with the Iron Rhine, Dutch steamship companies lowered their fares to Rotterdam.[22] Many Antwerp-bound passengers still used the waterways through Rotterdam where local agents often convinced them to

---

[20]Pasionomie, law number 271, 14 March 1843; and ABMFA, 2020, Emigration I: 1834-1848, correspondence, 5 April 1843-16 June 1844.

[21]ABMFA, 2020, Emigration I: 1834-1848, correspondence, letter, 10 June 1843, and Consul M. Muhlens, Nachricht fur Auswanderer nach Amerika, February 1844 and letter, 20 May 1845; and Fouché, *Émigration Alsacienne*, 144-156.

[22]Mack Walker, *Germany and the Emigration, 1816-1885* (Cambridge, MA, 1964), 81; and ABMFA, Catalogue par matières, Emigration 2020, I-X: 1834-1914, letter, 25 June 1845.

leave from Dutch ports. The regulations protecting migrants received praise, yet a strict application of these rules increased prices to 110 Belgian *francs* including food. To overcome these obstacles, the commission recommended several things. First, it suggested giving shippers the freedom to adapt their food supplies to the taste of the passengers and to reduce the quantity during spring and summer from ninety to seventy-five days.[23] Next, it proposed relaxing passport controls which added ten or twelve *francs* to the cost, and many migrants did not bother to acquire one.[24] Infrastructure to handle the baggage in Antwerp needed to be improved, and cheaper accommodation had to be provided by the community council. An emigration inspector was needed to protect migrants from abuse. Finally, the cost for direct access to the port had to be reduced to prevent passage through Rotterdam.[25]

These events exemplify the aspects on which competition for the migrant trade centred; trade, maritime and migration policies; the cost of inland and ocean transport; transit facilities and accessibility to the port; the reputation of the port and quality of service; and port infrastructure and technological evolution. The Congress of Vienna, which abolished the slave trade and helped launch a new tradition of diplomatic consultation, created an international regime that stimulated cooperation, free trade, economic integration and international migration. The transition from protectionism to free trade led to numerous renegotiations of trade and navigation treaties. Speculation on the outcome of these negotiations could temporarily influence trade and migration routes, as those between Belgium and US in 1844 illustrated. Shippers also feared that the strict application of measures, such as those mandating provisions or requiring passports, which regulated migrant transport would increase costs or hinder transit. It is impossible to measure how well the laws were enforced, but at any rate we know that shipowners and migrant brokers found means to circumvent them, often with the consent of the authorities, to protect the competitive position of the port.[26] Price competition brought down the basic rate

---

[23]The commission suggested the substitution of biscuit and potatoes for rice, beans and peas to provide a diet with which Germans were more familiar. The regulations brought the cost of provision to forty *francs* which, according to the Chamber of commerce, was much more than at other ports. ABMFA, Catalogue par matières, Emigration 2020, I-X: 1834-1914, letter, 17 August 1842.

[24]The maritime police denied that passports were required, stating that they also accepted birth certificates or any official document on which they could put a visa before embarkation. They claimed that three-quarters of the migrants had no passports. *Ibid.*, letter, 28 January 1846.

[25]*Ibid.*, letter, 30 January 1846.

[26]Carl Strikwerda, "Tides of Migrations, Currents of History: The State, Economy, and the Transatlantic Movement of Labor in the Nineteenth and Twentieth

for a berth to eighty *francs*, excluding provisions, sleeping gear and cooking utensils. Competition also moved to the inland transport. To counter Rotterdam, authorities obtained a thirty percent reduction from the Cologne Steamship Company for migrants heading for Antwerp. On top of free transport of luggage, migrants using the Iron Rhine also received a thirty percent reduction on the fare, which later was increased to fifty percent for groups.[27] The expanding railroad network and decreasing costs stimulated direct access.

The frequent advertising campaigns illustrate the importance of information about the port and its reputation. The Belgian authorities used the consular corps to promote Antwerp in foreign regions where out-migration was high. They discussed the advantages of scheduled sailing dates, new legislation, railroad connections and special migrant fares. Consuls also kept an eye out for negative publicity in the local press, such as reports of migrant abuse, shipwrecks or unsuccessful colonization attempts such as Santo Thomas de Guatemala. Smear campaigns were viewed as attempts by German authorities to direct their citizens to Bremen and Hamburg. Consuls refuted rumours about the mistreatment of migrants in Antwerp and backed this up with publicity about the appointment of an official emigration inspector to protect migrants, provide them with information and handle their complaints. The reputation of the port also needed to be defended overseas. The New York consul Henri Mali coordinated advertising campaigns in the American press to convince immigrants to guide friends and relatives through the port.[28] New York migrant brokers like Francis Thompson enabled settled immigrants to transfer funds to friends and relatives so that they could follow in their footsteps, pio-

---

Centuries," *International Review of Social History*, XLIV, No. 3 (1999), 374-375; Pierre-Henri Laurent, "Antwerp versus Bremen: Transatlantic Steamship Diplomacy and European Port Rivalry, 1839-1846," *Journal of World History*, IX, No. 4 (1966), 951; and Eric Spelkens, "Belgian Migration to the United States and Other Overseas Countries at the Beginning of the 20th Century," in Ginette Kurgan and Eric Spelkens, *Two Studies on Emigration through Antwerp to the New World* (Brussels, 1976), 83-101.

[27]The thirty percent reduction was introduced in November 1844. Nonetheless, the steamboat passage from Mayence to Cologne cost 5.75 *francs*; when added to the 10.5 *francs* for the railroad leg to Antwerp, this totalled 16.25 *francs*. Dutch companies, on the other hand, offered transportation from Mayence to Rotterdam for 7.5 *francs*. The commission urged that transit costs be reduced to eleven *francs* to end indirect migration through Rotterdam. ABMFA, Catalogue par matières, Emigration 2020, I-X: 1834-1914, letter, 25 June 1845.

[28]*Ibid.*, Ministry of Foreign Affairs (MFA) to Henri Mali, 30 January 1844; and Linda Maesens, "De Regeringsbemoeiing in de organisatie van de emigratie via Antwerpen naar Latijns-Amerika (1843-1913)" (Unpublished MA thesis, Ghent University, 1978), 33.

neering a practice that later developed into the sale of prepaid tickets.[29] The campaigns also fit in with the drive by Belgian authorities to create goodwill in the US for the opening of transatlantic steamship lines, which they hoped would end the dependence on favourable winds to enter or clear Antwerp.

Opening of a Transatlantic Steamship Line

The simultaneous arrival in New York of *Sirius* and *Great Western* from Liverpool in 1838 gave rise to intense competition among European and American ports to open up transatlantic steamship lines. Initially, steam was concentrated on the British-North America route. The first continental port to challenge this dominance was Antwerp.[30] The Belgian government believed that, like railroads, maritime connections powered by steam that required large investments needed the financial support of the state.[31] The reasons for this active policy were summarized in a report which led parliament to pass a special bill to subsidize a line between Antwerp and New York:

> With the industrial evolution the wealth of nations will greatly depend on its commercial importance and its ability to force other nations to trade through them. The geographical position of Belgium enhances her development as a nodal point for trade. By stimulating this, the government will give the young nation more political power. Nations that enjoyed the benefits of Antwerp could later be lobbied to push for the free navigation of the Scheldt.[32] It's the best way of fighting

---

[29]Albion, *Rise of New York Port*, 339-340.

[30]*Ibid.*, 313; G.J. de Boer, *125 jaar Holland-Amerika Lijn, 1873-1998* (Rotterdam, 1998), 8; and Laurent, "Antwerp versus Bremen," 938-952.

[31]The intervention of the Belgian government was also stimulated by a European economic crisis which made investment credits for new technology hard to obtain. This crisis tempered the elaborate plans of the Société Générale Belge de Bateaux à Vapeur, which had been organized by Antwerp merchants to build fourteen ships for lines to various European and transatlantic destinations. See Laurent, "Antwerp versus Bremen," 939; and Karel Veraghtert, "The Slow Growth of Steam Navigation: The Case of Antwerp, 1816-1865," *Collectanea Maritima*, V (1991), 209.

[32]To enhance the trade through Antwerp, the Belgian government refunded the tolls levied by the Dutch. As trade increased, this policy started to weigh heavily on the government's funds. Moreover, with the liberalization of trade, there was a tendency to eliminate such tolls. The Sont and Stade toll had been bought out by the maritime nations. In 1863, the last remaining Scheldt toll followed as the Belgian government and other maritime nations agreed to pay the Dutch thirty-six million *francs* to

> off the influence of our natural rival, the Netherlands and contesting its dominant position in the German transit-trade because of its natural advantages through the Rhine and the Meuse. If we succeed we'll obtain the sympathy of the powerful German State and become less dependent of France. Moreover, strong trade relations with the US will result in an important political alliance with the nation which is predestined to rule the waves. A steamship connection with New York is a complementary link to our railroad network, and vital to globalize our depository function in this economic transit system. The dependency of favourable winds to enter and leave Antwerp has hampered regular and fast services to the US which are essential to attract manufactured goods for export. Steam shipping solves this problem and will stimulate American and Belgian merchants to examine the opportunities for increased trade between the two nations, travelling time being reduced to two weeks. Finally it would improve the competitive position of the port of Antwerp.[33]

Also, if a country questioned the right of the young nation to exist by force, the national merchant marine could be used to retaliate. The report clearly reflected Belgium's geopolitical orientation. Plans in Rotterdam and Le Havre to open lines doubtless spurred the decision to adopt this policy.

The Belgian ambassador in London, Sylvain van de Weyer, acquired *British Queen* and *President* from the British and American Steam Navigation Co. In the meantime, the government sought someone to manage the line. Candidacies came from both sides of the Atlantic and included David Colden, a New York businessman, and the Bostonian Edward Derby, chairman of the Western Rail Association. The latter stressed that the emerging rail connections allowed easy access inland for migrants and that his port would provide the necessary infrastructure. In the end, the government preferred to entrust the management to Belgian entrepreneurs, but for all candidates raising capital remained the biggest obstacle, despite a yearly subsidy of 400,000 *francs*.[34]

---

make the navigation of the Scheldt free. Karel Veraghtert, "De havenbewegingen te Antwerpen tijdens de negentiende eeuw: een kwantitatieve benadering" (Unpublished PhD thesis, Catholic University of Leuven, 1977).

[33]Belgium, General State Archives (BGSA), I 215, 4052, report on the Opening of a Steamship Line between Antwerp and New York, 25 April 1840.

[34]Laurent, "Antwerp versus Bremen," 939-941; BGSA, I 215, 4052, anonymous letter, n.d.; ABMFA, 2241, Steamshipping, Antwerp-New York, 1839-1889,

The Atlantic world tumbled into the grip of an economic crisis, throwing existing steamship lines into disarray and dampening the enthusiasm of investors.[35] Despite the failure of existing lines, J.-F. Catteaux-Wattel, J. Lejeune and G. Jullie established the Belgian Steam Navigation Service Antwerp-New York. The enterprise projected migrant transport as a source of revenue. Unlike Cunard, which offered only first-class passage, the new company believed that a second class had to be available to make transatlantic passages accessible to travellers from all social classes.[36] To compete with other ports, rates for cabin passengers and valuable goods had to be ten percent lower than those of Cunard and could not exceed the prices of the prospective French line.

The venture received a serious blow when *President* sank just prior to its delivery, seriously damaging the reputation of its sister ship, *British Queen.* To make matters worse, B. Basteyns announced an agreement with one of the biggest New York merchant houses to open a regular sail connection from Antwerp leaving every two weeks. Catteaux-Wattel and Jullie resigned even before the maiden voyage.[37] Because passenger volumes had dropped considerably due to the crisis, Lejeune began to question the notion of transporting migrants. Conversely, George Schuyler, who unsuccessfully applied for the head agency in New York, tried to convince the company to focus on migrants after studying the market on both continents.[38] The company opted for a mixed service, including cabin passengers and upper-class migrants; the two, however, had to be separated to protect the line's reputation. *British Queen* left on its maiden voyage with fifty passengers but due to bad weather only arrived in New York twenty-four days later. The poor results raised the question of opening the passenger service to the lowest class of migrants for 100 *francs*. After two more loss-making crossings, the line was suspended.[39]

---

letters, 5 July and 9 October 1840, and report presented at the Belgian Chamber of Representatives, 1 June 1840.

[35]The British government raised the subsidies for the Cunard Line and the Royal Mail Steam Packet Co. to prevent bankruptcies. Meanwhile, the Great Western and the British and American Steam Navigation Co. ceased their activities. BGSA, I 215, 4052, Séance, 10 March 1843.

[36]*Ibid.*, navigation law of 29 June 1840.

[37]ABMFA, 2241, Steamshipping Antwerp-New York, 1839-1889, letters, 18 June 1841 and 1 and 15 February 1842.

[38]BGSA, I 215, 4052, letter, 31 January 1842.

[39]De Boer, *125 jaar Holland-Amerika Lijn*, 8; Veraghtert, "De havenbeweging," 13-25; and ABMFA, 2241, Steamshipping Antwerp-New York, 1839-1889, reports, 15 March and 10 June 1842; and 30 May 1847.

The lack of connections with American businessmen and bad publicity overseas contributed to the failure. Another factor was that negotiations for a trade agreement between Belgium and US failed to materialize, thus subjecting the line to high tariffs.[40] The most notable factor is that the venture was ahead of its time. Indeed, as Gerald Graham argued, the introduction of steam spurred technological innovation in sail shipping in its attempt to remain competitive. Size and speed crept steadily upwards after the introduction of steamships.[41] The French consul in New York, in collecting information for the opening of a steamship line, observed that "sailing ships anticipated the feared competition of steamships for the emigrant transport by lowering the prices from 150 *francs* to 120 *francs* and even 100 *francs*. Moreover, the accommodation on sailing ships improved considerably."[42] Price cuts for steerage berths in sailing vessels to protect this lucrative market have been noted by other scholars.[43] In Antwerp it led to the establishment of packet sailing ships leaving on a set schedule. The government subsidized such lines with premiums per ton while imposing maximum rates. This policy proved successful, and by 1844, eight regular long-distance services sailed to New York.[44] The increased competition lowered the cost of migration and improved the level of service, which may have delayed the transition of migrant transport to steam.

Migrant Transport Policies versus Migration Policies

By the time Europe was hit by the economic and agrarian crisis midway through the 1840s, there were well-established, competing networks assisting people to relocate overseas. Yearly arrivals in the US quadrupled during the

[40]Laurent, "Antwerp versus Bremen," 941-942.

[41]Gerald S. Graham, "The Ascendancy of Sailing Ship 1850-1885," *Economic History Review*, 2nd ser., IX, No. 1 (1956), 74-88; and Albion, *Rise of New York Port*, 333.

[42]The exchange rate for US $1 amounted to 5.3 French *francs*, making the price drop from US $28.30 to US $22.60 and US $18.90. Diplomatic Archives, Nantes (ADN), Consulats, New York, 7, letter, 12 August 1842.

[43]Simone A. Wegge, "Chain Migration and Information Networks: Evidence from Nineteenth-Century Hesse-Cassel," *Journal of Economic History*, LVIII, No. 4 (1998), 957-986; and Engelsing, *Bremen*, noted that transport costs from Bremen varied from US $21 to US $28 in 1839, dropping to between US $14 and US $19.60 in the early 1840s.

[44]Veraghtert, "Slow Growth," 210-211.

decade 1845-1855, with average arrivals going from 76,675 to 309,572.[45] European authorities, weighed down by a growing population dependent on poor relief, started to use migration networks as security valves. Although the share of migrants receiving direct assistance from recruiting agents and state authorities remained relatively low, their impact on bringing Europe and the US closer in the mental maps of Europeans cannot be overlooked. The Belgian case is used to analyze assisted migration and its links to migration and maritime networks.[46]

During the economic crisis the problem of destitute migrants being stranded *en route* re-emerged. At the request of the Prussian government, Belgium adopted the French measure requiring the possession of 200 *francs* at the border to prevent destitute migrants from entering.[47] The authorities were immediately submerged by complaints of migrant brokers and ship-owners. The Antwerp Chamber of Commerce, outraged by the lack of communication and hearing about the measure only through the German press, wrote the following which reveals the importance of the trade and the extent that local authorities and the transport sector jointly organized assisted migration:

> Often contracts between migrant brokers at the port and German migrant agents or communities stipulate that the payment for transportation is to be carried out on instalment, not by the emigrant but by the communities, agents or another designated third party. Such contracts which have been concluded for thousands of emigrants are now under review. It is impossible for the communities to give the sum to the emigrant because frequently they still need to sell the migrant's possessions to cover part of the cost. We would like to remind that these shippings stimulate our maritime trade and relations with transatlantic countries. That they multiply export possibilities to the advantage of our national industry, procuring an outbound cargo for ships using our port, these

---

[45]Imre Ferenczi and Walter F. Willcox, *International Migrations, Vol. I: Statistics* (New York, 1929), 399.

[46]Many Belgian opinions about migration also circulated in the German states where the debate was more prominent given the large numbers moving overseas. The debate centred on whether restrictive, encouraging or non-intervention policies should be adopted. Prussia's intention to restrict migration in the wake of the 1848 revolution was successfully opposed by the Hanseatic cities that were defending their interests in the migrant trade. Walker, *Germany and the Emigration*, 103-178.

[47]ABMFA, 2020, Emigration I: 1834-1848; letters, 10 January and 13 February 1847.

> shippings lower the incoming freight rates of cotton, tobacco, cereals and other products...Each migrant stays on average 5 to 6 days spending about 70fr. on provisions, lodging, and utensils which times 13000 for 1846 gives the lump sum of 910000fr. If the berth price of 80fr. is added, in which the national marine takes an important part, the business yields a profit of 1950000fr. Tolls and taxes collected on ships involved in the traffic surpassed one million francs. Also, despite the reduction the railroads are benefiting from the trade. Our trade relations with the US have already increased to such extent thanks to the passage of emigrants that the government no longer considers the premiums favouring the lines to be needed.[48]

The measure was immediately repealed, and migrant brokers stood as surety for the crossing.[49] Even if the "thousands" mentioned by the Chamber of Commerce was likely an exaggeration, the letter illustrates how migration networks adapted to the needs of communities in assisting their members to relocate and reconfirms the importance of migrant transport for trade in general. The German practice stimulated Belgian authorities to use migration networks as security valves for an increasingly impoverished population.

The fiasco of Santo Thomas de Guatemala had planted doubts about state-directed migration. The colony had been established to stimulate trade and to increase political influence through territorial expansion. Mismanagement and high mortality rates left the Belgian government with a financial hangover and a blackened reputation.[50] The public and parliamentary debates were divided between the belief that the state always had to take care of its nationals - considering every migrant as a loss for the military and the workforce - and the Malthusian fear of overpopulation. As a report on the crisis, which hit the Flemish countryside hardest, demonstrated, in provinces with the highest population densities about one of every four inhabitants depended on charity support, while in the province with the lowest population density the

---

[48]*Ibid.*, reports, 14 January and 6 March 1847.

[49]*Ibid.*, letters, 8 March and 12 May 1847.

[50]Luc Schepens, *Van vlaskutser tot Franschman: Bijdrage tot de geschiedenis van de Westvlaamse plattelandsbevolking in de 19e eeuw* (Bruges, 1973), 86-92; Eddy Stols, "Latijns-Amerikaanse vurigheid, utopieën en luchtspiegelingen," in Anne Morelli (ed.), *Belgische emigranten: oorlogsvluchtelingen, economische emigranten en politieke vluchtelingen uit onze streken van de 16de eeuw tot vandaag* (Berchem, 1999), 234; and Stefan van den Bossche, *Een kortstondige kolonie: Santo-Tomas de Guatemala (1843-1854): een literaire documentaire* (Tielt, 1997), 1-12.

ratio was one in seventy.[51] Exporting part of the population offered a safety valve and opened ways of enhancing trade relations by using migrants as ambassadors and consumers of Belgian products abroad.

Politicians favouring migration used the successful Irish and German flows to sway opponents.[52] The crisis over which two governments fell in as many years called for immediate action, so the government financed new attempts to establish colonies. Demographic motives, now taking precedence over political or economic issues, influenced both the location and the type of colony. The authorities intended to establish an exemplary and self-sufficient agricultural colony which would induce local authorities and charity institutions to invest in similar projects as an alternative to the existing poor relief. The initiators chose the US based on a report by Auguste-Gabriel van der Straeten-Ponthoz who by order of the Belgian government examined the opportunities the country offered for trade and migrants.[53] Forty years later, his report was still cited in Belgium as *the* reference work on opportunities in America. It was also used for similar purposes in Germany and the Netherlands. Hendrick Scholte translated the report into Dutch and published it for

---

[51]ABMFA, Emigration, 2946, III, letter, 1847.

[52]For the parliamentary debates, see Belgium, Chambre de Représentants, Compte rendu de l'emploi du crédit extraordinaire de 1,000,000 ouvert au département de l'intérieur par la loi du 21 juin 1849 séance du 5 février 1852; Annales parlementaires, Chambre de représentants, séance du 15 février 1845, 814-816 séance du 31 mai 1849, 1522-1585, et séance du 9 mai 1854, 1652-1660. The contemporary literature reflected the diverse views on migration; see, for example, Jean-Louis Cartuyvels, *Aux émigrants belges: Colonie de Sainte-Marie, canton d'Elk, dans l'état de Pennsylvanie* (Saint-Trond, 1850); Victor de Ham, *Conseils à l'émigrant Belge aux États-Unis de l'Amérique du nord* (Brussels, 1849); Pierre Hansen, *Des questions relatives à l'émigration aux Etats-Unis d'Amérique du Nord: situation de Belgique en 1849 et moyens d'améliorer* (Mons, 1849); and Auguste-Gabriel van der Straeten-Ponthoz, *Rapport sur un voyage d'exploration dans les États-Unis d'Amérique du Nord* (Brussels, 1846).

[53]The five main topics he needed to investigate outline the purpose of the mission: (1) What advantages does the American government offer to attract emigrants? (2) How are the colonists that settle in the country doing and what are their moral and material conditions? (3) Where do they settle? Why? What is the influence on the trade relations between the country of emigration and immigration? Do the emigrants still have ties with their home country? What are the consequences for commerce? (4) What is the best place for Belgian emigrants to settle for their own good and for the good of trade relations between Belgium and the United States? (5) In what way does the Belgian government need to intervene domestically and in America? Could the government, in collaboration with the American government, regulate emigration to protect the emigrants and to make this movement as efficient as possible? ABMFA, Emigration, 2020, I, Emigration 1834-1848, letter, 15 April 1844.

potential migrants in the Netherlands, while Kollmann did the same in Germany.[54] Reliable information was crucial for the migrant's success, and the authorities recognized the need to provide alternatives to the often biased material circulated by migrant agents, philanthropic organizations, recruiting agents and the like. Even letters from immigrants were sometimes forged to influence migrant decisions.[55] Exploratory missions complemented the consular reports and provided the emigration inspector and the Ministry of Foreign Affairs with trustworthy information which was transferred to anyone who asked for it.

The authorities subsidized two colonies, New Flanders in Pennsylvania and Kansas in Missouri. New Flanders was established in collaboration with the American Association for the Colonization of Sainte-Marie, one of many "philanthropic" associations seeking to sell land. A government official, Victor De Ham, headed the project, leading fifty-nine volunteers who previously had depended on poor relief. The volunteers signed a contract binding them to contribute to the development of the colony for three years. In exchange, transport costs, land and the necessary materials to cultivate it were provided. Every year, fifty new colonists sponsored by the government and coordinated by emigration inspector Jean-François Thielens would join them. A similar arrangement was made with Guinotte, Magis and Co., which managed the colony in Missouri. Contracts binding the migrants to periods of servitude resembled the Redemptioner System and the subsequent Padrone System. In the former, American state officials registered the contracts to provide a legal framework which protected both employers and migrants.[56] Subsequent assisted movements financed by European governments could not count on the same support from US states, many of which prohibited the entrance of paupers. Hence, the servitude contracts had no legal standing in the United States, placing such ventures in a vulnerable position. Colonists took advantage of the fierce competition among land speculators to move to places where better

[54]Torsten Feys, "The Emigration Policy of the Belgian Government from Belgium to the U.S. through the Port of Antwerp, 1842-1914" (Unpublished MA thesis, Ghent University, 2003), 5-43; Pieter R.D. Stokvis, *De Nederlandse trek naar Amerika, 1846-1847* (Leiden, 1977), 126; Van der Straeten-Ponthoz, *Rapport*; and Antoine de Smet, *Voyageurs Belges aux États-Unis Du XVIIieme sciècle à 1900* (Brussels, 1959), 164.

[55]Marie-Rose Thielemans, "De Waalse emigratie naar Wisconsin," in Anne Morelli (ed.), *Belgische emigranten: oorlogsvluchtelingen, economische emigranten en politieke vluchtelingen uit onze streken van de 16de eeuw tot vandaag* (Berchem, 1999), 131.

[56]Torsten Feys, "Radeloosheid in crisistijd: pogingen van de Belgische regeringen om een deel van de arme bevolking naar de Verenigde Staten te sturen, 1847-1857," *Belgisch Tijdschrift voor Nieuwste Geschiedenis*, XXXIV (2004), 204-210; and Grubb, "End of European Immigrant Servitude," 797.

terms were offered. As a result, the continued existence of such colonies depended greatly on the ability to tie pioneers to the land, hoping that their success would trigger chain migration. The Belgian colonies failed in this regard, forcing the government to abandon such projects.

Another network of assisted migration was set up by the Antwerp governor Jan T.F. Teichmann, emigration inspector Thielens and the migrant broker Adolphe Strauss to send beggars, ex-convicts and convicts overseas. The project was designed to relieve the overcrowded beggar workhouses where condemned vagabonds and beggars stayed at the expense of their community. The Community Council of Antwerp pioneered the alternative strategy of paying for the ocean crossing to the US.[57] Teichmann tried to convince other communities in his province to follow the example:

> By sending detainees of beggar workhouses, the community gets rid of miserable individuals who inevitably would have spread the begging to their families. The community offers them a new chance for a better future and to get new morals in a country where the salary is much higher and where the immigrant escapes from the shame of his past and the influence of his disruptive companions. The crossing, food included, costs on average between 160fr. and 180fr. per adult, which is only a bit more than the price of confinement for one year. This sum also includes the expenses for the equipment and some pocket money to get through the first days of their stay. The emigration inspector Thielens has already sent you a brochure. He keeps an eye on the embarkation of the beggars. Only moments after their liberation beggars get convicted again to be sent once more to the beggar workhouse which they consider to be a permanent shelter. In case of interest you can get directly in touch with Thielens.[58]

The reaction of the communities varied; some needed to be reminded that the candidates had to volunteer, while others expressed concern about whether they would indeed be better off overseas. The latter was not totally without reason considering the history of the migrants as beggars and the limited resources that were given to make a fresh start: "a shirt, two pairs of socks, two

---

[57]René Boumans, "Een onbekend aspect van de Belgische emigratie naar Amerika: De gesubsidieerde emigratie van bedelaars en oud-gevangenen, 1850-1856," in *L'expansion Belge sous Léopold 1er, 1831-1865* (Brussels, 1965), 470-504; and Feys, "Radeloosheid in crisistijd," 211-219.

[58]Provincial State Archive of Antwerp (PSAA), Provinciaal Bestuur, Bedelaarsgestichten, 78, I, Emigratie, letter, July 1850.

handkerchiefs, a pair of pants, a pair of shoes, a hat, a cardigan, a towel, a suitcase, a brush, a comb, smoking tobacco and pipes, chewing tobacco, Dutch gin, white soap, cooking materials, straw mattress, pillow, blanket and 15fr. pocket money."[59] Still, all the communities eventually cooperated. When a request to emigrate came from a detainee with no fixed residence, the Ministry of Justice financed the move. The intervention of the national authorities spread the practice to other provinces around the country.

The Committee for Aftercare and Resettlement of freed Prisoners assisted ex-convicts to reintegrate into society by helping them to find work, sometimes as sailors. It was a logical progression to incorporate ex-convicts and pardoned criminals into the network. Minister of Justice Victor Tesch provided them with passports and special certificates which masked their history of incarceration. Teichmann handled the correspondence with the communities, while Thielens arranged practical details with Strauss. Thielens' close relations with Strauss suggest that he also had a financial interest in the business. The migrant broker signed an exclusivity contract for these movements in exchange for a fixed price of 180 *francs*; eighty *francs* for the berth, forty *francs* for provisions and sixty *francs* for the equipment. For the poorest communities, they made special arrangements for beggars to work as sailors. The costs to outfit a beggar as a sailor only amounted to about 115 *francs*. It was unlikely that any of these men would return to Belgium since no steerage berths were available on the eastbound leg, and cabin berths cost about 500 *francs*.[60] Indeed, only two percent ever returned.

These examples of assisted relocation show how the networks through which transatlantic migrants moved expanded and became increasingly complex. The organization of transport was in the hands of migrant brokers at the port of embarkation, a situation which became increasingly institutionalized not only because of the authorities' concern for the well-being of the migrant but more especially for the trade it generated. The Belgian case illustrates that increasing contacts between migrant brokers and authorities were not limited to transport. Indeed, Antwerp migrant brokers drew migrants from the hinterland in collaboration with German local authorities who paid for the crossing of their poorest residents in instalments. This inspired the Belgian government to follow suit. Through Thielens, local and national authorities were directly connected to the networks that sent passengers overseas. The emigration inspector also gathered and distributed information on opportunities through the diplo-

---

[59] *Ibid.*, Correspondence, September 1850-June 1851, contract signed by J. Veezen, Charles Vasteneer and [unknown], 27 December 1850.

[60] Boumans, "Een onbekend aspect," 485; and PSAA, Provinciaal Bestuur, Bedelaarsgestichten, 78, I, Emigratie, correspondence between Thielens and Teichmann, 1850-1855.

matic corps. Bremen and Hamburg copied Antwerp by appointing a government inspector with similar responsibilities.[61]

New York as Nodal Point for the American Foreland

Recent port histories have stressed that ports have to be studied as nodes between the hinterland and foreland which shape maritime routes. During the nineteenth century, competition among ports intensified, making this an important feature.[62] In the case of the transatlantic migrant transport, the foreland had an important impact upon who migrated and how. While European ports competed to export migrants, an equally keen competition existed between Atlantic ports in the US to receive them. The Erie Canal provided New York with the best connections to the interior, which were complemented with railroads and coastal shipping. As James Bennett, the owner of the *New York Herald*, noted, infrastructure and technological innovation were key elements in maintaining an edge over rival ports. He advocated the development of railroad networks and pressed for New York to become the American terminus of transatlantic steamship lines. Of equal importance was the city's development as the financial capital of the country, allowing New York merchants to gain control of many of the eastbound trades. In a system where, for example, New York financers bought cotton before it was planted or flour before it was milled American planters and farmers were placed in a chronic state of debt. Financers collected interest in return and directed a large share of American exports to the port. The money they advanced also attracted the nations' storekeepers to New York, where they replenished their stocks with imports and domestic products. By controlling these trades, traffic to the port increased and so did the migrant flow. Prior to the Civil War, two-thirds of all migrants landed in New York, leaving its rivals to compete to be a distant second.[63] Due to the importance of the migrant trade, the financers tried to gain control of the networks that supplied this "commodity." The lack of this control had driven large parts of the tobacco business into the hands of Bremen tradesmen.[64] Therefore, American migrant brokers, such as Finlay in Le Havre, established themselves in Europe. Others remained to meet the demands of the growing stock of immigrants and prospered from the booming markets for remittances

---

[61]Gelberg, *Auswanderung nach Übersee*, 12-13.

[62]Reginald Loyen, *et al.* (eds.), *Struggling for Leadership: Antwerp-Rotterdam Port Competition, 1870-2000* (Leuven, 2003), 3-6.

[63]Albion, *Rise of New York Port*, 94; and James L. Crouthamel, *Bennett's New York Herald and the Rise of the Popular Press* (Syracuse, NY, 1989), 92.

[64]Engelsing, *Bremen*, 66-76.

and prepaid tickets. Land speculators, employers, railroad companies and state authorities tried to direct the new arrivals according to their own needs. The competition spread to Europe through the transport networks. Debates on ways to regulate transport and on whether to restrict immigration led to a variety of laws.

Chain Migration and Business Networks

The failures of the colonies at Kansas and New Flanders contrasted with the apparent success of the unsubsidized migration of Belgians. A movement starting off with a collection by a parish minister to fund the emigration of ten families that depended on poor relief turned into an outflow of approximately 10,000 Belgians between 1852 and 1857. Relocation to the American Midwest was spurred by letters from pioneers about inexpensive and abundant land. The authorities in Wisconsin, like many others, offered land on credit at low interest rates to attract future taxpayers. They appointed immigration officials in New York and Europe to recruit migrants for the state. The chain-migration patterns which developed attracted all sorts of people. The American Association for Property and Land financed the return trip of a pioneer who easily convinced 250 people in his native region to settle in the US; for his trouble, the returnee received a commission for each migrant he recruited. For those who booked their ocean passage through Strauss, the Association advanced the funds. Thielens and Strauss set up a promotional campaign for Wisconsin to entice migrants. Information circulating through migrant letters, state officials and migrant and recruiting agents convinced others to follow.[65]

This movement exemplified various influences which steered migration. Adherents of the sociological approach to migration history have argued that chain-migration patterns were the principal determinant of migrant flows. According to this theory, the personal decision to migrate was predominantly made within the family. Villagers, acquaintances and family members who had previously emigrated were the main sources of information. Indeed, the informants often advanced the funds required for the crossing, provided a provisional place to stay and helped the newcomers find work. This theory stresses the importance of the foreland, or countries of destination, to the path dependency of migrants. Yet what it fails to acknowledge is that chain-migration patterns were built around commercial networks which originated from the profitability of migrant transport. Because of the fierce competition for this lucrative trade, these networks expanded and adapted quickly to stimulate and meet the

---

[65]Thielemans, "De Waalse emigratie," 123-137; Antoine de Smet, *La communauté belge du nord-est du Wisconsin: ses origines, son évolution jusque vers 1900* (Brussels, 1956), 24-25; and Jean Ducat, *et al.*, *From Grez-Doiceau to Wisconsin: contribution a l'étude de l'émigration Wallonne vers les États-Unis d'Amérique aux XIXe siècle* (Brussels, 1986).

needs of the migrants. All parties interested in migration were eventually connected through the business networks which shaped chain-migration patterns. It is true that most migrants travelled without the assistance of governments or land speculators. But it is important to remember that migrants using the assistance of family, acquaintances, governments, land speculators and employers, or even using their own resources, had to pass directly or indirectly through the migrant broker. This privileged position allowed the brokers to use the various actors to their advantage. Their inside position in the market enabled them to adapt quickly to the changing needs of the newly arrived migrants. As the business became specialized, an increasing range of services were offered through the migrant agent network.

The efforts of migrant brokers to enable and encourage communities to assist their poorest residents to emigrate to the United States illustrate how they developed new market opportunities. They did the same to enhance chain-migration patterns. Initially, the only way for an immigrant in America to finance the passage for someone joining them was by giving the money to people travelling to Europe, often shippers or captains, or by transferring the funds through banks. The banking business generated by mass migration remains largely unexplored, but Farley Grubb has found that a third of all Irish and German migration before 1834 was financed through remittances, putting an end to the Redemptioner System. The Remittance System could only be sustained if the flow grew, allowing regular banking and merchant connections to be established. Only then could the reputation for honesty that repeat business created give enough guarantees to immigrants to entrust their brokers. The increased shipping traffic and banking connections also decreased the transaction cost of remittances. Finally, the expansion of industrial employment made loans secured by future wages possible as a means to finance the crossing of friends or relatives while also providing jobs for the newcomers to help in paying off the debt.[66]

New York merchants quickly noted the potential of expanding the market by selling ocean passages across the Atlantic. The connections between Liverpool and New York merchant houses, and entrepreneurs such as Samuel Thompson in Britain and Caleb Grimshaw in the US led to the establishment of the first Emigration Office in New York. Other businessmen soon followed suit. Human freight was assured through contacts with migrant brokers in European ports and recruiting agents travelling to Europe, while they also offered prepaid tickets to settled migrants.[67] The Remittance System encouraged migrant brokers and agents to combine banking and the passage business. The banking world profited from the monetary exchanges and transfers generated

---

[66]Grubb, "End of European Immigrant Servitude," 816-818.

[67]Albion, *Rise of New York Port*, 339-341.

by mass migration; again, the migrant brokers served as go-betweens. As the competition for business in the US increased, networks of migrant agents spread inland, further stimulating the sale of tickets for inland transport in America. Although ticket frauds were not uncommon, this did stimulate the creation of a door-to-door service and in the long run created an integrated Atlantic transport network. The improved organization fuelled the developing chain-migration patterns.

American Migration Legislation and the Rise of Nativism

As in Europe, American shipowners and migrant brokers tried to shield their businesses from regulations which might impede further growth. The main concern for American authorities was that migrants not become public charges. On the one hand, federal-state differences about the value of migration allowed the shipping interest to play one against the other. On the other hand, port competition helped shipowners obtain concessions from the authorities. Calling migrant transport a form of international commerce meant that the trade fell under federal authority, yet preventing the admission of paupers and convicts was deemed a police matter and hence under state control. The role of the seaboard states, federal government and shipping industry in shaping American immigration policy by attempting to control the quantity and quality of migrants is often ignored by migration historians.[68]

Aristide Zolberg characterized the pre-Civil War period as the "rehearsal of remote control" era. The best way to avoid undesirable aliens entering the US was to prevent them from leaving Europe.[69] The humanitarian ideals of the Passenger Act of 1819 were betrayed by the concept of increasing the cost of migration to block the entry of the poorest. The law set the standards for European migrant transport legislation on all long-distance routes, including those from Bremen and Antwerp. Yet the means to implement the laws were limited, while the methods to circumvent them were numerous. For instance, Belgian inspectors could not prevent ships leaving Antwerp from picking up additional passengers in Flushing.[70] On arrival in America, passengers could easily be transferred to smaller vessels before facing inspection. Moreover, on both sides of the Atlantic, port interests advocated lax controls

[68]Brendan Mullan, "The Regulation of International Migration: The US and Western Europe in Historical Comparative Perspective," in Böcker, *et al.* (eds.), *Regulation of Migration*, 30; Aristide Zolberg, "The Archaeology of Remote Control," in Fahrmeir, Faron and Weil (eds.), *Migration Control*, 195-221; and Zolberg, *Nation by Design*, 99-125.

[69]Zolberg, "Archaeology," 197.

[70]ABMFA, 2020, Emigration I: 1834-1848, letter, 19 August 1846.

for fear that a strict implementation would drive business to rival ports. The legislation also was slow to adapt to the rapidly evolving technological improvements of ships.

Information on the transport of criminals and paupers to the US reached the American government through its consuls, yet attempts to pass legislation to deal with the matter were blocked by the Supreme Court. The only way for the federal government to restrict the flow was by decreasing the capacity of ships, thus increasing the costs. The second Passenger Act of 1847 did this, but pressure from the shipping lobby led to a new law which reset capacity requirements to the old standards, albeit with slight modifications to the advantage of American vessels. The booming American shipping industry increased its carrying capacity five-fold between 1830 and 1860, in the process expanding its influence on legislators. The readjustment safeguarded the competitive position of American ships which, in contrast to British vessels, were often built for speed rather than capacity. It allowed the construction of three-decked rather than two-decked passenger ships, increasing capacities to 1000 passengers, nearly double what the 1847 regulations permitted. This type of vessel dominated the migrant trade on the Le Havre and Liverpool routes during the next decade. In 1855, the shipping lobby again blocked a new Passenger Act from affecting its profits.[71]

In the meantime, a growing segment of the American populace was beginning to see migrants, especially Irish Catholics, as threats to the country's values and institutions. Sporadic uproars against the foreign-born developed into an organized xenophobic movement known as the Know Nothings. The movement fed on the widespread assumption that European countries sent their worst subjects, including paupers and criminals, to the US. State authorities drew up measures to prevent migrants from becoming public charges and levied head-taxes to improve immigrant controls at the ports. But the constitutionality of the head-tax was successfully challenged by shippers as interference with international commerce. Attempts by states along the eastern seaboard to pass tighter immigration controls were countered by immigrant-hungry southern and western States. The seaboard states used their right to require bonds from captains landing passengers who were likely to become public charges to pressure shipping interests. A system was set up whereby captains paid com-

---

[71]Roosevelt Study Center, Middelburg, Diplomatic Archives (RSC), M 42, dispatches from US ministers to the Netherlands, roll 17, April 1845-September 1850; ABMFA, 2020, Emigration I: 1834-1848, letters, 7 February and 30 June 1847; Dutch National Archives (DNA) 2.05.13, Gezantschap in de Verenigde Staten, letter, 27 May 1847; John G.B. Hutchins, *The American Maritime Industries and Public Policies, 1789-1914: An Economic History* (Cambridge, MA, 1941), 272; Zolberg, *Nation by Design*, 131; and Maldwyn Allen Jones, "Aspects of North Atlantic Migration: Steerage Conditions and American Law, 1819-1909," in Klaus Friedland (ed.), *Maritime Aspects of Migration* (Cologne, 1989), 324-326.

mutation fees - essentially head-taxes - which released them from bond obligations. Yet competition among Atlantic ports soon undermined the measure. Cuts to the charges were made frequently to avoid ships unloading passengers in rival ports with lower fees.[72]

The powerlessness of American authorities was exploited by the Belgian government both to get rid of undesired nationals and to attract assisted migrants from other European countries. Inspired by the German flow of assisted migrants, the Belgian Consul-General in Bern, M. de Gremus, was ordered to try to deflect similar networks of indigent Swiss to Antwerp.[73] State authorities in New York pioneered measures for the stricter implementation of the laws to fight these tactics. Their policies centred in the first place on the well-being of the migrant. They took charge of the costs for migrants who became public charges and appointed an Emigration Commission to protect newcomers from abuse. The conviction grew that controls assuring good quality of service and a good reputation attracted rather than drove away passengers. With the commutation fees and the help of the shipping industry, several health, employment and control institutions, such as Castle Garden, were built to improve the screening of migrants.[74] To counter the increased controls, Thielens appointed a special agent to welcome, direct and find jobs for assisted Belgians on arrival. The agent recommended sending small groups after failing to place a batch of fifty. By lingering in New York they could attract attention, so Consul Henry Mali paid for their transport inland to avoid a scandal. The consul strongly opposed his government's attempts to circumvent the rules, an approach which he believed threatened his year-long efforts to promote the reputation of Antwerp as a migrant gateway. Mali also feared that this could compromise the success of the long-awaited steamship line connecting Antwerp with New York. The practice lasted until a letter implicating the Belgian authorities fell into the hands of the American press leading to the arrest of twelve alleged paupers in 1854. Finally, the New York Emigration Commission was able to prove its suspicions that Antwerp, through migrant broker

---

[72]Benjamin J. Klebaner, "State and Local Immigration Regulation in the United States before 1882," *International Review of Social History*, III, No. 2 (1958), 272-283.

[73]PSAA, Provinciaal Bestuur, Emigratie, 275, Landverhuizers, Kolonies, letter, 5 September 1855.

[74]Charlotte Erickson (ed.), *Emigration from Europe, 1815-1914: Select Documents* (London 1971), 269-272; and Klebaner, "State and Local Immigration Regulation," 274-275.

Strauss, was a centre for the shipment of the lowest class of emigrants from Belgium, Germany and Switzerland.[75]

These events coincided with the apex of the nativist movement and created a diplomatic incident between the two countries. The case received a good deal of coverage in the American press and reopened the Congressional debate about federal restrictive laws. But the federal government's powers remained restricted only to the regulation of transport, a problem that led to the passage of the ineffective Passenger Act of 1855. Meanwhile, the detained paupers in New York were eventually released after a writ of *habeas corpus* led to a Supreme Court decision.[76] Yet Antwerp's reputation was blackened. The vessels were held up for extra controls, and the authorities threatened to impose extra taxes on ships coming from Antwerp. Alvis Gall, the American consul in Antwerp, required that all emigrants pass through his office to solemnly swear that they were not paupers or convicts; he also charged them one *franc* for his services. Although Teichmann doubted Gall's authority to do this, he refrained from protesting in order to avoid more controversy. The American consul briefly pioneered the delicate enterprise of transferring remote control measures to the European continent.[77]

Nonetheless, all of this endangered the competitive position of Antwerp as a migrant gateway and demanded immediate action. The network though which at least 750 paupers and criminals migrated between 1850 and 1856 was diverted to Canada and Brazil before being dismantled. An investigation by American diplomats found that other European authorities also terminated programs of assisted migration to the US.[78] The Belgian authorities launched a new propaganda campaign to regain American confidence in Antwerp. This was crucial because the long-awaited opening of a new steamship line relied predominantly on migrant transport as a source of revenue. But as Raymond Cohn has noted, the nativist surge led to the downfall of the first

---

[75]PSAA, Provinciaal Bestuur, Emigratie, 275, Landverhuizers, Kolonies, letter, 13 December 1851; *New York Times*, 25 and 27 December 1854; 1 January, 15, 16 17 and 27 February and 5 February 1856; Feys, "Radeloosheid in crisistijd, 211-220; and ABMFA, 2020, Emigration, IV, letter, 15 February 1855.

[76]Edward P. Hutchinson, *Legislative History of American Immigration Policy, 1798-1965* (Philadelphia, 1981), 39-42; and Boumans, "Een onbekend aspect," 493-494.

[77]Six months later, when the storm of protest finally blew over, Belgian authorities objected to Gall's behaviour. With the support of American captains, Gall was denounced for acting solely to enrich himself and was forced to stop his interference. ABMFA, 2020, Emigration, IV, letter, 24 May 1855.

[78]*New York Times*, 5 February 1856.

mass-migration movement.[79] The subsequent economic recession and the onset of the Civil War brought the flow to a practical standstill.

Opening of American Steamship Lines

Of the pioneering steamship companies, only the Cunard Line managed to stay afloat due to considerable government subsidies. The prestigious British line offered a bi-weekly service between Liverpool, Halifax, Boston and New York. A growing number of Americans called for an alternative that flew the "Stars and Stripes." The apprehension among financers to invest in a capital-intensive business that was undergoing the growing pains of technological innovation remained the biggest obstacle. To stimulate such investments, Congress moved temporarily to subsidize steamship navigation to Europe. Consuls quickly spread the news across the Atlantic, triggering keen competition among various ports to serve as the terminus for such a line.[80]

The importance of consuls as sources of information on legal, commercial and political developments abroad has only recently been stressed by maritime historians. Consuls established contacts with local authorities and merchants to promote trade relations with shipping enterprises based in their homelands. Especially in new markets, where uncertainties and hence transaction costs were considerable, consuls played a vital role. In the nineteenth century, there were two systems to manage the rapidly-expanding consular corps. The system of honorary consuls consisted of merchants who received no remuneration other than the fees derived from certain official duties. They lived off the profits of trade, but the title of "consul" conferred a certain prestige within the business community. The Netherlands, Belgium and the Hanseatic cities used this system, albeit with some salaried consuls in key locales. France and the UK used a system of salaried officials, career consuls who were forbidden to engage in trade.[81] The role of consuls in gathering and spreading

---

[79]Raymond L. Cohn, "Nativism and the End of Mass Migration of the 1840s and 1850s," *Journal of Economic History*, LX, No. 2 (2000), 361-383.

[80]Albion, *Rise of New York Port*, 314-335; and Hutchins, *American Maritime Industries*, 325-356.

[81]Leos Müller and Jari Ojala, "Consular Services of the Nordic Countries during the Eighteenth and Nineteenth Century: Did They Really Work?" in Gordon Boyce and Richard Gorski (eds.), *Resources and Infrastructures in the Maritime Economy, 1500-2000* (St. John's, 2002), 23-41; Müller, "Swedish-American Trade and the Swedish Consular Service, 1780-1840," *International Journal of Maritime History*, XIV, No. 1 (2002), 173-188; Müller, *Consuls, Corsairs and Commerce: The Swedish Consular Service and Long Distance Shipping, 1720-1815* (Uppsala, 2004), 17-32; Charles S. Kennedy, *The American Consul: A History of the United States Consular Service, 1776-1914* (Westport, CT, 1990), 72-85; Ginette Kurgan-van Hentenryk,

information on possible migrant destinations and routes, as well as actively directing flows has already been noted. What follows is an analysis of the efforts of diplomatic representatives to convince the American authorities to use certain ports for their subsidized line.

The ports of Bremen, Hamburg, Antwerp, Le Havre, Brest, Lisbon, Southampton, Bristol and Liverpool made the American government's shortlist as potential terminals. The absence of Dutch ports reflects the decline of commercial relations between the two countries.[82] Dutch maritime interests between 1815 and 1850 centred manly on trade with its colonies in the East Indies. Government intervention in colonial trade, through the Nederlandse Handels Maatschappij (NHM), offered high freight rates and guaranteed return cargoes. It also placed no premium on speed, so merchants used sailing vessels rather than investing in costly steamers. Hence, the Dutch institutional structure delayed the transition from sail to steam. It also caused the Dutch business community to develop an aversion to the German transit trade. The laws restricting the movement of German migrants through the country corroborate this observation. From the 1830s onwards, however, the German states forced the Dutch government to liberalize transport on the Rhine to facilitate the transit of goods. The colonial trade brought tropical goods to the Dutch ports which were traded further up the Rhine and with other European ports. The focus on these trades also hindered entry into the transit traffic. It allowed merchants to do most of the transactions on their own, avoiding middlemen and paralyzed the development of large-scale enterprises. Moreover, the NHM favoured Amsterdam over Rotterdam which had better inland connections for the German transit trade. It sent just enough ships to obtain the support of local Rotterdam interests. The Rotterdam Chamber of Commerce opposed modernization into technologies such as steam shipping and railroads and considered transit traffic a threat. The city council shared this conservatism, which explains the deplorable state of the port's public services and infrastructure. Under these circumstances, G.M. Roentgen found no support in 1839 for his project to open a steamship line to New York with the principal revenue to be derived from migrant transport.[83] For these reasons, the once thriving com-

---

"Belgian Consular Reports," *Business History*, XXIII, No. 3 (1981), 268-270; and C.A. Tamse, "The Netherlands Consular Service and the Dutch Consular Reports of the 19th and 20th Century," *Business History*, XXIII, No. 3 (1981), 271-275.

[82]Frank Broeze, "Connecting the Netherlands and the Americas: Ocean Transport and Port/Airport Rivalry," in Rosemarijn Hoefte and Johanna C. Kardux (eds.), *Connecting Cultures: The Netherlands in Five Centuries of Transatlantic Exchange* (Amsterdam, 1994), 86-87.

[83]Roentgen planned to transport migrants for as low as 100 *francs*; Rotterdam Community Archives (GAR), Holland-America Line Archive (HAL), 318.14, Wentholt Archief, 6, letter 3 April 1839. See also Jochen Bläsing and Ton Langenhuyzen,

mercial relations between Rotterdam and the US deteriorated as did the direct migrant flow. Most migrants that used the Rhine to the port embarked on ships to Antwerp, Le Havre or Liverpool, all of which had more frequent sailings.

Failing to make the shortlist for the American subsidized line served as a wake-up call for the Dutch, whose primary concern was to avoid Antwerp being chosen. To try to ensure that this did not happen, the Dutch government launched a publicity campaign in Europe and the US to counter its poor reputation as a transit country. It blamed the Hanseatic ports for spreading malicious rumours to attempt to divert traffic away from the Netherlands.[84] In the US, the campaign centred on the advantages Dutch ports offered for migrant traffic and the opening of a steamship line.[85] Upon discovering that the Americans had opened negotiations with authorities in Antwerp and Bremen, the Dutch consuls redoubled their efforts, pointing especially to the advantages of Rotterdam over its two competitors.[86]

Although the company failed to materialize, the effort revived Dutch interest in the North Atlantic, especially in the migrant trade. This was spurred by the increasing flow of nationals going to the US. The growing internal market led to an intensified competition in which the migrant broker Johan Wambersie, the American consul in Rotterdam, occupied a dominant position. The Dutch migration movement was triggered by an intolerant religious policy that drove away repressed Seceders and was intensified by the declining economy in the mid-1840s. Suggestions for state-sponsored emigration gained momentum and led to the founding of an agricultural colony in Surinam in 1846. High death rates, however, deterred the government from continuing to actively support this movement. On the contrary, it passed a law to monitor the emigra-

---

"Dutch Sea Transport in Transition: The Influence of the German Hinterland, 1850-1914," in David J. Starkey and Gelina Harlaftis (eds.), *Global Markets: The Internationalization of the Sea Transport Industries since 1850* (St. John's, 1998), 103-126; Thimo de Nijs, *In veilige Haven: Het familieleven van het Rotterdamse gegoede burgerij, 1815-1890* (Nijmegen, 2001), 39-53; Horlings, *Economic Development*; and Johan G.J.C. Nieuwenhuys, *De haven Rotterdam in Verleden en Heden* (Rotterdam, 1952), 48-72.

[84]DNA, 2.05.13 Gezantschap Verenigde Staten, letter, 3 October 1844; and Stokvis, *De Nederlandse trek*, 154-170.

[85]According to the consul, the main advantages of Dutch ports included a daily, speedy, comfortable and inexpensive inland steamship service based on the Rhine; easy transfers of passengers and luggage to transatlantic ships; regular departures to the US; quick access from the ports to the sea; and a supervisory committee to protect migrants and to control shipowners and brokers. DNA, 2.05.13 Gezantschap Verenigde Staten, letter, 11 January 1845.

[86]*Ibid.*, letters, 18 February 1845 and 20 January 1846.

tion of nationals to the US and to enable government intervention if the movement got out of hand. Authorities even secretly spread anti-emigration propaganda because the liberal opposition portrayed the migration of nationals as a sign of bad governance, blaming high taxes for the loss of compatriots.[87] The movement did not result in better protective measures for migrants. The Dutch envoy in Washington even advised nationals to go through Bremen where migrant brokers included food in the price of the passage. In Rotterdam, migrants were overcharged and received very poor quality in return. He also denounced the lack of decent, affordable lodging and railed against abuses regarding monetary exchange.[88] Calls to adapt the Bremen model remained unanswered. In short, the renewed interest in the North Atlantic trade was in no way powerful enough to turn the tide from the colonial maritime policies.

Unlike Rotterdam, Antwerp was a serious contender in the contest to become the European terminal for the prospective American steamship line. Previous efforts by the Belgian government had not gone unnoticed on the other side of the Atlantic. Improved diplomatic relations between Belgium and the US led to a liberal trade agreement. Belgian diplomats exerted all possible influence on members of the Commerce and Post Office committees in Congress. They placed articles in the American press praising the advantages of Antwerp over Le Havre and Bremen. Antwerp's railroad and steamboat connections guaranteed the timely redistribution of mail, goods and passengers. Bremen, on the other hand, had poor railroad connections and no liner service to London. It depended on Hamburg for the English trade, while contacts between the Hanseatic towns diminished. Moreover, ships had to cross the feared North Sea to reach the port. Le Havre had better connections, yet these were not as good as Antwerp's and did not offer the same promising prospects regarding the transit trade with the German states. Belgium's new trade agreements with the US and the *Zollverein* opened more possibilities. The Iron Rhine offered the ideal connection for the German migrants, according to these

---

[87]Robert P. Swierenga, "The Journey Across: Dutch Transatlantic Emigrant Passage to the United States 1820-1880," in Hoefte and Kardux (eds.), *Connecting Cultures*, 114-115; and van der Valk, "Landverhuizers," 157; Swierenga, *Faith and Family: Dutch Immigration and Settlement in the United States, 1820-1920* (New York, 2001), 9-15; Jacob Hinte, *Nederlanders in Amerika: Een studie over landverhuizers en volksplanters in de 19de en 20ste eeuw* (Groningen, 1928), 166-199; Gerald F. de Jong, *The Dutch in America, 1609-1974* (Boston, 1975), 129-153; Stokvis, *De Nederlandse trek*, 160; Hans Krabbendam, *Vrijheid in het verschiet: Nederlandse emigratie naar Amerika, 1840-1940* (Hilversum, 2006), 58-66; and Henri van Stekelenburg, *Landverhuizing als regionaal verschijnsel van Noord-Brabant naar Noord-Amerika, 1820-1880* (Tillburg, 1991), 82-86.

[88]DNA, 2.05.13 Gezantschap Verenigde Staten, Envoy of Washington to MFA, 11 December 1845.

articles.[89] The plans of the French government to open its own steamship connection strengthened the conviction of the Antwerp bidders that the Americans would not pick a route with a new competitor. Too confident about Antwerp's advantages, the Belgian authorities underestimated the importance of lobbying, something with which Bremen's merchants were much more familiar.

The Hanseatic city dispatched as lobbyist-negotiators Theodor Gevekoht and A. Dudley Mann, the American consul in Bremen awaiting reappointment. They were authorized to deal directly with US authorities and especially with businessmen who remained sceptical about the profitability of such a venture. Only subsidies kept the Cunard Line afloat, and investors doubted that the US government would invest similar amounts. The main advantage of Bremen was the port's strong orientation toward North Atlantic trade and its well-established commercial networks in the US. The first plans to open a steamship line date back to 1840 when Carl Keutgen projected a line to carry mail, fine goods and first-, second- and third-class passengers. Keutgen counted on German national pride to remain ahead of the French and Belgians, but without success. Five years later, the bidders for the American subsidy still played on the same sentiment, but on both sides of the Atlantic. With the continuous migrant stream, the German community in the US gained importance and organized a petition to Congress in support of the Bremen bid.[90] The Prussian *chargé d'affaires* in Washington, Friedrich von Gerolt and the Bremen consul in Baltimore assisted Gevekoht and Mann in launching propaganda campaigns in the American press.[91] The dominant position in the migrant trade and the booming commercial relations between Bremen and the US were used as the main arguments for the Bremen bid. In the meantime, the Bremen Senate worked on the weakness of the bid. It pressured the Hannover authorities to complete the railroad connecting the port to the southwestern German states and Eastern Europe. The Senate, which had already made significant efforts by building Bremerhaven, continued to invest in a new space to handle large steamships. A new trade agreement between the *Zollverein* and the US also helped the cause. Hannover stopped levying tolls on American products coming through Bremen and lobbied to extend this to the whole *Zollverein*, follow-

---

[89]BGSA, I 215, 4052, report 1846.

[90]ABMFA, 2241, Steamshipping, Antwerp-New York, 1839-1889, letters, 27 September and 15 October 1845 and 4 November 1846; and Bremen Staatsarchiv (BSA), 2-R-11, Dampschiffahrt, post- und Packetschiffahrt zwischen Bremen und VS, prospectus Carl Keutgen, 31 October 1840.

[91]Mann led the lobbying campaign and later was made an honorary citizen of Bremen for his efforts. BSA, 2-R-11, Dampschiffahrt, post- und Packetschiffahrt zwischen Bremen und VS, letters, 30 September 1845 and 18 August 1846.

ing Belgian success in obtaining this for Antwerp.[92] Some Bremen senators feared that their independence from the *Zollverein* and commercial future was at stake. As Arnold Duckwitz put it, "if Antwerp is chosen, Bremen would probably be forced into the *Zollverein* which would be negative for the commerce with the US, would imply higher duties on tobacco and would lead to a decline of its use."[93]

To foment division among the German states, the Belgian envoy in Berlin obtained assurances from Prussian authorities that it would support the Antwerp bid after concluding the toll agreement with the *Zollverein.* Many German merchants, especially from the Rhine district, preferred Le Havre or Antwerp for commercial and geographical reasons. So did the Prussian consul in New York, John W. Schmidt, but he could not go against Gerolt, who was his superior. The German-American community was equally divided. To prevent increasing discord, Prussian authorities broke their promise and instead of backing Antwerp, distanced themselves from the subject.[94] In the US, the Belgian envoy in Washington, Charles Serruys, concluded a new trade agreement based on "most favoured nations" principles, exempting future steamship lines from all transit duties and pilotage expenses. Cave Johnson, the postmaster general, agreed to lower the mail tariffs between the two countries, favouring a future mail service. Mali used his previous experience as New York head-agent for *British Queen* to influence local capitalists. His successful merchant house earned him a good reputation in the American business community, but the lack of fellow compatriots in the US hampered his efforts. The appointment of Adolphe Moxhet as consul-general of New York did little for their fight against the more experienced and better established Bremen lobby. With shipments of exquisite old German wines, the latter obtained goodwill from the German Society in New York and gained the favour of congressmen, the postmaster general and the President.[95] Mann even convinced Henry Hillard, a former American envoy in Brussels and a member of the House committee in

---

[92]*Ibid.*, various newspaper articles, June 1847; and letters, 17 January and 7 October 1845.

[93]Mann also concluded a treaty between the US and Hannover in 1846 which, some believed, would allow the North Sea states to remain independent from the *Zollverein. Ibid.*, letters, 10 November 1845 and 26 March 1846.

[94]ABMFA, 2241, Steamshipping, Antwerp-New York, 1839-1889, letters, 26 January, 28 February and 4 June 1846.

[95]For wine connoisseurs, the shipment comprised eighty-one bottles of 1727 Rudesheimer Berg Rosewein, twenty-five bottles of 1822 Rudesheimer Berg Ausstich Cabernet and fifty bottles of 1783 Johanisberger Cabernet. BSA, 2-R-11, Dampschiffahrt, post- und Packetschiffahrt zwischen Bremen und VS, letters, 29 September, 7 and 14 October and 2 November 1845.

charge of the project, to give his vote to Bremen.[96] The Bremen lobby bribed the American press to stop publishing pro-Antwerp material, effectively derailing the bid.[97] The Belgian lobby then tried to promote the use of Antwerp as a port of call instead of terminus, but to no avail.

The French envoy, backed by his British colleague and the majority of New York merchants, turned Le Havre into Bremen's main rival. Johnson, from the tobacco state of Virginia, helped Congress pass a compromise favouring the Bremen tobacco lobby by choosing Edward Mills' bid over those of well established entrepreneurs such as R. Forbes, M. Sloo, Edward Collins and J. Smith. Mills who was virtually unknown in American maritime circles, received $200,000 a year for a bi-weekly service to Bremen via Southampton and subsequently was given $150,000 for a bi-weekly service to Le Havre. The lack of support from New York investors and merchants made it impossible for Mills and Gevekoht to raise the necessary capital. The lobbyist was forced to return home to seek financial support which allowed the opening of the Bremen service with *Washington* and *Hermann* offering first- and second-class crossings for $120 and $60, respectively, in June 1847.[98] Yet the ships proved no match to the Cunard Line service. Due to Mills' inability to raise the funds for the Le Havre service, American authorities assigned the subsidy to Mortimer Livingstone and his Havre Steam Navigation Company. Despite the subsidies, both lines were only qualified successes and never developed or expanded during their ten-year existence. Only the subsequently subsidized Collins Line raised American hopes of rivalling the British fleet.

Breakthrough of Transatlantic Steamshipping

If the 1840s were characterized by the growing pains of steamshipping and sceptical capitalists who refrained from investing in this branch of the shipping

---

[96]They also convinced Thomas Green, the American consul in Antwerp to support Bremen. Only the envoy in Brussels, Thomas Clemson, supported Antwerp. *Ibid.*, letters 13 and 29 December 1845; and ABMFA 2241, Steamshipping, Antwerp-New York, 1839-1889, letter, 14 April 1847.

[97]ABMFA 2241, Steamshipping, Antwerp-New York, 1839-1889, letters, 7 May and 24 June 1846.

[98]The authorities in Bremen and Prussia each contributed US $100,000, while Sachsen, Hannover, Baden, Oldenburg, Frankfurt, Nassau, Darmstadt and Hessen added US $200,000. The national pride attached to the line was reflected by the names chosen for the ships: *Hermann* alluded to the liberator of Germany from Rome, just as Washington was seen to have liberated America from England. *Ibid.*, various newspaper articles, 1847; ABMFA 2241, Steamshipping, Antwerp-New York, 1839-1889, letter, 10 May 1847; and BSA, 2-R-11, Dampschiffahrt, post- und Packetschiffahrt zwischen Bremen und VS, letter, 29 January 1846.

industry, the 1850s were marked by a turnaround with the commercial success of unsubsidized lines drawing their revenues from migrant transport. The analysis of the various prospects for the opening of a transatlantic steamship line during the 1840s illustrated the extent to which this breakthrough had been anticipated. Efforts by owners of sailing vessels to protect this lucrative market delayed but did not prevent the transition. Plans for long-distance steamship lines within the Hamburg-Le Havre range continued because of the growing awareness that a lack of such services endangered the competitive position of the ports, especially since trade through Liverpool thrived because of its steam connections. The success and failures of these ports would have an important impact on their prominence as migrant gateways in subsequent periods.

Anglo-American Rivalry

Under pressure from New York merchants, Congress awarded another contract to Edward Collins for a line to Liverpool in direct competition with Cunard.[99] The British Admiralty responded by increasing its subsidy to the market leader to allow it to expand and modernize its fleet. The rivalry quickly evolved into a matter of national prestige, fuelled by eager reports in the popular press on the battle for the blue ribbon, a distinction awarded to ships making the fastest transatlantic crossing.[100] The popular attention for the Anglo-American struggle for maritime supremacy was used by both lines to maintain or increase their subsidies.[101] The rivalry spurred technological innovation, yet behind the scenes the lines concluded a secret agreement that neutralized the competition. A month before the Collins Line's first sailing, both companies established the first steamship cartel by pooling revenues and setting minimum rates for both passengers and cargo. Cunard took the initiative to avoid a rate war out of fear that Collins might outdo him. Those fears were not unfounded because by 1852, Collins' faster and bigger ships carried more passengers than Cunard. Despite occasional price cuts, the agreement was respected and worked to the advantage of the British line by giving it protection against the superior American service. In the long run it allowed Cunard to consolidate its position in cabin passage and mail transport on the North Atlantic.

---

[99]Collins, operating a sailing passenger service with the Dramatic Line, began to lobby for subsidies in 1841 and was finally rewarded by an Act of Congress on 3 March 1847 which awarded him US $385,000 for twenty round-trip sailings per year.

[100]Crouthamel, *Bennett's New York Herald*, 39 and 87.

[101]Collins' lobbying efforts culminated in a huge inauguration party in Washington for *Baltic* which was attended by the President and 2000 prominent officials. It resulted in an increase in the subsidy to US $853,000. Cunard used the rivalry to maintain his subsidy because he was still being challenged by non-subsidized British lines.

The success of Collins' fast crossings in attracting passengers also had drawbacks, pushing the company into taking on increased costs and risks. The speed was obtained through heavy coal consumption and by straining the engines so that they were in need of constant repairs. More importantly, because of the rivalry the line suffered two shipwrecks with heavy passenger losses.[102] On the other hand, the more conservative Cunard Line never lost a ship prior to 1915, earning an impeccable reputation based on the regularity of its service and the safety of its ships, two crucial elements in the passenger business. While Cunard paid dividends to its shareholders, Collins never returned anything to his investors and was forced out of business by 1858. Collins' failure had important repercussions for American maritime policy, ending all direct financial support for deep-sea steamship lines on the Atlantic. Policies aimed at protecting domestic shipbuilders and seamen put American shipowners at such a disadvantage that the American flag virtually disappeared from the North Atlantic. With the subsequent transition from sail to steam, the lucrative migrant business, which had been dominated by American sailing packet companies, would be left almost entirely in the hands of foreign steamship enterprises.[103]

The conservative policy of the Cunard Line, combined with the Admiralty's requirements regarding shipbuilding, delayed the adaptation of technological innovations used by unsubsidized rivals. In 1850, the Inman Line introduced the iron hull and screw propellers in contrast to Cunard's wooden paddle-wheel steamers. Wooden ships were limited in size, whereas iron enabled ships of virtually any size to be built. Increased capacity permitted lower prices and hence opened steamship travel to less wealthy migrants. Engine improvements reduced coal consumption, further decreasing costs and increasing capacity. In the meantime, Liverpool had developed into *the* nodal point for transatlantic migrant traffic, attracting British, Irish, German and Scandinavian emigrants at cheap rates through feeder services via Hull. William Inman opened the market for migrant transport by steam in 1852, focussing on the quality of service and building separate compartments for women, men and

---

[102]*Artic* sank in 1854 with the loss of 300 lives. The loss without a trace of *Pacific* in 1856 signalled the beginning of the end for the American Line.

[103]Hutchins, *American Maritime Industries*, 325-357; Albion, *Rise of New York Port*, 312-335; Edward W. Sloan, "Collins versus Cunard: The Realities of a North Atlantic Steamship Rivalry, 1850-1858," *International Journal of Maritime History*, IV, No. 1 (1992), 83-100; Francis E. Hyde, *Cunard and the North Atlantic, 1840-1973: A History of Shipping and Financial Management* (London, 1975), 38-52; and Jeffrey J. Safford, "The Decline of the American Merchant Marine, 1850-1914: An Historiographical Appraisal," in Lewis R. Fischer and Gerald E. Panting (eds.), *Change and Adaptation in Maritime History: The North Atlantic Fleets in the Nineteenth Century* (St. John's, 1985), 51-85.

families while offering individual berths for each steerage passenger, three cooked meals per day, an onboard doctor, towels, soap and decent washing facilities. Despite charging £8, twice the price of sailing vessels, the line had no problem finding migrants prepared to pay the difference for the many advantages it offered. The crossing could now be made in less than two weeks, while sailing packets averaged five.[104] No longer dependent on the wind, the regularity of sailings also increased. This shortened the time during which migrants remained without income and reduced the risks of contracting disease at sea. The unsubsidized company also gained ground in the mail transport and cabin passenger markets.[105] Inman became the first long-term challenger to Cunard's monopoly and forced the line to enter the steerage business in 1860. Inman's success proved the profitability of steamshipping without subsidies based on migrant transport and inspired many new lines to follow suit. In 1856, only one in twenty-eight migrants arrived in the New World by steam, while four years later the proportion was one in three. By then increased competition had reduced the price to £5.[106] The most important impact of Inman's innovations on migration patterns was that migration became less definitive. An increasing number of migrants started to leave with the intention of returning, further reducing the barriers separating Europe and the US.

Migrant Transport by Steam in the Hamburg-Le Havre Range

Rotterdam

The unsuccessful effort to convince American authorities to include Rotterdam as a port of call caused some local merchants to change their views. The Chamber of Commerce, which initially opposed the idea, later gave its support. It also moved some prominent Rotterdam entrepreneurs to take matters into their own hands by establishing the Rotterdam-American Steamship Co. in

---

[104]Nicholas J. Evans, "The Role of Foreign-born Agents in the Development of Mass Migrant Travel through Britain, 1820-1923," in Torsten Feys, *et al.* (eds.), *Maritime Transport and Migration: The Connections between Maritime and Migration Networks* (St. John's, 2007), 51; Hyde, *Cunard*, 72; Drew Keeling, "The Transport Revolution in Transatlantic Migration, 1850-1914," *Research in Economic History*, XIX, No. 1 (1999), 41; Albion, *Rise of New York Port*, 346; and Terry Coleman, *The Liners: A History of the North Atlantic Crossing* (New York, 1977), 25-27. The first-class clippers reduced the crossing to three or four weeks, yet many migrants still made the crossing on chartered ships rather than liner services.

[105]Collins and Cunard suffered from Inman's £20 first-class rates while they were charging £35. GAR, HAL, 318.14, Wentholt Archief, letter, 7 May 1854.

[106]Albion, *Rise of New York Port*, 349; and Keeling, "Transport Revolution," 42.

1850.[107] The new company negotiated with the same shipbuilders as the Inman Line and also targeted migrants as the main source of revenue. Raising capital again proved the major obstacle as efforts to find investors in Germany, England and the US failed. The New York merchant house Boonen and Graves advised against investing in the line because of the murderous competition from Cunard; the lack of financial support from the Dutch government; and the limited volume of high-value German and Dutch goods which made the enterprise too dependent on steerage passengers.[108] Baltimore and Norfolk interests tried to induce the founders to use their ports as US terminals, but the entrepreneurs feared it would compromise their fundraising efforts since New York dominated the transatlantic trade.[109] Repeated applications for national and local subsidies were unsuccessful. The company even turned to the Prussian government, which declined because of the support it had given to Bremen. The lack of capital forced the entrepreneurs to shelve their plans.[110]

The Dutch finally awoke from their commercial daze in the 1850s. The country's colonial trade policies had led to economic stagnation and the decline of the once dominant Dutch merchant marine. Seriously lagging behind its neighbours, the government started to invest heavily in infrastructure, modernizing port facilities and expanding the railroad network. It also liberalized its commercial policies, ending a decades-long dispute with the German states over the Rhine trade. Tolls on the Voorne Channel were decreased considerably. A new trade agreement with the US put an end to the high tariffs which harmed trade between the countries. A transatlantic propaganda campaign promoted a new orientation towards the German transit trade which would be a catalyst for Dutch industrialization.[111]

---

[107]DNA, 2.05.13 Gezantschap Verenigde Staten, correspondence, 1846-1848; and GAR, HAL, 3.04.14, Wentholt Archief, 7, letters, 1850-1855.

[108]Graves was related to the Cunard family, and the merchant house collaborated with the Havre Line which underlines its expertise in the passenger business. GAR, HAL, 318.14, Wentholt Archief, 7, letter, 14 May 1851.

[109]Baltimore interests argued that its railroad connections offered the best prospects for migrants; that the company would receive much more support from local authorities; and that it would not have to deal with competitors. The American consul in Amsterdam pointed out that by using Norfolk the line would profit by freeing southern states of their dependence on Liverpool and New York. *Ibid.*, letter, 24 April 1851.

[110]M. Mees, *Geschiedenis der stoomvaart van Nederland op Amerika* (Rotterdam, 1883), 5-12; and De Boer; *125 jaar Holland-Amerika Lijn*, 7-10.

[111]DNA, 2.05.13 Gezantschap in de Verenigde Staten, correspondence, 1840-1865; Bläsing and Langenhuyzen, "Dutch Sea Transport," 102-108; and Horlings, *Economic Development*, 194-197.

Although Dutch authorities reviewed the migrant transport regulations, it was not until 1861 that a law based on Belgian and German legislation was enacted. The new law no longer required passports but toughened the inspection of ships and adapted the space requirements in US laws. A new Committee of Supervision controlled boarding houses, handled migrants' complaints and provided them with information. Its main task was to improve Rotterdam's reputation abroad in concert with the consuls.[112] But the laws came too late (table 1): in 1863, only 938 migrants passed through Rotterdam, of which a mere thirty-nine travelled directly to the US. Dutch ports only managed to redirect migrant flows with the establishment of transatlantic steamship connections, yet they would never catch their German and English rivals.

Table 1
Emigration through Continental Ports, 1846-1914 (thousands)

Year	Bremen	Hamburg	Le Havre	Antwerp	Rotterdam
1846-1850	150.4	32.1	163.8	56.1	44.7
1851-1855	262.6	140.2	224.5	72.2	13.5
1856-1860	161.5	107.0	112.4	31.3	2.5
1861-1865	122.3	127.1	59.5	17.4	8.6
1866-1870	312.6	217.6	101.9	22.3	17.2
1871-1875	67.6	81.8	137.6	17.8	15.9
1876-1880	70.2	78.7	89.0	49.8	23.7
1881-1885	126.9	190.3	131.7	169.5	52.5
1886-1890	271.7	300.1	165.7	180.2	53.2
1891-1895	303.3	285.3		177.8	108.3
1896-1900	307.4	225.2		124.5	83.0
1901-1905	680.9	479.3		330.9	235.9
1906-1910	749.5	540.8		423.3	229.8
1911-1914	577.0	460.8		266.4	229.8

Notes: Antwerp's 1911-1914 figures do not include emigrants in 1914.

Sources: Leo A. van der Valk, "Landverhuizers via Rotterdam in de negentiende eeuw," *Economisch en Sociaal historisch jaarboek* (Amsterdam, 1976), 151, based on data in Imre Ferenczi and Walter F. Willcox, *International Migrations, Vol. I: Statistics* (New York, 1929), 613, 678, 693, 703 and 740.

Antwerp

Conversely, the Belgian government had invested heavily in port infrastructure and railroad connections. Its orientation to the German transit trade paid off as

---

[112]DNA, 2.05.10.04, Gezantschap in duitse Bond Fankfurt, Nassau, Hessen en Keur-Hessen, 14, correspondence, 1861-1866; and van der Valk, "Landverhuizers," 159-160.

twenty-seven percent of the volume of its transport came from the German hinterland. Efforts to attract migrants to Antwerp resulted in a steady increase in numbers (figure 2). The governor believed that the port's commercial future rested on the decent organization of migrant transport. He pleaded for lines to invest their subsidies in measures to attract migrants, claiming that steerage passengers would make subsidies superfluous.[113]

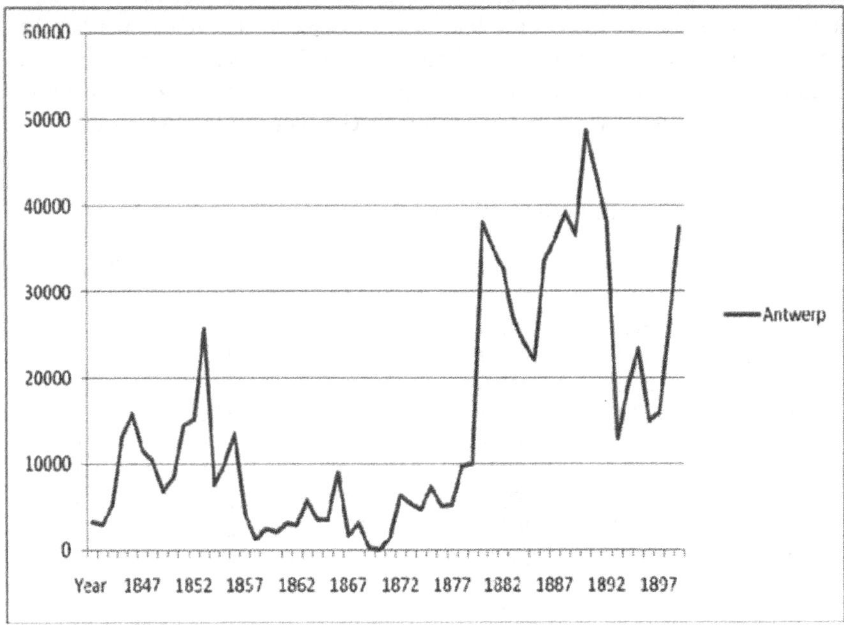

Figure 2: Number of Emigrants from the Port of Antwerp, 1843-1900

Sources: Karel Veraghtert, "De havenbewegingen te Antwerpen tijdens de negentiende eeuw: een kwantitatieve benadering" (Unpublished PhD thesis, Catholic University of Leuven, 1977), table LXI.

The Belgian government felt that the opening of a steamship line remained the top priority, especially once the rival ports of Le Havre and Bremen inaugurated their transatlantic steam services. Antwerp was falling behind in technological innovation, a race it had once led. Antwerp's conservative merchant community believed that the port's position relative to the German hinterland was in danger, and this spurred them to undertake various initia-

---

[113]Bläsing and Langenhuyzen, "Dutch Sea Transport," 108-109; Horlings, *Economic Development*, 208; and ABMFA, 2020, Emigration, II, letter, 14 January 1847; and 2241, Steamshipping, Antwerp-New York, 1839-1889, letters 17 October and 9 November 1846.

tives. Consuls tried to obtain the support of the Rhine states and Prussia for a new steamship line. Hearing about the opening of a state-sponsored line from Denmark, Belgium's envoy in Washington negotiated with his Danish colleague about possibly joining to establish an alternating service from Antwerp and Glückstadt to New York. Backed by English investors, the Antwerp migrant broker Antoine Laane planned to open a specialized service for migrant transport. J. Claes, travelling on a Belgian subsidy to promote trade connections with the US, reported on two similar American prospects. Yet the outbreak of the 1848 revolution and the poor results of the Bremen and Le Havre Line tempered enthusiasm.

Table 2
Third-Class Prices, Sail versus Steam, and Estimates of Revenues

Month	**Sail (*Francs*)**	**Steam (*Francs*)**	**Number of Steerage Passengers**	**Revenues in *Francs***
January	100	115	125	14,375
February	100	115	250	28,750
March	120	130	500	65,000
April	150	180	500	90,000
May	130	150	500	75,000
June	120	130	500	65,000
July	120	130	375	48,750
August	130	150	500	75,000
September	135	155	500	77,500
October	120	140	500	70,000
November	110	125	250	30,000
December	100	110	125	13,750

Sources: Archives of the Belgian Ministry of Foreign Affairs (ABMFA), 2241, Steamshipping, Antwerp-New York, 1839-1889, letters 1846-1849; and Rotterdam Community Archives (GAR), Holland-America Line Archive (HAL), 318.14, Wentholt Archief, 7, statutes of the Compagnie Belge-Rhéneane de Navigation Transatlantique.

Laane gained the support of Antwerp merchants but had to compete with Adolphe Le Hardy de Beaulieu for government subsidies and interest guarantees. The difficulty of raising capital pushed Laane and Le Hardy to join forces to travel through Europe and the US in an unsuccessful search for investors. The declining migrant flow and transit trade pushed the authorities to outline conditions for supporting a steamship line. Lacking the means to compete for mail and passengers with first-class steamers, the authorities opted for slower and smaller ships specialized in migrant and freight transport. From among proposals based on the draft, the government chose the one from E. Weber, C. Spillaerdt and G. Nothomb. It differed little from other proposals which illustrated clearly the ongoing shift to migrant transport by steam. The capital required for their venture was about five million *francs*. This would provide five small steamers accommodating fifty first-class and 500 steerage berths, with limited room for freight, operating on a fortnightly service. The prices in the table 2 include provisions, estimated at ten *francs*, and the head-tax, hospital and New York port costs estimated at thirty *francs*.[114]

An important competitive advantage for steam over sailing was their speed, which of course reduced the cost for provisions. Sailing vessels needed to provide food for ninety days, and laws compelled captains to distribute the remainder of the supplies among steerage passengers upon arrival to avoid these being withheld for sale after the trip.[115] The laws were not adapted to include steamships, giving them an important advantage in undercutting on price. Table 2 also shows that prices fluctuated seasonally, peaking in the spring and summer. The Minister of Foreign Affairs defended the project in Parliament, describing migrant transport as one of the catalysts of maritime business. Despite fears of setting a dangerous precedent, government granted the company a guarantee of four percent on the capital besides a subsidy of 1200 *francs* per sailing and an exemption from all port dues.[116] Emigration Inspector Thielens was appointed as government commissioner of the company while Consul Henri Mali represented the line in New York where he was responsible for obtaining freight for the eastbound leg and selling passenger tickets in the US. The Société Générale, which functioned as a national bank, bought 1000 shares; combined with 1500 stock options taken by Antwerp merchants, this allowed the company to start operations in 1853. The consular corps promoted the opening, but again the project failed. Shoddy shipbuilding delayed the line's opening to 1856, and the poor quality of the ships and mistaken cost estimates led to serious losses. After the Crimean War, many vessels returned to transatlantic service, creating a tonnage glut and depressing prices; this combination forced the company to fold in 1858. With this failure Antwerp began to decline as a migrant gateway. Despite government aid, the port could not gain a prominent position in the trade. The Bremen lobbyist De

---

[114]ABMFA 2241, Steamshipping, Antwerp-New York, 1839-1889, correspondence, 1850-1853; and prospect of the company, 1853.

[115]In Belgium, the laws were revised in 1855 to include steamships and required provisions for thirty-five days (lowered to twenty in 1858).

[116]ABMFA, 2241, Steamshipping, Antwerp-New York, 1839-1889, summary of parliamentary debates, 10 June 1853; BGSA, TO 74, 36, Scheepvaart, correspondence 1853.

Mann's assessment of Antwerp as "the frog on the table, which wished to reach the size of an ox" seemed true for the time being.[117]

Le Havre

Like the Netherlands, France lagged behind Belgium, Germany and England in the provision of infrastructure. Due to a lack of capital and unsympathetic government policies, the railroad network remained under-developed up to the 1850s.[118] The same was true for transatlantic steamshipping which despite government aid failed to be a success. Two state-funded attempts to open a Le Havre-New York line in 1841 and 1847 were short-lived. The French merchant marine lost ground on England, the US and the German states. Indeed, American merchants controlled nearly the entire Franco-American trade: figures for 1841, for example, show that eighty-six percent of the trade was carried in US vessels.[119]

After the 1848 revolution, reformers attempts to revive the economy were obstructed by a political stalemate which only ended with the *coup d'état* by Louis-Napoleon Bonaparte. The banking revolution which began in the previous decades with the introduction of joint-stock companies and limited liability took a decisive turn when the Pereire brothers founded Crédit Mobilier in 1852. This institution, like the Société Générale in Belgium, provided the means to finance industrial development, making capital available to modernize port infrastructure and expand steamship lines and railroads. The Pereire brothers were the driving force behind the establishment of the transatlantic shipping company Compagnie Générale Maritime in 1855. It included a line to New York which targeted third-class westbound and second-class eastbound passengers as the primary source of revenue. Nonetheless, after a few sailings the service was discontinued.[120] It took another nine years before the opening

[117]ABMFA, Consuls et Consulats, New York, 623, and letters, 1852-1861; and BSA, 2-R-11, Dampschiffahrt, post-und Packetschiffahrt zwischen Bremen und VS, letter, 13 December 1845.

[118]Michael S. Smith, *The Emergence of Modern Business Enterprise in France, 1800-1930* (Cambridge, MA, 2006), 64-65.

[119]Albion, *Rise of New York Port*, 320-324; ADN, New York, 7, letters, 18 August 18 and 16, 19 and 24 September 1842; ABMFA, 2020, Emigration, II, letter, 20 May 1847, and 2241, Steamshipping, Antwerp-New York, 1839-1889, letter, 27 September 1845.

[120]Smith, *Emergence*, 67-69; ADN, New York, 11, letters 26 March 1856 and 12 November 1860; and Centre d'Archives du monde du Travail, Roubaix (CAMT), 9AQ, 2-7, dossiers des assemblées générales, 1855-1865.

of a successful Le Havre-New York service with the establishment of the Compagnie Générale Transatlantique (CGT).

Until then, various American entrepreneurs provided first-class sailing and steam connections on the route. The ships of the subsidized service provided by M. Livingstone proved no match to the Collins and Cunard steamers. Cunard opened a feeder service from Le Havre to compete with the new line for continental goods. Meanwhile, a law protecting British ships in the transport of national goods prevented Livingstone from competing for British goods. His line made losses and could not meet the requirements for the American mail subsidy. The Belgian envoy in Washington, backed by a group of American entrepreneurs headed by Ambrose Thompson, used the opportunity to buy out the line and convince the postmaster general and Congress to sail to Antwerp instead. An intensive lobbying campaign led by Livingstone and the French envoy to Washington delayed the transition thanks to the fact that the line started to make profits.[121] Those results inspired Cornelius Vanderbilt to compete on the route with a new steamship line. The American Civil War, however, forced both companies to fold.

In the meantime, the French government amended its migrant transport laws which had remained relatively unchanged since the 1830s. The old policies tended to restrict the movement as the three-month closure of the French borders to all migrants during the cholera scare of 1849 illustrated. Some years later, the Prussian government used the lack of any legislation protecting migrants as an excuse to prohibit the transatlantic migration of nationals through French ports, diverting them to Bremen and Hamburg instead. This led the French to modify the migrant transport polices to facilitate rather than obstruct the transit. The imperial decree and laws of 1855 and 1860 brought French regulations closer to the German and Belgian models. The laws facilitated the subsequent takeover of migrant transport by the CGT.[122]

Hanseatic Cities: Bremen and Hamburg

With its active efforts to attract the American subsidized steamship line, Bremen characterized itself as *the* port of the *Zollverein* with direct connections

[121]Thompson later tried unsuccessfully to obtain subsidies from the Belgian and Dutch governments. ABMFA, 2241, Steamshipping, Antwerp-New York, 1839-1889, letters, 23 May 23 1852-12 February 1854.

[122]This included establishing commissions to supervise transport on land and at sea. Emigration agents now had to obtain a concession. The rules included measures regarding contracts, provisions, space allocations and the like. See Fouché, *Émigration Alsacienne*, 69-78; and Marie-Françoise Vannoise-Pochulu, "La politique de la Compagnie Générale Transatlantique et l'émigration vers les États-Unis à partir du Havre (1875-1914)" (Unpublished MA thesis, University of Paris XII, 1993), 138-142.

worldwide, much to the dismay of Hamburg. Initially, the Hamburg Senate opposed the migrant trade, passing a law which blocked the entry of migrants to the port. Trade relations centred upon Britain rather than the North Atlantic, but Bremen's success led to a policy change in the 1840s. Hamburg ships started to call at Bremen to load migrants on their way to Britain. The Senate also passed laws based on the Bremen model to stimulate direct migration from the port. The Hamburg Patriotic Society established a bureau to gather and spread information on opportunities abroad and to assist migrants during their journey. Yet because of the strong trade relations with the British Isles, the majority of this traffic was indirect. The laws failed to include the indirect passage, which was cheaper but more arduous, earning Hamburg a poor reputation as a migrant gateway. Indirect migration patterns persisted throughout the century, obstructing the efforts of Hamburg shippers to open direct lines.[123]

As migration fever spread to Hamburg's northern and eastern hinterland, the port's commercial relations with the US improved. Fuelled by the increasing rivalry with Bremen, Hamburg merchants founded the Hamburg-Amerikanischen Packetfahrt-Actien-Gesellschaft (HAPAG). Its New York-bound sailing vessels offered room for twenty first-class and 200 steerage passengers. The company went to great lengths to expand the migrant agent network and soon developed into a first-class company. This success was crowned by the inauguration of a steamship service in 1855 with ships offering fifty-four first-, 136 second- and 310 third-class berths, illustrating the growing diversification of the migrant trade. The cornerstones were laid for what would grow to become the biggest shipping company in the world.[124]

Bremen, however, retained a leading role in migrant transport from the continent despite its natural disadvantages and inferior geographic location. Its pioneering role in migrant transport laws bore fruit when it consistently had lower mortality rates than Rotterdam and Hamburg. As Raymond Cohn has noted, there was a direct correlation between port sanitary conditions and mortality.[125] The Belgian envoy in Berlin attributed this to the dynamism of the

---

[123]ABMFA, 2241, Steamshipping, Antwerp-New York, 1839-1889, letter, 28 June 1842; Gelberg, *Auswanderung nach Übersee*, 10-16; Bretting and Bickelmann, *Auswanderungagenturen und Auswanderungsvereine*, 28; and Walker, *Germany and the Emigration*, 88-92.

[124]As in other ports, numerous failures preceded HAPAG's successful steamship service. ABMFA, 2241, Steamshipping, Antwerp-New York, 1839-1889, Consul of Hamburg to MFA, 31 March 1851; Hans-Jürgen Witthöft, *HAPAG: Hamburg-Amerika Linie* (Herford, 1973), 9-18; and Susanne Wiborg and Klaus Wiborg, *Unser Feld ist die Welt, 1847-1997: 150 Jahre Hapag-Lloyd* (Hamburg, 1997), 16-48.

[125]Raymond L. Cohn, "Mortality on Immigrant Voyages to New York, 1836-1853," *Journal of Economic History*, XLIV, No. 2 (1984), 298.

Bremen migrant brokers who did not wait until migrants arrived at the port but energetically took the migrant at the point of departure and guided him until his final destination.[126] The interdependence between their success in the migrant trade and the development of the flourishing tobacco industry may explain the extra zeal of Bremen merchants. This dynamic activity also won them the battle for the subsidized American line which was fuelled not only by commercial but also by political motives. Success in North Atlantic trade offered a way to remain outside the grip of the *Zollverein* which increased its pressure to gain control of the Hanseatic ports and their merchant marines after the 1848 revolution and the Danish-German war.

The poor results of the American line did not deter Bremen merchants from opening new steamship services which specialized in the port's prime commodity. A. Fritze and Company managed one such service, yet its outdated wooden paddle steamers did not produce the same results as Inman's iron screw-propelled ships. The appearance of Vanderbilt's European Line and the North German Lloyd (NGL) using modern steamers drove Fritze from the North Atlantic route. Only the NGL maintained its position after the US Civil War, monopolizing the Bremen migrant trade to the US and in the process becoming the fourth biggest shipping company globally.[127]

Breakthrough of Steam in the Low Countries

In 1863, Belgium and many of the nations trading with Antwerp bought the free navigation of the Scheldt. The Dutch used the lump-sum payment to modernize the infrastructure and bring it on a par with its neighbours.[128] The abolition of the toll triggered a keen rivalry between Rotterdam and Antwerp for North Atlantic trade. Entrepreneurs from Amsterdam, Rotterdam and Flushing battled to open the first steamship line to New York at the end of the 1860s. Despite the support of the local merchant community for each project, raising capital remained difficult. The traditional way of spreading the risk - using a large investor base and dividing the shares into sixty-four parts - had been replaced by a system based on a limited number of investors. Specialized shipowners who both managed and owned ships began to appear. Yet the large

[126]ABMFA, 2241, Steamshipping, Antwerp-New York, 1839-1889, Jean-Baptiste Nothomb (envoy to Berlin) to MFA, 13 June 1849.

[127]Armgort, *Bremen-Bremerhaven-New York*, 46-47.

[128]Gustaaf Asaert, *et al. Antwerpen een geschenk van de Schelde: De Antwerpse haven door de eeuwen heen* (Brussels, 1993), 93-97; and Karel Veraghtert, "State Policy and Maritime Business in Belgium, 1850-1914," in Randi Ertesvåg, David J. Starkey and Anne Tove Austbø (eds.), *The North Sea: Maritime Industries and Public Intervention* (Stavanger, 2002), 73.

sums needed for steamships, which were more costly to construct and operate than sailing vessels, required new structures. The introduction of joint-stock companies facilitated the accumulation of capital, but only after limited liability replaced private partnerships in the 1860s did large-scale steam liner services develop. The maritime world only slowly adopted the new legal structures, fearing that they might encourage opportunistic behaviour. The ventures that did adopt them usually consisted of private networks bound together by business or personal ties. Steamship entrepreneurs still relied heavily on personal contacts to raise capital.[129] The Holland-America Line exemplified this.

Antoine Plate, whose father was behind the Rotterdam attempt to found a transatlantic steam line in the 1850s, was unable to raise the funds needed to operate a service with four steamers. He then set up a limited partnership with Rotterdam merchant Otto Reuchlin and ordered two small steamers to transport goods and steerage passengers. The opening of the line resulted in the refusal of the government to subsidize the Flushing entrepreneurs, who soon shelved their project. Clearly, the authorities did not want to compromise the success of the two non-subsidized lines in Amsterdam and Rotterdam. The success of the first sailings by the Rotterdam line attracted not only new local investors, such as the directors of the Rotterdam Trade Union and the Rotterdam Bank, but also outsiders, such as the Groningen entrepreneur Willem Scholten, who became the biggest shareholder. Plate, Reuchlin and Co. expanded and restructured in a public limited-liability company under the name Netherlands-American Steamship Company, popularly known as the Holland-America Line (HAL).[130] The company shared many characteristics with similar British enterprises. A wealthy businessman was identified with the project, something unique to liner shipping. The founders had been shipping agents, and the majority of the investors came from the same port community. The major difference was the weak interests of shipbuilders in HAL. British shipyards dominated steamship construction and developed strong ties with British shipowners through local networks. Operating outside the local networks, Dutch owners took longer to establish strong relations with British

---

[129]Gordon Boyce, *Information, Mediation and Institutional Development: The Rise of Large-Scale Enterprise in British Shipping, 1870-1919* (Manchester, 1995), 27-33; and Simon P. Ville, *Transport and the Development of the European Economy, 1750-1918* (London, 1990), 85-89.

[130]Antoine Plate, "Onze Stoomvaart," *De Economist*, XVIII (1869), 558-571; van der Valk, "Landverhuizers," 161-162; Cees Zevenbergen, *Toen zij uit Rotterdam vertrokken: emigratie via Rotterdam door de eeuwen heen* (Rotterdam, 1990), 39-40; De Boer, *125 jaar Holland-Amerika Lijn* 10-19; A.D. Wentholt, *Brug over den Oceaan: een eeuw geschiedenis van de Holland-Amerika Lijn* (Rotterdam, 1973), 25-33; and Henri Reuchlin, *Zeil strijken, stoom op* (Rotterdam, 1975), 68-72.

shipbuilders, yet the latter eventually played an important role in the further development of the company.[131]

The quality of a line's management was reflected by a strict regularity and ability to maximize capacity utilization while minimizing costs by attracting a constant flow of cargo and passengers in both directions. Both cargo and passenger booking agents played key roles in these activities.[132] HAL's managers put an emphasis on steerage passengers and wanted a broker who committed to sell for the company exclusively. Brokers who booked for various lines directed most of their business to companies offering the best service and lowest price, something established lines could offer more easily than new lines. Unable to find an established German broker, the HAL directors contracted the biggest Dutch migrant brokers who formed the firm Van Es, Wambersie and Ruys which was committed to positioning agents in European out-migration regions to promote the line and contract migrants in exchange for a commission per booking. John Wambersie, the former American consul in Rotterdam, played a prominent role as his shipbroking firm Wambersie and Son also booked the cargo for the westbound leg. As passenger brokers, they combined the sale of ocean and railroad passage, receiving a 12.5 percent commission on each ticket sold for the American Erie Railroad Company.[133]

The economic downturn midway through the 1870s tempered the optimism about steamship companies when the construction boom overreached itself. Many companies had been founded simultaneously, thus increasing competition in a falling market. This created a permanent overcapacity on the North Atlantic and led to rate wars.[134] Confronted with the fluctuations characteristic of the migrant trade, the HAL struggled more than the longer-established, first-class liners that carried mail and cabin passengers and were less sensitive to business cycles.[135] In 1877, the HAL reorganized and took over the passenger business in Europe, approaching new migrant brokers and

---

[131]De Nijs, *In veilige Haven*, 34-58; and Boyce, *Information, Mediation*, 56-60.

[132]Boyce, *Information, Mediation*, 36.

[133] GAR, HAL, 318.14, Wentholt Archief, 9-2, minutes of annual meetings, May 1871-January 1872, and letters, 27 March and 26 June 26 1872; Swierenga, "Journey Across," 107 and 114-117; and van der Valk, "Landverhuizers," 156-158.

[134]HAPAG's prices dropped from fifty-five *thalers* midway 1873 to thirty a year later. British lines offered rates of £2 from Liverpool; Jean Heffer, *Le port de New York et le commerce extérieur Américain, 1860-1900* (Paris, 1986), 319-320.

[135]Derek H. Aldcroft, *Studies in British Transport History, 1870-1970* (Newton Abbot, 1974), 287; and Hyde, *Cunard*, 62-68.

agents to book directly through the company. One of them, Prins and Zwanenberg of Groningen, drew their passengers from the Dutch and German hinterland but also had representatives among Dutch settlements in the US selling prepaid tickets. Through the American representatives, the brokers expanded their activities to land speculation in order to direct migrants to their properties.[136] Prins and Zwanenberg underline the diversity and transatlantic dimension of migrant brokers' activities.

The Royal Netherlands Steamship Co (RNS) in Amsterdam and the Red Star Line (RSL) in Antwerp, rival lines that began at the same time as the HAL, also struggled. The RNS refused to cooperate with the HAL and paid dearly for its audaciousness by having to suspend its New York service.[137] With the RSL, Belgian authorities saw their lengthy efforts to open a direct steamship line from Antwerp finally rewarded. When the migration flow came to a complete standstill in 1871, the government appointed a commission to revive the migrant trade and propose new laws reconciling business interests with public order and humanity. A new law granted a mail subsidy of 500,000 *francs* for a direct steamship line to the US, trying to lure foreign lines as previous domestic attempts had failed.[138] It drew the attention of the Pennsylvania Railroad Company (PRR) which wanted to shift the interest of the American fleet back to the North Atlantic where it had once thrived. The PRR's main objective, however, was to divert part of the lucrative passenger business from New York rivals to its home port of Philadelphia. Considering maritime lines as natural extensions of its services, it provided substantial financial backing for an American-flag steamship line known as the American Line. Still doubting the success of a line under the American flag, the PRR also supported another venture, the International Navigation Company (INC), launched by shipbrokers Peter Wright and Sons. Because vessels built in American shipyards cost approximately thirty percent more than those built in Europe; combined with the high wages of domestic crews, these constituted important sur-

---

[136]GAR, HAL, 318.14, Wentholt Archief, 18, letter January 31, 1877; Paul Gottheil, "Historical Development of Steamship Agreements and Conferences in the American Foreign Trade," *Annals of the American Academy of Political and Social Sciences*, LV, No. 1 (1914), 59; and Swierenga, "Journey Across," 116-117.

[137]De Boer, *125 jaar Holland-Amerika Lijn*, 10-20; and GAR, HAL, 318.14, Wentholt Archief, 18, letter, 4 May 1881.

[138]Spelkens, "Belgian Migration," 87-89; Greta Devos, "Belgische Overheidssteun aan scheepvaartlijnen, 1867-1914," in Kaerl Degryse and Christian Koninckx (eds.), *Bijdrage tot de internationale maritieme geschiedenis* (Brussels, 1988), 81-97; Veraghtert, "State Policy," 72-84; and BGSA, I 215, 4054, House of Representatives, session 252, 5 July 1887.

charges.[139] Peter Wright's close ties with Antwerp merchants, the port's central location and the favourable predisposition of the Belgian government led to an agreement for a Belgian-flagged service.

The Belgian authorities granted a yearly subsidy of US $100,000 for postal services; provided free wharfage at Antwerp; granted exemptions from light and pilotage dues; gave a rebate on Belgian coal used by the company; and agreed that Belgian train stations would serve as selling points for ocean passages free of charge. In return, Clement Griscom, representing the American interests, agreed to split the service between Philadelphia and New York. The consular corps and American owners organized huge advertising campaigns to make the line known to the public. Despite the depressed business conditions and keen competition, the RSL produced encouraging results while the American Line accumulated losses. The PRR board therefore entrusted the responsibility for operating the American ships to Peter Wright and Sons in 1874. The combination allowed cost-cutting and the operation of ships on a complementary service. A decade, later the INC took over the American Line which continued to sail as a wholly-owned subsidiary of the company.[140]

Migration as an International Trade Issue

Carl Strikwerda has refuted the claim that demographic and economic causes were the most important determinants of migration flows in favour of an argument that stressed the role of the state. He correctly points out that during the last two centuries, international regimes in the Western world have strongly affected the "tides of migration," despite the lack of an international migration regime, through trade and diplomacy: "the significant degree of international cooperation, free trade and economic integration which arose in the nineteenth century was only possible because of this diplomatic transformation which created the first modern international regime."[141] What seems to have

---

[139]Salaries of British crews were half those of American seamen. When adding the higher cost of coal, supplies and insurance, an American ship annually cosy US $50,000 more to operate; Vernon E.W. Finch, *The Red Star Line and the International Mercantile Marine Company* (Antwerp, 1988), 35.

[140]BGSA, I 215, 4055, letters, 17 September 1871; and 4056, I 215, letter, 4 April and 14 August 1873, agreement between the International Navigation Company (INC) and Belgian government, n.d., and report, 1877; William H. Flayhart III, "The Expansion of American Interests in Transatlantic Commerce and Trade, 1865-1893," in Starkey and Harlaftis (eds.). *Global Markets*, 129-137; Flayhart, *The American Line, 1872-1902* (New York, 2000), 41 and 79-85; Finch, *Red Star Line*, 23-37.

[141]Strikwerda, "Tides of Migrations," 375; and Carl Strikwerda and Camille Guerin-Gonzales, "Labor Migrations and Politics," in Guerin-Gonzales and Strikwerda

escaped the attention of both migration and maritime historians is the central role of transatlantic migrant transport. The growing flow converted the migrant into a lucrative product, determining trade movements on the North Atlantic. Some authorities backed the development of the migrant trade to support the national economy through which they tried to increase their political influence, and in the case of the US, Bremen and Belgium, aimed to consolidate their political independence. In the wake of this, European and American authorities signed new liberal trade treaties spurring Atlantic economic integration. Based on the lack of laws restricting or encouraging nationals from moving or foreigners from entering, it has been wrongly assumed that nineteenth-century governments had little impact on migration. For authorities with ports involved in the North Atlantic trade, the main preoccupation was not so much who moved, but much more how and through what ports they moved.

In the US, legislation regulating how people moved was increasingly used to control the quality and quantity of migrants, yet port competition and the shipping lobby prevented these issues from have a great impact on the trade. In Europe, as was the case for Antwerp, Bremen and later for Hamburg, authorities made conscious efforts to facilitate the transit of migrants, reconciling this with initial fears of burdening the public welfare system. Authorities supported the opening of new routes to the ports and adapted border controls to allow the greatest flow possible to pass. The consular corps assisted migrant brokers in expanding their agent network and advertised migrant gateways, swelling the information flow about the "New World" and ways to reach it. These diplomatic agents transferred information on the organization and legislation of the trade in rival ports, spurring the spread of efficient measures to attract the flow. With the growing awareness of the importance of good service and sterling reputation to attract the trade, governments passed laws protecting the migrant during the crossing but also while travelling to, and during their stay in, the port. These measures contributed to the low death rates among passengers heading to the US, which were barely higher than the rates on land.[142] The laws together with the increasing organization of migrant transport from place of departure to the final destination reduced the costs, risks and fears in moving. The effect of these measures is best illustrated by comparing the passenger numbers of the above- mentioned ports with the former natural gateway, Rotterdam, where the authorities refrained from attracting trade.

Early migration policies were embedded in maritime and trade policies. As the Belgian case illustrates, the movement through Antwerp inspired authorities to encourage the migration of nationals. Yet this practice was

---

(eds.), *The Politics of Immigrant Workers: Labor Activism and Migration in the World Economy since 1830* (New York, 1993. Rev. ed., New York, 1998), 3-45.

[142]Cohn, "Mortality," 289-300.

stopped as soon as it threatened Antwerp's competitive position as a migrant gateway. The importance of the international migrant trade outweighed that of emigration policies of citizens in countries of departure. It also outweighed that of immigration policies toward aliens in the countries of arrival, as the lack of American restrictions and the reluctance to implement them during the first half of the nineteenth century indicate. Yet that this does not diminish the impact of governments on the flows is illustrated by their involvement in the opening of transatlantic steamship lines. With little capital available, government subsidies were crucial for the establishment of the pioneering transatlantic steamship connections. The aid given out of commercial, political and naval considerations triggered a fierce competition that became the object of national prestige. The diplomatic corps played a key role in the opening of such lines by lobbying for foreign state support; finding foreign investors; promoting the line; renegotiating new trade and postal treaties; or acting as shipping agents for the lines. During the steamship era, consuls retained their importance as informers about newly developing markets that could lead to the opening of new routes.[143] Yet the difficulties of successfully applying technological innovations spurred by this rivalry are illustrated by the many failures. These show that from the beginning steamship lines had targeted migrants as a source of revenue. Sailing vessels took measures to protect this lucrative business but could not prevent steamship lines from penetrating the market in the 1850s. In Hamburg, Bremen and Liverpool, where authorities supported the development of the trade, successful lines opened before the US Civil War allowed them to obtain a dominant position in the migrant trade. Despite government support, Antwerp failed to open a line until the 1870s and fell behind. So did Le Havre, as the trade shifted from sail to steam, driving out the American ships to which it had owed its dominant position. The delay in discovering that the trade was in the national interest, as in Rotterdam, created a disadvantage that would never be overcome during the steamship era.

[143]Nicolas Manitakis, "Transatlantic Emigration and Maritime Transport from Greece to the US, 1890-1912: A Major Area of European Steamship Company Competition for Migrant Traffic," in Feys, *et al.* (eds.), *Maritime Transport and Migration: The Connections between Maritime and Migration Networks* (St. John's, 2007), 63-74.

Part II
The Impact of Steamshipping on Transatlantic Migration, 1870-1914

Introduction

The impact of steamshipping on migration patterns has not gone unnoticed by migration historians. Steam propulsion reduced the duration of the crossing to less than two weeks and increased the regularity of sailings. The shorter transit and travelling times limited the period during which the migrant remained without income. Mortality rates dropped to below one percent. With the reduced costs, time and risks, migration became less permanent. A growing number of single individuals made the crossing with the intention of accumulating a certain amount of capital before returning, instead of moving permanently with the family. Steamships gained so much popularity with migrants that by the end of the Civil War in 1865 the fleet could not meet the demand. Attracted by the high dividends paid out by steamship lines, new ventures mushroomed, driving sailing ships off the main North Atlantic routes by 1873.[1]

Yet as Francis Hyde has noted, "the real point to grasp is that it was the steamship which changed the whole nature, organization and profitability of the migrant trade."[2] Only because of the increased organization and commercialization of this trade was the transatlantic migration movement able to attain the sheer volume it did. Maritime and migration networks have too often been considered as parallel webs, but the commercialization of migrant transport firmly connected both of them. These networks encompassed the entire Atlantic world, connecting state authorities, business and labour interests with the individual migrant. The works of Rolf Engelsing and Marianne Wockek in

---

[1]Raymond L. Cohn, "Mortality on Immigrant Voyages to New York, 1836-1853," *Journal of Economic History*, XLIV, No. 2 (1984), 299; Cohn, "The Transition from Sail to Steam in Immigration to the United States," *Journal of Economic History*, LXV, No. 2 (2005), 469-495; and Jean Heffer, *Le port de New York et le commerce extérieur Américain, 1860-1900* (Paris, 1986), 316-318. During the so called "record years" (1860-1873), the returns on invested capital reached heights of as much as twenty percent in 1865 and 1866 for some German companies.

[2]Francis E. Hyde, *Cunard and the North Atlantic, 1840-1973: A History of Shipping and Financial Management* (London, 1975), 23.

analyzing how the business was organized during the golden age of sail have not been followed up by studies analyzing the true impact of steam on the organization of the migrant trade.[3] With the transition from sail to steam and the subsequent concentration of the migrant transport business in the hands of one or a limited number of steamship companies in major European ports, a shift from port to company competition took place. In the following chapters we will discuss how company agents of the Holland-America Line (HAL) took over the efforts of consuls abroad to attract the migrant flow to Rotterdam. In the process, promoting the good reputation of Rotterdam as a migrant gateway became ever-more associated with the services offered by the HAL. Migrants no longer migrated through a specific port but rather with a particular company whose reputation often reflected that of the harbour. The brand of Rotterdam as migrant gateway was used and eventually usurped by the HAL.

Due to the lack of interest in passenger transport in much of the scholarly literature, our knowledge about these maritime giants is sparse, and no one has analyzed their impact on the migrant trade. The existing literature is mainly of the popularizing genre and often has been sponsored by the company.[4] Robin Bastin's work on the organization of migrant transport by the Cunard Line is a notable exception, although the archives did not allow an in-depth analysis. In particular, the formation and functioning of shipping cartels remained unexplored until recently.[5] The work of Erich Murken is still the only study encompassing the working of the various shipping cartels regulating

---

[3]Rolf Engelsing, *Bremen als Auswandererhafen, 1683-1880* (Bremen, 1961); and Marianne S. Wokeck, *Trade in Strangers: The Beginnings of Mass Migration to North America* (University Park, PA, 1998; reprint, University Park, PA, 2003).

[4]See, for example, Marthe Barbance, *Histoire de la Compagnie Générale Transatlantique* (Paris, 1955); G.J. de Boer, *125 jaar Holland-Amerika Lijn, 1873-1998* (Rotterdam, 1998); Dick Schaap, *Brug naar de zeven zeeen: Holland Amerika Lijn 100 jaar* (Rotterdam, 1973); Vernon E.W. Finch, *The Red Star Line and the International Mercantile Marine Company* (Antwerp, 1988); Nico Guns, *Holland-Amerika Lijn: een beknopte geschiedenis van een rederij* (Rotterdam, 2004); William H. Miller, *Going Dutch: The Holland America Line Story* (London, 1998); Charles Offrey, *Cette Grande Dame qui fut la Transat* (Paris, 1994); Robert Vervoort, *Red Star Line* (Antwerp, 1999); and A.D. Wentholt, *Brug over den Oceaan: een eeuw geschiedenis van de Holand-Amerika Lijn* (Rotterdam, 1973).

[5]Robin Bastin, "Cunard and the Liverpool Emigrant Traffic, 1860-1900" (Unpublished MA thesis, University of Liverpool, 1971). Two important exceptions appeared simultaneously to the present work and hence could not be incorporated: Drew Keeling, *The Business of Transatlantic Migration between Europe and the United States, 1900-1914* (Zurich, 2012); and Per Kristian Sebak, "A Transatlantic Migratory Bypass: Scandinavian Shipping Companies and Transmigration, 1898-1929" (Unpublished PhD thesis, University of Bergen, 2012).

the traffic of freight, cabin and steerage passengers on the North Atlantic. He focussed on the negotiations that led to the agreements without looking at their impact on the price of the crossing, the relationship between shipping companies and the migrant agent network, the further integration of the Atlantic transport network (including inland transfers), their influence as a lobby group on migration policies on both sides of the Atlantic, the means used by these companies to circumvent restrictive regulations, and many other similar issues.[6] The following chapters, based predominantly on the archives of the HAL, intend to fill that lacuna in the literature. The main object of this study is the American market for ocean passages - hence the selling of prepaid and return tickets. The particular nature of the migrant transport business was shaped by chain-migration patterns based on a vast network of agents on both sides of the Atlantic which created market-specific features that turned the foreland into an important catalyst for the passenger lines. The HAL archives shed new light on the working of the migrant agent network, the formation of shipping cartels, the activities of the shipping lobby and their impact on the enforcement of migration laws.

---

[6]Erich Murken, *Die grossen transatlantischen Linienreederei-Verbande, Pools und Interessengemeinschaften bis zum Ausbruch des Weltkrieges: Ihre Entstehung, Organitsation und Wirksamkeit* (Jena, 1922).

Chapter 1
The Role of Middlemen

As Michael Miller has observed, Atlantic migration only reached a fever pitch as a result of the business networks comprising lodging house owners, local agents, recruiters, labour agencies, migrant brokers and trading, railroad and shipping companies.[1] Yet most migration studies treat the vast networks of migrant agents as parallel entities existing beside chain-migration patterns and having little or no impact on migrant flows. Migrant agents are treated as mere travelling agents, facilitating demographic movements without stimulating them. Such studies, however, neglect the fact that transatlantic migration patterns developed around pre-existing maritime trade routes and networks which reinforced these chains. How passenger liners integrated the widespread pre-existing networks of migrant brokers and agents remains unclear. Hartmut Bickelmann and Agnes Bretting suggest that migrant brokers and agents lost their influence when shipping companies gained control of the forwarding business by separating freight and passenger services with the transition from sail to steam.[2] The records of the Holland-America Line (HAL) which employed these agents will shed new light on the working relations during the steamship era.

With the introduction of steam, the American market for ocean passage tickets gained importance as the expanding return, prepaid and remittance markets demonstrate. The concentration of migrants in ethnic communities generated demands for specific products and services, which in turn created opportunities for immigrant entrepreneurs with unique qualifications to fill.[3] Ethnic ties played an important role for newcomers who often found in immi-

---

[1]Michael B. Miller, "Pilgrims' Progress: The Business of the Hajj," *Past and Present,* No. 191 (2006), 205.

[2]Hartmut Bickelmann, "The Emigration Business," in Günter Moltman (ed.). *Germans to America: 300 Years of Immigration, 1683-1983* (Stuttgart, 1982), 135; and Agnes Bretting and Hartmut Bickelmann, *Auswanderungagenturen und Auswanderungsvereine im 19. und 20. Jahrhundert* (Stuttgart, 1991), 84-90.

[3]Douglas Massey, "Why Does Immigration Occur? A Theoretical Synthesis," in Charles Hirschman, Philip Kasinitz and Josh DeWind (eds.), *The Handbook of International Migration: The American Experience* (Chicago, 1999), 39; and Dirk Hoerder, *Cultures in Contact: World Migrations in the Second Millennium* (Durham, NC, 2002), 17.

grant entrepreneurs emissaries "to America within America." Yet despite the important role of ethnicity on the formation and function of the American business community, it has received little attention in business history.[4] Jared Day's cross-ethnic analysis describing the general features of "immigrant bankers" still awaits a detailed investigation.[5] This chapter reassesses the key role of agents in the migration process, connecting the individual migrant to shipping companies. They were the middlemen working on what Dirk Hoerder labelled the "meso-level," mediating networks and linking individuals to world systems.[6] To understand these middlemen, we first need to look at the debate about their impact in the migration and maritime literature. The terminology of migrant brokers, expedients, agents, runners, etc., will be discussed to deconstruct the various layers of the vast agent network. European and American legislation will be compared, followed by an in-depth analysis of the American network, discussing the profile of these agents, the services rendered, advertising strategies and the pressures they suffered at the turn of the century. This will highlight the significance of ethnic ties in the migrant business where banking services and ocean passage sales were of crucial importance.

Primary Sources and the Debate on Migrant Agent Activity

Dillingham Commission

The mania for the collection of information by legislative committees during the Progressive Era culminated in the forty-one volumes compiled by the Dillingham Commission (DC), a congressional committee charged with investigating the "immigration question." One volume in particular (volume thirty-seven) dealt with the causes of emigration from Europe and the influence of shipping companies and migrant agents. The conclusion did not differ much from the prevailing view: "To say that steamship lines are responsible, directly or indirectly for this unnatural immigration is not the statement of a theory, but

---

[4]Charles Dellheim, "The Business of Jews," in Kenneth Lipartito and David B. Sicilia (eds.), *Constructing Corporate America: History, Politics, Culture* (New York, 2004), 229-231.

[5]For an overview on the sparse historiography about immigrant banks, see Jared N. Day, "Credit, Capital and Community: Informal Banking in Immigrant Communities in the United States 1880-1924," *Financial History Review*, IX, No. 1 (2002), 65 and 77-78.

[6]Dirk Hoerder, "Migration in the Atlantic Economies: Regional European Origins and Worldwide Expansions," in Hoerder and Leslie Page Moch (eds.), *European Migrants: Global and Local Perspectives* (Boston, 1996), 84.

a fact."[7] The continuous advertising campaigns by shipping companies and the spread of propaganda on opportunities in America by migrant agents caught the Commission's attention as the assistance given by the latter in advancing funds or auctioning the migrant's property was stressed.

These findings have been dismissed by most migration historians for a variety of reasons. Some point to the biased nature of the source, influenced as it was by a new wave of nativism which found in foreign steamship companies convenient scapegoats for the increasing numbers of migrants. Yet while rightly noting the bias, no one has yet produced any direct evidence to refute the claims. On the other hand, advocates of the concept of chain migration have been less critical about the DC's statistical information, which showed that between 1908 and 1910, seventy-nine percent of the migrants stated that they had come to the US to join family and fifteen percent mentioned friends, leaving only six percent without contacts. Moreover, thirty percent of the arrivals claimed to have travelled on prepaid tickets.[8] The numbers drawn from passenger manifests are one of the pillars of the transatlantic chain-migration theory and are confirmed by other smaller analyses.[9] Unfortunately, scholars have generally used the data without asking who gathered the information and the influence of immigration laws and nativist ideas on the data.

From 1893 onwards, the shipping manifests recorded how much money each migrant possessed; inspectors used this to turn away migrants likely to become public charges. The primary inspections at the various gateways were the responsibility of one lowly civil servant and only lasted a minute or two. Based on these rudimentary inquiries, between eighty and ninety-five percent of immigrants were admitted, while the others were deferred for further investigation.[10] The controls and impositions were less severe on people joining relatives or friends. The contract labour law prohibiting the entrance of migrants with work already arranged – meaning that future earnings

---

[7]Mark Wyman, *Round Trip to America: The Immigrants Return to Europe, 1880-1930* (London, 1993), 31.

[8]United States, Senate, 61st Cong., 2nd sess., Immigration Commission (Dillingham Commission, DC), *Reports* (41 vols., Washington, DC, 1911), III, 359-363.

[9]Annemarie Steidl, "The 'Relatives and Friends Effect:' Migration Networks of Transatlantic Migrants from the Late Habsburg Monarchy," in Torsten Feys, *et al.* (eds.), *Maritime Transport and Migration: The Connections between Maritime and Migration Networks* (St. John's, 2007), 75-95; and Simone A. Wegge, "Chain Migration and Information Networks: Evidence from Nineteenth-Century Hesse-Cassel," *Journal of Economic History*, LVIII, No. 4 (1998), 957-986.

[10]United States, National Archives, Washington, DC (NAW), Records of the Immigration and Naturalization Service, 1787-1993 (RINS), Record Group (RG) 85, 52495/18, problems with primary inspection, Ellis Island, report, 8 August 1912.

could not be used as an argument – made family and friends the best guarantee that a poor migrant would be allowed to enter.[11] Hence, many migrants may have mentioned the names of family and friends without having any intention of joining them. On the other hand, the lack of any way to check the veracity of such statements means that at least some of the contacts may have been fictional. A special investigation by Marcus Brown in 1904 showed that of 105 passengers on Cunard's *Pannonia* giving addresses in New York, forty-six could not be traced, either because the address was fictitious or the alleged relatives did not know the immigrant. Frustrated by his inability to verify much of the information, New York's Commissioner of Immigration, William Williams, reversed the policies during his second term to consider passengers with prepaid tickets as assisted migrants, thereby obstructing their landing.[12]

Information about these policies reached Europe through shipping companies and migrant agents. As deportations occurred at a cost to shipping companies, they spared no efforts to guarantee the landing of their passengers. Company personnel, or sometimes specially hired interpreters, prepared the passengers for the interrogations on board or at the port of departure, and in some cases they even advanced money.[13] For those passengers that risked detention, shipping lines contacted family or philanthropic organizations to facilitate the landing. Being responsible for filling out the manifests put them in a privileged position to manipulate them to their advantage which may well have affected the trustworthiness of the data. Immigrant inspectors only had time to complete or correct some of these. By the time the DC was formed, the importance of mentioning a contact had become common knowledge in the migrant business. As a result, the statistics may have seriously overestimated the importance of kin and acquaintances, as Dudley Baines has noted. Moreover, migrants who moved outside the chains are much harder to trace.[14] With the

---

[11]Rotterdam Community Archives (GAR), Holland-America Line Archive (HAL), 318.02, Directors, 112-121, correspondence, 1893-1910.

[12]NAW, RINS, RG 85/52599/16, investigation fictitious addresses, Marcus Braun, report, 16 November 1904.

[13]GAR, HAL, 318.04, Passage, 221-226, correspondence, 13 July 1909-27 May 1910; Herman J. Schulteis, *Report on European Immigration to the United States of America and the Causes which Incite the Same, with Recommendations for the Further Restriction of Undesirable Immigration and the Establishment of a National Quarantine* (Washington, DC, 1893), 43; and Marie-Françoise Vannoise-Pochulu, "La politique de la Compagnie Générale Transatlantique et l'émigration vers les États-Unis à partir du Havre (1875-1914)" (Unpublished MA thesis, University of Paris XII, 1993), 89.

[14]Dudley Baines, *Emigration from Europe, 1815 -1930* (Cambridge, 1991), 34.

focus on the prepaid ticket market, this study does not consider these and hence cannot prove or disprove chain-migration theories. Instead, I contend that shipping companies and migrant agents were in great part responsible for how they developed. To prove this, the volumes of the Dillingham Commission, especially those dealing with immigrant banks and steamship companies, are used to complement the findings taken from the HAL archives.

Scandinavian Sources

Berit Brattne and Sune Åkerman's work is the main point of reference on the impact of migrant agents. Using the archives of the Swedish migrant brokers Larsson Brothers, Brattne and Åkerman concluded that the extensive propaganda campaigns and pricing policies adopted by the transport sector had only a marginal effect on migration. The conclusions are based on the sparse bookings the brothers received through the direct actions of sub-agents. Moreover, an increase in sub-agents had little impact on passenger volume. Collaborating with more effective sales promoters - Swedish Americans - and bypassing sub-agents completely was more effective. Most propaganda spread by the Larsson Brothers contained information on the advantages of a particular line and port while only briefly touching on opportunities in the US, something that was prohibited by law in 1883. Correspondence with possible clients suggests that these had little influence on the decision to migrate. Finally, Brattne and Åkerman argued that price fluctuations did not affect the total volume.[15]

Yet Brattne and Åkerman fail to discuss the relationship between the migrant broker and the shipping company or the role of shipping conferences in regulating the agent network. These are crucial factors to comprehend the influence of the transport sector on migration. The dearth of studies on the subject contributed to the generalization of Brattne and Åkerman's findings. Historians such as John Gould have stressed the regional differences in migration patterns.[16] Swedish migration in the 1880s, for example, had market-specific characteristics. Swedish migration polices aimed to slow the flow while its maritime policies, imposing outrageous space requirements on national ships, impeded its merchant marine from profiting from the trade and

---

[15]Berit Brattne and Sune Åkerman, "The Importance of the Transport Sector for Mass Migration," in Harald Runblom and Hans Norman (eds.), *From Sweden to America: A History of the Migration* (Minneapolis, 1976), 176-200.

[16]John D. Gould, "European Inter-Continental Migration, 1815-1914: Patterns and Causes," *Journal of European Economic History*, VIII, No. 3 (1979), 593-679; Gould, "European Inter-Continental Migration - The Road Home: Return Migration from the USA," *Journal of European Economic History*, IX, No. 1 (1980), 41-112; and Gould, "European Inter-Continental Emigration: The Role of 'Diffusion' and 'Feedback,'" *Journal of European Economic History*, IX, No. 2 (1980), 267-315.

allowed British companies to control the market.[17] A study of the expanding Italian market, which was served by many competing lines during this period, attributed a much more active role to the transport sector. Agents not only sold tickets but also loaned funds for the passage or helped to auction the migrant's property. These were spurred by the Italian government, which favoured migration and used the movement to stimulate its merchant marine.[18]

Another Scandinavian scholar, Kristian Hvidt, agreed that pricing policies had little short-term influence on migration flows, yet he questioned the meagre impact of agents based on a study of Copenhagen police records. The so called "Yellow Book" containing conference regulations of the British lines which organized agent activities in Denmark was put forward as a key to understanding the working of the transport system.[19] Hvidt expressed concern over the neglect of the transportation system on mass migration, while Brattne, Åkerman Charlotte Erickson pointed to the lack of sources in Bremen, Hamburg, Hull and Liverpool.[20] Drew Keeling has provided a good survey on how the debate unfolded, albeit based on second-hand sources. Agents became increasingly stigmatized as mere travel agents. Keeling corroborates this view, only conceding, as did Maldwyn Jones or Dirk Hoerder, that during the beginning of mass migration, agents stimulated pioneers to move. He placed more importance on shipping companies in the process, yet he did not explicitly state

---

[17]Brattne and Åkerman, "Importance of the Transport Sector," 188; Francis E. Hyde, *Cunard and the North Atlantic, 1840-1973: A History of Shipping and Financial Management* (London, 1975), 200-202; and Odd S. Lovoll, "For the People Who Are Not in a Hurry: The Danish Thingvalla Line and the Transportation of Scandinavian Emigrants," *Journal of American Ethnic History*, XIII, No. 1 (1993), 60.

[18]Wyman, *Round Trip to America*, 22-36; Schulteis, *Report*, 36-48; Amoreno Martellini, "Il commercio dell' emigrazione: intermediari e agenti," in Piero Bevilacqua, *et al.* (eds.), *Storia dell' emigrazione Italiana: La Partenza* (Rome, 2002), 292-304; and Augusta Molinari, "Porti, trasporti, compagnie," in Bevilacqua, *et al.* (eds.), *Storia dell' emigrazione Italiana*, 239-251.

[19]Kristian Hvidt, *Flight to America: The Social Background of 300,000 Danish Emigrants* (New York, 1975); and Hvidt, "Emigration Agents: The Development of a Business and Its Methods," *Scandinavian Journal of History*, III, No. 2 (1978), 178-202.

[20]Magnus Mörner, "Divergent Perspectives," in P.C. Emmer and Magnus (eds.), *European Expansion and Migration: Essays on the Intercontinental Migration from Africa, Asia, and Europe* (New York, 1992), 283; Brattne and Åkerman, "Importance of the Transport Sector;" and Charlotte Erickson (ed.), *Emigration from Europe, 1815-1914: Select Documents* (London, 1971).

how this occurred except by reducing the risks of the move.[21] Before refuting this, however, the various layers in the agent network will be deconstructed.

Various Layers of the Agent Network

The plethora of terms used for the various actors in the agent networks requires some clear definitions. Scandinavian scholars failed to observe that the roots of the networks dated back to the golden age of sail. Indeed, Hvidt claimed that prior to steam, "migrants were recruited in a haphazard way often by a captain of a sailing ship or a recruiting agent of an American company."[22] His division into agents, sub-agents and Yankee recruiters failed to reflect the complexity of the networks or the maritime background of the participants. This study instead classifies the various actors as migrant brokers, agents, sub-agents and recruiting agents, a schema used by many German scholars.[23]

The Migrant Broker

The first link below the shipping company was the migrant broker. Based in migration gateways, these men began as shipping brokers who added the mi-

---

[21]Dirk Hoerder, "International Labour Markets and Community Building by Migrant Workers in the Atlantic Economies," in Rudolph J. Vecoli and Suzanne M. Simke (eds.), *A Century of European Migrations, 1830-1930* (Urbana, IL, 1991), 79; Drew Keeling, "Costs, Risks, and Migration Networks between Europe and the United States, 1900-1914," in Feys, *et al.* (eds.), *Maritime Transport and Migration*, 118-122; and Maldwyn Allen Jones, *American Immigration* (Chicago, 1960; 2nd ed., Chicago, 1992), 157.

[22]Hvidt, "Emigration Agents," 180.

[23]The German literature on agent networks and the laws regulating it is very dense. These include Bretting and Bickelmann, *Auswanderungagenturen*; Rolf Engelsing *Bremen als Auswandererhafen, 1683-1880* (Bremen, 1961); Klaus J. Bade, *Europa in Bewegung: Migration von späten 18. Jahrhudert bis Gegenwart* (Munich, 2000); Dirk Hoerder, "The Traffic of Emigration via Bremen/Bremerhaven: Merchants' Interests, Protective Legislation, and Migrants' Experiences," *Journal of American Ethnic History*, XIII, No. 1 (1993), 68-101; Birgit Gelberg, *Auswanderung nach Übersee: Soziale Probleme der Auswanderungbeförderung in Hamburg und Bremen von der Mitte der 19. Jahrhunderts bis zum Ersten Weltkrieg* (Hamburg, 1973); Mack Walker, *Germany and the Emigration, 1816-1885* (Cambridge, MA, 1964); and Axel von der Straeten, *Die Rechtsordnung des Zweiten Kaiserreiches und die Deutsche Auswanderung nach Übersee, 1871-1914* (Berlin, 1997). They generally sub-divide the layers into *makler* (broker), *expedienten* (agents), and *unteragenten* (sub-agents); Bickelmann, *Emigration Business*, 136. Although the works of Engelsing and Bretting and Bickelmann are especially valuable for the sailing ship era, the implementation of the laws and changes in the networks during the steam era remain unexplored.

grant trade to their portfolios and eventually specialized in it as the movement swelled. During the sailing ship era, they chartered and outfitted the 'tween decks, contracted passengers through agents and coordinated sailing dates. With the shift from tramp ships to liners specially outfitted for migrant transport, the brokers' organizational tasks decreased, while managing the agent network became their main activity. Keen competition spurred bookings inland rather than at the port, yet the proportion remains uncertain. Studies indicate that by the steamship era the majority booked their passage where they lived. Early legislation requiring migrants to have a ticket booked before crossing borders contributed to this evolution.[24]

Most brokers advertised themselves as a "Banking Exchange, Passage Forwarding, Insurance and Foreign Express Company," answering the demand for other services that the movement generated. In Europe, the activities of the migrant brokers became a concern for the authorities. To safeguard the reputation of migration gateways, brokers had to pay a deposit to ensure their good character; licences to do so had to be renewed yearly (shipowners often advanced the money for this). The authorities used the funds to compensate abused migrants or to protect travellers when the brokers were unable to fulfil their contract. The German states pioneered these laws which gradually spread across the continent. Remarkably, though, they never crossed the Atlantic; in the US, the migrant business remained practically unregulated up to World War I.[25]

---

[24]Agnes Bretting and Hartmut Bickelmann, *Auswanderungagenturen*, 85, argue that bookings at the port increased with the transition to steam based on an agreement between HAPAG and the Hamburg brokers. Yet the agreement does not reflect an increase of direct business done at the port. The numbers given by Philippovich for the 1880s are not comparable with figures for the previous period. The arguments for an increase of the so-called *Platzgeschäft* are not conclusive. It is true that improved transport connections and increased sailings it became easier to bypass the migrant agents, but it is questionable whether migrants did so because agents provided special railroad fares, organized lodging at the port and provided useful information on opportunities in the US, the organization of the trip, the inspections and relevant legislation.

[25]Bretting and Bickelmann, Bickelmann, *Auswanderungagenturen*, 31-40; Bickelmann, "Emigration Business," 136; Nicole Fouché, *Émigration Alsacienne aux États-Unis, 1815-1870* (Paris, 1992), 74-81; Gelberg, *Auswanderung nach Übersee*, 10-17; Hoerder, "Traffic of Emigration," 74; Hvidt, "Emigration Agents," 180-190; Eric Spelkens, "Belgian Migration to the United States and Other Overseas Countries at the Beginning of the 20th Century," in Ginette Kurgan, and E. Spelkens, *Two Studies on Emigration through Antwerp to the New World* (Brussels, 1976), 83-96; Leo A. van der Valk, "Landverhuizers via Rotterdam in de negentiende eeuw," *Economisch en Sociaal historisch jaarboek* (Amsterdam, 1976), 158-161; and Vannoise-Pochulu, "La politique," 44-47.

Brokers generally had first-hand experience as migrants. The main broker in Rotterdam, Johan Wambersie, was born in Savannah but later returned to his parents' homeland. His appointment as American consul boosted his reputation.[26] Four of the five of the Larsson Brothers spent time in the US during their youth to become familiar with the business and acquire language skills.[27] This was common practice in the shipping world, relying heavily on personal networks to obtain reliable information. To consolidate ties with overseas shipping agencies, young family members were often sent overseas as apprentices. Hvidt observed the same process in Copenhagen where contacts established by brokers abroad with railroads and employment bureaus created additional income.[28] During the steamship era, the biggest brokers opened branches or established partnerships with brokers across the Atlantic to increase their grip on the market.

With the transition to steam, the most successful brokers guaranteed the exclusivity of sales to a steamship line to become their passage agents. For instance, the Cunard Line engaged the migrant brokers Williams and Guion when it entered the steerage business. Cunard profited from the brokers' wide network of agencies built up while running a sailing packet service targeting migrants. Francis Hyde stressed that shipping companies were "largely dependent on the efficiency and goodwill of their agents, especially for steerage passengers because they were more responsive to skilful sales talk than cabin class travellers."[29] Just as with cargo brokers, successful migrant brokers sometimes climbed the ladder and became shipowners. Their success in attracting steerage business for the Cunard Line inspired the brokers to open the Guion Line which soon carried more steerage passengers than their ex-employers.[30] Conversely, various brokers were forced to take a step down, especially when steamship companies moved towards vertical integration, taking the passage business into their own hands. Some brokers did so reluctantly and used their networks against their former employers. As Erich Murken

---

[26]Van der Valk, "Landverhuizers," 157; and Robert P. Swierenga, "The Journey Across: Dutch Transatlantic Emigrant Passage to the United States 1820-1880," in Rosemarijn Hoefte and Johanna C. Kardux (eds.), *Connecting Cultures: The Netherlands in Five Centuries of Transatlantic Exchange* (Amsterdam, 1994), 114.

[27]Brattne and Åkerman, "Importance of the Transport Sector," 182.

[28]Hvidt, "Emigration Agents," 181.

[29]Hyde, *Cunard*, 77.

[30]*Ibid.*, 77-78; Robin Bastin, "Cunard and the Liverpool Emigrant Traffic, 1860-1900" (Unpublished MA thesis, University of Liverpool, 1971), 28; and Gordon Boyce, *Information, Mediation and Institutional Development: The Rise of Large-Scale Enterprise in British Shipping, 1870-1919* (Manchester, 1995), 36.

stressed, migrant brokers managing an independent agent network were often more powerful than the shipping companies.[31]

Migrant Agents, Sub-agents, Newlanders and Runners

Migrant agents were commissioned by various brokers seeking to attract a sufficient amount of business to open permanent offices in main transit points. Fluctuations in migration flows made it risky to rely solely on passage sales, yet the side industries the movement generated allowed agents to develop other trades. Migrant agents booked passengers both directly and indirectly through sub-agents who connected them to the rural areas. As the first link to someone willing to book passage, the sub-agent played an important role. As well, since many migrants preferred booking through someone familiar, local sub-agents were more likely to earn the trust of purchasers than random recruiters. The sub-agent also gave important advice on where and how to travel.[32]

The division between agent and subagent was not always clear. In the HAL records the terms are often used synonymously. What initially differentiated them was that agents managed more business and dealt directly with the shipping company. As the companies tried to increase their influence over a network, conference rules prohibited agents from hiring sub-agents. Although this proved difficult to enforce, it contributed to the trend of referring to anyone working as a middleman as an agent. Although agents preferably were people who came into frequent contact with locals or travellers, they varied considerably from religious leaders to mayors, innkeepers, shopkeepers, schoolteachers, hotel owners, notaries, tradesmen, craftsmen, farmers, barbers, shoemakers and the like.[33] When recruiting agents in Europe, the HAL described the profile and tasks of candidates as follows:

> Agents have to be recruited from people who are held in high regards by their community and need to possess administrative skills. Knowledge on the living conditions in the US is an important asset. They have to thoroughly brief the passen-

---

[31]Erich Murken, *Die grossen transatlantischen Linienreederei-Verbande, Pools und Interessengemeinschaften bis zum Ausbruch des Weltkrieges: Ihre Entstehung, Organitsation und Wirksamkeit* (Jena, 1922), 15.

[32]Bretting and Bickelmann, *Auswanderungagenturen*, 65-66.

[33]Wyman, *Round Trip to America*, 26; Bickelmann, "Emigration Business," 136; Nicholas J. Evans, "The Role of Foreign-born Agents in the Development of Mass Migrant Travel through Britain, 1820-1923," in Feys, *et al.* (eds.), *Maritime Transport and Migration*, 57; Hvidt, "Emigration Agents," 186; and Martellini, "Il commercio dell' emigrazione," 301-302.

> ger before the departure, make the arrangements for their luggage, fill out the required forms and point to the advantages of the HAL hotel in Rotterdam. The agents need to be familiar with the American immigration laws and sanitary requirements to inform third class passengers and avoid deportations. They have to warn passengers against fraudulent land and colonization companies. Special attention has to be drawn to advertising matters such as billboards in train stations and public places or ads in the popular press. They are responsible for organizing the publicity campaigns in their regions. Finally the agents have to send in reports on the status of the business on a regular basis.[34]

By 1890, the HAL managed a network of more than two thousand agents spread across Europe.[35] Exclusivity of sales in these networks was exceptional, as only the combined sale for different companies generated enough business to make it appealing for middlemen. Recruiting agents for railroad trusts, real estate companies, state authorities or other employers complemented the network.[36] Agents often were migrants travelling back home to convince fellow countrymen to emigrate. Also known as "newlanders" or "Yankees," they negotiated special passage rates for their recruits with migrant brokers or directly with shipping companies. Able to provide first-hand testimony about conditions in the US and to serve as guides during the journey, these recruiters reduced the uncertainties of the move.

Because of this network, people considering a move usually did not have to leave their village to arrange the crossing. On payment of the fare, the agents or sub-agents issued a provisional shipping ticket, printed and numbered by the migrant broker. They sent a copy to the broker containing the name of the buyer, number of passengers, port of departure, shipping company and money received. Some weeks before the departure, the agent proposed a ship to the broker based on the list of departures circulated by shipping companies. The broker then made the reservation and advised when the passenger needed to leave home. At the port, the provisional ticket was exchanged for one issued

---

[34]GAR, HAL, 318.04, Passage, 1, letter, 5 November 1897.

[35]Van der Valk, "Landverhuizers," 163.

[36]Except in the east where migrants were concentrated, states advertised the opportunities they offered for settlers; Wisconsin, Minnesota and Iowa were especially successful. They competed with land-grant railroads which offered greater inducements through fare reductions for transport, work upon arrival, land to be cultivated and long-term financing. Jones, *American Immigration*, 161-162.

by the shipping company.[37] Agents usually combined the sale of ocean passages with inland travel for which they earned an extra commission. Inland transport companies offered special migrant fares or organized special trains since they shared interests with the port and shipping companies in attracting migrants who in turn benefited from this increasingly integrated transatlantic transport network.[38] Migrant and railroad agents helped the *émigré* during the journey to the port of embarkation, and others did the same from the port of arrival to the final destination, triggering keen competition and special rates for migrants. Already during the 1840s, the battle for the migrant trade between American inland transport companies had moved to Europe. While US authorities pressured European governments to prohibit these sales because of widespread fraud, only Prussia did so temporarily.[39] Port authorities though soon realized the importance of protecting migrants from crooks trying to defraud migrants for lodging, money exchanges, travelling utensils and inland travel. To protect Antwerp's reputation, migrant brokers advised the police of new arrivals in order to arrange an escort from the station to their lodging house. Representatives of the migrant brokers working under police supervision subsequently took over the task. Other European migrant ports took similar measures.[40] The same was done on the other side of the Atlantic to protect migrants at the port of arrival and to assist them to their final destination.

---

[37]Michael Just, *Ost und südosteuropäische Amerikawanderung, 1881-1914* (Stuttgart, 1988), 49.

[38]Belgian railroads offered a thirty percent discount to Antwerp-bound migrants and later increased this to fifty percent. Railroad companies connecting Switzerland to Le Havre not only gave migrants discounts but also organized special trains. The same was true for trains connecting Hull with Liverpool. Boats on the Rhine connecting Rotterdam with the hinterland (and railroads in a later period) also had special fares. Bickelmann, "Emigration Business," 138, states that German railroads stopped giving reductions after they were nationalized in the 1850s when new policies stipulated that emigration should not be encouraged. Despite this, records in the HAL archives show that both North German Lloyd (NGL) and the Hamburg-America Line (HAPAG) kept special migrant fares at least up to the end of the 1880s.

[39]The Belgian and French governments considered prohibition but did not implement it; see Fouché, *Émigration Alsacienne*, 68-72; and Torsten Feys, "The Emigration Policy of the Belgian Government from Belgium to the U.S. through the Port of Antwerp, 1842-1914" (Unpublished MA thesis, Ghent University, 2003), 71.

[40]Archives of the Ministry of Foreign Affairs, Brussels (ABMFA), 2020, Emigration, I, letter, 17 January 1847; Gelberg, *Auswanderung nach Übersee*, 10-40; Spelkens, "Belgian Migration," 71-81; and Cees Zevenbergen, *Toen zij uit Rotterdam vertrokken: emigratie via Rotterdam door de eeuwen heen* (Rotterdam, 1990), 38-40.

Migrant agents also provided other services, but it is hard to know to what extent the facilities offered can be generalized. It is clear that they helped in obtaining official travel documents. Passports were not a prerequisite to board ships or to enter the US, but the tendency of the European authorities during the second half of the century to increase their grip on the movement spurred their use. Russian, Hungarian and Italian authorities in particular tried to control emigration through passports long before World War I. This created new market opportunities for agents assisting migrants to travel clandestinely. A law requiring nationals to have passports when sailing from Italian ports opened opportunities for Swiss agents to send those who could not obtain one through northern ports.[41] Indeed, they advertised this service, as the circular of the Swiss agency Carecco and Brivio to Italian sub-agents illustrates:

> We will accept your passengers for New York at net rates of 120 *Francs* from Chiasso through Antwerp with RSL or English steamers. Make sure your passengers arrive in Chiasso on Tuesday. Migrants coming through Milan have to go the *trattoria* which address has previously been sent. We accept passengers without passports guaranteeing their embarkation. Instruct your passengers not to confide in anyone, never tell that they are going to America and hide any addresses or papers linking them to their destination. If someone inquires about where they are going they should frankly respond that they are on their way to Switzerland looking for work. To make reservations you need to send us beforehand their names, address, etc. and a bond of 50 *Lire* for each migrant.[42]

In countries like Russia, which opposed migration, a semi-clandestine network of agents arranged transport and smuggled migrants over borders. Although it exposed the migrants to many abuses when crossing the border, this assistance proved crucial for most Russian Jews bound for the US. The agents worked clandestinely or bribed local authorities at the risk of being ex-

---

[41]As John Torpey observed, Italian lawmakers wanted to reduce deportations and facilitate the emigration of nationals with these passports, which had to be issued within twenty-four hours after a request The measure was aimed at creating goodwill with American authorities by preventing the emigration of "excludables." John Torpey, "Passports and the Development of Immigration Controls in the North Atlantic World during the Long Nineteenth Century," in Andreas Fahrmeir, Olivier Faron and Patrick Weil (eds.), *Migration Control in the North Atlantic World* (New York, 2003), 83.

[42]GAR, HAL, 318.04, Passage, 221-226, letter, 19 April 1894.

iled to Siberia. As many agents also combined notary functions, they assisted clients in selling their property and procured all kinds of official certificates.[43]

John Gould stressed the importance of information flows and the impact of "diffusion" and "feedback" mechanisms on the patterns of European inter-continental migration. First-hand information about the US from pioneers, kin and fellow villagers often shaped the volume and impacted how the fever spread from village to village.[44] The Bielefeld migrant letter collection illustrates the detailed information these contained on conditions, opportunities and other kinds of advice.[45] Yet because of the stress on information flows from family and kin, the role of migrant agents has been downplayed by migration historians. For example, in their studies of the impact of the diffusion of information on migration, Yuzo Murayama, John Rice and Robert Ostergren do not even consider the role of the transport sector.[46]

Information about transatlantic destinations also received wide coverage in the popular press, which profited from advertisements placed by recruiters, agents and shipping companies. Techniques used to promote the migrant trade predated modern practice and were extremely forceful in their approach.[47] Migrant agents distributed brochures and circulars promoting the advantages and sailing dates of the lines they represented. These contained sound advice to migrants and details of the services but very little on opportunities in the US. Agents also advertised through pamphlets. Federal and local authorities, employers, railroads and landowning companies all used agent networks to spread their propaganda. But Brattne and Åkerman found that the

---

[43]Just, *Ost und südosteuropäische*, 54-55; GAR, HAL, 318.02, Directors, 112-121, letter, 23 November 1900; and YIVO Institute for Jewish Research (New York, RG 102/1-397, autobiographies; Wyman, Round Trip to America, 27; and Marie-Rose Thielemans, "De Waalse emigratie naar Wisconsin," in Anne Morelli (ed.), *Belgische emigranten: oorlogsvluchtelingen, economische emigranten en politieke vluchtelingen uit onze streken van de 16de eeuw tot vandaag* (Berchem, 1999), 129.

[44]Gould, "European Inter-Continental Migration, 1815-1914," 614-616; and Gould, "European Inter-Continental Migration – The Road Home," 41-112.

[45]Walter D. Kamphoefner, Wolfgang Helbich and Ulrike Sommer (eds.), *News from the Land of Freedom: German Immigrants Write Home* (Ithaca, NY, 1991), *passim*.

[46]Yuzo Murayama, "Information and Emigrants: Interprefectual Differences of Japanese Emigration to the Pacific Northwest, 1880-1915," *Journal of Economic History*, LI, No. 1 (1991), 125-147; and John G. Rice and Robert C. Ostergren, "The Decision to Emigrate: A Study in Diffusion," *Geografiska Annaler*, LX, No. 1 (1978), 1-15.

[47]Bastin, "Cunard," 11; and Hyde, *Cunard*, 65.

repetitious and often monotonous ads had little influence on the decision to migrate, especially once Swedish authorities placed limits on what could be said about opportunities.[48] Yet in Austria-Hungary and the German states, where authorities forbade such propaganda much earlier, pamphlets and booklets published by Belgian and Dutch printers circulated clandestinely through the agent network.[49] Gould attributed much more importance to the role of agents as information diffusers:

> At least, the constant representation to the public on the opportunities in other countries and the proffer of practical information about ways and means must have been a factor in the diffusion of the habit of emigration...Any advertising expert knows that, it is constant repetition rather than reasoned (or valid) argument which sells the product.[50]

Agents also were crucial diffusers of information on migration laws. Indeed, American authorities integrated the network into their policies by requiring that US immigration laws be displayed in the agents' offices on both sides of the Atlantic. Not surprisingly, the agents also provided information on how to circumvent restrictive laws. For instance, they often assisted young males to migrate to avoid military service in their native land. They also prepared their clients for interrogations at American landing stations by supplying the right answers to pass immigration inspections. If they judged the risks to be too high, agents were often ready to discuss alternative routes of entry by sea or by land through Canada or Mexico.

As Michael Just concluded, agents stimulated migration, especially by pioneers. Once the movement from a region persisted, their job was easier because word-of-mouth publicity constituted an excellent (and inexpensive) means of inducing new departures. It is difficult, however, to estimate their true impact on the migrant's decision. Agents could with difficulty motivate

---

[48]Brattne and Åkerman, "Importance of the Transport Sector," 191.

[49]Just, *Ost und südosteuropäische*, 37; and Schulteis, *Report*, 23. Towards the end of the century, shipping companies tried to avoid direct associations with landowning or colonization companies for fear that stories about the abuses and failures of the latter might blacken their reputation. The HAL tried to discourage the spread of information about these companies through their agents, and it screened pamphlets put at the disposal of its clients. Nonetheless, it still secretly gave special fares for large groups recruited by these ventures. GAR, HAL, 318.04, Passage, 1, letter, 5 November 1897.

[50]Gould, "European Inter-Continental Emigration: The Role of Diffusion," 275.

someone to leave or could win over people who were already contemplating such a move,[51] but none of this was determinative.

Still, agents constituted a vital link in the transatlantic transport network. Combined with technological innovations in transport and communication, they helped to lift many of the legal and psychological barriers to migration, making a potentially long and fearful journey across the ocean seem less threatening than, say, a trip to Rome for Italians. For many Irish, this move was much less of a journey into unknown territory than looking for work in another Irish city.[52] The availability of agents across Europe with their constant advertising campaigns brought America a lot closer in the mental map of many Europeans.

The integration of both worlds was further enhanced by the American agent network. Strangely enough, in a field stressing the importance of chain migration, this has received no consideration. The next section discusses this in detail. Because an important difference between the European agent network and that in the US was the complete lack of regulations in the latter, before crossing the Atlantic we need to look briefly at the relevant laws in Europe.

European Laws Regulating the Agent Network

The first regulations in Europe dated to the 1830s when Baden introduced surety bonds for migrant agents at the same time that Bavarian authorities added formalities regarding the contract. The other German states followed suit; Württemberg and Hessen (1847); Mecklenburg (1852); Prussia, Sachsen, Frankfurt and Kuhresen (1853), and so on. The laws enabled the authorities to monitor both the number and activities of agents. Although the free ports of Hamburg, Bremen and Lübeck did not follow suit, they established institutions to control the activities of brokers and agents. In all states, the privilege to act as a migrant agent could be withdrawn and in some was subject to annual renewal. Surety bonds ranged from 300 *thaler* to 30,000 *marks*. The efforts of Prussia to standardize the regulations for all states in the late 1840s only bore fruit in 1897 when a united Germany decided that concessions to act as agents needed to be obtained from the central government and were granted only to nationals. Further, they needed to live where they worked and required authorization from a licensed entrepreneur for whom they acted. Agents acting without concessions risked a year's imprisonment and a heavy fine.[53]

---

[51]Just, *Ost und südosteuropäische*, 60-61.

[52]Gould, "European Inter-Continental Emigration: The Role of Diffusion," 294-295.

[53]Bretting and Bickelmann, *Auswanderungagenturen*, 31-40; Gelberg, *Auswanderung nach Übersee*, 10-14; and Hoerder, "Traffic of Emigration," 75.

It took the Belgian government until 1875 to adopt a law controlling the morality and solvency of brokers and agents. The law required a deposit of 20,000 to 40,000 *francs* from brokers who obtained a concession which was subject to yearly renewal. Agents had to meet their clients at the railroad station in Antwerp and guide them to lodging houses to prevent unlicensed runners from deceiving them. An 1890 law made shipping companies responsible for the actions of their brokers, agents and sub-agents. They needed to submit a list of all authorized agents to enable the emigration commissioner to investigate their character. Yet on several occasions the biggest company, Red Star Line (RSL), refused to release its agents' names, claiming that this could be used by rivals to lure them away. The authorities did not press the RSL on this, which reflects both the company's power and the priority of economic rather than humanitarian concerns in regulating the trade.[54]

Similar laws were passed elsewhere. A Dutch law of 1862 included a clause requiring deposits from brokers and agents to be collected and supervised by local authorities. In 1855, a French decree stipulated that shipping companies transporting migrants and agencies recruiting them needed a concession from the Department of Agriculture, Commerce and Public Works on payment of a deposit ranging from 15,000 to 40,000 *francs*. The license could be withdrawn in case of abuses. Agencies were responsible for their sub-agents, who needed to obtain an authorization from the emigration bureau of the Department of Interior. The law also regulated the contracts used by agencies. Unlike Belgium, French authorities strictly enforced the laws. From the 1880s, despite strong protests by migrant brokers fearing for their competitive position, the price had to include board and lodging at Le Havre according to French law.[55]

The Danish authorities imposed a security bond of 10,000 *riksdaler* on migrant brokers. They had to provide the police with the names of agents working for them and for whom they were responsible. Between 1868 and 1876, the number of brokers rose from six to twelve, and agents from 126 to 571. At the peak of Danish migration, fifteen brokers managed a network of 1053 agents, but the number decreased to eight and 300 during a subsequent slump. Their numbers finally stabilized at ten and 700 at the turn of the century. Nonetheless, migrant agents remained largely beyond police control. Sub-agents and recruiting agents seemingly escaped Danish vigilance.[56]

---

[54]Spelkens, "Belgian Migration," 94-96; and Feys, "Emigration Policy," 144-146.

[55]Van der Valk, "Landverhuizers," 157-161; Fouché, *Émigration Alsacienne*, 76-81; and Vannoise-Pochulu, "La politique," 44-47, 68-72 and 139-144.

[56]Hvidt, "Emigration Agents," 180-190.

European countries affected by the first wave of mass migration passed laws to control the agent network by the time the steamship companies took control of the market. This shows that the distinction between brokers, agents and sub-agents was not always clear even to lawmakers. The French and German authorities imposed the same surety bond on brokers and agents. Danish police limited this to brokers but do not seem to have distinguished between agents and sub-agents. In France and Germany only a small number could afford a surety bond, increasing the number of sub-agents, whereas in Denmark many of what the Germans and French would call sub-agents were classified as agents. The measures adopted in countries where migration fever spread after the introduction of steam, such as Italy (1888), Hungary (1900) and Austria (1904) reflect a decreasing differentiation between various layers.

As the organizational participation of the brokers receded with the transition to steam, the overall distinction between broker, agent and sub-agent became vague. Most brokers retained a network of agents and sub-agents but could not prevent some inland agents from breaking away and dealing directly with the shipping companies since nothing in their role in migrant passage bookings differentiated them any longer. A hierarchy persisted nonetheless, based on volume of business and the geographic area the middleman controlled. Brokers, inland or at ports, became middlemen on whom shipping companies relied to obtain their share from one of their sub-markets. The geographical delimitation varied from provinces to entire countries. The rest came from other brokers or agents with whom the shipping lines increasingly dealt directly. Agents limited their business to local regions. To make the network manageable, shipping companies tried not to deal with sub-agents directly.

But neither laws nor shipping companies could prevent a wide network of unauthorized runners, peddlers, sub-agents and agents from operating beneath the network of official representatives. The various layers connecting the migrant with the shipping companies made it difficult to implement the laws. For this reason, in 1901 the Italian authorities revoked the concessions to migrant brokers, granting permission to contract migrants only to shipping companies departing from Italian ports. The companies could appoint agents for whom they were directly responsible. By reducing the layers of middlemen, the authorities tried to make the market more transparent, obviating the possibilities for sub-agents, agents, brokers and shipping companies to shirk responsibility for violations.[57] Yet the goal proved illusive. Formally, the law limited the actors to shipping companies and their agents, yet in practice the old structures persisted.

---

[57]Martellini, "Il commercio dell' emigrazione," 294-302; and Murken, *Die grossen transatlantischen*, 362-364.

Importance of the American Ocean Passage Market

According to estimates, thirty to fifty percent of the market for third-class, westbound ocean passages was sold in the US through prepaid tickets.[58] Eastbound return tickets, sold exclusively in the US, amounted to thirty percent of the westbound sales.[59] These figures reflect the direct impact of the American market. Gustav Schwab, the New York head agent of North German Lloyd (NGL), estimated that when adding indirect business resulting from prepaid tickets the market was responsible for at least sixty percent of westbound sales:

> The ticket is sent to John Smith to some village of Germany, and the whole village knows that he has a ticket from his brother to come over; that he is working on a farm, not subject to military duty, paying very little taxes, and generally believing that he is in a pretty good country and would like his brother to come. His brother tells all his friends and neighbours, and brings with him, two, three, or four men to this country they heard of. So this prepaid business is of immense importance.[60]

Since some people preferred to send money instead of prepaid tickets, the number of crossings financed through remittances remains unclear.

The market also gained in importance as an increasing number of European countries used the migrant transport laws to favour national companies. For instance, German authorities moved to prohibit agents from booking for foreign lines, but fearing diplomatic repercussions a concession was given to all major lines except the HAL. The line lobbied for redress through Dutch diplomats and its German trade partners, and the company even ordered two

---

[58]Murken estimated that prepaids comprised twenty-five to thirty-five percent of the total westbound market. The DC corroborated these figures. There were great variations depending on place of origin, something illustrated by the high percentages of Russian Jews. The percentage of Scandinavian migrants leaving from Gothenburg fluctuated between thirty-five and fifty-five percent for the period 1883-1889. Other figures show that in 1882, 57.6 percent of the Allan Line's Scandinavian passengers travelled on prepaids in 1882, which increased to 73.9 percent in 1892. The combined average of prepaid sales of the British lines for that year amounted to forty-seven percent of the westbound movement; Murken, *Die grossen transatlantischen*, 48; Lovoll, "For the People Who Are Not in a Hurry," 56; and Brattne and Åkerman, "Importance of the Transport Sector," 185.

[59]Gould, "European Inter-Continental Migration, 1815-1914," 609.

[60]Testimony of Gustav Schwab during the hearings before the DC in New York, 25 July 1899, quoted in Erickson, *Emigration from Europe*, 232.

new passengers ships from German shipbuilders to regain favour with the German government, but to no avail. Some German federal states had already banned the Dutch company from its turf during the 1880s because agents advertised Rotterdam as the best route for people looking to evade their military obligations; at Dutch ports no military papers or passports were required. But German authorities could not prevent the HAL from selling prepaid tickets in the US and sending instructions on how to evade German border controls to migrate illegally through Rotterdam.[61]

Prepaid tickets also provided steamship lines with effective means to circumvent laws restricting emigration from Europe. Russian authorities obstructed migration by restricting the issue of passports and the sale of ocean passages. The HAL relied more heavily on the prepaid market to contract Russian passengers who received assistance from a network of official and clandestine agents to leave the country.[62] They either migrated legally through Libau, where the migrant brokers Hoffmann and Bielby provided them with the necessary passports to join a ship in Rotterdam, or illegally overland where smugglers helped them to "steal the border," as one Russian migrant put it.[63] The Austro-Hungarian government intercepted letters from America in an attempt to screen them for prepaid tickets; this led the HAL to order its American agents not to contact these passenger themselves but to leave it to its Vienna office to make the arrangements for the trip.[64] Prepaid tickets gave companies a means to circumvent both laws favouring the transport of migrants through national lines over foreign lines and those restricting emigration from Europe. This also increased the importance of the American market for shipping lines where the HAL sold fifty percent of its tickets.[65] The prepaid tickets sold over the winter served as an indicator of the annual westbound migrant traffic, which peaked between April and September.

---

[61]Bretting and Bickelmann, *Auswanderungagenturen*, 40-62; and GAR, HAL, 318.04, Passage, 221-226, letters, 14 March and 18 October 1894, and A1, correspondence with Berlin office, letter, 14 January 1898.

[62]Officials abused their power to levy a surcharge for issuing a passport; the average price was twenty *rubles* or about US $10, while it took three months to deliver. Hasia R. Diner, *A Time for Gathering, 1820-1880: The Second Migration* (Baltimore, 1995), 43.

[63]YIVO, RG 102, autobiographies, 274; and GAR, HAL, 318.04, Passage, 221-226, letter, 24 October 1893.

[64]*Ibid.*, letter, 24 March 1891.

[65]Murken, *Die grossen transatlantischen*, 47. By comparison, HAPAG and the NGL booked forty percent of their steerage passengers in the US, while the Guion and National Line booked a third. *New York Times*, 26 June 1888.

Despite the importance of return migration, little is known about the organization of the eastbound traffic. The high return rates during American recessions in the 1870s, 1890s and 1900s underscore Russell King's observation that economic rather than non-economic factors weighed more heavily on the decision to return, and that unfavourable economic conditions in the recipient country were determinant.[66] Although an increasing number of migrants arrived with the intention of returning, American business conditions largely influenced whether they eventually did as well as the timing of the return.[67] By reducing time and the cost of the crossing, steamships reinforced seasonal transatlantic migration patterns described by contemporaries as "birds of passage." Return and repeat migration already occurred during the first mass-migration movement, but technological innovations intensified this pattern among eastern and southern Europeans. Many left right after winter to return as early as the next autumn. The growing re-migration also served as a new encouragement for emigration: you could always come back.[68]

The return movement was also spurred by market forces in the transport sector. Permanent westbound overcapacity after the steamship boom of the 1870s was much more pronounced on the return leg. This eastbound overcapacity kept prices lower than westbound fares.[69] Moreover, rate wars among shipping companies tended to start when the westbound market collapsed, generally due to economic recessions. These periods were used to measure the strength of the rival companies before renegotiating the agreements when the westbound trade picked up again. Rate wars always spread to the eastbound

---

[66]King, "Generalizations," 18-21.

[67]Although this study focuses on economic factors, it is important to stress the influence of personal, social, ethnic, cultural and political factors in shaping the return movement; see Russell King, "Generalizations from the History of Return Migration," in Bimal Ghosh (ed.), *Return Migration: Journey of Hope or Despair*. (Geneva, 2000), 7-56; Ewa Morawska, *For Bread with Butter: The Life-Worlds of East Central Europeans in Johnstown, Pennsylvania, 1890-1940* (New York, 1986; reprint, New York, 2004); Morawska, "Return Migrations: Theoretical and Research Agenda," in Vecoli and Simke (eds.), *Century of European Migrations*, 277-292; and Morawska, "Labour Migrations of Poles in the Atlantic World Economy, 1880-1914," *Comparative Studies in Society and History*, XXXI, No. 2 (1989), 237-272, reprinted in Dirk Hoerder and Leslie Page Moch (eds.), *European Migrants: Global and Local Perspectives* (Boston, 1996), 170-208.

[68]Dudley Baines, "European Emigration, 1815-1930: Looking at the Emigration Decision Again," *Economic History Review*, New ser., XLVII, No. 3 (1994), 533-536; Michael J. Piore, *Birds of Passage: Migrant Labour and Industrial Societies* (New York, 1979), 148-154; and Wyman, *Round Trip to America*, 31.

[69]Murken, *Die grossen transatlantischen*, 52-54.

market, drastically lowering prices just when business conditions in the US favoured re-migration. Only during the Panic of 1907 did the high demand for return passage manage to neutralize this tendency. Shipping lines maintained high rates for some months despite a rate war for westbound passages. This underlines the growing market forces of return migration, but these never managed to compensate for the loss on westbound traffic during the American recession. The cheap rates must have facilitated the decision to return.

So called extra "Christmas sailings" that responded to the increasing demand of migrants to rejoin their family for Christmas illustrates how the movement became institutionalized. Shipping companies did not passively wait for clients to make up their minds to return, as a letter from HAL's New York head agent anticipating a break up of the conference agreement and a subsequent rate war illustrates:

> We need to prepare pamphlets targeting Germans for whom the American experience has been a bitter disappointment inciting them to return home. The leaflets need to promote Rotterdam as ideal gateway for the Rhine region. Dutch are hard to agitate since most of them are farmers who are stuck to their lands.[70]

The letter emphasizes the difference between agrarian settlers and industrial labourers in terms of their propensity to return. The ascendancy of industrial society throughout the nineteenth century significantly increased transatlantic mobility. The HAL's New York head agents underlined the difficulties in estimating the number of eastbound bookings which only came in shortly before departure, making it hard to fill the extra capacity with goods instead. With the overcapacity and daily departures from New York to Europe there were no risks of congestion at the port. Many return migrants bought their ticket only after their arrival in New York. The large concentration of shipping lines, migrant brokers, agents and runners turned the port into the best place to find a cheap homeward journey. Many did so through correspondence beforehand.

Because of its superior hinterland connections and its control over eastbound trades, New York outdistanced its Atlantic competitors. The dominance increased in the 1860s when the National Currency Act turned the city into the nation's banking centre, further stimulating money to flow towards New York. In the meantime, the immigrant landing station at Castle Garden opened its doors, providing assistance for inland travel, food and lodging, currency exchange, employment and housing. It reduced the activity of swindlers

[70]GAR, HAL, 318.02, Directors, 112-121, letter, 21 November 1883.

abusing the naivety of new arrivals and enhanced the reputation of the port.[71] The major passenger lines gave direct first-class steam connections to Europe, which greatly contributed to New York's supremacy.[72] Up to 1914, New York's share of the migrant flow normally was around eighty-five percent, with some peaks as high as ninety-five percent.[73] The concentration of branch offices for all the major passenger lines turned the port into the nodal point of the migrant trade.

HAL's Agency in New York

To represent the HAL in the US, the directors appointed the Dutch consul in New York who also ran a shipping agency, Burlange and Co. R.C. Burlange had a lot of experience in trade from New York to the Low Countries, and his position as consul added prestige which helped the line to establish local contacts.[74] American contacts underlined the importance of regular sailings leaving on a fixed day of the week. They also suggested choosing ship names with a special characteristic, such as Dutch towns ending with "dam" to impress the HAL in the memory of people. Good treatment of passengers with little niceties such as a decent pint of claret on Sundays made the difference. They warned that newspapers could make or break a line, especially in case of accidents, and advised the HAL to appoint a Dutch official at Castle Garden. HAL's directors followed the advice but dithered over the appointment of a passage agent despite the important revenues the German lines retrieved from the prepaid business. Initially, the activities in New York were limited to securing cargo for the eastbound trip through the shipbrokers Funch and Edye.[75]

Burlange, whose shipping agency may have created a conflict of interest with the HAL, was soon replaced by Cazaux van Staphorst who received

---

[71]Karl E. Born, *International Banking in the 19th and 20th Centuries* (Stuttgart, 1977), 92-93; and Erickson (ed.), *Emigration from Europe*, 270-272.

[72]Jean Heffer, *Le port de New York et le commerce extérieur Américain, 1860-1900* (Paris, 1986), 156-173. The number of transatlantic passenger lines in 1890 based in US east coast ports were: New York, twenty-nine; Boston, six; Philadelphia, four; and Baltimore, two.

[73]Swierenga, "Journey Across," 120.

[74]GAR, HAL, 318.14, Wentholt Archief, 9-2, letters, 22 July and 14 November 1871. R.C. Burlange was consul in New York from 1855 to 1881; Hans Krabbendam, *Vrijheid in het verschiet: Nederlandse emigratie naar Amerika, 1840-1940* (Hilversum, 2006), 167-181.

[75]GAR, HAL, 318.14, Wentholt Archief, 6, anonymous letter, n.d; and 9-2, letters, 27 March and 26 June 1872.

a salary of 10,000 *guilders* and committed to not getting involved in other commercial activities. He had to establish contacts with export and import houses, supervise the ships in New York and watch over the activities of Funch and Edye.[76] He also supervised the newly appointed passenger agency L.W. Morris and Co. which sold third-class and cabin berths for the HAL.[77] By 1884, Morris coordinated the activities of 1400 agents and sub-agents selling third-class passages nationwide.[78] The cabin business was handled by a parallel network of agencies which mushroomed in big cities during the steamship era. Wealthy Americans rather than Europeans sustained the booming transatlantic tourism industry. Both networks sold second-class passages which responded to the demands of low-budget business travel and an upgraded service for wealthier migrants. Second-class cost approximately US $10 more than steerage and had the advantage for passengers of not having to pass through immigrant inspections upon arrival. Drew Keeling has estimated that Cunard drew half its revenues from migrant transport, while freight and non-migrant transport accounted for nearly a quarter each. The share of migrant business for smaller lines like the HAL, initially must have been larger because cabin passengers were more sensitive to reputation than were migrants.[79]

These numbers emphasize the responsibility of the external firms managing the passage business for the success of a line. The renewed competition with the Amsterdam-based Royal Netherlands Steamship Co. (RNS) corroborates this. After the HAL refused to split its service between Amsterdam and Rotterdam, the RNS resumed its sailings to New York. The HAL directors favoured the idea of serving both ports in the long run but in the short term refused to divide its fleet, offering only a weekly service between Rotterdam and New York. Except for the two biggest lines, the others kept to their home ports. For the HAL, Rotterdam's connection to the German hinterland made it

[76]*Ibid.*, 44, contract between Cazaux van Staphorst and Netherlands-American Steamship Co. (NASM), 1874.

[77]Whether this New York agency had any relation with the one in Hamburg where Albert Ballin started his career could not be established. Birgit Ottmüller-Wetzel, "Auswanderung über Hamburg: Die HAPAG und die Auswanderung nach Nordamerika, 1870-1914" (Unpublished MA thesis, Freie Universität Berlin, 1986), 14.

[78]GAR, HAL, 318.02, Directors, letters, 21 November and 16 December 1884.

[79]Drew Keeling, "The Transport Revolution in Transatlantic Migration, 1850-1914," *Research in Economic History*, XIX, No. 1 (1999), 40; Keeling, "Costs, Risks, and Migration Networks between Europe and the United States, 1900-1914," in Feys, *et al.* (eds.). *Maritime Transport and Migration*, 122-128; and Abraham Cornelis, "Dromen tussen Europa en de VS: een cultuurhistorische studie van 100 jaar luxevervoer aan boord" (Unpublished MA thesis, Leiden Univerity, 1993), 57-64.

the logical choice over Amsterdam.[80] In 1881, the first full year of service, the RNS transported 10,000 passengers compared to the HAL's 16,000. To drive the RNS out of the passenger market, the HAL opened a competitive service from Amsterdam the following year. Despite this the RNS still carried 15,000 passengers to the HAL's 18,000. The competition forced the HAL to give in the following year and agree to divide its sailings equally between Amsterdam and Rotterdam for the next ten years, while RNS promised to leave the North Atlantic.[81] The boom in migrant traffic through Amsterdam indicates the secondary importance of superior access routes to out-migration regions and points to the primary importance of migrant agents in directing clients to certain ports.

When selling prepaid tickets for the HAL, these agents contacted Morris and Co. The passage agent passed on the information to the shipping company's head agent who sent weekly lists of those who needed travelling instructions to the Rotterdam directors. The purchaser was handed a receipt and a numbered shipping ticket on which the name of the shipping company or migrant broker, port of embarkation, names of the passengers and amount paid had to be mentioned. The agent sent the ticket to the passenger to start preparing for the trip and to await instructions from the shipping company. The recipient was then contacted by the nearest local agent or by the shipping company directly to arrange travel to the port of embarkation. Through the network, companies could arrange this according to sailing dates, minimizing the time a passenger spent at the port and minimizing extra costs for the passenger. Shipping lines promoted the sale of railroad tickets to the port of embarkation and from the port of arrival to the final destination which facilitated the transit and enabled migrant agents to earn an extra commission. The passenger was given up to a year to prepare for his trip after purchasing the ticket.

The HAL was forced to restructure midway through the 1880s after its reputation was tarnished by four shipwrecks. The directors sent W.H. van den Toorn from Rotterdam to replace van Staphorst as head agent.[82] The latter left in a huff, slamming the office doors, taking all the archives and using his influence to blacken the reputations of his successor and the HAL. Being from outside New York, van den Toorn had some difficulty in becoming established in the local business community, but with the help of Dutch consul, John Rutger Planten, and through his membership in the Holland Society of New York, an elitist group which traced its Dutch roots back to seventeenth century, he began to make a name for himself. To cut costs van den Toorn took more as-

[80]GAR, HAL, 318.14, Wentholt Archief, 18, letters, 2 and 4 May 1881.

[81]G.J. De Boer, *125 jaar Holland-Amerika Lijn, 1873-1998* (Rotterdam, 1998), 10-20.

[82]GAR, HAL, 318.02, Directors, 53, letter, 2 November 1884.

pects of the business into its own hands, including the loading and unloading of ships in the harbour. He suggested taking over the freight business in Rotterdam from Wambersie and Son and the American passage business from Morris and Son. Mr. Krummeich received training in Rotterdam before crossing the Atlantic to run the passage business under van den Toorn. Rather than recruiting locally to fill openings in its US offices, the HAL increasingly sent over employees from the Netherlands where they had time to become familiar with the company's philosophy. The directors trusted Dutchmen more than foreigners. Overseas service became a *sine qua non* for those interested in being promoted in a company which was still dominated by family ties.[83]

The reasons for the takeover of Morris and Son were two-fold. First, it allowed the HAL not only to save on commissions but also to predict costs more accurately. Commissions fluctuated depending on the level of competition. For example, in August 1885, when the lines had just signed an agreement neutralizing competition and reducing commissions, Morris received US $6.50 per cabin and US $6.25 per steerage passenger he booked directly. On tickets sold through agents, the broker earned US $2 for cabin and US $2.25 for steerage bookings. Morris sold twenty-five percent of the cabin passages directly, but ninety-three percent of the steerage tickets were sold through agents. In total, Morris and Son earned an average of US $10,675 in commissions per year. Second, Morris' son, Frank, did not manage the business with the same zeal as his father and lost control of his agents. To ensure a smooth transition, Morris let Krummeich do an internship at his office before the HAL took control of the business in 1886. In exchange, Morris shared in the company's profits for the next two years. Van den Toorn defended this expense, stressing that parting acrimoniously would have cost a lot more.[84] The Hamburg-Amerikanischen Packetfahrt-Actien-Gesellschaft (HAPAG) proved the head agent right when it encountered serious trouble with a similar transition. When the German line took over the passage business from C.B. Richard and Co., which had represented HAPAG for four decades, the migrant broker used all his influence to tarnish his former employer's reputation. He contracted passengers for rival British lines and took the head agencies of new lines competing on the same routes as HAPAG. Oscar Richard also challenged his for-

---

[83]The following New York head agents joined the board of directors; W. Van den Toorn (1899-1906), J.R. Wierdsma (1906-1936) and A. Gips (1912-1933). The following completed the board's membership before World War I; W. van der Hoeven (1873-1884); A. Plate (1874-1880), J.V. Wierdsma (1881-1916), O. Reuchlin (1873-1919) and J. Reuchlin (1906-1912). The list emphasizes the predominance of the Wierdsma and Reuchlin families. A.D. Wentholt, *Brug over den Oceaan: een eeuw geschiedenis van de Holland-Amerika Lijn* (Rotterdam, 1973), 14-15.

[84]GAR, HAL, 318.02, Directors, 112-121, letters, 16 August 1885 and 23 June 1886.

mer employer in court for being a member of various shipping conferences allegedly in violation of Sherman Antitrust Act.[85]

With the takeovers, van den Toorn supervised both the freight and passage businesses, the latter being divided into steerage and cabin departments. As business increased, the HAL opened new offices in key transit points on both sides of the Atlantic.[86] Van den Toorn replaced young passage personnel with more experienced men to strengthen relations with the migrant agents. He hired two "travellers" who visited the agents to ensure that they observed the conference rules and that the HAL received a fair share of the business.[87] Travellers pressured those agents that failed to produce satisfactory results to increase their bookings or be replaced. The reports they filed summarized local market conditions and commented on future business prospects. Whenever possible, travellers also tried to encourage migration.[88] Van den Toorn also appointed general passage agents to control the agents in specific districts.[89] The general agents were not allowed to book for other lines but earned a US $1 commission on each passenger booked in their district. Van den Toorn assumed that the HAL would lose a few agents during the takeover, but he banked on the fact that the HAL's membership in the continental shipping cartel assured them of having the best and most respectable agents. If they

---

[85]Richard first booked for rival lines and then took on the head agency of the Prince Line in 1897, the Christianson Line in 1898, the Austro-Americana Line in 1904, the Lloyd-Italiano Line in 1905 and the Russian Volunteer Line in 1906. Richard first denounced the conference system in 1898 which ended with the acceptance of the Prince Line into the Mediterranean cartel. The Continental Conference constantly feared a new complaint by Richard as representative of the Russian Volunteer Fleet. *Ibid.*, 318.04, Passage, 72-76, 221-226, correspondence, 1892-1911.

[86]These included Amsterdam, Leipzig, Paris and Vienna in Europe, and Chicago, Boston, St. Louis, Minneapolis, San Francisco and New Orleans in the US.

[87]They spent half the year travelling and the other half at the passage office in New York or Chicago to prevent them from deviating from the business policies. GAR, HAL, 318.02, Directors, 112-121, letters, 1 February and 8 April 1886 and 30 August 1895.

[88]For instance, when strikes broke out in the Pennsylvania coal mines, Henry Schleissner travelled to the area to ensure that the HAL got its share of bookings. Similarly, when visiting the Dutch colonies in California, the HAL traveller stimulated the residents to write home and convince people to follow in their footsteps. *Ibid.*, 318.04, Passage, 221-226, letters, 26 November 1897 and 22 May 1902.

[89]Two were appointed for the western states, one for the Pacific coast, one for New England and another one for the southern states.

decided to leave the cartel, the directors knew that a wide network of less solid but active non-conference agents existed as a fall-back.[90]

Shipping companies generally failed to generate enough business for a broker or agent to be an exclusive representative. For their part, migrant entrepreneurs tried to obtain the agency of as many shipping companies as possible to boost both their prestige and income. Agents spread their sales among the lines they represented in order to retain their agency, yet the company offering the best incentives normally obtained the biggest share of their business. The keener the competition among the lines, the more advantages middlemen could obtain. They exploited the rivalry among shipping lines to increase their grip on the market, which proved much harder to control than the HAL had anticipated. Van den Toorn quickly realized that the measures within the firm to control the agents were inadequate. Shipping companies needed inter-firm collaboration if they wanted to hold on to their profits. The establishment and operation of shipping conferences will be discussed in detail in the following chapters. What follows here is a profile of the services rendered by American agents.

Role of the Immigrant Banker/Migrant Agent in the Migration Process

Despite the fact that migrants contributed to the rapid growth of savings banks during the nineteenth century, these institutions initially did not value the new clients fully because of the way they used their accounts. The increasingly mobile migrants opened accounts for short-term accumulations as part of their migration strategy, often either moving elsewhere in the US or returning home after attaining their goals. They engaged in more transactions and closed their accounts more rapidly than natives. New migrants built up their balances and closed their accounts more quickly than did those who had been in America longer. Savings institutions were generally hostile to short-term depositors. Partly due to legal constraints, these banks reinvested deposits in long-term placements, so migrant accounts which could be closed on short notice threatened their stability. Some banks, like the Philadelphia Saving Fund Society, attempted unsuccessfully to change the way migrants used their accounts. Because migrants' accounts required a lot of paperwork in return for small earnings, savings banks made no special efforts to attract migrants and often were unwelcoming and unaccommodating toward them. They did not invest in language skills or provide the special assistance many migrants required.[91]

---

[90]GAR, HAL, 318.04, Passage, 563, letter, 30 April 1885; and Wentholt, 18/3, letter, 21 November 1884.

[91]DC, *Report*, XXXVII, 215-216; George Alter, Claudia Goldin and Elyce Rotella, "The Savings of Ordinary Americans: The Philadelphia Savings Fund Society in the Mid-nineteenth Century," *Journal of Economic History*, LIV, No. 3 (1994), 735-

As a result, many migrants, especially the first generation who depended on personal and ethnic relations, entrusted their savings to migrant agents selling ocean passages. The majority of agents only sold tickets as a sideline and to make contacts with potential clients for other businesses, of which banking quickly developed into the predominant activity. Migrant entrepreneurs often entered banking accidently, but having the same background helped them to earn the trust of their clients. Language skills and specialized services, especially administrative ones, allowed them to establish lasting links with others of the same ethnicity and often to establish immigrant banks. The fact that American financial institutions proved reluctant to hire migrant entrepreneurs seeking to enter the banking business further spurred the profusion of immigrant banks. The success of such entrepreneurs depended on their ability to obtain the agency of shipping lines since the sale of ocean passages was an indispensable part of immigrant banking. Because for the new immigrant savings was a primary goal, immigrant banks multiplied wherever migrant communities were established. The lack of legislation regulating these private banks enhanced their rapid growth.[92]

In 1897, 2625 official (and innumerable unofficial) immigrant savings banks were active.[93] As the market expanded, American bankers tried to get their hands on the business by investing in the foreign departments of their banks. Financial institutions today are rediscovering ethnic banking, using culture and ethnicity on a micro-level for both client orientation and market differentiation. For instance, the Spanish-American community has become a very competitive market for banks offering specialized services in which ethnic ties provide a strategic advantage.[94] Due to the lack of primary material on

---

767; and Rohit Daniel Wadhwani, "Banking from the Bottom Up: The Case of Migrant Savers at the Philadelphia Saving Fund Society during the Late Nineteenth Century," *Financial History Review*, IX, No. 1 (2002), 46-62.

[92]John Bodnar, *The Transplanted: A History of Immigrants in Urban America* (Bloomington, 1985), 131-132; Day, "Credit, Capital and Community," 68-70; Wyman, *Round Trip to America*, 59-60; Isaac A. Hourwich, "The Economic Aspects of Immigration," *Political Science Quarterly*, XXVI, No. 4 (1911), 632; and Piore, *Birds of Passage*, 56.

[93]Dino Cinel, *The National Integration of Italian Return Migration, 1879-1929* (New York, 1991; reprint, New York, 2002), 31; and David Gerber, "Internationalization and Transnationalization," in Reed Ueda (ed.), *A Companion to American Immigration* (Oxford, 2006), 237.

[94]David Armstrong and Peter R. Heiss, "Ethnic Banking: Identifying the Capacity and Future Implications of the Ethnic Banking Market" (Unpublished paper presented to the Oxford Business and Economics Conference, Oxford University, June 2007), 1-11; and Born, *International Banking*, 176.

immigrant banks, the discussion here relies on volume 37 of the Dillingham Commission. Material in the HAL archives, especially sporadic reports on the migrant agent network, is used to complement the findings.

Profile

The Dillingham Commission described immigrant banks as follows:

> These banks bear little resemblance to regular banking institutions. They are without real capital, have little or no legal responsibility, and for the most part are entirely without legal control. Immigrant bankers, as a rule, are also steamship-ticket agents, and usually conduct some other business as well. Consequently the "banks" are, for the most part, located in groceries, saloons, or other establishments which are natural gathering places for immigrants.
>
> Besides handling the savings of his patrons, the immigrant banker performs for them many necessary services. He writes their letters, receives their mail and is their general adviser...The ability and willingness of the banker to render such services naturally gives him an advantage over regular banking institutions...In this way immigrant banks and immigrant bankers are important factors in the life of the newer immigrants.[95]

According to the Commission, these banks concentrated in new immigrant communities, and their predominant feature was the connection between banking and selling steamship tickets. Of the 116 banks it investigated, ninety-four percent combined both activities. Migrants entrusted their money to steamship agents rather than American banks. They did this for safekeeping rather than investing and hence did not expect to earn interest. Because of this trust, steamship agents quickly accumulated capital and developed banking functions. The steamship agency was the most typical antecedent of the immigrant bank.

The DC described these representatives as intelligent men possessing considerable influence in immigrant communities who provided essential services to new and often illiterate immigrants because of their good command of English. Involvement in the local church or ethnic society increased their prestige in the community.[96] Sharing ethnic ties with patrons was essential. Some-

---

[95]DC, *Report*, XXXVII, 204.

[96]HAL appointed Frank Burszynski because of his involvement in several Polish societies in Buffalo. A. Rusin was appointed because he lived together with his brother, the priest of the Polish Roman Catholic Church in Syracuse. Rusin claimed

times these ties needed to go as far back as the province of origin, yet most bankers' potential to draw clients depended more broadly on their language skills. Compatriots represented the easiest targets, but the longer the banker stayed in business, the easier it became to break through ethnic barriers. The location of the office in official buildings helped with this.[97] The longer an immigrant remained in the US, the less importance was attached to ethnic ties.

Besides ocean passage sales and migrant banking, the majority of these entrepreneurs also carried out some other type of related business. A sample of banks found a combination with one or more of the following; notaries office (forty); real estate, rental, insurance and collecting agencies (twenty-seven); saloon keepers (twenty-one); grocers, butchers, and fruit vendors (fourteen); labour agencies (thirteen); book, jewellery and foreign novelty stores (twelve); postal substations (eleven); general merchants (nine); boardinghouse keepers (eight); wholesalers and importers (seven); barbers (two); printers (two); poolroom keepers (two); furniture dealer (one); and undertaker (one). Eighty percent of these banks were not only privately but also individually and locally owned. Only a dozen New York banks had branches in the interior of the US. Others seldom did, but always in the vicinity of the main office. The DC emphasized that shipping conference rules restricting the agents' sale of steamship tickets to the office to which he had been appointed limited the spread of branch offices. The shipping cartel imposed these restrictions to limit competition, combat instability and keep commission rates as low as possible.[98]

The Commission divided immigrant banks into three groups. The first, a minority, consisted of those incorporated under state law, highly organized and thoroughly responsible. Second, there were the steamship, labour and real estate agencies that advertised banking services without legal authorization. The third (and largest) group consisted of grocers, saloonkeepers and the like for whom banking activities were incidental and often conducted in a very irresponsible way. In some cases these classes overlapped.[99] What the DC did not underline was that most banks in the second and third category were run as

---

that 5000 Poles were connected to the church which assured him a good base on which to draw. Sometimes the link was even more direct as the appointment of Vladimir Alexandrov, a Russian priest of the local church in Ansonia, illustrates. GAR, HAL, 318.04, Passage, 72-77, letters, 2 November 1906 and 9 February 1909.

[97]The agents Westerhoff and Poelstra, who controlled the Dutch business in Patterson, New Jersey, reported that opening a branch in the Post Office building allowed them to establish contacts with Poles and Russians. *Ibid.*, letter, 29 July 1910.

[98]DC, *Report*, XXXVII, 205-220.

[99]*Ibid.*, 206-214 and 222-226.

family businesses. Sons, daughters and spouses played an important role assisting in, or even managing, the business.[100] Also, shipping lines avoided appointing land speculators because if their colonization attempts failed, the line risked being associated with it, damaging its reputation.

Services Rendered: Money Transfers, Deposits, Loans and Labour Agencies

The four main banking services offered were money exchange, deposits, loans and remittances. Most of the money exchange business was based in New York. Prepaid passengers exchanged their money before continuing their journey inland, while return passengers often waited until reaching the port of departure before converting their dollars into another currency. The keen competition greatly reduced profit margins on the exchanges.[101]

Other than savings banks, only a minority of the immigrant banks paid interest on deposits. Patrons deposited their money for safekeeping until enough was accumulated for a remittance or the purchase of a steamship ticket. Migrants rarely left their money for longer than a year - three months was the average - while US $100 appeared to be the limit of accumulation in savings accounts. Being unregulated, the bookkeeping practices of these banks often was extremely basic, while they disposed of money more or less as they wished. The migrant had very little protection against abuses. As proof of his deposit, he usually only received a receipt. Immigrant bankers reinvested the money in their own businesses; re-deposited it at two to four percent interest with regular banks; or invested in real estate and stocks. Nevertheless, banks claimed that all deposits were available for immediate withdrawal on demand. This was usually done only when returning to Europe. When moving somewhere else in the US, migrants often continued using the same bank through correspondence. Located in the main port of arrival, New York bankers were in an ideal position to bind the newcomers to their business. Many migrants settled in New York or remained there temporarily to earn extra funds before

---

[100]Agent Rainke of Frankford was hardly ever home, leaving the business to his wife. After the death of agent Roth in Mckeesport, his sons and son-in-law took over the business. J. Klauck, the biggest agent in Buffalo, received assistance from his son and two daughters. In the same city the daughter of F. Grosky managed the business, yet when she remarried and left her parents, sales rapidly decreased. Mrs. de Booy assured that all the Dutch business in the surroundings of Kenosha went through the HAL. Mrs. Dejaegher of Moline arranged the travels of the local Belgian community. Finally, traveller C. Van de Stadt labelled Mrs. J. Chemma as the best HAL agent in South Chicago. GAR, HAL, 318.04, Passage, 72-77, letters, 28 September, 18 October 18 and 2 November 1906, 24 and 30 July 1907 and 4 April 1908.

[101]DC, *Report*, XXXVII, 237-258.

moving elsewhere. This may explain the much higher concentration of immigrant banks in that state than in any other.[102]

Immigrant banks also offered loans. The most common form consisted in advancing money for steamship tickets, and in a few cases for a remittance home or for food. The banker required no security for the transaction because it was of a personal and private nature. Only the biggest banks charged interest (usually five to seven percent), but these were exceptional.[103] In 1893, Herman Schulteis, who investigated the causes of Italian migration for Congress, discovered that a significant number of Italian bankers concentrating on Mulberry Street in New York advanced the money for prepaid tickets and controlled a great part of the Mediterranean passage market. The tickets were sold in instalments as low as US $2 a month, and often the passenger helped to pay off his ticket with the first money earned in the US. Schulteis claimed that Italian bankers had become prosperous on the interest collected from the money advanced for prepaid tickets, and that the system was used on a large scale by American employers to violate the contract labour laws which prohibited the entry of immigrants who had made previous arrangements for work.[104] Being an advocate of immigrant restrictions, Schulteis may have exaggerated the scale of the practice, but van den Toorn corroborated it by stating that on the continental market tickets were bought at the direction of private persons or firms while part was paid for by the migrant in Europe.[105]

The *padrone* system, a popular form of often indentured apprenticeships in the Mediterranean was exported to the US. Labour agents, the so-called *padrone*, recruited unskilled labourers on contract at a fixed wage for American employers. They generally also managed or had close connections with an immigrant bank and often advanced the money for the crossing with credit tickets, thereby placing the migrant in a form of debt peonage.[106] Directly or indirectly, immigrants often secured work through the immigrant banks. Many unskilled migrants filled seasonal occupations and could rely on

---

[102]*Ibid.*, 213. In the state of New York, a special commission estimated their number at around 1000, excluding grocers, shopkeepers, barbers, etc., doing banking transactions. The DC counted 575 immigrant banks in Illinois, 410 in Pennsylvania, 175 in Massachusetts, 150 in Ohio, eighty in New Jersey, sixty in Wisconsin, sixty-five in Connecticut, and approximately fifty in the other states.

[103]*Ibid.*, 237-258.

[104]Schulteis, *Report*, 32-34.

[105]GAR, HAL, 318.04, Passage, 221-226, letter, 5 July 1893.

[106]Erickson (ed.), *Emigration from Europe*, 216-17; Donna R. Gabaccia, *Italy's Many Diasporas* (Seattle, 2000), 62-65; and Jones, *American Immigration*, 164.

immigrant banks for credit between jobs. Greeks, Syrians and Italians combined immigrant banking with labour agencies more often than Slavs and Jews.[107] Yet even in the latter communities the practice of selling tickets in instalments was also well established.

Jewish immigrant bankers/migrant agents, concentrated in Grand and Canal streets in New York, got their hands on the Continental market.[108] As seventy-five percent of the two million Jews who immigrated between 1881 and 1914 remained in New York, the brokers had a solid and expanding client base of co-religionists.[109] Yet by corrupting the prepaid ticket market through orders issued by overseas migrant brokers at lower European rates, they quickly pierced through the ethnic barriers (see below). Continental migrant agents with non-Jewish backgrounds lagged behind in getting their hands on such orders and remained under-represented in New York. During the 1890s, van den Toorn divided the Jewish Canal Street immigrant bankers into two groups. One comprised bankers who only issued tickets when the full amount was paid. The other consisted of bankers who used peddlers to sell tickets on credit, allowing relatives, friends or third parties to pay for the crossing in instalments at rates that exceeded the price fixed by the shipping cartels. Five or six dollars was enough to buy a ticket on credit. Such agents became dependent on peddlers to recover the money and bring in the necessary cash. Some went bankrupt and disappeared, leaving outstanding debts with the steamship lines. To protect against this, some lines substituted prepaid blanks with receipt books to prevent agents from disappearing with unaccounted for prepaid blanks.[110]

Yet the practice also undermined the attempts of shipping companies to decrease internal competition through price agreements. Although the rules imposed by the shipping cartels on agents made it more difficult to exceed the prices fixed by the lines (and also to use peddlers or to issue tickets before receiving the full amount), the combination of ocean passage sales with banking made it very difficult to check this practice. That some agents openly advertised the sale of tickets on instalments indicates this. It not only undermined the control of shipping companies over the agent network but also harmed the reputation of the lines, which were often confronted with stranded passengers

---

[107]Day, "Credit, Capital and Community," 72.

[108]GAR, HAL, 318.04, Passage, 221-226, letter, 11 November 1892.

[109]The majority came from Russia; the rest were from Hungary, Galicia and Romania. See Frederick M. Binder and David R. Reimers, *All the Nations under Heaven: An Ethnic and Racial History of New York* (New York, 1995), 114-115.

[110]GAR, HAL, 318.04, Passage, 221-226, letters, 19 February and 24 April 1889 and 15 May 1891.

at the port of embarkation because agents cancelled their tickets when the amount due by the purchaser had not been paid. Despite the efforts of the shipping lines to hire detectives to catch abusers, the practice persisted. Only the bank crash of 1907 curtailed the practice somewhat.

Remittances

For deposits, exchanges, ticket sales and loans, immigrant banks acted autonomously, but for transmitting money to Europe, the most important transaction of their business, they relied on other institutions. A number of large banking houses in New York City dominated the remittance business because of their extended network of foreign correspondents through which they offered immigrant banks ready facilities for transmission to small European towns. This way the small bank did not need to maintain balances or clearing reserves abroad. They provided immigrant banks with printed money order forms, allowing them to use their name and reputation without taking any responsibility for their actions, seeing them as mere correspondents rather than as agents. The system used for prepaids also applied to money orders, consisting of a stub to be retained by the immigrant bank as a record; an advice or direction slip to be returned to the banking house; an advice slip to be sent to the payee; and a receipt for the purchaser. To attract this business, New York banking houses and some steamship lines advertised in newspapers, employed solicitors and sent circulars. The DC's 1907 estimate indicates the importance of this business. Migrants remitted approximately US $275,000,000 to Europe, half of which went through immigrant banks. This amount was equal to twenty percent of the net annual growth in the individual deposits in all American banks and trust companies combined for the same year. The banks involved earned commissions of anywhere between one to three percent.[111]

As van den Toorn noted during the rate war in the 1890s, the primary goal of migrant agents was to get their hands on savings or the remittances sent to Europe to practice usury. Due to the fierce competition for ocean passage sales, they shared part of the commission with peddlers and often returned the other part as a discount to the purchaser to increase their sales. As van den Toorn noted, they sold tickets with a profit margin as low as twenty-five cents. This keen competition also drastically reduced the profit margin on money exchanges.[112] Yet the system of prepaid tickets allowed agents to draw profits by speculating on the market in two ways. Since prepaid tickets were valid for a year, when prices were low, especially during rate wars, agents ordered pre-

[111]DC, *Report*, 1911, XXXVII, 260-284; and Wadhwani, "Banking from the Bottom Up," 48.

[112]GAR, HAL, 318.04, Passage, 221-226, letters, 3 April 1888 and 15 May 1891.

paid blanks in bulk, writing these out to fictional people. When prices increased, these were sold with an extra profit margin. If prices dropped or tickets could not be sold in time the agents' loss was limited to the five percent cancellation fee.

Moreover, as some migrant brokers extended their networks on both sides of the Atlantic, cheaper European cash rate orders started to circulate in the US during the second half of the 1880s. Ocean passage rates in Europe were lower than prepaid rates and the commissions were higher, resulting in an important difference of net rates on both sides of the continent. Jewish migrant brokers in Hamburg opened branch offices in New York or collaborated with well-established American brokers and started issuing their own passage orders drawn on the European houses at cash rates. Such orders were then exchanged by the migrant broker for the shipping lines' European cash rate tickets in Hamburg.[113] The difference between prepaid and cash rate balanced between $3 and $5 during the 1880s allowing the brokers to seriously undercut the prepaid price.[114] The keen rivalry among shipping companies allowed the migrant brokers to play out the lines against each other. Conference rules supposedly stimulating the collaboration between the lines to control the agent-network were flagrantly violated. Brokers obtained all kinds of incentives spurring the development of the order system. Slowly but surely, orders drawn on European houses at cash rates drove out the prepaid tickets.[115]

Instead of taking control over the American passage business van den Toorn was forced to leave it in the hands of Louis Scharlach's Banking Exchange, Passage Forwarding, Insurance and Foreign Express Company. The migrant broker, with offices in Hamburg and New York, received 'carte blanche' to use all possible means to attract as many passengers as possible. It ruined van den Toorn's efforts to strengthen the ties with American migrant agents and to have them book directly through the HAL's New York passage department. American agents had to establish contacts with migrant brokers such as Scharlach to get their hands on cash orders and alienated from the shipping companies. The Red Star Line (RSL) had a similar agreement with Sender Jarmulowsky and the North German Lloyd (NGL) with Friedrich Missler. Scharlach forwarded passengers from Hamburg to Rotterdam despite

---

[113]This was also used by Italian bankers. *New York Times*, 26 June 1888.

[114]This estimate is based on the repeated calls to increase the cash rate and decrease the prepaid rate by a combined amount of two to five dollars. In January 1890, the difference on net ocean rates was US $4.7, with prepaids at US $19 while Hamburg cash rates were at sixty *marks*. This difference was reduced only gradually. GAR, HAL, 318.04, Passage, 221-226, letters, 20 January 1890 and 15 July 1892.

[115]The HAL archives indicate that orders began to circulate in 1885 and did so on a large scale by 1888.

the fact that transport between the ports cost US $2.25 while the price differential of HAL ships with the cheapest direct service of HAPAG was only US $1. Thus, including railroad fare, the passage through Rotterdam imposed extra travel and cost US $1.25 more than the lowest class of HAPAG steamers. This refutes the assumption that passengers chose to travel on the cheapest and most convenient route and underlines again the importance of migrant agents and brokers in persuading purchasers of ocean passage to travel on certain routes.

Another problem for the HAL, apart from alienating the American agents, was that indirect migration through Hamburg strengthened patterns that contributed to the development of a rival port while obstructing the promotion of Rotterdam as a gateway.[116] Hamburg migrant brokers like Scharlach, with interests in local boarding houses, banks, etc., showed little inclination to change the migration pattern. The HAL therefore started a parallel collaboration with the migrant broker Bruno Weinberger to forward passengers directly to Rotterdam. The agreement included a clause revealing how brokers directed their passengers via certain routes. It stressed that the HAL consented to bribe - but not to swindle or extort - border agents to direct passengers to Rotterdam. The Hamburg migrant brokers corrupted the business on both sides of the Atlantic, in the process increasing their grip on the market to the detriment of the shipping companies.[117] Of all the shipping companies, HAPAG suffered most as the indirect passage increased through the company's home port.

Because of the lack of coordination among shipping lines over how to regain control of the business, Albert Ballin, the manager of the HAPAG, attacked the Jewish migrant brokers at the heart of their business, competing directly with them by opening a bank and passage office on Canal Street. The HAL lacked connections with the Jewish community to find a person of trust to do the same.[118] Instead, van den Toorn suggested moving into the money transfer market to counter the brokers. By including advertisements for the HAL with the remittance, they would reach people who were most likely to migrate. As people buying prepaid tickets often transferred money for the extra costs on the crossing, both services seemed inseparable. Purchasers might prefer a line where they could do both at once, while some still chose to transfer money instead of buying prepaid tickets. It might be a mere coincidence,

---

[116]Ports tried to attract passengers directly overland, but it took time before companies became known in new out-migration regions and organized the routes, let alone appoint agents at transit points to guide passengers. Rotterdam had the extra difficulty for eastern Europeans of only having the right to appoint agents for the transit in Leipzig because the concession in Berlin had been withdrawn in 1883. GAR, HAL, 318.04, Passage, 221-226, 1887-1896.

[117]*Ibid.*, letters, 16 September 1889 and 5 August 1892.

[118]*Ibid.*, letters, 12 August 1890 and 15 May 1891.

but it is worth noting that the average remittance in 1907 amounted to US $35.18, approximately the cost of a steamship ticket. The White Star, Guion and Red Star lines had entered the market with success. Schumacher and Co. and Richard and Co., the passage agents for NGL and HAPAG, respectively, were also doing big business. If the restrictionist movement managed to prohibit the sale of prepaid tickets as proposed in the Stump Bill, the HAL risked losing ground to rivals involved in money transfers. HAL's directors agreed to a test but quickly pulled back.[119] The objections by the New York head agent to the proposals of the Vienna office to re-enter the business explain why:

> Opening a money transfer department would never become sufficiently important to compensate all the trouble and responsibility attached to it. We can't merely advise agents that we will accept money for transmission to addresses on the other side, but in view of the care, accuracy and promptness that the business requires we would have to establish a full-fledged money department. HAPAG some years ago maintained a money sending department for a time, but did away with it due to unsatisfactory results. The RSL still maintains such department more as a part of the IMM traveller cheques and money order branch, than as a typical RSL institution. The RSL have their money order business in the hands of most of their agents, and handle enough business to pay two experienced clerks employed constantly at the department. There is positively no financial profit in it, as the competition with other money order firms and the post offices, forces the exchange rate to the lowest level, while on the other hand they run the additional risks if an agents remains in default or fails, to lose the money not only for the outstanding tickets but also of the money orders. Yet RSL does believe that it helps the business in a general way and the Antwerp offices cherishes the idea that it allows them to collect addresses, giving the opportunity to get in touch with them and secure whatever cash business, connected with it, but the sale of prepaids does not seem to profit from that. In regards to draw up a database with interesting addresses we could obtain this by having the purser collect these from all eastbound passengers whereto they are returning in Europe.[120]

---

[119]DC, *Report*, XXXVII, 277. According to van den Toorn, Richard was wiring more than US $8,000,000 to Europe every year. GAR, HAL, 318.04, Passage, 221-226, 1887-1896, letters, 25 July 1891 and 23 September 1892.

[120]*Ibid.*, 318.03, Passage, 168, letter, 2 April 1914.

This statement illustrates the far-reaching connections between the shipping and banking worlds. Despite the fierce competition of important New York banking houses, J.P. Morgan's shipping merger, the International Mercantile Marine Co. (IMM), managed to maintain its position on the money transfer market. That the IMM persisted sits well with the business philosophy of financers who pursued vertical integration through direct marketing. The DC corroborated that it did not stand alone in mentioning an Italian line being active on the remittance market as well. Yet not all lines agreed on the profitability of the system. When the British lines entered the continental pool of the Nord-Atlantische Dampfer-Linien Verband (NDLV) in 1895, shipping companies managed to re-establish order on the prepaid market, taking away an important inducement for money transfers.

Legal Advisors and Boarding Bosses

The variety of parallel business activities engaged in by immigrant bankers reflected the extra services rendered to newcomers and explains why they attracted immigrants. The agents were also an important link with the fatherland by managing the correspondence of their patrons. As legal advisers and notaries, they assisted immigrants in settling disputes both at home and in the US. They obtained all sorts of legal documents, such as birth, death and marriage certificates and leaves of absence for military service; they also settled wage, heritage and property disputes. For instance, when travelling through Pennsylvania, Henry Schleissner reported that agents frantically helped patrons obtain naturalization papers before the more restrictive state laws went into effect.[121] Through shipping companies and migrant agent networks on both sides of the Atlantic, information on immigration and naturalization regulations spread quickly, allowing migrants to be very responsive.[122] These mediators often carried a line of novelty products from the home country which strongly appealed to the newcomers. Through the services, they developed a paternalistic attitude which was especially pronounced among boarding bosses.[123]

Newly arrived migrants working in industrial communities usually relied on the "boarding boss" system for accommodation. This group household offered washing, cooking and lodging for US $2 or $3 a month. Willing to be

---

[121]*Ibid.*, 318.04 Passage, 72-77, letter, 28 September 1906.

[122]The responsiveness of migrants to regulations and their impact on chain migration patterns has been underlined for later periods in Guillermina Jasso and Mark R. Rosenzweig, "Using National Recording Systems for the Measurement and Analysis of Immigration to the United States," *International Migration Review*, XXI, No. 4 (1987), 1212-1244.

[123]DC, *Report*, XXXVII, 206-214 and 222-226.

crowded into a room, which was mostly used for sleeping, allowed them to reduce the cost per capita. By buying food and preparing it in groups, immigrants kept monthly living expenses below US $15. The DC found that the average annual wage of more than 22,000 immigrants amounted to US $455.[124] An unskilled newcomer, right off the boat, earned less than this average of $38 a month, yet by denying himself many comforts a thrifty migrant could save relatively quickly. A Croatian boarding boss testified to the DC that his boarders deposited US $10 to $20 a month with him. A Bulgarian banker even mentioned US $30. At the turn of the century, Hungarian government official Perenyi Bela claimed that Hungarians sent back sixty percent of their wages, a fact later confirmed by Ewa Morawska. By the turn of the century, higher wages allowed Europeans to finance their crossing by working for one year in Europe, yet in America this was reduced to two to three months.[125]

In short, migrant agents tried to meet all the possible needs of migrants. The profits triggered a keen competition which resulted in various marketing strategies to attract and bind patrons.

Advertisements

Like other shipping lines, the HAL's advertising campaigns focused mainly on promoting cabin-class passages.[126] These advertisements added prestige to the line and indirectly increased third-class bookings. The same went for securing

---

[124]W. Jett Lauck, "The Real Significance of Recent Immigration," *North American Review*, CXCV, No. 2 (1912), 207. German migrant letters show that boarding houses offered good housing alternatives for migrants travelling outside their family network. Prices for board and lodging mentioned by Martin Weitz in Rockville, CT. of US $9 in 1855 and by Matthias Dorgathen of US $15 in mine districts in 1881 do not show great fluctuations; Kamphoefner, Helbich and Sommer (eds.), *News from the Land of Freedom*, 344 and 428. Edith Abbott's estimates of unskilled labourers' daily wages fluctuated between US $1.37 and US $1.57 in 1890; Edith Abbott, "Wages of Unskilled Labor, 1850-1900," *Journal of Political Economy*, XIII, No. 3 (1905), 358.

[125]Hourwich, "Economic Aspects of Immigration," 632-633; DC, *Report*, 1911, XXXVII, 242 and 316; NAW, RINS, 54152/77, Special investigation Hungarian migration, booklet Perenyi Bela, 1903; Keeling, "Costs, Risks, and Migration Networks," 136; and Morawska, "Return Migrations," 280.

[126]Ballin attached such importance to advertising that he established a "literary department" which constantly provided the German and foreign press with positive material about the firm. According to Johannes Merck, a HAPAG director, it was impossible to open a German newspaper before 1914 without seeing something about the company. All other advertising material, including rate sheets, posters and pamphlets were looked after by a separate printing office. Hamburg Staatsarchiv, HAPAG, 622-1, Erinnerungen Merck.

delegations attending transatlantic conferences and organizing excursions on board HAL ships for the Knights Templar or Magyar excursions; the Young Men's Christian Association conference in Basel; the Americanists conference in New York, etc. These excursions and conferences received attention in the press, giving the company extra publicity and contributing to build a reputation among certain target groups. The daily articles on the Magyar excursion published by Mr. Kohany, agent for the HAL in the US and editor of *Szabadsag*, also found their way into the Hungarian press, increasing the popularity of the HAL in the Hungarian community.[127]

The company only explicitly promoted steerage passages on rare occasions for limited time periods and specific market segments usually linked to ethnic groups. For instance, to counter the attacks of the insubordinate migrant agent Frank Zotti, targeting the South Austrian market, the HAL advertised in those American foreign language newspapers that reached ethnic groups from this region. Or when new shipping companies tried to penetrate the market, such as the Russian Volunteer Line, targeting Russian Jews in particular, the HAL placed ads in the four biggest New York Hebrew dailies. The conference agreements regulated ads in the foreign language press to neutralize excessive campaigns caused by competition. The members handed a list of the papers in which they advertised to the secretary. Any line could freely advertise in any of these papers. If they wanted to enlarge the list, the secretary needed to be informed. When one company advertised in a paper, others usually followed, especially if the owner also acted as migrant agent for the lines. This way of creating goodwill with agents was a hidden form of extra commission which the conference agreements tried neutralize. In 1908, the conference decided that "no lines should advertise in any publication of any sort published directly or indirectly by agents."[128] The rules also stipulated that papers attacking a line would lose the support of all the members.

Migrant brokers and agents generally took responsibility for advertising their business, including the sales of passage tickets and the steamship lines they represented. The lines provided the agents with pocket books, agendas, show cards, beer coasters, posters, steel plates, pamphlets, guides, almanacs, time and rate sheets and the like. Up to 1907, HAL's directors still printed most of these materials in various languages in Rotterdam, despite the repeated requests of the New York head agent to give him *carte blanche* on these matters. If migrant agents advertised through means other than the materials provided, such as newspaper ads, they did so at their own cost. Most agents also printed their own booklets and rate sheets. The boom of the foreign press, with

---

[127]GAR, HAL, 318.04, Passage, 72-77, 221-226, letters, 2 November 1897, 14 January 1898, 24 April 1902 and 15 May and 26 October 1906.

[128]*Ibid.*, 318.03, Passage, 49-58, letter, 4 April 1912.

3500 new papers appearing between 1883 and 1920, was spurred by migrant entrepreneurs trying to gain influence among ethnics. Conference rules stipulated that agents could not make any comparisons between the lines in their ads. As well, the names of the lines they represented needed to be included.[129]

That many agents also published their own newspaper did not escape the attention of the DC, which strongly opposed the combination of banks, employment and steamship agencies with the foreign language press, accusing the banks of using the papers to delay Americanization in order to protect their source of income. According to the Commission, advertisements aimed to stimulate migration by emphasizing favourable labour conditions and offering to advance funds for the ocean passage. The papers spread information on the situation in the home country and also on how and when to return or have friends and family travel to the US. Agents also mailed packages of printed matter to regular and prospective customers containing general paternalist circulars offering free advice in all matters to gain the confidence of countrymen; a second circular explaining how to transfer money home through the bank; a third including a money-forwarding rate list; an address book to fill out the names and addresses of countrymen living in his locality; transmission slips for deposits and withdrawals; post office money order application blanks; business cards; a steamship ticket poster; a sailing list; and return address cards and envelopes. Their offices were decorated with numerous posters of steamship lines, even if they did not represent them, to attract clients for other businesses. For cabin passengers, the HAL sent out its own circulars. But promoting the steerage business remained in the hands of migrant agents.[130]

This way of advertising through correspondence helps to explain how ninety-five percent of HAL's bookings took place through Chicago, Boston and New York. With this form of direct marketing, keeping address lists of former and potential clients was of prime importance for migrant agents. The Hungarian non-conference agents Lengyel and Kraus had a list of 10,000 names. We can only guess how long the lists of well-established conference agents were. Spreading little address books was one way of enlarging the list,

---

[129]*Ibid.*, Passage, 564, meeting, 4 October 1900, minute 598; and Passage 72-77, letters, 7 and 10 December 1906; Jones, *American Immigration*, 195; and William H.S. Stevens, "The Administration and Enforcement of Steamship Conferences and Agreements," *Annals of the American Academy of Political and Social Science*, LV (1914), 125.

[130]DC, *Report*, XXXVII, 228-231. The HAL started doing this on a large scale in 1907 by sending 32,000 individualized circulars to prospective clients with high incomes nationwide. Another 30,000 circulars were addressed to selected German tradesmen enclosing second cabin pamphlets with rates and sailings. In the meantime, it had also started printing its own "Holland America Line Monthly" for the same purposes. GAR, HAL, 318.04, Passage, 72-77, letter, 13 December 1906.

but newspapers acquired through subscription also helped. The importance of address lists is illustrated by the reluctance of the HAL to appoint Olin Brothers as conference agents when fighting the Uranium Line, which was trying to establish itself in Rotterdam. Being cousins and having received their training in the banking and passage business of the conference agent, A. Mandel, the Olin Brothers started on their own after stealing Mandel's address lists. They actively recruited from the list for the Uranium Line. Their appointment as conference agents meant that the Uranium Line would lose one of its best agents, yet the HAL stayed loyal to Mandel, who generated an average of US $50,000 worth of business annually. Along with the use of peddlers and runners, the sending of circulars based on a meticulous database of potential clients were the two most important ways for migrant agents to attract customers. The DC estimated that the number of peddlers in the business in New York alone ranged between 3000 and 6000.[131]

Growing Pressures on Immigrant Banks

Foreign Departments of Commercial Banks and Trusts

As immigrant banks thrived, American financial institutions started to regret their negligence of the migrant clientele. Reports of the HAL travellers show that a growing number of American trusts, commercial and savings banks started targeting migrants at the turn of the century, opening foreign departments staffed by managers and clerks from the targeted ethnic clienteles. The Philadelphia Saving Fund Society, for instance, started off by hiring a clerk to assist migrants with money transfers. By 1916, it ran a foreign department with clerks able to assist migrants in fifteen different languages. It adapted its investment policies on a short-term basis to meet the needs of this market.[132]

Their efforts concentrated on big cities and industrial centres, whereas in rural areas immigrant banks retained their position. For example, in Newcastle, where the tin plate industry employed 8000 men at an average wage of US $1.90 a day, the Lawrence Savings and Trust Company represented the HAL. When the factories needed more workers, the foreign department asked for extra copies of the HAL's third-class pamphlet, which it found very useful to increase their sales. The sales of ocean passages also attracted the booming travelling public of Americans and successful migrants. The names of the cabin agents in Cincinnati, which traveller C. van de Stadt labelled as a "German city," illustrate both the growing interest of bigger banks and the lasting

[131]GAR, HAL, 318.04, Passage, 72-77, letter, 15 June 1911; and DC, *Report*, XXXVII, 228.

[132]Day, "Credit, Capital and Community." 70; DC, *Report*, XXXVII, 316; and Wadhwani, "Banking from the Bottom Up," 60-61.

importance of ethnic identification. The foreign departments of the First National Bank, German National Bank, Western German Bank, Atlas National Bank and Brightson German Bank competed for cabin passengers and even organized their own excursions.[133]

The DC documented this evolution by pointing to Pittsburgh, where national and state banks absorbed the immigrant bank's business in less than a decade. Their foreign departments were primarily directed to the sale of steamship tickets and the handling of remittances. Their aggressive marketing strategies included advertising in foreign newspapers, sending broadcast circulars and pamphlets in different languages, employing solicitors to travel the country and opening branch offices. All these measures contributed to their rapid ascendancy. Traveller Nyland stated that the First National Bank in Pittsburgh had a foreign department with a workforce of about forty. It quickly positioned itself as the most important actor in the city's steamship business, controlling sixty percent of the first-class traffic. This illustrates how serious American banks were about acquiring the business and explains why some banks, like the Provident Savings Bank and Trust Company (founded in 1902), developed into one of the largest American travel agencies still operating as a subsidiary in the 1970s and selling worldwide trips to this day.[134]

Yet the national banks' dependence on the goodwill of the steamship companies for agencies put them in a weak position. As the manager of the foreign department of a leading bank declared to the Dillingham Commission:

> The steamship and immigrant banking business are almost inseparable. As a matter of fact, the sale of foreign exchange follows upon the establishment of a steamship agency and rarely comes before. In view of this important relation it would appear that the steamship companies are entirely too free in the manner in which they establish agencies. A public suggestion to that effect might be a healthy one.[135]

As part of their vertical integration strategy, the shipping lines experimented with opening offices of their own while reducing the number of agents. This explains why most applicants, even prestigious ones such as American Express, were refused the agency of conference lines. The company had managed to obtain the concession to do all the money transfers from Ellis

---

[133]GAR, HAL, 318.04, Passage, 72-77, letters, 18 and 26 October 1906 and 5 June 1909.

[134]DC, *Report*, XXXVII, 219-220; GAR, HAL, 318.03, Passage, 97, letter, 21 February 1913; and Born, *International Banking*, 178.

[135]DC, *Report*, XXXVII, 318.

Island, yet it is likely that J.P. Morgan used the IMM to obstruct the further growth of a rival. Subsequently, American Express lobbied in Albany to convince state representatives to withdraw the right of steamship companies to draw money orders and to sell travellers cheques.[136] If they were unable to get their hands on ocean passage sales, it would prevent the lines from getting into banking. The efforts remained unsuccessful, and the authorities could not be convinced to interfere with the shipping line's freedom to appoint agents. More successful were the banks' lobbying campaigns urging strict regulations for immigrant banks to enable them to move in the market more rapidly.

Legislation

What really stands out regarding the legislation regulating American ocean passage sales and immigrant banking is the lack of it. American authorities did not copy European laws regulating agent networks by imposing nationality and residency restrictions or requiring annual licenses requiring expensive bonds. As these were also used to favour national lines, the predominantly foreign passenger lines preferred to leave sleeping dogs lie and take matters in their own hands. After the British companies joined the NDLV, the lines began to require bonds from their New York agents, a practice which later extended to other states.

Only when American banks started to take an interest in immigrants did some states consider the matter, but it was the Panic of 1907 that exposed the weaknesses of the system of immigrant banking and the need for legislation. Escaping any legal supervision, most immigrant banks started without much capital and maintained small reserves. Without restrictions on how to reinvest the money, many bankers were unable to meet the liquidity demands of the great number of people withdrawing their deposits. Many bankers closed their doors or absconded as there were no laws to prevent this. The panic demonstrated that the speculative banks' assets fell well short of their liabilities. The New York head agent of the HAL, Adrian Gips, reported that many Jewish banks on the East Side and in Brooklyn crashed. As the line had developed the habit of requiring their agents to post bonds and only handing out books of five or ten steamship tickets at a time, it was covered.[137]

On the contrary, the immigrants enjoyed no protection. The DC found that most immigrant banks behaved honestly and noted that the better managed ones continued to lend money during the panic while American banks no

---

[136]GAR, HAL, 318.04, Passage, 564, meeting, 9 March 1901, minute 615; 72-77, letter, 1 July 1908; and 318.03, Passage, 48-59, letters, 19 September and 18 October 1912 and 7 March 1913.

[137]*Ibid.*, 318.04, Passage, 72-77, 221-226, letters, 10 September 1897 and 10 March 1908.

longer could. Yet the lack of a legal base to support the system made it impossible for migrants to pin responsibility on someone in the case of abuses. The DC contended that the events of 1907/1908 showed the urgent need to regulate the business. The National Liberal Immigration League also pleaded for regulations to protect migrants, asking the government to promote the use of the safer postal service among the foreign-born communities.[138]

Although many states had laws regulating private banking, few had the means to enforce them. Only New Jersey (1907), Massachusetts (1905), New York (1907) and Ohio (1908) had laws specifically for immigrant banking.[139] They proved effective in the first two states, but not in the latter two which had no measures for supervision. In general, the laws stipulated that if steamship or labour agents wanted to combine their business with banking, they needed a certificate from the authorities and had to post a bond for up to US $20,000. The bond needed to be executed by two sureties, owners of real estate. The four states set fines for people doing banking business in violation of these laws. Fearing that they might harm private banking interests, the authorities were reluctant to pass more restrictive and effective laws.

The economic crisis eventually convinced New York to follow the DC's recommendations to collect license fees which would only be issued after an audit of the books and proof of property ownership of a certain value; to require cash guarantees deposited with the state; to mandate frequent examinations of the books; and to require the maintenance of specified reserves. With the amendment of the private banking statute on 23 May 1910, only those meeting these requirements could call themselves banks. Simultaneously, the state amended the Wells Laws of 1907 which required ticket agents to have licenses to sell "transportation tickets or orders for transportation to or from foreign countries." These needed to be obtained annually from the comptroller upon proof of good moral character and payment of US $25. A surety bond of US $1000 to $2000 was also required. If found guilty of fraud, misrepresentation or failure to account for money, the comptroller could revoke the license. People doing such business without a license were guilty of a misdemeanour. Pennsylvania soon followed suit.[140]

---

[138]DC, *Report*, XXXVII, 248, 305-314; and NAW, RINS, 51632/13, Immigration Legislation, 1907, National Liberal Immigration League, memorandum, February 1909.

[139]Surprisingly, the DC forgot to mention Connecticut which passed a law requiring agents handling money orders to take out a bond for $10,000. It forced some agents like Herman Baurer of Union City out of both the money order and steamship ticket business. GAR, HAL, 318.04, Passage, 72-77, letter, 9 February 1908.

[140]*Ibid.*, 6 December 1911; Day, "Credit, Capital and Community," 75; DC, *Report*, XXXVII, 317-333 and 349-357; and *New York Times*, 26 May 1910.

The requirement of bonds made it harder for smaller agents to remain in the business, driving it into arms of the bigger concerns. But sometimes these laws backfired against American financial institutions. After the passage of new laws in Pennsylvania, the First National Bank was forced to close its doors because of a misinterpretation of the valuation of securities, assets and reserves. The steamship lines saw the market leader in the region disappear, but most of the outstanding business was covered and they immediately appointed Mr. Rovensky, manager of the steamship department in the failed bank, to take over the business. With former colleagues, Rovensky founded the National Steamship Agency of Pittsburgh to take care of all the bookings made by the First National Bank and swiftly entered the market. The laws hurt the agents but not the shipping companies which strengthened their position.

Only seventy-five years after European authorities started controlling migrant agents and brokers, American authorities followed suit. The need to regulate the banking business, which had developed around the sales of ocean passages, led to the passage of these laws. Most steamship companies welcomed the measures, increasing the supervision of their sales forces without giving a competitive advantages to American shipping lines.[141] Why it took so long for a country, which during the 1840s pressured European governments to prevent abuses in the sales of steamship and railroad tickets, to regulate ticket sales at home is remarkable. That the abuses did not really affect nationals and that business interests did not exert pressure were certainly factors, but further research is needed to explain the lacunae.

Much More than Mere Facilitating Agents

Reducing the activities of migrant brokers and agents to mere travel agencies greatly underestimates their roles. The transatlantic agent network managed by the steamship lines did much more than organize the trip from place of departure to final destination. The agents spread information on where, when and how to move. They also often helped with legal matters before the move. As barriers on emigration and immigration were raised around the Atlantic world, these middlemen offered ways to circumvent them. After the introduction of steam, the American migrant agent network continuously increased its importance as the market of prepaid and return tickets expanded.

American migrant agents/bankers not only sold tickets and offered financial services such as money transfers, money exchanges, safeguarding earnings and giving credit to finance the move but also became

> in a larger sense the economic and social gatekeepers of the American dream, whether that dream was bringing over

[141]GAR, HAL, 318.04, Passage, 72-77, letter, 30 August 1907.

> family and friends from the old country, buying a property, getting a job, saving money or simply finding a place to live. They were central actors in the social networks that coordinated the process of immigrant relocation.[142]

The many business opportunities created by mass migration allowed established entrepreneurs to prosper from the relocation of ethnic groups. The sale of ocean passage tickets and the development of banking operations played central roles in this "migrant business market." The disinterest of American banks in this business and the lack of legislation spurred the development of an unofficial banking network based on ethnic ties. This changed when American banks realized the profits being made from migrants and forced their way into that market at the turn of the century.

That the sale of ocean passage tickets was an essential element to penetrate the market triggered a struggle to acquire the agencies of steamship companies. The difficulties of passenger lines in controlling the agent network refutes the assumption that those agents and brokers lost their influence in the migrant transport market with the transition from sail to steam. Conversely, increased rivalry among shipping lines during the 1890s allowed Jewish brokers to prosper as they never had before. The next chapter analyzes how shipping companies tried to neutralize the competition through conference agreements and how, by doing so, they tried to control the agent network. The horizontal collaboration in the form of cartels was typical in the steamship industry. Business historians have emphasized that in this sector the logic of vertical integration did not pertain.[143] Yet the analysis of the HAL seems to weaken this argument somewhat as it shows clear signs of vertical integration which were more pronounced in the passenger than in freight business. By taking the passenger trade into its own hands and opening an increasing number of company offices at key transit points on both sides of the Atlantic, the Dutch line tried to move forward into the market. Yet to do so and to acquire control over the agent network required the collaboration of other steamship lines, especially in the US where in the absence of legislation they had great scope to operate. As will be argued in the following chapter, the success of passenger conferences significantly influenced the structures of the companies and their tendencies towards vertical integration.

---

[142]Day, "Credit, Capital and Community," 67.

[143]Alfred D. Chandler, Jr., *The Visible Hand: The Managerial Revolution in American Business* (Cambridge, MA, 1977), 189-192; Gordon Boyce, *Co-operative Structures in Global Business: Communicating, Transferring Knowledge and Learning across the Corporate Frontier* (London, 2001), 15; and Boyce, *Information, Mediation,* 6.

Chapter 2
Competition and Collusion: The Growing Pains of Passenger Shipping Conferences

The introduction of steamships had a major impact on the carriage of goods and people in the Atlantic world. Organizational and technological improvements led to sharply decreased freight rates.[1] Jeffrey Williamson, Kevin O'Rourke and Timothy Hatton demonstrated that this was the main reason for the convergence of the commodity market before 1914. As well, they highlighted the importance of migration in the development of the Atlantic economy.[2] Unlike freight rates, we have little information on passenger fares, but the figures available indicate that the price for passenger transport stabilized after the transition from sail to steam.[3] This is generally attributed to inter-line agreements known as shipping conferences or rings that mitigated competition and reduced the effects of trade fluctuations in order to regulate prices and market shares. Only during periodic rate wars did rates plummet. Knick Harley and Drew Keeling reconstructed yearly averages for the Cunard Line from Liverpool to New York, showing that rates on the North Atlantic fluctu-

---

[1]Douglass C. North, "Ocean Freight Rates and Economic Development, 1740-1913," *Journal of Economic History*, XVIII, No. 4 (1958), 537-555; and C. Knick Harley, "Ocean Freight Rates and Productivity, 1740-1913: The Primacy of Mechanical Invention Reaffirmed," *Journal of Economic History*, XLVIII, No. 4 (1988), 851-876.

[2]Jeffrey J. Williamson and Timothy J. Hatton, "International Migration and the Labour Market: Integration in the Nineteenth and Twentieth Centuries," in Hatton and Williamson (eds.), *International Labour Market Integration and the Impact of Migration on the National Labour Markets since 1870* (Milan, 1994), 214-215; Hatton and Williamson, *The Age of Mass Migration: Causes and Economic Impact* (New York, 1998), 14-21; and Williamson and Kevin H. O'Rourke, *Globalization and History: The Evolution of a Nineteenth Century Atlantic Economy* (Boston, 1999), 29-57.

[3]Timothy J. Hatton and Jeffrey G. Williamson, *Global Migration and the World Economy: Two Centuries of Policy and Performance* (London, 2006), 36; Francis E. Hyde, *Cunard and the North Atlantic, 1840-1973: A History of Shipping and Financial Management* (London, 1975), 109-112; and Drew Keeling, "The Transport Revolution in Transatlantic Migration, 1850-1914," *Research in Economic History*, XIX, No. 1 (1999), 42.

ated between £3 and £6 in the period 1885- 1914.[4] An incomplete series reconstructed by Kristian Hvidt for the same years was in broad agreement.[5] Because rate wars triggered by depressed business conditions did not lead to an increase in the volume of migrants, the influence of transport price on migration flows was minimal.[6]

None of these studies, however, considered how the market was organized or what elements influenced prices on the North Atlantic. While they do mention conferences, they do not discuss their operation or effectiveness. To fill this gap we will analyze the New York Continental Conference (NYCC) which regulated the prepaid and return business, based on its minutes and correspondence between the Holland-America Line (HAL) head agent in New York and the board of directors. These documents allow us to construct a price series of westbound prepaid tickets and eastbound return tickets for the Red Star Line (RSL), Hamburg-America Line (HAPAG) and North German Lloyd (NGL) for the period 1885-1902, and for the HAL from 1883 to 1914. They also provide details on how the conference tried to neutralize internal and external competition. Even more revealing is the head agent's correspondence which provides an inside look at the organization of the passenger business. This is especially important because, as Robert Greenhill noted, the meetings in various European locales left few written records, which helps to explain why the literature on conferences is so sparse.[7]

---

[4]C. Knick Harley, "North Atlantic Shipping in the Late Nineteenth Century: Freight Rates and the Interrelationship of Cargoes," in Lewis R. Fischer and Helge W. Nordvik (eds.), *Shipping and Trade, 1750-1950* (Leuven, 1990), 74-83; Drew Keeling, "Transatlantic Shipping Cartels and Migration between Europe and America, 1880-1914," *Essays in Economic and Business History*, XVII, No. 2 (1999), 65-66; and Simon P. Ville, *Transport and the Development of the European Economy, 1750-1918* (London, 1990), 95. The rate of exchange used by bankers in 1909 was US $4.866 to the pound. Kristian Hvidt used an exchange rate of US $6 to the pound, hence the prices roughly varied from US $14.50 to $36. United States, Senate 61st Cong., 2nd sess., Immigration Commission, *Reports* (41 vols., Washington, DC, 1911) (Dillingham Commission, DC), XXXVII, 242; and Kristian Hvidt, *Flugten til Amerika, eller Drivkræfter i masseudvandringen fra Danmark, 1868-1914* (Aarhus, 1971).

[5]Hvidt, *Flugten til Amerika*, 409-479.

[6]Berit Brattne and Sune Åkerman, "The Importance of the Transport Sector for Mass Migration," in Harald Runblom and Hans Norman (eds.), *From Sweden to America: A History of the Migration* (Minneapolis, 1976), 199; Keeling, "Transatlantic Shipping Cartels," 42; Hatton and Williamson, *Age of Mass Migration*, 14-21; and Hatton and Williamson, *Global Migration*, 35-40.

[7]Robert G. Greenhill, "Competition or Co-operation in the Global Shipping Industry: The Origins and Impact of the Conference System for British Shipowners

Unlike Europe, head offices in the US were concentrated on or near Broadway in New York City, which meant that conference meetings could be held easily whenever needed. Since most decisions of the NYCC required approval by the directors and depended upon regulations pertaining to a European business, it generated a dense correspondence. As David Genesove and Wallace Mullin found in their work on the sugar cartel, conference correspondence provides insights into the reasoning behind a firm's actions and the ways agreement among the lines was reached.[8] The success of the NYCC in regulating competition and fixing prices will be analyzed, and Dale Osborne's cartel formation model will help us to reconstruct the external and internal pressures on the conference.[9]

Shipping Conferences on Long Distance Routes: Their Real Origins?

Shipping conferences were among the earliest cartels in international trade. Their origins are generally ascribed to the need for shipping companies to ease the pressures of destructive competition which lowered prices and profits due to overcapacity. Most scholars agree that the first shipping ring was the UK-Calcutta Conference which was established in 1875 to regulate the tea trade. The practice spread quickly and is still in use today; indeed, more than 150 conferences were operative in 2001.[10]

Research on shipping conferences has concentrated on freight and neglected passenger transport.[11] The only substantial research on how shipping

---

before 1914," in David J. Starkey and Gelina Harlaftis (eds.), *Global Markets: The Internationalization of the Sea Transport Industries since 1850* (St. John's, 1998), 55.

[8]David Genesove and Wallace P. Mullin, "Rules, Communication and Collusion: Narrative Evidence from the Sugar Institute Case," *American Economic Review*, XCI, No. 3 (2001), 379-398.

[9]Dale K. Osborne, "Cartel Problems." *American Economic Review*, LXVI, No. 5 (1976), 835-844.

[10]Ville, *Transport*, 95; Daniel Marx, *International Shipping Cartels: A Study of Industrial Self-Regulation by Shipping Conferences* (Princeton, 1953; reprint, Westport, CT, 1969), 3 and 46; Greenhill, "Competition or Co-operation," 58-59; Brian M. Deakin and T. Seward, *Shipping Conferences: A Study of Their Origins, Development and Economic Practices* (Cambridge, 1973), 1-3; and William Sjostrom, "The Stability of Ocean Shipping Cartels," in Peter Z. Grossman (ed.), *How Cartels Endure and How they Fail* (Cheltenham, 2004), 82.

[11]A notable exception is George Deltas, Richard A. Sicotte and Peter Tomczak, "Passenger Shipping Cartels and Their Effect on Trans-Atlantic Migration," *Review of Economics and Statistics*, XC, No. 1 (2008), 119-133, on the effect of pas-

rings regulated passenger traffic was conducted by Erich Murken almost a century ago. Murken analyzed the pool agreement between the RSL, HAL, NGL and HAPAG known as the Nord Atlantische Dampfer Linien Verband (NDLV). Over the years the NDLV made arrangements with other companies and conferences, and by 1914 it was a horizontal alliance including twelve separate agreements among thirty North Atlantic passenger lines.[12] The lack of subsequent studies led to the misconception that North Atlantic conferences only appeared in the late nineteenth century, but Edward Sloan has shown that competition between the Cunard and Collins lines in the 1850s pushed them to collude. When discussing Sloan's findings, David Williams wrote that "perhaps its significance lies in the field of national rivalry, for it does not have much significance in the history of cartels: the agreement did not last long, ensure successful operations, or set a precedent."[13] Yet because the North Atlantic was the busiest and most competitive long-distance route, as well as the arena where technological innovation was introduced and spread most quickly, all the factors necessary to set a precedent were present. Moreover, the Cunard-Collins agreement was sufficiently beneficial for the former that it would have been surprising had the company not sought to extend it when new challengers - such as the Allan Line (1854) and Anchor Line (1856) in Glasgow or the Inman Line (1852), Guion Line (1862), National Line (1863) and White Star Line (1869) in its home port of Liverpool - tried to usurp its dominance.

As a number of scholars have noted, the British merchant marine dominated long-distance trade and was primarily responsible for bringing the conference system to life. In fact, agreements of this sort can be traced back to the introduction of liner shipping in the 1820s.[14] By focusing on personal net-

---

senger shipping cartels on transatlantic migration for the period 1899-1914. They disagreed with the argument that conferences had only a minor impact on migrant flows, claiming that the workings of the conferences may have reduced volumes by a fifth.

[12]Erich Murken, *Die grossen transatlantischen Linienreederei-Verbande, Pools und Interessengemeinschaften bis zum Ausbruch des Weltkrieges: Ihre Entstehung, Organitsation und Wirksamkeit* (Jena, 1922), *passim.*

[13]Edward W. Sloan, "The First (and Very Secret) International Steamship Cartel, 1850-1856," in Starkey and Harlaftis (eds.), *Global Markets*, 29-52; and David M. Williams, "Forum: Globalization and Sea Transport," *International Journal of Maritime History*, XI, No. 1 (1999), 206.

[14]Frank Broeze, "At Sea and Ashore: A Review of the Historiography of Modern Shipping since the 1970s," *NEHA Bulletin*, XII, No. 1 (1998), 17; Malcolm Falkus, *The Blue Funnel Legend: A History of the Ocean Steam Ship Company, 1864-1973* (Basingstoke, 1990), 117-133; and K.A. Moore, *The Early History of Freight Conferences: Background and Main Developments until around 1900* (London, 1981), *passim.*

works and inter-firm communications, Gordon Boyce underlined their importance for the expansion of British maritime enterprises.[15] Non-economic variables, such as group cohesion based on social background or locale, ensured stability and facilitated the formation and operation of conferences.[16] The concentration of passenger lines in Liverpool assisted the formation of conference agreements, which were preceded by the work of the Liverpool Steamship Owners Association in defending common interests. Francis Hyde found indirect evidence that by 1868 an agreement to fix freight rates and establish minimum passenger fares was concluded among the steamship companies based in Glasgow and Liverpool. This suggests strongly that the Cunard-Collins agreement did in fact set a precedent that paved the way for the creation in 1872 of the North Atlantic Passenger Steam Traffic Conference (NAPSTC).[17]

The main incentive to establish shipping conferences is the pressure on rates caused by excess capacity due to increased competition. Up to the 1870s the construction of new steamers could not keep up with the increasing demand for steamship berths, but the price remained fairly stable at between £5 and £7 for the period 1855-1874.[18] Other than locality and personal networks, what can explain the establishment of the NAPSTC? As I will argue, the reason can be found in the specific characteristics of the passenger market. Boyce emphasized the cooperative dimension of conferences and their importance in shaping relations among shipping companies and between shippers and shipowners. He criticized economists for focusing on market power and the cost- and service-driven necessity of conference regulation.[19] As will see, the cooperative dimension played an even bigger role in the passenger trade. The major difference between carrying cargoes and passengers is that the former was supplied by shippers in the port while the latter was provided by a broad network of migrant brokers and agents that encompassed the hinterland and the foreland. Models explaining the viability of conferences are based on an as-

---

[15]Gordon Boyce, *Information, Mediation and Institutional Development: The Rise of Large-Scale Enterprise in British Shipping, 1870-1919* (Manchester, 1995).

[16]Greenhill, "Competition or Co-operation," 66-67.

[17]Hyde, *Cunard*, 94; Derek H. Aldcroft, *Studies in British Transport History, 1870-1970* (Newton Abbot, 1974), 289; and Kristian Hvidt, "Emigration Agents: The Development of a Business and Its Methods," *Scandinavian Journal of History*, III, No. 2 (1978), 193.

[18]Raymond L. Cohn, "The Transition from Sail to Steam in Immigration to the United States," *Journal of Economic History*, LXV, No. 2 (2005), 483.

[19]Boyce, *Information, Mediation*, 161.

sumption about the community of interests between shippers and shipowners.[20] Regardless of the rationality of such an assumption, it is clear that a mutuality of interests hardly existed between shipowners and the various middlemen who supplied them with passengers. These go-betweens worked on a commission basis for various shipping companies, and these commissions increased when competition among lines intensified; for this reason, agents had no particular reason to favour a stable market. Hence, to increase their profits, the lines needed to tighten their grip on the agent network, and they did so by establishing conference agreements. Hvidt pointed to the importance of these agreements in regulating the agent network and found evidence that in 1871 the British conference members set up a sub-conference in Copenhagen to organize the local market by imposing rules on Danish migrant agents.[21]

The HAL Archives show that the British lines organized a similar sub-conference for the US market in 1872. The evidence indicates that elaborate conference agreements for the North Atlantic passenger trade predate even the Calcutta Conference. This allowed British lines to monopolize the traffic from the British Isles and Scandinavia while gaining ground elsewhere on the continent. The only continental lines to challenge British dominance early on were HAPAG and NGL, while those founded during the post-Civil War steamship boom never caught up with the dominant British and German lines. Competitors in turn organized to prevent the British lines from penetrating further into the continental market, as the German companies brought together in a conference those lines carrying migrants directly from Europe to the US.

The Establishment of the New York Continental Conference

The increased competition for migrant transport and the economic slump of the 1870s created a chronic overcapacity which favoured collusion. Drew Keeling pointed out that the incentives for cartelization were stronger in migrant than in freight transport because demand was both more sensitive to economic swings and less dependent on transport prices. Economic downturns had bigger impacts on the migrant flows than on freight movements.[22] In this context, the first NYCC was established in 1885 by the directors of European lines. A sub-conference, founded in New York, depended on the agreements in Europe. The HAPAG, NGL, RSL and HAL had tried to join forces in 1883, but direct outside competition in Hamburg from the Carr Line and in Antwerp from the

---

[20]Stephen Craig Pirrong, "An Application of Core Theory to the Analysis of Ocean Shipping Markets," *Journal of Law and Economics*, XXXV, No. 1 (1992), 89-131; and Sjostrom, "Stability," 88-95.

[21]Hvidt, "Emigration Agents," 193.

[22]Keeling, "Transport Revolution," 199.

White Cross Line made the conference disintegrate after only a few months.[23] Under the pressure of declining migration flows in 1884, the NAPSTC dissolved as well.[24] A general rate war ensued during which prepaid prices fell from approximately US $20 to anywhere between US $6 and $12, meaning that migrants were being carried at cost or below cost.[25] HAPAG and the RSL needed to discover how to neutralize the competition at their home ports. As it had done in the 1870s with the Adler Line, HAPAG orchestrated a takeover of the new Union and Carr lines in Hamburg. In 1885, the three lines reached an agreement under which Albert Ballin, who had managed the passage business for the Carr Line, entered HAPAG. In Antwerp, the White Cross Line was forced to leave the North Atlantic that same year. This relieved some of the external pressures on the NYCC, allowing it to be renewed after lengthy negotiations.[26]

The agreement included minimum rates based on the quality of service and port of call (appendix 1). The HAL, running the oldest and slowest steamers, obtained differentials to their advantage. Less popular routes, such as the RSL's Philadelphia and the NGL's Baltimore services, were included at lower rates. To prevent port competition from undermining the agreement, the lines decided that all of them could use the New York ocean rates to book passengers to and from Boston, Baltimore and Philadelphia. This means that the HAL was allowed to give free railroad transport between New York and Boston, Baltimore or Philadelphia. Otherwise, charges for overland transport could not be included, and rate sheets of the overland fares used had to be sent to the secretary. Ocean fares could only be changed if the differentials were maintained. The prices quoted were gross, including all relevant commissions. The agent's commission was set at US $3 covering all expenses except advertising in newspapers, which was left to the agent. Advertisements could not contain comparisons with services offered by other members. The companies

---

[23]Rotterdam Community Archives (GAR), Holland-America Line Archive (HAL), 318.02, Directors, 112-121, letter, 23 November 1883.

[24]Hyde, *Cunard*, 193. The Conference was dissolved in March 1884 and reorganized under the North Atlantic Passenger Conference in January 1886.

[25]Van den Toorn mentioned gross prices of US $12 for the HAL and US $10 for the German Lines. GAR, HAL, 318.02, Directors, 112-121, letter, 16 January 1886. Bernhard Huldermann, *Albert Ballin* (Berlin, 1922; reprint, Bremen, 2011), quoted rates as low as US $6, but he did not specify whether these were net or gross. According to Murken, *Die grossen transatlantischen*, lines started making profits on migrants when selling above forty or forty-five *marks* (US $10).

[26]Birgit Ottmüller-Wetzel, "Auswanderung über Hamburg: Die HAPAG und die Auswanderung nach Nordamerika, 1870-1914" (Unpublished MA thesis, Freie Universität Berlin, 1986), 146-157.

also agreed to withdraw advertisements from any paper that attacked a member. The lines appointed general agents for the Pacific, western states and southern states who worked exclusively for one company, supervising the local agents in exchange for a commission of US $1 on every ticket sold in their districts. The cancellation fee for a ticket was set at five percent. Every breach was reported to the secretary who, if necessary, passed it on to William Booker, the British consul in New York who also acted as arbitrator for the British lines. Booker was empowered to look at the books of the companies, and his decision was final. To ensure compliance, a US $1000 bond was required. The agreement was valid for six months, and withdrawal necessitated ed one month's notice.[27] The secretary contacted the British lines to jointly advance steerage rates, reduce the commission to US $2, set the children's age for reduced fares and increase the infant rate to US $2.[28] The New York representatives met monthly to coordinate affairs, and decisions required unanimity.

The agents received a circular with the new conference regulations. No returns or divisions of the commission would be given, nor could "improper inducements" be offered. Agents were not allowed to engage subagents and runners or share their commission with third parties. The actual amount received for a passage had to be stated on the ticket, and no credit could be given. Shipping companies would only pay commission when the ticket was actually issued and the money was received by the agent. Agents were not allowed to issue certificates, orders or tickets for prepaid passage drawn on any person or company other than the line employing him. The selling of tickets was restricted to a specified area so that agents could not invade each other's territory. Violations by other agents had to be reported, with evidence, to the secretary. The punishment depended on the infraction and could vary from a minimum fine equal to the value of the ticket to the disqualification of the agent. Lines agreed not to re-engage disqualified agents.[29] On paper the agreement looked promising but in practice proved difficult to implement.

The Operation of the NYCC up to the Formation of the NDLV

The evolution of the ocean fares serves as a good indicator of the cartel's success. But to what extent were members able to overcome internal and external

---

[27]This was first extended to two months and later reduced to sliding periods of fifteen days to one week, depending on the number of companies giving notice of withdrawal. GAR, HAL, 318.04, Passage, 563, meetings, 14 April 1887 and 25 May 1890.

[28]*Ibid.*, meeting, 15 May 1885, minutes 1-27, "Articles of an Agreement Entered into, by and between the Managers of the Continental Lines for the Purpose of Regulating Rates of Passage and the Business Connected Therewith."

[29]*Ibid.*, copy of circular to agents, 15 May 1885

pressures to raise the prices? Applying Osborne's model, the external problem can be reduced to the ability of the lines to predict and limit the market share of outsiders to keep the agreements viable. Internal problems consisted of agreeing on a workable and profitable contract; making sure that the agreement generated the expected shares for each member; and deterring and detecting cheating. For both Osborne and George Stigler, the detection of cheating was crucial. Secret violations, especially in the form of price cuts, gave the lines the possibility of increasing market share. According to Stigler, if detection mechanisms were weak, prices could not rise much above the competitive level. The basic method of detection was to note when price cutters obtained business which a line did not otherwise obtain.[30] For the NYCC, information on each line's market share was readily available because American ports registered all incoming third-class passengers. Fluctuation in sales by migrant agents also served as a barometer. The biggest problem, however, was to prove that lines obtained an increased share by cheating. What follows is an analysis of the external and internal pressures during the first seven years of the cartel, up to the division of the market with the formation of the NDLV.

Harmonizing the External Pressures

Connections among the British-Scandinavian, Continental and Mediterranean Markets

The external pressures on the conference were considerable. As migration fever spread across Europe, the migrant market was divided into three submarkets; the British-Scandinavian, the continental and the Mediterranean (see appendix 3). The British-Scandinavian market was predominantly in the hands of the British lines. The British Board of Trade (BT) imposed extensive controls on foreign ships to prevent continental lines from transporting British and Irish migrants on the westbound voyage.[31] This internal market represented the

[30]Osborne, "Cartel Problems," 835-844; and George J. Stigler, "A Theory of Oligopoly," *Journal of Political Economy*, LXXII, No. 1 (1964), 44-61.

[31]Murken, *Die grossen transatlantischen*, 58, fails to explain why the American Line was exempted from these time-consuming inspections. The fact that the NGL received British mail subsidies in 1874, using Southampton as port of call, seems to be in conflict with the Board of Trade's intentions. Furthermore, Derek H. Aldcroft, *The Development of British Industry and Foreign Competition, 1875-1914: Studies in Industrial Enterprise* (London, 1967), 348-349, suggests that a special agreement was concluded in 1886 allowing HAPAG to take passengers from British ports. Material in the HAL archive does corroborate the continuing difficulties for continental lines to attract British passengers. During rate wars, efforts to attack the British lines in their home markets centred on the eastbound return route. Midway through the 1890s, the source

majority of the revenues of the British lines, which also had a strong foothold in the Scandinavian market through well-established feeder services, such as the Hull-based Wilson Line. Through these feeders, British lines took advantage of the strict Swedish Passenger Acts which obstructed the development of direct lines under the Swedish flag. Although Swedish authorities adapted the Passenger Acts to allow the entry of national lines in 1883, it took nearly three decades for Swedes to launch a direct service.[32] The German lines and the Copenhagen-based Thingvalia Line also tried to invade the market but found it hard to convince Scandinavians to renounce the well-established migrant route using the British lines. Attempts to convince the Irish and British to emigrate indirectly via continental ports were even less successful.

Conversely, the British lines had always been able to attract continental passengers to migrate indirectly through British ports. The strong trade relations between Hamburg and England and the lack of interest in becoming involved in the trade during the early years of mass migration by local merchants transformed Hamburg into the most important continental hub for indirect transatlantic migration.[33] The ties between migrant brokers and agents in Liverpool and Hamburg were well established and institutionalized by British and Hamburg laws.[34] Other continental ports managed to reduce indirect mi-

---

explicitly mentions controls impeding the continental lines from embarking British steerage passengers on the westbound route. See also ABMFA, Emigration, 2959 I, correspondence, 16 February-28 July 1883.

[32]Brattne and Åkerman, "Importance of the Transport Sector," 176-202; Nicholas J. Evans, "The Role of Foreign-born Agents in the Development of Mass Migrant Travel through Britain, 1820-1923," in Torsten Feys, *et al.* (eds.), *Maritime Transport and Migration: The Connections between Maritime and Migration Networks* (St. John's, 2007), 52-55; and Hyde, *Cunard*, 60-62.

[33]Frank Broeze, "Albert Ballin, the Hamburg-Bremen Rivalry and the Dynamics of the Conference System," *International Journal of Maritime History*, III, No. 1 (1991), 1-3; and Birgit Gelberg, *Auswanderung nach Übersee: Soziale Probleme der Auswanderungbeförderung in Hamburg und Bremen von der Mitte der 19. Jahrhunderts bis zum Ersten Weltkrieg* (Hamburg, 1973), 10-13.

[34]Migrant brokers and agents in Liverpool needed a certificate from the authorities agreeing to abide by English law. For those who worked with brokers in Hamburg, from 1855 onwards a copy had to be deposited with the Hamburg consul agreeing to abide by both Hamburg and English laws. The following contracts existed: between Michols and Co. (Liverpool) and Morris and Co. (Hamburg); Sable and Searle with L. Scharlach and Co.; Stern with Falck and Co.; W. Inman and J. Kirsten; Hartmann and O. Moeller; D. MacIver and G. Hirschmann; and Magnus Ballin and Morris and Co. Hamburg Staatsarchiv, Consulaat Liverpool: Auswanderungsangelegenheiten 1851-1868, no. 8.

gration by opening direct lines, yet Hamburg did not.[35] During the 1880s, indirect migration from the German port via England often totalled fifty percent or more of the number travelling directly, constituting the Achilles heel of the NYCC.[36] Although continental traffic only represented a small percentage of their total business, it allowed the British lines to exert constant pressure on their continental rivals which to a large extent were dependent on their goodwill to raise prices or lower commissions.[37] Government protection of the internal market, combined with a foothold in the continental market, gave the British lines the edge they needed.

The Mediterranean market, which was just starting to expand, consisted mainly of Italians. Some lines, such as the Fabre and Italian lines, opened direct services to New York. British and other continental lines also tried to lure Italians to their ports. The Havre-based Compagnie Générale Transatlantique (CGT), drawing migrants mainly from Germany and Switzerland with special railroad services, saw the Mediterranean market as a natural territory for expansion.[38] Members of the NYCC took the initiative to organize the direct and indirect lines and fix rates on this route. It also founded the Mediterranean Conference (MC) consisting of the Fabre Line, Italian Line, the HAL and the RSL in November 1885.[39] The main reason behind the conference was that if rates for the Mediterranean route differed significantly from those on the continental route, Swiss and Austrians migrants might choose to travel through the Mediterranean instead of using continental ports. If Scandinavian rates were lower than continental rates, Germans and Poles would be

---

[35]Indirect migration also persisted in Rotterdam and Antwerp but on a much smaller scale after the opening of direct lines. The Inman Line suspended its feeder service from Antwerp immediately after the establishment of the RSL. Leo A. Van der Valk, "Landverhuizers via Rotterdam in de negentiende eeuw," *Economisch en Sociaal historisch jaarboek* (Amsterdam, 1976), 162; and William H. Flayhart III, *The American Line, 1872-1902* (New York, 2000), 113.

[36]Günter Moltmann, "Steamship Transport of Emigrants from Europe to the United States, 1850-1914: Social, Commercial and Legislative Aspects," in Klaus Friedland (ed.), *Maritime Aspects of Migration* (Cologne, 1989), 314.

[37]In 1894, the British market share of steerage passengers comprised seventy percent English and Irish, twenty-two percent Scandinavian and eight percent continental. GAR, HAL, 318.04, Passage, 223, letter, 9 May 1894.

[38]Marie-Françoise Vannoise-Pochulu, "La politique de la Compagnie Générale Transatlantique et l'émigration vers les États-Unis à partir du Havre (1875-1914)" (Unpublished MA thesis, University of Paris XII, 1993), 10-17.

[39]GAR, HAL, 318.02, Directors, 112-121, letter, 16 January 1886; and 318.04, Passage, 563, meeting, 25 May 1885, minute 41.

booked at the lowest price. If the rate difference between the continent and Great Britain was too large, continental migrants would travel to Liverpool. In short, the relationship among the various conferences was symbiotic.

Outside Rivals on the Continent

The continental market ranged from Spain to Russia and was rapidly expanding eastward. The NYCC had been drawn up to include both the Thingvalia Line and the CGT. The Danish line focused on Scandinavia, but its base in Copenhagen allowed it to target the continental market as well. Nonetheless, the Danes could not be convinced to join the NYCC. The exclusion of the CGT had even greater repercussions. Because the CGT to a great extent had the same hinterland as members of the NYCC, the latter could not fix rates or introduce commissions that differed much of the French line without risking the loss of market share. Moreover, the British lines required the CGT to be included in order to raise prices jointly as requested by the continental lines when the NYCC was founded. After months of futile negotiations, the continental lines took measures to force the CGT to join the NYCC. They did not use so-called "fighting ships," a practice that entailed special sailings at drastically reduced rates whenever an outside line scheduled a departure.[40] Neither did they cut the ocean rate, which would have affected all of their continental business. Instead, they cut railroad rates to and from destinations popular with the CGT's clientele. They also matched the French line's increased commission of US $4 on eastbound tickets. Furthermore, they notified agents that unless they relinquished the agency of the French line, ticket books of NYCC lines would be withdrawn. This forced the CGT to rely on a parallel network of non-conference agents. The British lines also used their agent network to put pressure on the French. The CGT finally gave in after reaching an agreement with the RSL and the HAL on through rates, including the railroad fare, to Switzerland, France and northern Italy. This cleared the path to enter further negotiations with the British lines on rates and agent regulations.[41]

The Network of Migrant Brokers and Agents

One of the NYCC's priorities was to impose "city rules" in New York where seventy-five percent of the American passage market was transacted. Chaos

[40]*Ibid.*, 318.04, Passage, 563, meeting, 15 July 1885, minutes 63 and 67. By sharing the costs, conferences often used "fighting ships" to drive out an outside line from a certain route or force it to enter the agreement.

[41]*Ibid.*, meetings, 3 May 1885, minute 39; 15 July 1885, minute 63; and 20 August 1885, minutes 74 and 85; 318.14, Wentholt Archief, 18/3, letter, 11 November 1884; and 318.02, Directors, 112-121, letter, 16 January 1886.

reigned because of the proliferation of agents and runners and the sale of tickets over the counter by innkeepers, boarding houses, peddlers, etc. With "city rules" the lines wanted to do away with the middleman and restrict the sale of ocean tickets to the company's office. This would greatly increase control over the business and eliminate commission costs. To do so without important losses of market share, all the lines had to adhere to the system. Anticipating an agreement with the British lines, the members of the NYCC limited the number of agents in the city, but they still had to await the collaboration of all the lines to move forward in the New York market.[42]

The lines also wanted to counter the developing system of orders drawn on Hamburg migrant brokers' agencies at lower European cash rates. These orders allowed brokers to undercut the lowest continental prepaid rate by US $4. The British lines stimulated the order system to increase their continental market share. HAPAG informed the continental conference members that unless the British lines could be forced to raise the European cash rates, they would have to break up the prepaid rate agreement to meet the competition. The German line opened a low-cost New York-Baltic service to and from Copenhagen, Göteborg and Stettin to put pressure on the British lines. It also negotiated an agreement with the Hamburg migrant brokers to reduce indirect migration through England. At the end of 1886, HAPAG, the Hamburg migrant brokers and the British lines reached an agreement. HAPAG withdrew its direct Scandinavian service, while the British lines agreed to limit their share of the traffic through Hamburg to thirty-five percent. All agreed that he price difference to the advantage of indirect British routes could not exceed five *marks*, and they established a clearing house to control traffic through Hamburg.[43]

Although an agreement was reached that agents of all three conferences could make bookings for all the members except for the outside lines, the distrust between German and British lines remained, impeding the imposition of "city rules" and a significant price rise. The mistrust also led to the payments of secret commissions on top of the agreed fixed rate to gain the favour of the agents. Still, he tensions gradually receded, allowing the conferences jointly to lower the commission to US $2, to mutually discuss changes in ocean rates and to prepare to implement "city rules." Yet an internal conflict that made the MC fall apart early in 1888 disrupted the increased harmony. An arbitrator found the RSL guilty of cutting rates and giving special incentives to

[42]Testimony of HAPAG head agent Emil Boas before the Ford Committee, quoted in *New York Times*, 26 June 1888; and GAR, HAL, 318.04, Passage, 563, meetings, 25 May 1885, minute 38; and 25 January 1886, minutes 164-166.

[43]GAR, HAL, 318.04, Passage, 563, meetings, 29 March 1886, minute 197; and 26 June 1886, minute 250; Murken, *Die grossen transatlantischen*, 19; and Otmüller-Wezel, "Auswanderung über Hamburg," 195.

agents, upon which the Fabre and Italian lines left the conference. In the meantime, the Italian government passed laws to direct migrant traffic through national ports, thereby hindering re-negotiations. It also put an end to the plans to pool traffic in the Mediterranean and to open joint offices in New York so that all lines would be represented by an independent agent whose books would have been accessible to members at all times. Subsequently, the agreement among the British lines was also discontinued due to internal tensions; this led to a rate war in the British-Scandinavian market. The continental lines managed to prevent the rate war from spreading to the continent, but they could not prevent continental rates from falling.[44]

Internal Pressures

Internal Mistrust and Duration of Agreements

Distrust among members who for a long time considered each other to be rivals constantly weakened the NYCC. The underlying suspicions were reflected in the duration of the agreements. During the first five years, agreements were never renewed for longer than seven months.[45] Sometimes renewal negotiations, during which the old pacts usually continued, took longer than the duration of the agreement. The reason was that the agreement to fix prices had shifted the competition from rates to the quality of service. During the first five years, the HAL in particular greatly improved its fleet.[46] As differentials among lines were based on quality of service, they were subject to constant renegotiations. The RSL insisted that initial differentials should be adapted and led the conference into its first crisis less than a year after its creation.[47]

---

[44]GAR, HAL, 318.04, Passage, 563, circular, 14 April 1887; meetings, 31 May, minute 31, 26 June, minute 50, 15 August, minute 61, 6 September, minute 64, 20 September, minutes 69-70, and 25 October 1887, minute 77; 31 January 1888, minute 165; 2 October 1891, minute 370; Passage 221-226, letters, 3 and 20 January 1888, 10 September, 3 and 17 October and 19 November 1890; 16 July, minute 165, 2 October, minute 370, 2 and 23 December 1889, minutes 375-379, 382; and Passage, 221-226, letters, 11 and 15 October 1889, 21 January 1890 and 10 December 1891.

[45]Except in 1889, when agreements were renewed for one year. *Ibid.*, 318.04, Passage, 221-226, letter, 11 December 1889.

[46]Between 1886 and 1889, the HAL bought seven second-hand ships totalling 27,000 tons.

[47]GAR, HAL, 318.04, Passage, 563, meetings, 11 December 1888, minute 214, and 13 June 1889, minute 273. The HAL eventually relented and agreed to reduce its differential with RSL steamers by fifty cents. GAR, HAL, 318.04, 221-226, letter, 11 October 1889.

Failing to obtain its expected market share, the RSL refused to renew the agreement, triggering a rate war in which prepaid rates plummeted by US $10. The HAL reacted by notifying its agents that it would attempt to meet any new reduction to maintain the differential it had before the rate war. Conference agents were at liberty to dispose of their commissions as they saw fit, yet they had to stop selling RSL tickets or send back the ticket books of the conference lines. The limit on the number of agents in New York was lifted. This rate war to force RSL back into the fold lasted eight months during which agents were allowed to ignore many regulations. When they were caught violating those still in force, fines were lower. Agents still selling tickets for the RSL received a warning before being disqualified in order to retain as many as possible. When a new agreement was finally signed, a circular reminded the agents of the old regulations as well as a few new ones. The cancellation fee was increased to ten percent, and flat-rate commissions were replaced by commisssions of ten percent of the price of the ticket. Although the new commission structure gave the agents and shipowners a reason to raise prices, the small lines feared that percentage commissions would induce agents to sell-more expensive services on the bigger lines. Their protests eventually led to the reintroduction of fixed commissions.[48] This was only one disadvantage of the lack of product homogeneity.

Lack of Product Homogeneity

The operation of the cartel was further complicated because some lines offered slow and fast services and routings to alternate arrival ports at different rates. Negotiations about whether to include new services offered by conference members added to the internal tensions. For instance, the HAL opened a Baltimore service to combat the increasing competition for freight between Rotterdam and the US, to take advantage of cheaper railroad rates from that port and to press for more leniency in the application of immigration laws. The Dutch line previously was the only company serving just one destination with no variety in the standard of service. It was well known that companies sometimes booked passengers at regular service to be transported on express steamers, or passengers were booked at lower Philadelphia and Baltimore rates but landed in New York. Although this was against the conference rules, it was difficult to prove such abuses. Companies gave these facilities to their most reliable agents who, to avoid fines and disqualification, operated with the utmost secrecy. As passengers were reluctant to file affidavits about fraud, the lines hired private detectives when they suspected a member was evading the

---

[48]GAR, HAL, 318.04, Passage, 563, meetings, 26 July, minute 258 and 2 August 1886, minutes 265-269; Passage, 767, circular to agents, 3 August 1886; and Passage, 563, new series, minutes 1-109, meetings, March-December 1887.

regulations on a large scale. All kinds of tricks were used to prevent the sleuths from uncovering evidence; indeed, the HAL even hired an extra bookkeeper to cover up violations.[49] To prove cheating with upgraded services, the detectives actually had to travel on these tickets.

Whenever violations were too difficult to prove, the HAL tampered with the rules as well, which explains the opening of the Baltimore service. The NGL, which practically monopolized passenger traffic in the port of Baltimore, radically opposed the inclusion of the new service in the NYCC. In theory this meant that the HAL's agents were not allowed to book passengers for its Baltimore service. In practice, however, by paying extra commissions the HAL found many agents willing to risk fines or disqualifications since they had the means to prevent other lines from proving the violations. The fact that the HAL's Baltimore service was not included permitted the company to quote low rates and pay higher commissions, thus attracting more passengers and eventually forcing its acceptance into the NYCC.[50]

Railroad Rates

Fixed ocean rates also had the effect of shifting competition to railroad rates because ocean and inland passages were often sold together. The differentials on ocean rates could easily be cancelled out by railroad fares. Trying to fix through rates, the conference secretary required the lines to hand in lists of actual inland fares obtained from railways on both sides of the Atlantic. Any cut in these rates was considered a conference violation, yet again it was difficult to prove this. In fact, the lines constantly negotiated with railroads to obtain special rates. On American soil the lines used the keen competition between railway lines to obtain all kinds of reductions. Yet the establishment of the Interstate Commerce Commission (ICC) in 1887 dampened price competition among railroads. The ICC opened an Immigrant Clearing House to coordinate migrant railroad transport and allowed the railways to increase their rates and cut the commissions on tickets sold in connection with an ocean passage. Plans by steamship lines to open Joint Railroad Offices to regain control

---

[49]In 1890, rates from Baltimore and Philadelphia to the west cost on average US $1.94 and US $1.24, respectively, less than from New York. *Ibid.*, 318.04, Passage, 221-226, letters, 20 December 1890 and 21 August 1891.

[50]*Ibid.*, letters, 17 March, 12 June, 22 July and 25 September 1891. Other new services eventually included were HAPAG's Union Line, specializing in migrant and freight transport; HAPAG's Express Line and its Stettin and Baltimore services, although its Hansa service to Montréal was excluded. NGL's Roland Line, specializing in migrant and freight transport to Baltimore and New York, was accepted.

over the railway end of the business never materialized. Secret reductions persisted but were far less significant.[51]

European inland tariffs caused even greater instability. The HAL's low overland tariff had a particularly demoralizing effect. Dutch railway and Rhine steamboat companies reduced their fares in 1887, giving the HAL an important differential in the price of inland transport. The other conference members questioned the validity of the rates and brought the case to arbitration. During the investigation the members ignored the rule requiring them to quote the actual tariff obtained and offered the HAL's tariff instead. Tensions increased when the arbitrator ruled in favour of the HAL, and the RSL refused to stop using the HAL tariff. The HAL attributed the low rates to the geographic advantage of Rotterdam which it was not prepared to relinquish and in its view was worth a rate war. After protracted negotiations, the lines reached a compromise, reducing the differentials on ocean rates. Yet even with the agreement the CGT calculated that the average differential, including railroad and ocean rates, at thirty-five popular European locations amounted to US $9.25 in favour of the RSL and US $11.35 in favour of the HAL. To prevent the French line from leaving the conference, the HAL and the RSL reduced the differentials on through rates to French, Swiss and northern Italian points to US $2. A special sub-committee, formed to tackle the problem of European overland fares, established a list of 300 points from where passengers could be booked at fixed rates.[52]

The Hamburg Migrant Brokers

The most important internal pressure was the competition among the lines to gain the favour of migrant brokers by providing special facilities. Such competition enabled a group of predominantly Jewish entrepreneurs to corrupt the prepaid market out of Hamburg by issuing their own orders. The pool agreement for Hamburg traffic between HAPAG, the Hamburg brokers and the British lines did not end this practice. Net European cash rates remained US $4

---

[51]Torsten Feys, "Where All Passenger Liners Meet: The Port of New York as a Nodal Point for the Transatlantic Migrant Trade, 1885-1895," *International Journal of Maritime History*, XIX, No. 2 (2007), 249-251; Gabriel Kolko, *Railroads and Regulation, 1877-1916* (Princeton, 1965), *passim*; and GAR, HAL, 318.04, Passage, 563, meetings, 22 and 30 December 1890, minutes 384 and 390.

[52]GAR, HAL, 318.04, Passage, 563, meetings, 31 May, minute 32, 17 November, minute 87 and 27 December 1887, minute 104; 31 January, minute 109, 24 April, minute 143, and 7 July 1888, minutes 174-176; and 22 January 1889, minute 224; 318.04, Passage, 221-226, letters, 16 and 22 June 1888; Passage, 563, meetings 27 June 1889, minutes 272-276, 27 February, minute 329 and 30 December 1890, minute 390, May 21, minute 432; and 1 July 1891, minute 449.

to $5 cheaper than net prepaid rates; only after repeated requests from New York was the gap reduced to US $2.50.[53] Yet this still offered enough margin for Hamburg's migrant brokers - who in the meantime had opened branch offices in New York - to undercut the prepaid rate. Although it was against conference rules, it was an open secret that HAPAG had made special arrangements with some brokers who had been using their orders to counter the British lines. Because of this rivalry the practice spread quickly, and other continental lines made similar arrangements through branch offices in New York to get their hands on the order business. Instead of imposing "city rules" and closing the gap between shipping companies and their clients, the discord allowed brokers to take control of ocean passage sales. They drove migrant agents out of the business of selling regular prepaid tickets and forced them to sell orders for these brokers instead. When caught cheating, offenders paid their fines but protested against disqualification by claiming that the conference afforded no protection for regular business. By 1889, the CGT, which because of its orientation towards the Mediterranean did not have the same connections with Jewish migrant brokers who initially specialized in the eastern European market, saw its continental prepaid sales come to a standstill.[54]

During the next eight months, lines renegotiated the agreements allowing Jewish brokers to increase their grip on the market. The order business spread to Baltimore, Philadelphia, Chicago, St. Louis and Milwaukee. Because of the restrictions of the Hamburg pool, brokers opened branches in Bremen, Rotterdam and Antwerp to expand their businesses. The migrant brokers Louis Scharlach, Friedrich Missler and Sender Jarmulowsky obtained control of the prepaid business of the HAL, RSL and NGL, respectively. To increase their market share the companies gave them all sorts of facilities in violation of conference agreements, ranging from cheating with upgraded service to not charging cancellation fees, paying extra commissions, allowing name changes on tickets, hiring subagents, dividing the commission or offering part of it as a

---

[53]No price series of European cash rates is at hand, but the net price difference must have balanced at around US $4 to $5 based on the repeated calls of agents to raise the cash rate by ten or fifteen *marks* or cut prepaid rates by US $2 to $3. In 1889, the CGT was still urging a reduction on prepaid rates of US $3.50 despite a previous rise in the cash rate of ten *marks*. In 1890, the gap was reduced further but still left a gap of US $2.90; the cash rate was sixty *marks*, which at the exchange rate of 4.2 *marks* to the dollar used by the companies gave a net rate of US $14.10 while the prepaid net rate was US $17.00. *Ibid.*, meetings, 25 October 1887, minute 72; 28 February, minute 127, and 16 June 1888, minute 165; and 10 March, 10 April and 2 and 10 May 1889; and Passage, 221-226, various letters.

[54]*Ibid.*, 318.04, Passage, 563, meetings, 25 October 1887, minute 72; 28 February, minute 127 and 16 June 1888, minute 165; 29 August 1889, minutes 284-285; and Passage, 221-226, letter, 19 November 1889.

reduction to the buyer. Scharlach ensured that purchasers did not receive actual documents that might be used against him at conference meetings; instead of receiving the receipt attached to the ticket, an outsider issued a proof of payment while the originals were sent to the European houses. Despite such precautions, proof of abuses surfaced which led to various fines and his disqualification on two occasions. Yet Scharlach always managed to be reappointed because conference members feared that with his control over the market he could do more damage to their business by working for rival lines.

The Hamburg pool, created to control indirect migration through the port, boomeranged with the opening of new indirect routes, increasing tensions among members of the NYCC and the British lines. Much to HAPAG's dismay, the RSL and the HAL had to be included in the Hamburg pool to stop the abuses from escalating. As a result, HAPAG's share of the traffic through its home port was reduced. Tensions between HAPAG and the HAL reached the point where each made preparations to open services through the other's home port. When conference agreements failed to provide stability, a general rate was seemed unavoidable unless members found a new arrangement.[55]

An Evaluation of the First Seven Years of the Continental Conference

The interdependence among the conferences that led to the division of North Atlantic passenger traffic into three sub-markets to raise prices, fix commissions and implement conference rules governing the network of agents undermined the stability of the NYCC. Although the cartel managed to prevent rate wars in other sub-markets from spreading to the continent, the turmoil prevented the lines from significantly raising fares to prevent continental passengers from using alternative routes. With their foothold in Hamburg, the British lines managed to maintain the upper hand. HAPAG's efforts to neutralize competition in its home port backfired and affected the internal cohesion among continental lines. The difficulty of detecting and discouraging cheating on the agreements, especially those regulating sales through the migrant agent

[55]RSL and HAL, former rivals, joined forces to strengthen their negotiating position against the German lines. On admission into the Hamburg pool, lines had to cease paying extra commissions to their Hamburg agency but were assured a fixed number of passengers (or compensation if the number was not reached). The number of passengers would decrease but they would be booked at a better price. Moreover, the Hamburg pool was an excellent way to put Ballin under pressure during negotiations. With the agreement, HAPAG's share of the traffic through Hamburg decreased from sixty-five to 57.8 percent. *Ibid.*, 318.04, Passage, 563, meetings, 29 August, minutes 284-285, 17 September, minute 291 and 8 October 1889, minute 298; 23 January, minute 317 and 27 February 1890, minute 328; Passage, 221-226, letters, 2 October and 19 November 1889; 31 January, 30 July, 19 August and 10 September 1890; and 8 June, 14 July and 12 September 1891.

network, hampered the cartel's efficiency. Instead of becoming more transparent, transactions became even more corrupt. Where violations were too difficult to prove, members made sure they were able to cheat as well, further encouraging abuses. This supports the argument of game theorists about conditional cooperation among firms: as soon as one acts opportunistically, the others will follow, thereby reducing the level of mutual support.[56] Most evidence of cheating was collected by company personnel and private detectives. But the use of detectives, who found it difficult to obtain affidavits, proved an inefficient way to verify cheating. Agents hardly ever denounced colleagues since cheating was so widespread. Shipping companies were unable to enforce the rules designed to eliminate differential treatment of customers by migrant agents. Neither could they prevent companies from only awarding facilities to some brokers. When violations by agents were recorded, the conference failed to use retaliation to deter repetition. Fines were not high enough, while lines refused to disqualify agents lest they do more damage by working for non-members. Members caught cheating also got away with only moderate fines; as W.H. van den Toorn observed, this only had a slight effect on the line's position during the next round of negotiations. These factors prevented the companies from raising prepaid rates.

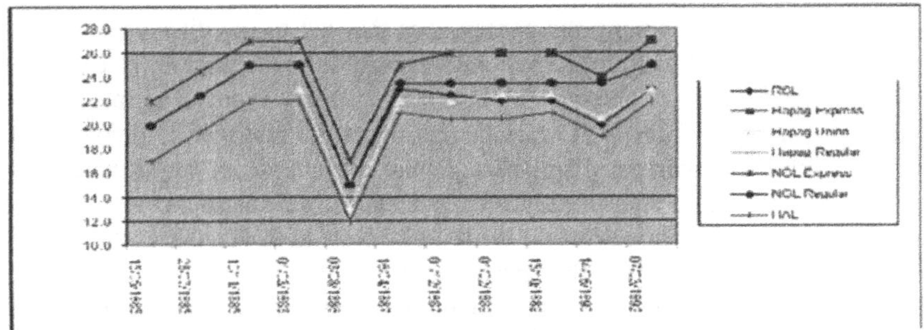

Figure 2.1: New York Prepaid Fares of Continental Lines, 1885-1892

Source: GAR, HAL, 318.04, Passage, 563-565, 767, minutes of NYCC; 72-77, 221-226, correspondence; and 318.02, Directors, 112-121, correspondence.

The cost per passenger was approximately US $10, yet considering the cheating by using cheaper European cash orders, payment of extra commissions and cuts on railroad rates, the HAL's net prices can only have exceeded this cost slightly. The indirect price cuts varied according to competi-

[56]Gordon Boyce, *Co-operative Structures in Global Business: Communicating, Transferring Knowledge and Learning across the Corporate Frontier* (London, 2001), 8.

tive pressures, causing net rates to be far less stable than the graph showing gross rates suggests (figure 2.1). Conference membership failed to increase the HAL's profits while it invested heavily in its fleet. This worked to the advantage of the agents and especially the migrants. Extra commissions were often returned to passengers to enable agents to increase their sales. Hence, migrants enjoyed better and faster service at rates barely covering costs.

Pooling the Traffic: The NDLV

Fixing market shares is the most efficient method of combating secret price cutting.[57] Experience in the initial years of the NYCC convinced members of the need to reduce competitive pressures to control both agent networks and transport fares. Albert Ballin, the manager of HAPAG which suffered most due to the instability, became the driving force behind the expansion of the agreements. Core members divided the market into shares and used compensation schemes to balance shortages or excesses. To reduce external price cutting, agreements were made with other lines to divide the North Atlantic market geographically. Although the American antitrust movement gained momentum at the time, shipping lines felt protected by the thought that US jurisdiction did not extend into international waters, a belief which vanished in the mid-1890s.

Founding the NDLV

Negotiations for a westbound pool between the RSL, HAL, NGL and HAPAG began early in 1890. As the CGT refused to join these talks, the members considered France, Switzerland and Italy as a special territory for which they organized a separate "money pool."[58] The situation in Hamburg made the inclusion of the British lines highly desirable, if not indispensable. Market shares were based on the number of continental steerage passengers carried in the previous decade from ports north of Cádiz to the US and Canada; this gave the HAL eight percent, the RSL 13.5 percent, the NGL 39.7 percent and HAPAG 24.8 percent. A separate agreement with the British lines established their combined share at fourteen percent. The percentage could be altered depending on changes in the tonnage of vessels employed either by permitting more frequent sailings or the introduction of new vessels. Companies exceeding their

---

[57]Stigler, "Theory of Oligopoly," 44-61.

[58]The lines contributed a fixed amount per passenger from these territories which was then divided into shares at the end of the year. The CGT did remain in the NYCC, adhering to the rules and adapting its rates to the members' interests. GAR, HAL, 318.04, 221-226, Passage, letter, 29 January 1892; and Passage, 563, meeting, 1 April 1892, minute 537.

share had to compensate the lines which fell short by a fixed amount per passenger which fluctuated according to the ocean fare. To limit such compensation, members with a surplus during the year would raise their rates to allow companies that were short to book passengers at more profitable prices instead of having to lower their rates. Gross rates and agent commissions were fixed between six and twenty *marks* in Europe and US $2 to $5 in North America. Members agreed that prepaid gross rates should, as far as possible, be equal to European cash rates. No commission was allowed on overland European transport. All members paid high deposits as a disincentive to drop out of the agreement. The contract was valid for four years. Only if alterations proposed by two or more members were rejected did a company have the right to withdraw from the agreement.[59] As van den Toorn observed, there was a good deal of apprehension among members regarding the outcome:

> No one knows what the pool will bring and why HAPAG was so compliant with the NGL. Possibly it is a conspiracy to destroy us and the RSL, however I'd rather believe that both urgently need money and want to clear out the steerage business from innumerable abuses, being weighed down by the restless actions of agents, or should we say parasites.[60]

The contract shows that the continental lines learned from the weaknesses of previous agreements. The quotas guaranteed that rates would no longer be cut to obtain larger market shares. Linking prepaid and cash rates put an end to the order system. Efforts were made to fix rates for overland travel, and the HAL's Baltimore service was included. The duration of four years without the possibility of exiting the agreement unilaterally put an end to continual renegotiations and constant threats of withdrawal. Separate agreements neutralized the competition from the CGT and the British lines. Despite the enactment of the Sherman Antitrust Act, the lines did not fear interference from the American authorities. As anti-immigration feelings intensified, the lines believed that an agreement increasing the price for the passage would be welcomed.[61]

The NDLV's Achilles Heel

According to van den Toorn, collaboration with the British lines had been bought dearly, yet internal divisions among the thirteen British lines delayed

---

[59]GAR, HAL, 318.04, Passage, 580, contract of the Nord-Atlantische Dampfer-Linien Verband, 19 January 1892.

[60]*Ibid.*, Passage, 221-226, letter, 20 December 1891.

[61]*Ibid.*, letter, 12 September 1891.

the signing of the contract. Cunard in particular distrusted the Germans. The International Navigation Company (INC), with the American Line in the British-Scandinavian conference and the RSL in the NDLV, was critical during the negotiations.[62] The verbal agreement which was to be enforced in February 1892 remained pending. Two months later the lines went ahead without the National Line and Cunard for a three-month trial. They jointly increased rates to unprecedented levels. Yet with Cunard and National quoting US $19 and $15, respectively, via Hamburg, while the HAPAG's lowest rate was US $25, the German line was forced to pay a secret extra commission of US $3.50 to its agents to reach its pool share. Whatever scheme Ballin put together to increase HAPAG's profits, the money ended up in a pocket other than his own. He concluded special agreements with agents on the Prussian-Russian border and the Jewish Aid Committee of Berlin and lobbied the German government to end the Hamburg brokers' business.[63] This forced the Hamburg Agents' Association (HAA) to negotiate a new three-year pool agreement, setting minimum rates for all the lines. Fixed commissions for cash passengers were pooled by the HAA. A clearing house controlled the validity of all prepaid tickets to prevent evasion using order tickets. The margin between the cheapest HAPAG direct service and the British indirect service was reduced to two *marks*.[64] Overall, the NDLV led to satisfactory results and was extended to eastbound steerage as well.[65] When everything seemed to be falling into place, cholera broke out in Hamburg, disrupting traffic for six months.

When business resumed, both the westbound and eastbound pools were extended until the end of 1893, and rate agreements were reached with the British lines. In the meantime, due to the cholera in Hamburg, Jewish migrant brokers had opened branch offices in other continental ports, thereby strengthened their position.[66] As the brokers increased their influence in Rot-

---

[62]The term "British lines" refers to those lines serving from Great Britain and thus includes the American Line from 1885 onwards.

[63]GAR, HAL, 318.04, Passage, 221-226, letters, 1 and 15 July 1891, and 11 and 27 May 1892; and Passage, 563, 1 April 1892, minute 541.

[64]The fare to embarkation ports such as Liverpool, Southampton or Glasgow through Hull, Grimsby, London or West Hartlepool was fixed at twenty-six *marks* (17.5 *marks* for the ocean and 8.5 *marks* for overland transport). *Ibid.*, 318.04, Passage, 580, contract between HAPAG and Vereinigung Hamburgischer Passagier-Expedienten, 1 June 1892.

[65]GAR, HAL, 318.04, Passage, 221-226, letters, 22 June, 12 July and 5 August 1892.

[66]Spiro and Co., Scharlach and Co. and Karlsberg and Co. opened offices in Rotterdam.

terdam, they exposed the HAL to difficulties regarding indirect migration through England which HAPAG unsuccessfully tried to control. Yet as Erich Murken showed, some migrant brokers became more powerful than the shipping companies due to inter-line rivalries which the pool did not bring to an end.[67] Because of the ability of these brokers to direct migrants to certain routes, even if this meant extra travel and additional costs, the HAL preferred to see them settle in Rotterdam rather than in Antwerp. If the pool failed, the brokers were an asset in ensuring part of the migrant flow to Rotterdam. Moreover, this would promote the direct route through the Dutch port, which was a much more desirable migration option than Hamburg. If Ballin managed to circumvent the brokers, it would take time to alter the routing of migrants.

Because of the continuing distrust among the continental lines and particularly the failure to get all British lines into the fold, the brokers regained special facilities from the lines which corrupted the market. The HAL gave Scharlach a special rebate of ten *marks* on cash rates which allowed him to undercut prepaid tickets by US $5. Scharlach was also at liberty to change the name on the ticket, omit the price and avoid paying cancellation fees. The broker could freely speculate by writing out orders when he expected prices to increase. Furthermore, if he obtained better conditions from the British lines, passengers destined for the HAL could easily be forwarded indirectly. Scharlach quickly gained control over the HAL's prepaid sales and corrupted the Rotterdam traffic. As van den Toorn put it, "not only do they corrupt the inland, prepaid and cash rates or alienate the agents from us; they also blacken our reputation by mistreating the passengers."[68] Moreover, the Dutch and American authorities started imposing stricter border controls on HAL passengers because Scharlach supplied a growing number who were in poor health and needed assistance. The migrant brokers posed a very serious threat, especially when Oscar Richard joined their ranks after being disqualified by HAPAG as a passenger agent. To try to regain control, the HAL withdrew all facilities from Scharlach, who responded by joining forces with Richard to charter a ship, completely bypassing the lines. The ship was quarantined for carrying many sick passengers, forty of whom were deported which created significant costs and deterred the brokers from renewing their charter. For their part, shipping companies increasingly moved into the migrant banking and remittance market to put pressure on agents.[69] When again not all the British lines could be convinced to join the pool agreement in 1894, a rate war seemed inevitable.

---

[67]Murken, *Die grossen transatlantischen*, 19.

[68]GAR, HAL, 318.04, Passage, 221-226, letter, 29 May 1893.

[69]*Ibid.*, letters 17 and 27 March, 7 April, 29 May, and 14 and 19 July 1893.

Remaining Internal and External Pressures

Despite failing to neutralize the external pressures, the NDLV did improve cohesion among its members as joint action to regulate aspects of the passenger business became more common. Yet two aspects of the agreement still caused a lot of friction. The first arose because of the tonnage clause which allowed members of the pool to increase their market percentage if they increased their capacity compared to other members. The lines used various means to expand their fleets, which decreased the capacity utilization of their ships (see table 2.1).[70] This spurred the introduction of new high-tonnage services, such as the NGL's Roland Line, carrying freight and steerage passengers only at lower rates, which encouraged cheating. HAPAG converted sections of cattle steamers to carry the minimum number of migrants. To make the tonnage count for the recalculation of market share, companies needed to book fifty passengers westbound and fifteen eastbound. When lines feared they might not meet the quota, passengers could obtain last-minute deals. The HAL secretly booked passengers as low as US $5 net, while HAPAG even transported some free of charge. Fearing not to be able to book enough passengers to make some sailing count for the tonnage clause, members with a surplus were reluctant to raise prices. This prevented members who failed to meet the quota to book at more profitable rates. Tonnage increased by fifty-one percent during the first six years of the pool; combined with declining migrant flows due to the economic recession, this led to a capacity decrease per 1000 tons from 119 passengers to thirty-eight which allowed HAPAG to increase its share (WB, +1.84; EB, +5.18) to the detriment of the NGL (WB, -1.59; EB, -3.21) and the RSL (WB, -0.79; EB, -1.11), while the HAL basically maintained its share (WB, +0.54; EB, -0.86). Instead of reducing overcapacity, this clause in fact stimulated the tonnage glut, encouraging lines to cut rates and preventing them from raising them. Accordingly, in 1895 the lines lowered the increase in market share attributed to the rise in tonnage. Three years later, the clause was revoked and fixed, unchangeable market shares were introduced. It put an end to the lines' artificial increase of tonnage, as the immediate withdrawal of the German lines' specialized freight and third-class services illustrated.[71]

---

[70]Murken, *Die grossen transatlantischen*, 80-86; and Richard A. Sicotte, "Competition and Cartels in Liner Shipping Industry: A Historical Perspective," in Ulf Olsson (ed.), *Business and European Integration since 1800: Regional, National and International Perspectives* (Gothenburg, 1997), 152-153.

[71]Westbound/Eastbound: HAPAG, 30.71/26.47; NGL, 44.14/41.53; RSL, 15.37/18.68; and HAL, 9.78/13.32. The percentages remained unchanged with the exception of a slight concession (Westbound, 0.5 percent; Eastbound, one percent) of the NGL towards the HAPAG in 1908; Murken, *Die grossen transatlantischen* 80-86;

Table 2.1
Tonnage and Capacity Utilization of NDLV, 1890-1898

Westbound	Joint NDLV Tonnage	No. Passengers	No. Passengers per 1000 tons
1890	1,775,839	210,598	119
1892	1,505,209	214,753	143
1893	2,123,899	211,656	99
1894	2,051,720	84,610	41
1895	2,114,212	127,111	60
1896	2,383,881	129,554	54
1897	2,480,718	83,699	34
1898	2,686,050	102,886	38

Source: Erich Murken, *Die grossen transatlantischen Linienreederei-Verbande, Pools und Interessengemeinschaften bis zum Ausbruch des Weltkrieges: Ihre Entstehung, Organitsation und Wirksamkeit* (Jena, 1922), 80-86.

The second problem was due to the limited duration of the agreement. The refusal of the Cunard and National lines to join led the NDLV members to conclude an agreement for one year instead of four. This undermined the stability of the cartel as members were constantly preparing for renegotiations. The members initially felt that lines which fell short of their market share and which accepted financial compensation from those with a surplus weakened their negotiating position during the annual discussions to renew the agreement and would eventually lose part of their quota. Therefore, lines paid extra commissions to ensure that the quotas were filled. This practice was reinforced because the rate agreements with the British lines did not diminish the keen rivalry and violations persisted. For example, the HAL paid US $3848 in extra commissions in 1892 and US $21,918 the following year. The continental lines did propose to withdraw completely from the British eastbound steerage market and to give up twelve percent of continental traffic if, in exchange, the British lines would not quote prices below the lowest rate of continental members and would cede a share of the Scandinavian market. Anticipating the signing of what seemed an imminent agreement, the head agents of the continental lines introduced "city rules" in New York, limiting ticket sales to joint company offices. Migrant agents tried to stay in business by attempting to direct all their clients to the British lines. Van den Toorn was confident that the short-term loss would largely be compensated by the long-term gain of putting an end to the abuses and allowing the overland agencies to increase their sales. But again, the lack of unity among the British lines, in particular between Cunard and the White Star Line, prevented the signing of the contract. When

---

and GAR, HAL, 318.04, Passage, 221-226, letters 2 October 1896 and 6 June and 9 September 1897.

negotiations collapsed, the continental lines decided to start a rate war to force the British to a compromise. The fact that the market had collapsed because of the American financial crisis spurred this decision. To limit the losses caused by rate wars, lines usually waited for recessions to force the weakest companies to make concessions.[72]

All the agents in New York were reinstated and paid extra commissions ranging from US $2 to $5. The continental lines opened a regular service to Ireland touching at Queenstown, alternating sailings on the eastbound route and quoting net rates of US $10. They also increased sailings to and from Southampton. For their part, the British lines used orders from migrant brokers in European ports to undercut continental fares, quoting US $15 from Rotterdam to New York.[73] The war also spread to Scandinavia, where the German lines reopened a direct service, and to the booming Mediterranean market where the bigger continental and British lines had opened direct services. Improved collaboration among the continental lines as a result of the pool strengthened their position relative to the British lines whose collaboration was still based on less complex rate agreements. The American Line joined forces with the NDLV lines, allowing them to attack the British on their internal westbound market.[74] For continental traffic, the NDLV initially responded to the British price cuts with extra commissions rather than by lowering rates. This had the advantage of binding agents to the lines and preventing agents and brokers from speculating by issuing large numbers of prepaid blanks to be used when prices increased. Still, it was impossible to prevent eastbound continental passengers from taking advantage of the low British rates quoted by the NDLV lines and returning indirectly to Europe. As the British lines increased their share of the westbound traffic, a drastic cut of US $8 on prepaid and eastbound continental rates followed.[75]

The slump in the market combined with the rate war put a lot of strain on both the pool and the British lines with the Guion and National Line being forced out of the passenger business. In 1895, negotiations resumed and the

---

[72]GAR, HAL, 318.04, Passage, 221-226, letters, 10 and 20 March, 14 July and 22 December 1893; 18 January and 2, 10, 11, 20 and 24 April 1894; and Passage, 563, meetings, 4 and 20 January, minutes 669-672, 30 March 30, and 4 April 1894, minutes 717-739.

[73]*Ibid.*, Passage, 563, meetings, 30 March and 4 April 1894, minutes 717-739; and Passage, 221-226, letters, 2, 10, 11 and 24 April 1894.

[74]Agreement was reached at a conference in Cologne. *Ibid.*, Passage, 221-226, letter, 27 April 1894.

[75]*Ibid.*, letters, 11 May, 5 September and 10 December 1894; and Passage, 563, meeting, 26 July 1894, minutes 775-777.

lines agreed to stop the war and jointly raise fares. If both parties came to an agreement, agents and brokers would no longer be able to play out the rivalry to their advantage. Fearing exclusion from the market, the principal American agents formed the New York City Agent Association, headed by A. Falck to discuss a suitable arrangement for agents and shipping lines. Agents agreed to abide by all conference rules and to stop drawing orders on European houses in exchange for a guarantee of a minimum amount of business and protection from the lines against the abuses of non-conference agents. The Hamburg brokers also signed a new agreement with the continental and British lines to end the abuses originating from the German port. The long-awaited pool agreement finally materialized. British lines agreed to keep away from the Mediterranean market and to limit their share of continental traffic to six percent for which net rates could not go below the lowest continental fare. Continental lines for their part withdrew from the British and Scandinavian markets.

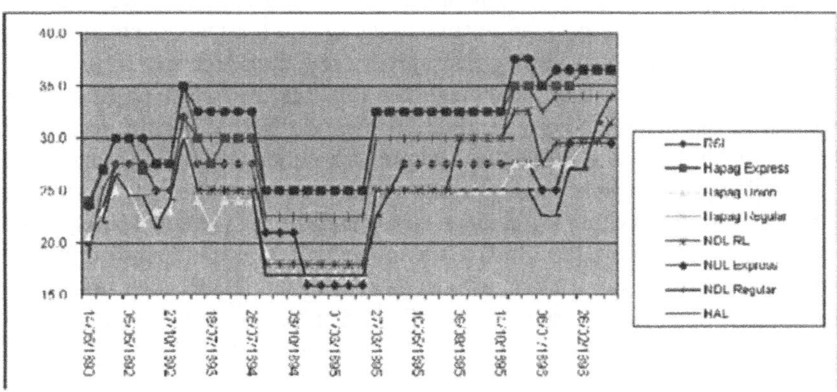

Figure 2.2: New York Prepaid Fares of Continental Lines, 1890-1896

Source: GAR, HAL, 318.04, Passage, 563-565, 767, minutes of NYCC; 72-77 and 221-226, correspondence; and 318.02, Directors, 112-121, correspondence.

This consolidation of the NDLV at the end of 1895 made it possible to impose regulations on agents and brokers with important repercussions for transatlantic steerage fares. As figure 2.2 illustrates, the pool agreement allowed the continental lines to increase prepaid prices significantly in 1892. Yet discord among the British lines delayed further increases and forced the lines to pay high commissions which cut into profits. Prices plummeted during the war but recuperated when negotiations resumed. When the extended pool agreement was signed, prices reached unprecedented levels. Compared to 1885, the HAL's prepaid prices doubled from US $17 to $34 by 1896. During the same period, consumer prices dropped by thirteen percent while nominal

GDP per capita and wages for unskilled labour remained the same. The agreement set new standards for fixing ocean fares and greatly increased the cost of migration. Yet the steady increase of the migrant flow in the following years does not seem to indicate any direct impact.[76]

Expansion and Consolidation of the NDLV

Releasing the Competitive Pressures in Other Trade Departments

The agreement for third-class westbound passage was a landmark for the cartels competing for North Atlantic traffic. The competition for eastbound passages could quickly increase tensions, however, undermining the westbound agreement. To ease the pressure, lines agreed to regulate the entire North Atlantic passenger traffic. Freight traffic posed fewer problems since it was not profitable for British lines to call at continental ports for goods, while continental lines only took or delivered mail and cabin passengers at English ports. Internally, the NDLV fixed minimum rates for westbound freight and pooled the revenue.[77] This allowed passenger ships to face the stronger external competition for freight. Their superior speed enabled them to acquire the traffic in luxury goods, while freight lines and tramps competed for other cargo. The passenger lines' specialized freight ships improved their competitive position for these. But since it consisted mainly of raw materials and cereals, eastbound traffic market fluctuated much more and impeded pool or rate agreements.[78]

Cabin traffic had a bigger influence on inter-line relations. The competition for first-class passengers between the continental and British lines was keener than for migrants. Tourists had fewer financial restrictions, were more sensitive to technological innovation and were less concerned about a particular route. The large number of subdivisions (and changes) at different prices within first-class obstructed lasting rate agreements. Second-class accommoda-

---

[76]*Ibid.*, Passage, 563, meetings 19 June, minute 843, 13 August, minutes 861-871 and 4 September 1895, minute 875; Passage, 223, letters, 3 April and 15 June 1895; 318.04, 221-226, letter, 15 September 1895; and Samuel Williamson, "Six Ways to Compute the Relative Value of a U.S. Dollar Amount, 1790 to Present," http://www.measuringworth.com/uscompare.

[77]In 1894, freight traffic was divided based on the three preceding years, giving HAPAG 37.5 percent, the HAL eighteen percent, the NGL 23.5 percent and the RSL 20.5 percent. Murken, *Die grossen transatlantischen*, 127.

[78]Solomon S. Huebner, "Steamship Line Agreements and Affiliations in the American Foreign and Domestic Trade," *Annals of the American Academy of Political and Social Sciences*, LV (1914), 77; Murken, *Die grossen transatlantischen*, 119-141; and J. Russell Smith, "Ocean Freight Rates and Their Control through Combination," *Political Science Quarterly*, XXI, No. 2 (1906), 249-253.

tion, targeting mainly wealthier migrants, gained popularity but could easily interfere with third-class agreements as the price difference between the two averaged about US $10 (table 2.2). Attempts by the continental lines to pool cabin traffic without agreements with the British lines failed. Members of the NDLV, however, reached a rate agreement that fixed the difference between second- and third-class passages at US $10. In the wake of the third-class westbound agreement, the British and continental lines concluded minimum rate agreements for cabin passage midway through 1896. Due to the greater fluctuations in cabin rates, these were subject to constant renegotiation, but the main carriers of North Atlantic cabin passenger traffic did manage to neutralize the competition.[79]

Table 2.2
HAL Second-Cabin Passengers and Rates, 1886-1895

Year	Passengers	Average Price (*Guilders*)	Average Price (Dollars)
1886	1374	63.3	25.3
1887	1606	63.9	25.5
1888	1919	65.1	26
1889	2106	62.2	24.9
1890	2553	63.4	25.4
1891	2877	67.5	27
1892	3448	81.3	32.6
1893	4202	92.6	37
1894	1561	93.7	37.5
1895	1241	94.3	37.7

Note: The source did not specify whether these were net or gross prices.

Source: GAR, HAL, 318.04, Passage, 221-226, letter, 15 September 1896.

Due to overcapacity and the lack of agreement with the British lines for eastbound steerage traffic, return migrants paid approximately US $10 less to return home than to reach the US (see figure 2.3). The NDLV's eastbound pool did not produce the anticipated results because members could not adapt prices for fear of losing passengers to British lines (see figure 2.4). Members that exceeded their quota refrained from raising prices to allow conference members in deficit to catch up. In 1896, negotiations with British lines led to an agreement, but the lack of consensus on how to pool the traffic did little to reduce competitive pressures. The continental lines remained relatively re-

[79]GAR, HAL, 318.04, Passage, 580, NDLV agreement, January 1892; and meeting, 12 December 1895, minute 182; and Murken, *Die grossen transatlantischen*, 90-118.

stricted in setting the prices, and the gap with the westbound rates hardly decreased. To their dismay, British lines acquired nearly ten percent of the eastbound continental market. The German lines reduced their rates which, combined with the overland fare, made most eastern European destinations cheaper to reach than when travelling with the HAL (appendix 1), which refrained from lowering its rates because the price agreement allowed British lines to do the same (see table 2.5). The continental lines increased their bookings for the eastbound pool in this way, yet because the HAL accumulated an important deficit it received financial compensation from the German lines. This strategy was profitable for the HAL, but in the long run it threatened to drive the company out of the eastbound market.[80] New rate agreements between the British and continental lines, containing differentiations for each continental port rather than an entire range, allowed the HAL to lower rates and re-establish a differential with the German lines without fear of losing passengers. Still, eastbound prices remained below westbound due to discord over second-class rates. Only when all the lines raised eastbound rates by US $2 in 1901 did the gap narrow. Thereafter the differential was reduced even further until finally rates were equalized.[81] This also allowed the lines to set prices according to their position in the pool quotas. Previously, rates for all companies followed the same pattern, but now they diverged more frequently (see figure 2.4).

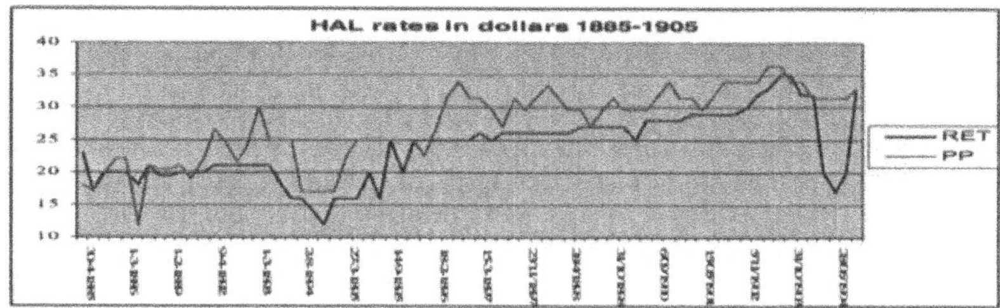

Figure 2.3: HAL Prepaid and Return Steerage Prices, 1885-1905

Source: See figure 2.2.

[80]Murken, *Die grossen transatlantischen*, 63; and GAR, HAL, 318.04, Passage, 221-226, letters, 11, 15, 16 and 18 September and 27 October 1896; and 580, meeting, 12 December 1892, minute 53. The HAL received US $20 compensation per passenger. Its eastbound rate was US $25, and the cost per passenger was US $10, which left an approximate financial gain of US $5. The compensation had gradually increased from US $10 to $15 in 1893. GAR, HAL, 318.04, Passage, 221-226, letters 18 September 1896 and 30 July 1897; and Passage, 580, meetings, 16 February, minute 59 and 18 December 1893, minute 95.

[81]*Ibid.*, 318.04, Passage, 580, agreement between British lines and NDLV, 7 June 1898; and Passage, 221-226, letters, 6 February 1900 and 3 and 16 July 1901.

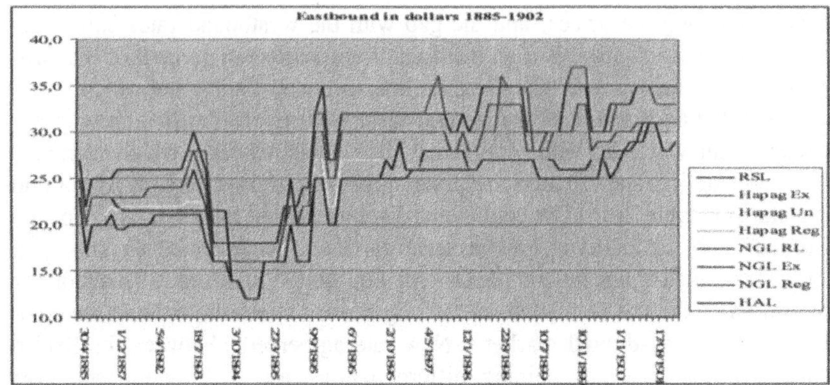

Figure 2.4: Eastbound Dollar Rates of NDLV Members, 1885-1902

Source: See figure 2.2.

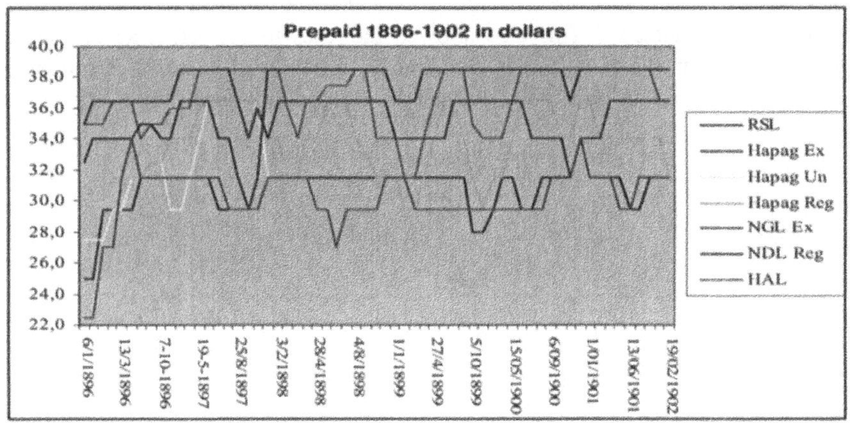

Figure 2.5: Prepaid Rates of NDLV Members, 1896-1902

Source: See figure 2.2.

The Inclusion of the CGT and Other Outside Lines

The non-inclusion of the French line in the NDLV pool agreement meant that special low fares persisted for northern Italy, France, Switzerland and the "Orient" (Asia, Africa, Turkey and Greece). As prices for other continental points increased, travel to or from some places in France and Switzerland, including overland transport, became cheaper than, for instance, the HAL's ocean fare from Rotterdam. It became difficult for lines to avoid special rates being abused for other continental destinations. Negotiations with the CGT led to its inclusion in the NYCC, yet it continued its own course by violating the rules whenever it judged that opportunistic behaviour might lead to greater returns. For example, it offered special return fares through Greek consuls in the US to enable Greeks to return to defend their homeland when tensions with the Ottoman Empire increased. The CGT also cut into railroad rates, paid extra commissions and allowed some brokers, such as Fugazi, Zotti and Zwilchenbart, to continue using cash orders instead of prepaids.[82] It obstructed the NDLV's attempts to make the market more transparent, but when the CGT expanded to the east and began to affect rates in the Austrian market, its inclusion in the pool became essential.[83] The NDLV managed to block the CGT from expanding further east into what one of its agents labelled as the "holy northern pool territory." The CGT eventually gave in and joined the westbound pool. Because of its close ties with both Mediterranean and continental markets, its share of 11.7 percent was divided into continental and Mediterranean passengers. Satisfied with the outcome, the CGT subsequently joined the eastbound pool, acquiring a share of 15.21 percent. At last, all the major lines in the Hamburg-Le Havre range were united by a pool agreement.[84]

The CGT's eastward expansion was spurred by growing competition in the Mediterranean. The HAL failed to open a direct service to Italy because it lacked vessels and could not attract enough cargo to make it profitable.[85] With their larger fleets and better contacts, the German lines could more easily react to new market opportunities and hence did open direct services to Italy. Under the new NDLV agreement the British lines, except for the Anchor Line, remained excluded from the market. But the NGL and HAPAG could not prevent the establishment of other outside lines. This process was aided when the techniques conferences used to block new lines from entering a market were questioned by the Supreme Court's new interpretation of the Sherman Antitrust Act which declared that all combinations regulating commerce or keeping

---

[82] *Ibid.*, letters, 14 and 25 May. 25 June and 6 July 1897; and 25 February 1898; and 31 March and 4 April 1899; and 318.04, Passage, 580, meeting, 19 February 1892, minute 9.

[83] In 1901, prepaid tickets from Rotterdam cost US $34, while from Innsbruck, including the inland fare, the cost on the same ship was US $30.95. Other Austrian passengers could avail of the low South Austrian rate as they all were forwarded through Vienna. *Ibid.*, letters, 22 June and 13 September 1901, and 25 March 1902.

[84] *Ibid.*, 318.02, Directors, 112-121, letter, 21 November 1900; and 318.04, Passage, 580, Agreement G and L between NDLV and CGT, 1903-1904.

[85] *Ibid.*, 318.02, Directors, 112-121, letters, 26 September and 16 October 1891.

prices high and stable were unlawful. Mounting public concern about big business led Congress to try to curb monopolies. Yet in the Sherman Act lawmakers had failed to specify when and how to implement it, leaving the interpretation to the courts. The 1897 ruling that all restraints of trade, reasonable or not, were illegal threatened the viability of shipping conferences.[86]

The NYCC lines hence became liable for prosecution. Fears that the system might be declared unlawful led the lines to modify their policies, especially towards new entrants. The corollary was that new firms, such as the Prince Line which opened a direct service from Naples, used the ruling to force their way into conferences. The Prince Line appointed Oscar Richard, manager of C.B. Richard and Co., as its New York head agent; the year before, he had represented the Atlantic Line, a failed attempt to sustain a service from Genoa. He used the court decision to denounce the MC in the press for illegally blocking the line. He challenged the right of conferences to prohibit agents from selling tickets for non-conference lines, a practice to which he attributed the failure of the Atlantic Line. The attack was fuelled by a personal vendetta with his former associate, Emil Boas, who became HAPAG's head agent when it took the passage business away from C.B. Richard and Co. Despite Boas' strong opposition, the MC allowed the Prince Line to join if only to avoid a trial which might lead to the collapse of the conference.[87]

The Dominion Line used the same strategy two years later to abolish the clause which blocked British lines from the Mediterranean market.[88] The British lines quickly realized their misjudgments about future market growth in the subdivisions of North Atlantic passenger traffic. Having settled predominantly for the shrinking British-Scandinavian market, they were left with little *marge de maneuvre* in the growing continental and Mediterranean markets. When the Dominion Line forced its way into the latter, other British lines soon followed, joining various new Italian lines which gained access to the MC due to protectionist measures imposed by the Italian government that guaranteed

---

[86]George Bittlingmayer, "Antitrust and Business Activity: The First Quarter Century," *Business History Review*, LXX, No. 3 (1996), 375-378; Mansel Blackford and K. Austin Kerr, *Business Enterprise in American History* (Boston, 1986; 3rd ed., Boston, 1993), 222-224; Alfred D. Chandler, Jr., *The Visible Hand: The Managerial Revolution in American Business* (Cambridge, MA, 1977), 172; and James Weinstein, *The Corporate Ideal in the Liberal State, 1900-1918* (Boston, 1968; reprint, Westport, CT, 1981), 66-68.

[87]GAR, HAL, letters, 8 July 1896; 27 March, 6 April and 15 May 1897; and 25 October 1898; *Journal of Commerce*, 22 October 1898.

[88]The Dominion Line opened an Italian service from Boston. It used the same arguments as the Prince Line, and to gain local support it portrayed conferences as a scheme of New York interests against other Atlantic ports.

national companies a share of the market.[89] The new lines and the inferior quality of ships in the Mediterranean kept rates low. Moreover, a 1901 Italian law gave the commissioner of migration the authority to play a role in setting steerage prices. The differential with continental rates attracted Europeans to Italian ports, blocking further increases in continental rates.[90] Gradually, the MC allowed prices to rise and began to reduce the gap with continental prices, although the differential never fully disappeared. The growing collaboration among the lines and sub-conferences led to a relatively well respected gentlemen's agreement that Mediterranean rates would not be used for continentals.

Railroad Rates, Quality of Service, Quality of Migrants

In the US, the ICC supervised railroad rates while a clearing house at Ellis Island divided the migrant traffic with rail connections. Shipping companies no longer gained competitive advantages on inland passenger rates, and some railroads reduced or withdrew commissions on railroad tickets sold in connection with ocean passages. The railroad migrant tariffs increased, and shipping companies found it harder to obtain free transport for its representatives visiting the American agent network. The accord among railways underwent various crises before 1914, but the ICC prevented shipping companies from exploiting them. Such control helped to stabilize shipping conferences, unlike European overland rates which remained a point of contention among NDLV members.

The plan for all members to quote the same overland fares never materialized. The list reducing the through booking facilities to 300 popular destinations, from which forwarding would be organized by the lines rather than by migrant brokers, was meant to curtail the influence of the latter on the traffic. Nonetheless, rate cutting persisted, and the HAL lacked the means to arrange through booking properly. The biggest problem was making sure that luggage followed the migrant. Often, the company could only send money to the passenger who had to buy the train ticket to one of the main transit points himself. Because of poor service, prepaid through-bookings plunged from an average of sixty-five percent (1888-1892) to twenty-five percent (1893-1896). Although the lines eventually improved the logistics, van den Toorn unsuccessfully sug-

---

[89]Augusta Molinari, "Porti, trasporti, compagnie," in Piero Bevilacqua, *et al.* (eds.), *Storia dell' emigrazione Italiana: La Partenza* (Rome, 2002), 240. The Mediterranean Conference included Navigazione Italiana, HAPAG, NGL, Bordeaux Line, Fabre Line, CGT, Anchor Line, HAL and RSL. It expanded as follows: 1901, La Veloce; 1902, Dominion Line; 1904, Austro-Americana, Compagnia Transatlantica, Cunard, White Star; 1905, Lloyd Italiano, American Line; 1907, Hellenic Line, Sicula Americana, Italo-New York Line, Lloyd Sabaudo; and 1909, National Greek Line.

[90]Murken, *Die grossen transatlantischen*, 63, quotes an average difference of twenty-five *francs*.

gested limiting through-bookings for all lines to major transit points in order to end the continuous rate-cutting and to establish prices based on distance. The RSL and the HAL in particular cut railroad rates below cost to remain competitive with the German lines which enjoyed a geographic advantage as the market expanded eastward. HAL's overland fares spiralled downward and only stabilized at the turn of the century when the NDLV settled on the differentials to the main transit points (see tables 2.3 and 2.4, and appendix 4).

Table 2.3
HAL Overland Rates in Dollars from Main Transit Points to Rotterdam

Destination	1893	1895	1900	1907/1909
Agram	14.15	11.50	8.40	8.40
Budapest	11.95	8.78	7.55	7.55
Chur		6.03		6.70
Debrecen	13.60	10.18		9.00
Kaschau	13.60	7.90	7.90	7.55
Oderberg	5.87		5.60	5.60
Oswiecim	6.07		5.70	5.70
Prague	8.95	7.55		4.60
Szegedin	13.60	11.20		8.75
Temesvar	13.60	11.60		9.15
Trieste	12.20	11.25	9.55	9.35
Vienna	7.18	7.18	6.00	6.00

Note: The Uranium Line used the same rates as HAL.

Source: GAR, HAL, 318.04, Passage, 221-226, letters, 14 August 1894, 6 December 1895 and 6 February 1900; Zotti, circular, October 1905; HAL, rate sheet, 12 April 1907; and Uranium Line, rate sheet, 29 November 1909.

Table 2.4
Continental Lines' Overland Fare from Home Port to Main Transit Points, 1902

Destination	CGT	RSL	HAPAG	NGL	HAL
Agram	13.55	9.60	7.40	8.00	8.40
Budapest	12.60	8.05	5.80	6.85	7.55
Fiume	12.00	9.90	7.30	9.05	8.40
Innsbruck	8.80	6.90	6.20	6.35	5.95
Karlstadt	14.95	9.85	7.00	8.00	8.40
Laibach	11.70	8.60	6.80	7.40	8.50
Oderberg	12.25	6.05	3.90	4.10	5.60
Oswiecim	12.45	6.30	4.00	4.25	5.70
Trieste	12.00	9.70	7.90	8.45	9.35
Vienna	9.00	6.50	4.65	5.30	6.00

Source: GAR, HAL, 318.04, Passage, 221-226, letter, 15 July 1902.

With both prices and quotas fixed, competition moved towards the quality of service provided from the place of departure to the final destination. Arrangements ensuring a fluid transit to and from the ports was an important component. To assist its passengers, the HAL opened offices at key transit points and built hotels in Leipzig and Rotterdam. The hotels allowed the line to control lodging costs and to reduce the cost of migrating via Rotterdam. It also helped to protect its clients from scalpers while in transit and from abuses in private lodging houses. This helped to improving Rotterdam's reputation as a migrant gateway. On board, more companies adapted steerage accommodation to second-class standards. By the turn of the century, the HAL converted its steerage dormitories into closed staterooms for a maximum of six passengers. This gave guests more space and privacy while the sanitary conditions and ventilation were also improved. The company stressed the good treatment of passengers by its personnel. About thirty people attended the third-class passengers, serving them abundant and good food and keeping the steerage compartments clean.[91] In the more spacious dining rooms, the HAL started to provide entertainment. Occasional stories of weakened migrants arriving in New York because of malnutrition at sea disappeared from the tabloid press with the introduction of steam. For many steerage passengers, the quality and quantity of the menu on board exceeded the rations they had at home.[92] Interests involved in the migrant business had always been aware of the importance of the reputation of a migrant route. In a system dominated by chain migration, word of mouth played a crucial role in deciding if, when and how to travel. Shipping companies tried to provide the best possible service which improved with the growing competition among lines and the subsequent conference agreements. The HAL's advertising campaigns centring on "good treatment, good food, comfort and convenience" underline this.[93]

Competition also moved towards the quality of the passengers, something that depended on the means of the migrants and the likelihood of being deported. Ethnic background played an important role when American authorities sharpened controls for Mediterranean and eastern European passengers. Jews, particularly those from Russia, enjoyed the worst reputation among continental passengers, especially after the outbreak of cholera in Hamburg. Many

---

[91]The cost of the food per passenger per day fluctuated between US $0.35 and US $0.5 per day from 1883 to 1914. *Ibid.*, 318.16 Museum, 53, Staten van voedingskosten van passagiers, 1883-1919.

[92]A random example of the daily menu on a German line consisted of cereal, coffee, white bread, butter or prune jam for breakfast; coffee and dried bread as an afternoon snack; sausage, potatoes, a vegetable mixture and white bread for dinner; and pickled herring, potatoes, tea and black bread for supper. DC, *Report*, XXXVII, 24.

[93]GAR, HAL, 318.03, Passage, 49-58, 97, 160, 190, letter, 1 February 1914.

were poor or ill, relying on the assistance of aid societies to migrate.[94] These passengers spent less in port or on the ship and frequently could not even afford room and board before embarking. They were also more likely to be refused entry to the US and returned home at the line's expense. Moreover, Jewish passengers initiated the majority of legal proceedings against shipping companies for lost luggage and accidents. Some lines, in particular NGL and the RSL, made conscious efforts to recruit from regions other than Russia. In 1895, the RSL introduced discriminatory prices for Russian Jews while launching a major propaganda campaign in Austria. This coincided with the end of the "Wiener cartel" in which the RSL and the HAL pooled business transiting through Vienna. Both initially feared that the NDLV was a scheme by the German lines to usurp the migrant business, and they joined forces to prevent it. The HAL had a share of forty-four percent and the RSL fifty-six percent in the Wiener cartel. After terminating the agreement, the RSL's efforts in Austria paid off as it increased its market share to 69.5 percent. Conversely, the HAL disapproved of discriminating against certain markets because with the increasing interference of European governments in the trade, lines could be shut out of a market, thereby increasing the risks of specialization.[95] It also denounced discriminatory prices as being against the spirit of a pool. Instead, the HAL introduced special prices for Russians, charging an extra US $2 which, however, included board and lodging before departure. This way it ended the practice of withholding the luggage of passengers who failed to settle their lodging bills. The other lines copied the strategy, which gradually spread to other ethnic groups.[96] The popularity of the Rotterdam route among Russians is illustrated by table 2.6.

---

[94]The average amount possessed by Jews on arrival in the US from 1903 to 1909 was US $13.93, making them among the poorest ethnic groups. DC, *Report*, IV, 39; and GAR, HAL, 318.04, Passage, 221-226, letters, 12 and 26 October, 9, 19 and 30 November and 17 December 1897.

[95]For instance, HAL feared that government support for Oesterreichs Colonial Gesellschaft might disrupt the Austrian market. The RSL and the HAL also formed a cartel for the Benelux region. GAR, HAL, 318.04, Passage, 221-226, letters, 15 September 1896 and 13 July 1899; and Passage, 235, file, 1892-1896.

[96]GAR, HAL, 318.04, Passage, 221-226, letters, 6 August 1897; 28 July 1898, 15 February 1899 and 16 January 1907.

Table 2.5
Emigration via Rotterdam According to Nationality, 1887-1914

Year	Dutch	German	Austrian	Hungarian	Russian	American	Other	Total
1887	2659	3754	1135	0	314	822	2451	11,135
1888	2162	3316	685	0	515	315	2616	9609
1889	5862	4378	397	421	743	700	2751	15,252
1890	2057	2640	1589	946	1111	117	1439	9899
1891	3169	4985	2727	4314	7312	428	1737	24,672
1892	5182	4860	1207	5729	2582	147	1284	20,991
1893	4598	6737	11,275	679	10,826	301	1492	35,908
1894	983	1748	3166	277	6072	128	659	13,033
1895	1156	1737	2588	3012	5048	115	487	14,143
1896	1251	1196	2587	2105	3633	31	260	11,063
1897	611	804	1934	762	2599	75	220	7005
1898	746	959	4725	1751	3862	49	467	12,559
1899	1227	951	6569	2301	6820	42	1052	18,962
1900	1854	1938	7450	3072	13,261	98	5708	33,381
1901	1791	1874	5803	4506	14,352	107	4472	32,905
1902	2201	2251	8408	8026	19,148	173	5328	45,535
1903	2835	2571	8592	8439	24,976	184	5233	52,830
1904	2224	1446	5403	4391	31,835	228	3489	49,016
1905	1965	1511	6105	8809	34,878	235	2071	55,574
1906	2069	1354	4794	6587	31,944	171	2002	48,921
1907	3435	1729	8084	13,794	27,521	255	4484	59,302
1908	1695	821	2681	1874	8269	373	1366	17,079
1909	1600	1101	6131	6569	24,506	409	3245	43,561
1910	2605	1175	10,206	5873	35,290	439	5309	60,897

Year	Dutch	German	Austrian	Hungarian	Russian	American	Other	Total
1911	2165	865	9146	4182	20,837	405	2773	40,373
1912	1555	1315	11,415	6949	39,115	456	6585	67,390
1913	1817	1958	17,252	9312	44,299	380	7452	82,470
1914	1779	882	8276	3663	12,567	3842	2336	33,345

Note: Figures do not reflect the total number carried by the HAL up to 1892 because it also ran a service from Amsterdam. Similarly, from 1906 onwards other lines operated from Rotterdam targeting the Russian market.

Source: Rotterdam Emigration Commission, as published in Leo A. van der Valk "Landverhuizers via Rotterdam in de negentiende eeuw," *Economisch en Sociaal-Historisch jaarboek* (Amsterdam, 1976), 165.

The German lines had an impotant advantage in selecting the quality of the passengers because they managed the border control stations built in the wake of the Hamburg cholera outbreak. Border agents discriminated in favour of HAPAG and NGL because most of the so-called ticketless "*Anschluss*" passengers, traveling with friends or relatives with tickets, were generally directed to Bremen or Hamburg even if their travel companions held tickets through Antwerp or Rotterdam. Many tickets were sold at the border stations, as this was a condition to enter Germany. Some HAL agents complained that German lines sometimes rebooked their passengers through Hamburg or Bremen. Also, migrants holding tickets of German lines, but showing a high probability of being debarred in the US at the control station, were sometimes rebooked for the HAL or the RSL. It allowed German lines to avoid risking deportation costs but prevented the passenger from being lost for the pool. As the costs of exploitation of the control station were shared by all conference lines, the HAL protested against the practice. At the same time, it feared that stations would be used as the original decree had foreseen, allowing only HAPAG and NGL passengers to cross the borders. The control stations remained a pressure point among the members. Only at the outbreak of World War I would HAL's passengers be refused entry and forced to use well-prepared alternative routes through Libau or Austria.[97]

Steerage Price Formation on the North Atlantic: A Complex Story

The transatlantic networks of migrant agents undermined the ability of shipowners to fix the fares for ocean passage. Agents favoured an unstable market because the keener the competition between the lines, the higher their commissions and the more facilities they obtained to increase their sales. The lack of a common interest between migrant agents and shipowners forced the latter to rely on conference rules to police the former. Shipping conferences which regulated passenger transport were as much a means of horizontal integration regulating competition among shipping companies as they were a means of vertical integration to gain control over the agent network. It took the NYCC lines a decade to find a workable equilibrium. The distrust among members prevented them from making long-term arrangements. The constant renegotiations of ocean rate differentials and the fact that fixed rates pushed the competition increasingly towards quality of service, railroad rates and the tying of migrant brokers and agents to a line impeded the conference from relieving the

---

[97]*Ibid.*, letters, 18 July 1896 and 6 January 1901; Passage, 1, correspondence with Berlin agent, 1898-1903; 318.02, Directors, 121-121, letter, 23 June 1914; and Katja Wüstenbecker, "Hamburg and the Transit of East Europeans," in Andreas Fahrmeir, Olivier Faron and Patrick Weil (eds.), *Migration Control in the North Atlantic World* (New York, 2003), 234-244.

internal pressures among lines. Such internal pressures were intensified by the external pressures.

The success of the NYCC depended on the imposition of similar arrangements in the other sub-markets into which the North Atlantic passenger market was divided; the British-Scandinavian and the Mediterranean. The British conference lines held a dominant position on the North Atlantic passenger market because of government protection of the home market from foreign competition and the strong foothold in the continental market via Hamburg. Continental lines therefore depended on the collaboration of the British lines to fix continental fares and commissions, as well as to impose rules on the migrant agent network to regulate sales. The lack of harmony among lines allowed migrant brokers to play off the rivals to their advantage, thereby increasing their control over the market. In particular, the price difference between European cash and American prepaid tickets allowed them to undercut the shipping lines on the American market by issuing their own orders. Instead of making the market more transparent, the level of abuses expanded during the first seven years of the NYCC. Cheating on conference agreements was too hard to detect, and no effective means were put into place to deter lines and agents from trying.

By dividing the market into shares with the formation of the NDLV, the continental lines neutralized the internal incentives to cheat on the agreements and greatly improved the level of harmony among the members. The increased collaboration helped to pressure the British lines to reach a compromise. When the British lines joined the pool agreement, the continental lines finally managed to tame the migrant agents, raise the gross rates and limit the price cuts. This significantly increased profits on the sales of steerage passages while raising the cost for migrants to cross the Atlantic. Before the agreement, excluding the lows of US $10 during rate wars, the HAL's net prices varied between US $15 and $20. In 1896, the rate reached US $34, which set the standard for the next decade.

The westbound steerage agreement served as a platform to consolidate the North Atlantic transport business on various levels. Rate agreements between the conferences for cabin passage soon followed, preventing the competition from these markets from affecting westbound steerage rates. Finding a workable equilibrium for the eastbound steerage market was a lot more difficult due to overcapacity, the concentration of the lines in the same port and the divergent return patterns of the various ethnic groups. All of which stimulated interference among the sub-markets. Return prices remained significantly lower than westbound passages. Rate wars underline the greater susceptibility to competitive pressures of return fares, which fell lower and more rapidly than pre-paids. Agreements on through rates also gradually closed.

The expansion of conference agreements reduced the external pressures on the NDLV pool, which in the meantime was consolidated. By striking out the tonnage clause, members put an end to the excessive competition of introducing new and larger vessels. Also, the intensified pressure that fixed ocean rates had generated on inland railroad fares stabilized. The inclusion of the CGT in the NDLV pool ended lower fares for some parts of the continental market. The competition over quality of service and passengers could not spoil the growing market stability that allowed lines to increase their profits as migration picked up again after 1895. In the five years following the agreement, HAPAG averaged a dividend of 7.6 percent, while the NGL earned an average of 6.8 percent.[98] The increased cost for the passenger was partly compensated by the improved service. The success of passenger lines attracted the interest of new investors like J.P. Morgan, who planned to take consolidation a step further. His appearance on the scene did not help the conference lines to escape the attention of the growing trust-busting climate in the US, putting the legality of the conference system in jeopardy.

[98]Murken, *Die grossen transatlantischen*, 190.

Chapter 3
The IMM Merger and Further Consolidations in the Shipping Industry

Conference agreements in the shipping industry boomed at the end of the nineteenth century. On the eve of World War I, over 100 agreements and consolidations regulated American foreign and domestic waterborne commerce. As contemporaries noted, despite the healthy market, only a few new passenger lines were established on the North Atlantic after 1890, and they did not play an important part in the general expansion of trade.[1] The long-term trend towards consolidation and the legal uncertainty engendered by American legislation favoured mergers. J.P. Morgan extended his business philosophy to the shipping industry with the establishment of the International Merchant Marine (IMM), and its impact on the organization of the steerage market will be analyzed in this chapter. The chapter also takes a closer look at the strategies conferences used against outside lines. How successful was the New York Continental Conference (NYCC) in preventing new or established lines from enlarging or acquiring market share? How did this affect the internal relations among conference members and what was the impact on steerage rates? How did it affect shipping companies' efforts to rationalize the migrant agent network through conference agreements? As well, the connections among the submarkets and the impact of increased government interference in the organization of migrant traffic will be examined. In the end, the antitrust campaign caught up with the shipping industry during the Progressive Era. The strategies used by the lines to defend the conference system during the federal investigation shed light on the growing fusion among public opinion, business, legislators and academics during this period.

Taking Horizontal Combinations a Step Further: The IMM Merger

The Supreme Court's new interpretation of the Sherman Antitrust Act in 1897 had a boomerang effect, pushing many cartel-like agreements to evolve into great corporate consolidations by way of merger. Looser agreements that

[1]Solomon S. Huebner, "Steamship Line Agreements and Affiliations in the American Foreign and Domestic Trade," *Annals of the American Academy of Political and Social Sciences*, LV (1914), 75; and Paul Gottheil, "Historical Development of Steamship Agreements and Conferences in the American Foreign Trade," *Annals of the American Academy of Political and Social Sciences*, LV, No. 1 (1914), 49.

looked like pools or cartels became much more vulnerable before federal courts.[2] The shipping industry did not escape this trend, but as Alfred Chandler has noted, economic rather than legal reasons led to the administrative centralizations.[3] Political reasons matter as well, as the interest for shipping in the United States grew after the Spanish-American War had exposed the shortcomings of domestically owned fleet. It triggered speculation about the approval of several important ship subsidies being considered by Congress. The continuous lobbying for such subsidies by Clement Griscom, the manager of the Internaational Navigation Company (INC) seemed to have borne fruit. Anticipating the approval of subsidies, Griscom looked for capital to expand his fleet, a quest that led him to J.P. Morgan who orchestrated the merger of the INC with the Atlantic Line, the only other American-flag service on the North Atlantic. Through the efforts of Lord William Pirrie, manager of the Belfast shipyard Harland and Wolff, the merger expanded to Europe. Pirrie, who operated the world's leading builder of passenger ships, had contacts which led to the incorporation of the Leyland Line, Dominion Line and White Star Line (WSL).[4] The German lines, Hamburg-Amerikanischen Packetfahrt-Actien-Gesellschaft (HAPAG) and the North German Lloyd (NGL), feared that the merger and Morgan's strong ties with American railroads might disrupt the equilibrium in the North Atlantic trades. As a result, they concluded a profit-sharing agreement with the IMM that included many clauses guaranteeing the continuation, renewal and direction of the pool agreements. The merger in many ways was a logical consequence and expansion of the conference agreements. To neutralize the remaining causes of friction, the German lines worked to include the Holland-America Line (HAL) in the venture, while the IMM worked on taking over the Cunard Line.[5]

---

[2]James Weinstein, *The Corporate Ideal in the Liberal State, 1900-1918* (Boston, 1968; reprint, Westport, CT, 1981), 67-68.

[3]Alfred D. Chandler, Jr., *The Visible Hand: The Managerial Revolution in American Business* (Cambridge, MA, 1977), 334.

[4]Thomas R. Navin and Marian V. Sears, "A Study in Merger: Formation of the International Mercantile Marine Company," *Business History Review*, XXVIII, No. 4 (1954), 291; and Vivian Vale, *The American Peril: Challenge to Britain on the North Atlantic, 1901-04* (Manchester, 1984), 55-57. Harland and Wolff provided ships to the WSL, HAPAG, the Dominion Line and the HAL. Its involvement in the IMM opened promising prospects to expand the list.

[5]Gordon Boyce, *Information, Mediation and Institutional Development: The Rise of Large-Scale Enterprise in British Shipping, 1870-1919* (Manchester, 1995), 105; and Erich Murken, *Die grossen transatlantischen Linienreederei-Verbande, Pools und Interessengemeinschaften bis zum Ausbruch des Weltkrieges: Ihre Entstehung, Organitsation und Wirksamkeit* (Jena, 1922), 199.

Early in 1898, the HAL received a joint offer from the Pacific Mail Co. and the Vanderbilts, owners of the New York Central and Hudson Railroad Company, to take over the line. The scheme was presented as a form of vertical integration to further rationalize global freight and passenger transport. The plans were spurred by the speculation about ship subsidies; the establishment of the Joint Traffic Association by a consortium of eastern American ports and railroads to end the dominance of New York; and the uncertainty about Griscom's intentions to redirect his ships to Philadelphia.[6] Given the nature of the conference system, buying an existing line was often much cheaper than starting a new one and fighting for inclusion in a conference. The Vanderbilts were not the only ones considering taking over the HAL; HAPAG had used this strategy in its home port, taking over smaller lines to eliminate competition and to establish itself on new routes, in the process becoming the biggest shipping company in the world. In order not to destabilize the Nord Atlantische Dampfer Linien Verband (NDLV) pool, HAPAG considered that taking over the HAL was the best option to continue its expansion.[7]

For their part, the directors of the HAL had no intention of being taken over by Vanderbilt or HAPAG, and they adapted the company's statutes to safeguard its Dutch character. The line also strengthened its national character by increasing its capital by two million *guilders* and placing most of it with an Amsterdam financer. The HAL used the capital to enlarge its fleet, doubling its carrying capacity in short order. The new tonnage was used for the Rotterdam/Amsterdam-New York route in part because it was the most profitable and in part because it feared that dividing the fleet on various routes would increase its vulnerability to a takeover. The service to Buenos Aires was suspended, as the firm had done previously with the route to Baltimore. This strategy enabled the HAL to become a first-class steamship company and to quadruple its cabin business during the following decade. The HAL no longer lagged behind other lines and remained competitive even during slumps.[8]

---

[6]By offering important differentials, the Joint Traffic Association successfully did divert some traffic from New York. To combat this, New York interests renovated the Erie Canal; a successful lobbying campaign, co-financed by the shipping companies, got an appropriation bill approved. Rotterdam Community Archives (GAR), Holland-America Line Archive (HAL), 318.04, Passage, 221-226, letters, 17 December 1897, 25 January 1898 and 18 September and 6 November 1903.

[7]Frank Broeze, "Shipping Policy and Social Darwinism: Albert Ballin and the *Weltpolitik* of the Hamburg-America Line, 1886-1914," *Mariner's Mirror*, LXXIX, No. 4 (1993), 419; Murken, *Die grossen transatlantischen*, 165; Vale, *American Peril*, 68; and GAR, HAL, 318.02, Directors, 112-121, letters, 23 September, 13 October, and 22 and 25 November 1898.

[8]Vale, *American Peril*, 85-87; A.D. Wentholt, *Brug over den Oceaan: een eeuw geschiedenis van de Holand-Amerika Lijn* (Rotterdam, 1973), 118; GAR, HAL,

The conference system, which was based on having regular meetings among its members, greatly improved the *esprit de corps* among the managers of passenger lines, most of which largely were not confined to operations in a single set of ports. The fact that Albert Ballin became the godfather of Henri Reuchlin, the son and grandson of the HAL directors Johan and Otto, demonstrates that the relationships among steamship managers reached far beyond corporate levels. As Robert Greenhill has noted, the success of shipping conferences depended to a great degree on the personalities of their leaders, and a sense of group loyalty could be extremely important in their success.[9] The capabilities of Albert Ballin ensured the success of the conference and earned him a great deal of respect. HAL's directors acknowledged this but always remained suspicious of the intentions of the man whose motto was *mein feld ist die Welt*. They gladly cooperated with the consolidation efforts from which the company prospered but had no intention of becoming absorbed by HAPAG.

The HAL's directors were well aware that it could not remain outside an agreement between the IMM and German lines because the latter's connections with American railroads which combined with control over the German border stations put the Dutch company in a weak competitive position. Moreover, the directors favoured a consolidation guaranteeing the continuation of the pool as they were well aware that small members profited more from these agreements than did the larger members. The IMM finally convinced the directors through Pirrie to transfer fifty-one percent of the HAL's shares by guaranteeing the preservation of the line's Dutch character and by paying bonuses to the HAL directors upon signing. To facilitate the takeover, the company's capital was increased by fifty percent to twelve million *guilders*.[10] Some months later, the IMM transferred half these shares to the German lines. The directors did not understand why the IMM gave up its control and denounced the hypocrisy of the German lines which had concluded an agreement behind their backs. Despite the increased tensions, the directors realized that they

---

318.02, Directors, 112-121, letters, 18 December 1898; 17, 24 and 30 January and 28 February 1899; and 15 February 1901; and 318.14, Wentholt Archief, A 12, annual report, 1898.

[9]Robert G. Greenhill, "Competition or Co-operation in the Global Shipping Industry: The Origins and Impact of the Conference System for British Shipowners before 1914," in David J. Starkey and Gelina Harlaftis (eds.), *Global Markets: The Internationalization of the Sea Transport Industries since 1850* (St. John's, 1998), 66-67.

[10]Murken, *Die grossen transatlantischen*, 206; and GAR, HAL, 318.02, Directors, 112-121, letters, 20 December 1901, and 3 and 10 January and 22 April 1902.

"needed to attune the German companies to HAL's interests which also have become theirs."[11]

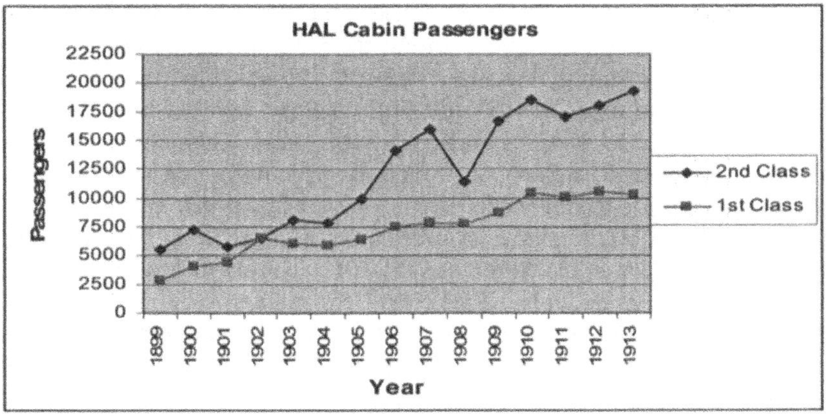

Figure 3.1: HAL Cabin Passengers, 1899 and 1913

Source: Rotterdam Community Archives (GAR), Holland-America Line Archive (HAL), 318.04, Passage, 578, conference statistics, 1899-1914.

Frank Broeze argued that the HAL did not have to join the combination by selling more than half its shares. Indeed, he refuted the common conception in Dutch historiography that the company, by remaining under the Dutch flag retained full entrepreneurial control. The contract of the takeover stipulated that the HAL's policy would be in accord with the general directions of the IMM's board; in other words, it would continue to respect the pool agreements. In exchange, the powers of the HAL directors remained intact except for increases in capital, opening new services and mergers, all of which required the permission of the Joint Committee in which the German lines had a voice. Broeze claimed that this clause trapped the Dutch line in Ballin's *Weltpolitik*.[12] Yet as Erich Murken argued, the clause remained a dead letter as the company rapidly expanded its operations during this period while neutralizing the competition on the Rotterdam-US Atlantic route.[13] This was particularly noticeable in the cargo trade, where the HAL gained control over the

[11]*Ibid.*, letter, 14 October 1902.

[12]Frank Broeze, "Dutch Steamshipping and International Competition: The Holland-America Line under Foreign Control, 1902-1917," in Gordon Jackson and David M. Williams (eds.), *Shipping, Technology and Imperialism: Papers Presented to the Third British-Dutch Maritime History Conference* (Aldershot, 1996), 107-117.

[13]Murken, *Die grossen transatlantischen*, 207-208.

traffic between Rotterdam and the Atlantic coast. It forced the Holland Boston Line out of business, opened a service to Newport and took control of the Cosmopolitan Line (Philadelphia), Neptune Line (Baltimore) and Burg Line (Savanah). As for the passenger business, the HAL managed to hold off the competition of the Russian Volunteer Fleet (RVF), which had not yet the become the Uranium Line. In 1907, the HAL planned to inject new capital to increase the size of its fleet; it claimed that based on its contract with the IMM and its own statutes it could do so without the approval of the German lines. The economic crisis that year hindered its plans to raise new capital, yet despite this and HAPAG's protests it placed an order for a new 24,000-ton ship and another one for a 32,000-ton ship in 1912. Unable to control the company's behaviour, as Ballin had hoped, the German lines resold their shares to the HAL in 1915. In the meantime, the Dutch company consolidated its position on the North Atlantic while earning greater profits than any other line involved in the IMM merger. Between 1903 and 1913, the HAL's average annual dividends were eleven percent, far outperforming the other members (HAPAG, 7.6 percent, and the NGL, 4.7 percent; the IMM did not pay any dividends in this period.)[14]

The Exclusion of the Cunard Line from the IMM

Another company which profited from the establishment of the IMM was Cunard. During the formation of the IMM the pioneering British line, which had been losing market share, was busy renegotiating its subsidy with the British Admiralty. These talks were influenced by press reports about the Leyland, Dominion and White Star lines passing to American control. Although British maritime supremacy remained unchallenged around the turn of the century, with two-thirds of the world's ships being built in Britain and half of global steamship tonnage sailing under the Union Jack, the rise of the German lines and the creation of the IMM alarmed the British public. Although Morgan and his associates only managed to acquire about 300,000 of a total of 12,000,000 tons, the quality of the tonnage used on the North Atlantic, which was vitally important for naval purposes, was being eclipsed by ships owned elsewhere. In 1897, a German ship had taken the "Blue Riband" for the fastest North Atlantic crossing. British lines, which had long dominated this most prestigious shipping route, were being challenged. As the British press noted, if Cunard accepted the IMM's offer to buy a controlling share of the company, four-fifths of the country's finest steamers would fall under American control.

---

[14]Gottheil, "Historical Development," 60-61; GAR, HAL, 318.14, Wentholt Archief, 8, correspondence between Wierdsma and Pirrie, 18, 20, 24 and 26 July, and 1 August 1907; 20 and 25 July 1908; 13 October 1910; and 14 and 22 February 1914; and Murken, *Die grossen transatlantischen*, 206.

Along with the pending American ship subsidy bills, the tonnage could soon be sailing under the Stars and Stripes. To prevent this became an urgent matter of national security. The Cunard Line used this situation to regain the driver's seat on the North Atlantic. With subsidies and a cheap loan backed by the Admiralty, the Cunard Line was able not only to retain its independence but also to re-take the Blue Riband. The Admiralty also reached an agreement with the IMM to prevent it from transferring its newly acquired British tonnage to another flag. If the IMM were to be successful, Morgan needed to block the withdrawal of existing subsidies to the WSL and to prevent other discrimination against the IMM regarding naval and mail subsidies. The fact that the expected support of the American authorities became less likely over time made some kind of arrangement with Britain more important. The IMM also guaranteed that the majority of the directors of the British companies incorporated into the IMM would remain intact, that ships be manned by British sailors and that half of future tonnage be registered under the Union Jack.[15]

This agreement took away many of the incentives the IMM had to press for concessions from the American authorities for US-flag ships, while it obstructed any far-reaching rationalization of the administration of the various IMM lines. The failure of the IMM to include Cunard would destabilize the North Atlantic passenger market rather than consolidating it. Having reinforced its position, Cunard gave notice that it intended to withdraw from the British and continental agreements in May 1903 to prepare to fight for a bigger slice of the Mediterranean and continental markets where it only controlled zero and 0.38 percent, respectively. On the continent, Cunard lowered its rates from Hamburg and Antwerp. It also promised a big salary to Lawson Sandford, the secretary of the NYCC, to head the passage and freight department of its new Mediterranean service. By hiring Sandford, Cunard acquired valuable information about his rivals and about how to penetrate markets.[16]

---

[15]Boyce, *Information, Mediation*, 100-102; Francis E. Hyde, *Cunard and the North Atlantic, 1840-1973: A History of Shipping and Financial Management* (London, 1975), 142-148; Murken, *Die grossen transatlantischen*, 223-230; and Vale, *American Peril*, 103-181.

[16]With the establishment of the Atlantic Conference in 1908, Sandford returned to his position as conference secretary. Another similar appointment took place in 1911 with Hermann Winter, who led NGL's passage department. When word got out that he was unhappy in Bremen, Cunard, HAPAG and the HAL tried to contract him. Offering him an annual salary of US $7500, the British line ensured itself of inside information on the NGL, which could be especially useful during conference negotiations. GAR, HAL, 318.04, Passage, 221-226, letters, 23 June and 30 October 1903; and Cunard Line Archives, Liverpool (CLA), Chairman correspondence, C 1, 63, letters, 22, 25 and 28 April 1911.

But perhaps the biggest blow to the continental lines was the agreement that Cunard reached with the Hungarian government. As part of a larger trend in Europe, Hungarians began to think about using out-migration to stimulate the merchant marine and national ports. The central idea was that passport regulations would be used to force citizens to travel with a national company from Fiume to New York. Due to a lack of interest by domestic shipowners, the authorities turned to HAPAG and the NGL. But the German lines declined to open a route that went against the interests of its home ports (Hamburg and Bremen, respectively), was 1200 sea miles longer and offered faint prospects for freight and cabin passengers. Indeed, the Germans coerced the conference members into refusing to accept any Hungarian concessions. What the Germans had failed to consider, however, was that another shipping company might view the potentials of Hungary more positively. Freed from conference obligations, Cunard seized the opportunity to increase its share of continental passengers by opening a direct service from Fiume to New York backed by a Hungarian guarantee to compensate the line if passenger numbers failed to reach 30,000 annually. Cunard's move inspired the Austro-Americana Line, at the time operating a freight service from nearby Trieste to the US to launch into the passenger market. It did so in part to compensate for the losses in revenue from freight transport which was then in a deep crisis. With the support of the Austrian government and Oscar Richard, it diversified its service. The location on the Adriatic allowed the company to attract both Mediterranean and continental passengers. Fearing a scenario similar to that in Hungary, the German companies acceded to Austro-Americana's request for support and supplied an important part of the capital even though this went against the self-interest of its home ports.[17]

Austrians and Hungarians, who previously had migrated through northern ports, now had two alternatives on the Adriatic. The competition forced the continental lines to reduce their rates for this market. The IMM and Cunard also cut their fares in the British-Scandinavian market. The HAL's agent in New York stated that these moves affected bookings in general because people were waiting to buy tickets as the press predicted that a general rate war imminent and might reduce transatlantic fares to as low as US $10. Despite such warnings, the continental lines managed to keep the rate cuts to a minimum and to limit them to the Austrian-Hungarian market while the British battled to hold on to the British-Scandinavian market. The NYCC allowed the American agents to keep booking for Cunard in order to prevent the conflict from escalating to cabin business. The fear of violating the Sherman Antitrust Act also influenced the decision, as did the belief that Cunard would use the situation to try to obtain more favours from the British government. Yet the

[17]Murken, *Die grossen transatlantischen*, 247-262; and GAR, HAL, 318.04, Passage, 221-226, letters, 15 April, 10 and 13 May and 4 October 1904.

mounting pressures since Cunard's withdrawal from the conferences culminated in a general rate war for the eastbound market in the summer of 1904. Despite pressures caused by low westbound Mediterranean, British and Austro-Hungarian rates, the NDLV managed to stop the contagion from spreading to the westbound continental market. Even when Cunard targeted the Russian market by circulating orders for the passage from Libau at $10 in the US, the NDLV lines maintained their rates until the rate war ended in November 1904. Instead, to meet the competition the German lines diverted Cunard passengers at their border control stations. Moreover, diplomatic pressures from countries having interests in the migrant trade forced the Hungarians to lift the barriers at its borders and to stop refusing to issue passports to citizens choosing to migrate via northern ports.[18]

During the previous rate war in the 1890s, the continental lines depended on their British counterparts to set rates. Now they managed to contain the war to certain sub-markets while keeping rates at profitable levels where they had strong footholds. The NDLV lines continually adapted their rates in competitive areas to limit the impact of the conflict on total earnings. Table 3.1 shows the monthly prepaid bookings at special rates in these areas. These applied predominantly to Hungry and Croatia, and to a lesser extent to Romania, Bulgaria, Serbia, Istria and Dalmatia.

Table 3.1
HAL Prepaid Tickets Sold at Special Rates during Rate War, 1904 (US $)

	$24.50	$19	$12	$21	$26.50	$10
April	257					
May	165					
June	69	84				
July	3	234				
August	1	224				
September	102	332	8			
October	196	145	138	33	93	183
November				59	186	498

Source: GAR, HAL, 318.04, Passage, 221-226, letters, 29 August, and 1, 7, 9, 16 and 27 September 1904.

Everywhere else the HAL maintained gross rates of US $31.50 for continentals and US $33.50 for Russians, including board and lodging. Despite the rate war, its position in the continental market allowed the HAL to increase its prepaid sales in 1904 to an average net price of US $29.71, only US $4 less than in 1903. The average eastbound rates dropped from US $30.23 to $21,

[18]GAR, HAL, 318.04, Passage, 221-226, letters, 25 March, 15 April, 20 and 27 May and 15 June 1904; and *Mail and Express*, c. 25 March 1904.

showing that this market remained more sensitive to outside competition. Cunard was transporting continentals below cost, but it could not drag the continental lines into a general price war. The latter wanted to prolong the more limited war but they acceded to their IMM partners which competed on all fronts. The bottom line, however, is that the HAL and the NGL still managed to pay low dividends while Cunard and IMM passed in 1904.[19]

Table 3.2
HAL Rate Changes, Eastbound and Westbound, 1904

1904	East-bound	West-bound
1 Jan	32	34
21 Jun	20	34
28 Jun	17	31.5
16 Sep	20	31.5
14 Nov	33	33

Source: GAR, HAL, 318.04, Passage, 72-77, correspondence; and 318.02, Directors, 112-121, correspondence.

The effectiveness with which the NDLV contained westbound predatory pricing to certain regions contrasted with its inability to exclude new lines from the continental pool, as the Austro-Americana, Cunard and Canadian Pacific (CPL) lines acquired a share in 1904. Since the 1880s, improved collaboration among the continental lines allowed them to monopolize the traffic through their home ports and dissuade new lines from becoming established on the continental routes. North Atlantic passenger conferences were of the "closed" variety, admitting new applicantss only with the consent of existing members and not trying to enlarge the select group. The high cost required to enter the specialized passenger service on the very competitive North Atlantic routes deterred new initiatives. The few entrepreneurs who took the risk, such as the North Atlantic Transport Company, were driven out by the NDLV. By using the agent network to boycott new lines and through the use of fighting ships, it blocked their entry. By scheduling a fighting ship as close as possible to the new entrant's sailing, the conference cut rates and prevented the rival from making profitable crossings.[20] Fiona Scott-Morton analyzed the use of

---

[19]GAR, HAL, 316.04, Passage, 221-226, letter, 14 February 1905; and Murken, *Die grossen transatlantischen*, 278.

[20]Brian M. Deakin and T. Seward, *Shipping Conferences: A Study of Their Origins, Development and Economic Practices* (Cambridge, 1973), 1; William H.S. Stevens, "The Administration and Enforcement of Steamship Conferences and Agreements," *Annals of the American Academy of Political and Social Science*, LV (1914),

predatory pricing by British cargo carriers, noting that a lot depended on the characteristics of the new entrant, particularly its age, financial resources, experience and customer base. Government subsidies affected the share a new entrant was likely to receive but not whether there would be a fight.[21]

Subsidies and other forms of government support played a much bigger role in the migrant transport sector. There were several reasons for this. First, companies receiving subsidies were likely to be able to withstand rate-cutting for a longer period. When this type of financial support was given to a giant company, such as the Canadian Pacific Railroad Co. (CPR), the use of predatory was extremely risky. As a reaction against the IMM, Canadian authorities facilitated the takeover of the Beaver Line by the CPR to enable the CPL to gain access to Antwerp and Liverpool. Through its railroad network, the CPL could affect the Canadian and American markets. Instead of fighting, the continental lines immediately entered into negotiations to reach a compromise and ceding 5.429 percent of the NDLV westbound traffic to the CPL.[22] Second, governments tended to use population movements to support its merchant marine. As continental lines transported migrants from or to countries which supported new national initiatives, such as Austria and Canada, it feared that when fighting these lines governments could take measures to exclude them from its territory, as the Hungarian authorities tried to do. The Austro-Americana Line acquired its membership with a quota of four percent of NDLV's westbound traffic in order to dissuade the Austrian authorities from following its neighbour's example.

Yet the Hungarian case showed that shipping companies were much better equipped to direct migration than were national authorities. Despite efforts to impede migration through northern ports, the NDLV lines still attracted seventy-five percent of Hungarian migrants. The Hungarian policy failed dramatically because it led to the opening of an Austrian line, while the ten-year contract with Cunard impeded the establishment of a national line. Instead of reducing migration, the increased competition and rate war accelerated it. Diplomatic pressures to lift these barriers illustrate that migration also remained a trade issue. Yet the NDLV could not prevent Cunard from increasing its footing in the continental market through its agreement with the Hungarian government. The NDLV had to recognize the agreement which ensured 32,500 continental passengers for Cunard's Fiume service for five years. This

---

126; and William Sjostrom, "The Stability of Ocean Shipping Cartels," in Peter Z. Grossman (ed.), *How Cartels Endure and How they Fail* (Cheltenham, 2004), 96.

[21]Fiona Scott-Morton, "Entry and Predation: British Shipping Cartels, 1879-1929," *Journal of Economics and Management Strategy*, VI, No. 4 (1997), 679-683.

[22]Boyce, *Information, Mediation*, 117; and Murken, *Die grossen transatlantischen*, 241-245.

amounted to a share of six percent to eight percent of the continental traffic.[23] For the first time in two decades, the continental lines had to tolerate three new competitors in 1904. This forced them, however, to rethink the policies with which they had attempted to deter new entrants.

The Battle for the Russian Market

The 1904 annual report of the Jewish temporary shelter in Whitechapel noted that due to the rate war prices through England were reduced to £2, while from the continent rates of 120 *marks* persisted. As a result of this discrepancy, Jewish migration through England rose by 242 percent. During the rate war, Cunard dramatically increased its market share of continental migrants from 0.38 percent in1902, to 1.4 percent in 1903 and 7.48 percent in 1904. It refused to re-enter a pool agreement where it had to share six percent of the traffic with other British lines, but it agreed to join the NYCC which regulated agents and fixed prices. With the surge of Russian migration following the Russo-Japanese War, Cunard booked 2.34 percent of the continental traffic via Liverpool on top of the 39,626 passengers via Fiume. The other British lines also increased their shares, but the continental lines did little to prevent this penetration.[24]

With the immigrant influx into the US exceding one million per year, market forces neutralized conference strategies. Prices remained high despite the lack of pool agreements between the British and continental lines. At the end of the Russo-Japanese War, the heavily subsidized RVF, which had transported troops to East Asia, redirected its steamers to New York from Libau via Rotterdam. The Libau network of migrant brokers and agents hoped to increase their sales through this direct service. They obstructed Ballin's attempts to include the RVF in the NDLV pool, but Oscar Richard announced the new direct service in New York as the fastest and cheapest from Russia, offering the major advantage of avoiding the humiliating experiences at German border control stations. The RVF's passengers did not need to apply to their district governors for passports, a time-consuming process, but obtained one through the Minister of the Interior at Libau. The line served kosher food, and Richard boasted that inland fares to and from any Russian place were much cheaper from Libau than from any other European port. To promote the

---

[23]Murken, *Die grossen transatlantischen*, 261 and 275.

[24]*Ibid.*, 283-296; and National Archives, Washington (NAW), Records of the Immigration and Naturalization Service, 1787-1993 (RINS), Record Group (RG) 85, 52011/A, investigation, Marcus Braun, report, 1904.

line among New York shippers and migrant agents, he organized a dinner aboard *Smolensk*.[25]

When the British Lines matched the RVF rates, they had a differential of US $12 compared with the HAL rates, so the Dutch line urged the NDLV members to take some drastic measures. Instead of fighting ships, the NDLV established a fighting line. HAPAG acquired a controlling interest in the Russian East Asiatic Co (REA) and opened a service on the same route, at the same rates, using similar sailing dates as the RVF. The NDLV members shared the costs for the service. To fight the growing competition from the British lines, they opted for special rates from the border control stations rather than reinforcing migration patterns through Libau by running a feeder service to the continental ports from there. The battle with the RVF reflected the growing fusion between company and pool interests. The HAL's permission to the HAPAG-owned REA to call at Rotterdam for goods to make the sailings more profitable was not without risk and points to the increasing trust among the lines. Indeed, the Dutch line, despite having an important surplus in the westbound pool when the RVF began its service, did not reduce its rates until the NGL and HAPAG made up for their deficits. Due to its strong ties with Rotterdam shippers, the HAL felt confident that they would not risk supplying the RVF with freight which it would not have found in Libau and jeopardizing the profitability of the venture. The HAL also praised the speed by which the decisions had been made. Previous experience had shown the importance of prompt action, since preventing a line from gaining a foothold was crucial in future negotiations, either to convince the line to look elsewhere or to limit the entrant's share.[26]

The RVF proved a tough competitor. Richard advertised widely in the New York Jewish dailies, forcing the continental lines to follow suit. He hired an "army" of peddlers whom he bonded and allowed to sell tickets on instalments, giving three months' credit. The cheaper rates, higher commissions and fewer restrictions allowed the RVF's agents to gain ground in New York quickly. The Russian line also distributed posters and ticket books to conference agents whose contact details were readily available to Richard as a representative of the Prince Line, which was a member of the Mediterranean Conference. Richard destabilized the conference lines' efforts to discipline agents. When ordered to distribute RVF material, Mr. Cooper, the HAL agent in

[25]HAPAG and the WSL served kosher food, as did the RSL and the NGL by 1912. The HAL did not, but this does not seem to have affected its popularity among Russian Jews. GAR, HAL, 318.03, Passage, 48, letter, 22 April 1912; 318.04, Passage, 72-77, letters, 22 and 30 June and 10 and 11 July 1906; and 318.02, Directors, 112-121, letters, 27 and 30 July 1906.

[26]*Ibid.*, 318.04, Passage, 72-77, letters, 30 June and 12 and 17 July 1906; and Murken, *Die grossen transatlantischen*, 297-301.

Denver, exposed one of the weaknesses of the system by asking how Richard could represent both the Prince Line and the RVF.[27] The conference seemed incapable of driving well-established migrant brokers, such as Richard, out of business or of preventing them from forcing their way into conferences. Richard systematically accepted the head agency of every new line which tried to penetrate the North Atlantic passenger market, sometimes with success, as with the Prince Line, Lloyd-Italiano and Austro-Americana, and sometimes not, as with the Atlantic Line.[28] This ambiguous position limited him somewhat, as when he denounced the boycott of the RVF by the agent network in the press, yet as a member of the Mediterranean Conference he refrained from filing a lawsuit in which he might have had to appear both as plaintiff and accused.[29] The conference's lawyers reassured them that if each line advised the agents separately, instead of using a joint circular, the RVF had no legal basis on which to fight clause 9 which stipulated that "agents are prohibited from booking passengers for any steamer, except those of the lines, members of the Continental, Mediterranean or North Atlantic Passenger Conference." Yet the HAL directors were still uncomfortable about the rules regulating the agents:

> Similar matters, if brought before a court, may lead to further investigation of the present methods employed by the steamship companies, which in many respects would cause unsatisfactory results. The course followed by the steamship companies to maintain control of the agents under their supervision is in many ways very arbitrary, and although for the steamship companies perfectly justifiable may be condemned if brought before an investigation. Proceed slowly![30]

With the case of H. Thomson, *et al.* vs. Union Castle Steam Co., *et al.*, the trust-busting climate reached the shipping industry, explaining the cautiousness of the HAL's directors. The first judgment favoured the shipping conferences, questioning only the legality of the fighting steamers.[31] But other

---

[27]GAR, HAL, 318.04, Passage, 72-77, letters, 17 June and 21 October 1904; 15 June, 17 August, 18 and 28 September, 18, 20, 25, 26 and 27 October and 21 and 31 December 1906.

[28]The German lines seemed to have ousted Richard from Austro-Americana.

[29]GAR, HAL, 318.04, Passage, 72-77, letters, 16 September 1896, 12 April 1904, 4 April and 2 and 9 June 1905 and 13 September 13 October 1906.

[30]*Ibid.*, letter, 7 September 1906.

[31]*Ibid.*, letter, 16 January 1907 and copy of court decision.

court cases soon followed, inspiring Richard to commence action against clause 9 of the NDLV.[32] In the meantime, the continental lines discontinued the REA service, opting for separate fighting steamers at equal or lower rates instead. For the eastbound route, the conference lines in New York voted for which steamer depending upon sailing dates and whether a line was in surplus or deficit in the pool agreement. They also appointed another steamer to transport any overbookings. The lines usually announced the fighting steamer about a week before its sailing. Because the bulk of eastbound steerage bookings occurred within ten days prior to sailing, publishing the fares too early meant that the steamer could be overbooked at a time when its effect was most needed. The managers of the RVF responded by secretly taking over the REA and reopening the service under the same name. As the representative in New York they appointed Alexander Johnson, an experienced British-Scandinavian migrant broker who hoped to penetrate the market. With the extra competition from the British lines in Libau, the popularity of the port among Russians began to outstrip other European ports, according to the New York agents who claimed to be in an untenable position with respect to the conference rules.[33]

Management of the Agent Network

From the beginning, the NYCC prohibited the use of sub-agents and only allowed the sale of tickets in an agent's office. In theory, this reduced brokers to simple agents, yet in practice the system was never truly implemented. A clear hierarchy based on turnover persisted in the agent network and was reinforced by Hamburg migrant brokers who delocalized the prepaid market. American agents had to entrust their remittance and passage business with an expedient in Europe upon whom they drew orders. Expedients chose how to forward passengers unless the agent specified a route. With the 1895 NDLV consolidation, the main brokers and agents established associations in Chicago and New York to strengthen their negotiating positions with the shipping lines.[34] While they feared that the lines might open their own offices, they also were interested in purging irregularities from the market. When founding the New York City Agents Association (NYCAA), A. Falck and M. Rosett seized the opportunity to halt the proliferation of agents and runners which affected their prof-

[32]*Ibid.*, letters, 27 April, 4 June, 18 October and 3 December 1907; and complaint before Interstate Commerce Commission (ICC), Cosmopolitan Line vs. HAPAG.

[33]*Ibid.*, Passage, 72-77 and 221-226, letters, 9 February, 8, 26 and 27 March, 8 and 14 April, 28 May, 5 and 8 June, 17 July, 18, 21 and 28 August and 4 September 1908.

[34]Other cities such as Minneapolis and St. Louis soon followed. *Ibid.*, Passage, 564, meeting, 16 July 1897, minute 238.

its. The main agents agreed to enforce the conference rules strictly in exchange for concentrating the business in a limited number of hands. The reduced network made it more manageable for the lines and allowed them and members of the NYCAA to increase their profits.[35] Moreover, many American agents wanted to end the order business which put them at the mercy of European expedients. If correspondents refused to honour orders drawn on them, passengers could be stranded in transit. To uphold their reputations, the New York agents had to rebook such passengers as prepaids at their own expense.[36] Nothing protected them from opportunistic behaviour by the Europeans except keeping the business within the family on both sides of the Atlantic through branch offices, as Jarmulowsky, Scharlach and a number of others did. If this was impossible, they had to recruit someone they trusted, generally of the same ethnicity because such ties were the second-best guarantee against opportunism. Trust was essential in a business where distance and the lack of international rules exacerbated principal-agent problems.

Managing markets through a multi-ethnic migrant agent network was challenging in an enterprise where, as Gordon Boyce observed, social and cultural affiliations were important in generating mutual trust between principals and agents.[37] The agreement with the NYCAA allowed the lines to re-impose the use of prepaid tickets and retake control over passenger routing. To ensure adherence to the rules, the continental lines established Standing Complaint Committees (SCC) in New York for the east and Chicago for the west. They relied on agents to be self-policing and on private detectives to detect abuses. The SCC was a link between the lines and the migrant agents. The continental, British-Scandinavian and Mediterranean conferences agreed that an agent who was disqualified for rules violations would have to return the ticket books belonging to every conference line. Only a few smaller lines remained outside these agreements, meaning that disqualification in practice excluded them from selling ocean passages, a crucial part of immigrant banking. This was a more important deterrent to cheating than the US $250 bond required.[38] Still, some recurrent abuses proved hard to eradicate.

---

[35]*Ibid.*, Passage, 221-226, letters, 14 June, 6 and 23 August and 5 September 1895.

[36]See the case of New York agent Max Kobre and Rotterdam expedient Karlsberg Co. *Ibid.*, letter, 19 September 1895.

[37]Gordon Boyce, *Co-operative Structures in Global Business: Communicating, Transferring Knowledge and Learning across the Corporate Frontier* (London, 2001), 4-5.

[38]GAR, HAL, Passage, 221-226, letter, 18 October 1897; and Passage, 564, meetings, 26 September 1895-6 December 1896, minutes 1-138.

The Credit System and the Sale of Tickets through Peddlers

Falck strongly recommended allowing the sale of tickets on credit because this practice was too entrenched to eradicate. This was especially true among Jewish agents who used peddlers to sell tickets on the instalment plan. Peddling was a common employment for newly arrived Jews who willingly added the sale of ocean tickets to their trade.[39] The shipping lines did not approve because this undermined the price agreements. Yet the cases of abuses brought before the SCC show that the practice persisted. Thomas Fitchie, the director of Ellis Island, corroborated this, stating that a growing number of passengers arrived with debts due to having to pay off a ticket bought on instalments. Pinkerton detectives conducting a wide-ranging investigation found that the principal Jewish agents added a surcharge of about one-third of the ticket price if it was bought on instalments. They usually required a down payment of US $5 to $10 followed by weekly instalments of one dollar. Fines equalling the price of the ticket did little to deter the agents.[40]

A circular which threatened fines of US $500 and six-month suspensions had a greater impact. The Pinkertons discovered that some agents had up to US $15,000 outstanding for peddler tickets. The agents petitioned the lines to reconsider, stating that a ban on credit would drive the business to Europe. Moreover, the British lines had lowered their rates following Cunard's withdrawal from the conference which once again encouraged the order business. Jewish agents would book their passengers whose tickets were bought on instalments with British lines instead of with the NYCC conference lines. Indeed, some agents transacted eighty percent of their business in this fashion. In order not to drive agents to Cunard, the continental lines tolerated the peddler business in New York only. From their part, the agents agreed to cease their order business connections in Russia. They also promised to take care of those prepaid passengers in transit whose tickets were cancelled by a peddler for being behind in their payments, thus removing the biggest problem with the

---

[39]*Ibid.*, Passage, 564, meeting, 26 September 1895, minute 6; Passage, 221-226, letters, 17 September 1897 and 23 July 1901; Barry E. Supple, "A Business Elite: German-Jewish Financers in Nineteenth-Century New York," *Business History Review*, XXXI, No. 2 (1957), 143-178; Rowena Olegario, "'That Mysterious People:' Jewish Merchants, Transparency, and Community in Mid-Nineteenth Century America," *Business History Review*, LXXIII, No. 2 (1999), 161-189; and Arcadius Kahan, "Economic Opportunities and Some Pilgrims' Progress: Jewish Immigrants from Eastern Europe in the U.S., 1890-1914," *Journal of Economic History*, XXXVIII, No. 1 (1978), 235-258.

[40]GAR, HAL, 318.04, Passage, 221-226, letter, 8 July 1899; and Passage, 564, meetings, 22 October 1896, minute 122, 15 August 1900, minute 574 and 28 February 1903, minute 765.

peddler system. When dealing with such stranded passengers, the HAL tried to locate the unauthorized agent responsible and urge him to remit the deposit. The purchaser then had the option of buying new tickets or having the passengers sent home. If they had the means most chose the first option rather than leaving loved ones or friends stranded or taking a chance on suing the vendor in American courts.[41]

A side effect of the agreement was to give official recognition to peddlers, who soon chose a representative to defend their interests before the SCC. For their part, the continental lines were unhappy that they were unable to restrict the use of credit to New York. When joining the battle for the business, American banks employed canvassers to solicit deposits for steamship tickets. For eastbound return passages, the conference rules in fact allowed such deposits. Indeed, the sale of steamship tickets and the use of credit seemed inextricably linked. With the opening of the RVF and Richard's recruitment of two hundred peddlers, the practice escalated. In response, the continental lines tried to revoke the option of using peddlers. This proved to have the unintended consequence of giving a competitive advantage to RVF agents who quickly gained ground in the money transfer and ocean passage sales markets. In the end, conference agents regained the right to use peddlers, and some were even allowed to book for the RVF temporarily.[42] This underlines the weak position of the conference lines relative to the agents. It was a vicious circle: strict implementation of conference rules in periods of sharp competition weakened the agents but was difficult to enforce; as a result, peddlers, canvassers and runners maintained their positions, stimulating increased competition which the conferences again tried to contain.

The Problem of Outside Agents

The agreement with the NYCAA shut a significant number of agents out of the market. Most tried fruitlessly to regain the concession from the conference lines while seeking other ways of participating in the sale of ocean passages, which Jared Day described as "the most common service and the most power-

---

[41]*Ibid.*, GAR, HAL, 318.04, Passage, 564, meetings, 13 April 1898, minute 334, 20 December 1898, minutes 415-417, 23 February 1899, minutes 421-432, 5 February 1903, minute 770, 26 March 1903, minute 777, and 2 July and 3 August 1903, minutes 810-822; and Passage, 221-226, letters, 2 August and 7 September 1906.

[42]*Ibid.*, Passage, 564, meetings, 24 October 1899, minute 456, 24 April 1904, minute 849, 27 October 1904, minute 891, 11 May 1905, minutes 911 and 923, and 17 January-5 August 1907, minutes 1015-1047; and Passage, 221-226, letters, 14 February 1904, 30 December 1906, and 10 September and 26 October 1907.

ful anchor of private ethnic bankers."[43] Two options were available; representing one of the few non-conference lines or selling illegally for authorized conference agents as a sub-agent. The agency of Pollowe, Mogilewsky and Werner illustrates the creative methods by which ethnic bankers sold ocean passage. The three men started as clerks for Louis Scharlach, but when the latter moved from 391 to 362 Grand Street, the trio opened their own banking, exchange and passage office (the Austro-Russian Bank) in the old offices of their former employer. Scharlach used his influence to prevent their appointment as passage agents from all lines except for the dissident Atlantic Line. Scharlach then gathered testimonies of unsatisfied Atlantic line customers which he passed to local newspapers. The Atlantic Line's poor results left the Austro-Russian Bank with the sole option of selling orders drawn on Hermer and Knie in Libau and Haimsohn and Co. in London, both of which undercut prepaids by US $2.

Still, only an agency from the conference lines offered the desired growth opportunities. To buy their way in, the three outsiders supplied the HAL and HAPAG with correspondence linking Scharlach to abuses of the conference rules (this was not a unique strategy; other outside agents did the same thing).[44] This created a certain amount of goodwill, but the conference's most important criteria for acceptance was the amount of new business agents could contribute. The Austro-Russian Bank tried to increase its business by working as a sub-agent for the authorized agent A. Kass. Again, this was typical, for many official agents used networks of outside agents to increase their sales. The unauthorized agents contracted clients for Kass who in exchange either sent the bank clients who wanted money exchange or remittances or gave Pollowe, Mogilewsky and Werner a share of the commissions. Working outside the conference rules gave the Austro-Russian Bank some competitive advantages, and it gradually gained in popularity. Through the Beaver Line it was able to book ocean passages via Canada. It also secretly worked for the Compagnie Générale Transatlantique (CGT) which was trying to gain a foothold in Russia. The refusal of Cunard to renew the NDLV pool agreement offered more opportunities. To prevent the bank from seizing them, as well as to force the Beaver Line back into the conference and to prevent the CGT from moving into the Russian market, the continental lines appointed the bank as an official agent. It went on to become one of the biggest continental agents in New York

---

[43]Jared N. Day, "Credit, Capital and Community: Informal Banking in Immigrant Communities in the United States 1880-1924," *Financial History Review*, IX, No. 1 (2002), 67.

[44]For example, the former clerk Harry Oppenheim offered to disclose Kobre's connections to the Beaver Line in exchange for a conference agency. GAR, HAL, 318.04, Passage, 221-226, letters, 28 August and 10 September 1901 and 12 September 1907.

and survived the deaths of Pollowe and Mogilewsky because their widows maintained their interests, but it finally failed during the Panic of 1907.[45]

Many entrepreneurs acquired expertise in the business at established banks before opening their own. Yet not all left their former employers on bad terms. For instance, Mr. Kraus started off as a clerk at Falck and Co. before joining Mr. Lengyel, the owner of the newspaper *Magyar Trasulat*, to open an immigrant bank.[46] Kraus remained on good terms with Falck, for whom he continued to contract passengers as an outside agent. Falck was caught several times by the SCC and paid his fines, but he never relinquished his ties to the agency. This points to the profitability of working with outside agents and shows how entrenched the practice was. Although Lengyel and Kraus eventually obtained a conference agency, their story illustrates the difficulty of doing business according to conference rules: they were disqualified shortly after their appointment for sending 10,000 circulars to correspondents across the country advertising tickets on instalments.[47]

Despite the geographic expansion of business activities across the US, the growing ethnic diversity and the increase of passengers transported, the HAL succeeded in limiting the number of authorized agents, which totalled approximately 1400 in 1884, 2000 in 1893, 1264 in 1895 and 1700 in 1906.[48] It was not alone in this, for in New York the continental lines managed to con-

---

[45]*Ibid.*, letters, 7 and 18 May, 28 June, 17 September and 29 October 1897; 21 January and 1 April 1898; and 27 October and 30 December 1899; Passage, 564, meeting, 24 October 1899, minute 444; and Day, "Credit, Capital and Community," 76.

[46]Some worked their way up by returning to the home country where they started an agency to work as correspondents for New York contacts, as did C. Nekritz, who returned to open an office in Slutz, Russia. GAR, HAL, 318.04, Passage, 221-226, letter, 2 February 1901.

[47]*Ibid.*, letters, 30 March 1898 and 24 October, 11 November and 12 December 1899; and Passage, 564, meeting, 23 August 1900, minutes 453-477.

[48]The figures are approximate, except for 1895; subdividing the agencies; east, 577; west, 595; Pacific, thirty-six; and New York, fifty-six. Based on the number of circulars sent to the agents containing updates of the conference rules, it is possible to estimate the number of other companies. In 1905, the HAL printed 2500 circulars while Gips stated a year later that there were 1700 agents. The other companies printed the following amount in 1905; Cunard, 5400; Austro-Americana, 750; CGT, 2000; RSL, 4000; HAPAG, 4500; NGL, 4000; and NGL Baltimore, 1000. Maldwyn Allen Jones, *American Immigration* (Chicago, 1960; 2nd ed., Chicago, 1992), 160, mentioned 3200 HAPAG, 1800 RSL and 1500 Anchor Line agents in 1890. GAR, HAL, 318.04, 72-77 and 221-226, Passage, letters, 25 November 1893 and 10 December 1906; Passage, 564, meeting, 10 August 1905, minute 930; and Passage, 154, report, 1895.

tain the number of agents notwithstanding the numerous applications (appendix 5). Some of these were hard to refuse, as was that of Joseph Senner, the former director of Ellis Island and president of the Austro-Hungarian Immigrant Home who had provided great services to the lines as president of the Immigration Protective League. In spite of this, the lines refused his application, fearing that he might destabilize the Austro-Hungarian market.[49] For the same reason they refused the application of the Transatlantic Trust Company - which was opened by the Hungarian government - in order to protect their agents and to prevent governments from controlling the steamshipping, money transfer and exchange business between the countries. While favouring concentration, the shipping lines did not want migrant banks or outside firms to control too much business, even blocking important companies such as American Express.[50] Their success in containing authorized agents, however, contrasted sharply with their failure to prevent outside agents and peddlers from getting their hands on shipping tickets. Limiting the armada of middlemen between the company and the purchasers remained an extremely difficult task.

The Circulation of European Cash Orders in the US

The SCC imposed its heaviest fines for drawing orders. Agent S. Baros was the first to get caught and fined US $100. The HAL had suspicions about many others, but it lacked proof. Pollowe showed that Scharlach did a lot of business through orders and that HAL and HAPAG passengers sometimes were rerouted through England. Although it was highly unusual for clients to make their way to the SCC, Mr. Hauptmann testified that the passengers he booked on instalments from Scharlach arrived through Canada instead of directly to New York. The committee imposed a US $150 fine together with a warning of disqualification. Kobre, who was caught using orders to route Russian passengers via Canada with the Beaver Line chose disqualification rather than granting the lines access to his books. This refusal suggests (but does not prove) widespread violations of conference rules. To cover such transgressions, agents no longer drew their own orders but used receipts of regular money transfers. The European correspondent then forwarded the passenger according to the amount received. Kobre's disqualification pushed him to the verge of bankruptcy. He was reinstated after paying a US $160 fine because the continental lines feared that he might associate himself with the Austro-Russian Bank and divert a lot of business to the Beaver Line. But it was not only Jew-

---

[49]GAR, HAL, 318.04, Passage, 564, meetings, 31 October 1901, minute 688; and 30 April 1903, minute 780.

[50]*Ibid.*, meeting, 9 March 1901, minute 615; Passage, 221-226, letter, 1 July 1908; and Passage, 48-59, letters, 19 September and 18 October 1912, and 7 March 1913.

ish agents that continued using orders, so did the biggest Hungarian and Swiss brokers, M. Rosett and Zwilchenbart Grasser and Co., both of whom forwarded prepaid passengers at European rates. Despite using equal net rates for Europe and the US after 1895, the discrepancy in commissions and the high rate of exchange used (which overestimated the real value of the dollar relative to the *mark*) combined for a differential of US $2. Van den Toorn, who repeatedly expressed his incomprehension of the differential, stated that a profit margin of sixty cents was enough for brokers to use orders rather than prepaids. Because setting equal prices seemed impossible, the HAL's New York head agent urged the directors to make European houses liable for disqualification if they maintained connections for drawing orders in the US. What started as a local phenomenon in Hamburg had spread across Europe. The HAL boycotted those houses which were established in its home port, such as Karlsberg and Co., and reached an agreement with the Red Star Line (RSL) to do the same in eastern Europe.[51]

Yet Karlsberg continued to book passengers on the indirect route through Rotterdam and England thanks to the facilities offered by the Beaver Line. Despite being a conference member, the line violated the rules to increase its share of the continental market without validating the revenues for the pool. The continental members were well aware of the practice, but their detectives encountered many difficulties in obtaining the affidavits of passengers booked in violation of the pool agreement. When they did, the Beaver Line withdrew from the agreements, finding it more profitable to increase its number of passengers at lower rates through expedient houses than settling for the fixed share at higher conferences rates. The line also granted special rates to Baron Hirsch to attract the business of the Hebrew charity associations in Canada. It constantly tempted conference agents to violate the rules and managed to attract a good number of continental passengers. The continental lines could not convince the Beaver Line to rejoin the conference, so Beaver remained a thorn in the side until the CPR took it over in 1903.[52]

It is clear that outside agents - and even some conference agents - continued to sell orders and that the resort to this practice increased whenever competition from the non-conference lines intensified. The frequent references to the order system disappeared after the Panic of 1907 which indicates that with the establishment of the Atlantic Conference, orders stopped circulating in

---

[51]*Ibid.*, Passage, 221-226, letters, 14 June 1895; 31 July 1896; 2 and 23 March, 7, 14 and 25 May, 17 September and 15 October 1897; 4 April 1899; and 6 January and 20 March 1900; and Passage, 564, meetings, 5 and 11 May 1897, minutes 188, 194, 195 and 215; and 30 March 1898, minute 329.

[52]*Ibid.*, Passage, 72-77 and 221-226, letters, 21 May, 2 and 11 June, and 21 and 28 September 1897; 14 February 1901; and 2 August and 7 September 1906; and Passage, 564, meeting, 10 February 1902, minute 699.

the US. Yet the biggest question is why the lines, which could easily have put an end to the system by setting equal rates and commissions on both sides of the Atlantic, never did. No organizational benefits or financial gains are apparent on the American side of the transatlantic market; indeed, the opposite seems to be the case. A plausible reason might be that the directors of conference lines were reluctant to delegate control over the majority of sales in the expanding American market to outside agents or the companies' head agents overseas. With the differential they stimulated sales in Europe, while with the order system some American sales were transacted through European agents on whom they could keep a close eye. More research on the organization of the European market should shed light on whether this tactic was used to resist vertical integration and the ongoing managerial revolution.

Interference of the Mediterranean Market: The Case Study of Zotti and Co.

On the Mediterranean market European agents also received nearly twice as much commission (twenty *lire*) as their American counterparts (US $2).[53] Nonetheless, the HAL mistrusted Italian agents for their opportunistic behaviour as much as it did Jewish ones. Opportunistic agents, government interference and the continuous entry of new lines into the booming market made the transatlantic migrant trade less stable than the British-Scandinavian or continental markets. In turn, the unstable market kept prices lower than continental fares despite the fact that the route was much longer and more costly for the shipping lines. From 1897 to 1899, the cheapest gross prepaid and eastbound prices quoted by Mediterranean Conference lines from/to Naples ranged from US $16 to $21 and US $14 to $17. During the same period, the HAL offered the cheapest continental prepaid and eastbound service at rates from US $27 to $31.50 and US $25 to $27, respectively.[54] A gentlemen's agreement existed between the conference lines so that Mediterranean rates would only be used for certain ethnic groups. For instance, Croatians were considered to be continentals and hence had to pay much higher rates than their neighbours across the Adriatic. This opened opportunities for scalpers to move in on the market. When emigration fever hit the region, Frank Zotti, the owner-editor of *Narodni List*, moved into immigrant banking by booking Croatian and Dalmatian eastbound passengers at Mediterranean rates.[55] As an outside agent, Zotti

[53]One *lire* equalled 19.3 cents. *Ibid.*, Passage, 221-226, letter, 25 April 1899.

[54]*Ibid.*, Passage, 565, telegrams with rates from 1896-1905.

[55]A newspaper with the same name, *Narodni List*, also circulated in Dalmatia (and still does). The paper highlighted the positive aspects of emigration. Whether both papers were linked remains to be explored. Antić correctly noted that newspapers still contain a lot of information for migration researchers; Ljubomir Antić, "The Press as a

initially got his hands on tickets through conference agents. Thanks to influence among his co-ethnics, he rapidly increased his sales. By establishing contacts with European correspondents, Zotti obtained orders to move in the westbound market.

The south Austrian market when in full expansion intensified the competition between shipping lines to gain a foothold, putting a lot of strain on the gentlemen's agreement. Suspecting the CGT and the NGL of breaking the agreement, the HAL allowed Zotti to secretly book for it to prevent getting shut out of the market. The CGT had not yet joined the pool agreements and sought to increase its continental passengers, so it allowed Zotti to book eastbound Croatians at Mediterranean rates through Genoa instead of at continental rates through Le Havre. Conversely, the HAL refused to let Zotti chose the routing to direct passengers via Modane and withdrew its ticket books. The NDLV lines closed ranks and organized a propaganda campaign against Zotti through their newly appointed Dalmatian agent, Frank Sakser, editor of *Glas Naroda*. But because the CGT gave Zotti the freedom to use orders at cash rates and to route his passengers as Mediterraneans, they could not prevent Zotti from gaining ground. The CGT did this while negotiating entry into the pool. The more continental passengers it attracted, the stronger its position. There was a breakthrough in 1903 when the CGT entered the westbound pool based on the passengers it had transported over the past three years, a period that coincided with its collaboration with Zotti. Fearing that he would lose his business, Zotti took the first steamer to Paris where arrangements were made to redouble efforts for the eastbound market. Zotti used Italian rates to forward Agram-bound passengers through Genoa and retained privileges to book westbound passengers for the CGT.[56]

To constrain his activities, the continental lines appointed Zotti as a conference agent. Refusing to give up his network of sub-agents, his appointment was short-lived. Cunard's withdrawal from the agreements and the opening of direct services from Fiume and Trieste complicated matters. The CGT refused to break with Zotti because of the increased competition, a situation which the Croatian banker eagerly played to his advantage, secretly obtaining ticket books from other lines including the HAL. The Dutch line accepted business at regular rates, paying commissions at the end of the year to reduce

---

Secondary Source for Research on Emigration from Dalmatia up to the First World War," *South-East Europe Review for Labour and Social Affairs*, IV (2004), 25-35. This study shows that a thorough check of an editor's background is useful in determining whether the paper is biased by connections to the migrant transport business.

[56]GAR, HAL, 318.04, Passage, 221-226, letters, 1 December 1899; 2 January and 10 February 1901; 24 April and 1 May 1903; and 19 February 1904; Passage, 564, meetings, 31 October 1901, minute 679, 31 July 1902, minute 731, 12 May 1903, minute 795; and Passage, 578, agreement G between NDLV and the CGT, 1903.

the risk of being caught working with a non-conference agent. In four months, Zotti sold six hundred tickets for the HAL, underscoring his grip on the market. Yet his power decreased when an eastbound pool agreement including the CGT was established after the rate war with Cunard. The continental lines obtained the right to verify whether the CGT and the American Line had booked eastbound continental passengers at special Italian rates. As these lines did not have separate ships serving their continental and Mediterranean services, the controls occurred at quayside before embarkation. Conference agents received a circular stipulating that: "only bona fide Italian and Oriental passengers can be booked through Italian ports, no Austrians, Germans, Hungarians, Dalmatians, Croats, Galician, Russians or Slovenians." The lines also monitored brokers known for abusing these rates.[57] The CGT withdrew the facilities from Zotti, who did not hesitate to denounce the price discrimination:

> Imposition upon common sense and against the Law! A Frenchman going home has to pay $34 for Le Havre with a CGT steamer, while an Italian, on the same ship pays $20 for Genoa or Naples. In other words the French Line contracts to transport an Italian on one of their steamers from New York to Havre, from Havre to Marseille by rail, and from Marseille to Naples by boat for the sum of $20 and a Frenchman himself must pay $14 more for his transport only to Le Havre. While the rate from New York to Milan is only $21.75 and another $5 to Trieste by rail, the French rate to Trieste is $45.55.[58]
>
> No law in this country allows asking a certain price for one passenger while charging a much higher one for another. Such discrimination has been going on for years unnoticed and must stop! We invoke the American press, to right wrongs, to investigate the matter affecting the poorest class of American citizens, greatest sufferers and with no protection against the monopoly of such big Line.[59]

---

[57]*Ibid.*, Passage, 221-226, letters, 14 December 1903, 8 January and 29 April 1904, and circular, 25 May 1905; and Passage, 564, meetings, 11 November 1903, minute 825, 17 December 1903, minute 829, 3 February 1904, minute 842 and 28 April 1904, minute 869; and Passage 242, agreement L between NDLV and the CGT, 1904.

[58]*Ibid.*, Passage, 72-77, letter, 25 July 1905.

[59]*Narodni List*, 5 June 1905.

The large rate difference was unusual. After the rate war the continental lines raised their rates before the Mediterranean lines had reached an agreement. When they did, the CGT quoted US $34 to Naples, while the cheapest Fabre and Anchor Line service nearly doubled their rates compared to 1899 at around US $30. As stipulated by the conference rules, all lines withdrew their ticket books from Zotti. From his part, Zotti hired a lawyer for a test case and forced the CGT to board eight Croatians at the Italian rate. Through his offices in Pittsburgh, Chicago and New York at prime locations, Zotti was moving a huge volume of money transfers.[60] For the passage business, he bought his own ship, christened it *Brooklyn* and founded the Frank Zotti Steamship Company. The HAL did not foresee any problems for him in finding passengers for the first sailings, but running a regular service was much more complicated. The Dutch line had secretly continued accepting bookings from Zotti. Johan Wierdsma, who in 1899 succeeded van den Toorn as the HAL's head agent in New York, praised Zotti for being reliable, prompt and honest. He defended using him by claiming that otherwise the business would go to Cunard or the Italian lines and be lost to the continental pool. Anticipating that Zotti would fail as a shipowner, the HAL kept contact with him in hopes of taking over his bookings when that happened. A year later, mainly because of the refusal of the Italian authorities to grant him a license to call at domestic ports, Zotti sold his ship and flirted with bankruptcy. The CGT categorically opposed his reappointment as a conference agent despite all the other lines being in favour to get him under control and prevent the RVF from hiring him. Zotti proceeded to attack the conference lines in his new paper *Rail and Sail* and recruited passengers for the RVF. Tensions among the conference lines built up over the reappointment issue. When Cunard finally ignored the CGT's opposition and hired Zotti, the French line stopped consulting with the conference when appointing its agents. Zotti survived the economic downturn but never regained his pre-eminence in the south Austrian market.[61]

Zotti's saga demonstrates that shipping companies still depended on migrant brokers to direct business from the sub-markets. Owning a newspaper was an important asset to gain trust from co-ethnics and to attract immigrant

---

[60]The rent on Smithfield Street in Pittsburgh was US $8000 a year. The offices on Dearborn Street in Chicago, on Greenwich Street and in the Bowling Green Building point to the significant amount of business he was doing.

[61]GAR, HAL, 318.04, Passage, 72-77, letters, 9 June, 14 September and 8 December 1905; 9 January, 9 September, 26 October and 12 December 1906; 6 July, and 13 September 1907; and 16 April 1909; and Passage, 564, meeting, 7 July 1907, minute 1030.

ocean passage and banking business.[62] These middlemen continued to influence the routing of migrants and hence tempted shipping companies to break conference rules. Yet no matter how much business the middleman managed to control, it proved impossible to bypass the established shipping companies. Zotti's attempt to do so failed, just as did the attempt of the Hamburg brokers in the 1890s. Despite the tensions Zotti created among the lines, the case study illustrates above all that shipping lines extended their control over the North Atlantic transport market through conferences. What is striking is not that brokers defrauded the lines by routing continentals at special Italian rates, but rather that the lines contained the abuses and maintained the price differentials between continental and Mediterranean rates - even on the same ship.

Remaining Re-occurring Conference Violations

Another recurring violation of conference rules was the booking of cattlemen. Shipping companies took advantage of the increasing return movement by finding people willing to work their way across the ocean. The lines were particularly anxious to recruit men for the cattle trade because the US Department of Agriculture required a certain number of so-called "cattlemen" for a certain number of animals carried.[63] Some migrants agreed to pay US $6 to $8 for their return journey on which they cared for cattle. An estimated 3000-5000 people left New York annually as emergency workers. Passenger liners hired them directly or through specialized agencies. These agencies started posing problems when they launched advertising campaigns luring away eastbound passengers from the migrant agents. They convinced some people to accept a cattleman's position while all they wanted were eastbound tickets. By sharing their commission with migrant agents, cattlemen agencies widened their networks. As these agencies continued to abuse conference rules, the lines opened a joint agency to recruit personnel autonomously.[64]

---

[62]Another example is John Boras, who acted as an agent for the HAL in the "Oriental" market and published the *Forward*, a Yiddish newspaper in which he ran ads for the HAL free of charge. *Ibid.*, Passage, 221-226, letter, 14 February 1901.

[63]Passenger liners usually managed cargo services, such those as supplied by HAL's "dyk" ships. Most cattle transport used these ships, yet sometimes it took place on passenger ships for which lines quoted special rates, usually US $1 less than the regular price.

[64]The specialized agencies were Jacobs (Canal Street), International Shipping Company (Clinton Street) and Johnson (Hoboken). GAR, HAL, 318.04, Passage, 564, meetings, 5 February 1900, minute 496; 4 October 1900, minute 572; 3 March 1903, minute 773; 30 April 1903, minute 778; 14 June 1906, minute 955; and 20 December 1906, minute 1002.

Another abuse that persisted were price cuts, although after 1895, they were less common and much smaller, ranging from fifty cents to one dollar. The main reasons were that commissions stabilized at US $2 and lines greatly reduced the practice of paying extra commissions, thereby limiting the agent's margin for giving rebates. The system of having a line with a surplus in the pool raise its rates so that those in deficit could catch up improved, decreasing the incentives to reduce a deficit by paying extra commissions. Yet when outside competition intensified, the practice resurfaced. For instance, when fighting against Cunard the HAL exempted Kobre, Kass and the Austro-Russian Bank from paying the extra US $2 charged to Russians for board and lodging before embarking. This form of extra commission was granted to obtain the business these agents managed for the "Kischeneff Relief Committee," which helped to finance the passage of Russians in distress whose relatives in the US could not pay for the ticket in full. Applicants paid US $10 to the agents, and the relief committee paid the balance.[65] With Cunard undercutting continental rates by US $6.50, agents had difficulties in booking these passengers exclusively through the conference lines. The relief committee sought the lowest rates in order to help as many refugees as possible. The cut of US $2 and the loyalty of the agents helped to safeguard this business for the HAL and HAPAG. Agents convinced most applicants to pay the extra charge for using these lines. In return, shipping companies continued to give agents free or reduced passages to Europe for their personal use, organized fancy dinners onboard new steamers and gave gifts to create goodwill among agents. Nonetheless, the practice diminished after the 1890s. Extra commissions remained the most effective way to increase sales, but the HAL only sometimes resorted to these and never exceeded US $2 after the 1895 NDLV consolidation. The sporadic use improved the effectiveness of the measure. This contrasts with the period prior to the agreements when an extra commission of US $2 was common and at times reached as high as US $7.[66]

The NYCAA and its secretary, M. Rosett, initially extolled the adherence of the agents to the conference rules and successfully encouraged them to denounce transgressors. Yet sometimes the system of open criticisms was abused by agents to take over the business of a rival. For instance, Hugo Lederer obtained the disqualification of his next-door rival on Avenue B, H. Schnitzer, thanks to his brother Emil, the head of HAPAG's steerage depart-

[65]GAR, HAL, 318.04, Passage, 221-226, letter, 30 August 1903.

[66]*Ibid.*, Passage 564, minutes 1-1052; 318.02, Directors, 112-121, letters, 2 February 1902 and 20 November 1907; Passage, 221-226, letters, 12 January and 27 May 1898; 21 May and 24 June 1902; 25 March, and 1 and 24 April 1904; and 4 January, 10 February and 20 December 1905.

ment and his nephew Arthur, an employee of the RSL.[67] Both represented their respective companies on the SCC and show that family ties of at least some migrant agents held important positions in shipping companies. Schnitzer's main clients, the NGL and the HAL, managed to redress the decision by exposing Lederer's motives and fabricated evidence. Despite the odd abuses, shipping lines welcomed the initiative of agents because they still were reluctant to track down abusers themselves. For instance, van den Toorn hesitated to denounce Rosett for cutting rates through European overland transport orders because to do so would have greatly harmed the line's popularity with one of the biggest brokers in the city and with New York agents in general. Therefore, when they suspected widespread abuse the lines shared responsibility by jointly hiring detectives. This proved an efficient way to discipline agents.[68]

Delimiting the territory of American agents remained a difficult issue. On rare occasions lines encouraged agents to expand their territory if it was to recruit directly in Europe. For instance, the HAL gave its California agent, H. Bier, free steerage passage to Europe to recruit migrants in the lower Volga region. The HAL gave a commission per recruit and provided assistance to cross the German-Russian border.[69] In the US, conference rules restricted ticket sales to the agent's office, yet they managed to expand their territory through peddlers and unauthorized agents. Many New York agents also did a lot of business through correspondence, sending out circulars advertising their agency to potential clients. Some opened branch offices, as A. Kass did in Philadelphia. The HAL even supported this initially by giving him an extra commission of US $1 to enable him to move into the market. By delimiting territories the lines hoped to restrict excessive competition. Yet as Adrian Gips, the substitute for the New York head agent Wierdsma in 1906, observed, this tended to discourage efficient agents while contributing to the inefficiency of others. Attempts to attract the business of an agent outside his area should not be restricted, Gips believed, even if it interfered with a local agent. Being on the spot the latter had an advantage; if he failed to meet the competition, it proved his inefficiency. Fines for selling tickets outside their office were low. In general, if New York agents observed the through-booking rule that obligated agents to book railroad passage to the final destination along with the prepaid passage, the lines tolerated the practice. As lines sought to restrict the armada of agents, concentration of the business was easier to su-

---

[67]Emil Lederer worked as a traveller for the HAL until 1895 when HAPAG lured him away. *Ibid.*, Directors, 112-121, letter, 8 July 1895.

[68]*Ibid.*, letters, 2 February and 9 and 20 July 1897; and 318.04, Passage, 564, minutes 1-1052.

[69]The same went for agent Klay in Rock Valley, Iowa. *Ibid.*, Passage, 221-226, letters, 19 May 1902 and 8 May 1906.

pervise at the place where they had their headquarters. By not strictly implementing the conference rules, shipping companies allowed the New York agents to retain their dominant position.[70]

Joint Ticket Offices

Despite being unable to implement conference rules strictly, control over the agents greatly improved thanks to closer collaboration among the lines. There was still room for opportunistic behaviour, but a lot less than before the NDLV consolidation. Passenger lines also continued to open new offices in big cities, underscoring their desire for vertical integration and to concentrate business. They partly recouped the extra costs by increasing direct bookings, thereby saving on commissions. Smaller companies, such as the HAL, trailed the bigger companies in doing this. With the opening of new offices, general agents often were cast aside, creating opportunities for smaller lines to hire them. In Boston, for instance, F. Houghton and Co. was relegated from general to regular agent by the WSL when it opened its own offices. The RSL then appointed the company to manage its business in New England until it merged all general agents with the American Line. The HAL then hired Houghton, who tried to retain as much business as possible through his long-standing networks, in the process allowing the HAL to increase its bookings in the region. Just like the other HAL general agents, Thomas Cook and Son (San Francisco) and Bartlett Catrow (Philadelphia), Houghton received US $2 per cabin and US $1 per steerage passenger booked in New England. The HAL made an annual contribution of US $500 for advertisements, telegram, postage and other expenses. The International Bank (St. Louis) only received $100 for such expenses, while commissions were set at 2.5 percent on first-class, US $1.5 on second-class and US $1 on third-class bookings.

Dissatisfied with the results of the International Bank, van den Toorn suggested appointing R. Bain, the general agent of the WSL and Thomas Cook. The predominantly British-Scandinavian business of the WSL did not conflict with that of the HAL. Collaboration with a first-class steamship line added prestige to the HAL while allowing both companies to reduce costs. Cook contributed US $1000, the HAL US $1500 and the WSL US $5500 to cover the expenses for a joint office. The majority of the WSL's agents in the region were supplied with HAL ticket books. Van den Toorn dispatched HAL's travellers to promote the line with new agents and to explore business opportunities in the unexploited Oklahoma region where the WSL was already established. In the long run, the collaboration could lead to the one like that between the RSL and the American Line which honoured each other's tickets.

---

[70] *Ibid.*, letter, 21 April 1904; and Passage, 564, meetings, 5 February 1900, minute 501, and 5 September 1901, minute 663.

The agreement was valid for a year and extended the cooperation between the companies which began a decade earlier when the HAL bought its first second-hand WSL steamer. Others followed until the HAL began to have its own ships built at Harland and Wolff, the WSL's shipbuilders. Both companies shared a successful policy centring on service rather than speed. The son of HAL's director Johan Wierdsma served an apprenticeship at the WSL in Liverpool under Bruce Ismay. This experience proved useful during his period as head agent in New York and underlines the strong working relationship between the lines. Encouraging results of the partnership led to the foundation of another joint agency in the northwest. To gain a solid footing in the area west of Chicago, the HAL hired a traveller who was responsible to appoint the right kind of agents and push them to book for the Dutch line. Frequent visits to Bain were also necessary lest most of his bookings go to the WSL. Working in the shadows of a prestigious liner company clearly also included some risks.[71]

The IMM took the rationalization of administration a step further. The members of the combine agreed on the interchangeability of cabin-class tickets, giving demanding tourists more flexibility in organizing their trip.[72] These could be exchanged at the growing number of joint offices on both sides of the Atlantic. Instead of appointing commission-based general agents, the combine encouraged the appointment of salaried managers to run the offices. The IMM pressured the HAL to join, yet the Dutch line was reluctant. Giving up the New York and Chicago offices was out of the question, but even in Boston the HAL felt inclined to use its own agents. The company secured ninety-five percent of its bookings through these three offices. Unlike the WSL-HAL agreement, the IMM's offices joined lines targeting the same market. Wierdsma feared losing business, especially to the RSL in New England where the HAL booked many more passengers. The Dutch line agreed to a trial in other territories, opening joint offices in St. Louis, Minneapolis, San Francisco and New Orleans for which the companies divided the expenses according to the business received.[73] To further cut costs, they placed joint advertisements in news-

---

[71] *Ibid.*, 318.02, Directors, 265, letter, 14 October 1888; and 112-121, letters, 5 October 1888, 29 October 1889, 28 April 1891, 10 September 1895, 1 April and 25 November 1898 and 3 June 1901; and Passage, 221-226, letters, 2 February and 19 April 1901.

[72] *Ibid.*, Passage, 211-226, letters, 20 February and 17 April 1903.

[73] The territory was divided as follows: Toronto (Province of Ontario), Montréal (rest of Canada), San Francisco (Oregon, California, Nevada and southern part of Idaho), St. Louis (Kansas, Missouri, Arkansas, Texas, Indian territory, Arizona, Oklahoma and New Mexico), Minneapolis (North and South Dakota, Washington, Minnesota, Montana, Idaho, northern part of Wisconsin and Michigan), Chicago (all the territory reporting to Minneapolis plus southern part of Wisconsin and Michigan, Illinois,

papers. The relatively satisfying results convinced the HAL to reach a compromise for Boston where it retained F. Houghton as the general agent but moved him to the IMM buildings under the supervision of the salaried management of Maynard and Child. Both could book for all the lines represented in the joint office. Montréal, Toronto and Winnipeg soon followed.[74]

Yet the enthusiasm for the joint offices rapidly soured as bookings decreased. The HAL increasingly mistrusted the IMM of using the joint agencies to increase its market share. This sense of apprehension spread as the HAL declined to participate in a new Pittsburgh office and withdrew from the Minneapolis and Boston joint offices to open its own. It also appointed David Brattstrom and Co. as general agents in Seattle for the states of Idaho, Washington and Oregon.[75] The HAL also mistrusted J.P. Morgan personally for trying to introduce the same business structures that proved successful for railroads into steamshipping. Sensing that both forms of transport were related and encountered many similar problems regarding principal-agent relations and the delegation of power, Morgan wanted to appoint salaried managers to replace general agents and introduce the managerial revolution into shipping. Yet the limitations of extending a horizontal combination with the IMM merger obstructed the further vertical integration that was needed to slash the various layers of middlemen from the ocean passage trade. The German lines and the HAL could never be convinced to centralize administration for the American market fully, and they were even less sold on trying to do this in Europe. Even the lines forming part of the IMM remained a federation of mostly autonomous lines. Technological innovations like the telegraph and the steamship reduced distances between directors and head agents, allowing the former to retain their predominance in decision making. Alfred Chandler pointed out that the volume of the railroads' operations greatly surpassed those of any other industry.[76] Yet

---

Iowa, Nebraska, Colorado, Utah, Wyoming and Indiana) and Boston (New Brunswick, Prince Edwards Island, Nova Scotia and parts of New England). *Ibid.*, letter, 17 February 1902.

[74]*Ibid.*, Passage, 72-77 and 221-226, letters, 27 January, 20 February, 24 March and 8 December 1903; 8 December 1904; 12 and 15 December 1905; 7 and 14 December 1906; 16 December 1907; 18 December 1908; 20 August 1910; and 14 January 1911; and 318.02, Directors, 112-121, letters, 4 January 1904 and 14 March 1911.

[75]*Ibid.*, 318.03, Passage, 49-58, letters, 6 December 1912 and 21 February 1913; and 318.02, Directors, 112-121, letters, 14 March 1911, and 4 and 10 April and 6 June 1913.

[76]Alfred D. Chandler, Jr., "The Organization of Manufacturing and Transportation," in David T. Gilchrist and W. David Lewis (eds.), *Economic Change in the Civil War Era* (Greenville, DE, 1965), reprinted in Thomas K. McGraw (ed.), *The*

unlike the railroads, the gains from administrative coordination were far less significant in shipping.

As Drew Keeling has noted, those horizontal combinations already in place when Morgan founded the IMM were much more successful than similar entities organizing American railroads in the 1870s and 1880s.[77] Railroad agreements suffered earlier and more significantly from government pressures than did shipping companies. Although the Interstate Commerce Act facilitated collusion between railroads, it prohibited pools. Shipping companies that received more time to fine tune conference agreements did not have these restrictions. The success of these pool agreements allowed the predominantly European shipowners to retain most of the decision-making in "family" hands, limiting the need to delegate power to salaried managers. The rise of managing directors also took place in Europe, albeit at different paces from country to country and sector to sector. The ascendancy of Albert Ballin clearly illustrates this for the shipping world, yet family ties still dominated the pre-1914 European business world.[78] Therefore, the success of shipping conferences and the organizational features of the ocean passage trade may explain why the merger movement in shipping was only a pale imitation of what occurred in the railroad industry. The IMM may also have failed because there was little to rationalize. The sale of ocean passage tickets was so cheap that vertical integration should have brought only small benefits. Why would a company want to move forward into a market where agents battled to sell the product; advertised in local newspapers, hired canvassers and sent personal circulars to promote the product; opened offices nationwide wherever the demand for the product was centred; provided market specific language skills and ethnic ties; operated more or less independently and posted a bond protecting shipping companies from losses; and supplied information on rival lines and fellow salesmen for a US $2 commission or a mere ten percent of the profit made per ticket? Another dollar commission ensured that a general agent took charge of the supervision and efficiency of the network. The financial benefits of opening joint offices, run by salaried managers, were negligible and certainly did not outweigh the organizational difficulties of guaranteeing equal returns for all

---

Essential Alfred Chandler: Essays Towards A Historical Theory of Big Business (Boston, 1988), 215-218; Chandler, *Visible Hand*, 189-192; and Gottheil, *Historical Development*, 74.

[77]Drew Keeling, "Transatlantic Shipping Cartels and Migration between Europe and America, 1880-1914," *Essays in Economic and Business History*, XVII, No. 2 (1999), 198.

[78]Youssef Cassis, "El Empresario," in Ute Frevert and Heinz-Gerhard Haupt (eds.), *El hombre del Siglo XIX* (Madrid, 2001), 63-88.

lines, a problem which did not exist with general agents working under exclusive patronage.

Foundation of the Atlantic Conference

The success of the NYCC was reflected in the price fluctuations of the HAL between 1903 and 1908. Despite the failure to renew the pool agreement with the British lines and the competition from new entrants, the HAL maintained its high prices. Comparing the HAL's average westbound rates to Cunard's shows the former's superiority in containing price fluctuations and increasing rates, thereby underlining the success of the price policies of the continental pool (figure 3.2).

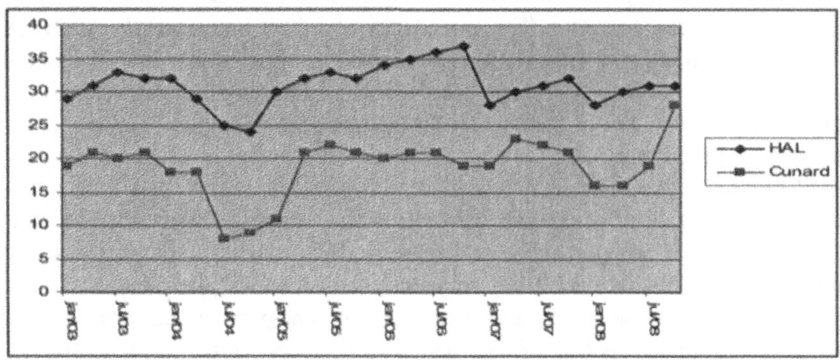

Figure 3.2: HAL and Cunard Westbound Steerage Rates, 1903-1908 (US dollars)

Note: Head taxes may have influenced the discrepancy by US $2 before 1907; thereafter, all lines agreed to collect it separately when it was raised to US $4. There was a little cost for the extra sea miles to Rotterdam than Liverpool, but not enough to explain a gap of US $10 and more.

Source: Drew Keeling, "Costs, Risks, and Migration Networks between Europe and the United States, 1900-1914," in Torsten Feys, *et al.* (eds.), *Maritime Transport and Migration: The Connections between Maritime and Migration Networks* (St. John's, 2007), 164-165.

The NDLV pool suffered from the profit-sharing agreement between the IMM and the German lines; when the former failed to be profitable, the Germans were forced to pay important annual contributions. Relations deteriorated when Bruce Ismay of the WSL replaced Griscom as president of the IMM. Griscom had often acted as mediator between the British and the continental lines and knew how to balance the interests of both markets. Conversely, Ismay favoured the WSL, the most profitable unit in the IMM, to the detriment of the continental lines. Moreover, tensions between the German lines for the South American trade and the cruise business also affected relations among the NDLV's members. The fight with the RVF put more strain on the NDLV, as HAPAG and the HAL, depending largely on the Russian market, favoured far-reaching measures, while the NGL and the RSL, relying more on the Austro-Hungarian market, wanted to limit expenses.[79]

The continual high demand for steerage berths neutralized the unresolved differences among the lines, preventing these from greatly affecting ocean fares. Yet when the market collapsed, tensions between the lines surfaced, driving down the rates (figure 3.2). The depressed market stimulated shipping companies to compromise with aggressive strategies before establishing a new equilibrium. Again, the British lines gave in first, sinking the British-Scandinavian market into a rate war. Cunard spread the war to harm the IMM which had much larger interests in the freight market. The low British rates affected the continental and Mediterranean markets where lines eventually met the price cuts. Eastbound gross passage prices hit lows of US $12.[80]

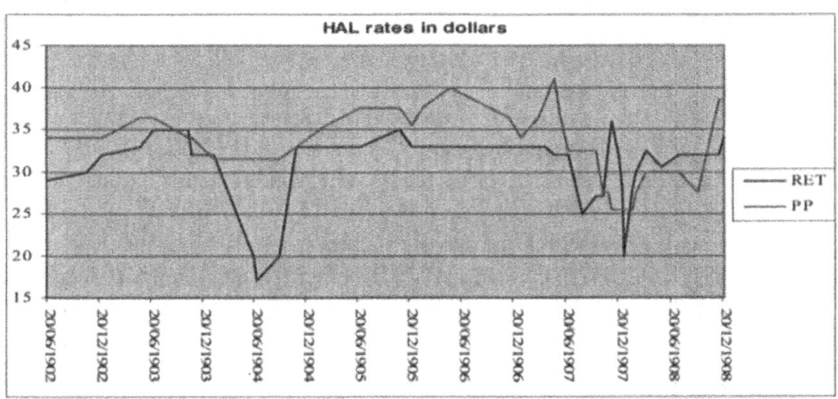

Figure 3.3: HAL Prepaid and Eastbound Rates, 1902-1908

Source: See figure 3.2; GAR, HAL, 318.04, Passage, 72-77, correspondence; and 318.02, Directors, 112-121, correspondence.

[79]William H. Flayhart III, *The American Line, 1872-1902* (New York, 2000), 350-352; Murken, *Die grossen transatlantischen*, 308-316; Kurt Nathan, *Die deutsches Schiffahrtskampf* (Kiel, 1935), 16-28; and GAR, HAL, 318.04, Passage, 72-77, letters, 17 February, 10 and 14 May, 6 and 21 June, 20 September, 28 October and 1 November 1907.

[80]GAR, HAL, 318.04, Passage, 72-77, letters, 10, 17 and 31 January and 3, 10 and 15 April 1908; 318.02, Directors, 112-121, letters, 15 and 20 January 1908; and CLA, Chairman correspondence, C 1, 63, letter, 7 July 1910.

The IMM and the NDLV lines laid the foundation for a new equilibrium with a preliminary agreement for a pool including the British, Scandinavian and continental steerage business midway through 1907. HAPAG and the NGL settled their dispute, the latter conceding 0.5 percent westbound and one percent eastbound from its quota to the former in exchange for concessions in the freight market. This allowed the NDLV agreement to be renewed until 1912. In February 1908 a new agreement including the Allan, Anchor and Cunard lines was reached. The Atlantic Conference pooled the British, Scandinavian and Continental steerage traffic as follows.

Table 3.3
Shares of Traffic Allocated by the Atlantic Conference, February 1908

	WB	**EB**
HAPAG	19.61	12.35
NGL	26.53	18.79
HAL	6.63	6.10
RSL	9.71	8.56
Anchor	3.40	3.93
Cunard	13.75	15.12
American	6.68	8.72
WSL	8.60	15.49
Dominion	4.47	1.50
Allan	0.62	4.95
CPL		4.49

Source: Erich Murken, *Die grossen transatlantischen Linienreederei-Verbande, Pools und Interessengemeinschaften bis zum Ausbruch des Weltkrieges: Ihre Entstehung, Organitsation und Wirksamkeit* (Jena, 1922), 313-343.

This brought the conference system to a new level of complexity and effectiveness. The separate regional British (NAPC) and continental (NDLV) cartels persisted but were now subordinate to the Atlantic Conference. With the new agreement the British lines acquired 11.9 percent of westbound continental traffic, excluding the Cunard service to Fiume that increased its share to 50,000 passengers (another 6.7 percent of the traffic).[81] When adding the con-

[81]The continental lines proposed that the Hungarian government establish the Hungarian American Line from Fiume; the authorities could be compensated by a head tax for each person travelling through the port, as was done in Italy. Cunard's stiff demands to buy out the contract ended talk of the deal. Murken, 1922, *Die grossen transatlantischen*, 298-299.

tinentals that the CPL (3.9 percent), Austro-Americana (2.1 percent) and the Russian lines (4.3 percent) acquired, the market share of the continental lines was greatly reduced over the last five years. Yet in spite of this, the RSL, the NGL, HAPAG and the HAL doubled the number of steerage passengers transported to New York (appendices 2 and 3). With the continental market expanding while the British-Scandinavian market contracted, this concession seemed necessary to prevent a costly global rate war whose outcome was unpredictable and likely to have forced the continental lines to concede a share anyway. The agreement strengthened the continental lines' acquired dominance over the steerage market

Table 3.4
Steerage Passengers Landed in New York by Various Groups of Lines

Year	Continental Lines	British-Scandinavian Lines	Mediterranean Lines	Total
1906	410,995	179,278	371,883	964,062
1907	485,230	183,523	395,485	1,066,145
1908	145,330	82,883	90,579	318,792
1909	329,388	131,483	329,083	791,863

Source: CLA, Chairman correspondence, C 1, 214, letter, 11 October 1916.

The Atlantic Conference also concluded through-rate agreements for cabin-class passengers. It augmented the pressure on the Russian lines which depended heavily on steerage passengers and struggled as westbound traffic reached a near standstill and eastbound prices collapsed. The RVF suspended its sailings and the REA made significant losses; nevertheless, they persevered thanks to the subsidies and support of the Russian government which was preparing a law exempting their passengers of passport charges and offering special railroad fares. The NDLV, wanting to avoid similar scenarios as in Italy and Hungary, conceded 4.3 percent of the westbound and eastbound traffic to the Russian lines, which merged into the Russian American Line (RAM).[82]

The interference of the Italian government continued to undermine the effectiveness of the Mediterranean conference and obstructed an agreement to pool traffic. The policies led to the establishment of six new national lines on the North Atlantic between 1900 and 1905. During the following three years the Italian lines built thirty-five new vessels, mainly at national shipyards, rep-

[82]Gottheil, "Historical Development," 60-61; Solomon S. Huebner, "Recommendations of the Committee of the Merchant Marine and Fisheries," *Annals of the American Academy of Political and Social Sciences*, LV (1914), 78; Murken, *Die grossen transatlantischen*, 351-353; GAR, HAL, 318.04, Passage, 72-77, letters, 9 February, 8, 26 and 27 March, 8 and 14 April, 28 May, 5 and 8 June, 17 July, 18, 21 and 28 August and 4 September 1908.

resenting a gross carrying capacity increase of 242,000 tons. Confident that its ascendancy could be pressed further, the Italian lines gave notice to the Mediterranean conference, plunging the market into a rate war. After the formation of the Atlantic Conference, foreign companies feared measures that would shut them out of Italy and wanted to safeguard the stability of other markets, so they conceded to the Italian lines which acquired half of the direct Italian steerage traffic (49.13 percent westbound; 49.49 percent eastbound). Parallel agreements were concluded to divide the indirect traffic. The direct lines refrained from transporting continental passengers, while all lines agreed not to abuse the Mediterranean rates for other markets. Inspired by the Italian success, Greek authorities helped national lines to acquire a slice of the cake soon there after.[83] Peace on the Mediterranean was bought dearly, but it prevented the market from affecting other interests.

The Antitrust Movement Reaches the Shipping Cartels

Compared to other nations, the Dutch authorities did little to protect the interest of the HAL, turning Rotterdam into a natural port of call for new outside competition. The New York Continental Line, failing to obtain a licence to transport passengers at German ports, moved its operations to Rotterdam. By appointing fighting steamers, conference members prevented the line from making profits, yet its founders persevered, hoping to attract enough passengers to force the conference lines to buy them out or to convince a third party to take them over. Not wanting to stimulate similar speculative ventures, the conference lines refused, yet the line attracted the interest of the Canadian Northern Railway. The new service, baptized the Uranium Line, also called at Halifax. The losses on the ocean passage now could be compensated by profits on railroad tickets. The conference lines intensified measures to drive the line out of business. It hired the most successful Uranium Line agents, but the low rates enabled new agents to move easily into the market. Enlarging the corps of conference agents did not reduce the Uranium Line's bookings but only divided the business, encouraging abuse and hampering control. Fighting steamers could not prevent the line from increasing its market share either.[84] The Uranium Line often postponed its eastbound sailing once the conference lines named their fighting steamer, forcing them to appoint another one and increasing the cost of the practice. High costs, poor results and the risk of legal sanctions by US authorities caused the British and German lines to with-

[83]Murken, *Die grossen transatlantischen*, 360-412.

[84]Uranium Line steerage passengers: 1910: WB, 19,642, EB, 10,016; 1911: WB, 5846, EB, 13,286; 1912: WB, 13,938, EB, 10,836; 1913: WB, 10,046, EB, 4316; and 1914: WB, 1171, EB, 2404. GAR, HAL, 318.04, Passage, 578, passenger statistics.

draw from the fighting steamer agreement. The HAL deplored the decision, underlining the fact that the principal reason for appointing fighting steamers was to allow conference agents to remain competitive with Uranium Line agents. Without protection, the conference agents would not abide conference rules very long. To prevent the Uranium Line from corrupting the agent network, the NDLV lines reached a compromise to limit the fighting rates to eastern states. Nevertheless, the conference failed for the first time to prevent the entry of an outside line at one of the core members' home port. This failure reflected the weakness of the conference, which showed signs of disintegration as World War I approached.[85]

The legal threat in the US continued to weigh on the conference agreements. The cases initiated before the Panic of 1907 remained without consequence because the Interstate Commerce Commission (ICC) declared seaborne trade to be beyond its jurisdiction, while Richard's complaint in the name of the RVF was settled outside the courtroom. Yet the Supreme Court's decision to dissolve Standard Oil and American Tobacco, and President William Howard Taft's tightening of antitrust policies, created a sense of insecurity in the American business community. The conference lines were especially concerned because a letter book belonging to Gips with details on the use of fighting steamers and freight rebates from railroads had leaked to the press in 1910. The Dutch envoy in Washington intervened to halt the prosecution instituted against Gips and the HAL for violating the Sherman Act. The next year, however, the Uranium Line denounced shipping conferences for violating the antitrust act in the New York Circuit Court.[86] This moved Congress to appoint a special committee, named after its chairman, Joshua Alexander, to examine whether pooling, rebating and special agreements regarding overseas and coastal shipping violated international agreements and US laws.[87] The congressional decision was influenced by the IMM's failure to revive the American

---

[85]*Ibid.*, Passage, 72-77, letters, 19 March, 16 and 27 April, 16 and 20 May, 4, 11, 17 and 25 June, 9 July, 3, 17 and 20 August; 29 September, 8 and 22 October, 5, 12 and 17 November and 10, 21 and 28 December 1909; 11, 18 and 25 January, 1, 11 and 15 February, 11 March, 6, 8 and 19 April, 10, 24 and 30 June, 15 July, 4 August, 23 September, 21 October and 5 and 18 November 1910; 318.02, Directors, 112-121, letters, 23 June 1911 and 24 February 1914; 318.03, Passage, 49-58, letters. 19 April and 25 September 1912; and CLA, Chairman correspondence, C 1, 63, letter, 13 May 1911.

[86]Henry R. Seager, "The Recent Trust Decisions," *Political Science Quarterly*, XXVI, No. 4 (1911), 611-614; George Bittlingmayer, "Antitrust and Business Activity: The First Quarter Century," *Business History Review*, LXX, No. 3 (1996), 386-388; and Weinstein, *Corporate Ideal*, 78-85.

[87]GAR, HAL, 318.02, Directors, 112-121, letters, 18 December 1911; and 18 January, 4 and 5 March, 6 and 12 April and 18 June 1912.

merchant marine. Some congressmen, led by William Humphrey, had fruitlessly lobbied for shipping subsidies and hoped that the Alexander Committee, for which they obtained an appropriation, would create support for their cause. They portrayed the conference system as a scheme of foreign lines, led by Albert Ballin, against US national interests, reminding the public that German lines had sold tonnage to Spain when that country was at war with the US. The conference line's lawyer, Lucius Beers, warned of growing hostilities against foreign lines in congress and among the public. He advised the lines to moderate their campaigns to influence maritime and migration policies because it would greatly compromise them if these came to light.[88] The lines prepared a protest claiming that American authorities had no jurisdiction on agreements concluded outside its territory and which were in accordance with European laws. Yet as national sovereignty gained importance in international commercial relations, European representatives in Washington were never ordered to file an official protest.

The fear that corporate officials risked actual prison sentences, as Taft threatened, was tangible among the New York head agents who all received subpoenas from the District Attorney, creating a lot of mistrust about what information each agent passed along to the authorities and whether one would compromise the others to save his skin. The tension drove Gustav Schwab (NGL) to commit suicide and Emil Boas (HAPAG) to have a nervous breakdown with fatal consequences. The concurrent sinking of *Titanic* increased the pressures and dramatically reinforced the feeling against foreign lines. The shipwreck symbolized and accentuated the crisis that the shipping conference system was undergoing. With the growing number of members and the numerous parallel agreements, it became increasingly difficult for directors to please all interested parties which led to constant renegotiations of the agreements. Despite the crisis the lines jointly agreed to fight for their right to conclude rate and pool agreements. They hired journalists to conduct a US $70,000 propaganda campaign to refute the common prejudices that politicians and newspaper editors had spread about shipping cartels.[89] The conference lines maintained the use of fighting steamers and continued their lobby campaigns against immigration restrictions. They contemplated bringing the Uranium Line prosecution to an early conclusion by accepting a judgment on the fight-

---

[88]CLA, Chairman correspondence, C 1, 11, 63, letters, 13 September 1909; and 11 and 15 March, 17 June and 10 October 1910; and *New York Times*, 17 June 1910.

[89]The costs were divided as follows: Transatlantic lines, sixty percent; long-voyage lines, twenty-five percent; and Caribbean and the West Indian Group, fifteen percent. GAR, HAL, 318.02, Directors, 112-121, letters, 19 and 22 April 1912 and 26 April 1913; CLA, Chairmen correspondence, C1, 7, 63, letters, 10 May 1912, and 25 April, 7 and 15 July and 15 December 1913.

ing ship question. The man on the street could accept the decision of the lines not to compete, but all condemned conspiracies among big corporations to put smaller lines out of business. For its part, the government was likely to welcome the idea of making some political capital from a quick settlement which it could claim as a victory. Giving up fighting steamers, whose advantages were questionable, could save much expense and anxiety.[90]

In the end the lines decided to defend the whole case on its merit, including the fighting steamers. The secrecy of conference agreements had created a lot of suspicion around shipping cartels. To erase these, the lines provided all the information the commission requested, including a copy of all existing agreements.[91] W.G. Sickel and Philip Franklin, both Americans and vice-presidents of HAPAG and the IMM, respectively, represented the lines at the public hearings and clarified the information gathered independently by the Alexander Committee. Typifying the Progressive Era, the committee had contracted expert academics, such as Professor Solomon Huebner, for this. During the hearings, steamship lines created much goodwill among the committee members by forming a "special committee of steamship lines engaged in foreign trade" to provide the legislators with all sorts of documents and advice for their final report. Aware of the sensibility of the public regarding the manipulation by corporations of legislators and the press, this was all done very discretly.[92] In the meantime, public sentiment surrounding shipping lines started to shift. The assumption had prevailed that cartels artificially increased prices by neutralizing market forces, which should guarantee the public reasonable prices based on supply and demand. The idea that conferences prevented the entry of new companies and obstructed the development of the American merchant marine was also widespread.

The propaganda campaign refuted these allegations and pointed to the benefits of the conference agreements for the American public. Shipping companies argued that the *raison d'être* of conferences was self-preservation in the midst of ruinous price competition. They allowed the companies to fix stable, yet reasonable, prices for freight and passenger traffic. This stability allowed the shift of the competition on services rendered to passengers and shippers.

---

[90]CLA, Chairmen correspondence, C1, 7, 63, letters, 10 May, 13 July, 21 August and 5 September 1912.

[91]GAR, HAL, 318.02, Directors, 112-121, letter, 21 September 1888; and daily reports on the hearing by C. Bennett, January and February 1913; and Hamburg Staatsarchiv, HAPAG, 622-1, Erinnerungen Merck.

[92]The committee consisted of W.G. Sickel (HAPAG), Philip Franklin (IMM), Paul Gottheil (Funch Edye aand Co.), H. Barber (Barber and Co), W. Boyd (Holder, Weir and Boyd) and A. Outerbridge (Quebec Line). GAR, HAL, 318.02, Directors, 112-121, letters, 10 March, 18 June and 4 and 5 September 1913.

They also stressed that conferences facilitated far-reaching progress in the comfort, quality and safety of steerage transport. The lines also claimed that it enabled a strict observance of American immigration and migrant transport laws. The conference lines strongly objected to the idea of establishing a commission to supervise foreign trade comparable to the ICC, arguing that this would greatly harm maritime trade to and from the US. Shipping conferences offered the best alternative, and the consequences of making them illegal could not be overlooked. It would condemn North Atlantic passenger traffic to continuous rate wars which would have a negative impact on the maintenance of the ships and the security of the passengers. They even used the arguments of the Immigration Restriction League (IRL) that low rates stimulated the flow of undesirable migrants. To deconstruct the David versus Goliath image, steamship men stressed that conferences protected, above all, the interests of small and weaker members which would be the first to suffer if these cartels no longer existed. They refuted the accusation that new companies did not stand a chance, insisting that any experienced manager with reasonable capital would not be fought off for long. Fighting steamers generally affected the business too much to allow its long-term use. Bernard Baker, the founder and operator of the Atlantic Transport Line until it merged with the IMM, took the stand to disprove the allegation that conference agreements were a foreign conspiracy against American shipping. He testified on his efforts to raise American capital for a national shipping company to trade through the Panama Canal which were obstructed by the transcontinental railroads until Ballin provided part of the capital and helped raise the rest in the US. Instead of harming the American merchant marine, Baker argued that Ballin was an important sponsor.[93]

The conclusions of the Alexander Committee closely resembled the ones reached by the British Royal Commission on Shipping Rings in 1906. It recognized that shipping conferences increased the security of capital invested in shipping, improving the quality and regularity of service. Conference agreements enabled members to rationalize their services, schedule sailing dates and ports of call and eliminate wasteful competition. Most shippers favoured the stability of rates it provided and hence supported the system which stimulated trade. The Alexander Committee found the rates fixed by the ship-

[93]Philip A.S. Franklin, "Rate Agreements between Carriers in the Foreign Trade," *Annals of the American Academy of Political and Social Sciences*, LV, No. 1 (1914), 155-163; W.G. Sickel, "Pooling Agreements," *Annals of the American Academy of Political and Social Science*, LV (1914), 143-154; Solomon S. Huebner, "Advantages and Disadvantages of Shipping Conferences and Agreements in the American Foreign Trade." *Annals of the American Academy of Political and Social Sciences*, LV (1914), 243-252); CLA, Chairman correspondence, C1, 7, 63, letters, 15 May, 5 June, 21 August and 5 and 19 September 1912; and 25 April and 7 July 1913; and GAR, HAL, 318.02, Directors, 112-121, daily reports on the hearing by C. Bennett, January and February 1913.

ping rings to be reasonable and not excessive. It also concluded that conferences offered protection to the weaker lines, something the British investigators, in Daniel Marx's view, had the good judgment to omit. The Committee's only criticism regarded the monopolistic nature of the system and the secrecy of its operations, fortifying suspicions about the excessive use of deferred rebates. The committee advised against prohibiting rate and pool agreements which would lead to a dangerous competition affecting trade in general. It did, however, support the idea of placing the agreements and rate-fixing under the ICC's supervision to prevent the passage of clauses that would harm US trade. It also suggested prohibiting the use of deferred rebates and fighting ships. These recommendations would form the basis of the Shipping Act of 1916.[94] With these conclusions, all charges against the shipping companies were dropped except for the one regarding fighting steamers. The Shipping Act created a Shipping Board to supervise the agreements and rates, as well as to revive the merchant marine. Yet it lacked the international authority to regulate foreign seaborne trade while unilateral interventions would cause sovereignty conflicts whose consequences were hard to predict. The efforts to revive the merchant marine only received significant political backing with the New Deal.[95] Until that time, foreign shipping cartels retained control over North Atlantic traffic.

The Success Story of the NDLV

Like the bulk of academic research, most of the attention of the Alexander Committee went to freight traffic, interviewing two thousand shippers yet failing to solicit the opinion of migrant or cabin agents. Previous studies of the pre-1914 conference system have underlined its ineffectiveness.[96] To quote Robert Greenhill, "even in the case of shipping conferences which appear to have lasted some time, their effectiveness in overcoming market forces and in promoting joint-profit maximization, may in fact have been negligible."[97] This

---

[94]Daniel Marx, *International Shipping Cartels: A Study of Industrial Self-Regulation by Shipping Conferences* (Princeton, 1953; reprint, Westport, CT, 1969), 57-67; and Huebner, "Advantages and Disadvantages," 243-263.

[95]Marx, *International Shipping Cartels*, 127-136.

[96]Robin Bastin, "Cunard and the Liverpool Emigrant Traffic, 1860-1900" (Unpublished MA thesis, University of Liverpool, 1971); Deakin and Seward, *Shipping Conferences*; Greenhill, "Competition or Co-operation;" Marx, *International Shipping Cartels*; and Douglass C. North, "Ocean Freight Rates and Economic Development, 1740-1913." *Journal of Economic History*, XVIII, No. 4 (1958), 537-555.

[97]Greenhill, "Competition or Co-operation," 71.

conclusion is largely due to a myopic focus on freight conferences. The downward spiral of freight rates from 1850 to 1910 and the decreasing profits of the industry sustained these theories. As Drew Keeling correctly noted, the passenger business presented a totally different picture which the gross rates of prepaid and eastbound steerage tickets of the HAL clearly corroborate.[98]

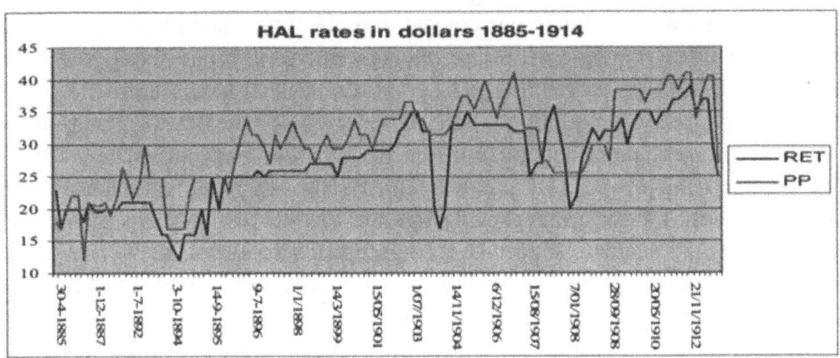

Figure 3.4: HAL Prepaid and Return Rates, 1885-1914

Source: GAR, HAL, 318.04, Passage, 72-77 and 221-226, correspondence and 318.02, Directors, 112-121, correspondence.

The cornerstone of this success story was the continental pool agreement for westbound steerage passengers of 1892. This profit-sharing agreement neutralized internal pressures among the continental members. The rivalry, fuelled by personal antipathy between the WSL and Cunard, obstructed any scheme to pool passenger revenues among British companies. Therefore, the Anglo-American route remained much more competitive than the European-American route where pool agreements led to the culmination of a series of consolidations.[99] Because of this internal division, British lines lost their dominance over the North Atlantic steerage market to continental lines. By forcing the British companies to join the continental pool, the NDLV put an end to the principal external pressure corrupting the continental market. It allowed the lines to conclude agreements for other segments of the passenger liner business. This relieved the competitive pressures and allowed a marked increase of net steerage prices as the achievement of market stability put an end to high extra commissions. With some exceptions the commission re-

[98]Keeling, "Transatlantic Shipping Cartels."

[99]Hyde, *Cunard*, 102-103; Murken, *Die grossen transatlantischen*, 223; and J. Russell Smith, "Ocean Freight Rates and Their Control through Combination," *Political Science Quarterly*, XXI, No. 2 (1906), 260.

mained fixed at US $2, reducing the possibility for agents to cut rates. The fixed railroad rates further helped to maintain profits. The continental lines started to adapt their rates according to their pool quotas which maximizing their profits even more. The steady increase of prices between 1896 and 1914 from US $34 to $41 (twenty-one percent) followed the consumer price index which rose by eighteen percent. The rise of unskilled wages (thirty-five percent) and nominal GDP per capita (eighty-five percent) indicates that prepaid tickets became more affordable.[100] In short, the agreements significantly increased the HAL's profits while stabilizing the price after 1895.

Scholars have put forward various reasons for the failure of the IMM to take the horizontal combination a step further by way of merger, such as the non-inclusion of the Cunard Line, the failure to obtain American vessel subsidies, the royal bonuses paid to executives and the huge overcapitalization of the merger. Vertical integration, a requirement for a merger's success according to Alfred Chandler, did not follow the horizontal combination as the IMM remained a federation of autonomous lines.[101] But scholars overlooked the successful conference system already in place which allowed the directors in Europe to retain control over decision-making while giving them a means to get a grip on the agent network. These proved important barriers to vertical integration while providing the lines with a cheap and widespread network of ticket agencies, leaving few profits to be drawn from further rationalization. With the NDLV consolidation drawing the British lines into the pool, the continental lines achieved two of the main objectives of collusion: namely, to use the keen competition among agents to their advantage and to contain the abuses which had previously corrupted the market. Since the sale of ocean passages was crucial to the development of other aspects of their migrant business, American agents became much more cooperative as the exclusive patronage clause of the three sub-conferences could easily have left them without official ticket books. The conference rules regulating the agent-network could finally be imposed, but not strictly because some violations proved impossible to eradicate, such as the sale of tickets on instalments, collaborations with peddlers and outside agents or the use of orders instead of prepaid tickets. Whenever the lines renegotiated a new equilibrium or new lines tried to penetrate the market, violations increased. To fight the competition of non-conference agents working for new lines, conference members proved more indulgent, sometimes looking the other way at the infringements of exclusive patronage. Lines did not strictly impose conference rules because to do so would have

[100]Samuel Williamson, "Six Ways to Compute the Relative Value of a U.S. Dollar Amount, 1790 to Present," http://www.measuringworth. com/uscompare.

[101]Chandler, *Visible Hand*, 189-192; Murken, *Die grossen transatlantischen*, 145-239; Navin and Sears, "Study in Merger," 291-328; and Vale, *American Peril*, *passim*.

risked losing business for the pool. Moreover, the means to do so were expensive and exposed them to accusations of violating the Sherman Antitrust Act. In short, the situation was more of containment than control, but the abuses of migrant agents never again affected the market as it did before 1896. The ability of the continental lines to prevent the low Mediterranean rates from significantly affecting the transatlantic market illustrates the increased control over the agents who provided the lines with many services in return for a small commission.

The main threat to equilibrium at the turn of the century was increasing government intervention in the trade on both sides of the Atlantic. The Cunard Line cunningly took advantage of this by obtaining important aids from both the British and Hungarian authorities. It allowed the line to start a rate war to increase its market share. Various new lines, such as the CPL, Austro-Americana and the RVF, successfully penetrated the market thanks to government support. More likely to resist ruinous competition for a longer period, the conference lines negotiated their entry before fighting them. As they transported migrants to and from nations that backed the new initiatives, conference lines feared government measures which could disadvantage or exclude them from these markets. As well, the market forces influenced the fighting strategies. As Fiona Scott-Morton observed, trade growth on a route negatively affected the probability of a price war.[102] Not only were the measures to fight outside lines very costly during such periods, but they also had less effect as the high demand made it harder to prevent outside lines from booking passengers. As Ballin put it, "I would much rather fight in a year when business is not good, than put it off to a year that is full of prosperity."[103] Rate wars were fought as much as possible when the market plummeted not only to reduce its impact on company profits but also because stronger lines were better armed to go through these slumps than weaker ones. The combination of freight, cabin and steerage traffic controlled by well-established passenger lines enabled them to pressure new lines such as the RVF which predominantly relied on steerage traffic. Freight brokers were tied to conference lines by loyalty contracts and deferred rebates, while cabin passengers, sensitive to the prestige of a line, made it hard for new lines to penetrate the market. Another limitation of diversifying sources of incomes of new lines such as the RVF was its dependence on one route, while HAPAG served 300 ports with eighty different services. In short, slumps represented an ideal opportunity for companies to flex their muscles before renegotiating new agreements and forcing outside companies to comply or go out of business. This refutes Robin Bastin's conclusion that passenger conferences were a "very inadequate rate defense mechanism; being at

---

[102]Scott-Morton, "Entry and Predation," 699.

[103]CLA, Chairman correspondence, C1, 49, letter, 13 May 1911.

its weakest when business was bad, while by the time the lines reached a new agreement trade was already improving anyway."[104]

The first two rate wars of the new century underline the increased control of the NDLV lines on the continental market. They managed to contain the rate war to specific regions, allowing the HAL to continue to reap profits that averaged about US $15 per ticket, while Cunard sold theirs slightly above cost. Only when Cunard re-entered the pool in 1908 did it manage to significantly raise its prices. It also exposed the inability of the Hungarian government to obstruct its citizens from migrating through northern ports. The barriers imposed by the Russian authorities also could not stop US-bound traffic from expanding despite the simultaneous eastward migration movement to Siberia. Through the long-established agent network, continental lines retained a stronger grip than the government authorities on routing migrants. Yet as the experience of the Uranium Line confirmed, despite the use of fighting steamers the conference lines had difficulties preventing new lines from penetrating the market which expanded and gradually moved away from their home ports. Nevertheless, the NDLV lines retained their dominance and increased the number of steerage passengers they carried. The control of these companies over a vast hinterland, stretching from Beirut to the steppes of Russia, was notable. Yet just before the outbreak of World War I, HAPAG initiated a new rate war, underlining that the aim of the NDLV was to reduce competition, not eliminate it. Shipping rings were not objectives but rather means to an end, in this case to be used by companies to strengthen their position. After turning HAPAG into the world's biggest shipping company, Ballin intended to end the NGL's claims for the largest share of the migrant market based on Bremen's pioneering role in the trade. The NDLV allowed the NGL to retain this claim despite falling behind HAPAG, and it enabled the HAL to pay the highest dividends among the North Atlantic passenger lines despite various attacks on its home port. Ballin's plan to claim greater benefits from the North Atlantic conference system he masterminded were disrupted by World War I, which totally changed the dynamics governing the transatlantic steerage market.[105]

As Gordon Boyce observed, the strength of the conference's internal ties not only depended on relations among shipping companies but also on its connections with brokers, agents and governments.[106] Because of their military

---

[104]Bastin, "Cunard," 104.

[105]Frank Broeze, "Albert Ballin, the Hamburg-Bremen Rivalry and the Dynamics of the Conference System," *International Journal of Maritime History*, III, No. 1 (1991), 11; Broeze, "Shipping Policy and Social Darwinism," 420; Greenhill, "Competition or Co-operation," 64 and 73; and Nathan, *Die deutsches Schiffahrtskampf*, 4-12.

[106]Boyce, *Information, Mediation*, 113.

importance, shipping companies usually maintained close relations with their national governments, turning them into symbols of national prestige. But as pioneering global companies, their relations with the authorities reached much further. The sovereignty vacuum over international waters offered a great deal of protection to the freedom of organizing their trade. Yet as national administrations gained control and responsibility over an increasing number of issues, they became an important external threat, not only to the conference system but even more to the migrant trade. The joint action of the conference lines to defend the legality of the system during the US federal investigation were only a small indication of their efforts to prevent the passage and enforcement of American maritime and migration laws which could harm their business interests. Volume LV of the *Annals of the American Academy and Social Science*, entitled *Government Regulation of Water Transportation*, compiled by the shipping representatives and academic members of the Alexander Committee, explained and defended the need for shipping conferences to the broader public. This characterized the increasing connections between corporations and legislators; the growing importance of public opinion and acting according to the "public interest;" and the growing significance of scientific opinions to assess policies during the Progressive Era. How this affected American maritime and migration laws will now be discussed.

Chapter IV
The Nationalization of American Migration Policies and the Visible Hand of the Shipping Lobby

During the Civil War, the federal government intervened directly in immigration matters for the first time. Once the Supreme Court moved all migration issues from the state to the federal level in the mid-1870s, the pressures on Congress to legislate grew. A reluctance to do so because of concerns over trade agreements and international relations based on reciprocity eventually ebbed as both in Europe and the US the conviction grew that it was a nation's right to control migration to protect its citizens and institutions and to preserve its sovereignty. The question quickly moved from whether to exclude certain people to how and which ones. In this debate, which became known for its strange coalitions, two main pressure groups advocated restrictions. First, there were the labour unions which claimed that employers used immigrants as strikebreakers and to keep down wages. Second, new nativist movements, particularly in California and Massachusetts, claimed that the ethnic composition of the new migrant stream, which consisted mainly of eastern and southern Europeans and Chinese, threatened the "purity" of the "American race." On the other side of the spectrum, various ethnic and religious communities defended liberal immigration policies that allowed co-ethnics and co-religionists to follow in their footsteps, while business groups were most often interested in increasing the size of the pool from which to recruit workers. A much neglected group in the debate were the shipping companies that earned the greatest part of their revenues from the transport of migrants. Aristide Zolberg and Maldwyn Jones acknowledged the importance of the shipping lobby in shaping American laws regulating migrant transport, but neither they nor any other scholar has paid much attention to their role in opposing immigration restrictions.[1] This chapter tries to shed more light on the position of the shipping

[1]Aristide R. Zolberg, "Reforming the Back Door: perspectives historiques sur la reforme de la politique américaine d'immigration," in Jacqueline Costa-Lascoux and Patrick Weil (eds.), *Logiques d'États et Immigrations* (Paris, 1992); Zolberg, "The Archaeology of Remote Control," in Andreas Fahrmeir, Olivier Faron and Patrick Weil (eds.), *Migration Control in the North Atlantic World* (New York, 2003), 195-221; Zolberg, *A Nation by Design: Immigration Policy in the Fashioning of America* (New York, 2006); Maldwyn Allen Jones, *American Immigration* (Chicago, 1960; 2nd ed., Chicago, 1992); Jones, "Immigrants, Steamships and Governments: The Steerage

lobby within the constellation of interest groups advocating liberal immigration policies. With the federalization of the issue and the growing reluctance of diplomats or other government officials to intervene on their behalf, shipping companies revised their strategies to focus more intently on Washington. The strategies will be discussed, while the role of shipping companies in shaping (and sometimes circumventing) immigration laws will be touched upon here and analyzed more thoroughly in the next chapter. The aim is to determine the lengths to which shipping companies went to ensure the right of entry of as many of their passengers as possible.

Migration: From International Trade to National Sovereignty

The Civil War and Acts to Encourage Migration

The American Civil War (1861-1865) created an important labour shortage, forcing federal authorities for the first time to intervene directly to increase immigration, which had slowed because of the conflict. In 1862, Congress passed the first of a series of Homestead Acts, offering 160 acres of land to anyone who committed to work it for at least five years. The American diplomatic corps in Europe advertised the act through the press and hired recruiting agents to induce potential migrants to consider the US. On the west coast, Chinese merchant associations and the Pacific Steamship Company formed a partnership to import Chinese migrants on a large scale, mainly (but not solely) to complete the first of four transcontinental railroads. Secretary of State William Seward convinced the Chinese government not to obstruct this movement, where many labourers paid their transport costs with the first money they earned in the US. These efforts ended the downward spiral, and the number of immigrants entered the US began to rise again in 1863. The following year, Seward successfully lobbied for the passage of an Act to Encourage Immigration which included a scheme to provide employers who advanced the money for the crossing with the legal means to enforce indenture contracts, which were now to be limited, however, to one year. The inability of land speculators and employers to enforce such contracts in the past had prevented the adoption of this system on a large scale. The American Emigration Company (AEC) coordinated the initiative and received support from the consular corps to tap into the European labour market. The AEC even planned to launch a steamship line to organize the transport of migrants, but a lack of funds forced it to abandon the idea and meant that it would never be able to encourage mi-

---

Problem in Transatlantic Diplomacy," in Harry C. Allen and Roger Thompson (eds.), *Contrast and Connection: Bicentennial Essays in Anglo-American History* (London, 1976), 178-204; and Jones, "Aspects of North Atlantic Migration: Steerage Conditions and American Law, 1819-1909," in Klaus Friedland (ed.), *Maritime Aspects of Migration* (Cologne, 1989), 321-331.

gration on the scale it intended. Because this initiative closely resembled the Redemptioner system, it encountered political opposition for resembling in some respects slavery, which many Americans viewed as the cause of the bloody Civil War. Elements of the American workforce, which were just considering the possibility of unionizing, also opposed the scheme. In the end, the AEC's activities were limited primarily to promoting immigration and arranging transport.[2]

Migration was also becoming a lively topic of debate in Europe. Some governments were starting to look with apprehension at transatlantic migration and mistrusted the American initiatives. Especially since the Union army was also recruiting in Europe at the same time, rumours spread that workers were being forced into the military upon their arrival in America.[3] In Belgium, the migrant agent Louis Dochez, who also recruited labourers to work in American mines, circulated advertisements which ironically fed these rumours:

> In America they look for 800, single, voluntary emigrants between 21 and 40 years of age to emigrate to the United States of America. It is of no use to present one's self without the certificate of militia. Address yourselves to L[ouis] Dochez, Bureau of Emigration, number 2, Brabant Street, Brussels.[4]

In collaboration with the notorious migrant broker Adolphe Strauss, Dochez contacted the governors of different provinces and the mayors of important cities to lobby for the reinstatement of the old practice of releasing the inmates of workhouses and shipping the beggars to the US. This time, however, the crossing was not paid for by the Belgians but rather by the American authori-

---

[2]Francis Balace, *En marge de la guerre de sécession: recrutements en Belgique par les troupes fédérales, 1864-1865* (Brussels, 1969), 2; Daniel J. Tichenor, *Dividing Lines: The Politics of Immigration Control in America* (Princeton, 2002), 65-67; and Zolberg, *Nation by Design*, 166-173.

[3]Folke Dovring, "European Reactions to the Homestead Act," *Journal of Economic History*, XXII, No. 4 (1962), 463-470. In 1862, Seward sent a circular to US diplomats about the promotion of immigration in which he suggested that unemployed Europeans could join the Union army. This kind of recruitment took place mainly in Ireland and Germany. Activities increased in 1864 as numerous soldiers were discharged after their three-year service commitment ended. A blockade of German ports followed when the authorities uncovered so many abuses that Seward was forced to ship his recruits through Antwerp. Balace, *En marge de la guerre de sécession*, 15.

[4]Belgium, General State Archives (BGRA), I 160, no. 154, enrôlements et recrutements de Belges pour l'étranger, letter, 7 July 1864; and advertisement published in *L'Etoile*, 7 April 1864.

ties. Efforts by men like Dochez and Strauss led to a diplomatic row between the two nations, but now it was the Belgian government which protested. An investigation revealed that recruits had been deceived, mainly because of Dochez's dual role. Some men, believing they would be placed in civilian jobs, were shocked to find that when they landed in the US they filled the ranks of the Union army.[5] The scandal ended such recruitment in Belgium and compromised other attempts to lure Belgian workers to the cross the ocean. With the end of the Civil War, a booming American economy caused migration to resume, but internal opposition in the US strengthened. In 1868, Congress repealed the law, ending the policy of actively encouraging immigration.[6]

Immigration and Immigrant Transport as a Federal Issue

In the meantime, attempts by the US authorities to regulate migration through passenger transport laws were also proving to be ineffective. Lawsuits over violations of the 1855 Passenger Act exposed its shortcomings. The first cases were won by shipowners based on the fact that the law only applied to passengers from the US and not to migrants who landed on American territory. The Civil War consigned the issue to the background, but the arrival of various ships in 1867 with high mortality and morbidity rates renewed the interest of the American government in the problem.[7] By then, most migrants arriving in the US came in steamships, but the courts ruled in several cases that the Passenger Act only applied to sailing vessels. Despite the fact that such decisions protected the interests of shipping companies, fears arose that the government might amend the law to their detriment. To protect the interests of their merchant marine, the British and German ambassadors to Washington, Edward Thornton and Baron Friedrich Gerolt, advanced a proposal to the American authorities that involved synthesizing the existing passenger laws of the three countries. Hamilton Fish, the American Secretary of State, welcomed the initiative and approached the other major maritime powers involved in the mi-

---

[5]Balace, *En marge de la guerre de sécession*, 19, estimated that 300 Belgians joined the ranks of the Union army in this way.

[6]*Ibid.*, 1-2; and Torsten Feys, "The Emigration Policy of the Belgian Government from Belgium to the U.S. through the Port of Antwerp, 1842-1914" (Unpublished MA thesis, Ghent University, 2003), 113-117.

[7]See the cases of *Guiseppe Baccarcich* from Antwerp and *Lord Brougham* and *Leibnitz* from Hamburg. Bismarck took advantage of such incidents to place emigration under federal supervision. Eric Spelkens, "Belgian Migration to the United States and Other Overseas Countries at the Beginning of the 20th Century," in Ginette Kurgan and Eric Spelkens, *Two Studies on Emigration through Antwerp to the New World* (Brussels, 1976), 92; and Jones, "Immigrants, Steamships and Governments," 180-183.

grant trade – France, Italy, Belgium, Denmark, Sweden and the Netherlands – about the advisability of passing uniform regulations for passenger transport and establishing international courts at American ports to prosecute abuses that occurred on the high seas. He believed that the latter was necessary because American courts lacked jurisdiction over foreign-flagged ships, while European courts lacked witnesses to exercise effective jurisdiction over national ships.

The composition and functions of the so-called "Emigrant Courts" constituted the main obstacle during the subsequent negotiations. Mixed tribunals with foreign representation (most likely the consuls) were almost certainly unconstitutional in the US, while foreign governments refused the concede jurisdiction over their ships to a court in which they were not represented. European shipping interests also opposed the idea and voiced their concerns through Gerolt, who was a shareholder in the North German Lloyd (NGL), and Gray Hill, the secretary of the North Atlantic Steam Traffic Conference. Hill feared an abuse of power because of American jealously about the ascendancy of the British merchant marine. He also criticized other measures proposed by Fish for unnecessarily increasing the fares for migrants. The Belgian government also opposed the scheme in order to defend Belgian migrant transport interests. Yet to prevent the US from making unilateral decisions, Belgian diplomats feigned good will towards Fish. They also adopted this position to protect the standing of Antwerp as a migrant gateway, which had suffered in recent years from publicity about *Rochembau* and *Guiseppe Baccarcich*. The fruitless negotiations over emigrant courts dragged on for six years while shipping interests gladly saw support to amend the Passenger Act wither and die.[8]

It was concern in the western states over Chinese labour that put immigration back on the national political agenda. The growing influx of Chinese workers led to a backlash among natives and to calls to restrict the entry of Asians. As a result, in 1875 Congress passed a law prohibiting the further import of prostitutes, convicts and Orientals migrating against their will. The next year, the Supreme Court ruled that the practice of states levying commutation fees as a substitute for a head tax usurped the power of Congress to regulate foreign commerce and hence was unconstitutional. This turned out to be a landmark decision for another reason: the Court went on to declare that immigration was a key method of regulating the labour force and hence an inherent component of commerce; the result was to place all migration issues under federal authority. There were other consequences. The decision deprived the State of New York and other seaboard states of an important source of

---

[8]Belgium, Archives of the Ministry of Foreign Affairs (ABMFA), Emigration, 2020, IX, Emigration, 1870-1895, letter, 5 January 1870; Feys, "Emigration Policy," 131-135; Spelkens, "Belgian Migration," 89-93; Jones, "Aspects of North Atlantic Migration," 326-330; and Jones, "Immigrants, Steamships and Governments," 178-204.

revenue for maintaining landing facilities for migrants, and the states did not manage to obtain federal compensation for many years.[9] Due to a lack of funds, New York State threatened to close Castle Garden. Along with continuing lobbying by western states to prohibit Chinese immigration, pressures grew for Congress to intervene. The lawmakers‘ previous reluctance to do so because of trade agreements and international relations based on reciprocity had faded as the conviction grew in both Europe and the US that it was a country's sovereign right to control migration. Hence, the main question was no longer whether a state had the right to exclude migrants but rather who it should exclude and how to do it. In 1882, Congress passed a Chinese Exclusion Act which barred the importation of Chinese labourers for the next decade. That same year, it also passed a law excluding convicts, lunatics, idiots and persons likely to become a public charge. These acts launched a new era: the regulation of immigration was now clearly a federal task, and racial distinctions increasingly mattered.[10]

Simultaneously, Congress approved a new Passenger Act to replace the outdated 1855 statute. But President Chester Arthur vetoed the law at the instigation of his mentor, former Senator Roscoe Conkling (R-NY), so that some of the features which the shipping industry opposed could be removed. For instance, a provision providing that the deportation of excluded migrants would be at the expense of the shipping companies was omitted. The amended Passenger Act imposed new requirements for migrant ships regarding sleeping space, the separation of men and women, light and ventilation, hygiene, food, physicians and medical facilities which reduced the number of passengers that could be carried. It also included a head tax of fifty cents levied on all third-class passengers. Maldwyn Jones has claimed that the authorities once again failed to enforce the Act, yet the correspondence of the Dutch envoy to Washington shows that inspections intensified. The law triggered a transatlantic debate about sovereignty during which the idea of an international convention to

---

[9]The competition among the seaboard states to attract the traffic reduced commutation fees in the 1870s. The state of Massachusetts even cancelled these to make Boston more competitive with New York.

[10]Marion T. Bennet, *American Immigration Policies: A History* (Washington, DC, 1963), 15-17; John Torpey, "Passports and the Development of Immigration Controls in the North Atlantic World during the Long Nineteenth Century," in Fahrmeir, Faron and Weil (eds.), *Migration Control*, 97; Jones, *American Immigration*, 214-215; Cheryl Shanks, *Immigration and the Politics of American Sovereignty, 1890-1990* (Ann Arbor, 2001), 39; Reed Ueda, "An Immigration Country of Assimilative Pluralism: Immigrant Reception and Absorption in American History," in Rainer Münz and Myron Weiner (eds.), *Migrants, Refugees and Foreign Policy: U.S. and German Policies toward Countries of Origin* (New York, 1997), reprinted in Klaus J. Bade and Myron Weiner (eds.), *Migration Past, Migration Future: Germany and the United States* (Providence, RI, 2000), 42-43; and Zolberg, *Nation by Design*, 185-193.

regulate migrant transport resurfaced.[11] The consular correspondence shows that once regular passenger lines were established, the role of the diplomats in the development of migrant transport decreased as shipping agents increasingly assumed the responsibility of providing reliable information on business opportunities, market fluctuations and competitive conditions, as well as defending the interests of the home port and the company. As the Holland America Line (HAL) illustrated when it appointed the Dutch consul in New York as its head agent, the transition was gradual. But although the long-term trend was against them, diplomats nonetheless remained important spokesmen in defending the commercial interests of the merchant marine with foreign authorities. They lobbied against laws and treaties which obstructed trade, including the new Passenger Act.

The Amsterdam-based Royal Netherlands Steamship Company (RNS) and the HAL approached the Dutch envoy in Washington, G. de Weckherlin, about the differences between Dutch and American passenger transport laws. Although a Dutch committee had concluded that these might weaken the protection of migrants, it praised the US for acting and expressed the hope that this might initiate a dialogue about unifying the legislation concerning migrant transport. As Weckherlin emphasized, it would be difficult to object to the Act for protecting the well-being of the needy, but he believed an argument could be made that Dutch ships at sea were not obliged to obey American laws. It was equally true, he concluded, that nothing prevented the US from refusing to allow ships to enter its waters that did not respect its laws. Instead of arguing against US jurisdiction, Weckherlin supported the Dutch committee's advice to reach an international agreement with all countries concerned. But the Dutch Minister of Foreign Affairs did not want to take the initiative for fear that it might give the impression that the Netherlands was organizing opposition to the US. The US therefore had to be moved to invite all the countries involved. Yet in the meantime, with the concurrence of the German and English passenger lines the governments of both countries drafted a joint resolution to adapt US laws to theirs. This in turn led to a congressional committee to study the unification of the passenger acts of the three countries.[12]

Weckherlin contacted the other countries to try to arrange a joint approach for an international convention. He omitted Sweden because, unlike other European nations, the Swedes had strict passenger acts with high space

---

[11]Jones, "Aspects of North Atlantic Migration," 329; and Zolberg, *Nation by Design*, 192-193.

[12]The Netherlands, National Archives (DNA), 2.05.13, Gezantschap Verenigde Staten, 210, letters, 4 May and 14 August 1882, 16 February and 16 March 1883, and 12 April 1884; and reports of Supervision Committee of Rotterdam and Amsterdam, 29 June and 3 July 1882; and ABMFA, Emigration, 2959 I, US migration laws, 1882-1898, letter, 16 February 1883.

requirements which had obstructed the development of national passenger lines. Moreover, the Swedish government was beginning to oppose emigration and was likely to increase rather than decrease space requirements, thus elevating the cost of migration.[13]

The other objectionable feature of the US law was that it set penalties for violating the capacity requirements that consisted not only of fines per excess passenger but also possible prison sentences for captains. Backed by the Belgians and Italians, the French and Dutch diplomats led the negotiations with the Department of State. Secretary of State Frederick Frelinghuysen favoured the idea of standardizing laws but claimed that his hands were tied because of the Republican majority in the House of Representatives. Weckherlin and Freylinghuysen promoted a convention jointly organized by the Dutch and American authorities.[14] Unfortunately, the discord among European states obstructed a joint line of action and ended hopes for an international convention.

Against Weckherlin's advice, the RNS continued using Dutch laws to calculate the allowable number of passengers. It also challenged the jurisdiction of American authorities over Dutch ships and the legality of the penalties imposed. When the chartered British vessel *Survey* arrived in the US, once again disregarding the new Passenger Act, the American authorities not only imposed a fine but also arrested Captain Bacon and the Dutch head agent of the RNS, Mr. Toelaar. Since *Survey* was a British ship, Weckherlin did not intervene directly but used his influence to avoid a trial. If this tactic failed, he was convinced that if Toelaar proved he acted in accordance with Dutch legislation the court would offer a settlement. The American consul in Amsterdam also intervened on his behalf. The head agent and Captain Bacon were released on bail of US $5000. The authorities seemed ready to abandon the case when another RNS ship arrived with twenty dead passengers. To further worsen the situation, that same week the HAL's *Edam* sank, attracting the attention of the American media which questioned the safety of Dutch ships. The Dutch diplomats suspected that the German lines were behind the media attacks and launched their own propaganda campaign to defend the national lines. Under media pressure, the authorities now set a trial date for Toelaar and Bacon. Weckherlin pleaded the case with the district attorney but did not base his defence on the argument that the RNS believed that Dutch laws had as much weight as American laws because he feared that a long trial would harm the

---

[13]Odd S. Lovoll, "For the People Who Are Not in a Hurry: The Danish Thingvalla Line and the Transportation of Scandinavian Emigrants," *Journal of American Ethnic History*, XIII, No. 1 (1993), 1-48; and DNA, 2.05.13, Gezantschap Verenigde Staten, 210, letters, 30 March, 18 April and 19 May 1883.

[14]ABMFA, Emigration, 2959 I, correspondence, 16 February-28 July 1883; and DNA, 2.05.13, Gezantschap Verenigde Staten, 210, letters, 28 February, 14 March, 5, 19 and 20 May, and 18 June 1883.

line's reputation. Instead, he pleaded that the company assumed that the act applied only to sailing ships, playing down the idea that the RNS had any criminal intent.[15]

While the sources do not reveal the verdict, the fact that the case went to trial demonstrates that the American authorities intended to impose the Passenger Act on foreign ships. To avoid international repercussions, Congress consulted the two most important maritime nations, Great Britain and Germany. While some American officials still welcomed the initiative to re-launch negotiations towards an international convention, they no longer took a leading role. The federal government, now empowered to pass legislation regarding immigration matters, would gradually feel more comfortable in making unilateral decisions about regulating immigration and migrant transport. The established notion of reciprocity among nations on matters involving shipping and migration was slowly replaced by the conviction that such issues belonged to the nation and had to be imposed to preserve and enhance sovereignty. The shipping lobby, which had successfully obstructed the effectiveness of state and federal laws that negatively affected its business, was forced to change its strategy when migration became a federal matter. Washington became the place for passenger liner companies to defend their interests and where they ran into opposition from labour unions and nativist organizations.

Labour Unions: From International Solidarity to America for Americans

The policy of the Knights of Labour (KL) to unite workers in different trades without discriminating on racial, religious or gender grounds helped it to expand rapidly to become the country's biggest union. The KL even made contacts abroad who became go-betweens for both employers and unions. For instance, some Belgian glass workers who migrated to Pittsburgh in the 1870s created a link with the Belgian glass industry at Charleroi. American employers used these contacts to attract Belgian workers to migrate, while the KL made contacts with the Belgian Union Verrière and began to expand worker solidarity across national borders. The unions supported each other financially during strikes. The KL expanded the network to glass workers in Germany, France and England, creating a "Universal Federation" to control the transatlantic labour market. Through these contacts, the KL hoped to increase European wages and hence slow transatlantic migration, but this hope vanished in the 1890s when craft solidarity began to splinter, and Belgian unions made secret arrangements with American employers to send over strikebreakers.[16]

---

[15]DNA, 2.05.13, Gezantschap Verenigde Staten, 210, correspondence, 24 April-20 August 1883.

[16]Feys, "Emigration Policy," 134-140; Tom Goyens, "Waalse glasarbeiders in de Verenigde Staten: Pennsylvania, West Virginia, Ohio en Indiana, 1870-1910"

These kinds of translational networks appealed to skilled migrants, who showed a greater willingness to unionize than did the unskilled labourers who comprised the bulk of the newcomers. Labour unions spread the notion that American employers tried to artificially induce immigration to depress wages. They also accused employers of importing workers as strikebreakers.[17] The KL's "Master Workman," Terence Powderly, denounced the monopolistic tendency of big corporations, claiming that this widened the gap between employers and employees. As leader of the largest labour union, he gained influence in economic and political spheres, lobbying for legislation limiting the power and formation of trusts. He also backed the demands of glassworkers and cigar makers to restrict the arrival of immigrants with labour contracts. His efforts bore fruit in 1885 with the passage of the Alien Contract Labor Law (ACLL), which prohibited the import of aliens to work in the US except for skilled workers in new industries, professional actors, lecturers, singers, domestic workers, relatives and friends.[18] The last two categories were included at the insistence of shipping lines to protect their prepaid market.

Scholars such John Higham and Daniel Tichenor have generally dated the support of labour unions for restricting immigration to the 1890s. Tichenor contends that the KL hardly differentiated between new and old immigration because "with its international orientation the union sought to enhance the solidarity among workers regardless of nationality and thus expressed no desire

(Unpublished MA thesis, Leuven University, 1982), 28-34; Ken Fones-Wolf, "Immigrants, Labor and Capital in a Transnational Context: Belgian Glassworkers in America, 1880-1925," *Journal of American Ethnic History*, XXI, No. 1 (2002), 63-68; and Fones-Wolf, "Transatlantic Craft Migrations and Transnational Spaces: Belgian Window Glass Workers in America, 1880-1920," *Labor History*, XLV, No. 3 (2004), 300-308.

[17]Jones, *American Immigration*, 214-215; Zolberg, *Nation by Design*, 192-195; and Terence V. Powderly, "A Menacing Irruption," *North American Review*, CXLVII, No. 2 (1888), 170. Researchers have shown that the image of migrants as strikebreakers and scabs was greatly exaggerated by the unions because migrants tended to concentrate in low-level segments of the labour market that were shunned by natives. For the most part, conflicts erupted on those few occasions when migrants undercut prevailing wages or introduced new technology. Dirk Hoerder, "International Labour Markets and Community Building by Migrant Workers in the Atlantic Economies," in Rudolph J. Vecoli and Suzanne M. Simke (eds.), *A Century of European Migrations, 1830-1930* (Urbana, IL, 1991), 90-96; and Hoerder, *Cultures in Contact: World Migrations in the Second Millennium* (Durham, NC, 2002), 9.

[18]Freidrich Notebohm, *Rapport sur la situation des ouvriers aux États-Unis* (Stockholm, 1905), 36-37; and ABMFA, Question ouvrières Etats-Unis, 3284, 1885-1912.

for sweeping restrictions."[19] Many American trade unions had been pioneered by migrants and with the exception of the ACLL did not demand far-reaching restrictions. Yet, as Aristide Zolberg also noted, the debates over the ACLL indicate a radicalization of the KL. Martin Foran (D-OH) had gained support for the bill by claiming that the new wave of migrants consisted mainly of single men who wanted to save as much as possible to be able to return home and were therefore willing to accept deplorable living and working conditions without any intention of becoming US citizens. This criticism dominated immigration debates for the next three decades. Powderly shared Foran's point of view, moving away from international solidarity towards the idea of "America for Americans." He openly criticized the new arrivals from southern and eastern Europe who he labelled as "semi-barbarous" for lowering the quality of life and working conditions in the US. Moreover, because the new wave of migrant sojourners did not show the same tendency to join unions as did their predecessors, the labour organizations began to lobby for increased barriers to entry.[20] Indeed, Powderly pressed to restrict immigration completely:

> It is still dangerous to say anything concerning the restriction of immigration for fear of being charged with Know-Nothingism. Whatever Know Nothingism meant in former years, the man who advocates restriction of immigration today is a patriot who loves his country better than the opinion of demagogues, or of those who will not speak the truth, because it may temporarily affect their interest.[21]

He advocated "remote control" measures by which the consular corps would screen the intentions of potential migrants before they left Europe and would issue certificates to those intending to become American citizens. While some labour organizations, such as the American Federation of Labour, only advocated general restrictions in the mid-1890s, Powderly's stance and the many petitions for restrictions from other labour organizations in the early 1890s underline labour's early commitment to reduce immigration.[22]

---

[19]Tichenor, *Dividing Lines*, 72.

[20]Powderly, "Menacing Irruption," 165-174; Feys, "Emigration Policy," 139 and 207; John Higham, *Strangers in the Land: Patterns of American Nativism, 1860-1925* (New Brunswick, NJ, 1955; reprint, New Brunswick, NJ, 2002), 112-113; Jones, *American Immigration*, 188-190; and Zolberg, *Nation by Design*, 194-196.

[21]Powderly, "Menacing Irruption," 166.

[22]*Ibid.*, 167-170; and Edward P. Hutchinson, *Legislative History of American Immigration Policy, 1798-1965* (Philadelphia, 1981), 105.

Powderly's radicalization may have been spurred by the ineffectiveness of the ACLL, which remained a dead letter until it was amended to put the Secretary of State in charge of enforcement in 1887. That year, the first passengers accused of violating the law were returned to Antwerp. The group of Turks were arrested at the port for vagrancy and attracted the concern of local authorities which feared getting stuck with deportees who could not finance the trip home. They requested guidelines from the government which was also unprepared to deal with the situation despite receiving copies of the bills from its New York consul, Charles Mali, who claimed that although the ACLL breached the Treaty of Commerce and Navigation signed by both nations in 1875, this was not the first time that US authorities passed immigration laws which violated international treaties. The Minister of Foreign Affairs, Joseph de Chimay, consulted with his colleague in the Department of Justice about how to prevent emigrants from being stranded in Antwerp. He wanted to lodge an official complaint and sought support from ten other European countries affected by the law.[23]

The replies show that most countries had no intention of opposing the ACLL. The German, Norwegian and Swedish governments considered emigration to be detrimental to their respective countries and thus favoured the measure. The Russian Minister of Foreign Affairs shared this position and stressed that his country had no intention of interfering with legislation passed by other nations. Other states, like Portugal and Great Britain, preferred to direct emigrants to their colonies rather than the US. The Swiss were neutral on the issue and refrained from stimulating emigration while protecting those who chose to leave from abuse. With the second industrial revolution in full swing, most European countries began to oppose the flow of migrants who were now needed for the development of the domestic economy. The Belgians, however, still leaned towards encouraging the movement which had failed to materialize as early as elsewhere and was only now starting to develop. It considered emigration as a security valve to temper protests in industrial centres during periods of social unrest. Moreover, the laws interfered with the commercial interests of the Red Star Line (RSL), which had revived the migrant flow through Antwerp.[24] Due to this general lack of support, Chimay chose not to lodge an official protest. In the meantime, Americans opposed to restrictions questioned the constitutionality of the law, but the Supreme Court rejected their complaints. All of this reinforced the conviction of the US government that migration was a national rather than an international issue.

---

[23]Hutchinson, *Legislative History*, 91; and ABMFA, 2961, part 1, Ouvriers Belges aux Etats-Unis, letters, 1 January and 6, 8 and 20 February 1888.

[24]ABMFA, 2961, part I, Ouvriers Belges aux Etats-Unis, various letters, 1888-1889; and Feys, "Emigration Policy," 163-168.

The ACLL created a paradox in that it required new arrivals to prove that they were not likely to become public charges while at the same time forbidding them from making arrangements for work before entering the US. It increased the importance for poor migrants of having family or friends in America who could guarantee that they would not become public charges and may have tightened chain-migration patterns. Yet both the shipping companies and the Belgian authorities took measures to avoid the deportation of contract labourers. Mali advised Chimay to inform the population fully about the law: "we would not dare to advise our labourers to come here without a bond or a support assuring them work, but it is important to inform the emigrants to keep this silent if they do not want to experience difficulties upon their arrival in New York."[25] Chimay ordered the provincial governors to spread this information to the public, while the emigration commissioner in Antwerp briefed Belgian emigrants before departure. When Belgians were detained, the consuls intervened on their behalf, as was the case for cigar makers, diamond cutters and glassworkers. In the case of Jean-Baptiste Saint, the consul managed to prove that immigrant inspectors had deceived passengers to obtain evidence. Contacts in Belgium had given the KL a list of names of glassworkers from the Charleroi region who headed to the US with a labour contract; the KL passed this information to immigration inspectors who screened all the Belgian passengers. As most labour arrangements were made orally, it was difficult for inspectors to prove violations except by obtaining a confession. In the case of the Belgian glassworkers, the consul forced the translator at the interrogation, Mr. Palmeri, to confess in court that migrants were told to state that they had work or they would otherwise be sent back. The glassworkers were also forced to sign compromising declarations in English which they could not read.[26] The consul obtained their release by showing that the inspectors had intimidated passengers. The British consul also fought deportations, while the HAL's New York head agent, van den Toorn, mentioned the lack of interest from Austro-Hungarian diplomats, reflecting that nation's tendency to restrict migration.[27] As Donna Gabbaccia has shown, the efforts (or lack thereof) by governments to protect the interests of citizens and to retain ties with the home country are

[25]ABMFA, 2961, part I, Ouvriers Belges aux Etats-Unis, letters, 1 March 1888 and 29 August 1889.

[26]*Ibid.*, letter and report about the trial of the Belgian glassworkers, 19 August 1890; and Feys, "Emigration Policy," 148-155.

[27]See the case of seven detained English passengers who arrived on *Obdam* and the apathy of the Austro-Hungarian consul towards the deportation of citizens travelling with the HAL. Rotterdam Community Archives (GAR), Holland-American Line Archive (HAL), 318.04, Passage, 221-226, letters, 24 May 1889 and 9 March 1892.

an area which has not yet been fully explored.[28] More research on consular efforts to fight deportations should shed more light on this.

Shipping companies also tried to prevent passengers from being rejected, but van den Toorn often complained about the corrupt, despotic and arbitrary management of the landing stations which hampered these efforts. Positions at the control stations were often used as rewards for political favours and were not necessarily based on the appointees' capabilities.[29] Commissioners of Immigration heading the local control stations never remained for long periods, and these shortened after 1895 when the president took charge of appointing them. As the immigration laws passed by Congress left a great deal of room for interpretation, their enforcement depended largely on the zeal of the commissioners and inspectors. But these were easily influenced by external pressures, and when elections were looming the controls became stricter. As van den Toorn reported:

> The government here is completely corrupted, to an extent which is hard to imagine for a European. Just as the examination procedure of passengers. Immigrants are often sent back with no valid reason but for the sole purpose of pleasing the labor party for upcoming elections.[30]

Shipping companies also used the venality of the immigration inspectors to their advantage. They appointed a representative at Castle Garden to build goodwill among the inspectors by providing all sorts of incentives and to assist passengers during the landing. For instance, the good contacts the HAL established with immigrant inspector Heinzmann prevented the deportation of eighteen Syrians for violating the ACLL. In exchange of unspecified presents and free third-class passage for Heinzmann's cousin, the case against the Syrians was dropped. The HAL also maintained good relations with Heinzmann's successor, Mr. Arkedy, who was responsible for Syrian, Arab and Egyptian immigrants who together with Polish Jews had the greatest risks of being excluded as contract labourers. In exchange for three second-class tickets for his children, the inspector facilitated the landing of seventy detained Syrians.[31]

---

[28]Donna R. Gabaccia, "Is Everywhere Nowhere? Nomads, Nations and the Immigration Paradigm of United States History," *Journal of American History*, LXXXVI, No. 3 (1999), 1125.

[29]GAR, HAL, 318.04, Passage, 221-226, letters, 26 December 1886 and 7 July 1891.

[30]*Ibid.*, letter, 8 March 1892.

[31]*Ibid.*, letters, 8 February 1888 and 8 September 1896.

Yet as Van den Toorn emphasized, most problems could be avoided by preparing migrants for the interrogations before they landed. The purser played a crucial role by filling out the passenger manifests used by American inspectors to track down excludables. He screened the answers and adapted those that might raise suspicions. For instance, groups of single men with the same final destination would raise suspicions that they were contract labourers. The HAL's stewards informed these passengers about this and gave advice on how to pass controls. For example, *Amsterdam*'s steward changed the manifests for twenty-five men who had given up the same address as their final destination. Yet by boasting that no passenger from his ship had ever been sent back for violating the ACLL, he attracted the attention of the newspapers which accused him of forcing passengers to claim that they had paid for their passage themselves, possessed at least US $30 and had not made any prior arrangements for work. Van den Toorn reprimanded the purser and told him to exercise the greatest secrecy and avoid such publicity which led to stricter controls for the HAL's passengers on arrival. Furthermore, the purser needed to limit his efforts to people who were risks, not to all passengers.[32]

Preparations for the interrogations began with the European migrant agents informing the migrants about the American laws and how to circumvent them. The HAL's directors praised the Vienna office for being especially successful in coaching passengers about how to evade the ACLL. It proved very hard for the HAL's personnel in Rotterdam, who screened passengers with the highest risks, to establish the truth about contract labour violators sent through Vienna.[33] Hence, the HAL screened passengers three times about the risk of being excluded; through their inland agencies, at the port of embarkation and on board the ship. Shipping companies went to great lengths to ensure that passengers knew the right answers to avoid deportation and used the greed of inspectors when possible to save those who failed.

Rising Calls for Restrictions and Improvements to Enforce the Laws

In the wake of the ACLL a new wave of nativism emerged. This was reinforced in 1886 by the Haymarket bombing which associated immigrants in the public mind with radicalism and threats to the foundations of American society. Immigration became a hot topic in public debates, especially with the founding of the American Economic Association (AEA). The concern economists had for labour reform made immigration an inherent part of their theories, and they provided "scientific" arguments for immigration policies to the authorities. In their battle to better the poor, they posited a human hierarchy

[32] *Ibid.*, letters, 2, 3 and 14 March, 15 June and 13 July 1894.

[33] *Ibid.*, letter, 14 March 1894.

based upon eugenics, a doctrine accepted by many of the prominent AEA members such as Edward Bemis, Richmond Mayo-Smith and Theodore Roosevelt. The AEA's essay contest on "The Evil Effects of Unrestricted Immigration," won by Bemis in 1888, launched the idea of a mandatory literacy test for selecting immigrants. That this measure would reduce the new influx from eastern and southern Europe while leaving the old flow from northern and western Europe unaffected was the goal of these men.[34]

In his articles on immigration control, Mayo-Smith formulated the basic scientific arguments for immigration restriction. Using statistical evidence he claimed that because of the exponential growth of immigration it was no longer possible to guarantee that the migrants would be assimilated into American society. He went on to claim that the high percentage of criminals and illiterates among the foreign-born affected the proper functioning of American institutions. The problem was as much about quality as quantity. Improvements in the transport sector decreased the cost and risks of the transatlantic voyage and removed the natural barrier which had kept the most undesirable immigrants at home. Remittances from previous migrants and government assistance further reduced the barriers. Moreover, the new stock of migrants, such as the Hungarians and Slovaks, had strikingly "inferior" features, while Italians subsisted in overly crowded living conditions on a diet of stale food until they saved enough money to go home again. Immigration reduced US wages and living standards which affected American birth rates. Mayo-Smith also questioned the economic benefits of immigration. Through remittances and return migrants, capital exports exceeded imports. As the country had moved beyond the pioneer phase and was becoming more industrialized, the need for unskilled labour decreased. The lure of the west was growing fainter, and most of the new arrivals concentrated in urban centres. Mayo-Smith stressed that the state needed to give priority to its own citizens and did not foresee any diplomatic repercussion from Europe by questioning the natural right of migration. He considered the lack of official protests against the previous restrictions as implicit approvals of nations that welcomed these precedents and which acknowledged the state's right to control migration.[35]

---

[34]Edward W. Bemis, "The Restriction of Immigration," *Andover Review*, IX, No. 1 (1888), 251-264; Peter G. Filene, "An Obituary for The Progressive Movement," *American Quarterly*, XXII, No. 1 (1970), 24; Michael Just, *Ost und südosteuropäische Amerikawanderung, 1881-1914*. Stuttgart, 1988), 191-196; Jones, *American Immigration*, 214-218; Thomas Leonard, "American Progressivism and the Rise of the Economist as Expert" (Unpublished working paper, Princeton University, 2006), 1-7; and Zolberg, *Nation by Design*, 199, 211.

[35]Richmond Mayo-Smith, "Control of Immigration I," *Political Science Quarterly*, III, No. 1 (1888), 46-77; "Control of Immigration II," *Political Science Quarterly*, III, No. 2 (1888), 197-225; "Control of Immigration III," *Political Science*

In contrast to Bemis, Mayo-Smith did not propose any innovative measures. He opposed wholesale restrictions which would disrupt the vast interests bound up with the transportation business and would affect American trade in general. He pleaded for a gradual decrease in numbers through a rigid enforcement of existing immigration laws and passenger acts. The latter had to cut the high profits generated by the traffic and decrease the activity of business interests which unnaturally swelled the flow. European governments and shipping companies had to be discouraged from shipping those from the excluded classes. Authorities had to require security bonds from the shipping lines to increase their responsibility for passengers. Mayo-Smith, like Bemis and Powderly, proposed using the consular corps to check the quality and finances of the migrants and their intention to become Americans before embarkation in collaboration with foreign authorities and shipping companies.[36]

These ideas coalesced politically with the foundation of the nativist American Party in California and the sharp increase in proposals for immigration restrictions in Congress. The rising popularity of the American Protection Association reflected concerns about defending "American values." Mayo-Smith's arguments and Bemis' literacy test comprised a platform on which calls for restrictions were based for the next three decades. They found their way to the Senate where Henry Cabot Lodge (R-MA) endorsed restrictions and literacy tests.[37] In Lodge's home state, which with California was a breeding ground for nativism, a group of young Harvard intellectuals, including Charles Warren, Robert Ward and Prescott Hall, institutionalized the movement in 1894 by founding the Immigration Restriction League (IRL) which endorsed "scientific" racial selections through the literacy test. Yet as Mayo-Smith's articles showed, there was a growing awareness of the need to enforce the laws already enacted rather than passing new ones. Migration policies in the early 1890s focused on this and on using the control stations better.

Immigration Law Enforcement

In 1889, special immigration committees were established in the House and Senate to study how well existing laws were working and to process the in-

---

Quarterly, III, No. 3 (1888), 409-424; These articles formed the basis of his book *Emigration and Immigration: A Study in Social Science* (New York, 1890).

36 Mayo-Smith, "Control of Immigration III," 409-425; and Zolberg, *Nation by Design*, 211.

37 Hutchinson, *Legislative History*, 89-95; Desmond King, *Making Americans: Immigration, Race and the Origins of the Diverse Democracy* (Cambridge, MA, 2000), 52; Henry Cabot Lodge, "The Restriction of Immigration," *North American Review*, CLII, No. 1 (1891), 27-32; and Zolberg, *Nation by Design*, 200.

creasing number of proposals for new bills. The committees opened doors for expert organizations and members of the executive branch to give advice and influence legislation.[38] The first act to pass through the committees in 1891 moved immigrant control stations under federal control by founding the Immigration Service under the Secretary of the Treasury. The Superintendent (later referred to as the Commissioner General of Immigration), William Owen, took charge of enforcing the laws and supervising the control stations from Washington. John Weber supervised the New York station and played a much more active role than his superior in suggesting improvements. Detained migrants now appeared before a Board of Special Inquiry whose decision on deportation was subject only to administrative appeal to the Secretary of the Treasury. Weber obtained the opening of twenty-four new stations on the Mexican and Canadian borders to control the loopholes through which an increasing number of migrants entered unchecked. The law added polygamists, people with contagious diseases and assisted migrants to the excluded list. Shipping companies were required to inspect, disinfect and vaccinate their passengers, to defray the costs of maintaining the detainees and deporting rejected migrants. Newcomers who became a public charge within the first year of arrival could now be deported. The law prohibited advertisements containing promises of employment except from state immigration agencies. Steamship companies had to refrain from soliciting immigrants, limiting their advertisements to rates, facilities and dates of sailing. They also needed to provide passenger manifests with names, nationalities, last residences and destinations for all passengers.[39]

These policies marked a clear shift by increasing the responsibility of the transport companies. Lodge suggested the literacy test for the first time in Congress during these debates yet it was not considered a priority. Instead, the emphasis went to improving the selection of immigrants rather than introducing new restrictions. Nevertheless, during a meeting with the shipping companies Weber's definition of "likely to become a public charge" (LPC) illustrates that racial selections had infiltrated at the gates:

---

[38]Keith Fitzgerald, *The Face of the Nation: Immigration, the State and National Identity* (Chicago, 1996), 126.

[39]Bennet, *American Immigration Policies*, 21-23; United States, Senate, 61st Cong., 2nd sess., Immigration Commission (DC), *Reports* (41 vols., Washington, DC, 1911), XXXIX, 35-48; Hutchinson, *Legislative History*, 100-102; Allan Kraut, "Bodies from Abroad: Immigration, Health and Disease," in Reed Ueda (ed.), *A Companion to American Immigration* (Oxford, 2006), 112; and Torpey, "Passports," 96. Until 1895, the title "Superintendent" was used instead of "Commissioner General" of Immigration. That year the Immigration "Service" was elevated to the "Bureau" of Immigration. GAR, HAL, 318.04, Passage, 221-226, letter, 7 July 1891; and *New York Times*, 5 June 1891.

> The best way to fight the increasing agitation against immigration in the US is by tightening controls at the port of embarkation on the 'desirability' of the migrants. 'Desirability' is a question of mentality and nationality which do not fit in the US; French, Belgians, Dutch, Germans, English Scandinavians etc. are desirable; Italians, Russian Jews, Arabs, Slovaks, etc. are undesirable...In America strong and healthy individuals willing to work yet arriving without means are not considered as likely to become a public charge. However, people with means but with a reputation to throw it away – a shabby fellow, is. If a migrant becomes ill and becomes a public charge he will not be sent back if he had no predisposition of catching the disease prior to arrival, otherwise he will. Idiots should be turned away yet when travelling with relatives this is not applied. Same goes for disabled although we rather not have them.[40]

The lack of clear standards for LPCs gave immigrant inspectors a good deal of leverage and allowed them to apply stricter controls to the "undesirable classes." As cases of contract labourers and polygamists proved difficult to prove, inspectors often refused such suspects as LPCs.[41]

To avoid extra costs and the negative publicity caused by transporting deportees, shipping companies went to great lengths to land their clients successfully. When they were given increased responsibility in the control process, the shipping companies also acquired a privileged position to help migrants pass the barriers. The HAL intensified the screening of its passengers in Europe; the information was used not only to refuse transportation but also to facilitate the landing of excludables. Company doctors examined the passengers at the port of embarkation. The sick were held for observation and cured before being allowed to sail. The incurable chose other destinations, alternative routes or returned home. The company telegraphed a list of passengers with potential risks of being detained to its staff in New York when the ship left Europe. The pursers continued to screen the manifests and prepare passengers for interrogations. Powderly and Herman Schulties accused some companies of hiring translators to assist with this.[42] The crew also encouraged the migrants

---

[40]GAR, HAL, 318.04, Passage, 221-226, letter, 8 October 1891.

[41]Joseph H. Senner, "How We Restrict Immigration," *North American Review*, CLVIII, No. 4 (1894), 499.

[42]Herman J. Schulties, *Report on European Immigration to the United States of America and the Causes which Incite the Same, with Recommendations for the Further Restriction of Undesirable Immigration and the Establishment of a National Quar-*

to wash thoroughly before arrival to make the best possible impression on the inspectors. Upon arrival clerks in the HAL's steerage department screened the passengers and collected information on those most likely to be detained while accompanying them to the control station. For these cases, as well as for those on the list sent from Rotterdam and the eventual detainees, they tracked down relatives and friends who by picking them up, sending money, posting bond or testifying before the board of special inquiry could facilitate entry. The shipping line helped to defend the passengers appearing before the board, petitioned for re-hearings when new evidence became available and filed appeals if necessary.[43] The HAL sometimes paid for rail transport to join family members already in the US.[44] Through the agent network, passengers were encouraged to book tickets to their final destination because this facilitated the landing process. In short, the importance of the shipping lines as links both in the chain-migration process and between the immigrant and the state in fighting deportations cannot be underestimated.

If relatives or friends could not be traced, the HAL often contacted charities to assist detainees. Jewish passengers in particular relied on a wide transatlantic network of charity organizations at main transit points and ports. These offered free lodging, paid medical expenses, financed part of the inland or ocean passage, contacted relatives or friends abroad for assistance, paid bonds, defended detainees and provided jobs.[45] Because the HAL attracted an important share of the Russian Jewish market, it often relied on these associations to guarantee the landing of its passengers and to spread information on

---

antine (Washington, DC, 1893), 41-43; and Hutchinson, *Legislative History*, 101. Powderly's interpreter on board an Anchor Line vessel from Genoa to New York confided that he had travelled to the US a few times for the line as an assistant interpreter to instruct passengers about what to say when going through American inspections.

[43]GAR, HAL, 318.04, Passage, 221-226, letters, 24 December 1894, 3 January 1895 and 4 June 1902.

[44]For example, van den Toorn contacted friends in Shanondock about ten Galicians who were being detained for being LPCs. He proposed paying their rail transport to Shanondock if the friends would post bonds for them. The friends refused, leading to the deportation of the Galicians *Ibid.,* letter, 1 February 1889. There are many other cases in the archives. *Ibid.*, Passage, 72-77 and 221-226.

[45]For instance, the Jewish Committee of Charlottenburg assisted many migrants with their journey in Berlin, while the Hebrew Charity Society of London collected money for ocean transport and posted bonds *Ibid.*, letters, 29 September 1890 and 1 July 1891; and United States, National Archives, Washington, DC (NAW), Records of the Immigration and Naturalization Service, 1787-1993 (RINS), Record Group (RG) 85, 52011/A, Investigation Marcus Braun, report on charity organizations, 29 July 1904; and 51720/13, Jewish charities, letters, 1907.

how to pass the inspections. For example, van den Toorn credited Jewish missionaries at Ellis Island for the successful landing of twenty-three of twenty-five detained passengers from *Edam* after the group had been declared to be LPCs. Missionaries representing various national, ethnic and religious groups were stationed at Ellis Island to assist those detained to pass the inspections and to help the excluded get safely back home. The officials could even discharge aliens under bond to the missionaries if they agreed to handle family reunification or to secure employment for them. The major problem was that many passengers were destitute and lacked the means to continue their journey. Because Jewish passengers often mistrusted interrogators, they lied about what they owned for fear that it would be taken from them. Van den Toorn urged the agents and charity institutions to ensure that Russian passengers had a ticket to their final destination and at least a minimum amount of money. He also told them to be sure that the migrants showed these things to the immigration inspectors.[46]

In theory, companies could no longer accept passengers who had received financial assistance from charitable institutions. In practice they continued to do so, although the HAL sent most of these people through Baltimore where controls were less strict than in New York. At Ellis Island the new Commissioner of Immigration, Joseph Senner, targeted assisted passengers just as his predecessor had done. Both, being first- and second-generation immigrants, considered immigration the life blood of the Republic, but they repeatedly labelled Russian Jews as the most undesirable class. After the suspension of the Baltimore service, the HAL resumed the practice of shipping groups of assisted passengers to New York. When allegations appeared in the American press that Montefiore, a Rotterdam-based Jewish charity, had already assisted approximately 1100 passengers, van den Toorn quickly denied that the HAL was in any way involved but that such people migrated indirectly through England. Internal correspondence proved that Montefiore paid full passage for eighty passengers, while for many others it received a reduction in rates from the HAL. The association also covered the lodging costs of Jews in Rotterdam. Due to the fact that Senner lacked conclusive proof, the HAL escaped sanctions, but its passengers did endure stricter controls in the short term.[47]

---

[46]NAW, RINS, RG 85, 51720/13, Jewish charities, letters, 7 and 11 December 1894.

[47]The practice of shipping companies quoting special eastbound charity rates thirty to fifty percent below regular fares was common. These were granted to consuls and charity institutions under special conditions for passengers they assisted. Each case had to be reported to the secretary of the continental conference; Hebrew Charity Associations were excluded in 1895 because of the many abuses. GAR, HAL, 318.04, Passage, 221-226, letter, 31 March 1891, 4 and 8 December 1893 and 27 September 1895;

In the fight to prevent the entry of assisted migrants into the US, the use of bonds was looked at more carefully. For instance, J. Pasmovska's brothers wanted to post bond for their sister and her son, but the authorities refused. Upon arrival in Rotterdam the HAL intended to rebook the lady through Baltimore and asked the brothers to meet her on arrival.[48] Deported passengers could return home, opt for another destination, or try entering the US through Canada, Mexico or other ports of entry or by travelling second class.[49] Second-class passengers were exempt from immigrant inspections; even though it cost about US $10 more than steerage, it was a much-used back door tactic. Senner's attempts to subject second-class passengers to inspections met with strong opposition, including large numbers of Americans; although US citizens were exempt from controls, they viewed an inspection as a humiliation and feared that European governments would adopt similar measures.[50] Despite these protests, immigration inspectors often boarded ships at the quarantine station to screen cabin passengers before reaching the dock. The percentage of detainees and deportees show that risks remained much smaller for second- than for third-class passengers. The privilege of avoiding the uncomfortable procedure at Ellis Island was especially appreciated by the growing number of repeat migrants for whom the companies introduced mixed tickets consisting of third-class passage to Europe and a second-class return to the US. Drew Keeling rightly noted that the expansion of second-cabin passage improved capacity utilization. Still, he underestimated the importance of stiffer immigrant inspections as a cause for the growth of second-class passengers.[51]

The use of this backdoor strategies was not an isolated occurrence. Some individuals upgraded from third class on board following the advice of other passengers or crew members. The Mormon traffic illustrates that this also happened on an organized scale. The clause barring polygamists from entry was due in part to a desire to end the recruitment of John Smith's fol-

---

318.02, Directors, 112-121, letter, 24 November 1893; and *New York Times*, 9 December 1892 and 10 May 1893.

[48]New York's 1851 laws set these bonds at US $500, an amount still in vogue in 1896. *Ibid.*, letters, 8 March 1892 and 25 October 1896; and DC, *Report*, XXXIX, 775.

[49]Although not serving Canada, the HAL assisted deported passengers through this alternative route when they were part of families which had been split at Ellis Island. GAR, HAL, 318.04, Passage, 221-226, letter, 31 July 1893.

[50]*Ibid.*, letter, 24 December 1895.

[51]Drew Keeling, "Transatlantic Shipping Cartels and Migration between Europe and America, 1880-1914," *Essays in Economic and Business History*, XVII, No. 2 (1999), 202-204.

lowers in Europe. The Mormons, however, did not object to paying the extra US $10 for its members to travel second class and avoid immigrant inspections. This differential was even reduced after migrant agent Spence of Salt Lake City, who was entrusted with the transport of new recruits, obtained a reduction on second-class rates from the Guion Line. Although the HAL matched this, it did not do so on the scale of its competitor: the Guion Line transported groups of up to 400 Mormons, but the Dutch line limited this to forty so they would not stand out as much. Despite the fact that it violated interstate commerce laws, Spence also obtained special railroad rates to Utah from railroad companies. Transport companies clearly had few fears of being caught by the authorities. Yet the HAL directors worried that the RSL might discover the discounts which went against the spirit of the cartel agreements and would increase mistrust and stimulate cheating among the lines. Despite van den Toorn's assurances that he would use the greatest secrecy in his correspondence, bookkeeping and bookings, the directors discontinued the agreement with Spence to avoid compromising the NDLV agreement in 1892. When the Guion Line was forced out of business a year later - and after discovering that the RSL had cut its second-class rates - the HAL renewed the agreement with Spence. This collaboration lasted until the conference lines agreed to pool the second-class business. The compensation price of 140 *marks* per passenger made it unprofitable for the HAL to give reductions. While the pool agreement did not last, Spence transferred his business to the Anchor Line.[52] The experience with the Mormons reminds us that shipping companies tried to land as many passengers as possible, often disregarding US laws to take advantage of business opportunities when they arose. For their part, the American authorities seemed to be aware of that problem and sought to eradicate it through improved inspections and supervision.

Consuls and Remote Border Control

With the introduction of the so-called "spoils system" in 1828, consular positions became rewards for supporters of the party that won the presidential election. Merchant-consuls, who often served for long periods, were replaced by salaried appointees whose term depended on election results. The system remained until a professionalized corps was introduced under Theodore Roosevelt early in the twentieth century. In the interim, the spoils system affected the effectiveness and quality of the diplomats who often were interested only in enriching themselves financially or socially. The use of consuls to regulate migration at the point of departure was first suggested in 1838 by Friederich

[52]GAR, HAL, 318.04, Passage, 221-226, letters, 1 July 1891, 2 February and 3 March 1892, 26 January, 16 February and 4 and 10 March 1893, 11 April 1894 and 14, 18 and 25 May 1897.

List, the American consul at Leipzig. It was first experimented with to regulate the entry of Chinese labourers from the 1860s onwards when applicants were required to have certificates issued by a consul. Calls to expand this form of long-distance border control to Europe increased. Proposals to do so were introduced in Congress and turned over to John Weber who was chairing a special commission investigating the causes of European immigration and the cost and feasibility of a consular certification system.[53] The commissioner of Ellis Island claimed that the consular system would be impractical, useless and costly. Instead, he proposed improving and enforcing the existing statutes, and to

> place the expense of all returned migrants upon steamship companies whom self-interest will force to look for reimbursement to their sub-agents who have a personal knowledge of the qualification of the intending immigrants, better than anyone else, and who would have a direct pecuniary concern in the return of a defective. Make sub-agents in this country responsible for the sale of prepaid tickets, estimated to be nearly 60 percent of the whole, that up to the time of acquiring citizenship hold all aliens liable to compulsory return.[54]

In response to a circular the majority of consuls also doubted the feasibility of controls in Europe and did not consider shipping companies to be important instigators of emigration. In contrast, Herman Schulties, another member of the commission, accused the shipping companies of deliberately facilitating the entry of excluded migrants and of corrupting consuls by involv-

---

[53]Hans Krabbendam, *Vrijheid in het verschiet: Nederlandse emigratie naar Amerika, 1840-1940* (Hilversum, 2006), 167-181; Charles S. Kennedy, *The American Consul: A History of the United States Consular Service, 1776-1914* (Westport, CT, 1990), 71-83; Thomas G. Patterson, "American Businessmen and Consular Service Reform," *Business History Review*, XL, No. 1 (1966), 77-97; Gerald L. Neuman, "Qualitative Migration Controls in the Antebellum United States," in Fahrmeir, Faron and Weil (eds.), *Migration Control*, 108; Torpey, "Passports," 90-101; Robert F. Zeidel, *Immigrants, Progressives, and Exclusion Politics: The Dillingham Commission, 1900-1927* (Dekalb, IL, 2004), 15; Zolberg, "Archaeology," 205; Zolberg, *Nation by Design*, 211; Hutchinson, *Legislative History*, 98-112; Zeidel, *Immigrants*, 16-17; and GAR, HAL, 318.04, Passage, 221-226, letter, 6 October 1891; and *New York Times*, 16 October 1891.

[54]John B. Weber and Charles Stewart Smith, "Our National Dumping-Ground: A Study of Immigration," *North American Review*, CLIV, No. 3 (1892), 429.

ing them in the business. Like John Noble, Schulteis believed in the viability of a simple and precise legal qualification plan through consular certificates.[55]

The arrival in New York of HAPAG ships with passengers affected by cholera in August 1892 increased the pressure for inspections on European soil. Although the cause of the outbreak in Hamburg is still a subject of debate, contemporaries quickly blamed Russian Jewish migrants.[56] The stir in the US press against this class of passengers, often labelled "undesirable" and "immigrants of the worse kind" by immigration officials, had started a year earlier. Van den Toorn reported that due to a typhus scare, authorities transferred Russians to the quarantine station at Hoffman Island for stricter controls. To avoid difficulties both the NGL and the RSL temporarily refused to transport Russians, while HAPAG and the HAL fumigated their luggage and subjected them to extra inspections by company doctors who issued health and disinfection certificates legalized by the American consul. These measures earned the Dutch line the goodwill of health inspectors who subsequently imposed shorter quarantine periods on HAL ships. The line's policy of hiring American doctors for its ships to facilitate communication with immigrant inspectors and the lobbying efforts of George Glavis in Washington also contributed to this preferential treatment. Nevertheless, the increased agitation for restrictions pushed authorities to increase quarantine periods up to twenty days on ships carrying alien steerage class passengers from Europe. The French line converted steerage into third-class cabins to circumvent the law, yet its ships still underwent the same quarantine period. The arbitrariness of quarantine made migrant transport unprofitable, pushing shipping companies to suspend the traffic altogether in January 1893. Van den Toorn feared that new laws containing vaguely defined barriers would soon follow. While he noted the increasing susceptibility of American authorities to diplomatic protests on immigration matters, he did not believe that they would impose a general prohibition which infringed upon treaties with European countries.[57]

Nevertheless, Senator William Chandler (R-NH), chairman of the Committee on Immigration, proposed a one-year suspension to give Congress time to pass adequate legislation and to prevent European cabin passengers

---

[55]Just, *Ost und südosteuropäische Amerikawanderung*, 244; John Hawks Noble, "The Present State of the Immigration Question," *Political Science Quarterly*, VII, No. 2 (1892), 238-239; and Schulteis, *Report*, 41-43.

[56]Katja Würstenbecker, "Hamburg and the Transit of East Europeans," in Fahrmeir, Faron and Weil (eds.), *Migration Control*, 227.

[57]GAR, HAL, 318.04, Passage, 221-226, letter, 16 February 1892; 318.02, Directors, 112-121, correspondence, August 1892-March 1893, and letters, 15, 18 and 29 November and 2, 12 and 21 December 1892, 2 June 1893, 11 January 1897, 5 September 1905 and 10 January and 23 March 1909.

from being deterred to come to the Chicago World Fair. President Harrison did not consider this to be contrary to international treaties. Yet Chandler feared that the increased activity of the powerful shipping lobby would prevent radical measures during the next sessions of Congress.[58] The law passed in February 1893 did not contain radical restrictions, yet it did empower the President to prohibit immigration from regions infected by contagious diseases for as long as he deemed necessary. This put an end to the common practice of taking out bonds to obtain the right to land LPCs which now could only be granted by the Secretary of Treasury. Shipping companies had to ensure that their agents in Europe posted the American laws in their offices and informed prospective migrants about them. Detainees appearing before the board of special inquiry now needed a favourable decision by three out of four inspectors to obtain the right to land. The law also added many questions to the passenger manifests that had to be certified by the American consul before departure to enhance the screening of the migrants.[59] Shortly thereafter, the head tax was raised to US $1 to finance the improved inspections.

The American authorities also took the remote border control policy into their own hands by appointing health inspectors at the ports of embarkation. New York's quarantine laws stipulated that passengers from infected regions had to be detained for five days at the port of embarkation under the supervision of the consul and a physician designated by him, preferably a member of the US marine hospital staff, and all their baggage had to be disinfected by steam. These measures were completed by federal quarantine regulations requiring a bill of health and a certificate of disinfection for such passengers. The new law also stipulated that the US consul had to certify a complete passenger list in which captains and ship doctors swore that after a personal examination of all passengers they did not detect any of the banned classes. The passenger lines shipped steerage passengers again after the new law eased the threat of radical restrictions. Although the authorities did not prohibit the entry of Russian Jews, it let shipping companies know that long quarantine periods would be imposed on ships carrying Russians because reports indicated that cholera persisted in the region. HAPAG and the NGL, eager to maximize

[58]William E. Chandler, "Shall Immigration be Suspended?" *North American Review*, CLVI, No. 1 (1893), 3; and *New York Times*, 1 December 1892.

[59]These asked for name, age, sex, marital status, occupation, literacy, nationality, physical and mental health, last residence, seaport of landing, final destination, whether in possession of a ticket to that destination, who paid the passage, whether in possession of money (if so, whether if it was over US $30), whether joining a relative (if so, name and address), whether ever in the US, in prison or almshouse and whether under contract to perform labour. DC, *Report*, XXXVII, 39; GAR, HAL, 318.04, Passage, 221-226, letter, 26 July 1894; and 318.02, Directors, 112-121, letter, 11 September 1894.

their capacity after months of inactivity, evaded the restrictions. The HAL followed suit, informing its American agents that while it could not risk assisting Russians travelling to Rotterdam, those who reached the port on their own would be transported. The RSL leaked this circular, prompting the HAL to cancel all Russian prepaid tickets and to make a great effort to convince the US authorities not to make a case of it. The line nonetheless continued to transport small groups of Russians.[60] Despite the new impositions, shipping companies found ways to evade them and were only obstructed by inter-firm rivalries.

The interference of American officials at European ports triggered instant complaints about their arbitrariness. The HAL denounced American consul Walter E. Gardner for overcharging the company for the issuance of certificates for which a rate had not been fixed. Subsequently, the government set rates of US $2.50 per bill of health, certificate of disinfection and certified passenger list, which included the costs for the inspection and disinfection service. The consul also received twenty-five cents for each certified passenger manifest which contained thirty or more names.[61] Nevertheless, complaints that consuls overcharged and imposed unwarranted controls to enrich themselves persisted. The HAL also denounced Dr. W. Woodward for his exaggerated zeal during health inspections, claiming that he and other doctors were inclined to refuse more people than they should in order to justify their function. For instance, Woodward extended the area designated as infected by cholera to the Austro-Hungarian Empire while doctors in Antwerp and Bremen did not. The extra inconvenience and cost generated by the five-day quarantine represented an important competitive handicap. Attempts by the HAL to gain Woodward's favour through presents and special favours failed. To prevent such arbitrariness, shipping lines offered to build special quarantine and disinfection facilities in New York so that all companies would be screened on the same basis, but local officials did not favour such installations. Similar control stations were being built on the eastern border of Germany because the sharp rise of illegal crossings by Russian Jews during the cholera outbreak had exposed the inability of the authorities to regulate migration. To protect their interests, the NGL and HAPAG covered the costs to manage border control stations where baggage was disinfected and passengers screened for diseases and compliance with the other US requirements for entry.[62]

---

[60]GAR, HAL, 318.04, Passage, 221-226, letters, 10, 27 and 31 March, and 7, 10, 20, 21 and 24 April 1893.

[61]When the number of manifests exceeded ten, only ten cents was charged for each addition.

[62]GAR, HAL, 318.04, Passage, 221-226, letters 21 January, 21 and 24 April, 5 May, 31 July and 22 August 1893; and Würstenbecker, "Hamburg," 224-234.

The continual complaints by the shipping companies led to a congressional investigation. Some consuls, including Gardner, were discharged for overcharging the companies. The HAL deplored this because it had finally established a good working relationship with Gardner who intended to take up his old job as a journalist in the US and had reached an agreement with the HAL to lobby against proposals to increase consular interference.[63] Together with George Glavis, Gardner voiced the shipping line's main objections against such measures as formulated by van den Toorn:

> ...measures that will fail in their purpose and expose the US to the danger of getting rebuked by foreign nations for an attempt to establish certain powers in foreign countries entirely against the principal of International Law, and what is infinitely worse, will make the US morally responsible for the many acts of cruelty and injustice on those, who by emigrating to the land of the free, intend to better their condition, and were prevented from doing so, not by the laws which the United States have the perfect right to enact for their protection, but by well meant, but ill-considered acts of an US official, who of necessity cannot be competent to be accuser, jury, judge and even Supreme Court all at once.[64]

Due continuing complaints by shipping companies about the arbitrariness of health inspectors, the system was finally changed. The consuls still supervised the medical inspections, but these were again done by the shipping lines.[65] When rumours of cholera outbreaks re-emerged, as in 1894, 1899, 1905 and 1909, New York health inspectors were sent to European ports to supervise the observance of the five-day quarantine periods. Shipping companies took charge of the quarantine and disinfection procedures dictated by American law.[66]

---

[63]Gardner's appointment was short-lived as other shipping companies refused to share the costs. GAR, HAL, 318.04, Passage, 221-226, letters, 19 May, 12 August and 16, 17 and 23 October 1893; 318.02, Directors, letter, 11 September 1893; and *New York Times*, 12 March, 29 June and 2 August 1893.

[64]*Ibid.*, 318.02, Directors, letter, 8 August 1894.

[65]*Ibid.*, letters, 11 November and 22 December 1893.

[66]Dr. Dotty advised shipping companies on extra measures to be taken on board and at the port when the threat of an epidemic disease loomed. Although not a legal imposition, shipping companies complied as much as possible and built up a good relation with him. Same went for Dr. Arthur Thomas, who was sent to Rotterdam. In

In a Presidential message at the end of 1893, President Cleveland stated that a new treaty with Turkey claimed that "the right to exclude any or all classes of aliens is an attribute of sovereignty."[67] Simultaneously, the opening of the first German border control stations in the hands of HAPAG and the NGL, as well as proposals for new laws prohibiting migrant agents from representing foreign shipping companies on German soil, show that at the turn of the century the US was not alone in considering immigration and migrant transport as national rather than international matters. This tendency would be reinforced in Europe in the decades that followed. Shipping interests would continue to play an important role in shaping transatlantic migration policies. For example, due to strong international protests backed by the shipping lines, the German law passed in 1897 did not impede agents from representing foreign lines. Yet it made an exception for Dutch lines, excluding the HAL from selling steerage tickets in Germany, mainly for assisting its passengers in circumventing the laws regarding military duties. Also, at the insistence of the shipping lobby, most of the American remote border controls implemented in the wake of the cholera scare were listed. They hampered the attempts of Senator William J. Stone (D-KY) to gain passage of a law extending the authority of consuls to issue individual immigration certificates. The Secretary of State and the Secretary of the Treasury supported the idea but believed that the consular corps was too understaffed to carry out the inspections, preferring instead to delegate the responsibility for refusing excludables to the transportation companies. By doing this, they avoided international complications for granting consuls authority over non-citizens on foreign soil.[68] Increasing the pressure on steamship companies by increasing the costs of carrying undesirables became "the" regulatory policy.

Migration as a Lobby Issue

As Claudia Goldin has observed, the perplexing thing about the history of immigration restriction in the US is that it took so long to close the gates. During the Progressive Era, bills requiring literacy tests passed either the House or the Senate no fewer than seventeen times without becoming law. In the meantime, seventeen million migrants, most from eastern and southern Europe, landed in

---

1900, American authorities required the purchase of new disinfection machines which worked with steam instead of the sulphur used by Europeans. *Ibid.*, Directors, 112-121, letters, 6 October 1891, 10 October 10 and 27 November 1899, 27 January and 6 April 1900, 1 August 1902, 5, 11 and 29 September and 27 December 1905, 18 April 1907, 27 August 27 and 1 September 1909, and 30 June 1911.

[67]Hutchinson, *Legislative History*, 109-110.

[68]*Ibid.*, 112; and Higham, *Strangers in the Land*, 101.

the US. Goldin examined the influence of the foreign-born population in each state, economic fluctuations and the actions of the various interest groups (labour unions, capitalists, immigrants and agriculturalists) on the voting behaviour of congressmen on this issue. She ascribes the absence of radical restrictions before World War I to shifting political interests, generally favourable economic times and sheer luck.[69] Yet because she did not differentiate within the capitalist group, Goldin overlooked an important sub-lobby which played a key role in opposing restrictive measures. Prescott Hall, the secretary of the IRL, noted that "this test has already been adopted by the commonwealth of Australia and by British Colombia, and would have certainly been adopted here long since but for the opposition of the transportation companies." [70]

The role of steamship companies in obstructing immigration restrictions may have been exaggerated by the IRL. Depicting business as interfering with national welfare was a popular way to gain support in the Progressive Era. Nevertheless, the IRL's constant reference to the shipping lobby as its main opponent has strong factual roots. The influence of shipping on American migrant transport laws was pointed to by Maldwyn Jones and Aristide Zolberg, but it reached much further than they believed. The cartel among passenger lines enhanced collaboration in defending common interests. The shipping lobby expanded its activity once federal authorities tightened their grip over migration and foreign diplomats proved reluctant to intervene on behalf of the migrants. This happened while party politics declined and important institutional changes materialized, offering new means for interest groups to influence policy.[71] How the lines reacted to these, mobilized public opinion and organized lobbying campaigns against restrictions will be discussed here. At the same time, the influence of the IRL, which too often has been boiled down to a failure to impose the literacy test prior to 1917, will be reassessed.

Yet the hand of the shipping lobby was notable in another area. Perhaps even more astonishing than the tardy attempts to restrict immigration is that policies to reverse the decline of the American merchant marine during the

---

[69]Claudia Goldin, "The Political Economy of Immigration Restriction in the United States, 1890-1921," in Claudia Goldin and Gary D. Libecap (eds.), *The Regulated Economy: A Historical Approach to Political Economy* (Chicago, 1994), 223-252.

[70]Prescott F. Hall, "Selection of Immigration," *Annals of the American Academy of Political and Social Science*, XXIV, No. 2 (1904), 183; and NAW, RINS, 51762/1, Immigration Restriction League, circular "Literacy Test: Why It Should Be Adopted?" 1916.

[71]Jones, "Aspects of North Atlantic Migration," 326; Gabriel Kolko, *The Triumph of Conservatism: A Reinterpretation of American History, 1900-1916* (Chicago, 1963; reprint, Chicago, 1977), *passim*; Tichenor, *Dividing Lines*, 45-47; Zolberg, "Archaeology," 195-220; and Zolberg, *Nation by Design*, 99-125.

steamship era were only adopted during the New Deal in the 1930s. Neither the Spanish-American War nor the formation of the International Merchant Marine moved Congress to alter its passive policy and revive the US fleet. This failure occurred despite the fact that two presidents supported ship subsidies.[72] But foreigners dominated the lucrative migrant trade and went to great lengths to keep it that way. Their opposition to laws favouring American ships sheds more light on the composition of the shipping lobby and the things it stood for.

Maritime Policies and the Division of the Shipping Lobby

Once European governments stopped pressuring the US to reach an international migrant transport agreement, the intervention by Dutch diplomats on behalf of the HAL diminished. The imposition of stricter controls on the observance of the Passenger Act in 1887 underline: the company now relied on lawyer Philip J. Joachimsen and former New Jersey governor Leon Abbett to defend its interests before the courts and the Treasury Department. At US $50 per excess passenger, and with captains risking six-month imprisonments, the law had important repercussions. For instance, when *Edam* arrived with fifty-eight excess passengers, the HAL had to post a bond of US $2500 as bail for the release of Captain Taat and was assessed a US $2900 fine. Van den Toorn reassured the directors that prison sentences were never imposed and that by making arrangements with the district attorney the fine would be greatly reduced or dropped. Nevertheless, the proceedings were time consuming, and the lawyer's fees weighed on the budget. While this pushed the HAL to make a greater effort to refit its ships to conform to American laws, it did not stop the carriage of excess passengers. Van den Toorn entrusted the new cases to George Glavis, who he described as "the lobbyist of the Conference Lines knowing all the inside tracks." The attorney, based in the *Washington Post* building, charged less and could pull more strings. He became the spokesman in Washington for the HAL, the NGL and HAPAG, but also for other cargo lines trading with continental Europe. The British lines for their part relied on Mr. Sandford to defend their interests, although on some issues both lobbyists collaborated. Finally, the International Navigation Company (INC), which managed the Red Star Line (RSL) and the American Line (AL) hired their own lobbyist because of the divergent interests of its American owners in US migration and maritime policies. The conferences regrouping the continental and British lines had to keep their lobbying efforts secret from the RSL and the

---

[72]Vivian Vale, *The American Peril: Challenge to Britain on the North Atlantic, 1901-04* (Manchester, 1984), 51.

AL, both of which tried to obtain support from the American government to the detriment of foreign lines.[73]

Post-Civil War US maritime policies aimed at protecting shipbuilders by preventing foreign-built ships from registering under the American flag. This policy disadvantaged American shipowners, who were forced to buy domestically built ships and hire American crews which increased the cost by thirty percent compared to Europeans. Moreover, the US authorities did not associate their military needs with the merchant marine as much as European governments did. This contributed to the decline of the American merchant marine on the North Atlantic: just before the Civil War, the US fleet transported two-thirds of American trade, but only one-third by 1866 and sixteen percent by 1881.[74] The INC's attempt to reposition the American flag on the North Atlantic did not receive the anticipated support from a Congress which remained indifferent to the lobbying campaigns for ship subsidies. It also failed to get any preferential treatment from the Postmaster General who entrusted American mail to the fastest line regardless of the nationality of the ship. In 1887, the INC lost its British mail subsidies during the takeover of the Inman Line and saw the Belgian subsidies for the RSL reduced.[75] This pushed Clement Griscom, the manager of the INC, to lobby in the press for government assistance. In Congress, Senator William Frye (R-ME) led the campaign that resulted in the Postal Aid Act of 1891. The first piece of legislation to aid the merchant marine in thirty-two years, it empowered the Postmaster General to give mail subsidies to American citizens operating a line with American-built, owned and officered ships. The United States Navy (USN) would supervise the construction of these vessels to guarantee their usefulness for military purposes.[76]After pushing for some amendments, Griscom managed to register the Inman Line's ships under the American flag, and he committed to constructing two equivalent vessels at American shipyards. His twenty years of lobbying finally paid off when he obtained a subsidy of US $12,000 per voyage for

---

[73]GAR, HAL, 318.02, Directors, 112-121, letters 24 May 1887; 10 April, 4 May, 13 and 26 June and 7 September 1888; and 318.04, Passage, 221-226, letters, 24 October 1892 and 16 October 1893.

[74]Jeffrey J. Safford, "The Decline of the American Merchant Marine, 1850-1914: An Historiographical Appraisal," in Lewis R. Fischer and Gerald E. Panting (eds.), *Change and Adaptation in Maritime History: The North Atlantic Fleets in the Nineteenth Century* (St. John's, 1985), 58-61.

[75]William H. Flayhart III, *The American Line, 1872-1902* (New York, 2000), 31-36 and 126-127; and BGRA, I 215, 4056, correspondence, 1877; and I 215, 4054, 4059, convention for a service to New York, 10 March 1887.

[76]GAR, HAL, 318.02, Directors, letter, 10 April 1888.

these steamers.[77] Simultaneously, Griscom renegotiated the RSL's contract with the Belgian authorities. The government withdrew the direct subsidy but continued to give full "moral" support, including reductions on railroad fares, special rail connections to Paris, Basel and Cologne, the use of train stations to sell tickets, compensation for the carriage of mail and the like. Only half the fleet had to remain under the Belgian flag, while the a contract for an indefinite term could be ended by either party with three- months' notice. On the one hand, this gave Griscom the freedom to increase lobbying in Congress while also obtaining subsidies for the RSL's ships. On the other hand, the INC's manager could now threaten to move the line to a rival port as a means of acquiring favours from the Belgian authorities.[78]

The patriotic celebrations for the launching of *St. Louis* and *St. Paul* reflected the emergent feelings of Americanism at the close of the nineteenth century. The ships gave additional credibility to American jingoist pretensions, yet US naval power still lagged far behind many other nations. The INC used this argument to receive more support to the detriment of its foreign rivals. For instance, the INC lobbied to abolish the exemption from tonnage dues based on the most favoured nation treaties concluded with Germany and the Netherlands to divert trade to Antwerp. The issue received consideration in Congress because of the new tariffs that would have obstructed American imports proposed in the German *Reichstag*. The INC also used the commotion to gain advantages over the HAL. Van den Toorn reported that Griscom organized fancy dinners with congressmen and distributed free transatlantic passages for their families. The HAL's head agent arranged with Glavis and Weckherlin to oppose new tariffs among congressmen and the Secretary of Agriculture. He contacted Standard Oil which with its line of oil tankers on the Rotterdam route was directly concerned with the issue. Having a Standard Oil representative on the INC's board of directors proved useful. The next day James Wright, the INC's vice president, visited van den Toorn to deny the company's involvement as that would be against the spirit of the continental conference. Nonetheless, help from INC's lobbyist to oppose the bill was refused, quite logically according to van den Toorn, since he was the one who introduced it. Meanwhile the HAL refused, as in previous cases, to pay twenty-five to fifty percent of HAL's recuperated tariffs and taxes which Glavis was able to prove had been falsely charged. The HAL believed that Glavis was earning enough. To retaliate and show his power, the lobbyist failed to intervene on

---

[77]*Ibid.*, letters, 29 January and 6 May 1892; and Flayhart, *American Line*, 133-136.

[78]This strategy was used to make improvements to the infrastructure in Antwerp, building a dry dock, enlarging and deepening the Westerscheldt, acquiring new icebreakers, etc. BGRA, I 215, 4068, contract between the RSL and the Belgian government, 1892; letters, 12 August and 21 November 1892; and report, 1893.

two occasions when the new tariff bill was discussed in Congress and passed the House. Together with HAPAG's head agent, Emil Boas, van den Toorn travelled to Washington to lobby politicians. He came to terms with Glavis who arranged to contribute US $5000 to the campaign funds of both the Republican and Democratic parties if the Senate Committee on Tariffs made a negative recommendation on the bill. The costs were divided based on pool participation, amounting to US $735 for the HAL, $2085 for HAPAG and $2180 for the NGL. If the law was not reported out of the committee or did not pass, another US $3000 would be donated. Van den Toorn admitted that this created a dangerous precedent but fortunately the composition of the parties changed frequently. The adoption of new tariffs by the German *Reichstag* made the scheme fall apart and led to the abolition of exemptions from tonnage dues for German ships. The HAL still retained its most favourite nation privilege for Dutch ships.[79]

The tariff issue illustrates the venal atmosphere in Washington where congressional votes and reports were up for sale to replenish campaign funds for upcoming elections. It also shows the opportunities that special committees offered to influence legislation and the importance of Glavis as a mediator. Finally, it highlights the limitations of the conferences in harmonizing the interests of its members. The lines tried to obtain benefits from their national governments to gain competitive advantages against one another, which often created tensions. The HAL, depending on German legislation for the transit of its passengers and on American laws to land them, found itself in a weak position because other members did not depend on Dutch policies for migrant or cargo traffic. In Europe, the HAL joined forces with the INC to protest against German regulations obstructing their business.[80] The tendency to pass measures regulating migrant transport which favoured the national merchant marine over its foreign competitors was gaining ground in Europe. The British passenger acts prevented foreign lines from boarding steerage passengers westbound, while HAPAG and the NGL gained favours through the border control stations and the migration law of 1897. Italy, Greece, Russia, Austria and Hungary all followed suit after the turn of the century. Yet no European gov-

[79]Flayhart, *American Line*, 173-193; and GAR, HAL, 318.02, Directors, letters, 21 January, 14 and 28 February, 24 March, 3 April 3, 16 and 19 June and 4 December 1896.

[80]Van den Toorn used all possible means to maintain a good relationship with Griscom. When *St. Louis* saved all the passengers from the doomed *Veendam*, he urged the Dutch government to give Griscom a medal. Weckherlin, however. opposed honouring a man who had nearly robbed the country of its most favoured nation status. Van den Toorn badly needed Griscom's support at the next pool meeting and believed that the decoration would help; it was granted a few days later. GAR, HAL, 318.02, Directors, letters, 25 November 1897 and 11 and 15 March 1898.

ernment could favour its merchant marine by such measures as much as the United States. For instance, the INC backed a proposal in 1896 to increase the head tax for passengers landed by foreign ships to US $10 which would have given American ships a crucial advantage.[81] Avoiding this was a *sine qua non* for the foreign lines, which closed ranks in opposition. This explains the division in the shipping lobby in the US.

The increasing international tensions caused jingoism to supersede nativism as the most aggressive expression of late nineteenth-century nationalism in the US. Yet, as Sheryl Shanks observed, defending and controlling the borders fused into the issue of American sovereignty, a topic to which immigration restrictionists would increasingly appeal to defend their cause.[82] In the wake of the New Orleans lynching of Italians, diplomatic tensions between the US and Italy almost led to an armed conflict. A near conflict with Chile and Great Britain followed for seemingly unimportant motives.[83] Spain was next in line, and as van den Toorn wrote regarding the Cuba crisis:

> I believe that the odds for a war between both countries are very plausible if Spain does not act more wisely then the US Congress. The Americans take a pleasure in interfering with matters that do not concern them. If it wouldn't have such negative consequences for us, I wouldn't mind someone to teach them a serious lesson. Since the US acquired some war-vessels the "war party" has been reinforced and if a second or third rate opponent can be found, I am afraid a conflict will follow.[84]

The Republican Party made the revival of the merchant marine a plank in its platform in 1897. The bills in the previous session imposing a head tax of US $10 or an extra duty on all goods imported by foreign ships failed to get out of the committees. The proposals entailed negotiating thirty-three treaties with other nations robbed of their reciprocity clauses. Out of fear of retaliation, the Commissioner of Navigation, Eugene Chamberlin, who favoured

---

[81]*Ibid.*, 318.04, Passage, 221-226, letter, 23 May 1896.

[82]Shanks, *Immigration*, 39.

[83]Higham, *Strangers in the Land*, 75-76. Van den Toorn claimed that the subsidy lobby staged the threat of a potential conflict with Chile to obtain support for its cause. GAR, HAL, 318.04, Passage, 221-226, letters, 29 January and 6 May 1892, 16 June 1896, 5 and 18 March 1897 and 25 February 1898.

[84]GAR, HAL, 318.04, Passage 221-226, letter, 22 November 1896.

the revival of the merchant marine, did not support the bills.[85] Yet after the Republicans' electoral victory, Glavis reported on a "kind of love feast" in the Senate among representatives of American shipping interests, among whom were Griscom, Charles H. Cramp, Alfred Vanderbilt, Senators Mark Hanna (R-OH), William Frye (R-ME), George Perkins (R-CA), Stephen Elkins (R-WV) and Lodge. They inserted a plank in the Republican national platform for mail subsidies or tonnage bounties favouring American ships.[86] The foreign shipping lobby tried to obstruct this by lobbying for the appointment of free trade advocates to key positions. Glavis tried unsuccessfully to have Chamberlin replaced as Commissioner of Navigation.[87] Nonetheless, during the build up to the Spanish-American War Congress failed to alter US maritime policy.

The conflict laid bare the shortcomings of American maritime and naval policy. Initially, the USN relied as much as possible on ships owned by the American Line, Atlantic Transport Line and coastal shipping companies.[88] Due to the lack of first-class steamships, it had to explore the market for foreign ships. Because of the urgency, the foreign lines had a unique opportunity to sell their ships at very good prices. The HAL joined in the fierce competition and managed to sell *Obdam* through Glavis. In consultation with the Dutch government, the company made the transaction through a third party to circumvent the neutrality provisions.[89] When the New York press enquired about a possible violation of neutrality, van den Toorn clearly disassociated the HAL from the sale: "so careful are we to observe our duties as neutrals, that shortly before the war, when we saw it was imminent, we refused to sell to the Span-

---

[85]*Ibid.*, letters, 24 March and 19 June 1896, and 7 May and 23 July 1897; and *New York Times*, 10 December 1896.

[86]The shipbuilder of *St. Louis* and *St. Paul*, Charles Cramp, would receive more orders if the bill passed. The complete list of people present at the meeting: E.C. Bliss (Red D Line), Henry Prosper Booth (Ward Line) William P. Clyde (Clyde Shipping Co.), Frank J. Firth and C.H. Keep (Lake Carriers Association), Collis P. Huntington (shipbuilder), Thomas W. Hyde (shipbuilder) and Sumner Sewell (shipbuilder). GAR, HAL, 318.04, Directors, 221-226, letter, 19 April 1897; and *New York Times*, 8 April 1897.

[87]*Ibid.*, letter, 1 December 1897.

[88]The Atlantic Transport Line was founded by Bernard Baker in collaboration with the Pennsylvania and Baltimore and Ohio railroads. It operated a line between Liverpool and Baltimore, branching off to New York in 1891 when it began a passenger service. Flayhart, *American Line*, 277; and Vale, *American Peril*, 33-35.

[89]The HAL received US $230,000 for its old steamer after deducting Glavis' commission of US $20,000. GAR, HAL, 318.02, General Correspondence, 112-121, letters, 7 March, 15, 19 and 21 April, and 1, 10, 21 and 27 June 1897.

ish government, which wished to purchase ships from us."[90] Of course, careful listeners understood that he was really contrasting the actions of the HAL with those of the NGL and HAPAG, both of which did sell ships to Spain, thereby added to the growing anti-German sentiment in the US. The Dutch line hoped to capitalize on these feelings to attract more of the American travelling public.

With the end of the Spanish-American War, the US came into possession of Puerto Rico and the Philippines, and enjoyed almost complete hegemony over Cuba, thereby increasing the importance of the national merchant marine. Griscom pushed for more subsidies because the American Line, unlike other companies, had failed to pay dividends since the passage of the 1891 Postal Aid Bill, underling the unprofitability of an American-registered line. To meet the speed requirements in the contract, ships were pushed to the limit and broke down or were wrecked more often. Further, the subsidy did not compensate for the extra cost of sailing under the American flag. Moreover, Griscom urgently needed capital to modernize the fleet. This led him to J.P. Morgan who, speculating on congressional approval of important subsidies, prepared an ambitious plan to buy his way into the steel and shipping industries in order to create a transatlantic vertical merger. A growing number of capitalists started to speculate on the passage of the ship subsidy bill and joined Griscom's lobbying campaign. Similar bills were introduced in the House and Senate by Representative Sereno Payne (R-NY) and Senator Frye, respectively. If they passed and Vanderbilt had succeeded in taking over the HAL, he could have benefitted from an annual subsidy of US $1,000,000.[91]

Yet the HAL's owners showed no interests in being taken over. Together with HAPAG and to a lesser extent the NGL, the Dutch line prepared a strategy to oppose the bill. But the unexpected death of Glavis created an important vacuum in Washington. The lobbyist had also been on the payroll of the British lines, as the visit to New York of Bruce Ismay, president of White Star Line (WSL), to appoint a successor illustrates. The British and continental lines' interests usually coincided, yet both groups still tended to organize separate lobby campaigns. The continental lines asked Joseph Senner, former Commissioner of Immigration hired to agitate the popular press against immigration restrictions, to shape public opinion against ship subsidies. To lead the campaign in the press and Congress, HAPAG, the NGL and the HAL appointed John de Witt Warner, a member of the Reform Club. Under the guise of the Reform Club, foreign shipping lines that could not oppose the laws openly

---

[90]*New York Evening Post*, 25 June 1898.

[91]GAR, HAL, 318.02, General Correspondence, 112-121, letter, 23 August 1898 and 11 and 24 1899; Flayhart, *American Line*, 259 and 289-315; Thomas R. Navin and Marion V. Sears, "A Study in Merger: Formation of the International Mercantile Marine Company," *Business History Review*, XXVIII, No. 4 (1954), 302; and Vale, *American Peril*, 44.

found a cover to voice their protests. To divide Congress the campaign centred on portraying the bill as a scheme of eastern industrialists to centralize all transportation facilities and extend their control over southern and western states. If subsidies were granted, the two biggest eastern railroads could acquire an important advantage over southern and western railroads. The shipping lobby mobilized the latter to agitate against the bill in their states and to pressure their congressmen. Warner provided articles to journals, newspapers and magazines, and the majority took his side. He scorned the annual conferences of labour unions and manufacturers. Instead, he approached congressmen and found strong allies in Senators Alexander S. Clay (D-GA), Henry M. Teller (D-CO), Benjamin R. Tillman (D-SC) and James K. Jones (D-AR). The lobbyist provided them with amendments to weaken the bills or with arguments for filibustering sessions in Congress to prevent action at all. In the drive to influence congressmen he was helped by the Congressional Information Bureau, founded in 1897 by the lobbyist Claude N. Bennett, which published a daily newsletter about congressional activities relating to immigration and shipping. Bennett also prepared data for congressmen on these issues.[92]

By 1900, the bill still had not been brought to a vote in Congress. Nonetheless, the German lines stopped financing the lobbyist, claiming that the bill would not pass the next session and that Warner lacked the influence to prevent it if it did reach the floor. In contrast, the HAL praised Warner for his efficiency and moderate costs. The company covered all the costs for his services until 1902, and even then they paid Warner an extra bonus to make sure he would not leak their involvement to the press. The unusual disagreement between the HAL and HAPAG on lobbying strategies may have been influenced by Morgan's plans to monopolize the North Atlantic trade. The German companies had started to negotiate with the combine and perhaps did not want to compromise those talks. Moreover, the negotiations needed to remain secret so as not to compromise the passage of the bill. The trust-busting climate would kill the bill if the interests behind it were exposed, but as the talks dragged on, rumours, which the Reform Club gladly spread, appeared in the international press.[93] The basic agreement to establish the IMM was signed on

---

[92]GAR, HAL, 318.02, Directors, 112-121, letters, 17 and 21 February and 22 December 1899, 16 April 1900 and 23 December 1901; and *New York Times*, 1, 24 and 31 January and 6 February 1901. The Congressional Information Bureau still exists, and the current president, Bob Cazalas, provided useful information on the organization. See also *Marquis Who's Who* (1966), I, 84.

[93]GAR, HAL, 318.02, Directors, 112-121, letters, 7 March, 16 and 17 April and 16 November 1900, and 22 November and 23 December 1901; *New York Times*, 15 October and 17 November 1901, and 20 February 1902; and *New York Evening Post*, 22 November 1901.

4 February, leaving Morgan sixty days to make the deal official and for Congress to pass the ship subsidy bill.

His influential ally Mark Hanna, the chairman of the Republican Party who was renowned for his innovative propaganda campaigns, made sure that the bill passed the Senate. Morgan stayed in Washington using all possible means to get the bill approved by the House before mid-April. The Democrats had taken a clear stand against the bill, yet they played only a secondary role because the Republicans had majorities in both the House and the Senate. Yet the vote in Senate, where six prominent Republicans voted against the bill, showed that the party did not close ranks on the subject. Western Republicans in particular voiced their discontent because they feared electoral repercussions. The fierce struggle over the Cuban tariff question had increased the division between eastern and western members of the party, who were disinclined to risk a further split over ship subsidies. Charles Grosvenor (R-OH), chairman of the House Committee on the Merchant Marine and Fisheries and an outspoken advocate of the bill, did not find an opportunity to enact it. David Henderson (R-IA), Speaker of the House, killed the bill by prioritizing other matters. When the enormity of Morgan's US $170,000,000 shipping trust was made official, defending the idea of granting taxpayers' money to it became impossible.[94] In various speeches, President Roosevelt suggested amending the constitution to put restraints on trusts and combinations. As the *New York Times* observed, "It is, we think, increasingly improbable that after having signed a bill authorizing the Attorney General to take the trust bull by the horns, President Roosevelt would sign another bill instructing the Secretary of Treasury to increase the animal's ration."[95] Griscom and Morgan's aspirations to build a fleet under the national flag received a terrible blow. The subsequent signing of an agreement with the British authorities to retain their subsidies took away many of the IMM's incentives to press for concessions favouring American ships. Maritime policies would not change up to World War I, thereby leaving the migrant transport business to European lines.

Lobby Campaigns for and Against Immigration Restrictions

Migration became one of the topics of social reform during the Progressive Era during which the close ties between business and government were consolidated despite being contested. As Gary Freeman has noted, "immigration

[94]Flayhart, *American Line*, 338-342; Navin and Sears, "Study in Merger," 316; Neuman, "Qualitative Migration Controls," 321; *New York Times*, 24 January 1900; 21 and 24 November 1901; 17 and 22 January, 5, 8, 11, 12, 13, 14, 15, 18 and 21 March, 7, 20 and 21 April and 7 December 1902; and 19 and 24 February 1903; and GAR, HAL, 318.02, Directors, 112-121, letter, 14 March 1902.

[95]*New York Times*, 26 November 1902.

tends to produce concentrated benefits and diffuse costs, giving those who benefit from immigration greater incentives to organize than persons who bare its costs."[96] Among those that benefited from immigration, none did so as directly as passenger lines. Although splits within the conferences and American maritime policies divided the passenger shipping lobby, all sub-groups built on the industry's efforts dating back to the first half of the nineteenth century to prevent authorities to interfere with their main source of revenue. As the federal government gained control over immigration, the shipping lobby increased its activities in Washington. As part of this shift, Congress acquired a growing number of responsibilities and gradually began to rely on lobbyists to collect information. By the turn of the century, lobbyists invaded Washington *en masse*, becoming the main source of information for congressmen and congressional committees to decide on what and how to vote. For exceptional issues, special investigation commissions received appropriations to collect information and recommend legislation. The Senate and House immigration committees processed the bills and could kill them by keeping the bill from reaching the floor, but when they reported on a bill it usually formed the basis for action. These committees became the battlefield for restrictionist and pro-immigration lobbyists. Both sides stirred up constituents to put pressure on legislators through mail or press campaigns.[97] The impact of the lobby is hard to measure, yet the strategies used by the continental lines show that shipping companies had a strong foothold in Washington by the time the IRL opened its office on Capitol Hill.

Glavis distributed anti-restriction arguments among congressmen and organized the hearings of the pro-immigration lobby before the appropriate committees. When it seemed likely that a restrictionist law would pass, the lobby stalled it either by introducing amendments, bringing up other issues, filibustering or claiming the need for more information. If these tactics failed, the lines push congressmen to weaken the bill as much as possible. Glavis provided congressmen with amendments which safeguarded the interests of steamship companies. In the early 1890s, van den Toorn frequently attributed last-minute amendments to the efforts of the lobbyist, preventing, for instance, the adoption of the remote border control system. At the expense of the shipping

---

[96]Gary P. Freeman, "Modes of Immigration Politics in Liberal Democratic States," *International Migration Review*, XXIX, No. 4 (1995), 894.

[97]Elisabeth S. Clemens, *The People's Lobby: Organizational Innovation and the Rise of Interest Group Politics in the United States, 1890-1925* (Chicago, 1997), 30; Filene, "Obituary," 20-26; Edward B. Logan and Simon N. Patten, "Lobbying," *Annals of the American Academy of Political and Social Science*, CXLIV, No. 1 (1929), 56-60; Richard L. McCormick, "The Discovery that Business Corrupts Politics: A Reappraisal of the Origins of Progressivism," *American Historical Review*, LXXXVI, No. 2 (1981), 247-274; and Tichenor, *Dividing Lines*, 28-40.

lines, the lobbyist organized fancy dinners, distributed gifts and free first-class passages to Europe. Shipping interests also financed the election campaigns of friendly Republicans and Democrats. For example, when it seemed likely that Republicans would take control of the House and Senate in 1894, the HAL followed the NGL's example and contributed to their campaign fund. Much more could be obtained before the elections than when politicians were in office. During the subsequent presidential elections, the NGL, HAPAG and the HAL channelled US $5000 through Glavis to the Republican and Democrat campaign funds to prevent the passage of a literacy test for migrants and a differential tariff discriminating against foreign lines.[98]

As congressional missions to investigate the situation in Europe became common, the shipping lobby made sure someone defending their interests travelled with the party. For instance, when Weber investigated the feasibility of consular involvement in the migration process and the role of shipping companies as instigators of emigration, Charles Semsey of the New York Hungarian Association travelled along. Having an interest in the emigration of compatriots and contacts with the shipping companies, Semsey was committed to defending the interests of the latter. On the next mission, Glavis accompanied Assistant Secretary of State Oliver Spaulding and influenced his report.[99] The shipping lines also appointed a committee that screened the press for negative articles; the industry then withdrew all advertisements from papers that openly attacked a shipping company. They hired journalists to respond to hostile articles and to collect and write propaganda for distribution by the migrant agents, some of who were newspaper editors. Whenever Congress debated the topic, the press campaigns intensified. The advertising money paid by shipping lines helped gain the favour of papers which, according to the IRL's Prescott Hall, were "more or less muzzled by steamship advertising."[100] When the Chandler Bill prohibiting immigration following the cholera scare was discussed in Congress, van den Toorn reported the following:

> The Eastern gutter press predicts that the law will pass while more serious papers don't mention it. The secret agitation of the shipping lines out of Washington targeting the western

---

[98]GAR, HAL, 318.02, General Correspondence, 112-121, letters, 3 October 1894 and 3 April 1896.

[99]*Ibid.*, letters, 7 July 1891 and 6 July 1892; and 318.04, Passage, 221-226, letter, 28 July 1892.

[100]Prescott F. Hall, "The Recent History of Immigration and Immigration Restriction," *Journal of Political Economy*, XXI, No. 8 (1913), 748; and GAR, HAL, 318.04, Passage, 221-226, letter, 28 October 1892. For the annual amounts spent by the HAL, see appendix seven.

> voters through local western papers triggered an important wave of protest against restrictions. Western Senators and Representatives will not dare to vote in favor of the Chandler Bill unless a new wave of cholera brakes out again.[101]

The restrictionist organizations, on the other hand, lacked continuity and were too tied up in party politics, as was the case with the Know Nothing Party and the American Protective Association. The IRL, on the contrary, transcended party politics to create a solid and lasting platform for restrictionists using direct means to influence policymakers. The IRL brought together a group of upper-class academics, businessmen and politicians who considered the growing influx of new immigrants a threat to the nation's Anglo-Saxon character. Building on the work of Mayo-Smith and Bemis, the IRL openly expressed its xenophobic sentiments about the influx of Italians, Slavs and Jews. It claimed that the US could no longer safely assimilate these mass of migrants which it stigmatized as physically and mentally inferior and having a greater tendency towards criminality and pauperism. Moreover, they lowered American working and living conditions, slowed the natural growth of the US population and corrupted American institutions. The IRL quickly adopted the literacy test as its preferred tool to limit the influx.[102]

The IRL's main contribution was the use of new strategies to obtain policy changes. It used the same means as the shipping lobby to influence policymakers and public opinion. A screening of the American press produced a list of 500 papers willing to propagate their restrictionist ideals. Members organized speeches and distributed pamphlets claiming that the American "race" and its institutions were at stake. The IRL's close ties with the academic world contributed to the extensive use of scientific arguments to substantiate its claims and its active participation in the academic debate.[103] The league opened

---

[101]GAR, HAL, 318.04, Passage, 221-226, letter, 5 January 1893.

[102]Tichenor, *Dividing Lines*, 16-17 and 76; Chandler, "Shall Immigration Be Suspended?" 1-8; Prescott F. Hall, "Immigration and the Educational Test," *North American Review*, CLXV, No. 4 (1897), 393-402; Hall, "Selection of Immigration," 169-184;, Lodge, "Restriction." 602-612; and Noble, "Present State," 232-241.

[103]The "academic" battle between the liberalists and the destructionists is nicely illustrated be a series of articles in the *North American Review*. See, for example, Hall, "Immigration and the Educational Test" as a reaction to Simon Greenleaf Croswell, "Should Immigration be Restricted?" *North American Review*, CLXIV, No. 4 (1897), 526-536; Hall's "Italian Immigration," *North American Review*, CLXIII, No. 2 (1896), 252-254, vs. Joseph H. Senner, "Immigration from Italy," *North American Review*, CLXII, No. 6 (1896), 649-657; or Robert de C. Ward, "The Restriction of Immigration," *North American Review*, CLXXIX, No. 2 (1904), 226-237, vs. O.P.

an office in Washington headed by James Patten who distributed information and proposals for laws to congressmen. With Patten's appointment the restrictionist movement finally had a lobbyist to counter the transport and corporate lobby. Patten coordinated the speeches for restrictions in the House and Senate immigration committees. With outspoken restrictionist members such as Representative Samuel McCall and Senators Lodge and Chandler, the IRL had an excellent set of mouthpieces for which Patten wrote proposals and devised campaign plans. Helped by the ongoing economic recession, which started in 1893, and by the dominance of Republicans in Congress, they managed to secure the passage of an education bill containing a literacy test by overwhelming majorities in 1896.[104] Van den Toorn feared that the bill was likely to become a law; "American politics are hard to predict because Congress, at least the Senate, at times looks more like a lunatic asylum than a deliberating institution. Cleveland is likely to approve the law shortly."[105] The bills were sent to a conference committee to harmonize them, and the final draft included even more drastic measures than what had been proposed.

After the formation of the IRL, the shipping lobby redoubled its efforts. In 1895, the HAL, HAPAG and the NGL together hired two Washington journalists who worked as correspondents for various prominent American newspapers at US $80 per week to agitate in favour of migration. The lines rewarded Glavis' efforts with a pay increase to US $9000 per year including expenses, but excluding his legal fees when he represented them in court. The NGL, HAPAG and the HAL divided the cost in proportion to the number of passengers carried.[106] When in early 1896 the education bill was being considered in Congress based on the report of an immigration commission formed by Senner, his assistant Edward McSweeny and Commissioner General of Immigration Herman Stump, Van den Toorn wrote that "knowing that more than 20% of last years' arrivals would not have passed this test says it all. Most illiterates are transported by the Continental lines therefore I urgently recommend that the three pool-lines organize a propaganda campaign against it."[107]

Austin, "Is the New Immigration Dangerous to the Country?" *North American Review*, CLXXVIII, No. 4 (1904), 558-570.

[104]Zeidel, *Immigrants*, 17; Higham, *Strangers in the Land*, 103-107; Hutchinson, *Legislative History*, 112-116; Tichenor, *Dividing Lines*, 76-81; and GAR, HAL, 318.02, Directors, 112-121, letter, 25 January 1895.

[105]GAR, HAL, 318.02, Directors, 112-121, letter, 22 December 1896.

[106]Twenty-five percent was to be paid by the cargo lines and seventy-five percent by the passenger lines. *Ibid.*, letters, 16 October 1893 and 17 July 1895.

[107]*Ibid.*, letter, 28 January 1896.

Most of the British lines, whose market mainly consisted of literate Scandinavian, Irish and British passengers, saw little harm in the test and fended off requests to contribute to the lobbying costs.[108] Even the NGL hesitated, fearing a new escalation of costs which already weighed heavily on its budget. But when speculations about the passage of the bill started to affect the company's stock, it joined with HAPAG and the HAL to order Glavis to lobby against it, especially in the southern and western states. The lobbyist also introduced amendments that weakened the bill, such as limiting the test to women.[109] The lines used their connections with newspapers and the agent network to mobilize ethnic groups and associations throughout the US to pressure their congressmen, as the cable of the H. Claussenius, the NGL's general agent for the west, to the migrant agents in that region illustrates: "Immigration bill comes up in House on Wednesday; wire your congressmen, our expense, protesting against proposed exclusion and requesting bill be defeated, informing him that vote in favor means defeat in next election."[110] The influential German press joined the campaign and were followed by other foreign language newspapers where ready-made petitions appeared for readers to send to their representatives. Congress was flooded with petitions against the bill, especially from German associations. With elections in the offing, such efforts affected congressmen.[111]

Unfortunately for the shipping companies, the NGL's cable fell into Lodge's hands. The Senator promptly exposed the involvement of the steamship lobby, compromising their campaign. Glavis saw his efforts to defeat the redrafted bill fail in the House, where it passed by a small margin early in 1897. To his regret, the bill was sent again to the Senate/House conference committee. Glavis did not want this because he had President Cleveland's guarantee to veto the bill as it stood and hoped that it would not be stripped of its most objectionable features. The lobby's inside man in the House was none other than the chairman of the Immigration Committee, Richard Bartholdt (R-

---

[108]The DC calculated that between 1899 and 1909, 35.6 percent of new immigrants would have been excluded but only 2.7 percent of the old stock. Homer Hoyt, "The Relation of the Literacy Test to a Constructive Immigration Problem," *Journal of Political Economy*, XXIV, No. 5 (1916), 447.

[109]GAR, HAL, 318.02, Directors 112-121, letters, 17 July 1895 and 14 February 1896; and 318.04, Passage, 221-226, letter, 15 January 1902.

[110]Harvard Open Collection Program, Immigration to the United States, 1789-1930, IRL circular 22, "Foreign Steamship Agitation against the Immigration Restriction Bill," 22 February 1897.

[111]Higham, *Strangers in the Land*, 104; Just, *Ost und südosteuropäische Amerikawanderung*, 224; and Henry Beardsell Leonard, *The Open Gates: The Protest against the Movement to Restrict European Immigration, 1896-1924* (New York, 1980), 25.

MO). Apart from the continuous support of John Fitzgerald (D-MA), Bartholdt became increasingly isolated and could not prevent a new report on the bill from passing the House with an overwhelming majority. The veto was at stake. Glavis found more support in the Senate, especially form Arthur Gorman (D-MD), who was renowned for defending the interests of big business.[112] The bill only passed the Senate by a small margin, giving the President the signal that a veto would not be overridden. Helped by the improving economic conditions which decreased the pressure for restrictions, Cleveland vetoed the bill. Although the House overrode it, the Senate took no further action, meaning that restrictionists would have to start from scratch.[113] The lines praised Glavis for his excellent work. For his part, Glavis told his employers that he had "some friends at his house, among them several senators and members of the Immigration Committee, including Senator Charles J. Faulkner (D-WV). Promises were given that nothing would be done regarding immigration during the extra session."[114]

With the near-passage of the bill and the election of the Republican William McKinley who seemed more receptive to the IRL's demands, Glavis doubted whether to continue his opposition and run the risk of having radical measures adopted or to collaborate with the advocates and weaken the literacy test as much as possible. He proposed trying to exempt women, the immediate families of admissible migrants and men under the age of twenty-one from the literacy test. Yet the high rate of illiterates gaining entry to the US and the thought that collaborating gave no guarantees that a stricter test would not be adopted later led the shipping lines to decide that prevention was better than the cure.[115] McKinley's appointment of Terence Powderly as Commissioner General of Immigration and the replacement of Bartholdt as chairman of the House Immigration Committee by Lorenzo Danford (R-OH) confirmed the need for new measures, as van den Toorn reported:

---

[112]Hutchinson, *Legislative History*, 119-121; Leonard, *Open Gates*, 14-19; GAR, HAL, 318.04, Passage, 221-226, letters, 17 and 29 January and 5, 8 and 12 February 1897; *New York Times*, 19 July 1894 and 22 January and 10 February 1897. Gorman's proposal for tariff revisions in 1894 generated a huge controversy and earned him the description as "not a Democrat, not a Republican and only in legal form a Senator being in reality simply an agent of the Sugar Trust and the iron and coal interests of the country."

[113]GAR, HAL, 318.04, Passage, 221-266, letters, 18 and 25 February and 7 March 1897; and 318.02, Directors, 112-121, letter, 26 February 1897.

[114]*Ibid.*, 318.02, Directors, 112-121, letter, 5 March 1897; and 318.04, Passage, 221-226, letters, 18 February and 7 and 12 March 1897.

[115]*Ibid.*, 318.04, Passage, 221-226, letters 3, 9 and 15 April and 1 May 1897.

> Nothing good can be expected of both men. Hoping that the ameliorating economic conditions will turn the public opinion in favor of immigration, to influence it and go up against the IRL, the HAPAG and NGL elaborated a plan to establish a Pro-Immigration League. Dr. Senner, journalist and former Commissioner of Immigration of New York has been appointed to lead the League and set up branches nationwide. He will travel throughout the country, hold lectures and recruit members, especially in the West. The membership fee of $1 will be let off to recruit as many as possible. To cover up their involvement, the League will distance itself completely of the steamship lines and even create the impression to oppose us. The expenses of Senner have to be defrayed and he reached an agreement with the German Lines who will pay him $500 a month from October first till April first and that for the subsequent twelve months his salary would amount to $2000 plus expenses not surpassing $3000...The Germans asked to contribute, yet not to mention it to any other lines out of fear that it may leak out.[116]

Contrary to what leading scholars have assumed, it was not the associations representing various ethnic and national groups but HAPAG, the NGL and the HAL that formed the cornerstone of the anti-IRL group.[117] Being unable to openly oppose legislation, shipping companies established contacts with various ethnic groups to fight the IRL on humanitarian grounds. HAPAG and the NGL first turned to the German-speaking community, not only because of its close affiliation with the restrictionists but also because of the weight this community had in American politics. With fifty years of service as the main carriers of goods and passengers between Germany and the US, HAPAG and the NGL had acquired a lot of influence in the German-American community. This explains why the strongest protest against the bill originated from an ethnic community which would hardly have suffered from it.[118] Due to their more recent arrival, Slavs and Italians, who were among the main targets of the bill, lacked the organization and political power required for a successful campaign.

---

[116]*Ibid.*, letter, 16 November 1897.

[117]Higham, *Strangers in the Land*, 107; Tichenor, *Dividing Lines*, 81; Zeidel, *Immigrants*, 12; and Zolberg, *Nation by Design*, 222.

[118]The *New York Times*, 7 January 1898, mentioned that the following associations, among others, supported the IPL: the North American Gymnastic Union, the German Roman Catholic Society of North America, the Arion, the United Singers of Brooklyn and the German Catholic Central Union of Michigan.

The American Jewish community, predominantly from Western Europe, was divided about the influx of poor co-religionists from Russia. Some of them feared that the new influx would lower their social status and hence tended to support restrictions. Yet slowly but surely the new communities joined this cross-ethnic, nonsectarian and nonpartisan organization baptized as the Immigration Protective League (IPL). The appointment as vice president of Oscar Straus, a prominent German Jew who managed Hirsch funds to integrate new arrivals in the US, illustrated the IPL's intentions to incorporate new groups. The IPL President, Bourke Cockran, had to attract support from his native Irish community.[119] As a result of their long record of service in the migrant business, the shipping lines developed strong ties through their migrant agent network with the different ethnic communities. They also forged close relations with the foreign-language press.

The Austrian-born Joseph Senner had the perfect profile to lead the propaganda campaign as the former editor of the *New York Staatszeitung* and former Commissioner of Immigration at Ellis Island who was instrumental in introducing the idea of the literacy test in Congress.[120] During his first years as Commissioner he was known for bringing the shipping lines into disrepute and hence was the ideal person to counter suspicions about the shipping lines' participation. Initially, Senner followed Weber's views to decrease the influx of undesirables by putting the financial responsibility for them on the shipping companies. He did not urge restrictions because he believed that the existing laws, especially the clause referring to "persons likely to become a public charge" afforded "great opportunity to use the greatest discretion and good judgment not only as to the individual seeking admission, but also bearing in mind the general conditions of this country."[121] Senner even wrote an article defending Italian immigrants based on the rigorous collection of statistical data, sharing the notion evoked by Eugene Schuyler of Italians as "a desirable element to fuse with our motley population bringing to us the logical qualities of the Latin race, and they show in the long run the effect of an experience which no other people in Europe has had – of over two thousand years of civi-

---

[119]Leonard, *Open Gates*, 3-7, 28 and 39.

[120]Senner also was at some stage the vice-president of the *Liedekranz*, the president of the German-American journalists' organization and of the German Social Scientific Society. HAPAG's New York agent Emil Boas was married to the daughter of the owner of the *New-York Staatszeitung* and may have facilitated the collaboration between the two. This illustrates the close ties among the German-speaking community. Hamburg Staatsarchiv, HAPAG, 622-1, Erinnerungen Merck; and *New York Times*, 29 March 1893.

[121]Senner, "How We Restrict Immigration," 499.

lization."[122] The country would still need desirable immigrants for a long time to come, while the existing laws and improved controls managed to exclude a majority of undesirables. His statistics pointed to an increasing percentage of debarred undesirables, while the number of migrants sent back for becoming public charges within the first year of arrival was rapidly declining (see table 4.1). He also pleaded for the establishment of a national clearing house at Ellis Island to improve the distribution of the migrants according to their skills and the localities where they were needed. Nevertheless, he did favour a "moderate" educational test that would exempt people joining immediate family, fearing that too big an inflow of illiterates would lower the standards of living and wages.[123]

Table 4.1
Deportees from Ellis Island, 1891-1896

Fiscal Year	Immigration	Debarred at Gate	Percentage	Debarred after Landing
1891-1892	445,987	1727	0.39	637
1892-1893	343,422	817	0.24	577
1893-1894	219,046	2022	0.92	417
1894-1895	190,928	2077	1.09	177
1895-1896	263,709	2512	0.95	238

Note: Fiscal years run from 1 July to 30 June.

Source: Joseph H. Senner, "The Immigration Question," *Annals of the American Academy of Political and Social Science*, X, No. 1 (1897), 6-7.

When announcing the establishment of the IPL, Senner openly stated that its purpose was to oppose the "Lodge bill." The announcement underlined the strategy of instigating historical division between the eastern states and the rest of the country: "Western and Southern States, where immigrants are largely needed for their further development, have equal rights to decide on the policy as the East."[124] The IRL denounced the IPL for gaining the support of the German community by misrepresenting the bill as an Anglo-Saxon

[122]Eugene Schuyler, "Italian Immigration into the United States," *Political Science Quarterly*, IV, No. 3 (1889), 495; Senner, "Immigration from Italy," 655; and GAR, HAL, 318.04, Passage, 221-226, letter, 15 November 1895.

[123]Joseph H. Senner, "The Immigration Question." *Annals of the American Academy of Political and Social Science*, X, No. 1 (1897), 1-19; Senner, "How We Restrict Immigration," 493-499; and Senner, "Immigration from Italy," 649-657.

[124]*New York Times*, 7 January 1898.

scheme to ruin the German element politically and economically in the long run. It published a circular by Senner to German associations warning that the future of German schools, language, churches and newspapers was at stake. The restrictionists highlighted Senner's hypocrisy with quotations in which he advocated the literacy test and claimed to have introduced it on Ellis Island by sending back illiterates for being LPCs. The IRL insinuated that an outside influence was behind the IPL, but it lacked proof to link it to shipping interests.[125] The Lodge bill passed the Senate, but Glavis reassured the shipping lines that the President had called a meeting with the Republican members of the House Immigration Committee to urge them to go slowly on the matter. McKinley's rise to power was partly due to his tolerant stance towards the foreign-born and Catholics, electoral support which he did not want to lose. Pressures against the bill were also being felt from the influential Irish-Catholic community. Vernon Brown, the head agent of the Cunard Line, managed an "educational fund" for lobbying purposes in Washington and gaining the favour of the New York press.[126] Although initially giving the impression not to fear the educational bill, the British lines also campaigned to protect its interests in prospective markets as their own stagnated. The IRL's attempts to push the matter through suffered when Bartholdt got behind a bill to appoint a non-partisan commission to investigate the situation and recommend legislation to meet "the problems presented by labor, agriculture and capital."[127] This included the impact of immigration on labour markets, meaning that as long as the investigation lasted, far-reaching laws were unlikely to pass. The Industrial Commission, as it was called, took three years to complete its work.[128]

The Rise of the "Third House" or the "Assistant Government"

The economic convergence between the US and the European countries that had supplied it with migrants since the sailing ship era slowed down the out-

[125]Leonard, *Open Gates*, 37-38; Harvard Open Collection Program, Immigration to the United States, 1789-1930, IRL circular 27, "The Surprising Circular of the Immigration Protective League: Purpose and Operation of the Lodge Bill Greatly Misrepresented," 24 January 1898; and Senner, "Immigration Question," 15.

[126]Drew Keeling, "Costs, Risks, and Migration Networks between Europe and the United States, 1900-1914," in Torsten Feys, *et al.* (eds.), *Maritime Transport and Migration: The Connections between Maritime and Migration Networks* (St. John's, 2007), 150-153 and 172; Tichenor, *Dividing Lines*, 72-73; and Flayhart, *American Line*, 328.

[127]GAR, HAL, 318.04, Passage, 221-226, letters, 11 March and 13 May 1898; and *New York Times*, 15 December 1898.

[128]Hutchinson, *Legislative History*, 124-125; and Zeidel, *Immigrants*, 20.

migration from these areas.[129] When passenger shipping companies that specialized in the migrant trade saw their traditional markets dry up, they sought and found new ones in eastern and southern Europe. Yet they risked being shut out of these promising markets after the American federal government took control of immigration. The growing tendency to consider migration primarily as a national rather than an international matter, and the new wave of xenophobic feelings in the US that pressed for restrictions, became major concerns. These were reflected in the improved selection procedures where racist ideologies gained ground. As Aristide Zolberg pointed out, the Chinese Exclusion Acts and laws regulating the European influx from the 1880s onwards were "the first stones of a global wall erected by the rich industrial states to protect themselves from the 'invasion' by the world's poor."[130] But that this wall blocking the entry of Europeans took so long to be erected was to a great extent due to the efforts of the shipping interests. When permanent remote border controls in Europe proved unworkable, the authorities increased the responsibilities of shipping lines in the selection process. The latter used this position to redouble their efforts to guarantee the landing of as many passengers as possible. By the time immigration became a federal matter the shipping lobby was already well established, confirming Gary Freeman's theory of diffuse costs and concentrated benefits and explaining the lag of restrictionists and liberals to organize. Yet this has generally been overlooked by migration historians who often date a well-organized, pro-immigration platform as only developing after the foundation of the IRL.[131] The fact that initially the German and Irish communities led the protest against the literacy test rather than the targeted Jews, Italians or Slavs remained unexplained.

This problem can be clarified by looking at another difference between the anti- and pro-immigration lobbies. Labour unions and xenophobic associations could openly defend their ideals as being in the national interest, cloaking their arguments with slogans such as protecting the integrity of American institutions, defending decent working and living conditions, etc.

---

[129]Timothy J. Hatton and Jeffrey G. Williamson, *The Age of Mass Migration: Causes and Economic Impact* (New York, 1998), *passim*.

[130]Aristide R. Zolberg, "Matters of State: Theorizing Immigration Policy," in Charles Hirschman, Philip Kasinitz and Josh Dewind (eds.), *The Handbook of International Migration: The American Experience* (New York, 1999), 73.

[131]John Higham: "Of all the groups who, through confidence or conviction helped to turn back the tide of nativism, none was as resolute as the immigrants themselves." Higham, *Strangers in the Land*, 123. Or Maldwyn Jones: "Business interests were depicted as the chief defenders of an open gate policy. But this became only true after about 1905...the most strenuous opposition came from the immigrants themselves." Jones, *American Immigration*, 219 and 224.

Shipping companies needed to find alternative ways to convince the public and Congress of the benefits of immigration. They used the disequilibria of industrial development, population density and historical tensions between North and South to protect their interests. The shipping lobby centred its lobby campaigns in the western and southern states where they depicted restrictions as a scheme of the eastern and northern states to hinder their development. The IRL forced HAPAG, the HAL and the NGL to organize a well-structured campaign that could openly voice pro-immigration arguments. By establishing the IPL, the lines sought to institutionalize support from the influential German-American community and to expand this among other foreign-born communities. Through these immigrant communities, the shipping lines could fight the IRL on humanitarian grounds. Moreover, with the growing importance of the "migrant vote," they represented a good way to exert political pressure as the lines financed and provided them with the means to influence their congressmen. The shipping lobby was the driving force behind the liberal movement in an immigration debate known for its strange and shifting coalitions as the views of employers, capitalists, labour unions and congressmen from various regions changed overtime. As Elisabeth Clemens reminded us, how interest groups organize is equally as important as why.[132]

Nationalist interests divided the shipping lobby into American and foreign groups, with the latter being subdivided into British and continental due to the way in which the cartel was organized. Both sides advocated liberal immigration policies, yet they opposed each other in how best to influence American maritime policies. The INC's continuous efforts to obtain competitive advantages for American-flagged ships failed, despite the increasing nationalistic tendencies that were manifested through a decreasing loyalty to international treaties, unilateral decisions regarding immigration, changing tariff policies and the events culminating in the Spanish-American War. The subsidies granted in 1891 were insufficient to compensate for the extra costs of sailing under the American flag. The much-needed boost to the American merchant marine was compromised by the involvement of big business. Granting taxpayers' money to business was not popular given the rising antitrust sentiments. Yet that the US did not follow the more subtle example of European countries and use the migrant flow to favour the development of a national merchant marine is more surprising. As the principal receiving country, it was in a privileged position to do so, as was suggested by the discriminatory head tax. Again using the utmost secrecy under the guise of the Reform Club and through their lobbyists, the foreign lines strongly agitated against these ideas. When the IMM linked the interests of the INC with those of the foreign lines, the pressures to obtain competitive advantages decreased. This sheds more

---

[132]Clemens, *People's Lobby*, 6.

light on an ill-observed divergence between US and European maritime policies, a topic which deserves greater attention.

Chapter V
Shipping Companies' Interference with the Enactment and Implementation of Immigration Laws during the Progressive Era

Shipping companies were key actors in implementing immigration laws, especially with the growing trend to make the lines responsible for keeping "undesired" groups out of the US by making the cost of detention and deportation increasingly expensive. Previous studies of American immigration have too often focused on congressional debates and the bills enacted, but there are few discussions of their enforcement. The failure to introduce a literacy test has led many authors to conclude that the Immigration Restriction League (IRL), with its emphasis on eugenic theories, had little influence on policy. Yet statements by Ellis Island Supervisor John Weber show that "scientifically based" prejudices towards the "new" immigrants existed before the literacy test was even considered by Congress. Officials at the control stations designed ways to use existing laws to block the entry of "undesirables." The failure to enact a literacy test notwithstanding, the racist approach gained ground. The introduction of the "list of races and people" in 1898 further divided the growing influx of Europeans into various degrees of whiteness.[1] As the proportion of migrants from southern and eastern Europe surpassed those from northern and western Europe by 1896, calls for restrictions based on the racist notion that the new wave threatened the "integrity" of the American race and institutions became louder. While the efforts of the shipping companies to prevent the passage of restrictive legislation up to 1914 will be discussed in this chapter, the principal focus will be on how they blocked the implementation of the laws.

Immigration Policies as Implemented at Ellis Island

Policies under Herman Stump and Joseph Senner, 1893-1897

While fierce debates about further restrictions took place in Washington, the New York Commissioners of Immigration seemed quite happy to use laws

[1]Patrick Weil, "Races at the Gate: Racial Distinctions in Immigration Policy: A Comparison between France and the United States," in Andreas Fahrmeir, Olivier Faron and Patrick Weil (eds.), *Migration Control in the North Atlantic World: The Evolution of State Practices in Europe and the United States from the French Revolution to the Inter-war Period* (New York, 2003), 273.

passed in 1891 and 1893 to stem the influx of new migrants.[2] In particular, the "likely to become a public charge" (LPC) clause allowed inspectors to reject migrants they deemed undesirable without requiring too much evidence.[3] Under the leadership of Commissioner General of Immigration Herman Stump and his deputy, Joseph Senner, detentions and deportations increased in the mid-1890s. W.H. van den Toorn reported that tighter controls at Ellis Island were swelling their maintenance bills. For instance, at the end of 1894, 138 of the 230 passengers on *Amsterdam* were detained. Most were not paupers but were waiting either to be picked up by family and friends or for railroad tickets or money transfers to continue their journey. In the end, only two were excluded and four detained for further investigation. Migrant inspectors targeted poor Russian Jews in particular. By increasing maintenance and deportation costs, the authorities wanted to discourage shipping companies from carrying these "undesirable" migrants. Some lines, such as the Red Star Line (RSL) and the North German Lloyd (NGL), gave in to the pressures and avoided the market or introduced discriminatory fares for Russians. Others, including the Hamburg-Amerikanischen Packetfahrt-Actien-Gesellschaft (HAPAG) and the Holland-America Line (HAL) increased their share of the market; the Dutch company, however, started to doubt that the market was worth the extra trouble because it often needed to cover part of the lodging and railroad costs of Russians while in transit.[4] The HAL tried to recover these costs from charities that assisted such passengers despite being prohibited from doing so by US laws. Nonetheless, the decision to carry these migrants affected their relations with both the Dutch and American authorities. The HAL considered refusing Russians whose inland transport was not fully covered but finally opted to charge Russians an extra US $2, including board and lodging costs in Europe.[5]

---

[2]John B. Weber and Charles Stewart Smith, "Our National Dumping-Ground: A Study of Immigration," *North American Review*, CLIV, No. 3 (1892), 424-438; Joseph H. Senner, "How We Restrict Immigration," *North American Review*, CLVIII, No. 4 (1894), 494-499; and Senner, "The Immigration Question," *Annals of the American Academy of Political and Social Science*, X, No. 1 (1897), 1-19.

[3]This policy was still in force forty years later when President Herbert Hoover argued that there was no need for new laws to restrict immigration because strict enforcement of the "likely to become a public charge" clause would enable the influx to be easily regulated. Aristide R. Zolberg, "Matters of State: Theorizing Immigration Policy," in Charles Hirschman, Philip Kasinitz and Josh Dewind (eds.), *The Handbook of International Migration: The American Experience* (New York, 1999), 75.

[4]The need to adhere to Jewish dietary laws also added costs for the lines.

[5]Rotterdam Community Archives (GAR), Holland-America Line Archive (HAL), 318.04, Passage, 221-226, letters, 21 December 1894, 3 January and 27 September 1895, 17 January, 4 February and 19 May 1896, and 5 February 1897.

The main reason for deportation was that a migrant had "no money," but because American laws did not specify the amount required, shipping companies risked liability suits if they refused to transport passengers for that reason. Instead, the lines increased their efforts to contact family and friends in the US because having contacts boosted the chances that an immigrant would be admitted. The percentage of excluded prepaid passengers was lower than those who bought tickets in Europe. For those that were refused at the gates, the shipping lines tried to recoup the deportation costs from the purchasers of the ticket. An extra clause was added on prepaid tickets placing the responsibility for these expenses on the purchaser, but US courts ruled that this contravened American laws. The lines also attempted to force people who were high risks for exclusion to buy a return ticket before departure which would be reimbursed in the US if they gained entry, although this policy was the exception rather than the rule. Finally, the lines also tried to recover the costs from the agents that contracted the passenger. Yet the lack of a consensus among the shipping companies on such a policy limited the practice for fear that it would become a competitive disadvantage. They encountered similar problems in recouping maintenance costs at the landing stations. The HAL sometimes refused to pay these by claiming that by law the head tax should cover such expenses. Again, the lack of inter-line unity, as well as Senner's refusal to accept the HAL's passengers at Ellis Island - examining them instead on the ship and causing significant delays - forced the Dutch line to capitulate.[6]

Although they often appealed decisions made by Stump and Senner, the shipping companies generally tried to maintain good relations with them and other officials. The Commissioner General had broad powers to introduce new measures to improve controls. In his annual report he also suggested new laws to enhance the selection process. Congressional immigration committees frequently consulted him and his deputies when drafting new bills. Senner's detailed records for all third-class arrivals at Ellis Island provided statistical evidence to support their recommendations.[7] The procedures to restrict Russian Jews show the importance of the officials' interpretations of existing laws at Ellis Island and how they could be used to discriminate against certain groups. Both pro- and anti-immigration groups therefore tried to influence them and to have a say about future appointments. President William McKinley's nomina-

---

[6]Weber and Smith, "Our National Dumping-Ground," 429; and GAR, HAL, 318.04, Passage, 221-226, letters, 24 November 1892, 17 June and 12 August 1894, and 24 January, 4 February and 18 December 1896.

[7]*Ibid.*, letter, 15 November 1895. Senner registered who had been in the US before and who was joining immediate family. Instead of giving the total number of passengers, he divided them by nationality and the line which carried them. Senner, "Immigration Question," 5.

tion of Terence Powderly as Commissioner General and Thomas Fitchie as the leader at Ellis Island pleased the restrictionists.

The Rule of Terence Powderly and Thomas Fitchie, 1897-1902

The shipping companies viewed Powderly's appointment with great apprehension because he had repeatedly voiced his support for tougher restrictions. Despite his reputation, it is striking that nowhere in his annual reports did he recommend more restrictive measures. Together with Fitchie and his assistant, Edward McSweeny, he opposed both literacy and property tests. Instead, Powderly's main recommendations were to increase his authority to investigate contract labour violations, to boost the head tax to US $2 to pay for stricter inspections and to reinforce the health controls. For the first two, new laws were necessary which ongoing congressional investigations obstructed. Meanwhile Powderly concentrated on health inspections. Favus, a chronic skin disease, was the main reason for migrants being rejected for contagious diseases after the passage of the 1891 law. It was easy to identify and widespread among young immigrants regardless of nationality. It particularly affected families who risked separation at control stations as collective return often meant financial ruin. Health inspections intensified in the wake of cholera scares during which American inspectors were dispatched to European emigration ports. The HAL reported that passengers with even the slightest skin infection were being rejected by Dr. W. Woodward who was posted in Rotterdam. The company isolated them for special treatment and hired a dermatologist to treat them, sending those considered incurable back home. In some cases, as when the head of the family sent prepaid tickets to other members, one of whom showed incurable symptoms of favus, the company rebooked the affected member via Canada. The separation of families, however, caused uneasiness and embarrassment among the American inspectors both in Europe and in the US. Health inspectors' stays in Europe could not prevent some cases from passing through their controls; moreover, their appointments were temporary depending on cholera threats. Health inspectors at Ellis Island kept on detecting favus cases upon arrival. For families where only one member younger than fifteen was afflicted, the whole family was often transferred to the hospital until the affected member was cured. Heart-wrenching stories of family separation were eagerly covered by the New York press, creating an image of the inspectors as cold-hearted and inhuman. Ellis Island officials who tried to keep out of the public eye wanted to avoid such negative publicity. Yet this added to the maintenance costs charged to the shipping line that brought them in. Van den Toorn reported that expenses for the treatment of prepaid passengers at Rotterdam proved impossible to recover from the purchaser in the US, while efforts to recoup bills incurred at American control stations from family, friends or the passengers met with little success.[8]

When Powderly took office, trachoma was added to the excludable list. This contagious eye disease was associated with the growing influx of eastern and southern Europeans. Powderly ordered stepped-up controls, thus increasing hospital bills.[9] All infected migrants were transferred to city hospitals, which charged US $2 per day, compared with state hospitals, which charged US $1.[10] Between April and November 1897, fourteen infected HAL passengers incurred bills of US $540, but van den Toorn was only able to recoup US $100. The company wanted to refuse in Rotterdam to carry all suspicious cases, yet it feared legal proceedings for breach of contract for those with prepaid tickets. Liability suits against the HAL boomed in the US once its Jewish clientele began to grow. As the HAL was not subject to American authority in Rotterdam, and because US immigration authorities failed to take responsibility for refusing prepaid passengers affected with trachoma, the HAL preferred to transport affected prepaid passengers instead of being exposed to liability suits. If they were refused, van den Toorn tried to have them deported immediately to avoid high hospital bills. Exceptions were made for those for whom third parties agreed to cover these costs. Yet to avoid negative press about separated families, inspectors were more inclined to detain than to deport, to van den Toorn's great frustration. When minors were excluded, in theory a relative or guardian had to accompany them to the place of departure, yet in practice the inspectors lacked the means to enforce this. To avoid problems, they were often classified as LPCs who did not require chaperones.[11]

---

[8]GAR, HAL, 318.02, Directors, 112-121, letters, 1 and 7 August 1899; 318.04, Passage, 221-226, letters, 2 June and 31 July 1893, 18 October 1894, 24 December 1895, 22 November 1898, 31 October 1899 and 22 November 1901; and Terence V. Powderly, "Immigration's Menace to National Health," *North American Review*, CLXXV, No. 1 (1902), 58.

[9]Edith Abbott, *Immigration: Select Documents and Case Records* (Chicago, 1924; reprint, North Stratford, NH, 1969), 70-72; United States, Senate, 61st Cong., 2nd sess., Immigration Commission (Dillingham Commission, DC), *Reports* (41 vols., Washington, DC, 1911), XXXVII; and Allan Kraut, "Bodies from Abroad: Immigration, Health and Disease," in Reed Ueda (ed.), *A Companion to American Immigration* (Oxford, 2006), 114.

[10]For contagious diseases of adults and children, the charge was US $2 per day, while sick adults with non-contagious diseases were charged ninety cents per day (children, fifty cents) Burial costs ranged between US $14 and $24. The transport of sick migrants cost US $3. GAR, HAL, 318.04, Passage, 221-226, letter, 23 June 1898.

[11]*Ibid.*, letters, 12 and 26 October, 9, 19 and 30 November, and 17 December 1897.

The shipping lines considered contesting the inclusion of favus as a dangerous and contagious disease but refrained so as not to trigger Powderly's radical side. Indeed, Powderly tried, but failed, to add diseased children of naturalized Americans to the list of excludables. But children of immigrants who had started the citizenship process did not escape his zeal. He also considered imposing fines of up to a US $1000 on lines that brought in passengers belonging to the prohibited classes. The percentage of migrants detained or excluded for medical reasons increased rapidly (see table 5.1). Shipping companies and their lawyers discussed ways to reduce the maintenance bills, including the addition of a clause on prepaid tickets that protected them from breach of contract. The HAL ordered its agents to stop forwarding all favus patients, cash and prepaid passengers alike, and imposed extra screenings at the main transit points and at Rotterdam.[12]

Table 5.1
Reasons for the Refusal of Aliens at US Points of Entry, 1892-1910

Fiscal Year	Immigrants Admitted	Aliens Refused	Ratio	Loathsome/ Contagious Diseases	Other Physical or Mental Defects	Paupers and LPCs	Contract Labourers	Other
1892	579,663	2164	1:268	3.7	1.0	46.3	43.1	6.0
1893	439,730	1053	1:418	7.7	1.0	40.9	49.2	1.1
1894	285,631	1389	1:206	1.1	0.6	57.7	39.8	0.7
1895	258,236	2419	1:107	0.0	0.2	70.9	28.7	0.2
1896	343,267	2799	1:123	0.1	0.4	71.8	27.7	0.0
1897	230,832	1617	1:143	0.1	0.4	79.0	20.3	0.2
1898	229,299	3030	1:76	8.5	0.4	74.6	13.8	2.7
1899	311,715	3798	1:82	9.2	0.5	68.4	19.5	2.4
1900	448,572	4246	1:106	9.3	0.8	70.0	19.6	0.3
1901	487,918	3516	1:139	8.8	0.6	79.6	9.3	1.7
1902	648,743	4974	1:130	14.3	0.7	79.3	5.5	0.2
1903	857,046	8769	1:98	20.2	0.3	66.3	12.4	0.8
1904	812,879	7994	1:102	19.5	0.6	60.0	18.8	1.1
1905	1,026,499	11,879	1:86	18.5	1.1	66.5	9.8	4.1
1906	1,100,735	12,432	1:89	18.3	1.9	56.9	18.6	4.4
1907	1,285,349	13,064	1:98	29.3	1.7	52.6	11.0	5.5
1908	782,870	10,902	1:72	26.6	11.4	34.0	17.7	10.2
1909	751,786	10,411	1:72	22.9	7.0	42.3	11.3	16.6
1910	1,041,570	24,270	1:43	12.9	2.8	65.6	7.4	11.3

Note: Fiscal years run from 1 July to 30 June.

Source: United States, Senate, 61st Cong., 2nd sess., Immigration Commission (DC), *Report* (41 vols., Washington, DC, 1911), IV, 73.

---

[12]*Ibid.*, letters, 15 January and 9 February 1898.

Because it was much easier to reject migrants as LPCs, this category in table 5.1 includes an unknown number of excludables that truly belonged to other classes. Nevertheless, the impact of Powderly's policies is reflected by the sharp increase of debarred diseased aliens from 1898 onwards and especially by the data for 1907 on debarred passengers in Europe. It shows that the majority were refused for health reasons and that their number exceeded the total number of excluded aliens from American ports.[13] Powderly laid the foundation for this by further enforcing what Senner had set out as a fundamental principle of the immigration laws which placed "the full financial responsibility for all undesirable immigration directly on the steamship companies."[14] He introduced US $10 fines on shipping companies for each omission or error on passenger manifests; this greatly improved both their quality and the statistics derived from them.[15] His Immigration Bureau introduced new questions about ethnic and religious background to be asked by inspectors on arrival, allowing the establishment of a "list of races and people" that classifying new arrivals not only by nationality but also explicitly on ethnic backgrounds.[16] This permitted inspectors to refine their selections based on racial prejudices. Powderly tried to extend the use of passenger manifests to cabin-class passengers, but the advisory committee of the conference shipping lines pointed out that this class of passengers would take great offence if asked whether they were polygamists, beggars or ex-convicts. Due to the insur-

[13]During fiscal 1907, German border stations refused 11,814 passengers, of which 9916 were turned down for medical reasons, of a total of 455,916. In addition, many were refused at the ports for the same reasons as the figures illustrate for Bremen (3178), Hamburg (2694) and Le Havre (340) from 1 December 1906 to 31 December 1907. If the figures for other emigration ports were added, these would exceed the 13,064 migrants refused at all US landing stations in 1907. DC, *Report*, IV, 96-102.

[14]Senner, "Immigration Question," 8.

[15]GAR, HAL, 318.04, Passage, 221-226, letter, 21 February 1901.

[16]Weil, "Races at the Gate," 273. The four new questions were nativity, country and province; mother tongue, language or dialect; subject of which country; and religion. *Ibid.*, letter, 8 July 1899. The list of races remained in effect from 1 July 1898 until 1952 and included: African (black), Armenian, Bohemian, Moravian, Bulgarian, Serbian, Montenegrin, Chinese, Croatian and Slovenian, Cuban, Dalmatian, Bosnian and Herzegovian, Dutch and Flemish, East Indian, English, Filipino, Finnish, French, German, Greek, Hebrew, Irish, Italian (north), Italian (south), Japanese, Korean, Lithuanian, Magyar, Mexican, Pacific Islander, Polish, Portuguese, Russian, Ruthenian (Russnik), Scandinavian (Norwegians, Danes and Swedes).

mountable wave of national and international protests this would trigger, he abandoned the idea.[17]

Surprisingly, deportations for violations of the contract labour law decreased under the former union leader who had pushed for the passage of this bill. His subordinate at Ellis Island, Thomas Fitchie, no doubt influenced this because he considered those with labour contracts to be much more desirable than the penniless newcomers who were often forced to accept jobs for terrible wages. Fitchie had little sympathy for the new wave of immigrants and subjected Italians in particular to very strict examinations. His assistant McSweeny pleaded for a law denying the entry of "birds of passage" from such regions. While Powderly was the most active Commissioner General before World War I, Fitchie was much more passive and remained in the background of immigration policy debates, showing little initiative in innovating inspection procedures. This may have been influenced by the fire which closed Ellis Island for three years and forced inspections to be moved to the annex of the Barge Office and other nearby buildings. These gave new opportunities to scalpers and runners, groups which the officials at Castle Garden thought they had eradicated. Fitchie was constantly hounded by rumours of bribery, incompetence and brutality. Both Powderly and the Secretary of Treasury led internal investigations into these problems. Yet only when a steward of the French line was caught bribing an inspector to provide citizenship certificates to nine Italian passengers did a reorganization of personnel occur. A subsequent investigation showed that an illegal traffic in citizenship certificates and a scheme to exempt certain migrants from controls had been going on for months. Fitchie's successor, William Williams, wrote a devastating report on abuses ranging from rudeness toward immigrants and overcharging for their food to extortion and failing to reject many migrants who had been declared unfit by the medical inspectors. Some shipping companies also complained about preferential treatment being given to some lines. As in the past, the HAL used the venality of immigrant inspectors to its advantage. For instance, it gave free cabin passage to the brother of the newly appointed Greek and Arab interpreter, André Seraphic. Charged with registering the immigrants and also a member of the Board of Special Inquiry, he could render great services to the company.[18] Yet Theodore Roosevelt's appointments of Williams and Frank Sargent turned the situation around.

---

[17]GAR, HAL, 318.04, Passage, 221-226, letters, 7 and 20 November, and 20 December 1898.

[18]*Ibid.*, letters, 17 April and 20 June 1900, and 24 April 1901; and *New York Times*, 16 and 17 June, 2 and 15 July, and 28 September 1897; 10 March and 25 July 1899; 6 June, 31 August, 27 September and 3 December 1900; and 21 and 28 August, 28 November and 21 and 22 December 1901.

Implementation under Frank Sargent and William Williams, 1902-1905

Frank Sargent's appointment as Commissioner General of Immigration was generally seen as a change for the worse by the shipping companies. Although his views on immigration diverged little from Powderly's, he did favour the literacy test. Moreover, Sargent did not hide his antipathy for new immigrants, that "very undesirable class from southern and eastern Europe [that] is taking the place of the Teutons and the Celts." Rather than restricting migration, his priority was to ensure better distribution. He pleaded for an information bureau and exhibition hall at Ellis Island to direct migrants to locales where their skills could best be utilized. Under Sargent, the new hospital at Ellis Island opened its doors, ending the practice of using a variety of outside infirmaries. More formal procedures for deportation were adapted: representatives of shipping lines could no longer attend the first hearings of the Board of Special Inquiry but only the appeals. Friends and relatives were not allowed at appeals, and new evidence could no longer be introduced at this stage.

Sargent also obtained authority to dispatch officials across the Atlantic to investigate irregular migration schemes; this led to the appointment of Marcus Braun as special immigration officer for Europe. Braun's various missions consisted mainly of investigating organized schemes of illegal migration, such as the Hungarian emigration law, prostitution networks, the immigration of excludables and deportees through Mexico and Canada, contract labour networks and the migration of criminals. Braun returned with abundant proof that migrant agents were circulating information on how to pass or evade controls, in particular for contract labourers. These included pamphlets promoting alternative routes through Galveston, Baltimore, Canada and Mexico which "guaranteed" their landing. Some agents even advertised that they would reimburse the passage fare in case of deportation. Immigration inspector John Gruenberg found proof that local Bulgarian and Turkish agents advanced passage fares in return for promissory notes from the emigrants to repay the loans in three to six months. These notes were usually endorsed by family or friends with some property, but sometimes nothing more than the joint note of a small group of emigrants was required. This created a joint liability for the payment of the note which was relatively safe since most intended to return to their country. Braun also exposed networks of Syrians, Armenians, Japanese and Chinese who entered illegally through Mexico aided by traffickers in Yucatan and Mexico City who forwarded them to smugglers at Tijuana, El Paso, Eagle Pass, Del Rio or Laredo. Migrants sometimes headed for Canada via Antwerp and England to dodge the stricter American controls and cross the border by land. This route was popular with excluded passengers who the migrant agents often tried to prevent from returning home as they represented negative publicity about their business. Agents also tried to direct them to other destinations. Regarding prostitutes, there was a wide transatlantic network of women travelling on American passports or with US citizenship papers obtained at consulates through alleged American husbands. The reports of Braun and his successors convinced the commissioners of immigration to strengthen controls.[19]

With every new appointment of commissioners of immigration for New York the shipping lines anticipated increased tensions as these men initially tried to enforce the letter of the law and only with experience became more pragmatic. Yet with Williams, who made a clean sweep of Ellis Island and surrounded himself with lawyers, the lines feared a major clash. Williams rationalized procedures at the control station, clearly defining the tasks of the twelve divisions on the island. Sargent then drafted rules for inspectors and boards of special inquiry for uniformity.[20] When this occurred, the lines immediately reported a marked increase in deportations, especially of older migrants. As the HAL's head agent in New York, Johan Wierdsma, reported, people older than forty-five needed family ties in the US to gain admission:

> In case said immigrants have a close relation in this country namely parents, brothers or sisters, danger is less great, but they may be physically able, may have money and railroad tickets to destination, without relatives, in which case they exceed the above mentioned age under the present system, they are very likely to be debarred. Williams is of the opinion that immigrants of said age are not very desirable. Naturally an appeal can be taken but a re-hearing is not likely to be granted except with very strong arguments. It is rumoured that this action towards the 45+ is caused by chief clerk Mr. Lederhielger to create a bad feeling between the lines and the new commissioner in order to show them that the former immigrant authorities administered the laws to much greater satisfaction than the present.[21]

---

[19]Frank P. Sargent, "Problems of Immigration," *Annals of the American Academy of Political and Social Science*, XXIV, No. 1 (1904), 153, reprinted in *Population and Development Review*, XXXV, No. 4 (2009), 820; GAR, HAL, 318.04, Passage, 221-226, letters 17 May, 12 July and 18 October 1902, and 13 February 1903; and National Archives, Washington, DC (NAW), Records of the Immigration and Naturalization Service (RINS), Record Group (RG) 85, 52320/47, Marcus Braun, European investigation, 1903-1904; 52011/A, Marcus Braun, inspection in Europe, 1905-1906; 54411/1, Wheeler, immigration conditions, Europe and Mexico, 1906; 52066/003, alien contract labour evasions, Gruenberg investigation, 1908; and 51761/5, case of Herman Zalbert, 1907-1909.

[20]NAW, RINS, RG 85, 52116/1, rules and organization, Ellis Island, report, 1904; and 52495/18, problems with primary inspections, Ellis Island, report, 1903.

[21]GAR, HAL, 318.04, Passage, 221-226, letter, 13 May 1902.

The letter suggests that stricter controls were also retaliation against the shipping lines for their lack of support for the previous administration.[22] As the arrival of the HAL's *Noordam* illustrated, one group in particular was targeted: Italian birds of passage. Sixteen passengers over the age of forty-five were detained: one Russian, one Hungarian and fourteen Italians. Some of those rejected as LPCs had already been resident in the US.[23]

Williams also increased the financial responsibility of shipping companies that were negligent. For example, he fined the lines for every omission or mistake on passenger manifests; this quickly added up to fines of between US $100 and $500 per vessel. He also detained passengers with diseases in hospitals to increase the maintenance bills, as was the case with Mrs. Elterman and her two sons. The healthy son joined his father, while the sick boy was transferred to the hospital with his mother. Unable to get the father to pay the bills, Wierdsma tried to deport them. Williams blocked this until five months later, when young Elterman's trachoma showed no improvement and he returned to Europe with his mother, leaving the HAL with a bill of US $400. Williams opposed speedy deportations, stating that the shipping lines had not the slightest excuse for bringing in diseased passengers and that he was indifferent to what their illegal actions might cost them. Agents reported that this policy affected bookings, pointing to a drop in sales as purchasers became fearful of being refused at the gates. All of the conference lines joined forces to establish a special Ellis Island Committee (EIC) to improve dialogue with the Commissioner of Immigration. The committee tried to convince Williams that strict enforcement of the laws was impossible. They used their contacts, built up over the years, with various important people and institutions to exert pressure on Williams. In Washington, Edward van Ingen, chief counsel of the Bureau of Immigration, informed the committee that the administration deplored anything that would disturb the existing friendly relations with the steamship lines. Protests in the press against Williams' policies increased, and speculations about his dismissal appeared. These pressures forced Williams to open a dialogue with the shipping companies, and relations soon improved.[24]

Yet tensions reemerged with the passage of a new immigration law in 1903. The law empowered the commissioner to fine shipping lines US $100 if they flagrantly brought in diseased aliens who should have been detected before departure. Initially, Williams only made sporadic use of this law. In part

---

[22]Lederhielger was singled out as a corrupt inspector by newspapers which predicted his resignation in 1900. Yet he remained in his post until Williams fired him in September 1902. *Ibid.*, letter, 29 September 1902.

[23]*Ibid.*, letters, 16 May and 20 June 1902.

[24]*Ibid.*, letters, 6 and 10 June, 9, 12 and 14 July, 1, 22 and 29 August and 12 October 1902, and 6 January 1903.

this was because since the cholera scare shipping lines had greatly improved controls in Europe and tightened their relations with American health authorities. The incident-free presence of health inspectors in Rotterdam during the bubonic plague in 1899 underlines this. The HAL willingly complied with new requirements such as the acquisition of new disinfectant machines. With trachoma passing favus as the main cause for rejection, the company hired an eye specialist. Over the years, the Dutch line built up good relations with A. Dotty, the chief health officer of the port of New York, by giving free ocean passages to his brother's family and warmly welcoming him at Rotterdam when he arrived to inspect the port. Such actions earned the HAL a good reputation among immigrant inspectors and may explain why Williams initially only imposed a US $10 fine for wrongly listing diseased migrants as "healthy" on a manifest instead of US $100. Yet Williams' forbearance towards the line receded when cases of trachoma increased. He imposed a US $100 fine for passengers with advanced diseases that should have been detected at Rotterdam. The law did not permit an appeal against such fines, but Wierdsma advised against challenging it to avoid hostility from inspectors for seeming to undermine their decision. At the same time, Williams gave the inspectors more time to perform their checks, something which led to an increased number of detentions. Midway through 1903 *Statendam* returned to Europe with thirty-seven trachoma patients and eleven chaperones after being fined US $1000 for transporting these people across the ocean. Controls in home ports were subsequently sharpened. HAPAG, for example, introduced a bonus of five *marks* for each trachoma case spotted by its medical team. The HAL hired an extra doctor who was permitted to use new methods to detect diseases. Some lines even suggested appointing American doctors in European ports. Yet the majority of the lines, including the HAL, strongly objected to being dependent on the decision of a single doctor and to the apparent crackdown by American authorities.[25]

While the remote control system for diseased passengers started to function reasonably well, deportations for violating contract labour laws reached an all-time low. Suspicious of this, Sargent discharged van Ingen, who had advocated a liberal interpretation of the law. With his dismissal the lines lost an important ally in the Bureau of Immigration.[26] Williams soon began to target specific groups, such as young Greek bootblacks brought to the US through the *padrone* system. He systematically excluded all Greek boys between the ages of eleven and eighteen who lacked direct family ties in the US.

---

[25]*Ibid.*, letters, 21 April, 18 May, 8, 9, 15, 26 and 30 June, 24 July and 28 August 1903; and 318.02, Directors, 112-121, letters, 10 October and 27 November 1899, 29 January and 6 April 1900, and 7 July 1901.

[26]*Ibid.*, 318.04, Passage, 221-22, letters, 23 May, 4 and 22 June and 11 and 13 July 1902, and 22 June 1903.

Since minors could not be charged with violating the contract labour law, Williams excluded them as LPCs.[27] The screening of groups all claiming the same final destination also intensified. Certain nationalities raised greater suspicions. One was the Bulgarians, who were increasingly suspected of being contract labourers.[28] Williams also set new standards for defining LPCs, stating that:

> Aliens should not be landed without the sufficient funds for him to provide for himself until he secures employment; the vital point to be considered to determine whether an alien is a pauper or a person likely to become a public charge is whether or not he will be able to secure such employment and become self-supporting. The determination thereof involves a close inquiry into his real occupation, physical and mental aptitude therefore, the ability of residents in the US with the same occupations to secure employment at the time and place in question, the general conditions of the labor market and other material matters.[29]

Williams also introduced a financial test and detained all passengers possessing less than US $10, a sum he considered to be the minimum needed to get by initially while looking for a job or joining family. Yet the average amount possessed by immigrants in 1902 only amounted to US $5.50. This created a lot of extra work for the companies who had to track down family or friends through their agents to wire the amount to guarantee their landing. The HAL sent out a circular to its agents requesting them to recommend that purchasers of prepaid tickets also provide the passenger with US $10 as well as tickets for inland transport to the final destination.[30]

While the number of deportations increased, so did the number of immigrants arriving. This meant that proportionally fewer aliens were expelled

---

[27]Out of the 810 Greeks landed by the HAL in April, sixty-five were deported for these reasons *Ibid.*, letter, 24 April 1903.

[28]For example, thirty-seven Bulgarians travelling with HAPAG had an ad from a migrant agent promising work. Other examples included a group of Italians booked for Uniontown, and Welsh coal miners bound for the Ellsworth Coal Co. in Pennsylvania. Perhaps most obvious was the veto of the million dollar project of Duke de Litta Visconti to import Italian labourers to develop the silk industry in California. *Ibid.*, letters, 22 September and 20 October 1903, and 24 March and 12 April 1904.

[29]NAW, RINS, 52116/1, rules and organization, Ellis Island, 1904, rules for the registry division.

[30]GAR, HAL, 318.04, Passage, 221-226, letters 23, 28 and 31 May and 3 June 1904; and *Washington Post*, 3 January 1903.

by Williams and Sargent than by Fitchie and Powderly. Yet the financial burden on shipping companies increased due to the imposition of fines and the lengthy detention periods for medical reasons. Together with the American press, in particular the foreign-language newspapers, the shipping lines began to push for Williams' dismissal in early 1905. The publicity moved President Roosevelt to visit Ellis Island and to appoint a commission to investigate claims of irregularities. When the commission cleared Williams, the *New York Times* praised him for ensuring the "humane treatment" of immigrants and for ridding the control station of abuses. Williams used this opportunity to declare that the current immigration laws were inadequate and to press for the passage of the literacy test. Without strong public support for such a measure, the politicians failed to act on Williams' suggestion. Preferring to keep their electorate as broad as possible they went slowly, and even Roosevelt, a believer in eugenics who had previously advocated such a plan, altered his views and began to court the foreign-born vote. He appointed Joseph Murray as chief assistant to the Commissioner of Immigration to counterbalance the Commissioner of Immigration of New York. This was clearly a patronage appointment, and Williams, who had tried to eradicate such appointments, took this as an explicit repudiation and resigned. The President replaced him with Robert Watchorn, from whom he expected much less controversy.[31]

Migration as a Racial Issue

The role of the IRL in the establishment of immigration policy has often been downplayed because it failed in its bid to get the literacy test approved before World War I. Yet the influence of this group in keeping immigration restrictions on the agenda, in supporting the candidacy of restrictionists for key posts and in the propagation of social Darwinism has too often been overlooked. The establishment of a list of races and of differentiating newcomers by varying degrees of whiteness was based on William Ripley's *The Races of Europe*. Borrowing from Europeans the idea of subdividing the "white race" into "Teutonic," "Alpine" and "Mediterranean," Ripley attributed "superior" racial characteristics to old- stock immigrants.[32] The IRL used Ripley's book to back its most powerful ideological weapon. The culmination of its drive was Madison Grant's *The Passing of the Great Race* which claimed that the US was

---

[31]GAR, HAL, 318.04, Passage, 221-226, letters 13 and 20 January 1905; *New York Times*, 19 March 1903, and 15 January and 12 February 1905; and Daniel J. Tichenor, *Dividing Lines: The Politics of Immigration Control in America* (Princeton, 2002), 134-135.

[32]William Z. Ripley, *The Races of Europe: A Sociological Study* (New York, 1898), *passim*.

committing racial suicide by keeping the gates wide open to immigrants.[33] But this was a misinterpretation of Ripley's argument which had included the belief that racial qualities could be transformed by the American environment. Indeed, the Harvard economist had pleaded with politicians to curb child labour and to introduce a progressive social welfare programme including education, housing and social security.[34] The study by the noted anthropologist Franz Boas for the Dillingham Commission also refuted the notion that immigrants were a threat. Nevertheless, a congressional commission compiled a *Dictionary of Races* based on Ripley's divisions and advocated restrictions to block the entry of the "new" immigrants. The statistical information gathered at the gates showed that these new migrants had continuously increased their share after surpassing the old stock in 1896. Pressures for immigration restrictions based upon race mounted and gained the support of the majority in Congress, although no legislation was passed. In the meantime, the new migrants - the "in-betweens" as David Roediger has called them - initiated a long struggle to gain equality with their predecessors from northern and western Europe and to attain full "white status."[35] As Desmond King emphasized, the "whiteness" of American identity was sociologically and historically constructed.[36] But despite the various degrees of whiteness, Thomas Guglielmo pointed out that whether an "in-between" was considered to be white was something that was granted on arrival and hardly ever questioned thereafter. Admission to the US gave the newcomers unrestricted access to citizenship, allowed them to achieve political influence and permitted them to climb the "socio-ethnic" ladder.[37]

The efforts of shipping companies in Washington and at various points of entry helped to ensure that new immigrant groups continued to find a place in America and to gain political importance. The lines also stimulated these groups to use their influence to fight against restrictions. As the historians Gabriel Kolko, Martin Sklar and James Weinstein have noted, the rising

---

[33]Madison Grant, *The Passing of the Great Race, or the Racial Basis of European History* (New York, 1916; reprint, New York, 1922), *passim*; Charles C. Alexander, "Prophet of American Racism: Madison Grant and the Nordic Myth," *Phylon*, XXIII, No. 1 (1960), 73-90; and John Higham, "American Immigration Policy in Historical Perspective," *Law and Contemporary Problems*, XXI, No. 2 (1956), 224.

[34]Ripley, *Races of Europe*, 130-138.

[35]David R. Roediger, *Working towards Whiteness: How America's Immigrants became White* (New York, 2005), *passim.*

[36]Desmond King, *Making Americans: Immigration, Race and the Origins of the Diverse Democracy* (Cambridge, MA, 2000), 23.

[37]Thomas A. Guglielmo, *White on Arrival: Italians, Race, Color, and Power in Chicago, 1890-1945* (New York, 2003), 28-30.

corporate liberalism during the Progressive Era enabled big business to play an important role in shaping government policies. Being the target of Progressives who aimed to protect the population from the changing socio-economic conditions generated in part by the rise of big business, they needed to show that their economic interests coincided with the public interest.[38] The shipping lines relied partly on the various migrant groups to voice these claims. What follows is a brief overview of the lobbying strategies of the shipping lines to influence the new immigration laws passed after the turn of the century. Following this, we will examine their implementation at the gates.

The Immigrant Act of 3 March 1903

The growing importance of scientific expertise in policymaking characterized the Progressive Era. Special commissions, such as the Industrial Commission (IC), were formed to assess problems caused by industrialization and to suggest legislation. It consisted of nine congressmen and ten presidential appointees, assisted by two professors, Jeremiah Jenks and William Ripley, as experts on industrial combinations and transportation. The bill creating the IC was introduced by the shipping lobby's ally Richard Bartholdt (R-MO) and froze immigration debates, preventing Congress from passing new laws.[39] The completion of the nineteen-volume report coincided with the rise of Theodore Roosevelt to the presidency. Known for his trust-busting stance, Roosevelt also stressed the need for new immigration laws to exclude anarchists, illiterates and persons failing to meet certain economic standards. The IC recommended increasing the head tax to US $3, improving immigration inspections on overland border posts, inspecting cabin passengers, excluding anarchists, prolonging the Chinese exclusion, extending the period of deportability after entry to five years, prohibiting shipping companies from advertising and fining shipping lines US $100 per immigrant arriving with a contagious disease. These reflected the influence of Powderly, who was a key witness. Together with Egisto Rossi of the Italian Immigration Bureau and Prescott Hall of the IRL,

---

[38]Gabriel Kolko, *The Triumph of Conservatism: A Reinterpretation of American History, 1900-1916* (Chicago, 1963; reprint, Chicago, 1977); Kolko, *Railroads and Regulation, 1877-1916* (Princeton, 1965); James Weinstein, *The Corporate Ideal in the Liberal State, 1900-1918* (Boston, 1968; reprint, Westport, CT, 1981); Martin J. Sklar, *The Corporate Reconstruction of American Capitalism, 1890-1916: The Market, the Law, and Politics* (New York, 1988); and Sklar, *The United States as a Developing Country: Studies in U.S. History in the Progressive Era and the 1920s* (New York, 1992).

[39]GAR, HAL, 318.04, Passage, 221-226, letter, 12 December 1901; and *New York Times*, 24 February 1901.

Powderly was responsible for the bulk of the IC's immigration report. Despite Hall's efforts, only two members supported the literacy test.[40]

To influence the debates the shipping lines closed their ranks. The Immigration Protective League (IPL) had ceased to exist. As pressures for restrictions were reduced after the formation of the IC, shipping lines no longer considered the situation threatening enough to warrant significant expenditures and suspended their financial support. In the meantime, Claude Bennet of the Congressional Information Bureau (CIB) became the inside man for the German lines and the HAL in Washington after George Glavis' sudden death. He provided detailed reports on the congressional debates and on the personal opinions of congressmen. Yet they now relied on A. Anderson, the manager of the passenger business of the American Line, to defend the joint-interests of all the passenger companies before the congressional immigration committees. To coordinate their lobbying activities, the lines appointed a special Immigration Law Committee (ILC) consisting of one representative of the three sub-cartels into which the passenger market was divided; the British-Scandinavian, Continental and Mediterranean. This ILC increased the efficiency of the lobbying by the passenger lines. Other committees, such as the Immigration Inspection Committee (IIC), Railroad Committee and the EIC, reflected the closer collaboration among the lines. The ILC also mobilized the railroad companies that shared a common interest in opposing the bill. Hugh Fuller, the general passage agent of the Chesapeake and Ohio Railroad, represented the railroads in Washington where he collaborated with Anderson. He opposed restrictions to bar Canadian day labourers and measures to impose responsibility on railroads for migrants they brought in through Canada. The shipping lobby managed to mould most of the IC's suggestions to their liking because of their good relations with William Shattuc (R-OH) who chaired the House Committee on Immigration. Yet he could not prevent James Watson (R-IN) from adding an amendment providing for a literacy test to the bill which passed the House. The efforts by Charles Grosvenor (R-OH) and Rudolph Kleberg (D-TX) to block the amendment failed.[41]

The anti-restrictionists first tried to stall action on the bill in the Senate Immigration Committee. Anderson, S.C. Heal, the legal counsel of the International Mercantile Marine Company (IMM) and Senator Stephen Elkins

---

[40]Edward P. Hutchinson, *Legislative History of American Immigration Policy, 1798-1965* (Philadelphia, 1981), 127-128; Tichenor, *Dividing Lines*, 122-123; and Robert F. Zeidel, *Immigrants, Progressives, and Exclusion Politics: The Dillingham Commission, 1900-1927* (Dekalb, IL, 2004), 20-21.

[41]GAR, HAL, 318.02, Directors, 112-121, letter, 17 July 1896; 318.04, Passage, 221-226, letters 25 November and 6 December 1901, and 3, 15, 28 and 29 January, 3 and 8 February, 1 April, 7 and 19 May and 11 July 1902; New York Times, 7 December 1901 and 22 and 25 May 1902; and Hutchinson, *Legislative History*, 132.

represented the steamship companies, while Judge Fayson, James J. Hill and Mr. Dudley opposed the bill on behalf of the railroads. Both groups, however, lacked having a contact person of influence on the Immigration Committee whose chairman, Senator Boies Penrose (R-PA), championed the bill. Together with committee members Henry Cabot Lodge (R-MA) and Charles Fairbanks (R-IN), Penrose defied major corporations in his home state such as the Pennsylvania Railroad (PRR) and the IMM. He kept the hearings short in order to report the bill to the floor of the Senate so that even if opponents overloaded it with amendments, there would still be time to prevent it from going over into the next session. Besides railroad and shipping interests, a growing number of manufacturers and businessmen distributed pamphlets and pressured individual senators to prevent consideration for the bill or to convince them to vote against it. Claude Bennet suggested to Lodge that the educational test be omitted, but the Senator persisted even though he was aware that the clause jeopardized the bill. Senator Alexander Clay (D-GA) led the campaign against the bill. The IMM pressured Senator Mathew Quay (R-PA) to prevent consideration by prolonging debate on the Statehood Bill to admit New Mexico and Arizona to the Union. Senators Jacob Gallinger (R-NH), William Mason (R-IL) and Joseph Foraker (R-OH) also joined the opposition. Senator Elkins assured the shipping lines that he could defeat the bill, yet he was disarmed by the acceptance of any amendments they proposed. The educational test was struck out, the head tax set at US $2, and the constraints against Canadian immigrants were lifted.[42]

Both sides knew that the House would try to defend its version of the bill in the ensuing Conference Committee where amendments could be reinserted. With a president in the White House who had advocated the literacy test, the liberal immigration lobby could not count on a veto as it had in 1897. Representative Shattuc committed to oppose the literacy test strongly, while Senators Elkins and Gallinger pressured the Senate conferees to keep to their version. Otherwise, it was agreed that the senators would defeat the bill by filibustering it. This proved unnecessary as the bill passed on the last day of the session with the following provisions; exclusion of anarchists, prostitutes, the insane and epileptics; an increase of the head tax to US $2; US $100 fines for passengers landed with contagious and loathsome diseases whose illnesses should have been detected at the port of embarkation; prohibition of promises of employment in the US through advertisements in foreign publications; regulations for escorts for handicapped and minor debarred aliens; and the extension of the period of deportability of aliens unlawfully in the US to three years and of immigrants becoming a public charge from one to two years. Simulta-

---

[42]GAR, HAL, 318.04, Passage, 221-226, letters, 17 and 24 June, 11 and 12 July, and 3, 5, 8, 9 and 13 December 1902; and 7, 10, 16, 19, 24, 27 and 31 January, and 27 and 28 February 1903.

neously, another bill moved the Bureau of Immigration from the Treasury Department to the Department of Commerce and Labor. As Shattuc put it, "its passage is the best thing that could have happened to the shipping companies' interests because it prevents the passage of a measure by the next Congress which would have been much more objectionable to them." After the elections, shipping lines supported a movement to replace the restrictionist Senator Penrose with John Dryden (R-NJ) or William Dillingham (R-VT) as chairman of the Immigration Committee.[43]

It remains difficult to measure the influence of the shipping lobby, but Shattuc's reaction to some comments by Anderson after the bill was passed underlines their importance: "He [Anderson] wrote most of the bill, [so] he ought to be satisfied with it."[44] With the expansion of the shipping conference agreements, relations among the passenger lines improved as they joined to lobby against restrictions. Yet the danger of government measures giving advantages to the US merchant marine for migrant transport always loomed and threatened to undermine this equilibrium. The formation of the IMM and the agreements concluded by Cunard with the British and Hungarian authorities demonstrate this. The Hungarian contract triggered fierce international protests. American authorities objected in particular to the clause stipulating that the Hungarian government committed to pay a compensation of US $20 per passenger short of the annual minimum of 30,000 it guaranteed to Cunard's Fiume service. The IMM lobby misrepresented the clause as a scheme to stimulate emigration as Hungarian authorities would do everything in its power to avoid paying compensation. To obstruct its rival's service from Fiume and to obtain competitive advantages, the IMM supported Senator Dillingham's bill excluding those immigrants "encouraged by any government with a steamshipping company." Sereno Payne (R-NY), the Majority Leader in the House of Representatives, pointed to the laws in other European countries that favoured national lines and suggested a US $30 head tax on immigrants arriving in foreign vessels; Penrose and Lodge defended this in the Senate. As the congressional session came to a close, Anderson, Heal and J. Wright pleaded with the conferees to get the bill adopted quickly. Nonetheless, pressure from the foreign shipping lobby on various House conferees forced the senators to give in to save the renewal of the Chinese Exclusion Bill. In the meantime, under continuous international pressure the Hungarian government struck out the compensation clause and later lifted all barriers for nationals travelling through northern ports. The HAL, NGL and HAPAG rewarded the Hungarian-

---

[43]*Ibid.*, letters, 10 January, 6 and 28 February and 4 March 1903; and *New York Times*, 1 March 1903.

[44]Robert de C. Ward, "The New Immigration Act," *North American Review*, CLXXXV, No. 4 (1907), 590.

American newspaper *Szabadszag* with lush advertisements for its support in the campaign against the Hungarian government.[45]

These events put measures to revive the American merchant marine back on the political agenda. President Roosevelt favoured state intervention and appointed a special commission to investigate the issue. The American shipping lobby suggested direct subsidies and discriminatory duties, but the commission did not reach a unanimous agreement. This led instead to a moderate bill for the North Atlantic trade including minor discriminatory duties which affected the German lines but not the HAL. But the American shipping lobby managed to introduce an amendment through E.F. Chamberlin, the US Commissioner of Navigation, increasing the direct subsidy to the American Line to US $250,000 and cancelling the "most favoured nation clause" with the Netherlands. The HAL mobilized the Dutch envoy in Washington, Reneke van Swinderen, Claude Bennet and its legal representative, Mr. Putnam, to fight the law and retain its trading privileges. The foreign shipping lobby found a strong ally in Speaker of the House Joseph Cannon (R-IL) who opposed any form of direct subsidy. He used his power to appoint anti-subsidy conferees who, backed by the anti-trust climate, struck out the subsidy amendment and safeguarded the most favoured nation privileges of Denmark and the Netherlands.[46]

After this last surge of the pro-subsidy lobby, the IMM abandoned all hope of obtaining favours from the American government. The profit-sharing agreements with the German lines and the contract with the British government made these less attractive for the shipping giant. Only a far-reaching concession would warrant transferring the fleet to the American flag, but the anti-trust climate and public outbursts denouncing political corruption by big business impeded such legislation. Claude Bennett reported that in the following years, congressmen defeated ship subsidies on general principle rather than specific interests, making organized opposition superfluous. The general public showed less opposition to more subtle propositions such as discriminatory head taxes or forcing immigrants to travel on US-flagged ships, but the fear of repercussions by other nations concerned with the North Atlantic migrant trade

[45]NAW, RINS, 52011/A, investigation, Hungarian migration, Marcus Braun; and correspondence 1904; GAR, HAL, 318.04, Passage, 221-226, letters, 19, 20 and 22 April, 21 October, 4 and 10 November and 27 December 1904; *Washington Post*, 30 April 1904; and Erich Murken, *Die grossen transatlantischen Linienreederei-Verbande, Pools und Interessengemeinschaften bis zum Ausbruch des Weltkrieges: Ihre Entstehung, Organitsation und Wirksamkeit* (Jena, 1922), 254.

[46]GAR, HAL, 318.02, Directors, 112-121, letters, 10 and 18 January, 10 February and 13 December 1905, and 23 March 1906; 318.04, Passage, 221-226, letters, 19 January and 21, 25 and 29 November 1904, 14 December 1905, and 30 January, 25 May and 2 June 1906; and *New York Times*, 6 December 1903.

obstructed such measures. Well-established foreign shipping companies had developed strong business interests in the US and had expanded their influence well into the corridors of the Capitol. In a time when many other domestic industries obtained competitive advantages from the state, the American shipping industry did not. President Taft expressed his concern that foreign lines reaped the bulk of the profits from transporting American exports and immigrants in 1911, but the movement never acquired sufficient congressional backing to force legislation.[47]

The Immigration Law of 1907

Despite the new immigration law of 1903, the yellow press continued to agitate for restrictions on the dumping of European "riff raff" on American shores. Wierdsma reported that the campaign led by the *New York World* and the *New York Herald* backfired when other New York papers denounced the hypocrisy of both papers whose owners and founders were immigrants. The *New York Herald* had previously advocated liberal policies, and shipping lines traditionally spent more on advertising in this paper than in any other (appendix 6). The companies did not reduce these expenditures following the attacks which weakens the IRL's claim that steamship companies dictated the newspaper's stance on immigration by awarding or withdrawing their advertisements. Other lobbying groups went much further to monitor the press and assure their support against harmful legislation.[48] The IRL seemed more accurate in denouncing the shipping lines as the driving force obstructing immigration restrictions.

---

[47]Richard L. McCormick, "The Discovery that Business Corrupts Politics: A Reappraisal of the Origins of Progressivism," *American Historical Review*, LXXXVI, No. 2 (1981), 259-274; GAR, HAL, 318.02, Directors, 112-121, letters, 9 June 1909 and 7 December 1911; and NAW, RINS, 53139/5, bill for American vessels and immigrant transportation, 23 April 1911.

[48]James L. Crouthamel, *Bennett's New York Herald and the Rise of the Popular Press* (Syracuse, NY, 1989), 97; John Higham, *Strangers in the Land: Patterns of American Nativism, 1860-1925* (New Brunswick, NJ, 1955; reprint, New Brunswick, NJ, 2002), 127; Richard Kluger, *The Paper: The Life and Death of the New York Herald Tribune* (New York, 1986), 183; Tichenor, *Dividing Lines*, 115; and Edward B. Logan and Simon N. Patten, "Lobbying," *Annals of the American Academy of Political and Social Science*, CXLIV, No. 1 (1929), 6-7. For instance, in its fight against the Pure Food Bill in 1906 the Proprietary Medicine Association of America included a clause in its advertisement contract making it void if any law prohibiting the sale or manufacture of proprietary medicine was passed in the state where the paper circulated. Logan and Patten, "Lobbying," 7; GAR, HAL, 318.01, Directors, 1174, letter, 3 July 1903; 318.02, Directors, 112-121, letter, 8 December 1905; 318.04, Passage, 221-226, letters, 9 May and 9 June 1905; *New York Evening Journal*, 8 June 1905; and *New York Times*, 11 March 1906.

In pamphlets, scientific publications and in front of congressional committees the IRL's accusations grew ever shriller. The scientific racist discourse also gained prominence using Darwin's "survival of the fittest" theory. Science had proven that artificial selection leads to better breeds of animals and plants; the IRL claimed that the US could apply this to humans through restrictive immigration policies but instead left the selection of migrants to shipping companies which had artificially instigated the migration of the worst kind of people from southern and eastern Europe. According to the IRL, were it not for the shipping lines, a literacy test would have solved this problem long ago.[49]

Articles refuting these claims soon appeared in academic journals. Richmond Mayo-Smith, one of the first academics to question the racial benefits of immigration, later defended a nationality based on the unity of institutions, social habits and ideals rather than blood. These statements, however, seem to be in conflict with his subsequent appointment as vice-president of the IRL.[50] Other scientists used statistical data to refute the undesirability of "new" immigrants and to undermine the literacy test. Oliver Austin (Chief of the Bureau of Statistics in the Department of Commerce and Labor), Roland Falkner (Library of Congress) and Kate Claghorn (New York Tenement House Department) pierced the myth of their greater tendency towards pauperism than the old stock and showed that the second generation of unskilled illiterate immigrants was generally better off than skilled and literate newcomers. Hence, restrictions based on an educational test would have no effect on the growth of pauperism. Despite the growing influx, the percentage of immigrants in the total population was decreasing. Austin concluded that the so-called "objectionable" class of migrants contributed to the wealth of a nation which had not lost its power to assimilate newcomers. These conclusions were shared by the National Board of Trade's immigration committee, which urged better distribution policies in 1904. The year before, the Board still endorsed the literacy test. Northern businessmen, who had previously supported restrictions out of a

---

[49]GAR, HAL, 318.02, Directors, letter, 15 January 1902; Thomas Darlington, "The Medico-Economic Aspect of the Immigration Problem," *North American Review*, CLXXXIII, No. 6 (1906), 1262-1271; Prescott F. Hall, "Selection of Immigration," *Annals of the American Academy of Political and Social Science*, XXIV, No. 2 (1904), 169-184; Robert de C. Ward, "The Restriction of Immigration," *North American Review*, CLXXIX, No. 2 (1904), 226-236; and Ward, "Pending Immigration Bills," *North American Review*, CLXXXIII, No. 8 (1906), 1120-1133.

[50]Richmond Mayo-Smith, "Assimilation of Nationalities in the United States I," *Political Science Quarterly*, IX, No. 3 (1894), 426-444; and Mayo-Smith, "Assimilation of Nationalities in the United States II," *Political Science Quarterly*, IX, No. 4 (1894), 649-670.

fear of social unrest, now gave their full support to the unrestricted influx of unskilled labour.[51]

The shipping lobby also tried to take advantage of the increasing attempts to reconcile business with public and labour interests by groups such as the National Civic Federation (NCF). The founder, Senator Mark Hannah, had close ties with American shipowners, was one of the principle advocates of ship subsidies in Congress and was close to J.P. Morgan who helped finance the NCF. It organized a national conference to harmonize the standpoints of employers and labour unions on immigration. Yet the American Federation of Labor (AFL) leader, Samuel Gompers, could not be convinced to leave open the gates through which he had come. Being an immigrant or of immigrant descent clearly did not mean that one supported liberal immigration policies. The NCF established an immigration department to get labour unions and employers on the same wavelength, but Gompers refused to budge. To improve relations between the two groups, Roosevelt created the Department of Commerce and Labor to which the Immigration Bureau moved. The Secretary of the new department gained much influence on immigration policies at the expense of the Commissioner General of Immigration. Among other responsibilities, the Secretary dealt with deportation appeals. The appointment of Oscar Straus, a progressive German Jew who was a founder of the IPL, played to the advantage of the shipping lines. Yet as elections neared and the flow of newcomers swelled, the pressure on Congress to pass restrictions grew.[52]

Claude Bennet warned that the Senate Immigration Committee favoured a moderate bill but that the House Committee took a radical stance. The shipping lobby dispatched Anderson and Heal to the committee hearings but could not prevent Lodge from adding a literacy test to Dillingham's moderate bill which swiftly passed the Senate. House Committee member Augustus Gardner (R-MA), Lodge's son-in-law, reported a radical bill containing an educational test, a financial test and an increase in the head tax. The shipping lobby's allies in the Committee, William Bennet (R-NY) and Jacob Ruppert Jr.

---

[51]Oliver P. Austin, "Is the New Immigration Dangerous to the Country?" *North American Review*, CLXXVIII, No. 4 (1904), 558-570; Kate Holladay Claghorn, "Immigration in Its Relation to Pauperism," *Annals of the American Academy of Political and Social Science*, XXIV, No. 2 (1904),187-205; Roland P. Falkner, "Some Aspects of the Immigration Problem," *Political Science Quarterly*, XIX, No. 1 (1904), 32-49; Henry Beardsell Leonard, *The Open Gates: The Protest against the Movement to Restrict European Immigration, 1896-1924* (New York, 1980), 55; and John J.D. Trenor, "Proposals Affecting Immigration," *Annals of the American Academy of Political and Social Science*, XXIV (1904), 223-236.

[52]Higham, *Strangers in the Land*, 114-115; Weinstein, *Corporate Ideal*, 7-39; and Aristide R. Zolberg, *A Nation by Design: Immigration Policy in the Fashioning of America* (New York, 2006), 218-229.

(D-NY), attached a minority report to the bill. Speaker Cannon intended to block consideration of the bill. The power of the Speaker had increased with the revision of the House rules in the 1890s, and Cannon was the first beneficiary. Although Cannon was known as being anti-labour and pro-business, the President pressured him to get some kind of immigration law approved. Claude Bennett warned the lines that the Speaker might give in to a moderate literacy test and urged them to try to influence the President. Shortly thereafter, Representative Edward Morrell (R-PA) accompanied a delegation of the Philadelphia Italian Society on a presidential visit to voice their arguments against the test. William Bennet guided the visits of delegations representing the federation of Jewish organizations, the Southern Immigration Commission and the National Liberal Immigration League (NLIL) which met with the Speaker, the Commissioner General of Immigration and the President. William Bennet also helped to organize a mass meeting under the auspices of New Immigrants' Protective League where all organizations jointly voiced their protests. The German-American Alliance joined them and sent a delegation led by Bartholdt to plead with the President to have the idea of an educational test studied by a special commission. Representatives Benjamin Howell (R-NJ) and Joseph Goulden (D-NY) had suggested this to Cannon previously; Cannon opposed the idea then but became its strongest advocate six months later.[53]

As Robert Zeidel has noted, neither the traditional anti-restrictionist Bartholdt nor the Jewish Democrat Adolph Sabath (D-IL) led the charge in the House against the bill, but instead the leaders were the multi-generational American Republicans Cannon, Grosvenor and Watson. Zeidel ascribed their actions to pressure from President Roosevelt who did not want to expose his opinion on the literacy test openly. But what has been overlooked is that most of the actors can also be linked to shipping interests. Grosvenor had been one of the leading advocates of the ship subsidy bill and had already opposed an amendment containing the literacy test in 1902. That amendment had been introduced by Watson, who suggested excluding the Italians and preventing Hungarians and Russian Jews from filling up almshouses and jails. The reason for his radical change of heart cannot be linked directly to shipping companies and seems to confirm Zeidel's hypothesis. Claude Bennet, however, described Watson, who was in the chair during the House debates, as Cannon's legislative assistant and right-hand man. For his part, Cannon had fought the ship subsidies because they hurt foreign shipowners.[54] Shipping interests had also

[53]GAR, HAL, 318.04, Passage, 221-226, letters, 6 and 8 March, 22 and 23 May, and 6, 9, 12 and 15 June 1906; 318.02, Directors, 112-121, letters, 25 June and 3 July 1906; *New York Times*, 10 June 1906; Tichenor, *Dividing Lines*, 116; Higham, *Strangers in the Land*, 128; and Zeidel, *Immigrants*, 31.

[54]Zeidel, *Immigrants*, 27-32; To make his behaviour even more incoherent Watson reintroduced a literacy test at the end of 1907. Yet as William Bennet later

approached William Bennet who, like all the preceding congressmen from his state, defended migrant transport because it contributed to the dominant position of the port of New York. With the high concentration of foreign-born in his state, he also had strong electoral reasons to oppose restrictions. Only by abusing their crucial positions in the House and meticulously orchestrating their efforts did they manage to strike out the literacy test and introduce a new investigation commission. To avoid the test being reintroduced in the Conference Committee, Cannon appointed Bennet, Ruppert and Howell, all of whom represented the interests of the world's biggest migrant hub.[55]

Wierdsma's report on the work of the ILC, presided over by Gustav Schwab, underlines their influence but also indicates that some divisions within the lobby persisted:

> Thanks to the pressure on the Speaker and House Representative Ruppert the immigration bill has not been approved in its original form. Schwab warns to be very confidential with this information because if it leaked out that steamship lines are involved it would backfire against us. Rumor goes that advocates of the law hired private detectives to trace this. Due to the importance of the law the committee asks for more funds to fight it. So far, all lines except Cunard, spent $15,000 on the campaign and the German Lines would like to increase it to $60,000 based on a contribution of 10c per passenger transported in 1905. Do you agree? The committee is trying to involve Cunard that is contending to conduct their [sic] own campaign. The IMM has their personal representatives at Washington but is prepared to contribute.[56]

The shipping lobby used the same strategies as in 1897; forging key alliances in Washington to obstruct restrictive measures while mobilizing various foreign-born groups to intimidate politicians with the "migrant vote." The shipping lines, jointly with big businessmen such as Andrew Carnegie, financed the foundation of the NLIL in 1905. Initially a Jewish initiative, it was soon broadened to include representatives from German and Irish organizations. Through mass meetings and press campaigns it spread propaganda to mould public opinion. By appointing James Curley as its lobbyist and coordinating the

---

confided, Watson's personal actions on the floor proved crucial in preventing the passage of the literacy test. GAR, HAL, 318.02, Directors, 112-121, letter, 25 June 1906; and 318.04, Passage, 221-226, letter, 14 December 1907.

[55]Tichenor, *Dividing Lines*, 125-129; and Zeidel, *Immigrants*, 28-34.

[56]GAR, HAL, 318.02, Directors, 112-121, letter, 3 July 1906.

sending of delegations to national gatherings and to Washington, the NLIL was able to influence political debates. For instance, in 1908 it contributed to the suspension of the restrictionist plank at the Republican National Convention by providing its members with petitions to be sent to their representatives. At the Democratic Convention the plank was limited to Asiatic migration. Through assimilation and distribution programs they promoted positive solutions to immigration problems. The American Jewish Committee (AJC), which was founded in 1906, joined the fight which the Catholic Ancient Order of Hibernians and the German-American Alliance continued to support. In Oscar Straus, Louis Marshall and Jacob Schiff the AJC had three influential Republicans on board. Unlike the NLIL, which favoured aggressive strategies, the AJC used its influence discreetly on Capitol Hill. Other new immigrant ethnic groups also voiced their claims but were not as organized as their Jewish counterparts.[57] Their much higher return rates to Europe compared to the Jews may partly explain why they played a lesser role. The growing support of businessmen was highlighted by the National Board of Trade and the National Association of Manufacturers which organized pro-immigration campaigns of their own. The latter in particular opened branches throughout the country for the sole purpose of influencing state and federal legislation. It established legal, publicity and education bureaus to centralize and coordinate the efforts. The associations in the interior needed to ensure that "right-minded" legislators were elected. Its Washington lobbyist, James Emery, made sure that these right-minded men sat on House and Senate committees to defend its interests.[58]

The IRL fumed at the idea of another investigation commission freezing debate for the next couple of years. Nonetheless, to avoid a serious diplomatic conflict with Japan over a potential Japanese exclusion act the restrictionist Senate conferees Lodge and Anslem McLaurin (D-MS) went along with the House conferees.[59] The new bill appointed an investigation commission, raised the head tax to US $4; expanded the US $100 fine system to passengers with other diseases or handicaps; extended the period of deportability for illegal aliens and those becoming a public charge to three years; and gave the President authority to convene an international conference on immigration. A last-minute amendment suggested by Straus to review the Passenger Act of 1882 increased the minimum deck space requirement per passenger by twenty-

---

[57]Higham, *Strangers in the Land*, 123-126; Michael Just, *Ost und südosteuropäische Amerikawanderung, 1881-1914* (Stuttgart, 1988), 200 and 210; Zolberg, *Nation by Design*, 221-222; and NAW, RINS, 51632/13, immigration legislation, 1907, NLIL, 1905-1910.

[58]Logan and Patten, "Lobbying," 8-9.

[59]Tichenor, *Dividing Lines*, 127; Zeidel, *Immigrants*, 32; and GAR, HAL, 318.04, Passage, 221-226, letters, 12 December 1906 and 26 January 1907.

five percent. Due to the urgency with which Roosevelt wanted the bill passed, Lawson Sandford, Heal and Mr. Hartfield could not have the amendment dropped, but they did get the date of implementation postponed to 1909. These requirements predominantly affected older ships on the Mediterranean route.[60]

The IRL was very sceptical about the new law. The increase in space requirements and the rise in the head tax would not alter the fact that the US was in the "unenviable position of being about the cheapest place for Europeans to emigrate." Indeed, from its perspective the policies seemed to have been arranged for the accommodation of the shipowners.[61] Yet the IRL did obtain a small but important victory when the House Immigration Committee brought recruiting practices in South Carolina before Attorney General Charles Bonaparte who declared the activities illegal due to the involvement of private companies.[62] Aside from the New York representatives, southern congressmen had been the most loyal supporters of liberal policies during the 1897 literacy test debates. Since the early 1890s, the shipping lobby had directed its anti-restriction campaigns to the sparsely populated western and southern states where many believed migrants were needed for their development. They helped to propagate the idea that better distribution rather than restriction was needed, a position Senner, Powderly and Sargent also adopted. Yet the census of 1900 showed that only 620,000 foreign-born people lived in the South, a mere six percent of the total immigrant population. As federal initiatives to direct newcomers to these regions failed to materialize, state authorities took matters in their own hands, opening immigration bureaus which distributed propaganda, organized conventions and sent recruiting agents to Europe. Shipping and railroad companies willingly helped with special sailings and rates.[63]

---

[60]Of the 175 ships landing passengers in 1906, only seventy-five needed to make adaptations to conform to the new regulations. GAR, HAL, 318.04, Passage, 221-226, letters, 13, 15, 17 and 28 February 1907; and Hutchinson, *Legislative History*, 142.

[61]Ward, "New Immigration Act," 587-593.

[62]NAW, RINS, 51389/6, immigration to southern states, South Carolina, correspondence and printed documents, 1906-1908; GAR, HAL, 318.04, Passage, 221-226, letter, 28 February 1907; and *New York Times*, 12 March 1907.

[63]NAW, RINS, 51411/29, Allan Line advertisements, exhibits, southern states; GAR, HAL, 318.04, Passage, 221-226, letter, 10 January 1908; Claudia Goldin, "The Political Economy of Immigration Restriction in the United States, 1890-1921," in Claudia Goldin and Gary D. Libecap (eds.), *The Regulated Economy: A Historical Approach to Political Economy* (Chicago, 1994), 231; Joseph H. Senner, "Immigration from Italy," *North American Review*, CLXII, No. 6 (1896), 657; Sargent, "Problems of Immigration," 152-158; Walter L. Fleming, "Immigration to the South-

The lines also helped to organize the distribution of migrants, as a report of the ILC revealed:

> on lines favored by your committee a corporation has been established to carry on the work in the states of Virginia, Louisiana, Mississippi, Tennessee and North Carolina and a considerable amount of families have been located by the corporation which has been offered several 100,000 acres of land in various parts of the south...The lobby efforts of the committee of the last two years should be carried on. It is particularly desirable that the sentiment in the south be directed to the desirability of immigration, as upon the sentiment in the south will no doubt depend on the result in immigration legislation. Therefore the committee requests to renew its funds not exceeding [US] $15,000 to continue its activities which end on October first.[64]

South Carolina officials proved the most proactive by creating a Department of Agriculture, Commerce and Immigration (DACI) to attract investors and immigrants to stimulate industrial development. The commissioner, Ebbie J. Watson, was empowered to conclude agreements with steamship lines and migrant agents to lure immigrants. The DACI had a pronounced preference for recruiting from northern and western European countries, yet laws in France and Germany prohibited such recruiting. Instead, Watson targeted Belgium which still tolerated schemes to promote emigration and granted him permission to circulate his materials. The advertisements stated that South Carolina was looking for 10,000 farmers and 25,000 labourers, and that everything, including transport, would be advanced by the state authorities. Start-up capital for farmers and training for labourers would be provided.

Besides recruitment, the DACI worked to improve transport routes. It convinced the NGL to call at Charleston on its way to Galveston to drop off the recruits. The Gulf ports still depended on northeastern ports for long-distance trade, but by opening a direct route to Charleston the DACI wanted to stimulate both industry and migration. In his annual message, Roosevelt suggested prohibiting migration through northern ports temporarily to let the south catch up, but given the interests involved, especially in New York, this measure never had a chance. Although New York was losing its grip over exports, it had no intention of relinquishing control over imports and migration.

---

ern States," *Political Science Quarterly*, XX, No. 2 (1905), 277 and 286-287; and Higham, *Strangers in the Land*, 114.

[64]GAR, HAL, Passage, 221-226, letter, 26 October 1905.

Wierdsma reported on a special meeting in New York of railroads and steamship lines to devise tactics to oppose competition from the Gulf. This collaboration had already led to a successful propaganda campaign to secure state appropriations for work on the Erie Canal to counter increased competition from rival ports. Smaller passenger lines like the HAL preferred to concentrate on a single port because spreading the business made them more vulnerable. Moreover, the HAL doubted that conditions warranted the opening of a line to the Gulf because "the climate and the Negro population scare off immigrants." Some lines organized sporadic sailings in the low season, but only the NGL opened a regular passenger service to Galveston in 1902.[65] The promoter of the project, Israel Zangwill, correctly anticipated that although cotton and grain exports had begun to bypass New York, imports and immigrants would be much harder to divert. Southern ports demanded appropriations from the Immigration Bureau to build adequate landing facilities for immigrants, but Sargent proposed instead to establish an information bureau at Ellis Island to direct and assist migrants to the South. Southerners, however, suspected it would be used primarily to divert only undesirables to the south.[66]

This mistrust of the north and the federal government remained despite the fact that Straus and Sargent genuinely supported the distribution of migrants to the southern states. For their part, the IRL and the AFL challenged the schemes as violating the contract labour agreements. Straus refuted this, claiming that even though they were not explicitly mentioned the laws provided exceptions for state authorities to recruit labour according to their needs. The AFL and the IRL demonstrated, however, that such bureaus in Georgia, North and South Carolina were financed by employers for whom they often recruited directly. The decision of the Attorney General to reverse Straus' interpretation of the law greatly compromised the recruiting campaigns of the southern states. In compensation, the federal government established a Division of Information (DoI) under the Immigration Bureau headed by Powderly to improve the distribution of migrants. The former labour leader became a strong advocate of liberal immigration policies and an ally of the shipping

---

[65]*Ibid.*, letters, 9 November and 6 December 1905, and 18 June 1906; 318.02, Directors, 112-121, letters, 11 June 1895, 17 December 1897, 25 January 1898, 18 September 1 and 6 November 1903, and 10 February 1905; Belgium, Archives of the Ministry of Foreign Affairs, Brussels (ABMFA), Emigration, 2960, pamphlet, 11 November 1906; and RINS, 51389/6, immigration to southern states, South Carolina, correspondence and printed documents, 1906-1908.

[66]The Austro-Americana and Navigazione Italiana organized sporadic voyages in the winter, indicating that passengers were recruited by state or land agents for these sailings. *Times-Democrat* (New Orleans), 6 April 1905; *New York Times*, 4 January 1907; Jean Heffer, *Le port de New York et le commerce extérieur Américain, 1860-1900* (Paris, 1986), *passim*; and Fleming, "Immigration," 290 and 293.

companies, collaborating with them to spread information in Europe, on board ships and in the US about the American way of life, job and settlement opportunities, land prices, wages, rent, household expenses and education facilities across the nation. In its first year of operation the DoI assisted 2582 families directly, and the following year it helped 3951 while informing another 31,020. Powderly opened branches in big cities and organized annual meetings with immigration officials in thirty states to improve migrant distribution. The IRL and the AFL accused Powderly of enticing migrants and pressured Congress to close the DoI. In 1910, it reduced the DoI's activities to farm labourers and domestics, although Powderly continued to lead it until 1921.[67]

Many southerners mistrusted the DoI for relieving the northern states of their undesirable elements. That Watson recruited in Belgium underlines the general preference for old-stock migrants. Prejudices against new immigrants were also widespread in the south. The IRL agitated in the press to make sure that this did not change. After the court decision on South Carolina the south changed its stance on immigration, and many states passed resolutions to exclude Jews and Italians. The resolution of the General Assembly of Virginia was typical:

> That our representatives in both Houses of Congress be, and they are hereby requested to oppose in every possible manner the influx into Virginia of Immigrants from Southern Europe with their Mafia and Black-Hand and murder societies and with no characteristics to make them, with us a homogenous people, believing as we do, that upon Anglo-Saxon supremacy depend the future welfare and prosperity of this Commonwealth, and we view with alarm any effort that may tend to corrupt its citizenship.[68]

On the federal level, southern congressmen began to advocate restrictions. Representatives John Burnett (D-AL) and Oscar Underwood (D-AL) became the main spokesmen for the IRL on the House floor and before the House Immigration Committee after the failure to pass the literacy test in 1907. That they had little to fear from the immigrant vote is underlined by the 1910 census

---

[67]NAW, RINS, 52495/17, distribution of aliens in the US, 1904-1909; GAR, HAL, 318.04, Passage, 221-226, letters, 6 June, 7 July, 7 August and 16 and 21 September 1907, 2 December 1908, 7 January, 13 February, 13 and 14 June and 11 November 1909, 22 February 1910 and 17 November 1911; and 318.02, Directors, 112-121, letters, 16 November and 19 December 1906.

[68]NAW, RINS, 51389/29, immigration, Virginia, joint resolution to oppose in every possible matter the influx into Virginia of Immigrants from Southern Europe, 14 February 1908.

which showed that the foreign-born population in the south had decreased to 500,000.[69] After losing support from the western states, shipping companies also lost the battle for the southern states, making it increasingly difficult to find allies in Washington who were willing to vote against restrictions.

The Dillingham-Burnett Bill

After the approval of an investigation commission, lobby groups exerted pressure to secure the appointments of people they trusted. The congressional representation consisted of the conferees who reported the bill; Senators Dillingham, Lodge, McLaurin and Representatives Bennet and Howell. The liberal Ruppert, who did not run for re-election, was replaced by restrictionist John Burnett, shifting the balance in their favour. It was over the presidential appointment of the three commissioners that Lodge and Bennet had their first clash. Bennet prevented the appointment of the IRL lobbyist James Patten while Lodge vetoed the candidacy of Earl Hayward, a pro-immigration industrialist. In the end they settled for Charles Neill, Jeremiah Jenks and William Wheeler, all of whom were less opinionated on the issue. The next confrontation concerned the limits of the investigation. Lodge wanting to keep it as narrow as possible to enable the rapid consideration of new bills to restrict immigration. Conversely, Bennet's interests were best served by widening the investigation to include Europe. Despite having dispatched Powderly and a congressional commission to investigate the issue in Europe the previous summer, Europe was put on the Dillingham Commission's agenda.[70]

The commission sailed for Europe where members found no indications that governments wanted to use the US as a dumping ground for their undesirables. Nor did they find any evidence that shipping companies artificially swelled the number of migrants or that the numerous emigration associations financed crossings for the poor. Indeed, what they discovered was that by and large migrants still came from the "better class" of the population. The commissioners concluded that migration was mainly a function of economic conditions and that ticket agents, constrained by numerous laws, played only a minor role in inducing people to move. Their findings corroborated James Whelpley's study of European immigration policies which showed that these were favourable to US interests because they restrained shipping companies from instigating migration and regulated overseas traffic in accordance with

[69]Tichenor, *Dividing Lines*, 119-121; and NAW, RINS, 51632/13, immigration legislation, 1907, National Liberal Immigration League, correspondence, 1905-1910.

[70]GAR, HAL, 318.04, Passage, 221-226, letters, 19 January, and 23 and 25 February 1907; 318.02, Directors, 112-121, letters, 11 November 1906 and 3 May 1907; *New York Times*, 15 June 1906; and Zeidel, *Immigrants*, 48-53.

American immigration laws. The commissioners particularly praised the health inspections at border stations and emigration ports, although they found that the involvement of US officials varied from port to port.[71] In Rotterdam, inland migrant agents forwarded passengers from eastern Europe to arrive four or five days before the departure of a steamer. Migrants from nearby points arrived one day prior to the crossing. The HAL's personnel welcomed them at the railroad station and guided them to the company's hotel. Instead of putting them up in large dormitories, as in most other ports, the sleeping quarters were divided into small rooms. During their stay, the company's medical staff had plenty of time to check the migrants who often had passed examinations at the German border. The final examination occurred three-to-six hours before departure. It was attended by the American consul, a doctor appointed by him, the ship's doctor, an official of the Dutch emigration committee and a Rotterdam police officer on the lookout for fugitives. About 500 migrants annually were rejected at the port.

The procedures in Rotterdam resembled those at other ports, but there were big differences regarding the authority granted to American officials. In Naples the final medical inspection was left entirely to two surgeons from the US Public Health Service, assisted by the ship's doctor, a representative of the Italian emigration commission and Italian policemen who checked the compulsory passports for Italians. The delegation of authority made the presence of the American consul redundant. American health inspectors vaccinated all the steerage passengers and supervised the inspection and disinfection of the baggage. Inspectors rejected 10,222 steerage passengers between 1 December 1906 and 31 December 1907. On the other hand, Belgian authorities did not tolerate any interference by foreign officials in Antwerp, preventing American consuls from performing their duties and reducing American health inspectors to mere spectators. A Belgian Commission of Emigration supervised the examinations. Nonetheless, Antwerp had one of the best deportation records at US ports; significantly lower than the neighbouring ports of Rotterdam, Hamburg and Bremen or the Italian ports under American control.[72] The DC concluded that the remote health inspections worked well as only 0.36 percent of

---

[71]GAR, HAL, 318.02, Directors, 112-121, letters, 7 November 1907 and 20 March 1908; and James Davenport Whelpley, "Control of Emigration in Europe," *North American Review*, CLXXX, No. 7 (1905), 856-867. The commission inspected the ports of Antwerp, Boulogne-sur-Mer, Glasgow, Liverpool, Londonderry, Queenstown, Southampton, Cherbourg, Christiana, Copenhagen, Fiume, Bremen, Hamburg, Le Havre, Libau, Marseille, Patras, Piraeus, Rotterdam, Trieste, Naples, Palermo, Messina and Genoa.

[72]The percentage of rejected migrants due to disease at US ports between January and September 1907 was Antwerp, 0.18; Rotterdam, 0.36; Hamburg, 0.32; Bremen, 0.61; Palermo, 0.47; Messina, 0.34; and Naples, 0.36.

the total influx was refused in the US for health reasons. The rejections at Naples and German border stations for the fiscal year 1907 amounted to 5.5 and 2.2 percent, respectively. The DC used the case of Antwerp to refute the necessity of increasing US interference in Europe and incurring additional costs. The overall conclusion of this overseas adventure was very positive; as Zeidel summarized it, "if there was an immigration problem, the commission did not find the roots of it in Europe."[73]

The bulk of the research centred on the social, political and economic effects of the various ethnic groups in the US. How did each group influence general living and working conditions? How many criminals and paupers did they number? The DC needed to provide conclusive answers on whether or not ethnic groups from southern and eastern Europe were inferior and how (or if) they were assimilated? The DC eventually had sixteen committees at work, employing 300 people; this underscored its commitment to collect data and to use a scientific approach.[74]

In the meantime, the shipping lobby tried to reverse the amendment regarding space requirements. Philip Franklin (vice-president of IMM), Thorndike Spalding (from the White Star Line), Sandford, Heal and Chamberlin persuaded Straus to take existing European laws into account. Convinced that space requirements would not affect immigration, Lodge did not oppose this and even submitted the amendment prepared by Franklin to the Senate, where it passed swiftly. But Gardner and Burnett re-imposed the increased space provisions in the House, thereby returning it to the conferees. Rumours of the DC's findings on steerage conditions leaked to the yellow press which reported on the "horrendous travelling conditions." The DC's report later contradicted this, but it did note that conditions varied considerably according to the route, company and age of the steamer. On the Continental and British-Scandinavian routes, an increasing number of steamers accommodated steerage passengers in small staterooms, whereas on the Mediterranean route, served by older steamers, large dormitories prevailed. Nissim Behar, director of the NLIL who travelled in *Rotterdam* to experience the steerage class first hand, praised the conditions.[75] Nonetheless, negative press reports had turned the

---

[73]Zeidel, *Immigrants*, 68; and DC, *Report*, IV.

[74]Zeidel, *Immigrants*, 77-80; and GAR, HAL, 318.04, Passage, 221-226, letter, 18 September 1908.

[75]Steerage conditions on the HAL's ships were among the best on the North Atlantic. Moreover, because the line was aware of Behar's presence the purser was given strict orders to arrange for an impeccable crossing. GAR, HAL, 318.04, Passage, 221-226, letters, 11 and 14 August 1908; and NAW, RINS, 51632/13, immigration legislation, 1907, National Liberal Immigration League, Behar, report, August 1908.

tide against the shipping lines. The provisions for commodious toilets and dining, smoking and lounge rooms were dropped, but the space requirements were brought back from fifteen square feet of actual sleeping space to eighteen square feet for passengers below the waterline and from twelve to fifteen for all others. The new standards not only affected older ships on the Mediterranean route but also the ships of the German lines.[76] Despite reducing capacity, and hence increasing the cost for shipping companies, prices remained unchanged (see appendix 1). As Lodge suspected, the bill did not affect the cost and hence the decision to migrate.

Meanwhile, the lines' ILC continued its pro-immigration campaign to influence the DC. The Italian lines joined in contributing ten cents per westbound passenger. Franklin, Boas and Schwab, who conferred on the lobbying plans with the lawyers Lucius Beers, Judge Choate and Representative Bartholdt, no longer reported on their strategies to limit the chances of leaks. With the increasing anti-trust climate questions started to be raised on the legality of shipping conferences, and investigations into their activities loomed on the horizon. In the meantime, Representative Halvor Steenerson (R-MN) denounced the Merchant Marine League for hiring a detective to investigate his private life, in particular his past trips to Europe, and to link his voting behaviour against ship subsidies to foreign shipping interests in an attempt to pressure him to change his stance. The Merchant Marine League had attacked Steenerson on various occasions in its newspaper and denounced the foreign shipping lobby for hiring journalists to manipulate public opinion, making campaign contributions to political organizations and employing lobbyists to solicit them in office. Congress appointed a committee to investigate the alleged corruption of congressmen on the issue. Apart from the confession of Jerome Willburn, who as a member of the Associated Press in Washington also admitted to being employed by the German Lines, the investigators found little that compromised the foreign lines.

The investigation, along with the increasing hostility towards shipping trusts and the knowledge that the IRL had hired private detectives to uncover their involvement, made the lines consider moving the management of its "educational fund" to Europe. The fund was used to hire journalists, run a newspaper to educate the public, fund associations representing immigrant groups and for the personal compensation of an individual connected with a

[76]Much depended on the ships' promenade decks. For the HAL the changes did not have a radical impact yet, but for HAPAG and the NGL's Barbarossa and Kaiser-type ships it decreased capacity by forty percent. GAR, HAL, 318.02, Directors, 112-121, letters, 3 May, 21 June and 12 December 1907, 28 February and 19 and 28 December 1908, and 5 and 6 January and 15 December 1909; 318.04, Passage, 221-226, letters, 18 January, 14, 18 and 24 February, 20 March and 13, 14 and 16 April 1908; DC, *Report*, XXXVII; and Prescott F. Hall, "The Recent History of Immigration and Immigration Restriction," *Journal of Political Economy*, XXI, No. 8 (1913),741.

political organization. This individual, whose identity was not revealed in the correspondence and which for party purposes was interested in public questions such as immigration, used his influence directly on prominent officials in Congress and the administration to prevent the passage of certain immigration bills. The IMM and the Cunard Line withdrew their contributions, believing it to be safer to act on their own. Cunard worked with Senator James O'Gorman (D-NY) to oppose restrictions. The appointment in 1912 of the Alexander Committee to investigate shipping conferences made the lines even more cautious.[77]

For its part, the IRL focused on William Bennet, circulating pamphlets such as "Congressman Bennet Not a Progressive" and "Jews Attention" to discredit him, albeit with little success. The DC tried to fend off outside influences. It held no public hearings, relying solely on its staff to collect the necessary information. As long as the investigation proceeded, the commissioners resisted pressures from the press and Congress to provide preliminary conclusions. When the DC was to be dissolved early in 1910, it obtained a nine-month extension in exchange for reporting on the completed aspects of the investigation. The efforts by Patten and Representatives Robert Macon (D-AR) and Burnett to oppose any further delay failed in an election year.[78] Fearing that the DC might not recommend a literacy test, Patten and Arthur Holder of the AFL prepared a bill including a head tax of US $10 and an educational test. Representative Everis Hayes (R-CA) introduced it before the DC published its conclusions, but it failed to get consideration in Congress.

In the end, the IRL's fears proved unfounded as the DC concluded that the country could no longer safely assimilate the growing influx responsible for many social and political problems. It suggested a wide range of restrictions ranging from quotas limiting the number of immigrants by race, to the exclusion of unskilled labourers unaccompanied by wives and children, discriminatory head taxes and increasing the amount of money required on entry. With only one exception, all of the commissioners recommended a reading and writing test as the "most feasible single method of restricting undesirable migration." They disregarded Franz Boas' conclusions that denied the racial inferiority of the new wave of immigrants. The IRL's continuous de-

[77]GAR, HAL, 318.02, Directors, 112-121, letters, 28 December 1908 and 30 December 1910; Cunard Lines Archives, Liverpool (CLA), chairman's correspondence, C1, 11, 41, 63 and 69, letters, 13 September and 12 and 15 December 1909, 2 January, 3, 11, 15 and 23 March, 17 June, 3 August and 10 October 1910, and 8 March 1912; *New York Times*, 5, 6 and 15 April, 10 and 24 May and 27 November 1910, and 5 March 1911.

[78]Zeidel, *Immigrants*, 118; and GAR, HAL, 318.02, Directors, 112-121, letters, 9 December 1908, 6 January, 26 and 27 April, 15 June, 18 November and 15 and 16 December 1909, and 25 January, 3, 8 and 10 February and 22 October 1910.

nouncements of the impartiality of the anthropologist, appointed by Bennet, because he was the cousin of HAPAG's head agent Emil Boas may have influenced that decision. William Bennet refused to endorse the test because in his view the investigation showed that new immigrants were less addicted to alcohol, less dependent on charity and no more likely to engage in criminal activities than the native born. If there was a need to put a check on unskilled immigrants, the educational test in his view was the least appropriate way.[79]

The IRL ordered thousands of copies of the forty-one volume report and the summary of findings for distribution. The IRL's optimism received another boost when William Bennet was defeated in his bid for re-election in November 1910. That same year, James Clark (D-MO) replaced Cannon as Speaker of the House, and the position had been stripped of many of its powers and transferred to the committees, thus preventing a scenario like that of 1906 to reoccur. The enactment of the educational test seemed like a mere formality and could end the IRL's continuous claims that because of foreign communities, foreign shipping lines and foreign-language newspapers "there were much more stringent regulations to import cattle, sheep, hogs, dogs and horses than human beings." Yet because the publication of the conclusions came right before the closure of the congressional session, the IRL could not manage to get immediate consideration for the matter, giving the liberals some time to organize. Representatives of the AJC, the NLIL, the Union Committee of Hebrew Congregations, the Independent Order of B'nai B'rith, the Independent Order of B'rith Abraham, the National German American Alliance, the American Association of Foreign Language Newspapers, and the Italian Settlement and Aid Societies of Philadelphia all travelled to Washington to protest against the educational test. Mistrusting the findings of the DC, the AJC sponsored its own research led by Isaac Hourwich whose *Immigration and Labor* was an impressive refutation of the DC's conclusions. Hourwich criticized the DC for a lack of historical perspective noting that a strong economy would even out the short-term economic, social and political problems. He denounced the conceptual dichotomy of "old versus new" immigration as being based on racial prejudice. Hourwich defended the "birds of passage," stating that they adapted better to the fluctuations of American labour demands, preventing the congestion of a large unemployed contingent in cities during economic downturns. The use of his work in Washington at the hearings of the congressional immigration committees illustrates the growing fusion of scientific research, the agendas of various interest groups and policymaking during the Progressive Era.[80]

---

[79]DC, *Report*, I; King, *Making Americans*, 70; GAR, HAL, 318.04, Passage, 221-226, letter, 5 December 1910; and Zeidel, *Immigrants*, 101-114.

[80]Tichenor, *Dividing Lines*, 131-132; Prescott F. Hall, "The Future of American Ideals," *North American Review*, CXCV, No. 1 (1912), 94-102; Robert de

The pressures of the foreign-born vote in the upcoming presidential election did not leave Washington unaffected. The Democratic Congressional Committee convened to counter the successful Republican campaigns in attracting a growing share of the immigrant vote. Opposing immigration restrictions formed part of this strategy, which Republican President William Howard Taft also endorsed by declaring that he would veto any educational bill during his campaign for re-election. William Bennet arranged meetings for him with prominent members of the New York foreign-born community. To make sure his message reached foreign-born voters, Taft recruited Louis Hammerling, president of the American Association of Foreign Language Newspapers, which claimed to reach twenty million people. Nonetheless, Burnett gained support in the House Immigration Committee for a bill which only included the literacy test, while in the Senate Committee Dillingham proposed a general bill which included the test. Burnett suspected Dillingham of opposing the test by attaching it to a more general law which was much more likely to be stalled than a narrower bill. The Senate, however, quickly approved the bill and sent it to the House. Representatives of the shipping lines opposed the increase of the head tax to US $5, claiming that the Immigrant Fund was sufficient to cover the inspection costs and that it would deter families from migrating. William Bennet, hired by the shipping companies and representing various ethnic groups, tore the Dillingham bill to pieces. The former congressman also denounced the "LPC" clause for putting immigration inspectors in the "place of God Almighty." The attempt by Adolphe Sabath (D-IL) to get a motion voted on in the committee to prevent the bill's passage during the current session failed by one vote. Together with Speaker Clark he then moved other bills for consideration to delay action on the Dillingham bill. The lengthy petitions from immigrant communities kept pouring in. Burnett attached his literacy test to the Dillingham bill to speed up consideration, but because of a disagreement among the conferees on some amendments the bill was not reported.[81]

C. Ward, "National Eugenics in Relation to Immigration," *North American Review*, CXCII, No. 1 (1910), 56-57; Isaac A. Hourwich, "The Economic Aspects of Immigration," *Political Science Quarterly*, XXVI, No. 4 (1911), 615-642; Hourwich, *Immigration and Labor: The Economic Aspects of European Immigration to the United States* (New York, 1912); Jeremiah W. Jenks and W. Jett Lauck, *The Immigration Problem* (New York, 1911; 6th ed., New York, 1926); and Michael Berkowitz, "Between Altruism and Self Interest: Immigration Restriction and the Emergence of American-Jewish Politics in the United States," in Fahrmeir, Faron and Weil (eds.), *Migration Control in the North Atlantic World*, 260-261.

[81]Tichenor, *Dividing Lines*, 135; Zeidel, *Immigrants*, 124; GAR, HAL, 318.02, Directors, 112-121, letter, 23 April 1912; 318.03, Passage, 48-58, 97, 160 and 190, letters, 11, 12, 16 and 21 January, 7 and 21 May, and 4 June 1912; 318.04, Passage, 221-226, letters, 9 December 1910, and 13 January and 7 and 28 August 1911; and *New York Times*, 8 May 1912 and 25 January 1913.

The last chance for the advocates to pass the bill was during the final short session. The House approved Burnett's bill by a large majority. Party lines were severed during the vote. Republican Gardner and Democrat Burnett defeated the coalition of Henry Goldfogle (D-NY), Joseph Moore (R-PA) and James Curley (D-MA) that opposed the bill. Attempts to launch a filibuster in the Senate failed and could not prevent approval. Representatives of all ethnic backgrounds, but dominated by the new immigrant groups, went to the White House to argue against it. Despite having lost the election, President Taft kept his word and vetoed the bill.[82] The Republican Senate overrode his veto, but the Democratic House failed to do so by a small margin. This sent the restrictionists, two years after the DC's report, back to the drawing board. With the Democrat Woodrow Wilson, a former member of the NLIL, in the White House, Dillingham drafted a bill to impose national quotas rather than an educational test. In response, the shipping lines closed ranks and raised their lobbying budgets. Cunard Line joined the efforts led by the ILC on the condition that it be restricted to legal means.[83] The ILC decided to do the following:

> W.S. Bennet, who successfully defeated the Burnett bill last year, will be sent to Washington again for an undetermined period of time. He will keep us informed on the House and Senate Immigration Committees and openly represent us whenever needed proposing measures serving the interests of the steamship lines. Mr. Heal will assist him. Bennet's salary will be paid pro ratio based on the number of passengers carried by all the lines. According to Bennet there are five House committee members favoring and five opposing the bill while three others are still undecided. Hence there is chance to defeat the bill in the committee already, yet the economic downturn is not an ally. On the House floor Bennet counts on the support of the sixty-five catholic Representatives to counter the agitation of the Labor unions. Because of the dangers of a secret investigation on the shipping lobby

[82]Taft did so after consulting New York Commissioner of Immigration Williams, who remained neutral; Samuel Gompers, who opposed the veto; and Richard Bartholdt, William Bennet and Charles Nagel, all of whom backed it. *New York Times*, 7 and 14 February 1913.

[83]Hutchinson, *Legislative History*, 154; Tichenor, *Dividing Lines*, 137; GAR, HAL, 318.03, Passage, 48-58, 97, 160 and 190, letters, 17 and 18 December 1912, and 17 and 21 January, 4, 13, 15, 18 and 20 February 1913, 2, 13 and 19 June, 11 November and 5 December 1913.

> the lines decided to no longer maintain a particular fund against restrictive measures.[84]

After losing the support of western and southern congressmen, the shipping lobby forged alliances with Catholics who feared the rise of an anti-religious Socialist movement. By hiring William Bennet they secured an influential lobbyist with close ties to a number of foreign-born communities, and the lines continued to support organizations representing these communities. For instance, the HAL increased its contribution to the NLIL which was in financial difficulty. Moreover, a report by the Immigration Committee of the German-American Alliance mentioned that it would negotiate with the shipping lines for a contribution to support its upcoming campaign for liberal immigration laws.

But it was all in vain. After the House and the Senate again approved a literacy bill in 1915, the former failed to override President Wilson's veto by four votes.[85] Two years later, Congress finally overrode Wilson's veto and enacted the literacy test. This was soon followed by quota acts which selected migrants based upon their national and racial backgrounds. The Great War disrupted European mass migration, and the new acts made sure that the flow would not regain its former intensity after the signing of the peace agreements at Versailles. To what extent these laws were passed at least in part because of the war's devastating effect on the organization of the North Atlantic shipping cartel which weakened its influence in Washington, remains to be explored.

Immigration as a Gate Issue

Implementation under Frank Sargent and Robert Watchorn, 1905-1909

After Williams resigned in 1905, President Roosevelt entrusted the management of Ellis Island to Robert Watchorn. The former labour leader had acquired experience as Commissioner of Immigration in Montréal, where he improved Canadian-American border controls. His views on the desirability of migration differed substantially from those of Williams. He believed that every legal migrant, irrespective of race or nationality, contributed to the wealth of

---

[84]GAR, HAL, 318.03, Passage, 48-58, 97, 160 and 190, letter, 12 December 1913.

[85]Hall, "Recent History," 739; Higham, *Strangers in the Land*, 132; Tichenor, *Dividing Lines*, 136-138, and Zolberg, *Nation by Design*, 218. When news about the financial support from the lines leaked to the American press in 1915, the NLIL folded. GAR, HAL, 318.03, Passage, 48-58, 97, 160 and 190, letter, 3 November 1913; and NAW, RINS, 53288/8, conditions at Ellis Island, complaints by Germans, report, 10 October 1912.

the country.[86] Shipping lines initially hailed his appointment, especially because he gave priority to landing migrants on the day of their arrival, only detaining passengers when absolutely necessary. He also improved registration procedures to speed up the inspection process. He negotiated a less expensive catering contract. Finally, he let the shipping lines choose the hospital where diseased passengers were treated. This allowed the HAL, for example, to obtain charity rates from Saint Mary's Hospital instead of the standard rate imposed by Long Island College Hospital where Williams had sent all diseased passengers. All these measures cut the maintenance bills paid by the HAL.[87]

These improvements notwithstanding, in general Watchorn built on the work of his predecessors. He continued the efforts to close the "back doors" which had allowed some migrants to dodge inspections. Williams had denounced the practice of upgrading steerage passengers who risked deportation to second-class during to voyage; he required a list of all upgraded passengers but failed to impose manifests for cabin passengers. Watchorn improved the "casual inspections" of cabin passengers by adding surgeons to the inspection team. The figures for 1905, when twelve percent of the immigrants landing in New York travelled second class, underlines the importance of this particular back door. Only three percent were sent to Ellis Island, leading to the deportation of a mere 0.1 percent. The deportation ratio of steerage passengers for the same period was ten times higher. Hence, controls put an end to the guarantee of bypassing inspections by paying an extra $10 to travel second class, yet it still gave these passengers much better chances of passing through the entry procedures.

Another back door that Watchorn tried to close concerned abuses over American citizenship papers. He urged shipping companies to control passengers claiming citizenship, stressing that papers of intention were insufficient. This was especially important because Congress had delegated naturalization to any court in the land. This led to a great diversity of procedures and papers which made it difficult for inspectors to detect falsifications. Watchorn denounced the lack of uniformity in citizenship papers and pushed for the establishment of a Naturalization Bureau (NB). Attached to the Immigration Bureau in 1906, the NB gradually standardized procedures and moved the process from local and state to federal courts.

---

[86]*New York Times*, 11 March, 3 May and 19 November 1906.

[87]Fitchie reduced the catering costs per day from fifty to thirty-five cents; this was further cut to thirty cents under Williams and to twenty-two cents under Watchorn. The Long Island College Hospital treated adults at US $1.50 per day; those with contagious diseases needing isolation cost US $2 and the insane cost US $3. GAR, HAL, 318.04, Passage, 221-226, letters, 24 November 1903, 14 April and 2 June 1905, and 18 September 1908; and *New York Times*, 22 December 1901 and 19 January 1905.

Not all Watchorn's initiatives were successful, however. His attempt to make all American citizens in third-class go through Ellis Island elicited loud protests. Such passengers remained the responsibility of the boarding division where natives had to fill out an affidavit and the naturalized needed to present their certificates. While a passport was not considered proof of citizenship, nothing prevented people from passing on their citizenship certificates to aliens. Braun's proposal to require passports to contain a photograph would only be implemented after World War I. Still, those who met the requirements were registered in a book before being discharged; this enabled the authorities to trace cases of abuse. All others had to go through Ellis Island.[88]

The growing influx of immigrants arriving during his first months in charge of Ellis Island made Watchorn question his liberal convictions, and he began to implement the laws strictly to the chagrin of the HAL. As Williams had done in 1904, Watchorn tightened controls which led to an increase in fines.[89] He also sent a growing number of officials overseas to monitor the actions of shipping companies, although they did not find many abuses because the shipping lines were able to spot them and give them special treatment, including free tickets so that their families could accompany them.[90] Medical bills and fines increased as deportations for medical reasons reached unprecedented levels. Watchorn withdrew the privilege to choose hospitals. The HAL tried to gain goodwill by having its doctors in Rotterdam issue medical certificates, but the deportation rates still did not decrease. It then hired external specialists to refute the diagnoses made by the Ellis Island health inspectors and to pressure the authorities to drop the fines or loosen controls. The Dutch line usually contested the fines through their lawyers Lucius Beers and William Choate. The low sum collected for such violations, averaging around US $30,000 annually for all the lines, suggest that fines were not imposed for the

---

[88]GAR, HAL, 318.04, Passage, 221-226, letters 30 May, 4 and 13 June and 17 October 1902, 20 March 1903, and 12 and 13 April 1905; and *New York Times*, 12 October and 1 November 1905, and 11 March 1906; NAW, RINS, 52116/1, rules and organization, Ellis Island, report, 1904; 51632/5, Giovanni Guglio alias Raffaele Castrilli, 1907; 51830/26, international immigration conference, letter, 18 March 1909.

[89]NAW, RINS, 52332/13, steerage conditions, 1904-1909.

[90]This was the case for the wife and children of Dr. Stoner. *Ibid.*, letters. 22 August 1905, and 3 January, 1 June and 21 August 1906.

great majority of diseased aliens.[91] When it did pay, the HAL did so under protest, hoping to recoup the money in court.[92]

Litigations underline the troubled relation between immigration officials and the shipping lines. For instance, the lines contested the decision of Straus and Watchorn to apply the provisions for the unlawful landing of immigrants to sailors who deserted ships. Immigration laws placed the responsibility for preventing the landing of passengers before passing through inspection on the ship's captain. If passengers managed to escape before arriving at the inspection station, captains risked imprisonment and fines between US $100 and $1000. Nonetheless, until 1903 the barrier to prevent anyone from dodging inspections at the HAL's docks was limited to a rope separating steerage from cabin passengers. Only after the escape of a Greek passenger who jumped the rope and mingled with the second-class passengers did the HAL hire a guard and build a movable fence. The immigration authorities did not punish the HAL for this incident. Yet when officials started to suspect that excludable aliens were signing on as seaman only to desert upon arrival and avoid controls, it tried to impose fines and increase the responsibility of the shipping lines to avoid this. Sailors only underwent superficial screening by the boarding division and could freely land. Cunard was the first to challenge the tighter controls, going to court over a US $500 fine for the desertion of Mr. Taylor. All the lines contributed to the legal expenses, as was usual when a test case went to trial. After a long procedure, the Supreme Court ruled in favour of the lines. As Watchorn discovered, closing the back doors was not an easy task.[93]

Lawsuits also had to establish the financial responsibility for excluded aliens needing assistance, such as minors or diseased persons. The immigration authorities tried to assign these as much as possible to the shipping lines, while the latter claimed that the Immigrant Fund should cover the costs. These expenses could be considerable, especially for immigrants who became a public charge in their first years after landing. Transport to the port of embarkation had to be covered for both the migrant and the accompanying inspector; in the case of diseases, they had to provide for a nurse who also received compensa-

---

[91]The figures per fiscal year: 1904, $28,400; 1905, $27,300; 1906, $24,300; 1907, $37,200; 1908, $26,700; 1909, $27,400; and 1910, $29,900. DC, Report, IV.

[92]GAR, HAL, 318.04, Passage, 221-226, letters, 30 June and 15 August 1905, and 17 August, 24 September, and 19 October 1906; and *New York Times*, 25 May 1905.

[93]GAR, HAL, 318.04, Passage, 221-226, letters, 21 April 1903, 22 May 1906, and 25 October 27 December 1907; and NAW, RINS, 54166/112, escape of alien passengers. The Greek Line allegedly registered some passengers as personnel, allowing them to land without passing through Ellis Island; *New York Times*, 22 December 1910.

tion for her time. The 1907 law stipulated that the attendant had to be given an eastbound third-class and a westbound second-class ticket, as well as compensation of US $2 a day plus incidental expenses. When an attendant was needed, the HAL contacted the migrant agent who booked the passenger to try to convince relatives or friends to accompany the alien at their own cost. If that did not work, the line offered to cover the transport costs of the family to the final destination, generally avoiding the costs for second-class return tickets to America and the daily compensation for attendants.[94] Authorities let this happen until Watchorn began to implement the rules rigidly and appointed independent attendants. The shipping lines denounced the practice of procuring "leisure trips" for unqualified attendants while their medical personnel on the ships were perfectly qualified to attend to these patients during the voyage.

The EIC contested the lines' obligation to pay for European inland transport and second-class return tickets for attendants on the grounds that this breached European laws regarding the repatriation of excluded aliens. For instance, Dutch law required shipping companies to transfer a sick alien to the city hospital in Rotterdam where a determination was made about whether the patient was fit enough to continue the journey. If so, the shipping company contacted a family member to pick up the alien, or it appointed a delegate to accompany him back home. Wherever permitted by foreign governments, the HAL appointed a company employee as the attendant. All aliens declared unfit to continue the journey, as well as the insane, were sent to the state asylum where the Dutch authorities took charge of them and contacted the responsible foreign authorities to arrange repatriation. The EIC also demanded information on the qualifications of attendants appointed by the immigration authorities. Straus, Watchorn and Sargent eventually reached a compromise with the lines. Instead of attendants they required two reports; one from the ship's doctor about the voyage at sea certified by the American consul in Rotterdam, and one on the trip to the final destination with proof of arrival. The directors were not pleased about the interference of American authorities on Dutch soil, but they refrained from asking diplomats to intervene because their head agent in New York had agreed to the compromise. Through their agents the HAL continued its generally unsuccessful attempts to recoup the costs from the family, using great discretion to avoid difficulties with the American authorities.[95]

---

[94]GAR, HAL, 318.04, Passage, 221-226, letters, 1 and 7 July 1905, and 24 May, 13 July and 12 September 1907; and NAW, RINS, 54166/101, report, Babette Bosch, 1907.

[95]GAR, HAL, 318.04, Passage, 221-226, letters, 19 July, 8, 14, 20 and 28 August, 3 September, 18, 23, 24 and 25 October, 11 and 22 November and 3 December 1907, 2 February, 17 November and 16 December 1908, 27 September 1912, and 22 February 1913; NAW, RINS, 51758/3, shipping conference, letters, October 1907; and *New York Times*, 25 September 1907.

Watchorn's policy resulted in an increased deportation ratio, which reached 1.5 percent in 1908 (table 5.1). He blamed the shipping companies for carrying undesirables and American residents for bringing over immigrants without proper assistance. He lobbied to increase the financial responsibility of the shipping lines by extending the fine system to cover all deportees and making them refund the cost of their ocean passage to the US. In the meantime, Watchorn used the existing laws to increase the financial burden on the lines. On three occasions he imposed special five-day quarantine and luggage disinfection measures at European ports for Russian passengers because of cholera threats.[96] Watchorn was sceptical about attempts to divert immigrants to the south upon arrival in the US because by then the majority had decided where to go. Wages were the "honey pot that attracted the bees;" hence, if the south wanted to attract immigrants it needed to increase salaries and wages.

In short, his policies deferred little from those followed by Williams, but because of his lack of racial prejudice against the new immigrants, he was attacked constantly by the IRL which attempted to have him tried for abuse of power. The group also criticized the DC for not including Ellis Island in its investigation. This type of agitation blocked his reappointment, and the IRL urged President Taft to choose someone who shared its views on the desirability of immigrants. The shipping companies' efforts to reverse the tide in favour of Watchorn failed. Some months earlier they had seen their ally Oscar Straus replaced by Charles Nagel as Secretary of Commerce and Labor. Nagel and the IRL supported Taft's decision to reappoint his personal friend, William Williams, at Ellis Island. Sargent, who passed away in office, was succeeded by the former leader of the longshoremen's union, Daniel Keefe, an outspoken nativist and restrictionist. Liberal advocates and moderates were being replaced by restrictionists in key posts in the immigration system.[97]

Williams' Second Term under the Auspices of Nagel and Keefe, 1909-1913

Back in charge at Ellis Island, Williams tried to implement what Congress failed to enact; a system to raise the barriers of entry for the poor and illiterate migrants from southern and eastern Europe. He started by detaining every migrant arriving with less than US $25 on the suspicion that they were LPCs.

---

[96]These measures were implemented from September 1905 until June 1906, between October 1907 and the beginning of 1908 and again in September 1908. GAR, HAL, 318.04, Passage, 221-226, letters, 2 September 1905, 15 June 1906, 16 September and 3 December 1907, and 21 and 29 September 1908.

[97]NAW, RINS, 54167, improvements at Ellis Island, 1904-1907; *New York Times*, 11 March, 6 June, 16 September and 19 November 1906, 2 December 1908, and 6 and 9 January, 2 March, 25 April, 19 May and 19 June 1909; and Zeidel, *Immigrants*, 118.

Passengers with prepaid tickets, who previously had received preferential treatment, were now targeted as "assisted passengers." Jewish migrants in particular suffered from this measure. To circumvent the problem, the shipping companies urged the migrant agents to send US $25 along with the prepaid ticket. As Ellis Island did not have the facilities to detain large numbers of migrants, the lines obtained the release of about forty percent of the passengers for not having US $25, especially those with a *bona fide* address of family in the US. To give those rejected a fair chance, Williams allowed the shipping lines to look at the minutes of the board of special inquiry to prepare an appeal. The exponential increase in the number of detainees is best illustrated by the arrival of *Potsdam* in July 1909. Of the 679 third-class passengers, 304 were preliminarily detained, 186 while awaiting the arrival of additional money and 118 who were transferred to the board of special inquiry.

Williams' iron rule led not only to great congestion at the control station but also to a spectacular increase in deportations, which in the first weeks of July reached six percent. The press reported that Ellis Island was on the verge of a mutiny. Williams blamed the shipping companies, giving as an example the Uranium Line's *Volturno*, which brought in 231 passengers of whom 169 arrived with less than US $10 and ninety with less than US $5. Instead of protesting directly against the measure, the lines tried to organize a campaign through the NLIL. The agitation against Williams quickly escalated, and William Bennet brought the complaints of the Jewish community directly to President Taft. A delegation of foreign-language newspaper editors led by Louis Hammerling was invited to Ellis Island where they debated with Williams about the LPC clause and the defence of detainees by legal counsel. Max Kohler of the AJC used the exclusion of four Jews under the US $25 rule to bring a test case under a writ of *habeas corpus* to the US Circuit Court. He presented as evidence a circular by Williams in which he ordered all immigrant inspectors to implement the US $25 rule despite the absence of a statutory provision to do so. Kohler claimed that Williams had seriously exceeded his powers. Judge Hand accepted the case of the four men, yet limited the scope of the inquiry, declaring that he was not in a position to decide on the powers and good faith of the immigrant inspectors. The judge ruled in favour of the four detained, but not on the legality of US $25 rule.[98]

Following the case and the subsequent agitation Williams relaxed his policy somewhat, only to reinstate it even more strictly in 1910. The inspectors refused to consider money wired to Ellis Island by distant relatives or friends, only accepting transfers from members of the immediate family. How strictly this rule was enforced varied in the following years. Passengers with

---

[98]NAW, RINS, 52600/13, investigation at Ellis Island, 1909; GAR, HAL, 318.04, Passage, 221-226; letters, 21 June, and 1, 2, 9 and 16 July 1909; and *New York Times*, 5 June, and 10, 12, 14, 16, 17, 22, 26, 27 and 30 July 1909.

direct family ties in America remained exempt from the so-called "financial test." The lines considered compelling passengers to possess the required amount before embarking, especially cash passengers who generally had higher risks of being excluded for having weaker ties in the US than prepaid travellers. The passenger manifests for the arrivals in 1912 reflect the importance of these ties: eighty percent claimed to be joining family, fourteen percent were joining friends and only six percent had no point of reference at all. To reduce interference with deportations, Williams barred many charity and missionary organizations from Ellis Island. He was backed by Charles Nagel and the DC reports on the dubious character of some of these institutions. The Commissioner of Immigration even temporarily stopped the practice of discharging immigrants without funds in the care of homes which posted bonds for them. This represented a complete reversal of the approach of Straus and Watchorn, neither of whom ever imposed financial requirements except for having the means to reach their final destination. Strauss frequently overruled deportation decisions of the board of special inquiry and even administered a special fund to support those without means who could not get assistance from other institutions. Williams strongly criticized the preceding administration, particularly the discharging division, for being lax. Under his rule, the number of detained passengers reached twenty percent, whereas under Watchorn the number never exceeded seven percent. The number of debarred aliens increased to two percent. To alleviate congestion at Ellis Island, the commissioner repeatedly requested funds to enlarge the infrastructure. Wanting to encourage immigration though other ports, President Taft refused. The indirect impact of Williams' policies as a deterrent for migration is much harder to establish, although the HAL's agents reported that the strict implementation of the laws had a demoralizing effect on bookings.[99]

Through their lawyers, the shipping companies sought to mitigate the financial repercussions of Williams' reinstatement. The idea of taking out insurance to cover maintenance and deportation costs had been banned by the 1907 law which stated that "no charge for the return of any alien to be deported or any security should be taken for payment of said charge; any violation would be deemed as misdemeanour." The Supreme Court also ruled that debarred passengers possessing a return ticket needed to be reimbursed for the

---

[99]Max J. Kohler, "Some Aspects of the Immigration Problem," *American Economic Review*, IV, No. 1 (1914), 99; GAR, HAL, 318.03, Passage, 48-58, 97, 160 and 190, letters. 1 February, 1 March and 15 April 1910, and 11 September, 3 November and 5 and 23 December 1913; 318.04, Passage, 221-226, letter, 2 February 1911; NAW, RINS, 52116/1, rules and organization, Ellis Island, letter, 8 June 1909; *New York Times*, 16 September 1906, 11, 12, 13 and 29 August 1909, 19 and 20 October 1910, 3 and 14 November 1911 and 20 January 1914; DC, *Report*, XXXVII; Thomas M. Pitkin, *Keepers of the Gate: A History of Ellis Island* (New York, 1975), 42; and Tichenor, *Dividing Lines*, 122.

return and deported at the cost of the shipping line. The judgment came after the NGL was caught forcing an older couple with a high risk of being excluded to buy a return ticket as well - an indication that the practice persisted. As an alternative, the shipping lines started to question the legality of being billed for certain costs. They first stopped paying the medical bills for the treatment of diseases which were not a cause for deportation, such as scarlet fever and measles. They had paid in the past to show their good will, but they now claimed that these should be covered by the Immigrant Fund. By the end of 1909, these amounted to US $40,000, and Williams ran out of funds to pay for them.[100] To force the lines to capitulate, Williams carried out preliminary inspections for these diseases on board the ships and denied the transfer of affected aliens to Ellis Island. The shipping companies considered using section sixteen of the immigration law to force their landing, but they abandoned the idea after Williams threatened to use all means possible to delay landing procedures. To prevent the conflict from escalating, the lines began to pay the bills again. Yet the commissioner also insisted that they reimburse him for all the unsettled bills. For two year Williams tirelessly reiterated his claims, backed by all sorts of threats, but without success. He finally gave up his fear of losing in a legal battle and took the HAL to court. The HAL won the case, which also called the payment of all the food and maintenance bills by the lines into question. While the Department of Justice appealed the decision, the shipping lines won another case when the courts decided that the White Slave Trade Act of 1910 could not be applied retroactively. This decision exempted the lines from defraying the deportation costs of people violating the act and having resided longer than three years in the US. Nonetheless, another test case seeking to exempt the children of naturalized immigrants from exclusion under the contagious and loathsome disease clause was lost. This right was granted to wives but not extended to children. The NLIL's attempts to have a resolution passed in Congress to prevent the separations of families also failed. The court activity underlines the growing tensions. The lines started to refuse to pay food and lodging bills, denouncing the commissioner for overcharging them. When asking for explanations, Williams declared that he did not have time and suggested that "the steamship companies should not take cases to court because what he said was law."[101]

[100]The treatment of measles, for instance, could easily cost US $50 as it entailed hospitalization for four-five weeks at rates of US $1.50 to $2 per day.

[101]The White Slave Trade Act attacked prostitution abuses by immigrants. For the first time there was no time limit on deportation for those breaking this law. GAR, HAL, 318.02, Directors, 112-121, letters, 21 September, 20 October, 19 November and 21 December 1909, 17 December 1910, 10 February 1911, 21 June and 12 July 1912, and 19 May, 6 June, 18 July and 30 November 1913; NWA. RINS, 51460/121, case of Moische Wilenczik; 53137/394, NGL versus United States, 1910-1914;

Williams also continued to rationalize and professionalize Ellis Island, managing to increase inspection times per migrant. Yet he kept on denouncing the lack of sufficient personnel, especially medical staff, to do so more efficiently. He also noted that controls at the Canadian and Mexican borders had to improve. His authoritarian rule earned him the title of "Czar of Ellis Island" and made him many enemies in the foreign-born community. Although statistics on deportees do not include nationality or race, Williams' continual attacks on the new immigrants suggests that they constituted most of them. Besides the financial test, Williams also introduced new physical tests to determine a migrant's ability to earn a living, and he experimented with the Binet-Simon test to uncover feeblemindedness.[102] Jewish organizations accused him of abusing the right to exclude people who were physically unable to earn a living to discriminate against Jews. Marcus Braun, former special immigration inspector and president of the Hungarian Republican Club, and Hammerling established the American Immigration Society to advocate for new immigration laws and the proper administration of the existing ones. It also supported the better distribution of migrants, just like William Bennet's American Immigration Distribution League. Taft received them along with a delegation of thirty prominent figures in the foreign-language press whose transport was partly paid for by the shipping companies. They remonstrated against Williams' policies, backed by the National German Alliance which questioned his sanity and demanded his removal. Petitions appeared in the foreign-language press to be cut and sent to their representatives to push for an investigation. This campaign helped Congressman William Sulzer (D-NY) to pass his resolution for an investigation of the procedures at Ellis Island. The IRL mobilized labour unions and congressmen to defend the commissioner, blaming the shipping companies for promoting the scheme. As Representative Burnett testified:

51632/13, immigration legislation, 1907, National Liberal Immigration League, letter, 12 December 1910; and *New York Times*, 20 December 1909 and 10 September 1910.

[102]Homer Hoyt, "The Relation of the Literacy Test to a Constructive Immigration Problem," *Journal of Political Economy*, XXIV, No. 5 (1916), 460-462. The diseases affecting the ability to earn a living included abdominal tumours, ankylosis of various joints; arterial sclerosis, atrophy of the extremities, chronic progressive diseases of the central nervous system, chronic inflammation of the lymph glands in the neck, dislocation of hip joints with shortness and lameness, double hernia, goitre, poor physical development, locomotor athakia, psoriasis and lupus, valvular disease of the heart and well-marked varicose veins. The Binet-Simon test checked the ability to repeat numbers, the keenness of observation, native ingenuity, the ability to point out absurdities, etc. If applied consistently, these criteria would have debarred seven percent of the new entrants in 1912. NAW, RINS, 53531/67, medical inspections at Ellis Island, report, 30 March 1913.

> Whenever these shipping companies do not like a member of Congress, there is no mistaking it. I have felt their force in their last campaign. They will send their emissaries all through the country for the purpose of crushing any man who gets in their way. They do it in a secretive insidious manner. I have no doubt they are trying to crush Mr. Williams in his effort to do right.[103]

The investigation did not find any grounds to dismiss the commissioner. Indeed, Williams appointed a publicity agent at Ellis Island to improve the public perception of the control stations while continuing to use his position to select newcomers based on his racial prejudices. His second term underlines the importance of his position and the freedom that he and his predecessors had to interpret the law and impose new barriers. The revisions of the law over the years, extending the deportability of unlawful subjects and migrants becoming a public charge to three years after arrival, allowed him to extend his policy beyond Ellis Island. In his eyes there were clearly various degrees of whiteness, a standard he could now impose not only at arrival but also afterwards. This shows that the growing bureaucratization and institutionalization of the immigrant control system had a bigger impact than that most historians have believed. The shipping companies were well aware of this and tried to influence appointments and either change the views of unfavourable appointees or lobby for their removal. The first to come up for reappointment was Keefe, and after a scandal provoked by the acceptance of free tickets for his family from railroad and steamship companies, Nagel forced him to resign. The shipping lobbyists worked hard to prevent the appointment of the labour-friendly Anthony Caminetti as Commissioner General of Immigration, but without success. Shortly thereafter, Williams resigned and was replaced temporarily by his assistant, Byron Uhl, until the appointment of Frederic Howe. In the meantime the Department of Commerce and Labor was split, leaving Nagel, who had opposed racial selections, without a successor. The outbreak of World War I would greatly affect the work of the new administration.[104]

---

[103]*New York Times*, 9 October 1911.

[104]NAW, RINS, 53288/8, conditions at Ellis Island, complaints by Germans, correspondence, 1911-1912; 53321/73, press relations and publications, letter, 7 February 1912; GAR, HAL, 318.02, General Correspondence, 112-121, letters, 20 August and 15 November 1910, 6 January, 15 April and 11 July 1911, 23 February 1912, and 8 and 19 May and 6 June 1913; and *New York Times*, 14 November 1909, 12 June and 25 December 1910, 15 January, 23 April, 11 July, 8 October and 11 November 1911, 4 April, 24 May, 13 July and 1 September 1912, and 22 February and June 13, 1913.

Shipping Companies' Interference in Racist Immigrant Selections

Based on an econometric analysis of American immigration policies, Jeffrey Williamson and Timothy Hatton concluded "that racism and xenophobia did not seem to have been at work in driving the evolution of policy towards potential European migrants and that eugenics' motives never borne out at the end of the first global century." They also found a correlation between economic downturns and renewed attention for immigration restrictions in Congress and stricter enforcement of existing immigration laws. John Higham also noted a collapse of nativism with the economic recovery after 1898, only to reemerge in 1905. But the evidence presented here does not corroborate fluctuations in nativism or their supposed insignificance.[105] The IRL institutionalized a nativist movement which grew stronger from the 1880s onwards. As a driving force pleading for racial restrictions, the IRL never gave up influencing Congress and public opinion until the passage of the literacy test and the quota act. The so-called collapses were caused by the congressional investigation commissions which froze the debates for some years. The growing influx of migrants and the economic downturns helped to place their arguments higher on the political agenda, but they did not determine policy changes. As Daniel Tichenor noted, between 1880 and 1930 Congress enacted immigration laws when economic conditions were fairly healthy and not during downturns.[106] Instead, changes in institutional structures and elections seemed to have had a bigger impact on the enactment or not of new laws and policy changes. The shipping lobby was more successful than the IRL in using the openings that allowed interest groups to influence policies. It also proved more responsive to shifts in power both within and without national governing institutions.

The shipping companies also displayed enormous zeal in adapting existing laws to their interests. As the immigration control system developed, a lot of power fell into the hands of the Secretaries under which the Immigration Bureau fell, as well as the Commissioner General and the commissioners of immigration. Shipping companies tried to have a voice in these appointments because the ambiguity of the laws left a lot of room for personal interpretations on how to implement them. This allowed officials to tighten or loosen controls according to economic or political pressures. In this process officials put more

---

[105]Jeffrey G. Williamson and Timothy J. Hatton, "International Migration and the Labour Market: Integration in the Nineteenth and Twentieth Centuries," in Timothy J. Hatton and Jeffrey G. Williamson (eds.), *International Labour Market Integration and the Impact of Migration on the National Labour Markets since 1870* (Milan, 1994), 27; Hatton and Williamson, *Global Migration and the World Economy: Two Centuries of Policy and Performance* (London, 2006), 161-167 and 174-177; and Higham, *Strangers in the Land*, 110 and 158.

[106]Tichenor, *Dividing Lines*, 19-23.

responsibility on the shipping companies to keep out "undesirables." Who fell into that category depended a lot on the personal views of the Commissioner of Immigration at Ellis Island. Under Weber and Williams, racist, restrictionist ideologies infiltrated the control station. What Congress failed to pass, commissioners of immigration tried to impose by using existing laws and optimizing controls. This led to efficient remote border health controls, financial, mental and physical tests aimed at reducing the influx from eastern and southern Europe, elaborate deportation procedures, detailed statistical information and bigger appropriations to improve the implementation of the laws. Shipping lines served as moderators to limit the impact of the commissioners on their main source of revenue. If the dialogue did not help, the lines fought the commissioners' decisions in court, in the press or in Washington to obtain concessions or the removal of the commissioner. They went to great lengths to guarantee the right to land their passengers, keeping the barriers to entry low and preventing deportation rates from escalating. The lines and their migrant agents circulated information on how to pass through the tightening controls. Assistance to detained passengers improved. For those with high risks of exclusion or who failed the tests, they offered alternative routes to enter the US.

As the HAL's New York head agent of noted, "drafting a law is one thing, enacting and enforcing it still another."[107] The role of shipping lines both in enacting and implementing immigration policies explains why between 1897 and 1914 approximately ten million southern and eastern Europeans passed through the gates despite being considered racially inferior. While drastic restrictive laws blocking the entry of the European poor did not materialize, the increased bureaucratization and rationalization greatly improved the selection procedures. By the time Congress finally enacted the literacy test and the quota act to erect a restrictive wall, immigrant inspectors had laid the foundations to build it rapidly and manage it efficiently.

---

[107]GAR, HAL, 318.03, Passage, 48-58, 97, 160 and 190, letter, 18 August 1913.

Conclusion

Approaching nineteenth-century transatlantic mass migration as a trade issue adds to our understanding about the business structures that sustained chain-migration patterns, the structural development of passenger lines into cartels turning migrant transport into a big business and the origins, development and enforcement of early migration laws. Placing the steamship companies at the heart of the European mass migration story underlines their pivotal role in enabling, facilitating and stimulating the process.

Transatlantic business networks were entangled in the transnational chain-migration networks through which a majority of migrants moved. Migrant agents and brokers represent key "meso" level figures connecting both. The focus on the American market underlines the importance of established immigrant entrepreneurs in ethnic enclaves within this process. Sharing the same background put them in a privileged position to gain the trust of co-ethnics who depended on them for key services to fulfil their migration strategies. Bringing people from Europe formed part of these. Through prepaid tickets the agent connected the purchaser with the shipping company and local agents in Europe. Together they arranged inland transport to the port of embarkation and supplied the passenger with information on how to overcome barriers along the way. At these barriers and key transit points, other agents provided assistance to ensure that passengers arrived for their scheduled sailing. Besides assisting with the move, migrant agents played an important role as distributors of information on opportunities in the US, on ways to reach and finance the trip to various destinations, on laws regulating the passage and how to circumvent them and on conditions in the home country to stimulate sales in the US. They promoted ocean passage sales directly with continual advertisements in the popular press on both sides of the Atlantic at their own cost. Often migrant agents published their own newspaper whose subscriber lists served to extend their customer base. Lists of potential clients were used to send letters containing promotional material and to direct canvassers and peddlers. Personal contacts and forms of direct marketing were fundamental to gain the confidence of customers.

It was not so much the prospect of financial gains on ticket sales but rather the crucial importance of this migrant service to develop and attract other business opportunities that made this product attractive to migrant entrepreneurs in the US. The variety of services offered by immigrant agents demonstrates that their role was not limited to assisting migrants in crossing the ocean. They often also provided a job, a place to stay, land to start a new beginning, legal documents and products and news from back home. The number of these services varied from agent to agent, yet they all combined the sale of steamship tickets with migrant-specific banking transactions such as short-term deposits, loans and money transfers. The close ties between banking and ocean passage sales spurred the sale of tickets on credit. That steamship companies were unable to eradicate this practice indicates how common and useful it was. The exact scale remains unclear, just as does the extent to which entrepreneurs combining banking with steamship and labour agencies advanced the money themselves. Yet American authorities could not prevent employers and patrons from advancing funds for the crossing based on future wages, in particular on the Mediterranean market. The lack of legislation regulating the activities of immigrant bankers and ocean passage sales gave these entrepreneurs a free hand in the market. Only when American banking institutions started to target the migrant clientele by investing heavily in foreign departments did some states pass laws regulating the activities of migrant agents. The American banking lobby pressed for these laws to drive the many unofficial immigrant banks out of the market and to put an end to the power of shipping companies in freely choosing to whom they distributed their ticket books. The migrant agents maintained their position as middlemen on both sides of the Atlantic, lifting psychological barriers, reducing risks and financial restraints of the move before World War I. They brought the New World much closer in the mental maps of Europeans and constituted a vital link not only in the chain-migration pattern but also for the migrants travelling outside such networks. More research on European agents should further uncover these people and liberate them from the stigma of being mere facilitating agents.

Their influence is further underlined by the problems passenger lines encountered in controlling the agent network. Having pioneered the maritime networks long before the ascendency of major steamship companies, they retained control over the market for ocean passage sales well into the steamship era. Due to the commercial importance of the migrant trade, the competitive pressures between ports and shipping companies remained high. Lacking the shipping lines' common interest in stable fares, migrant agents stimulated competition among the lines in order to increase their commissions and their grip on the market. Migrants also profited from the keen competition which maintained pressure on ticket prices at the same time that service improved. To neutralize these pressures, the Holland-American Line (HAL) rationalized the organization of the business through both vertical integration and horizontal combination. The company took over the management of the passage business from independent passenger agents and opened new inland offices at key points on both sides of the Atlantic. It joined a cartel agreement with the main continental lines that sought to reduce competition among the members, fend off pressures from outside lines and impose regulations on the migrant agents. The ultimate goal was to end rate wars and allow the lines to set stable and more profitable rates. The firms gradually collaborated towards a workable equilibrium by neutralizing rivals at their home ports and by reinforcing internal ties to defy the dominance of the British lines. This British-continental rivalry polarized the North Atlantic passenger market into three sub-markets; British-Scandinavian, continental and Mediterranean.

By concluding profit-sharing pool agreements to divide the steerage market into quotas, the continental lines laid the foundation to dominate the British lines in the migrant transport market. Taking advantage of the greater disunity among the British lines which undermined their negotiating power, the continental lines forced their British rivals into a pool agreement through which they acquired control over the migrant agents. This allowed them to reduce commissions and significantly increase rates which could now be adapted to maximize profits. Success inspired the continental lines to consolidate and expand their cooperation to the freight and cabin businesses. By fixing through rates and striking out the tonnage clause, internal competitive pressures among the continental lines were further reduced. This far-reaching collaboration enabled the lines based within the Hamburg-Le Havre port range to control the growing continental market by moving eastwards. While freight rates plummeted, passenger fares peaked as the market boomed at the turn of the century. This attracted the interest of J.P. Morgan, who tried to lift the concept of consolidation to a higher level by way of merger. The International Mercantile Marine (IMM) did not fulfil the dreams of its founder, but it did put end to the fragile equilibrium among the British lines and undermine the entire North Atlantic passenger market. By containing the attacks of the Cunard Line to certain regions and by preventing any general rate reduction, the continental lines displayed the control they had achieved over the continental market.

The continuing high demand for steerage berths from Europe helped their cause at the same time that it incited governments to use the migrant movement to stimulate the merchant marine. Government support made it easier for new lines to penetrate the market. Pool members refrained from fighting such initiatives in countries from where they tapped migrants or transported them to. With the growing nationalistic tendencies, government took a firmer stance towards migratory movements, and increased bureaucratization provided the means to apply these, something the Hungarian case illustrated. Rather than risking both the implementation of new barriers on their trade and costly rate wars, the continental lines preferred to cede a small slice of the market to Austro-Americana and Canadian Pacific. When negotiations failed, as they did concerning the Russian market, predatory pricing strategies forced dissident outsiders either out of business or into the agreement. Although the core continental lines gradually lost market share, the growing number of passengers allowed them to increase their sales with high profit margins. This market stability allowed the continental lines to quote higher prices in Western and Eastern Europe than on the Mediterranean or British-Scandinavian markets. Migrant agents became more loyal because of the increased unity among pool members. Representing the conference lines was too important for the development of their business for migrant entrepreneurs to risk losing it. Exceptions remained and abuses of conference rules never disappeared, but these were contained successfully.

The success of the continental passenger conference and the cheap market-specific organization of ticket sales through migrant agents may explain why so little vertical integration occurred in this sector. Yet whether this validates Alfred Chandler's claim that steamship lines had little impact on the development of "modern business enterprise" is debatable.[1] The fact that conferences are still the most common way to organize international seaborne trade indicates that the managerial revolution was perhaps not the only response to changing business conditions. The shipping lobby managed to fend off the American antitrust storm and prevented far-reaching government intervention into the conference system. The delicate sovereignty issue of governing international waters allowed the lines to minimize government intervention and take advantage of the authority vacuum caused by globalization many decades before other industries. Future research analyzing the full scope of how these major companies combined cabin, steerage, delicate goods, cargo and mail business on the same ship while opening other services worldwide should reveal the true impact of these companies on the organization and development of "modern global business."

There were various direct impacts of the conference agreements on the migrants. The divisions into various markets and sub-markets defined the routes through which migrants moved from and to certain regions. Inland routes became cheaper as fixed rates for ocean passages increased the pressures on inland fares until agreements on through rates ended the downward spiral. The competition also moved to the quality of the service offered, which improved the inland travel experience as well as what the migrants experienced at the ports and on board the ships. Shipping lines turned the once unaccommodating, risky trip into a well-organized and relatively safe venture. They did not offer a full door-to-door service, but the competition for business spurred the integration of a transatlantic transport network. The impact of the conference on the HAL's gross prices shows that these doubled after the pool agreement and tended to stabilize thereafter. Net prices stabilized even more, greatly increasing the profits of the shipping lines and decreasing the cuts received by the migrant. Yet the absence of a correlation between migratory movements and third-class ocean passage fares in this study reflects the scepticism of whether it is worth looking for one. Based on the fact that rate wars failed to redress the downward spiral of migration during economic recessions,

[1] Alfred D. Chandler, Jr., *The Visible Hand: The Managerial Revolution in American Business* (Cambridge, MA, 1977), 189.

previous studies have tended to conclude that companies failed to accelerate the movement through price policies. Yet shipping companies used recessions to settle tensions and renegotiate agreements to limit the financial losses of rate wars, having no direct intention to try to encourage migration. Nothing indicates that shipping companies used price policies to stimulate migrant flows, as fluctuations were determined by economic forces far beyond their reach. The influence of shipping companies was much more on the organizational level and on greatly reducing the risks of the journey, spreading constant propaganda on how to reach the Americas and supplying migrants from emerging markets with ready-made means to fulfil their wish to relocate. Moreover, the market for prepaid and return tickets reinforced chain-migration patterns and lowered the financial barriers of the move. The sale of tickets on credit further undermined the correlations between price and migration fluctuations. Giving people the means to work off the move in the US cancelled out the financial barriers. The imposition of US $10 and later $25 as a requirement for entry had little to do with yearly fluctuations. All of this evidence corroborates Timothy Hatton and Jeffrey Williamson's findings that the price of ocean passages was unlikely to have caused many variations in migrant flows.[2] Yet this does not mean that shipping companies had no impact on the number of immigrants as they provided the means to circumvent immigration laws and played a leading role in preventing the enactment of far-reaching immigration restrictions.

Shipping companies went to great lengths to protect their trade. Because national governments also long considered migration as a trade explains why laws regulating their transport preceded those regulating the entry and exit of citizens and aliens. These laws, together with the opening of steamship lines, played a crucial role in the development of ports within the Hamburg-Le Havre range as migrant gateways. They set a clear hierarchy among the ports which was fixed by dividing the market into shares with the Nord Atlantische Dampfer Linien Verband (NDLV) agreement. The reluctance to take unilateral decisions regulating trade during the rise of mass migration explains the efforts to reach international agreements to standardize transport. Yet issues of jurisdiction prevented a consensus among countries with emigration gateways which tried to minimize regulations to prevent them from obstructing the trade, while receiving countries tried to maximize regulations to start controlling the quantity and quality of new arrivals. The visible hand of shipping companies was active throughout the long nineteenth century, adapting itself to the institutional changes to help shape these according to their interests. As nations gradually considered the movements of citizens and aliens as a matter affecting national sovereignty, recipient and donor countries began to take measures to

---

[2]Timothy J. Hatton and Jeffrey G. Williamson, *The Age of Mass Migration: Causes and Economic Impact* (New York, 1998), 14-16.

control migration. To impose these measures authorities increasingly relied on the shipping companies, in the process increasing their pivotal role between the migrant and the state. In Europe, legislation continued to centre upon directing the movement to national ports and companies rather than regulating the flows. As nationalist tendencies and bureaucratization grew, countries did so more openly and efficiently. Facing an increasing number of restrictions to carry out its business in regions through which migrants transited or from which they came, the HAL increasingly relied on the American prepaid market where it could freely contract passengers. Prepaid tickets offered an efficient way to circumvent laws restricting emigration and impeding their sales in Europe. To retain this freedom on American soil, the company joined forces with other foreign passenger lines to oppose attempts to revive the American merchant marine.

American laws regulating the shipping industry disadvantaged national shipowners on long-distance routes, making it very difficult to be competitive with foreign lines on the North Atlantic. The American Line was the only company flying the Stars and Stripes, but it continually struggled to be profitable. It never ceased to campaign for compensation either through direct subsidies or through discriminatory duties and head taxes. Especially during the 1890s, when American jingoism reached peaked without a marine force to enforce its imperial pretensions, the company managed to obtain the support of the Republican Party, the Commissioner of Navigation, the President and a majority of congressmen. Nonetheless, significant measures to revive the merchant marine did not materialize until the New Deal. Foreign shipping interests used their influence on Capitol Hill to fight any scheme which would grant a competitive advantage to the American Line. They turned the public against such measures by depicting them in the press as the efforts of big business to loot the treasury at a time when corporations were being denounced for monopolizing business and corrupting politics. This argument gained strength when J.P. Morgan's involvement in the scheme became known, making it impossible for Congress to grant subsidies to the IMM without losing its credibility in the antitrust battle. It buried the ship subsidy plan, leaving the control over migrant transport with foreign shipping cartels. Yet nationalistic resentment and the antitrust movement represented serious threats to the established equilibrium among the lines. These threats eventually materialized in federal prosecution, yet the long-established shipping lobby, knowing the inside tracks and how to bring public opinion and politics in line with their interests, successfully fought for the legality of the conference system, limiting government interference in their business.

In the meantime, the shipping lobby successfully prevented the federal government, which increased its grip on immigrant legislation and enforcement, from adopting radical restrictions. The shift from state to federal control over immigration policies, and the growing tendency to consider migration as a national rather than an international issue during the 1880s, constituted a turning point for global migration policies and controls. This transition materialized in an international climate in which nation-building processes spurred the urge to take unilateral decisions about migration. Shipping companies hired lobbyists to ensure that these did not obstruct their main source of revenue. Because of the institutional changes and shifts in party politics, lobbyist gained importance as middlemen between politicians and corporations. They positioned men inside special congressional investigation committees and the House and Senate Immigration Committees to supply recommendations about migration policies. They contributed to party campaign funds, distributed gifts and free transatlantic cabin passages and organized fancy dinners to create support for their cause among congressmen. Lobbyists organized the opposition against immigration bills in Congress to prevent their consideration and delay action. If unsuccessful, they introduced amendments to reduce the impact on their business. To influence congressmen, they agitated in the press to mobilize public opinion against restrictions. Pressures increased when the Immigration Restriction League (IRL) institutionalized the rising nativist movement by calling for a literacy test to stop the undesirable and inassimilable wave of new immigrants. With the IRL, the shipping lobby faced an organized opposition in Washington, while the battle moved increasingly into the public arena. Lobbyists and journalists no longer sufficed to safeguard their interests which they only managed to protect before the turn of the century by exploiting and amplifying the conflict of interests between coastal states and those in the interior. The shipping lobby therefore enlarged the interest group that was fighting restrictions. By founding the Immigration Protective League (IPL) they mobilized the old and new immigrant communities. As politicians became more sensitive to the "migrant" vote, it proved a very effective strategy to pressure them while covering up their involvement. Moreover, manufacturers and big businessmen rejoined the lobby for liberal policies. Shipping companies also closed ranks, merging and optimizing their efforts to oppose restrictions. Nonetheless, their congressional base was shrinking. By influencing people in key positions, the interest group frustrated the IRL's efforts. As the driving force opposing restrictions, the shipping lobby managed to delay far-reaching, racially inspired restrictive measures for more than two decades. We can only guess about the probable impact of the literacy test because a lot depended on how the laws were put into practice at the gates where the visible hand of the shipping companies was also at work.

By taking over enforcement, the federal government standardized the measures by appointing a Commissioner General of Immigration who was responsible for managing the border control stations. Together with the Ellis Island Commissioner of Immigration, the Commissioner General outlined the means to implement congressional decisions. The ambiguity of the laws left a lot of room for personal interpretations, giving these presidential appointees a lot of influence in carrying out the policies. The ambiguity of the phrase "likely to become a public charge" clause gave these men a lot of leeway to express their personal opinions on the "desirability" of immigration. By far the easiest way to exclude people, the officials often used this as a reason to reject suspects of other excluded classes as it proved very difficult to prove these suspicions at the gateways. Migrants with diseases constituted an exception to this rule. It was the only category for which the authorities managed to impose the much debated remote border control policies. For all the other categories, practical and juridical barriers hindered the transfer of controls to the country of origin or ports of embarkation. Instead, the authorities placed the responsibility on the shipping companies by augmenting the cost of maintenance and deportation and imposing fines for bringing over excludables. The immigration inspectors gradually improved controls and closed loopholes, yet at the same time shipping companies opened new ones and refined the assistance given to its passengers to guarantee their landing. Those with high risks of being returned were sent through Canada, Mexico or American ports other than New York where controls were less strict. Others were provided with information on how to pass interrogations at Ellis Island. The ones who did not pass received all kinds of assistance to facilitate their admission ranging from medical care to tracing family or friends, soliciting the assistance of philanthropic institutions and appealing the decision of detention and eventual deportation. Shipping companies also used all possible means to gain the favour and influence the appointment of inspectors, translators and commissioners of immigration working at the gateways. Despite their efforts, they could not avoid the selections of European migrants based on the various degrees of whiteness from infiltrating into the control stations. Depending on the commissioner in charge at Ellis Island, southern and eastern Europeans were not always considered white either before or at their arrival. They acquired this status only when they passed the gates. That so many eventually did is largely due to the lucrative business they represented for the steamshipping companies.

Appendices

Appendix 1:
Rates of the NDLV Members for the American Market

The price series presented here is based on the Continental Conference Minutes, 1885-1902, completed with letters of the New York head agent to the board of directors and telegrams sent regarding price changes. Conference minutes give a full account of price changes with the exact date of when these took effect except during rate wars when changes are not always taken up and for which the correspondence was used. The reconstruction of the HAL prices 1902-1914 are solely taken from the correspondence. The dates used are based on when the letter was written and are therefore less accurate. Whether the data are complete, especially for the period after 1902, remains questionable, yet the correspondence indicates that if there are gaps, these should be minor.

HAL Prepaid and Return Rates in US $ for Third-Class Passages between Rotterdam and New York, 1885-1914

Date	Return	Prepaid	Date	Return	Prepaid
30/04/1885	23	18	20/06/1902	29	34
15/05/1885	17	17	05/11/1902	30	34
28/07/1885	20	19.5	01/01/1903	32	34
10/11/1885	20	22	12/05/1903	33	36.5
01/03/1886	20	22	01/07/1903	35	36.5
03/08/1886	18	12	31/10/1903	35	34
16/04/1887	21	21	13/11/1903	32	34
01/12/1887	19.5	20.5	28/01/1904	32	31.5
01/02/1889	19.5	20.5	21/06/1904	20	31.5
15/10/1889	20	21	28/06/1904	17	31.5
14/05/1890	20	19	16/09/1904	20	31.5
07/03/1892	20	22	14/11/1904	33	33
09/04/1892	21	26.5	03/03/1905	33	35.5
05/05/1892	21	24.5	30/06/1905	33	37.5
01/07/1892	21	21.5	15/11/1905	35	37.5
27/10/1892	21	24	01/01/1906	33	35.5
01/03/1893	21	30	02/02/1906	33	37.5
04/04/1893	21	25	15/05/1906	33	40
29/06/1894	18	25	06/12/1906	33	36.5
26/07/1894	16	25	16/01/1907	33	34
02/08/1894	16	17	15/03/1907	33	36.5

Date	Return	Prepaid	Date	Return	Prepaid
03/10/1894	14	17	13/04/1907	33	38.5
10/12/1894	12	17	10/05/1907	32	41
21/03/1895	16	17	31/05/1907	32	37
27/03/1895	16	22.5	28/06/1907	32	32.5
05/04/1895	16	25	15/08/1907	25	32.5
10/05/1895	20	25	04/10/1907	27	32.5
06/06/1895	16	25	01/11/1907	27	27.5
14/09/1895	25	25	18/11/1907	33	27.5
14/10/1895	20	25	27/11/1907	36	25.5
05/12/1895	25	25	20/12/1907	32	25.5
06/01/1896	25	22.5	02/01/1908	28	25.5
18/02/1896	25	27	07/01/1908	20	25.5
13/03/1896	25	31.5	15/01/1908	22	25.5
19/03/1896	25	34	07/02/1908	28	25.5
09/07/1896	25	31.5	21/02/1908	30	27.5
15/03/1897	26	31.5	31/03/1908	32.5	30
08/08/1897	25	29.5	22/05/1908	30.5	30
27/08/1897	26	27	22/07/1908	32	30
15/10/1897	26	31.5	28/09/1908	32	27.5
23/11/1897	26	29.5	07/12/1908	32	38.5
10/12/1897	26	31.5	27/12/1908	34	38.5
01/01/1898	26	33.5	31/12/1908	30	38.5
23/02/1898	26	31.5	16/04/1909	33	38.5
28/04/1898	26	29.5	31/12/1909	35	38.5
01/07/1898	27	29.5	30/03/1910	35	36.5
13/07/1898	27	27.0	20/05/1910	35	38.5
23/07/1898	27	29.5	06/09/1910	33	38.5
31/10/1898	27	31.5	05/12/1911	35	38.5
14/03/1899	27	29.5	01/01/1912	35	40.5
10/07/1899	25	29.5	07/06/1912	37	40.5
01/07/1900	28	29.5	11/06/1912	37	38.5
06/09/1900	28	31.5	13/08/1912	38	41
01/11/1900	28	34.0	21/11/1912	39	41
01/01/1901	28	31.5	10/01/1913	35	34
23/01/1901	29	31.5	02/06/1913	37	38.5
15/05/1901	29	29.5	15/11/1913	37	40.5
12/09/1901	29	31.5	05/01/1914	29.5	40.5
01/12/1901	29	34.0	01/02/1914	25	27

RSL Prepaid and Return Rates in US $ for Third-Class Passages between Antwerp and New York, 1885-1902

	Return	Prepaid		Return	Prepaid
30/04/1885	25	20	05/12/1895	25	27.5
05/05/1885	20	20	08/01/1896	25	25
28/07/1885	23	22.5	18/02/1896	25	29.5
10/11/1885	23	25	10/03/1896	25	31.5
01/03/1886	23	25	01/05/1896	27	31.5
02/08/1886	21	15	01/07/1896	29	31.5
16/04/1887	23	23	02/10/1896	27	31.5
01/12/1887	22	22.5	12/10/1896	26	31.5
01/02/1889	21.5	22	12/12/1896	29	31.5
14/05/1890	21.5	20	31/01/1897	26	31.5
07/03/1892	21.5	23	08/05/1897	28	31.5
04/09/1892	21.5	27.5	17/07/1897	28	29.5
01/07/1892	21.5	25	09/12/1897	28	31.5
27/10/1892	21.5	25	02/02/1898	26	31.5
01/03/1893	21.5	32	01/07/1898	27	31.5
04/04/1893	21.5	27.5	07/10/1899	26	28
03/08/1894	21.5	21	09/01/1900	27	29.5
03/10/1894	14	21	05/04/1900	27	31.5
03/11/1894	14	16	14/06/1900	27	29.5
08/12/1894	12	16	29/08/1900	27	31.5
18/03/1895	16	16	01/101900	25	31.5
27/03/1895	16	25	01/11/1900	26	34
13/04/1895	20	27.5	01/01/1901	28	31.5
11/05/1895	25	27.5	13/06/1901	28	29.5
05/06/1895	20	27.5	01/071901	29	29.5
14/09/1895	25	27.5	28/07/1901	31	29.5
14/10/1895	20	27.5	27/11/1901	31	31.5

HAPAG Prepaid and Return Rates in US $ for Third-Class Regular, Union and Express Service between Hamburg and New York, 1885-1902

	Return Regular	Prepaid Regular	Return Union	Prepaid Union	Return Express	Prepaid Express
30/04/1885	25	20				
15/05/1885	20	20				
28/07/1885	23	22.5				
10/11/1885	23	25				
01/03/1886	23	25	21	23		
03/08/1886	21	15	19	13		
16/04/1887	24	24	22	22		
01/12/1887	23	23.5	21.5	22		
01/02/1889	23	23.5	22	22.5	26	26
14/05/1890	23	21.5	22	20.5	26	24

	Return Regular	Prepaid Regular	Return Union	Prepaid Union	Return Express	Prepaid Express
07/03/1892	23	25	22	23	26	27
09/04/1892	23	27.5	22	25	26	30
22/06/1892	23	24.5	22	22	26	27
01/03/1893	23	32	22	30	26	35
04/04/1893	26	27.5	22.5	24	28	30
13/07/1893	26	25	22.5	21.5	28	27.5
03/09/1893	26	27.5	22.5	24	28	30
26/07/1894	18	27.5	16	24	20	30
04/08/1894	18	22.5	16	19	20	25
21/08/1894	18	22.5	16	17	20	25
07/03/1895	18	22.5	16	17	20	25
27/03/1895	18	30	16	25	20	32.5
11/04/1895	18	27.5	16	25	20	32.5
15/04/1895	18	27.5	18	25	20	32.5
14/05/1895	20	27.5	20	25	22	32.5
03/07/1895	22	27.5	22	25	24	32.5
14/09/1895	30	27.5	27	25	32	32.5
14/10/1895	25	27.5	22	25	27	32.5
14/11/1895	25	30	22	27.5	27	35
05/12/1895	30	30	27	27.5	32	35
26/02/1896	30	31.5	27	29.5	32	36.5
21/03/1896	30	31.5	27	31.5	32	36.5
05/06/1896	30	31.5	27	31.5	32	34
01/07/1896	30	31.5	27	31.5	33	34
01/08/1896	30	31.5	27	31.5	34	34
20/09/1896	30	32.5	27	32.5	34	35
01/01/1897	30	34	27	29.5	34	36
18/03/1897	30	34	27	29.5	32	36
01/04/1897	26	34	27	29.5	32	36
04/05/1897	30	34	27	29.5	32	36
11/05/1897	30	34	27	31.5	32	36
19/05/1897	30	36	27	34	32	38.5
01/06/1897	30	36.5	27	36.5	32	38.5
11/10/1897	32	36.5	27	36.5	34	38.5
18/10/1896	32	36.5	27	36.5	36	38.5
04/11/1896	30	36.5	27	36.5	32	38.5
30/11/1897	30	36.5	27	36.5	32	38.5
06/12/1897	30	34	27	31.5	34	38.5
14/12/1897	34	34	27	31.5	34	38.5
29/1/1898	26	34	26	31.5	30	38.5
23/02/1898	26	31.5	26	31.5	30	36
10/03/1898	26	31.5	26	31.5	30	34
16/03/1898	26	34	26	34	30	36.5
28/05/1898	26	36.5	26	36.5	30	37.5
01/07/1898	28	36.5	28	36.5	30	37.5
04/08/1898	28	34	28	34	30	38.5

	Return Regular	Prepaid Regular	Return Union	Prepaid Union	Return Express	Prepaid Express
10/08/1898	29	34	29	34	30	38.5
22/08/1896	33	34	33	34	36	38.5
10/09/1898	33	33	33	33	36	38.5
27/09/1898	33	31.5	33	31.5	36	34
05/10/1898	30	31.5	30	31.5	35	34
09/01/1899	28	31.5	28	31.5	35	34
04/03/1899	27	29.5	27	29.5	35	31.5
09/03/1899	27	29.5			28	31.5
04/04/1899	27	31.5			28	34
27/04/1899	27	34			28	36.5
24/05/1899	27	36.5			28	38.5
28/08/1899	28	36.5			30	38.5
18/09/1899	28	34			30	38.5
05/10/1899	28	31.5			30	35
19/10/1899	28	31.5			35	35
27/10/1899	28	29.5			35	34
06/11/1899	28	29.5			37	34
13/11/1899	30	29.5			37	34
09/01/1900	27	31.5			30	34
15/05/1900	27	34			30	36.5
15/06/1900	27	36.5			30	38.5
29/09/1900	27	34			30	38.5
01/11/1900	30	36.5			33	38.5
14/01/1901	30	34			33	38.5
01/07/1901	31	34			35	38.5
17/08/1901	31	34			33	38.5
01/01/1902	30	34			33	36.5
19/02/1902	30	31.5			33	36.5

NGL Prepaid and Return Rates in US $ for Third-Class Regular and Express Service between Bremen and New York, 1885-1902

	Return Express	Prepaid Express	Return Regular	Prepaid Regular		Return Express	Prepaid Express	Return Regular	Prepaid Regular
30/04/1885	27	22	25	20	07/10/1896	32	36.5	30	34
15/05/1885	22	22	20	20	01/08/1896	32	36.5	25	34
28/07/1885	25	24.5	23	22.5	01/10/1896	32	36.5	28	34
10/11/1885	25	27	23	25	01/01/1897	32	36.5	30	34
01/03/1886	25	27	23	25	18/03/1897	32	38.5	30	36.5
03/08/1886	23	17	21	15	18/07/1897	32	38.5	30	34
16/04/1887	25	25			25/081897	32	36.5	30	31.5
01/12/1887	26	26			20/09/1897	32	34	30	29.5
01/02/1889	26	26	23	23.5	08/11/1897	30	34	28	29.5
14/05/1890	26	24			23/11/1897	30	36.5	28	31.5
07/03/1892	26	27	23	25	10/12/1897	30	38.5	28	34
09/04/1892	26	30	24	27.5	29/01/1898	30	38.5	28	34
01/03/1893	26	35	24	32	23/2/1898	26	38.5	28	36.5
04/04/1893	28	32.5	26	30	23/03/1898	26	38.5	30	36.5
18/07/1893	30	32.5	28	30	01/07/1898	30	38.5	35	36.5
30/09/1893	28	32.5	26	30	11/07/1898	33	38.5	35	36.5
29/06/1894	26	32.5	24	30	01/01/1899	33	36.5	35	34
26/07/1894	18	32.5	16	30	07/03/1899	28	36.5	30	34
03/08/1894	18	25	16	22.5	05/04/1899	28	38.5	30	34
01/03/1895	18	25	16	22.5	01/06/1899	28	38.5	30	36.5
27/03/1895	18	32.5	16	30	23/08/1899	30	38.5	30	36.5
15/04/1895	22	32.5	20	30	20/10/1899	30	38.5	35	36.5
03/07/1895	24	32.5	22	30	10/11/1899	33	38.5	35	36.5

	Return Express	Prepaid Express	Return Regular	Prepaid Regular
09/09/1895	24	32.5	22	30
14/09/1895	32	32.5	30	30
25/09/1895	35	32.5	30	30
14/10/1895	27	32.5	25	30
15/11/1895	27	37.5	25	35
05/12/1895	32	37.5	30	35
01/01/1896	32	35	30	32.5
12/02/1896	32	36.5	30	34
20/03/1896	32	36.5	30	34
15/06/1896	32	36.5	30	35

	Return Express	Prepaid Express	Return Regular	Prepaid Regular
09/01/1900	28	38.5	30	36.5
12/06/1900	29	38.5	30	36.5
31/07/1900	29	38.5	30	34
01/10/1900	29	38.5	33	34
04/10/1900	29	36.5	33	31.5
01/11/1900	30	38.5	33	34
18/01/1901	30	38.5	33	36.5
14/02/1901	30	38.5	33	36.5
01/07/1901	31	38.5	35	36.5

NGL Prepaid and Return Rates in US $ for Third-Class Regular Service between Bremen and Baltimore, 1885-1902

	Return	Prepaid		Return	Prepaid		Return	Prepaid
30/04/1885	25	20	01/03/1895	13	22.5	19/08/1897	30	29.5
15/05/1885	20	20	27/03/1895	13	27.5	20/09/1897	30	27
28/07/1885	23	22.5	15/04/1895	13	27.5	08/11/1897	28	27
10/11/1885	23	25	03/07/1895	19	30	23/11/1897	28	29.5
01/03/1886	23	25	09/09/1895	19	30	10/12/1897	28	34
03/08/1886	21	15	14/09/1895	27	30	12/01/1898	30	34
16/04/1887	23.5	23.5	25/09/1895	27	30	29/01/1898	28	34
01/12/1887	22.5	23	14/10/1895	22	30	11/07/1898	30	34
01/02/1889	22.5	23	15/11/1895	22	30	07/03/1899	27	34
14/05/1890	22.5	21	05/12/1895	27	30	19/09/1899	27	36.5
07/03/1892	22.5	23	01/01/1896	27	30	01/10/1899	30	36.5
09/04/1892	22.5	25	12/02/1896	27	31.5	09/01/1900	27	36.5
01/03/1893	22.5	32	20/03/1896	27	31.5	15/01/1900	27	34
04/04/1893	24.5	27.5	15/06/1896	27	35	01/08/1900	27	31.5
18/07/1893	26.5	27.5	01/08/1896	25	35	01/11/1900	30	34
30/09/1893	24.5	27.5	01/09/1896	28	35	18/01/1901	30	36.5
29/06/1894	24.5	27.5	16/09/1896	30	35	01/07/1901	31	36.5
26/07/1894	24.5	27.5	02/10/1896	30	34	01/01/1902	30	34
03/08/1894	24.5	22.5	16/06/1897	30	31.5			

Appendix 2:
HAL Total Passengers, 1873-1914

Year	Total Cabin	Total 3rd
1873	198	2820
1874	270	1511
1875	624	1815
1876	580	2622
1877	718	2149
1878	820	2880
1879	795	4132

Year	East-bound 1st	Eastbound 2nd	East-bound 3rd	West-bound 1st	Westbound 2nd	West-bound 3rd
1880	253		468	435		9558
1881	273		672	533		15,511
1882	293		1240	472		17,677
1883	348		1866	621		18,003
1884	218		3426	523		10,547
1885	838		3064	831		6530
1886	852	795	4089	1034	1374	9680
1887	860	876	2687	1092	1606	16,466
1888	734	1011	6183	1270	2106	16,298
1889	1376	1430	5102	887	1919	15,879
1890	1604	1545	6103	1660	2533	18,758
1891	1712	1699	9271	1710	2877	35,929
1892	1779	1083	7891	1857	3448	31,680
1893	1350	1325	12,402	1711	4192	30,216
1894	2052	1505	9696	1682	1552	11,207
1895	2020	1197	5997	1803	1238	13,729
1896	1004	2061	5215	1944	2330	13,343
1897	814	2003	4065	1044	1749	10,687
1898	715	2036	4260	843	2621	14,140
1899	1543	2672	3819	1259	2759	18,025
1900	2300	3541	7049	1829	3671	26,018
1901	2220	2543	6285	2233	3278	25,762
1902	3324	2593	8464	3122	3907	32,569
1903	2973	2817	10,971	3015	5398	36,812
1904	2839	2802	11,076	3029	5222	27,198
1905	3128	3380	10,277	3246	6623	41,319
1906	3704	4016	15,885	3833	9983	42,499
1907	3766	4830	22,105	4136	11,274	47,725
1908	3663	4369	20,721	4078	6947	11,720
1909	4219	4170	10,446	4415	12,382	29,738
1910	5115	4512	12,251	5336	14,146	36,270
1911	4684	4218	16,757	5335	12,812	22,758

1912	4961	4571	14,046	5575	13,081	33,782
1913	4968	4127	14,047	5315	15,132	48,820
1914	4980	3530	18,997	9781	14,279	22,918

Source: GAR, HAL, 318.14, Wentholt Archief, 1, 1-30.

Appendix 3:
Total Passengers of the Main Services on the North Atlantic and Number of Sailings, 1899-1914

The following statistics were made by Conference Secretary Peters based on the figures sent in by the passenger lines. See GAR, HAL, Passage, 580, conference statistics.

A) New York Services of Continental Lines and Main British Lines

AUSTRIA-AMERICANA

NY	3rd WB	3rd EB	3rd Total	2nd WB	2nd EB	2nd Total	1st WB	1st EB	1st Total	Total	WB	EB
1906	15,410	1836	17,246	284	54	338	200	55	255	17,839	36	27
1907	18,080	4490	22,570	0	0	0	0	0	0	22,570	32	29
1908	4646	14,046	18,692	0	0	0	0	0	0	18,692	28	34
1909	14,968	4222	19,190	0	0	0	0	0	0	19,190	37	34
1910	13,052	4321	17,373	0	0	0	0	0	0	17,373	36	31
1911	7952	6933	14,885	776	648	1424	266	337	603	16,912	31	32
1912	13,523	5278	18,801	1245	692	1937	436	569	1005	21,743	34	31
1913	20,035	6247	26,282	1638	842	2480	465	603	1068	29,830	36	31
1914	7015	5476	12,491	648	491	1139	194	568	762	14,392	20	18

Note: These are only the continental passengers of this line; for the Mediterranean, see below.

FRENCH LINE

NY	3rd WB	3rd EB	Total 3rd	2nd WB	2nd EB	2nd Total	1st WB	1st EB	1st Total	Total	WB	EB
1899	22,885	9994	32,879	3165	2331	5496	2958	3374	6332	44,707	54	52
1900	30,635	14,733	45,368	5186	3914	9100	3603	3874	7477	61,945	56	52
1901	35,973	11,970	47,943	4091	2586	6677	3159	2913	6072	60,692	54	54
1902	49,502	14,345	63,847	4787	3278	8065	3837	3711	7548	79,460	59	58
1903	51,445	10,666	62,111	7351	4115	11,466	4019	3938	7957	81,534	59	60
1904	34,665	9515	44,180	6914	4112	11,026	4549	4653	9202	64,408	54	54
1905	55,813	8448	64,261	6870	4074	10,944	4950	4576	9526	84,731	72	55
1906	62,400	27,622	90,022	9015	5437	14,452	5885	5825	11,710	116,184	79	63
1907	66,217	36,372	102,589	10,993	6093	17,086	5758	5575	11,333	131,008	86	67
1908	24,003	37,124	61,127	8157	5837	13,994	4557	4513	9070	84,191	69	72
1909	46,754	19,078	65,832	14,401	5905	20,306	4452	4271	8723	94,861	100	84
1910	50,934	11,391	62,325	16,275	7129	23,404	3122	4292	7414	93,143	109	97
1911	38,641	29,967	68,608	15,908	7957	23,865	4511	4219	8730	101,203	107	92
1912	49,777	32,781	82,558	16,378	7805	24,183	4621	4326	8947	115,688	101	90
1913	65,337	29,383	94,720	20,988	9416	30,404	5250	5456	10,706	135,830	109	97
1914	27,306	15,313	42,619	12,127	7467	19,594	3696	3858	7554	69,767	85	81

HAMBURG-AMERICA LINE

Regular

NY	3rd WB	3rd EB	3rd total	2nd WB	2nd EB	2nd total	1st WB	1st EB	1st total	Total	WB	EB
1899	32,674	6043	38,717	4559	3921	8480	2551	2898	5449	52,646	63	65
1900	49,057	6698	55,755	5679	5070	10,749	3499	3472	6971	73,475	61	57
1901	47,168	6066	53,234	5618	4578	10,196	2972	3032	6004	69,434	53	53
1902	68,471	10,164	78,635	8184	5224	13,408	4668	4628	9296	101,339	57	52
1903	65,354	9392	74,746	7083	3858	10,941	2785	2664	5449	91,136	48	45
1904	77,816	22,089	99,905	11,490	7645	19,135	6011	5838	11,849	130,889	77	78
1905	97,577	13,788	111,365	10,173	6634	16,807	7087	6114	13,201	141,373	76	67
1906	116,461	27,316	143,777	14,700	8972	23,672	12,046	10,161	22,207	189,656	83	76
1907	140,641	45,109	185,750	15,707	10,339	26,046	13,418	11,598	25,016	236,812	101	76
1908	36,599	36,972	73,571	12,790	10,338	23,128	10,598	9987	20,585	117,284	70	70
1909	89,799	18,410	108,209	19,631	9349	28,980	10,592	10,368	20,960	158,149	74	69
1910	96,250	27,662	123,912	23,798	11,415	35,213	11,348	10,557	21,905	181,030	82	71
1911	53,613	29,145	82,758	21,027	10,492	31,519	10,292	9404	19,696	133,973	75	64
1912	85,327	28,449	113,776	23,999	10,594	34,593	11,232	10,500	21,732	170,101	81	72
1913	122,467	26,872	149,339	26,826	11,662	38,488	13,307	11,635	24,942	212,769	87	78
1914	49,724	31,424	81,148	10,654	9052	19,706	7100	10,039	17,139	117,993	51	50

Note: HAPAG discontinued the Union service in 1906 and opened a limited monthly freight and westbound steerage passenger service to Philadelphia in 1910.

Express

NY	3rd WB	3rd EB	3rd Total	2nd WB	2nd EB	2nd total	1st WB	1st EB	1st total	Total	WB	EB
1899	5102	3554	8656	3216	2151	5367	3764	2666	6430	20,453	18	16
1900	10,155	8055	18,210	6988	5068	12,056	7180	6372	13,552	43,818	37	37
1901	10,463	6531	16,994	4870	3746	8616	6975	6425	13,400	39,010	32	30
1902	10,286	5941	16,227	3607	2561	6168	3649	3504	7153	29,548	26	25
1903	24,676	9997	34,673	6948	4115	11,063	5764	6125	11,889	57,625	37	35
1904	3292	2263	5555	2500	1352	3852	3023	2555	5578	14,985	11	9
1905	1369	2071	3440	1935	1590	3525	2200	2300	4500	11,465	7	7
1906	1491	1713	3204	1318	1227	2545	1448	1559	3007	8756	6	6
1907	2153	2073	4226	2045	1622	3667	1993	2050	4043	11,936	8	8
1908	1272	1649	2921	1243	1079	2322	1062	1163	2225	7468	7	7
1909	1238	1213	2451	931	584	1515	1062	905	1967	5933	5	5
1910	1020	1252	2272	829	633	1462	1143	793	1936	5670	4	4

Union

NY	3rd WB	WB
1899	4726	24
1900	6565	24
1901	5231	20
1902	5508	21
1903	5408	18
1904	0	0
1905	2421	6
1906	10,623	15

NORTH GERMAN LLOYD

Express

NY	3rd WB	3rd EB	3rd Total	2nd WB	2nd EB	2nd Total	1st WB	1st EB	1st Total	Total	WB	EB
1899	19,878	9946	29,824	4744	4672	9416	6750	6382	13,132	52,372	46	43
1900	22,961	13,886	36,847	6823	4846	11,669	8378	5994	14,372	62,888	51	45
1901	18,426	10,862	29,288	5455	3512	8967	6589	5291	11,880	50,135	32	31
1902	18,820	15,678	34,498	7149	4138	11,287	8272	7528	15,800	61,585	29	30
1903	22,896	21,049	43,945	9568	5110	14,678	10,375	8662	19,037	77,660	33	32
1904	21,926	18,288	40,214	9218	5140	14,358	9929	9060	18,989	73,561	31	31
1905	22,065	15,906	37,971	10,093	5903	15,996	10,527	9399	19,926	73,893	32	32
1906	21,369	22,848	44,217	10,435	6649	17,084	10,149	8910	19,059	80,360	31	31
1907	24,628	27,121	51,749	11,623	7346	18,969	11,350	9065	20,415	91,133	37	37
1908	12,705	20,788	33,493	8821	7151	15,972	11,080	9825	20,905	70,370	43	43
1909	24,036	11,116	35,152	8742	5190	13,932	10,374	8815	19,189	68,273	39	39
1910	21,106	15,522	36,628	8852	5198	14,050	9746	8561	18,307	68,985	37	38
1911	16,362	17,739	34,101	9088	5025	14,113	9085	7757	16,842	65,056	36	35
1912	25,547	18,334	43,881	9069	4903	13,972	8315	7935	16,250	74,103	34	35
1913	29,420	21,590	51,010	10,226	4738	14,964	9183	8553	17,736	83,710	38	38
1914	19,181	19,266	38,447	3068	1963	5031	2940	4089	7029	50,507	23	20

Regular

NY	3rd WB	3rd EB	3rd Total	2nd WB	2nd EB	2nd Total	1st WB	1st EB	1st Total	Total	WB	EB
1899	33,770	3489	37,259	3437	2406	5843	2828	3443	6271	49,373	53	48
1900	41,739	6126	47,865	4548	2921	7469	3585	3445	7030	62,364	51	42
1901	58,378	7818	66,196	4977	2965	7942	3383	3426	6809	80,947	54	44
1902	63,370	8241	71,611	6491	3475	9966	2742	3187	5929	87,506	57	39
1903	65,809	9520	75,329	8869	4518	13,387	3210	3725	6935	95,651	56	45
1904	53,621	14,250	67,871	9150	4534	13,684	3110	3535	6645	88,200	58	43
1905	66,367	7411	73,778	11,842	5461	17,303	2561	3763	6324	97,405	57	50
1906	80,563	12,535	93,098	13,557	5102	18,659	2647	3279	5926	117,683	64	50
1907	100,817	32,808	133,625	15,125	6028	21,153	2710	3225	5935	160,713	76	62
1908	26,014	31,257	57,271	9917	5133	15,050	3175	3105	6280	78,601	56	45
1909	67,656	14,327	81,983	14,148	5360	19,508	5190	4966	10,156	111,647	66	53
1910	57,889	22,194	80,083	14,437	5936	20,373	6538	5647	12,185	112,641	64	51
1911	35,437	24,262	59,699	14,384	6036	20,420	5813	6128	11,941	92,060	59	47
1912	64,509	21,131	85,640	17,341	6633	23,974	7775	6792	14,567	124,181	70	51
1913	101,676	16,037	117,713	18,115	6299	24,414	7085	6420	13,505	155,632	88	58
1914	28,772	11,507	40,279	6453	3977	10,430	2367	4418	6785	57,494	40	28

RED STAR LINE

NY	3rd WB	3rd EB	Total 3rd	2nd WB	2nd EB	2nd total	1st WB	1st EB	1st Total	Total	WB	EB
1899	20,129	6108	26,237	3422	2839	6261	897	1097	1994	34,492	52	52
1900	31,007	8778	39,785	4300	3618	7918	1261	1358	2619	50,322	50	51
1901	32,786	8541	41,327	4462	3332	7794	1800	1598	3398	52,519	52	50
1902	47,019	8325	55,344	4850	3269	8119	2035	2069	4104	67,567	54	52
1903	54,697	12,597	67,294	6375	3859	10,234	2597	2911	5508	83,036	51	51
1904	39,139	15,792	54,931	6511	4098	10,609	2918	2830	5748	71,288	50	50
1905	59,435	12,706	72,141	7560	4591	12,151	3816	3760	7576	91,868	53	51
1906	64,620	19,425	84,045	9551	4541	14,092	3556	3214	6770	104,907	58	49
1907	69,869	29,134	99,003	8438	5042	13,480	3324	3319	6643	119,126	55	50
1908	21,804	29,448	51,252	6514	4725	11,239	2566	2836	5402	67,893	53	53
1909	48,992	14,327	63,319	11,438	3866	15,304	3126	3285	6411	85,034	51	51
1910	50,351	18,779	69,130	13,027	4911	17,938	4014	4458	8472	95,540	53	52
1911	33,456	22,124	55,580	12,798	4147	16,945	3591	3347	6938	79,463	51	51
1912	52,822	18,623	71,445	14,352	4198	18,550	3737	3959	7696	97,691	53	53
1913	70,057	19,962	90,019	16,623	4246	20,869	3074	3106	6180	117,068	59	53
1914	24,927	17,158	42,085	6617	2382	8999	1129	2336	3465	54,549	33	31

RUSSIAN EAST ASIATIC / RUSSIAN AMERICAN LINE

NY	3rd WB	3rd EB	3rd Total	2nd WB	2nd EB	2nd Total	1st WB	1st EB	1st Total	Total	WB	EB
1906	2577	0	2577	233	0	233	0	0	0	2810	5	0
1907	10,001	4932	14,933	286	73	359	0	0	0	15,292	17	15
1908	6196	8082	14,278	335	282	617	20	38	58	14,953	17	17
1909	14,231	4581	18,812	765	229	994	0	0	0	19,806	21	19
1910	18,669	6316	24,985	2361	714	3075	0	0	0	28,060	24	25
1911	16,157	11,181	27,338	2982	921	3903	71	246	317	31,558	23	24
1912	20,363	11,639	32,002	3666	1297	4963	283	240	523	37,488	27	26
1913	23,169	17,130	40,299	5156	2101	7257	290	224	514	48,070	29	29
1914	9812	10,060	19,872	3401	1868	5269	97	245	342	25,483	22	25

URANIUM LINE / NEW YORK-CONTINENTAL LINE

NY	3rd WB	3rd EB	3rd Total	2nd WB	2nd EB	2nd Total	1st WB	1st EB	1st Total	Total	WB	EB
1908	278	2789	3067	12	27	39	7	12	19	3125	6	6
1909	9505	3341	12,846	332	172	504	0	0	0	13,350	22	21
1910	19,642	10,016	29,658	758	231	989	47	44	91	30,738	28	28
1911	5846	13,286	19,132	448	382	830	99	194	293	20,255	25	26
1912	13,938	10,836	24,774	531	575	1106	138	212	350	26,230	27	26
1913	10,046	4316	14,362	702	434	1136	54	0	54	15,552	21	22
1914	1171	2404	3575	728	315	1043	0	0	0	4618	15	13

RUSSIAN VOLUNTEER FLEET

NY	3rd WB	3rd EB	3rd Total	2nd WB	2nd EB	2nd Total	1st WB	1st EB	1st Total	Total	WB	EB
1906	5206	799	6005	0	12	12	28	8	36	6053	5	4
1907	21,277	14,290	35,567	290	129	419	159	78	237	36,223	21	21
1908	3537	8072	11,609	125	162	287	0	0	0	11,896	8	9

AMERICAN LINE

NY	3rd WB	3rd EB	3rd Total	2nd WB	2nd EB	2nd Total	1st WB	1st EB	1st Total	Total	WB	EB
1899	11,340	6512	17,852	5989	4234	10,223	8414	7275	15,689	43,764	46	45
1900	16,839	8597	25,436	7447	5296	12,743	6999	8990	15,989	54,168	44	44
1901	12,510	5606	18,116	6030	3146	9176	6180	4129	10,309	37,601	39	39
1902	20,651	7312	27,963	7095	4376	11,471	7388	4877	12,265	51,699	54	57
1903	16,027	9199	25,226	6084	3152	9236	4471	2793	7264	41,726	44	45
1904	28,030	12,422	40,452	4727	2807	7534	4106	3166	7272	55,258	48	48
1905	27,116	10,094	37,210	6731	3912	10,643	5626	4404	10,030	57,883	50	50
1906	26,612	12,701	39,313	8329	3667	11,996	5663	3872	9535	60,844	51	50
1907	23,064	15,635	38,699	8261	3951	12,212	5130	3955	9085	59,996	48	48
1908	6985	23,893	30,878	5528	3445	8973	3615	2633	6248	46,099	49	49
1909	18,974	12,565	31,539	7332	3176	10,508	3411	2372	5783	47,830	50	49
1910	14,313	12,252	26,565	7701	2997	10,698	3859	2968	6827	44,090	44	46
1911	9965	16,862	26,827	6539	2662	9201	3305	2107	5412	41,440	41	41
1912	11,525	11,147	22,672	5996	2474	8470	2625	1750	4375	35,517	40	39
1913	17,970	9327	27,297	6660	2421	9081	2019	1130	3149	39,527	40	40
1914	9881	9913	19,794	14,871	9263	24,134	0	0	0	43,928	50	51

CUNARD LINE

NY	3rd WB	3rd EB	3rd Total	2nd WB	2nd EB	2nd Total	1st WB	1st EB	1st Total	Total	WB	EB
1899	20,855	11,809	32,664	9160	7388	16,548	9856	10,828	20,684	69,896	62	62
1900	22,723	12,093	34,816	10,798	7296	18,094	9299	8847	18,146	71,056	51	50
1901	19,933	10,314	30,247	9394	6554	15,948	8388	8733	17,121	63,316	57	57
1902	23,650	9619	33,269	9070	6195	15,265	7238	7107	14,345	62,879	51	50
1903	33,781	12,273	46,054	11,863	7963	19,826	6578	6473	13,051	78,931	65	63
1904	38,929	22,260	61,189	12,197	8907	21,104	5948	5907	11,855	94,148	63	66
1905	38,062	14,387	52,449	10,928	7356	18,284	7618	8213	15,831	86,564	63	64
1906	62,298	18,472	80,770	13,899	9028	22,927	9104	8772	17,876	121,573	68	70
1907	61,744	27,533	89,277	17,620	11,404	29,024	10,957	9518	20,475	138,776	70	68
1908	32,396	33,688	66,084	17,650	13,493	31,143	12,893	11,783	24,676	121,903	80	80
1909	42,730	19,699	62,429	16,122	11,479	27,601	14,354	12,726	27,080	117,110	67	66
1910	32,413	21,994	54,407	17,940	12,039	29,979	15,657	13,666	29,323	113,709	63	62
1911	36,444	30,865	67,309	17,609	11,872	29,481	14,673	13,959	28,632	125,422	61	62
1912	40,611	26,986	67,597	17,243	11,194	28,437	13,976	12,022	25,998	122,032	59	54
1913	48,089	25,701	73,790	17,176	10,883	28,059	12,994	10,636	23,630	125,479	56	56
1914	25,223	27,948	53,171	13,742	9217	22,959	13,602	10,430	24,032	100,162	50	49

WHITE STAR LINE

Liverpool

NY	3rd WB	3rd EB	3rd Total	2nd WB	2nd EB	2nd Total	1st WB	1st EB	1st Total	Total	WB	EB
1899	25,145	13,004	38,149	4200	3396	7596	8514	8105	16,619	62,364	56	55
1900	29,365	16,227	45,592	5810	4548	10,358	9140	8152	17,292	73,242	50	50
1901	30,462	14,724	45,186	6865	4898	11,763	11,306	10,102	21,408	78,357	66	66
1902	40,215	15,727	55,942	7385	5737	13,122	11,018	9506	20,524	89,588	65	65
1903	45,468	25,300	70,768	9638	7231	16,869	12,451	11,724	24,175	111,812	81	80
1904	57,784	34,243	92,027	10,846	8643	19,489	13,022	12,625	25,647	137,163	70	71
1905	45,782	18,103	63,885	11,243	8053	19,296	13,527	11,569	25,096	108,277	66	64
1906	49,452	17,956	67,408	12,947	8265	21,212	11,914	9925	21,839	110,459	67	65
1907	41,807	20,324	62,131	12,238	6763	19,001	9110	7226	16,336	97,468	55	51
1908	13,674	21,350	35,024	9081	6659	15,740	6872	6161	13,033	63,797	45	45
1909	17,983	10,799	28,782	10,835	6534	17,369	6845	5959	12,804	58,955	45	42
1910	21,986	15,859	37,845	12,797	7995	20,792	7285	6766	14,051	72,688	44	45
1911	18,358	22,619	40,977	13,584	7933	21,517	7684	6584	14,268	76,762	46	45
1912	18,253	18,977	37,230	12,657	8006	20,663	6982	6186	13,168	71,061	47	46
1913	29,136	17,397	46,533	13,121	8490	21,611	6238	5920	12,158	80,302	47	47
1914	19,534	17,542	37,076	13,355	7116	20,471	7671	5105	12,776	70,323	45	46

Southampton

NY	3rd WB	3rd EB	3rd Total	2nd WB	2nd EB	2nd Total	1st WB	1st EB	1st Total	Total	WB	EB
1907	11,719	10,313	22,032	6604	3443	10,047	6376	5143	11,519	43,598	29	32
1908	10,121	24,282	34,403	6820	4403	11,223	7448	6644	14,092	59,718	49	50
1909	20,114	14,514	34,628	8246	4056	12,302	6735	5781	12,516	59,446	50	50
1910	17,364	10,407	27,771	9188	4334	13,522	7580	6345	13,925	55,218	44	43
1911	12,335	15,106	27,441	8132	5091	13,223	7891	7780	15,671	56,335	36	36
1912	12,465	9902	22,367	7233	3921	11,154	6031	6142	12,173	45,694	34	34
1913	23,035	13,902	36,937	10,257	5558	15,815	7770	7615	15,385	68,137	42	42
1914	10,399	10,665	21,064	5038	3247	8285	6083	5518	11,601	40,950	22	21

B) Main Non-New York Services of Continental and British Lines

AMERICAN LINE

PHIL	3rd WB	3rd EB	3rd Total	2nd WB	2nd EB	2nd Total	1st WB	1st EB	1st Total	Total	WB	EB
1899	6966	2284	9250	2714	2667	5381	0	0	0	14,631	46	45
1900	10,405	2656	13,061	3016	2431	5447	0	0	0	18,508	39	40
1901	8407	2509	10,916	3280	2494	5774	0	0	0	16,690	45	46
1902	13,254	2684	15,938	3961	2778	6739	0	0	0	22,677	49	48
1903	17,422	3632	21,054	3777	2656	6433	0	0	0	27,487	48	48
1904	18,428	6604	25,032	3459	2443	5902	0	0	0	30,934	43	44
1905	19,427	3407	22,834	4094	3061	7155	0	0	0	29,989	41	42
1906	24,838	3988	28,826	4078	2643	6721	0	0	0	35,547	38	40
1907	28,989	4608	33,597	5060	3103	8163	0	0	0	41,760	44	43
1908	7554	5292	12,846	3484	2938	6422	0	0	0	19,268	33	32
1909	13,618	2549	16,167	3386	2267	5653	0	0	0	21,820	29	29
1910	18,108	3525	21,633	4356	2650	7006	0	0	0	28,639	30	31
1911	11,216	4843	16,059	4014	2208	6222	0	0	0	22,281	26	26
1912	12,687	2497	15,184	3702	2214	5916	0	0	0	21,100	24	23
1913	15,645	2627	18,272	3491	1826	5317	0	0	0	23,589	23	23
1914	7053	2375	9428	3082	1622	4704	0	0	0	14,132	26	25

CUNARD LINE

Boston	3rd WB	3rd EB	3rd Total	2nd WB	2nd EB	2nd Total	1st WB	1st EB	1st Total	Total	WB	EB
1899	7611	1732	9343	767	606	1373	672	377	1049	11,765	29	29
1900	10,230	4214	14,444	1135	1124	2259	824	686	1510	18,213	22	22
1901	16,683	4787	21,470	2061	1368	3429	1291	1258	2549	27,448	30	30
1902	23,296	5045	28,341	2515	1604	4119	1676	1424	3100	35,560	29	30
1903	27,747	5665	33,412	3606	1736	5342	1639	1526	3165	41,919	31	31
1904	30,199	11,665	41,864	3564	2275	5839	1767	1869	3636	51,339	23	23
1905	26,750	6855	33,605	3938	2228	6166	1932	1619	3551	43,322	25	24
1906	30,897	7792	38,689	4458	2440	6898	1734	1656	3390	48,977	25	26
1907	31,538	10,357	41,895	5329	2811	8140	1915	1798	3713	53,748	25	26
1908	11,356	9023	20,379	4872	2922	7794	1643	1319	2962	31,135	25	25
1909	19,120	6523	25,643	6348	3028	9376	1887	1378	3265	38,284	24	24
1910	18,300	4999	23,299	5427	2525	7952	1688	1262	2950	34,201	17	17
1911	13,681	6313	19,994	5916	2565	8481	1706	1324	3030	31,505	16	16
1912	17,670	8027	25,697	6864	3280	10,144	2599	2331	4930	40,771	19	22
1913	20,822	6763	27,585	7048	2897	9945	2495	1817	4312	41,842	21	19
1914	12,310	6906	19,216	6074	2982	9056	2729	2120	4849	33,121	20	18

NORTH GERMAN LLOYD

Baltimore	3rd WB	3rd EB	3rd Total	2nd WB	2nd EB	2nd Total	1st WB	1st EB	1st Total	Total	WB	EB
1899	20,077	1535	21,612	895	675	1570	0	0	0	23,182	43	44
1900	19,712	2111	21,823	870	855	1725	8	343	351	23,899	33	31
1901	26,719	1408	28,127	843	722	1565	0	0	0	29,692	38	35
1902	48,153	2432	50,585	1278	1034	2312	0	0	0	52,897	50	41
1903	71,002	2741	73,743	2559	1409	3968	0	0	0	77,711	54	40
1904	38,209	2878	41,087	1814	1106	2920	0	0	0	44,007	42	32
1905	62,675	1762	64,437	2481	1531	4012	0	0	0	68,449	54	44
1906	63,951	3169	67,120	3431	1747	5178	0	0	0	72,298	56	41
1907	64,774	5400	70,174	3789	1591	5380	0	0	0	75,554	62	45
1908	8223	5593	13,816	1593	1874	3467	0	0	0	17,283	35	28
1909	24,930	1491	26,421	2643	1440	4083	0	0	0	30,504	36	26
1910	32,005	1971	33,976	3197	1887	5084	0	0	0	39,060	32	39
1911	16,759	3055	19,814	2768	1623	4391	0	0	0	24,205	27	42
1912	27,803	2599	30,402	2558	1513	4071	0	0	0	34,473	39	42
1913	39,299	2471	41,770	2751	1696	4447	0	0	0	46,217	49	40
1914	16,666	1823	18,489	980	1407	2387	0	0	0	20,876	24	21

Note: In 1902, the NGL also opened a monthly service to Galveston with the annual passenger numbers ranging between 2300 and 13,500 wetbound and between 800 and 1100 eastbound. Just like HAPAG right before the war, the NGL opened a service to Boston and Philadelphia.

RED STAR LINE

PHIL.	3rd WB	3rd EB	3rd Total	2nd WB	2nd EB	2nd Total	1st WB	1st EB	1st Total	Total	WB	EB
1899	4366	270	4636	0	0	0	0	0	0	4636	24	22
1900	4951	363	5314	0	0	0	0	0	0	5314	20	20
1901	4243	312	4555	0	0	0	42	5	47	4602	18	19
1902	5853	254	6107	0	0	0	0	0	0	6107	23	21
1903	7554	251	7805	0	2	2	0	0	0	7807	23	23
1904	2034	260	2294	0	0	0	0	0	0	2294	21	21
1905	0	0	0	543	20	563	0	0	0	563	8	5
1906	0	0	0	793	801	1594	0	0	0	1594	21	23
1907	0	20	20	0	847	847	0	0	0	867		26
1908	0	0	0	0	882	882	0	0	0	882		22
1909	0	0	0	1359	929	2288	0	0	0	2288		25
1910	0	0	0	1441	871	2312	0	0	0	2312		23
1911	0	0	0	1381	730	2111	0	0	0	2111		24
1912	0	0	0	1677	601	2278	0	0	0	2278		26
1913	0	0	0	1795	673	2468	0	0	0	2468	26	24
1914	0	0	0	617	363	980	0	0	0	980	17	15

WHITE STAR LINE

Boston	3rd WB	3rd EB	3rd Total	2nd WB	2nd EB	2nd Total	1st WB	1st EB	1st Total	Total	WB	EB
1903	489	210	699	96	41	137	105	18	123	959	4	2
1904	15,822	5088	20,910	2146	1053	3199	2073	1361	3434	27,543	27	25
1905	11,117	3678	14,795	2382	1258	3640	2761	1842	4603	23,038	23	24
1906	13,507	4373	17,880	2630	1235	3865	2651	1651	4302	26,047	23	25
1907	13,554	5261	18,815	2082	1151	3233	2026	1670	3696	25,744	19	19
1908	6862	5823	12,685	1386	746	2132	1558	1293	2851	17,668	18	18
1909	5499	1834	7333	0	0	0	775	634	1409	8742	11	11
1910	11,282	3672	14,954	2270	800	3070	1732	1294	3026	21,050	20	20
1911	8760	3826	12,586	1931	546	2477	1481	987	2468	17,531	17	17
1912	8433	2646	11,079	2685	1564	4249	679	524	1203	16,531	17	18
1913	9799	3716	13,515	4668	3262	7930	41	77	118	21,563	19	19
1914	7106	3899	11,005	3414	2523	5937	0	0	0	16,942	16	16

C) Mediterranean Services (to New York unless specified)

AMERICAN LINE

NY	3rd WB	3rd EB	3rd Total	2nd WB	2nd EB	2nd Total	1st WB	1st EB	1st Total	Total	WB	EB
1905	0	5907	5907	0	0	0	0	0	0	5907	0	50
1906	0	7749	7749	0	0	0	0	0	0	7749	0	50
1907	0	10,308	10,308	0	0	0	0	0	0	10,308	0	48
1908	0	9287	9287	0	0	0	0	0	0	9287	0	49
1909	0	5288	5288	0	0	0	0	0	0	5288	0	49
1910	0	1987	1987	0	0	0	0	0	0	1987	0	46
1911	0	4484	4484	0	0	0	0	0	0	4484	0	41
1912	0	4416	4416	0	0	0	0	0	0	4416	0	39

NY	3rd WB	3rd EB	3rd Total	2nd WB	2nd EB	2nd Total	1st WB	1st EB	1st Total	Total	WB	EB
1913	0	3844	3844	0	0	0	0	0	0	3844	0	40
1914	0	1295	1295	0	0	0	0	0	0	1295	0	28

ANCHOR LINE

NY	3rd WB	3rd EB	3rd Total	2nd WB	2nd EB	2nd Total	1st WB	1st EB	1st Total	Total	WB	EB
1899	13,696	971	14,667	0	0	0	14	6	20	14,687	28	23
1900	14,764	1266	16,030	0	0	0	38	13	51	16,081	25	24
1901	16,084	2133	18,217	0	0	0	68	27	95	18,312	33	24
1902	26,144	3777	29,921	0	209	209	87	55	142	30,272	33	22
1903	26,601	7289	33,890	0	0	0	90	90	180	34,070	32	20
1904	15,026	12,199	27,225	0	0	0	130	103	233	27,458	28	25
1905	21,129	4051	25,180	0	0	0	215	50	265	25,445	25	15
1906	25,835	6678	32,513	0	0	0	261	105	366	32,879	26	22
1907	21,833	9024	30,857	0	0	0	263	78	341	31,198	25	22
1908	2704	6475	9179	0	0	0	54	53	107	9286	14	13
1909	11,531	2085	13,616	0	0	0	164	50	214	13,830	19	13
1910	11,264	3347	14,611	0	0	0	154	66	220	14,831	19	19
1911	8560	6631	15,191	0	0	0	141	40	181	15,372	18	18
1912	9160	4865	14,025	0	0	0	120	48	168	14,193	18	16
1913	15,416	2972	18,388	0	0	0	143	45	188	18,576	19	19
1914	4563	3513	8076	0	0	0	96	24	120	8196	15	15

AUSTRIA-AMERICANA

NY	3rd WB	3rd EB	3rd Total	2nd WB	2nd EB	2nd Total	1st WB	1st EB	1st Total	Total	WB	EB
1904	4276	5142	9418	54	12	66	62	9	71	9555	8	8
1905	4106	2069	6175	71	35	106	54	23	77	6358	12	19
1906	14,254	4199	18,453	195	66	261	241	46	287	19,001	35	27
1907	16,577	9669	26,246	941	240	1181	441	106	547	27,974	31	29
1908	2472	11,411	13,883	1640	683	2323	353	282	635	16,841	32	34
1909	19,297	5347	24,644	3176	858	4034	691	520	1211	29,889	38	34
1910	16,940	5108	22,048	3260	938	4198	819	775	1594	27,840	36	31
1911	11,140	8481	19,621	2547	496	3043	421	382	803	23,467	32	32
1912	20,968	15,730	36,698	3514	1091	4605	670	629	1299	42,602	36	31
1913	13,750	11,310	25,060	5822	1333	7155	724	659	1383	33,598	38	31
1914	9108	3969	13,077	4371	685	5056	160	347	507	18,640	22	16

Note: Launched a limited service to New Orleans in 1908.

COMPAGÑIA TRANSATLÁNTICA

NY	3rd WB	3rd EB	3rd Total	2nd WB	2nd EB	2nd Total	1st WB	1st EB	1st Total	Total	WB	EB
1904	4312	1599	5911	25	14	39	21	23	44	5994	12	11
1905	6814	2267	9081	223	32	255	47	27	74	9410	12	11
1906	6400	3160	9560	130	27	157	84	32	116	9833	12	12
1907	6474	4525	10,999	333	108	441	235	157	392	11,832	13	12
1908	608	3861	4469	167	125	292	190	197	387	5148	12	12
1909	3088	2053	5141	233	176	409	362	274	636	6186	12	12
1910	1296	87	1383	247	80	327	303	138	441	2151	12	12

CUNARD LINE

NY	3rd WB	3rd EB	3rd Total	2nd WB	2nd EB	2nd Total	1st WB	1st EB	1st Total	Total	WB	EB
1903	240	3428	3668	0	0	0	74	166	240	3908	1	3
1904	0	15,237	15,237	0	151	151	0	850	850	16,238		18
1905	**39,388**	4423	43,811	1432	203	1635	578	1108	1686	47,132	24	19
1906	**50,363**	8674	59,037	2451	471	2922	1059	2009	3068	65,027	27	24
1907	**54,105**	14,048	68,153	3039	1051	4090	1156	2108	3264	75,507	30	27
1908	**13,823**	16,636	30,459	1646	965	2611	877	2784	3661	36,731	27	24
1909	**38,755**	5072	43,827	3215	876	4091	981	3111	4092	52,010	24	24
1910	**41,930**	5947	47,877	3574	645	4219	967	3321	4288	56,384	26	22
1911	**20,118**	11,744	31,862	1480	390	1870	196	2068	2264	35,996	25	23
1912	**31,854**	10,224	42,078	3723	621	4344	1351	3207	4558	50,980	28	27
1913	*37,205*	*20,187*	*57,392*	*7344*	*1502*	*8846*	*2089*	*5511*	*7600*	*73,838*	*32*	*33*
1914	*10,513*	*9080*	*19,593*	*6746*	*665*	*7411*	*1424*	*3390*	*4814*	*31,818*	*28*	*24*

Note: These are the figures of Cunard's Fiume service. Westbound steerage passengers were counted as Continental passengers here (represented in bold) while the rest were considered Mediterranean. From 1909 onwards, eastbound passengers are divided into Continentals and Mediterranean; 1908 includes 10,022 continentals; 1909, 3836; 1910, 4777; 1911, 7033; and 1912, 5875. For 1913 and 1914, the total passengers for both services are given.

DOMINION LINE

Boston	3rd WB	3rd EB	3rd Total	2nd WB	2nd EB	2nd Total	1st WB	1st EB	1st Total	Total	WB	EB
1902	14,018	3602	17,620	647	162	809	360	937	1297	19,726	14	14
1903	17,765	3265	21,030	1064	184	1248	715	1900	2615	24,893	21	19

FABRE LINE

NY	3rd WB	3rd EB	3rd Total	2nd WB	2nd EB	2nd Total	1st WB	1st EB	1st Total	Total	WB	EB
1899	14,121	1804	15,925	0	0	0	24	26	50	15,975	26	23
1900	15,648	1257	16,905	0	0	0	26	77	103	17,008	23	11
1901	14,157	694	14,851	0	0	0	23	9	32	14,883	28	10
1902	21,617	4262	25,879	0	0	0	77	74	151	26,030	27	13
1903	25,029	8987	34,016	0	0	0	168	255	423	34,439	29	17
1904	17,225	12,150	29,375	0	0	0	96	87	183	29,558	28	19
1905	30,178	8035	38,213	0	0	0	157	173	330	38,543	33	21
1906	31,757	12,306	44,063	0	0	0	210	272	482	44,545	34	23
1907	29,569	17,316	46,885	0	0	0	248	241	489	47,374	33	27
1908	6315	21,596	27,911	0	0	0	371	455	826	28,737	25	29
1909	18,287	6520	24,807	33	0	33	486	505	991	25,831	38	29
1910	20,853	10,159	31,012	317	77	394	720	670	1390	32,796	38	33
1911	13,399	13,434	26,833	771	497	1268	447	860	1307	29,408	40	39
1912	25,802	17,185	42,987	2017	1280	3297	690	1080	1770	48,054	42	42
1913	36,786	12,780	49,566	3214	2003	5217	1037	1332	2369	57,152	45	44
1914	15,189	13,395	28,584	2209	1813	4022	1122	1559	2681	35,287	45	45

FRENCH LINE

NY	3rd WB	3rd EB	3rd Total	2nd WB	2nd EB	2nd Total	1st WB	1st EB	1st Total	Total	WB	EB
1903	0	14,379	14,379	0	0	0	0	0	0	14,379	0	59
1904	0	14,599	14,599	0	0	0	0	0	0	14,599	0	54
1905	0	11,700	11,700	0	0	0	0	0	0	11,700	0	54
1906	0	15,966	15,966	0	0	0	0	0	0	15,966	0	60
1907	0	19,787	19,787	0	0	0	0	0	0	19,787	0	61

NY	3rd WB	3rd EB	3rd Total	2nd WB	2nd EB	2nd Total	1st WB	1st EB	1st Total	Total	WB	EB
1908	0	21,651	21,651	0	0	0	0	0	0	21,651	0	67
1909	0	11,214	11,214	0	0	0	0	0	0	11,214	0	67
1910	0	13,749	13,749	0	0	0	0	0	0	13,749	0	78
1911	0	16,251	16,251	0	0	0	0	0	0	16,251	0	77
1912	0	17,964	17,964	0	0	0	0	0	0	17,964	0	80
1913	0	8935	8935	0	0	0	0	0	0	8935	0	61

HAMBURG-AMERICA LINE

Regular

NY	3rd WB	3rd EB	3rd Total	2nd WB	2nd EB	2nd Total	1st WB	1st EB	1st Total	Total	WB	EB
1899	2540	3519	6059	0	0	0	424	1672	2096	8155	5	6
1900	2477	20	2497	0	0	0	0	0	0	2497	4	1
1901	10,815	844	11,659	0	0	0	0	0	0	11,659	18	13
1902	12,706	2753	15,459	248	19	267	187	348	535	16,261	17	11
1903	17,828	5568	23,396	727	68	795	194	467	661	24,852	16	15
1904	12,535	10,947	23,482	246	55	301	646	940	1586	25,369	17	18
1905	15,215	6699	21,914	655	42	697	824	1477	2301	24,912	20	21
1906	24,338	6887	31,225	1757	250	2007	1207	2645	3852	37,084	23	26
1907	21,479	16,850	38,329	2589	1248	3837	1579	2976	4555	46,721	23	25
1908	3822	9670	13,492	885	740	1625	514	1556	2070	17,187	12	12
1909	16,442	2928	19,370	2688	1179	3867	1072	2059	3131	26,368	20	20
1910	16,469	5718	22,187	1796	848	2644	1140	2066	3206	28,037	17	17
1911	8288	9817	18,105	2874	853	3727	924	2018	2942	24,774	15	16
1912	12,486	8307	20,793	2830	823	3653	981	2328	3309	27,755	14	15
1913	16,011	6002	22,013	4809	1108	5917	1460	1968	3428	31,358	16	16
1914	8188	2337	10,525	2284	728	3012	598	1762	2360	15,897	10	10

Express

NY	3rd WB	3rd EB	3rd Total	2nd WB	2nd EB	2nd Total	1st WB	1st EB	1st Total	Total	WB	EB
1900	4378	3584	7962	0	0	0	378	1914	2292	10254	7	8
1901	4487	3151	7638	0	0	0	442	1524	1966	9604	7	9
1902	1642	1316	2958			0	152	1181	1333	4291	3	6
1903	1447	1026	2473	0	0	0	217	515	732	3205	2	3
1904	566	591	1157			0	94	739	833	1990	1	2
1905	218	723	941	166	0	166	97	919	1016	2123	1	2

HELLENIC/GREEK LINE

NY	3rd WB	3rd EB	3rd Total	2nd WB	2nd EB	2nd Total	1st WB	1st EB	1st Total	Total	WB	EB
1907	3563	2299	5862	0	0	0	190	85	275	6137	3	3
1908	998	5088	6086	0	0	0	226	207	433	6519	6	6
1909	6518	4107	10,625	112	351	463	423	24	447	11,535	9	9
1910	11,439	4087	15,526	378	327	705	1119	280	1399	17,630	13	13
1911	5737	5444	11,181	0	707	707	2113	198	2311	14,199	13	13
1912	8568	4342	12,910	1144	389	1533	1053	253	1306	15,749	11	11
1913	3800	4591	8391	992	511	1503	443	265	708	10,602	7	7

ITALO-NEW YORK LINE

NY	3rd WB	3rd EB	3rd Total	2nd WB	2nd EB	2nd Total	1st WB	1st EB	1st Total	Total	WB	EB
1908	3073	3680	6753	0	312	312	595	349	944	8009	8	6
1909	14,137	1115	15,252	0	0	0	890	163	1053	16,305	18	8
1910	10,990	3779	14,769	304	111	415	758	510	1268	16,452	17	17
1911	8115	6373	14,488	1289	806	2095	255	218	473	17,056	18	14
1912	8935	7279	16,214	729	753	1482	319	199	518	18,214	10	10
1913	12,824	4245	17,069	923	615	1538	111	204	315	18,922	12	11
1914	3352	9723	13,075	940	473	1413	119	137	256	14,744	13	13

PHIL.	3rd WB	3rd EB	3rd Total	2nd WB	2nd EB	2nd Total	1st WB	1st EB	1st Total	Total	WB	EB
1908	112	8299	8411	0	0	0	3	36	39	8450	1	9
1909	8239	2369	10,608	0	0	0	164	219	383	10,991	18	18
1910	10,104	3268	13,372	70	12	82	340	152	492	13,946	17	17
1911	6054	7006	13,060	429	239	668	22	59	81	13,809	13	18
1912	5395	2794	8189	221	57	278	48	18	66	8533	8	8
1913	8583	2222	10,805	422	50	472	19	17	36	11,313	10	9
1914	3316	3758	7074	363	111	474	17	11	28	7576	9	9

Note: This is the Italia Societa di Navigazione a Vapore which was founded by HAPAG to operate between Italy and South America. In 1906, it sold its shares to Navigazione Generale Italiana which used the ships on the New York and Philadelphia route

LA VELOCE

NY	3rd WB	3rd EB	3rd Total	2nd WB	2nd EB	2nd Total	1st WB	1st EB	1st Total	Total	WB	EB
1901	13,532	3709	17,241	202	228	430	296	157	453	18,124	14	13
1902	20,167	5588	25,755	28	0	28	452	349	801	26,584	22	22
1903	31,172	10,162	41,334	0	0	0	786	444	1230	42,564	26	21
1904	18,894	13,968	32,862			0	671	401	1072	33,934	23	20
1905	32,476	5319	37,795			0	768	387	1155	38,950	29	22
1906	28,938	6040	34,978	156	73	229	780	486	1266	36,473	24	19
1907	29,822	11,993	41,815	254	181	435	1278	675	1953	44,203	26	25
1908	5049	9674	14,723	0	180	180	738	408	1146	16,049	13	13
1909	18,656	3695	22,351	145	72	217	1269	421	1690	24,258	18	14
1910	20,520	5339	25,859	0	0	0	2317	1067	3384	29,243	21	21
1911	13,376	9375	22,751	1457	411	1868	849	651	1500	26,119	17	17
1912	15,308	5233	20,541	1638	486	2124	123	199	322	22,987	10	9
1913	21,011	6798	27,809	1763	672	2435	104	405	509	30,753	14	14
1914	9858	15,578	25,436	2149	1135	3284	224	332	556	29,276	17	17

PHIL.	3rd WB	3rd EB	3rd Total	2nd WB	2nd EB	2nd Total	1st WB	1st EB	1st Total	Total	WB	EB
1912	454	1073		48	33			12			3	3
1913	3357	1048		115	37		3	10			6	6
1914	1945	2027		126	43		5	13			6	7

LLOYD ITALIANO

NY	3rd WB	3rd EB	3rd Total	2nd WB	2nd EB	2nd Total	1st WB	1st EB	1st Total	Total	WB	EB
1905	568	613	1181	0	0	0	0	0	0	1181	1	1
1906	19,958	6053	26,011	0	0	0	203	68	271	26,282	14	14
1907	26,355	10,354	36,709	0	0	0	314	134	448	37,157	20	20
1908	5902	9426	15,328	0	0	0	224	91	315	15,643	13	13
1909	17,564	2867	20,431	0	0	0	481	230	711	21,142	20	20
1910	14,721	6933	21,654	28	1	29	482	225	707	22,390	20	20
1911	7501	6984	14,485	493	159	652	0	53	53	15,190	15	15
1912	19,851	8429	28,280	1809	595	2404	217	292	509	31,193	18	18
1913	26,060	6547	32,607	1978	805	2783	137	158	295	35,685	18	18
1914	9874	12,735	22,609	1919	930	2849	349	269	618	26,076	17	17

PHIL.	3rd WB	3rd EB	3rd Total	2nd WB	2nd EB	2nd Total	1st WB	1st EB	1st Total	Total	WB	EB
1912	347	878	1225	21	13	34	0	0	0	1259	2	3
1913	1154	257	1411	44	21	65	4	0	4	1480	2	2
1914	601	798	1399	71	60	131	4	0	4	1534	3	3

LLOYD SABAUDO

NY	3rd WB	3rd EB	3rd Total	2nd WB	2nd EB	2nd Total	1st WB	1st EB	1st Total	Total	WB	EB
1907	15,862	8424	24,286	0	0	0	595	349	944	25,230	14	13
1908	4899	15,541	20,440	564	284	848	491	591	1082	22,370	13	14
1909	18,496	4591	23,087	119	125	244	1468	624	2092	25,423	18	19
1910	14,968	6005	20,973	89	207	296	1498	607	2105	23,374	19	18
1911	8542	4177	12,719	102	410	512	1244	149	1393	14,624	14	13
1912	7116	4428	11,544	0	0	0	652	376	1028	12,572	7	8
1913	19,762	4189	23,951	0	0	0	1268	492	1760	25,711	14	14
1914	4984	7563	12,547	728	54	782	1163	443	1606	14,935	12	12

NATIONAL GREEK LINE

NY	3rd WB	3rd EB	3rd Total	2nd WB	2nd EB	2nd Total	1st WB	1st EB	1st Total	Total	WB	EB
1909	5968	2715	8683	273	228	501	122	54	176	9360	6	6
1910	7513	2919	10,432	800	423	1223	10	171	181	11,836	8	8
1911	5473	4120	9593	727	413	1140	137	253	390	11,123	9	9
1912	11,113	6622	17,735	2528	903	3431	169	236	405	21,571	12	11
1913	2572	3896	6468	560	550	1110	196	190	386	7964	5	6
1914	5559	4727	10,286	1262	836	2098	564	242	806	13,190	11	11

NAVIGAZIONE GENERALE ITALIANA

NY	3rd WB	3rd EB	3rd Total	2nd WB	2nd EB	2nd Total	1st WB	1st EB	1st Total	Total	WB	EB
1899	8835	1981	10,816	0	0	0	76	48	124	10,940	11	11
1900	17,263	4724	21,987	0	0	0	285	265	550	22,537	18	18
1901	24,660	7091	31,751	68	49	117	465	429	894	32,762	27	26
1902	31,445	9697	41,142	683	408	1091	606	824	1430	43,663	34	30
1903	27,360	10,627	37,987	972	448	1420	581	769	1350	40,757	32	26
1904	17,315	14,535	31,850	903	538	1441	395	496	891	34,182	26	25
1905	35,617	8241	43,858	1086	542	1628	508	561	1069	46,555	34	27
1906	38,155	7344	45,499	997	677	1674	357	376	733	47,906	34	25
1907	34,295	13,085	47,380	1028	633	1661	178	211	389	49,430	24	24
1908	9314	19,293	28,607	416	305	721	452	391	843	30,171	18	17
1909	35,486	6933	42,419	946	535	1481	601	600	1201	45,101	38	37
1910	23,159	11,204	34,363	874	859	1733	695	832	1527	37,623	24	30
1911	20,067	16,611	36,678	930	1051	1981	914	717	1631	40,290	24	24
1912	24,272	12,875	37,147	1357	822	2179	547	611	1158	40,484	17	17
1913	29,816	11,250	41,066	2486	1168	3654	381	433	814	45,534	17	16
1914	16,790	22,950	39,740	3165	1732	4897	666	565	1231	45,868	23	21

Boston	3rd WB	3rd EB	3rd Total	2nd WB	2nd EB	2nd Total	1st WB	1st EB	1st Total	Total	WB	EB
1910	6003	223	6226	334	82	416	2	0	2	6644	9	6
1913	975	120	1095	81	4	85	0	0	0	1180	2	1
1911	1878	1584	3462	106	105	211	0	0	0	3673	4	4
1912	1388	1420	2808	49	50	99	12	24	36	2943	6	7
1913	3432	1728	5160	97	76	173	17	20	37	5370	7	7
1914	1028	698	1726	53	29	82	1	4	5	1813	3	3

NORTH GERMAN LLOYD

NY	3rd WB	3rd EB	3rd Total	2nd WB	2nd EB	2nd Total	1st WB	1st EB	1st Total	Total	WB	EB
1899	21,645	10,163	31,808	629	10	639	1606	3205	4811	37,258	29	31
1900	27,444	13,225	40,669	1040	0	1040	2187	4752	6939	48,648	36	36
1901	24,600	8738	33,338	724	0	724	1833	3712	5545	39,607	36	38
1902	29,617	11,299	40,916	747	5	752	2431	3775	6206	47,874	40	38
1903	29,576	14,165	43,741	1512	148	1660	2335	3299	5634	51,035	30	30
1904	22,902	28,968	51,870	3334	1082	4416	2409	3596	6005	62,291	31	32
1905	46,613	11,905	58,518	4907	1524	6431	2886	3946	6832	71,781	36	35
1906	47,469	13,635	61,104	5570	2134	7704	2770	3947	6717	75,525	33	33
1907	45,416	19,332	64,748	7107	3285	10,392	3058	3695	6753	81,893	38	38
1908	8536	29,436	37,972	4138	2278	6416	2624	3471	6095	50,483	30	30
1909	30,429	6143	36,572	5923	2238	8161	2736	3843	6579	51,312	31	33
1910	32,522	12,119	44,641	6192	3023	9215	3542	4371	7913	61,769	37	38
1911	21,746	12,311	34,057	4960	2265	7225	1996	3463	5459	46,741	25	27
1912	28,747	11,471	40,218	5287	1927	7214	2133	2641	4774	52,206	20	20
1913	33,452	12,196	45,648	6789	2463	9252	2080	2794	4874	59,774	21	20
1914	14,455	4079	18,534	3016	1209	4225	1254	1876	3130	25,889	12	12

PRINCE LINE

NY	3rd WB	3rd EB	3rd Total	2nd WB	2nd EB	2nd Total	1st WB	1st EB	1st Total	Total	WB	EB
1899	14,266	3465	17,731	0	0	0	221	377	598	18,329	17	16
1900	13,857	3768	17,625	0	0	0	246	519	765	18,390	17	18
1901	12,455	1592	14,047	0	0	0	159	311	470	14,517	17	15
1902	16,922	2466	19,388	0	0	0	59	61	120	19,508	18	15
1903	16,228	5331	21,559	0	0	0	93	19	112	21,671	19	17
1904	7937	6453	14,390	0	0	0	85	5	90	14,480	14	13
1905	14,179	4562	18,741	0	0	0	91	3	94	18,835	16	17
1906	15,942	5437	21,379	0	0	0	92	17	109	21,488	16	16
1907	8683	5808	14,491	0	0	0	159	3	162	14,653	13	12
1908	441	2295	2736	0	0	0	49	11	60	2796	3	4

SICULA AMERICANA

NY	3rd WB	3rd EB	3rd Total	2nd WB	2nd EB	2nd Total	1st WB	1st EB	1st Total	Total	WB	EB
1907	9314	6767	16,081	0	0	0	76	0	0	16,081	12	10
1908	3920	19,270	23,190	0	0	0	263	230	493	23,683	16	17
1909	14,576	2583	17,159	0	0	0	266	80	346	17,505	15	14
1910	10,594	4608	15,202	0	0	0	151	24	175	15,377	14	14
1911	7130	9504	16,634	209	180	389	191	17	208	17,231	12	15
1912	17,225	7023	24,248	1052	344	1396	71	40	111	25,755	17	17
1913	27,646	4007	31,653	1163	353	1516	81	32	113	33,282	16	16
1914	7990	11,231	19,221	2338	644	2982	256	79	335	22,538	16	16

WHITE STAR LINE

Boston	3rd WB	3rd EB	3rd Total	2nd WB	2nd EB	2nd Total	1st WB	1st EB	1st Total	Total	WB	EB
1903	0	1529	1529	0	0	0	0	133	133	1662	0	1
1904	14,119	8316	22,435	1166	100	1266	1214	3222	4436	28,137	17	18
1905	15,884	5980	21,864	1875	235	2110	1059	2542	3601	27,575	15	15
1906	18,733	7788	26,521	2227	414	2641	1104	2699	3803	32,965	16	16
1907	17,538	8560	26,098	2289	604	2893	1153	2962	4115	33,106	16	15
1908	6066	12,815	18,881	1553	506	2059	1145	2303	3448	24,388	15	16
1909	16,096	4622	20,718	2627	454	3081	1092	2416	3508	27,307	16	17
1910	11,862	4030	15,892	2127	619	2746	1316	2647	3963	22,601	15	15
1911	9951	9487	19,438	2716	570	3286	909	1711	2620	25,344	15	14
1912	14,802	7761	22,563	2672	687	3359	909	2019	2928	28,850	15	15
1913	18,128	8215	26,343	3510	745	4255	1055	2217	3272	33,870	14	14
1914	9334	8710	18,044	2444	471	2915	1259	1995	3254	24,213	13	13

New York

	3rd WB	3rd EB	3rd Total	2nd WB	2nd EB	2nd Total	1st WB	1st EB	1st Total	Total	WB	EB
1904	398	4886	5284	92	101	193	70	422	492	5969	2	4
1905	17,246	7562	24,808	2086	230	2316	1035	2697	3732	30,856	14	14
1906	25,480	10,918	36,398	2893	451	3344	1286	3165	4451	44,193	15	15
1907	22,938	12,120	35,058	2750	822	3572	1275	3418	4693	43,323	14	15
1908	4289	12,502	16,791	1244	486	1730	1193	2967	4160	22,681	13	13
1909	14,954	2147	17,101	2239	175	2414	984	2384	3368	22,883	12	11
1910	10,169	1622	11,791	1563	94	1657	803	2428	3231	16,679	8	9
1911	9922	8333	18,255	1621	480	2101	723	2235	2958	23,314	10	12
1912	5510	3267	8777	1072	96	1168	416	1827	2243	12,188	5	5
1913	6471	4633	11,104	1503	262	1765	583	1996	2579	15,448	5	5
1914	6390	2246	8636	1957	102	2059	449	1783	2232	12,927	6	6

Appendix 4:
HAL Through Rates to and from Hinterland Destinations, 1893-1907 (US $)

Destination	1893	1895	1900	1907	Destination	1893	1895	1900	1907
Aachen		1.29		1	Leeuwarden				0.9
Agram	14.15	11.5	8.4	8.4	Leipzig				3.05
Alexandria				12	Lille				0.9
Allenstein				5.3	Mainz		2.31		1.55
Bajohren				7.15	Mannheim		2.93		1.8
Basel		3.98		4.55	Marseille				2
Batoum				16	Milan				3.75
Belovar				9	Miskolcz				7.55
Bern		5.2		5.65	Mitrovicza				9.55
Berlin				3.1	Mohacs				9.6
Beyrouth				15	Munchen		5.93		4.85
Brunn				6	Munkacs				8.55
Budapest	11.95	8.78	7.55	7.55	Myslowitz				5.6
Bukarest				10.35	Naples				2
Budweis	9.4	6.52			Oderberg	5.87		5.6	5.6
Chiasso		8.28		8.35	Oedenburg				6.5
Chur		6.03		6.7	*Ostrowo*				4.9
Coblenz		1.8		1.25	Oswieczim	6.07		5.7	5.7
Cologne				0.95	*Ottolotschin*				5
Constantinople				12	Paris				1.8
Czernowitz				8.75	Peterwardein				9.55
Debreczin	13.6	10.18		9	Pilsen		4.91		
Dobricza				10.2	Pireaus				9
Dusseldorf				0.95	*Posen*				4.3
Eperjes	13.6	8.19		7.55	*Prostken*			6.55	6.55
Essegg				9.45	Prag	8.95	7.55		4.6
Eydtkuhnen				6.65	Saloniki				9

Destination	1893	1895	1900	1907	Destination	1893	1895	1900	1907
Franfurt a/M				1.75	Samsoun				14
Fiume		10.79	8.4		Sillein				6.25
Funfkircken				9.2	Smyrna				9
Genoa				2	Strassburg				2.9
Groningen				0.9	Stuttgart		4		2.85
Grosswardein				9.2	Szegedin	13.6	11.2		8.75
Hermannstadt				9.65	Temesvar	13.6	11.6		9.15
Illowo				5.65	*Thorn*				4.95
Innsbruck			5.95	6.55	*Tilsit*				6.6
Insterburg				6.35	Trebizonde				15
Jaffa				14	Triest	12.2	11.3	9.55	9.35
Jassy				10.15	Tripolis				16
Kaschau	13.6	7.9	7.9	7.55	Turin				3.65
Karlstadt			8.4	8.4	Ungvar				8.35
Klausenburg				9.2	Vukovar				9.5
Krakau			5.95		Wien	7.18	7.18	6	6
Kronstadt				9.2	Zombor				9.5
Linz	10.2	7.6			Zurich		6.34		5.45
Laibach			8.5	8.5					

Note: The destinations in italics are the border control stations. Between 1890 and 1897, the most popular through booking points of the company in order of importance were: Vienna, Groningen, Mannheim, Mainz, Leeuwarden, Marseille, Berlin, Stuttgart, Ludwigshafen, Basel, Cologne, Trier, Paris, Oderberg, Munich, Frankfurt, Strasburg, Crefeld, Posen, Düsseldorf, Aschaffenburg, Heilbronn, Pezsau, Dirschau, Leipzig, Kassau and Wurzburg.

Source: GAR, HAL, 318.04, Passage, 221-226, letters 24 August 1894, 6 December 1895, 23 March 1898 and 6 February 1900; Circular Zotti, October 1905; HAL rate sheet, 12 April 1907; and Uranium Line rate sheet, 29 November 1909 (the company quoted the same rates as the HAL).

Appendix 5:
New York Agents and Agents under Bond, 1897-1909

The three lists gathered – one of the New York City agents, Brooklyn and Williamsburg, and the other two of agents under bond for the New York territory – do not allow us to reaching conclusions because not enough is known about how inclusive the second and third lists are or about the true limits of the New York territory. Combining the lists seems to indicate that the number of agents in New York City decreased sharply from thirty-five in 1897 to twelve and eleven in 1906 and 1909, respectively.

List of Agents of the Continental Lines in New York City, 10 April 1897

NEW YORK	CGT	HA-PAG	HAL	NGL	RSL
S. Barasch, 74 Ridgeway St.		X	X		X
H. Birdsall, 187 West St.	X	X	X	X	X
H. Bischoff and Co. StaatsZeitung Bldg.	X	X	X	X	X
F. Brodsky and Co. 1331 2nd Ave	X	X	X	X	X
F. Budzynski, 122 Cedar St.		X	X	X	X
Geo. Deffas, 240 East 79th St.		X	X	X	X
Falck and Co. 26 Canal St.	X	X	X	X	X
A. Falck and Co. 127 Bowery and 156 East 125th St.	X	X	X	X	X
C. Foucart, 37 Desbrosses St.		X	X	X	
A. Germansky, 30 Canal St.		X	X		
M. Hauser and Co. 370 Grand St.		X	X	X	X
S. Jarmulowsky, 54 Canal St.		X	X	X	X
A. Johnson and Co. 27 Broadway	X	X	X	X	X
A. Kass, 78 Essex St.		X	X		X
J Keller, 117 Charlton St.	X	X	X		X
J. Kellerman, 49 Norfolk St.		X	X		X
M. Kobre, 40 Canal St.		X	X	X	X
Hugo Lederer, 58 Avenue B	X	X	X	X	X
W. Leuman, 18 Greenwich St.			X		X
Peter McDonnell, 2 Batterey Place	X	X	X	X	X
Markel Brothers, 94 Canal St.		X	X	X	X
Missler and Krimmert, 106 West St.	X	X		X	
M. Muller, 1 Broadway	X	X	X	X	X
O. Ott, 6 Greenwich St.			X		X
E. Pflugi, 130 Greenwich St.	X		X		X
A. Ragette, 2662 Third Ave		X	X		X
I. Rosenberg, 92 East 14th St	X	X	X	X	X
J. Rosenbaum, State Bank, 378 Grand St.		X	X	X	X
M. Rosett, 66 Greenwich St. 167 Stanton St.	X	X	X	X	X
J. Rosuck, 6 Market St.		X			
P. Rovnianek and Co. 25 Avenue A		X	X	X	X
L. Scharlach and Co. 362 Grand St.	X	X	X	X	X
A. Schleisinger and Son, 350 East Houston		X	X		X

NEW YORK	CGT	HA-PAG	HAL	NGL	RSL
H. Schnitzer, 141 Washington St.	X	X	X	X	X
H. Tamsen, 52 Avenue A		X	X	X	X
Zwilchenbart, Gasser and Co., 61 Greenwich St.	X	X	X	X	X
Mandel and Baros, 157 Rivington St.		X	X	X	
Total	**17**	**34**	**35**	**26**	**33**
BROOKLYN/WILLIAMSBURG		X	X		
Bernheim, 646 Broadway		X	X		
Epstein, 78 Graham Ave.		X	X		
Grochowski, 49 Grand St.		X	X		
Kellerman, Thatford and Belmont, Aves., Brownsville		X	X	X	X
Koch, 48 Broadway	X	X	X	X	X
Lehrenkrauss and Sons, 379 Fulton St.	X	X	X	X	X
Scheldt, 180 Graham Ave.	X	X	X	X	X
Schultz, 194 Ewen St.	X	X	X		
Siems, 131 Greenpoint Ave.	X	X	X	X	X
Total	**5**	**10**	**10**	**5**	**5**

List of Agents under Bond in New York Territory, 21 September 1906

Agent	Locality	Bond	Agent	Locality	Bond
Antonio Andretta	Hartford, CT	500	C. Litchman	Trenton, NJ	500
Joseph Bolcar	Passiac, NJ	500	I. Lewin	New Haven, CT	500
Max Beuchler	Bridgeport, CT	500	M. Leibschutz	Louisville, KY	500
M. Blitzstein	Philadelphia, PA	500	B. Litchman	Amsterdam, NY	500
Bowie and Co.	Bridgeport, CT	1000	V. Luczkowiak	Dunkirk, NY	500
Stephen Berleczky	Barberton, OH	500	H. Labowicz	New Haven, CT	500
Chas Bicsak	Garfield, NJ	500	Adolf Mandel	New York, NY	500
Joseph Bolcar	Boonton, NJ	500	Markel Bros.	New York, NY	500
S. Barasch	New York, NY	500	E. Mantel	Indianapolis, IN	500
S. Bronstein and Son	Baltimore, MD	500	A. Mitro	Lorain, OH	500
G. Dziadick	Derby, CT	500	A. Michalkiwicz	Elizabethport, NJ	500
Davis and Hurwitz	Syracuse, NY	500	R. Melville	Toronto, ON	3000
A.V. Dzubay	South Fork, PA	500	E. Nierenstein	Hartford, CT	500
Deutsch Bros.	New York, NY	1000	H. Norton	Vanderbilt, PA	500
Erdelyi and Weiner	Donora, PA	500	G. Oroszy	Lorain, OH	500
Josesoh Emory	Wilmington, DE	500	G. Prince	Rochester, PA	500
H. Epstein	Brooklyn, NY	500	Bela Pucky	Columbus, OH	500
B. Ewnowitch	Middletown, CT	500	A. Pirhalla	Jessup, PA	500
A. Friedman	Passaic NJ	500	E. Prokocimer	Newark, NJ	500
M. Friedman	Luzerne, PA	500	Polowe, Mogilewsky and Werner	New York, NY	1000
M. Fodor	New Brunswick, NJ	500	J. Rizsak	Passaic. NJ	500
S. Fleischhaker	Rochester, PA	500	N. Rizsak	Carteret, NJ	500
E. Germanus	Newark, NJ	500	P. Rovnianek and Co.	New York, NY	1000
A. Grochowski and Co.	Brooklyn, NY	500	C. Rainke	Philadelphia, PA	500
A. Greenbaum	Barberton, OA	500	N. Rizsak	South Carteret, NJ	500
B. Gross	Cresson, PA	500	J. Rojewski	Camden, NJ	500
T. Garbinsky	Auburn, NY	500	J. Reichman	Mt. Pleasant, PA	500

Agent	Locality	Bond	Agent	Locality	Bond
M. Gordon	Hartford, CT	500	A. Rudewick	Freeland, PA	500
M. Greenwald	Rondout, NY	500	M. Rakowsky	Conshohocken, PA	500
M. Gross	Avoca, PA	500	J. Rizsak	South Bethlehem, PA	500
M. Hirsch	Seymour, CT	500	N. Rizsak	Carteret, NJ	500
S. Holzmans and Sons	Johnstown, PA	500	W. Sawa	Wilkes-Barre, PA	500
P. Harbula	Ambridge, PA	500	J. Simon	East Toledo, OH	500
M. Hahn	Brooklyn, NY	1000	L. Sirotiak	Yonkers, NY	500
Aaron Hurwitz	Brooklyn, NY	500	F. Sakser	New York, NY	500
L. Hyman	Carbondale, PA	500	C. Scheid	New York, NY	500
P. Hegedus and Co.	Wet Seneca, NY	500	L. Sabow	Chrome, NJ	500
Aaron Hurwitz	Scranton, PA	500	M. Sameth	Yonkers, NY	500
M. and L. Jarmulowsky	New York, NY	1000	W. Szetela	Thompsonville, CT	500
J. Jacob	Canton, OH	500	J. Schneider	Providence, RI	500
Jubelirer Bros.	New Salem, PA	500	F. Savage	Durya Borough, PA	500
S. Kiernozycki	Plymouth, PA	500	P. Szewczyk	Niagara Falls, NY	500
Max Kobre	New York, NY	500	F. Szetela	Adams, MA	500
S. Kohan	New York, NY	500	A. Spiro and Co.	Ansonia, CT	500
Emil Kiss	New York, NY	500	J. Tonkay	Jacobs Creek, PA	500
E. Kaplan	Syracuse, NY	500	B. Trilecz	Canonsburg, PA	500
T. Knoblauch	Reading, PA	500	J. Tomcsanyi	Homestead, PA	500
M. Korlath	Scalp Level, PA	500	W. Teitelbaum	Johnstown, PA	500
S. Keltonik	Punxsutawney, PA	500	F. Trudnowski	North Buffalo, NY	500
A. Klein	Martins Ferry, OH	500	A. Ujhelyi	South Lorain, OH	500
K. Kazemekas	Waterbury, CT	500	M. Walenk	Scranton, PA	500
Krumholz and Zeisler	Trenton, NJ	500	L. Warady	Trenton, NJ	500
Abraham Kass	New York, NY	500	Zaruba and Durish	Clarksburg, WV	500
A. Klein	Yonkers, NY	500	A. Zemany	Windber, PA	500
N. Lusher	Montréal, QC	1000	G. Zavateson	Allegheny, PA	500

List of Agents under Bond in New York Territory, 5 January 1909

Agent	Locality	Bond	Agent	Locality	Bond
Joseph Bolcar	Passaic, NJ	500	S. Holzmans and Sons	Johnstown, PA	500
Max Beuchler	Bridgeport, CT	500	P. Harbula	Ambridge, PA	500
M. Blitzstein	Philadelphia, PA	500	J. Haarhay	Philadelphia, PA	500
Stephen Berleczky	Barberton, OH	500	I. Herz	Philadelphia, PA	1000
Joseph Bolcar	Boonton, NJ	500	A. Horbal	Derby, CT	500
F. Burszinski	Buffalo, NY	500	Aaron Hurwitz	Brooklyn, NY	500
J. Beda	Duquesne, PA	500	P. Hegedus and Co.	Wet Seneca, NY	500
J. Beler	Johnstown, PA	500	M. and L. Jarmulowsky	New York, NY	1000
J. Bertok	Toledo, OH	500	J. Jacob	Canton, OH	500
S. Blaustein	Baltimore, MD	500	S. Jex	Mt. Pleasant, PA	500
T. Coon	Wharton, NJ	500	J. Jacobson	Reading, PA	500
I. Cherokowick	Gilberton, PA	500	F. Jagocki	Brooklyn, NY	1000
I Csisarik	Duquesne, PA	500	Jubelirer Bros.	New Salem, PA	500
G. Dziadick	Derby, CT	500	S. Kiernozycki	Plymouth, PA	500
Davis and Hurwitz	Syracuse, NY	500	S. Kahan	New York, NY	1000
Deutsch Brothers	New York, NY	1000	Max Kobre	New York, NY	1000
O. Dobrovolsky	Barnesboro, PA	500	E. Kaplan	Syracuse, NY	500
Erdelyi and Weiner	Donora, PA	500	T. Knoblauch	Reading, PA	500
B. Ewnowitch	Middletown, CT	500	H. Korn	Brooklyn, NY	1000
L. Esiner	Trenton, NJ	500	M. Korlath	Scalp Level, PA	500
M. Fikete	Norton, VA	500	K. Kazemekas	Waterbury, CT	500
F. Fritsche	Long Island City, NY	500	M. Katzander	Stockertown, PA	500
S. Fischgrund	Wilmerding, PA	500	V. Kubelka and Co.	New York, NY	1000
A. Friedman	Passaic, NJ	500	Herman Kirch	New York, NY	1000
M. Friedman	Luzerne, PA	500	J. Karabinus	Martins Creek, PA	500

Agent	Locality	Bond	Agent	Locality	Bond
M. Fodor	New Brunswick, NJ	500	S. Keltonik and Co.	Conemaugh, PA	500
S. Fleischhaker	Rochester, PA	500	J. Kovacs	Brooklyn, NY	1000
S. Fleischhaker	Beaver Falls, PA	500	C. Kristupek	Ambridge, PA	500
L. Friedl	Mingo Junction, OH	500	I. Kline	Niles, OH	500
E. Germanus	Newark, NJ	500	M. Kosiolek	Niagara Falls, NY	500
A. Grochowski and Co.	Brooklyn, NY	1000	J. Kiss	S. Bethlehem, PA	500
A. Grochowski and Co.	Jamaica, NY	500	Krumholz & Zeisler	Trenton, NJ	500
A. Greenbaum	Barberton, OH	500	A. Klein	Yonkers, NY	500
B. Gross	Cresson, PA	500	E. Lenartowicz	Central Falls, RI	500
S. Glick	Clinton, PA	500	Lipschutz and Wurzel	Philadelphia, PA	500
J. Goodman	Manayunk, PA	500	W. Lucas	Minnersville, PA	500
S. Goodman	Coatsville, PA	500	N. Lusher	Montréal, QC	1000
T. Garbinsky	Auburn, NY	500	C. Litchman	Trenton, NJ	500
M Gordon	Hartford, CT	500	I. Lewin	New Haven, CT	500
D. Gordon	Paterson, NJ	1000	B. Litchman	Amsterdam, NY	500
P. Green	Bridgeville, PA	500	V. Luczkowiak	Dunkirk, NY	500
M. Greenwald	Rondout, NY	500	Adolf Mandel	New York, NY	1000
F. Gross	Buffalo, NY	1000	F. Mekszrunas	Manayunk, PA	500
M. Hirsch	Seymour, CT	500	L. Moeser Co	Pittsburgh, PA	500

Agent	Locality	Bond	Agent	Locality	Bond
J. McDonald	Harrisburg, PA	500	J. Radziwon	Buffalo, NY	500
G. Matyas	Treskow, PA	500	V. Rozuk	Newark, NJ	1000
C. Marz	Elizabeth, NJ	500	S. Ramonat	Shenandoah, PA	500
L. Markowitz	Buffalo, NY	500	A. Romanosky	Lawrence, MA	500
Markel Brothers	New York, NY	1000	J. Simon	E.Toledo, OH	500
Markel and Rosen	Brooklyn, NY	1000	D. Simon	Mansfield, PA	500
A. Miernicki	Shenandoah, PA	500	F. Sakser	New York, NY	500
E. Mantel	Indianapolis, IN	500	E. Sameth	Perth Amboy, NJ	500
A. Mitro	Lorain, OH	500	L. Sabow	Chrome, NJ	500
A. Michalowicz	Elizabethport, NJ	500	J. Schneider	Providence, RI	500
A. Michalowicz & Pankuch	Elizabeth, NJ	500	E. Schwartz	Pottstown, PA	500
E. Nierenstein	Hartford, CT	500	Stone and Zujawski	Northampton, MA	500
H. Norton	Vanderbilt, PA	500	J. Samley	Pittston, PA	500
J. Nagy	Toledo, OH	500	J. Slabinski	Plains, PA	500
A. Neubauer	Brooklyn, NY	1000	B. Sharfman	Hartford CT	500
H. Oppenheim	New York, NY	1000	E. Shurgot	Philadelphia, PA	500
W. Oliwiecki	Niagara Falls, NY	500	Sanditz and Traurig	Waterbury, CT	1000
G. Oroszy	Lorain, OH	500	Steiner Bros.	Kensington, PA	500
Bela Pucky	Columbus, OH	500	F. Savage	Durya Borough, PA	500
A. Pirhalla	Jessup, PA	500	J. Tomcsanyi	Homestead, PA	500
E. Prokocimer	Newark, NJ	500	J. Torok	Martins Ferry, OH	1000
N. Papp	Cleveland, OH	500	H. Torbet	Dillonvale, OH	500
K. Papp	Rankin, PA	500	J. Tetlak	Cleveland, OH	500
A. Pamer	Akron, OH	500	M. Tafel	Butler, PA	500
S. Payer	Pottstown, PA	500	E. Trochanowski	Mt Carmel, PA	500
J. Pacowsky	Ford City, PA	500	M. Tulenczik	Toronto, ON	500
Pollak Bros.	Lyndora, PA	500	A. Ujhelyi	South Lorain, OH	500

Agent	Locality	Bond	Agent	Locality	Bond
F. Prelewicz	North Tonawanda, NY	500	A. Ujhelyi	Klyria, OH	500
J. Rizsak	Passaic, NJ	500	C. Voelker	Atlantic City, NJ	500
J. Rizsak	Wharton, NJ	500	V. Willus	Jersey City, NJ	500
P. Rovnianek and Co.	New York, NY	1000	V. Willus	Kingsland, NJ	500
C. Rainke	Philadelphia, PA	1000	S. Wills	Auburn, NY	500
N. Rizsak	South Carteret, NJ	500	M. Woll	Lebanon, PA	500
J. Reichman	Scranton, PA	500	J. Whitelaw	Akron, OH	500
J. Recke	Punxsutawney, PA	500	Williams & Namanyi	West Seneca, NY	500
A. Rudewick	Freeland, PA	500	M. Walenk	Scranton, PA	500
M. Rakowsky	Concshohocken, PA	500	L. Warady	Trenton, NJ	1000
J. Rizsak	South Bethlehem, PA	500	S. Yasik	Wilmington, DE	500
J. Riszak	Alpha, NJ	500	Zaruba and Durish	Clarksburg, WV	500
N. Rutsek	South Carteret, NJ	500	A. Zemany	Windber, PA	500
A. Rusin	Syracuse, NY	500	G. Zavateson	Allegheny, PA	500

Appendix 6: Advertisements by the HAL in American Newspapers

The advertising expenses of the HAL were predominantly for cabin passages. If not specified, the advertisement was placed all year. If only for six months, this usually covered the period from March to September or the four months from 15 April to 15 August. The figures in bold show the contribution of the HAL to joint advertisements with other lines.

American Newspapers, Location and Duration	1894	1897	1903	1907	1910	1913
Dutch Papers						
De Nederlander, Chicago	50	40	40			
De Volkstem, De Pere, Wisconsin	40	40	40	40	40	40
De Wachter, Grand Rapids, Michigan		25	25	25		
De Standaard, Grand Rapids, Michigan	65	65	60	60	60	60
De Gids, Grand Rapids, Michigan		28	28	28	28	28
De Gids, De Pere, Wisconsin			20	20		
De Stem des Volks, Grand Rapids, Michigan		40				
De Vryheidsbanier, Grand Rapids, Michigan	40	40				
De Calvinist, Grand Rapids, Michigan						37
Onze Standaard, Green Bay, Wisconsin	60	60	60			
De Hollandsch-Belgische Amerikaan, De Pere, Wisconsin				60		
Onze Toekomst, Chicago, Illinois			36	36	36	36
De Hope, Holland, Michigan	60	60	60	60	60	60
De Grondwet, Holland, Michigan	60	60	60	60	60	60
De Hollander, Holland, Michigan	16					
De Hollandsche Amerikaan, Kalamazoo, Michigan	60	40	60	60	60	60
De Volksvriend, Orange City, Iowa	40	40	40	40	40	40
De Vrye Hollander, Orange City, Iowa				48	48	48
De Telegraaf, Paterson, New Jersey	60	60	60	60	60	60
Het Oosten, Paterson, New Jersey				60	30	30

American Newspapers, Location and Duration	**1894**	**1897**	**1903**	**1907**	**1910**	**1913**
Pella's Weekblad			25	25	25	25
Sioux Centre Nieuwsblad			25	25	25	25
Holland American, Rochester, New York				60	60	60
Boston						
Beacon 6m/6m/ /-/	21.67	24.37				
Globe / 4m/4m / /12m	40	32		***182.5***	***250***	
Herald /4m/4 m/ /12m	32	32		***273.8***		
Transcript /4m/4m / /12m	76.8	72.8		***138.1***	***138***	312
Journal /4m/4m/ /-/	43.2	43.2				
Boston Christan Science Monitor / 6m						390
Boston City Directory				***5.85***	***4***	
Boston Satchel Guide					***15***	
Chicago						
Stoelkers Guide	39	39				
Chicago Record Herald 6m/ 6 m/6m/4m/4m/4m	81.9	56.6	100	100	90	90
Chicago Tribune 6m/6m/ /12 m	95.55	98.35	375.3	417	403	461
Chicago Freire Presse		240	240	240	240	240
Illinois Staats Zeitung	329					
Interocean/ 5m		52.5				
New York						
Amerikanische Schweizer Zeitung				65	65	65
Badische Landes Zeitung /-/ /6m/12m				25	25	50
Courier des Etats Unis	100	100	164.8	199.8	181	173
Brooklyn Eagle			200.75	219	164	165
New York Herald	750	883.75	912.5	850	821	1551
New York Herald Directory			120	120	120	120
New York Evening Mail and Express /6m/6m/6m/6m/6m	91.2	96	243	156	210	211
New York Evening Post	241.6		312	300	337	655

American Newspapers, Location and Duration	**1894**	**1897**	**1903**	**1907**	**1910**	**1913**
New York Staats Zeitung	256.5	256.5	256.5	225	208	208
New York Sun /-/6m/6m/6m/6m			343.53	366	409	386
New York Tribune /6 m/6m/6m/6m/6m	136.8	144	182	180	246	246
New York Times /6m/ 6m/ 6m/6m/12m	138.5	144	300.3	274.5	328	659
Steam and Sail	120					
US. Post		222.3				
Pittsburgh						
Volksblatt	100	100				
Commercail Gazette 6m / - / 6m		62.5		***54.6***		
Pittsburgh Dispatch -/-/6m/-/6m/12m			196.04		***31***	91
St. Louis						
Anz. Des Westens	120	130	100	***100***	***100***	100
Globe Democrat 6m/6m/6m/4m/12m		103.95	165.45	***258.6***	***107***	501
Globe /8m					***152***	
St. Louis Amerika (joint with RSL)					***75***	75
Herold des Glaubens Amerika				***25***		
Struckhoff's (special advertisement)						50
Washington, DC						
Washington Evening Star 6m/6m/4m/4m/-/	60.5	45.37	61.1	34.67	35	
Washington Post 6m/6m/4m/4m/-/	80.67	57.2	46.8	39	39	
Washington DC Star / 4m						62
Washington Times	25.4					
Sentinel 6m		50				
Other						
Albany Argus			76.44			
Baltimore Sun/ 6m/6m/ 6m/6m/6m		52.5	57.2	81	95	164
Bridgeport Standard / 6m/6m					82	82
Buffalo Express 12m/6m/6m/12m			271.05	***46.8***	55	103

American Newspapers, Location and Duration	**1894**	**1897**	**1903**	**1907**	**1910**	**1913**
Buffalo Commercial 6m/6m/6m				***23.4***	31	43
Cambridge (MA) Harvard Monthly/6m		12				
Charleston News and Courier			30			
Cincinnati Freire Press	83.34	100	100	100	100	100
Cleveland Leader /6m			182			
Columbus Dispatch /-/6m/4m/4m/4m			65.52	75	98	97
Detroit Free Press /-/ /4m/4m/4m				108	136	180
Fresno Democrat				***18***		
Hartford Courant /-/6m/6m/6m/6m			30	30	51	52
Indianapolis News /-/6m/4m/4m/4m			117	132	147	160
Kansas City Star /6m			149.76			
La Incha (Havana) 4m			172			
Las Novedades	100					
Los Angeles Times					***75***	218
Meriden Record / 6m/6m					33	33
Milwaukee Herald			70	70		
Minneapolis Journal /-/6m/6m			128.4	***23.4***		
Minneapolis Tribune / 6m/6m					96	94
Montreal Gazette			92.4	48		
Montreal La Presse / 6m/6m					103	131
New Haven Journal and Courier /-/ /6m/6m/6m				28	28	40
New Haven Leader -/-/6m/-/-/-/			33.75			
New Orleans Times Democrat /-/6m/4m/6m/6m			110	70	70	70
New Orleans Picayune /-/ / 4m/6m/6m				70	70	94
Norfolk Public Ledger /-/ / 3m/ 3m/3m			81	36	33	33
Omaha Beach /6m			176.4			
Philadelphia Ledger /6m /6m/ 4m/4m /4m		163.8	323.4	160	158	156
Philadephia Record / 4m/4m					128	156

American Newspapers, Location and Duration	1894	1897	1903	1907	1910	1913
Providence Journal / 6m/6m/6m/6m			81.5	93.45	115	153
Rochester Democrat Chronicle -/-/6m/-/-/-			118.86			
Saint Paul Pioneer Press and Dispatch 6m/6m/6m			109.2	***29.28***	94	125
San Francisco Call				***37.44***	***37***	225
San Franciso Chronicle				***62.4***	***62***	187
San Francisco Democrat				***60***		
San Francisco Argonaut				***48.75***		
Springfield Republican /-/6m/6m/6m/6m			48	48	55	55
Syracuse Herald -/6m/-/-/-/			87.36			
Troy Record /3m / /-/		14.18				
Utica Herald Dispatch /6m			37.25			
Virginian Pilot /-/ / 3m/3m/3m				33	33	33
Winnipeg Free Press /6m						140
Winnipeg Telegram						100
Miscellaneous						
American Golf			180			
Annual Report Netherlands Chamber of Commerce				13	20	20
Badischer Volksfest Verein				25	25	25
Bischoff Calendar		10		25	25	25
By Rail and Water						75
Calender Morgen Journal			95			
Cooks Guide/Traveller's Gazette		125	125	150	150	150
Courier de France		12				
Detroit Journal			64.25			
Der Deutsche in Amerika			100			
Dutch Fare Program			50			
Eendracht maakt Macht			10	10	10	10
Glas Naroda			35			

American Newspapers, Location and Duration	**1894**	**1897**	**1903**	**1907**	**1910**	**1913**
Guide Franco-Americain			50	50	50	50
Grosser NY Burger and Bauer Calendar				45	45	45
Hotel America			30			
Kartford Lampoon			12.5			
Kawkab American	25	150				
Liedich's Traveller's Guide						100
L'union Francaise			10			
Medical Record			200			
Medical Times			180			
Minneapolis Beuer and Bauer Kal				*30*		
Nederlandsche Stamdag Programma						25
Ocean Sailings						50
Oldenburg Verein Journal				10	10	10
Old World Tourist Guide			30			
Plastic Catalogue				15		
Photo Era						125
Schweizer Calendar			50			
Stockler's Guide			39			
Szabadszag Calendar				275	250	
Toronto Art Club Catalogue				20		
Traveller's and Shipper's Mail Guide				39		39
Union Chretienne des Jeunes Gens				12	25	
US Tobacco Journal			250			
Women's Art Association of Canada					20	20
Yale Courant			25			
Extra Minneapolis			234			
Extra Advertising Steamship Rotterdam		502.2				
Total	3714.43	4582.8	9183.2	7867	8066	10,983

Bibliography

Primary Sources

BELGIUM

General State Archives, Brussels (BGSA)

BGSA, I 160: Archives du Ministère de la Justice: Administration de la sûreté publique du Régime français à 1914, 154, Enrôlements et recrutements de Belges pour l'étranger.

BGSA, I 215, Bestuur van Zeewezen, 4052-4056, Vaart der British Queen, eerste stoomvaart verbinding Antwerpen 1840-1847.

BGSA, TO 74, Ministerie van Financiën, 36, Scheepvaart.

Archives of the Ministry of Foreign Affairs (ABMFA), Brussels

ABMFA, Consuls et Consulats, New York, pers. 623.

ABMFA, Catalogue par matières, Enrôlements, 68, enrôlements militaires à l'étranger 1864.

ABMFA, Catalogue par matières, Emigration 2020, I-X: 1834-1914.

ABMFA, Catalogue par matières, Emigration, 2241, I-VIII, steam-shipping Antwerp New-York, 1839-1889.

ABMFA, Catalogue par matières, Emigration 2946, III, renseignements et documents fourni à la commission du travail 1886.

ABMFA, Catalogue par matières, Emigration, 2960, I-II, rapports consulaires sur les possibilités d'émigration en général.

ABMFA, Catalogue par matières, Emigration, 2960, III-XX, rapports consulaires sur les possibilités d'émigration par état 1885-1914.

ABMFA, Catalogue par matières, Emigration, 2961, I, ouvriers Belges aux États-Unis: généralités 1883-1908.

ABMFA, Catalogue par matières, Emigration, 2961, II, ouvriers Belges aux États-Unis: diamantaires 1895-1909.

ABMFA, Catalogue par matières, Question ouvrières, 3284, États-Unis 1885-1912.

Provincial State Archive of Antwerp (PSAA)

PSAA, Provinciaal Bestuur, Bedelaarsgestichten, 78, I-II, emigratie 1850-1855.

PSAA, Provinciaal Bestuur, Emigratie, 273, I-II, landverhuizers - kolonies 1817-1850.

PSAA, Provinciaal Bestuur, Emigratie, 274, I-II, landverhuizers - kolonies 1850.

PSAA, Provinciaal Bestuur, Emigratie, 275, landverhuizers - kolonies 1851-1860.

Miscellaneous

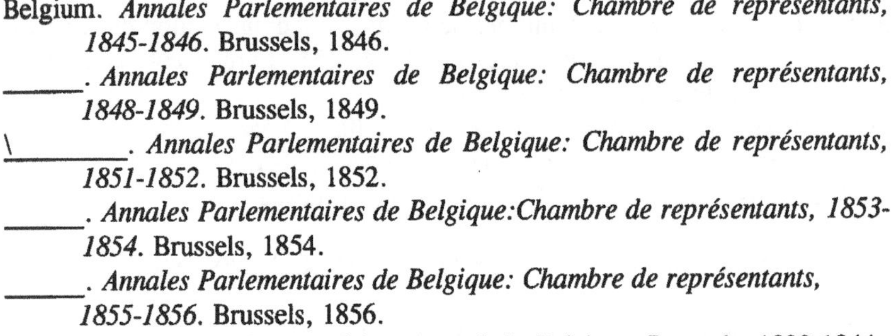

Belgium. *Annales Parlementaires de Belgique: Chambre de représentants, 1845-1846*. Brussels, 1846.

_____. *Annales Parlementaires de Belgique: Chambre de représentants, 1848-1849*. Brussels, 1849.

_______. *Annales Parlementaires de Belgique: Chambre de représentants, 1851-1852*. Brussels, 1852.

_____. *Annales Parlementaires de Belgique:Chambre de représentants, 1853-1854*. Brussels, 1854.

_____. *Annales Parlementaires de Belgique: Chambre de représentants, 1855-1856*. Brussels, 1856.

Bulletin officiel des lois et arrêtés royaux de la Belgique. Brussels, 1830-1844, *Recueil des lois et arrêtés royaux de Belgique*. Brussels, 1844-1914.

THE NETHERLANDS

Dutch National Archives (DNA), The Hague

2.05.10.04 Gezantschap in de Duitse Bond Fankfurt, Nassau, Hessen en Keur-Hessen, 1816-1867.

3; correspondentie met Ministerie van Buitenlandse Zaken over politieke zaken, 1857-1867.

9; stukken mbt de afdamming van de Schelde ivm de aanleg van de spoorweg naar Vlissingen, 1865-1867.

14; correspondentie over de doortocht van landverhuizers in Nederland, 1853-1866.

2.05.13: Gezantschap in de Verenigde Staten, 1814-1940.

14-47; correspondentie met het Nederlandse Ministerie van Buitenlandse Zaken, 1839-1881.

210; ingekomen brieven en uitgaande minuten over het vervoer van landverhuizers.

1158; stukken betreffende overtreding van Amerikaanse wetten bij het vervoer van landverhuizers, 1882.

Roosevelt Study Center, Middelburg, Diplomatic Archives (RSC)

M 42; dispatches from and to US ministers in the Netherlands, roll 17, 22 April 1845-30 September 1850.

Rotterdam Community Archives (GAR), Holland-America Line Archive (HAL)

318.01 Directie
1174; overeenkomsten en afschriften.

318.02 Directie
53; correspondentie privaat kopieboek, November 1884-April 1887.
112-121; corresspondentie, private brieven van hoofdagentschap. New York 1883-1914.
265; correspondentie Wierdsma.

318.03 Passage Department
49-58, 97, 160, 190; correspondentie kantoor, New York, 1912-1914.

318.04 Passage
1-5; kopieboeken algemeen 1897-1909.
42; brieven aan Reuchlin en van den Toorn, New York, 1902-1904.
72-77; brieven, orders, New York, 1904-1911.
221-226; brieven New York, 1887-1904.
232; Wiener cartel, 1892-1896.
243; minutes, NDLV, 1892-1914, part 1.
563; minutes, New York Continental Conference, 1885-1895.
564; minutes New York Mediterranean Conference, 1885-1906, and Standing Complaint Committee, 1896-1907.
565; minutes, railroad committee, 1896-1907, immigrant clearing house, 1886-1887 and others.
577; 581; minutes, NDLV, 1892-1914, part 2.
580; diversen van den Toorn en Willmink.
763; correspondentie NDL en zijn bedoelingen om de ander partijen uit te schakelen, 1914.
767; correspondentie met diverse stoomvaartlijnen, 1887-1888.

318.14 Wentholt archief
6; stoomvaart Amerika, 1839.
7; stoomvaart Amerika, 1850.
8; samenwerking met IMMCO Morgan trust.
9.2; Plate Reuchlin Co., notullen, vennootschap, vergaderingen.

9.3; NASM, 1869.
10.3; voorgeschiedenis van de oprichting NASM.
12.1-2; jaarverslagen.
18.3; correspondentie Scholten mbt kritiek op directie
20; Nord-Atlanticshe Dampfer Linier Verband.
43; corrspondentie mbt concurrentie NVSM Amsterdam, 1880-1882.
44; correspondentie met hoofdagent Cazaux van Staphorst, 1874-1884.

318.16 Museum
53; Staten van voedingskosten van passagiers, 1883-1919.

ENGLAND

Cunard Line Archives, Liverpool (CLA)

Chairman Correspondence, C, 1-75.

FRANCE

Diplomatic Archives, Nantes (ADN)

Consulats, New York, 7.

Centre d'Archives du monde du Travail (CAMT), Roubaix

Compagnie Générale Transatlantique, 9AQ, 1-13, Dossiers des Assemblées Générales

GERMANY

Bremen Staatsarchiv (BSA)

2-R-11; Shiffahrt zur See, 2a-2c Damp-, post- und Packetschiffahrt zwischen Bremen und VS, 1837-1867.
2-B-13; Verhaltnisse mit VS, generalia Auswanderung nach den VS.

Hamburg Staatsarchiv (HSA)

8; Consulaat Liverpool: Auswanderungsangelegenheiten, 1851-1868.
622-1; HAPAG, Erinnerungen Merck.

UNITED STATES

National Archives, Washington (NAW)

Records of the Immigration and Naturalization Service, 1787-1993 (RINS), Record Group 85

51389/6; Immigration to Southern States, South Carolina, 1906-1908.
51389/29; Immigration, Virginia ,1908.
51411/29;Allan Line advertisements, exhibits, southern states, 1904-1911.
51460/121; Moische Wilenczik case, 1906.
51632/5; Giovanni Guglio alias Raffaele Castrilli, 1907.
51632/13; Immigration Legislation 1907, National Liberal Immigration League, 1905-1910.
51830/26; International immigration conference, 1909.
51720/13; Jewish Charities, 1907.
51758/3; Shipping conference, 1907-1915.
51761/5; Herman Zalbert case, 1907-1909.
51762/1; Immigration Restriction League, 1894-1924.
52011/A; Investigation Marcus Braun, 1904.
52066/3; Alien contract labour evasions, Gruenberg investigation, 1908.
52116/1; Rules and organization Ellis Island, report, 1904.
52332/13; Steerage conditions, 1904-1909.
52495/17; Distribution of Aliens in the US ,1904-1909.
52495/18; Problems with primary inspection, Ellis Island, 1912.
52599/16; Investigation fictitious addresses, Marcus Braun, 1904.
52600/13; Investigation at Ellis Island, 1909.
53137/394; NGL versus United States, 1910-1914.
53139/5; Bill for American vessels and immigrant transportation, 1911.
53288/8; Conditions at Ellis Island, complaints by Germans, 1912.
53321/73; Press relations and publications, 1912.
53531/67; Medical inspections at Ellis Island, 1913.
54152/77; Special investigation, Hungarian migration, 1903.
54166/101; Babette Bosch case, 1907.
54166/112; Escape of alien passengers, 1903-1913.
54167; Improvements at Ellis Island, 1904-1907.
54411/1; Immigration conditions, Europe and Mexico, Wheeler investigation, 1906.

YIVO Institute for Jewish Research (New York)

Record Group 102, Autobiographies of Jewish Immigrants 1942-; 1-397.

Electronic Sources

New York Times Archive, 1851-1980. http://www.nytimes.com.

United States. Senate. 61st Cong., 2nd sess. Immigration Commission. Reports. 41 vols. Washington, DC, 1911. (Dillingham Commission). Available at Harvard Open Collection Program. Immigration to the United States, 1789-1930. http://ocp.hul.harvard.edu/immigration/dillingham.html and at http://lib.stanford.edu/digital-library-systems-services.

Williamson, S. "Six Ways to Compute the Relative Value of a U.S. Dollar Amount, 1790 to Present," 2009, http://www.measuringworth.com/uscompare/

Secondary Sources

Abbott, Edith. *Immigration: Select Documents and Case Records*. Chicago, 1924; reprint, North Stratford, NH, 1969.

______. "Wages of Unskilled Labor, 1850-1900." *Journal of Political Economy*, XIII, No. 3 (1905), 327-361.

Adams, Willi Paul. *Die Deutschprachige Auswanderung in die Vereenigten Staaten: Berichte uber Forschungstand und Quellenbestande*. Berlin, 1980.

Albion, Robert Greenhalgh. *The Rise of New York Port, 1815-1860*. New York, 1939. Reprint, Boston, 1984.

Aldcroft, Derek H. *Studies in British Transport History, 1870-1970*. Newton Abbot, 1974.

______ (ed.). *The Development of British Industry and Foreign Competition, 1875-1914: Studies in Industrial Enterprise*. London, 1967.

Alexander, Charles C. "Prophet of American Racism: Madison Grant and the Nordic Myth." *Phylon*, XXIII, No. 1 (1960), 73-90.

Alter, George; Goldin, Claudia; and Rotella, Elyce. "The Savings of Ordinary Americans: The Philadelphia Savings Fund Society in the Mid-nineteenth Century." *Journal of Economic History*, LIV, No. 3 (1994), 735-767.

Antić, Ljubomir. "The Press as a Secondary Source for Research on Emigration from Dalmatia up to the First World War." *South-East Europe Review for Labour and Social Affairs*, IV (2004), 25-35.

Armgort, Arno. *Bremen-Bremerhaven-New York, 1683-1960*. Bremen, 1992.

Armstrong, David and Heiss, Peter R. "Ethnic Banking: Identifying the Capacity and Future Implications of the Ethnic Banking Market." Unpublished paper presented to the Oxford Business and Economics Conference, Oxford University, June 2007.

Asaert, Gustaaf, *et al. Antwerpen een geschenk van de Schelde: De Antwerpse haven door de eeuwen heen*. Brussels, 1993.

Austin, Oliver P. "Is the New Immigration Dangerous to the Country?" *North American Review*, CLXXVIII, No. 4 (1904), 558-570.

Bade, Klaus J. *Europa in Bewegung: Migration von späten 18. Jahrhudert bis Gegenwart*. Munich, 2000.

_____. and Weiner, Myron (eds.) *Migration Past, Migration Future: Germany and the United States*. Providence, RI, 2000.

Baines, Dudley. *Emigration from Europe, 1815 -1930*. Cambridge, 1991.

_____. "European Emigration, 1815-1930: Looking at the Emigration Decision Again." *Economic History Review,* New ser., XLVII, No. 3 (1994), 525-544.

_____. "European Labor Markets, Emigration and Internal Migration, 1850-1913." In Hatton, Timothy J. and Williamson, Jeffrey G. (eds.). Migration and the *International Labor Market, 1850-1939*. London, 1994, pp. 35-54.

Balace, Francis. *En marge de la guerre de sécession: recrutements en Belgique par les troupes fédérales, 1864-1865*. Brussels, 1969.

_____ (ed.). *La guerre de sécession et la Belgique: Documents d'archives américaines, 1861-1865*. Leuven, 1969.

Barbance, Marthe. *Histoire de la Compagnie Générale Transatlantique*. Paris, 1955.

Barker, Theo. "Consular Reports: A Rich but Neglected Historical Source." *Business History*, XXIII, No. 3 (1981), 265-266.

Bastin, Robin. "Cunard and the Liverpool Emigrant Traffic, 1860-1900." Unpublished MA thesis, University of Liverpool, 1971.

Beelen-Driehuizen, Liesbeth J. and Kompagnie, Jan H. *Landverhuizers: Aanwijzingen over het doen van Onderzoek naar Nederlandse emigranten en transmigranten*. The Hague, 1996.

Bemis, Edward W. "The Restriction of Immigration." *Andover Review*, IX, No. 1 (1888), 251-264.

Bennet, Marion T. *American Immigration Policies: A History*. Washington, DC, 1963.

Berkowitz, Michael. "Between Altruism and Self Interest: Immigration Restriction and the Emergence of American-Jewish Politics in the United States." In Fahrmeir, Andreas; Faron, Olivier; and Weil, Patrick (eds.). *Migration Control in the North Atlantic World: The Evolution of State Practices in Europe and the United States from the French Revolution to the Inter-war Period.* New York, 2003, pp. 253-270.

Bickelmann, Hartmut. "The Emigration Business." In Moltman, Günter (ed.). *Germans to America: 300 Years of Immigration, 1683-1983*. Stuttgart, 1982.

Binder, Frederick M. and Reimers, David R. *All the Nations under Heaven: An Ethnic and Racial History of New York*. New York, 1995.

Bittlingmayer, George. "Antitrust and Business Activity: The First Quarter Century." *Business History Review*, LXX, No. 3 (1996), 363-401.

Blackford, Mansel and Kerr, K. Austin. *Business Enterprise in American History*. Boston, 1986; 3rd ed., Boston, 1993.

Bläsing, Jochen. and Langenhuyzen, Ton. "Dutch Sea Transport in Transition: The Influence of the German Hinterland, 1850-1914." In Starkey, David J. and Harlaftis, Gelina (eds.). *Global Markets: The Internationalization of the Sea Transport Industries since 1850*. St. John's, 1998, pp. 103-126.

Blom, Hans and Lamberts, Emiel (eds.). *Geschiedenis van de Nederlanden*. Baarn, 1995.

Böcker, Anita, *et al.* (eds.). *Regulation of Migration: International Experiences*. Amsterdam, 1998.

Bodnar, John. *The Transplanted: A History of Immigrants in Urban America*. Bloomington, 1985.

Bommes, Michael and Morawska, Ewa (eds.). *International Migration Research: Constructions, Omissions and the Promises of Interdisciplinarity*. Aldershot, 2005.

Born, Karl E. *International Banking in the 19th and 20th Centuries*. Stuttgart, 1977.

Boumans, René. "Een onbekend aspect van de Belgische emigratie naar Amerika: De gesubsidieerde emigratie van bedelaars en oudgevangenen, 1850-1856." In *L'expansion Belge sous Léopold 1er, 1831-1865*. Brussels, 1965.

Boyce, Gordon. *Information, Mediation and Institutional Development: The Rise of Large-Scale Enterprise in British Shipping, 1870-1919*. Manchester, 1995.

______. *Co-operative Structures in Global Business: Communicating, Transferring Knowledge and Learning across the Corporate Frontier*. London, 2001.

______ and Gorski, Richard (eds.). *Resources and Infrastructures in the Maritime Economy, 1500-2000*. St. John's, 2002.

Boyd, Monica. "Family and Personal Networks in International Migration: Recent Developments and New Agendas." *International Migration Review*, XXIII, No. 3 (1989), 638-670.

Brattne, Berit and Åkerman, Sune. "The Importance of the Transport Sector for Mass Migration." In Runblom, Harald and Norman, Hans (eds.). *From Sweden to America: A History of the Migration*. Minneapolis, 1976, pp. 176-200.

Brettell, Caroline B. and Hollifield, James F. (eds.). *Migration Theory: Talking across Disciplines*. New York, 2000.

Bretting, Agnes and Bickelmann, Hartmut. *Auswanderungagenturen und Auswanderungsvereine im 19. und 20. Jahrhundert*. Stuttgart, 1991.

Brinkmann, Tobias. "'Grenzerfahrungen' zwischen Ruhleben und Ellis Island: Deutsche Durchwanderkontrolle und Ost-West-Migration, 1880-1914." *Leipziger Beitrage Zur Judischen Gesichte Und Kultur*, II (2004), 209-229.

Broder, Albert A. "French Consular Reports." *Business History*, XXIII, No. 3 (1981), 279-282.

Broeze, Frank. "Albert Ballin, the Hamburg-Bremen Rivalry and the Dynamics of the Conference System." *International Journal of Maritime History*, III, No. 1 (1991), 1-32.

______. "Shipping Policy and Social Darwinism: Albert Ballin and the *Weltpolitik* of the Hamburg-America Line, 1886-1914." *Mariner's Mirror*, LXXIX, No. 4 (1993), 419-436.

______. "Connecting the Netherlands and the Americas: Ocean Transport and Port/Airport Rivalry." In Hoefte, Rosemarijn and Kardux, Johanna C. (eds.). *Connecting Cultures: The Netherlands in Five Centuries of Transatlantic Exchange*. Amsterdam, 1994, pp. 77-99.

______. "Dutch Steamshipping and International Competition: The Holland-America Line under Foreign Control, 1902-1917." In Jackson, Gordon and Williams, David M. (eds.). *Shipping, Technology and Imperialism: Papers Presented to the Third British-Dutch Maritime History Conference*. Aldershot, 1996, pp. 107-117.

______. "At Sea and Ashore: A Review of the Historiography of Modern Shipping since the 1970s." *NEHA Bulletin*, XII, No. 1 (1998), 3-37.

______. (ed.). *Maritime History at the Crossroads: A Critical Review of Recent Historiography*. St. John's, 1995.

Bruijn, Jaap R. "Recent Developments in the Historiography of Maritime History in the Netherlands." In Broeze, Frank (ed.). *Maritime History at the Crossroads: A Critical Review of Recent Historiography*. St. John's, 1995, pp. 193-211.

Caestecker, Frank. "The Changing Modalities of Regulation in International Migration within Continental Europe, 1870-1940." In Böcker, Anita, *et al.* (eds.). *Regulation of Migration: International Experiences*. Amsterdam, 1998, pp. 73-98.

______. "The Transformation of 19th Century Expulsion Policy, 1880-1914." In Fahrmeir, Andreas; Faron, Olivier; and Weil, Patrick (eds.). *Migration Control in the North Atlantic World: The Evolution of State Practices in Europe and the United States from the French Revolution to the Inter-war Period*. New York, 2003, pp. 120-137.

Calavita, Kitty. "US Immigration Policymaking: Contradictions, Myths and Backlash." In Böcker, Anita, *et al.* (eds.). *Regulation of Migration: International Experiences*. Amsterdam, 1998, pp. 139-154.

Cartuyvels, Jean-Louis. *Aux émigrants belges: Colonie de Sainte-Marie, canton d'Elk, dans l'état de Pennsylvanie*. Saint-Trond, 1850.

Cassis, Youssef. "El Empresario." In Frevert, Ute and Haupt, Heinz-Gerhard (eds.). *El hombre del Siglo XIX*. Madrid, 2001, pp. 61-89.

Chandler, Alfred D., Jr. *The Visible Hand: The Managerial Revolution in American Business*. Cambridge, MA, 1977.

_____. "Business History as Institutional History." In Taylor, George Rogers and Ellsworth, Lucius F. (eds.). *Approaches to American Economic History*. Charlottesville, VA, 1971, pp. 17-24. Reprinted in McGraw, Thomas K. (ed.). *The Essential Alfred Chandler: Essays Towards A Historical Theory of Big Business*. Boston, 1988, 301-306.

_____. "The Organization of Manufacturing and Transportation." In Gilchrist, David T. and Lewis, W. David (eds.). *Ecnomic Change in the Civil War Era*. Greenville, DE, 1965, pp. 137-165. Reprinted in McGraw, Thomas K. (ed.). *The Essential Alfred Chandler: Essays Towards A Historical Theory of Big Business*. Boston, 1988, pp. 202-224.

Chandler, William E. "Shall Immigration be Suspended?" *North American Review*, CLVI, No. 1 (1893), 1-8.

Cinel, Dino. *The National Integration of Italian Return Migration, 1879-1929*. New York, 1991; reprint, New York, 2002.

Claghorn, Kate Holladay. "Immigration in Its Relation to Pauperism." *Annals of the American Academy of Political and Social Science*, XXIV, No. 2 (1904), 187-205.

Clemens, Elisabeth S. *The People's Lobby: Organizational Innovation and the Rise of Interest Group Politics in the United States, 1890-1925*. Chicago, 1997.

Coene, Johan. "De Opvang van Landverhuizers te Antwerpen (1872-1914)." Unpublished MA thesis, Gent University, 1998.

Cohn, Raymond L. "Mortality on Immigrant Voyages to New York, 1836-1853." *Journal of Economic History*, XLIV, No. 2 (1984), 289-300.

_____. "Nativism and the End of Mass Migration of the 1840s and 1850s." *Journal of Economic History*, LX, No. 2 (2000), 361-383.

_____. "The Transition from Sail to Steam in Immigration to the United States." *Journal of Economic History*, LXV, No. 2 (2005), 469-495.

Coleman, Terry. *The Liners: A History of the North Atlantic Crossing*. New York, 1977.

Cornelis, Abraham. "Dromen tussen Europa en de VS: een cultuurhistorische studie van 100 jaar luxe-vervoer aan boord." Unpublished MA thesis, Leiden Univerity, 1993.

Croswell, Simon Greenleaf. "Should Immigration be Restricted?" *North American Review*, CLXIV, No. 4 (1897), 526-536.

Crouthamel, James L. *Bennett's New York Herald and the Rise of the Popular Press*. Syracuse, NY, 1989.

Darlington, Thomas. "The Medico-Economic Aspect of the Immigration Problem." *North American Review*, CLXXXIII, No. 6 (1906), 1262-1271.

Day, Jared N. "Credit, Capital and Community: Informal Banking in Immigrant Communities in the United States 1880-1924." *Financial History Review*, IX, No. 1 (2002), 65-78.

De Boer, G.J. *125 jaar Holland-Amerika Lijn, 1873-1998*. Rotterdam, 1998.

De Ham, Victor. *Conseils à l'émigrant Belge aux États-Unis de l'Amérique du nord*. Brussels, 1849.

De Jong, Gerald F. *The Dutch in America, 1609-1974*. Boston, 1975.

De Nijs, Thimo. *In veilige Haven: Het familieleven van het Rotterdamse gegoede burgerij, 1815-1890*. Nijmegen, 2001.

De Smet, Antoine. *Voyageurs Belges aux États-Unis Du XVIIieme sciècle à 1900*. Brussels, 1959.

______. *La communauté belge du nord-est du Wisconsin: ses origines, son évolution jusque vers 1900*. Brussels, 1956.

Deakin, Brian M. and Seward, T. *Shipping Conferences: A Study of Their Origins, Development and Economic Practices*. Cambridge, 1973.

Dellheim, Charles. "The Business of Jews." In Lipartito, Kenneth and Sicilia, David B. (eds.). *Constructing Corporate America: History, Politics, Culture*. New York, 2004, pp. 223-245.

Deltas, George; Sefres, Konstantinos; and Sicotte, Richard A. "American Shipping Cartels in the Pre-World War I Era." *Research in Economic History*, XIX, No. 1 (1999), 1-38.

______; Sicotte, Richard A.; and Tomczak, Peter. "Passenger Shipping Cartels and Their Effect on Trans-Atlantic Migration." *Review of Economics and Statistics*, XC, No. 1 (2008), 119-133.

Devos, Greta. "Belgische Overheidssteun aan scheepvaartlijnen, 1867-1914." In Degryse, Karel and Koninckx, Christian (eds.). *Bijdrage tot de internationale maritieme geschiedenis*. Brussels, 1988, pp. 81-98.

Diner, Hasia R. *A Time for Gathering, 1820-1880: The Second Migration*. Baltimore, 1995.

Dovring, Folke. "European Reactions to the Homestead Act." *Journal of Economic History*, XXII, No. 4 (1962), 461-472.

Ducat, Jean, *et al.* *From Grez-Doiceau to Wisconsin: contribution a l'étude de l'émigration Wallonne vers les États-Unis d'Amérique aux XIXe siècle*. Brussels, 1986.

Dunkley, Peter. "Emigration and the State, 1803-1842: The Nineteenth Century Revolution in Government Reconsidered." *Historical Journal*, XXIII, No. 2 (1980), 353-380.

Engelsing, Rolf. *Bremen als Auswandererhafen, 1683-1880*. Bremen, 1961.

Erickson, Charlotte (ed.). *Emigration from Europe, 1815-1914: Select Documents*. London, 1971.

Evans, Nicholas J. "The Port Jews of Libau, 1880-1914." *Jewish Culture and History*, VII, Nos. 1-2 (2004), 197-214.

______. "The Role of Foreign-born Agents in the Development of Mass Migrant Travel through Britain, 1820-1923." In Feys, Torsten, *et al.* (eds.). *Maritime Transport and Migration: The Connections between Maritime and Migration Networks*. St. John's, 2007, pp. 49-61.

Fahrmeir, Andreas; Faron, Olivier; and Weil, Patrick (eds.). *Migration Control in the North Atlantic World: The Evolution of State Practices in Europe and the United States from the French Revolution to the Inter-war Period*. New York, 2003.

Falkner, Roland P. "Some Aspects of the Immigration Problem." *Political Science Quarterly*, XIX, No. 1 (1904), 32-49.

Falkus, Malcolm. *The Blue Funnel Legend: A History of the Ocean Steam Ship Company, 1864-1973*. Basingstoke, 1990.

Fawcett, James T. "Networks, Linkages and Migration Systems." *International Migration Review*, XXIII, No. 3 (1989), 671-680.

______ and Arnold, Fred. "Explaining Diversity: Asian and Pacific Immigration Systems." In Fawcett, James T. and Cariño, Benjamin V. (eds.). *Pacific Bridges: The New Immigration from Asia and the Pacific Islands*. New York, 1987, pp. 455-473.

Ferenczi, Imre and Willcox, Walter F. *International Migrations, Vol. I: Statistics*. New York, 1929.

Fertig, Georg. "Eighteenth-Century Transatlantic Migration and Early German Anti-Migration Ideology." In Lucassen, Jan and Lucassen, Leo (eds.). *Migration, Migration; History, History: Old Paradigms and New Perspectives*. Bern, 1997. 3rd rev. ed., Bern, 2005, pp. 271-290.

Feys, Torsten. "The Emigration Policy of the Belgian Government from Belgium to the U.S. through the Port of Antwerp, 1842-1914." Unpublished MA thesis, Ghent University, 2003.

______. "Radeloosheid in crisistijd: pogingen van de Belgische regeringen om een deel van de arme bevolking naar de Verenigde Staten te sturen, 1847-1857." *Belgisch Tijdschrift voor Nieuwste Geschiedenis*, XXXIV (2004), 195-230.

______. "Where All Passenger Liners Meet: The Port of New York as a Nodal Point for the Transatlantic Migrant Trade, 1885-1895." *International Journal of Maritime History*, XIX, No. 2 (2007), 245-272.

______, *et al.* (eds.). *Maritime Transport and Migration: The Connections between Maritime and Migration Networks*. St. John's, 2007.

Filene, Peter G. "An Obituary for The Progressive Movement." *American Quarterly*, XXII, No. 1 (1970), 20-34.

Finch, Vernon E.W. *The Red Star Line and the International Mercantile Marine Company*. Antwerp, 1988.

Fischer, Lewis R. and Nordvik, Helge W. (eds.). *Shipping and Trade, 1750-1950*. Leuven, 1990.

______ and Panting, Gerald E. *Change and Adaptation in Maritime History: The North Atlantic Fleets in the Nineteenth Century*. St. John's, 1985.

Fitzgerald, Keith. *The Face of the Nation: Immigration, the State and National Identity*. Chicago, 1996.

Flayhart, William H. III. "The Expansion of American Interests in Transatlantic Commerce and Trade, 1865-1893." In Starkey, David J. and Harlaftis, Gelina (eds.). *Global Markets: The Internationalization of the Sea Transport Industries since 1850*. St. John's, 1998, pp. 127-147.

_____. *The American Line, 1872-1902*. New York, 2000.

Fleming, Walter L. "Immigration to the Southern States." *Political Science Quarterly*, XX, No. 2 (1905), 276-297.

Fones-Wolf, Ken. "Immigrants, Labor and Capital in a Transnational Context: Belgian Glassworkers in America, 1880-1925." *Journal of American Ethnic History*, XXI, No. 1 (2002), 59-80.

______. "Transatlantic Craft Migrations and Transnational Spaces: Belgian Window Glass Workers in America, 1880-1920." *Labor History*, XLV, No. 3 (2004), 299-321.

Fouché, Nicole. *Émigration Alsacienne aux États-Unis, 1815-1870*. Paris, 1992.

Franklin, Philip A.S. "Rate Agreements between Carriers in the Foreign Trade." *Annals of the American Academy of Political and Social Sciences*, LV, No. 1 (1914), 155-163.

Freeman, Gary P. "Modes of Immigration Politics in Liberal Democratic States." *International Migration Review*, XXIX, No. 4 (1995), 881-902.

______ and Betts, Katharine. "The Politics of Interests in Immigration Policy-making in Australia and the US." In Freeman, Gary P. and Jupp, James (eds.) *Nations of Immigrants: Australia, the United States and International Migration*. Melbourne, 1992, pp. 72-88.

Friedland, Klaus (ed.). *Maritime Aspects of Migration*. Cologne, 1989.

Gabaccia, Donna R. "Is Everywhere Nowhere? Nomads, Nations and the Immigration Paradigm of United States History." *Journal of American History*, LXXXVI, No. 3 (1999), 1115-1134.

______. *Italy's Many Diasporas*. Seattle, 2000.

Gelberg, Birgit. *Auswanderung nach Übersee: Soziale Probleme der Auswanderungbeförderung in Hamburg und Bremen von der Mitte der 19. Jahrhunderts bis zum Ersten Weltkrieg*. Hamburg, 1973.

Genesove, David and Mullin, Wallace P. "Rules, Communication and Collusion: Narrative Evidence from the Sugar Institute Case." *American Economic Review*, XCI, No. 3 (2001), 379-398.

Gerber, David. "Internationalization and Transnationalization." In Ueda, Reed (ed.). *A Companion to American Immigration*. Oxford, 2006, pp. 225-254.

Ghosh, Bimal (ed.). *Return Migration: Journey of Hope or Despair*. Geneva, 2000.

Goldin, Claudia. "The Political Economy of Immigration Restriction in the United States, 1890-1921." In Goldin, Claudia and Libecap, Gary D. (eds.). *The Regulated Economy: A Historical Approach to Political Economy*. Chicago, 1994, pp. 223-258.

Gottheil, Paul. "Historical Development of Steamship Agreements and Conferences in the American Foreign Trade." *Annals of the American Academy of Political and Social Sciences*, LV, No. 1 (1914), 48-74.

Gould, John D. "European Inter-Continental Migration, 1815-1914: Patterns and Causes." *Journal of European Economic History*, VIII, No. 3 (1979), 593-679.

______. "European Inter-Continental Migration - The Road Home: Return Migration from the USA." *Journal of European Economic History*, IX, No. 1 (1980), 41-112.

______. "European Inter-Continental Emigration: The Role of 'Diffusion' and 'Feedback.'" *Journal of European Economic History*, IX, No. 2 (1980), 267-315.

Goyens, Tom. "Waalse glasarbeiders in de Verenigde Staten: Pennsylvania, West Virginia, Ohio en Indiana, 1870-1910." Unpublished MA thesis, Leuven University, 1982.

Graham, Gerald S. "The Ascendancy of Sailing Ship 1850-1885." *Economic History Review*, 2nd ser., IX, No. 1 (1956), 74-88.

Grant, Madison. *The Passing of the Great Race, or the Racial Basis of European History*. New York, 1916. Reprint, New York, 1922.

Greenhill, Robert G. "Competition or Co-operation in the Global Shipping Industry: The Origins and Impact of the Conference System for British Shipowners before 1914." In Starkey, David J. and Harlaftis, Gelina (eds.). *Global Markets: The Internationalization of the Sea Transport Industries since 1850*. St. John's, 1998, pp. 53-80.

Grubb, Farley. "The End of European Immigrant Servitude in the United States: An Economic Analysis of Market Collapse, 1772-1835." *Journal of Economic History*, LIV, No. 4 (1994), 794-824.

Guglielmo, Thomas A. *White on Arrival: Italians, Race, Color, and Power in Chicago, 1890-1945*. New York, 2003.

Guns, Nico. *Holland-Amerika Lijn: een beknopte geschiedenis van een rederij*. Rotterdam, 2004.

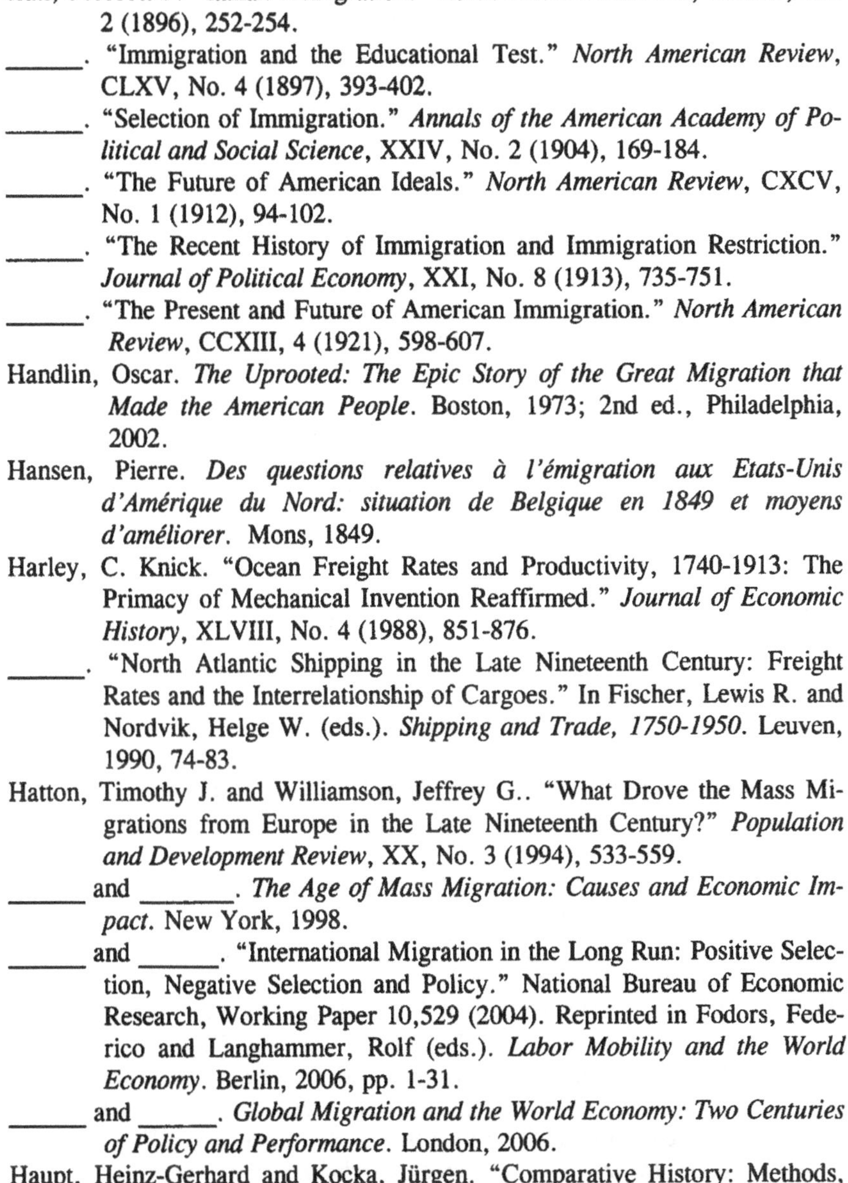

Hall, Prescott F. "Italian Immigration." *North American Review*, CLXIII, No. 2 (1896), 252-254.

_____. "Immigration and the Educational Test." *North American Review*, CLXV, No. 4 (1897), 393-402.

_____. "Selection of Immigration." *Annals of the American Academy of Political and Social Science*, XXIV, No. 2 (1904), 169-184.

_____. "The Future of American Ideals." *North American Review*, CXCV, No. 1 (1912), 94-102.

_____. "The Recent History of Immigration and Immigration Restriction." *Journal of Political Economy*, XXI, No. 8 (1913), 735-751.

_____. "The Present and Future of American Immigration." *North American Review*, CCXIII, 4 (1921), 598-607.

Handlin, Oscar. *The Uprooted: The Epic Story of the Great Migration that Made the American People*. Boston, 1973; 2nd ed., Philadelphia, 2002.

Hansen, Pierre. *Des questions relatives à l'émigration aux Etats-Unis d'Amérique du Nord: situation de Belgique en 1849 et moyens d'améliorer*. Mons, 1849.

Harley, C. Knick. "Ocean Freight Rates and Productivity, 1740-1913: The Primacy of Mechanical Invention Reaffirmed." *Journal of Economic History*, XLVIII, No. 4 (1988), 851-876.

_____. "North Atlantic Shipping in the Late Nineteenth Century: Freight Rates and the Interrelationship of Cargoes." In Fischer, Lewis R. and Nordvik, Helge W. (eds.). *Shipping and Trade, 1750-1950*. Leuven, 1990, 74-83.

Hatton, Timothy J. and Williamson, Jeffrey G.. "What Drove the Mass Migrations from Europe in the Late Nineteenth Century?" *Population and Development Review*, XX, No. 3 (1994), 533-559.

_____ and _____. *The Age of Mass Migration: Causes and Economic Impact*. New York, 1998.

_____ and _____. "International Migration in the Long Run: Positive Selection, Negative Selection and Policy." National Bureau of Economic Research, Working Paper 10,529 (2004). Reprinted in Fodors, Federico and Langhammer, Rolf (eds.). *Labor Mobility and the World Economy*. Berlin, 2006, pp. 1-31.

_____ and _____. *Global Migration and the World Economy: Two Centuries of Policy and Performance*. London, 2006.

Haupt, Heinz-Gerhard and Kocka, Jürgen. "Comparative History: Methods, Aims, Problems." In Cohen, Deborah and O'Connor, Maura (eds.). *Comparison and History: Europe in Cross-National Perspective*. New York, 2004, pp. 23-40.

Heffer, Jean. *Le port de New York et le commerce extérieur Américain, 1860-1900*. Paris, 1986.

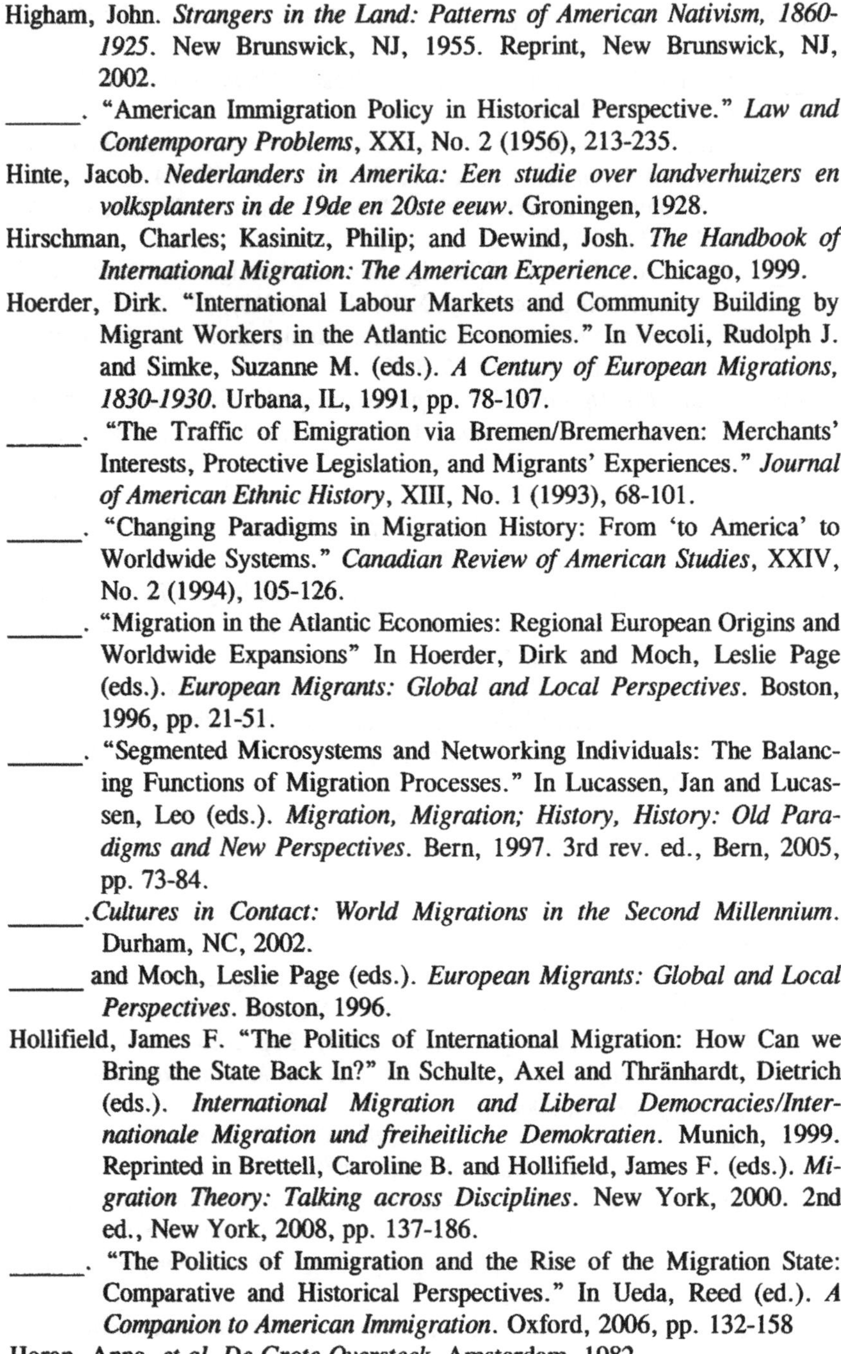

Higham, John. *Strangers in the Land: Patterns of American Nativism, 1860-1925*. New Brunswick, NJ, 1955. Reprint, New Brunswick, NJ, 2002.

______. "American Immigration Policy in Historical Perspective." *Law and Contemporary Problems*, XXI, No. 2 (1956), 213-235.

Hinte, Jacob. *Nederlanders in Amerika: Een studie over landverhuizers en volksplanters in de 19de en 20ste eeuw*. Groningen, 1928.

Hirschman, Charles; Kasinitz, Philip; and Dewind, Josh. *The Handbook of International Migration: The American Experience*. Chicago, 1999.

Hoerder, Dirk. "International Labour Markets and Community Building by Migrant Workers in the Atlantic Economies." In Vecoli, Rudolph J. and Simke, Suzanne M. (eds.). *A Century of European Migrations, 1830-1930*. Urbana, IL, 1991, pp. 78-107.

______. "The Traffic of Emigration via Bremen/Bremerhaven: Merchants' Interests, Protective Legislation, and Migrants' Experiences." *Journal of American Ethnic History*, XIII, No. 1 (1993), 68-101.

______. "Changing Paradigms in Migration History: From 'to America' to Worldwide Systems." *Canadian Review of American Studies*, XXIV, No. 2 (1994), 105-126.

______. "Migration in the Atlantic Economies: Regional European Origins and Worldwide Expansions" In Hoerder, Dirk and Moch, Leslie Page (eds.). *European Migrants: Global and Local Perspectives*. Boston, 1996, pp. 21-51.

______. "Segmented Microsystems and Networking Individuals: The Balancing Functions of Migration Processes." In Lucassen, Jan and Lucassen, Leo (eds.). *Migration, Migration; History, History: Old Paradigms and New Perspectives*. Bern, 1997. 3rd rev. ed., Bern, 2005, pp. 73-84.

______.*Cultures in Contact: World Migrations in the Second Millennium*. Durham, NC, 2002.

______ and Moch, Leslie Page (eds.). *European Migrants: Global and Local Perspectives*. Boston, 1996.

Hollifield, James F. "The Politics of International Migration: How Can we Bring the State Back In?" In Schulte, Axel and Thränhardt, Dietrich (eds.). *International Migration and Liberal Democracies/Internationale Migration und freiheitliche Demokratien*. Munich, 1999. Reprinted in Brettell, Caroline B. and Hollifield, James F. (eds.). *Migration Theory: Talking across Disciplines*. New York, 2000. 2nd ed., New York, 2008, pp. 137-186.

______. "The Politics of Immigration and the Rise of the Migration State: Comparative and Historical Perspectives." In Ueda, Reed (ed.). *A Companion to American Immigration*. Oxford, 2006, pp. 132-158

Horan, Anne, *et al. De Grote Oversteek*. Amsterdam, 1982.

Horlings, Edwin. *The Economic Development of the Dutch Service Sector, 1800-1850*. Amsterdam, 1995.

Hourwich, Isaac A. "The Economic Aspects of Immigration." *Political Science Quarterly*, XXVI, No. 4 (1911), 615-642.

______. *Immigration and Labor: The Economic Aspects of European Immigration to the United States*. New York, 1912.

Hoyt, Homer. "The Relation of the Literacy Test to a Constructive Immigration Problem." *Journal of Political Economy*, XXIV, No. 5 (1916), 445-473.

Huebner, Solomon S. "Advantages and Disadvantages of Shipping Conferences and Agreements in the American Foreign Trade." *Annals of the American Academy of Political and Social Sciences*, LV (1914), 243-252.

______. "Recommendations of the Committee of the Merchant Marine and Fisheries." *Annals of the American Academy of Political and Social Sciences*, LV (1914).

______. "Steamship Line Agreements and Affiliations in the American Foreign and Domestic Trade." *Annals of the American Academy of Political and Social Sciences*, LV (1914), 75-111.

Hutchins, John G.B. *The American Maritime Industries and Public Policies, 1789-1914: An Economic History*. Cambridge, MA, 1941.

Hutchinson, Edward P. *Legislative History of American Immigration Policy, 1798-1965*. Philadelphia, 1981.

Huldermann, Bernhard. *Albert Ballin*. Berlin, 1922. Reprint, Bremen, 2011.

Hvidt, Kristian. *Flugten til Amerika, eller Drivkræfter I masseudvandringen fra Danmark, 1868-1914*. Aarhus, 1971.

______. *Flight to America: The Social Background of 300,000 Danish Emigrants*. New York, 1975.

______. "Emigration Agents: The Development of a Business and Its Methods." *Scandinavian Journal of History*, III, No. 2 (1978), 178-202.

Hyde, Francis E. *Cunard and the North Atlantic, 1840-1973: A History of Shipping and Financial Management*. London, 1975.

Jackson, James H., Jr. and Moch, Leslie Page. "Migration and the Social History of Modern Europe." *Historical Methods*, XXII, No. 1 (1989), 27-36. Reprinted in Hoerder, Dirk and Moch, Leslie Page (eds.). *European Migrants: Global and Local Perspectives*. Boston, 1996, pp. 52-69.

Jansens, Marin Henri. *Een brug over den Oceaan: Stoomvaart op Amerika*. Amsterdam, 1869.

Jasso, Guillermina and Rosenzweig, Mark R. "Using National Recording Systems for the Measurement and Analysis of Immigration to the United States." *International Migration Review*, XXI, No. 4 (1987), 1212-1244.

Jenks, Jeremiah W. and Lauck, W. Jett. *The Immigration Problem*. New York, 1911; 6th ed., New York, 1926.

Johnson, Emory R. (ed.). *Government Regulation of Water Transportation*. New York, 1914.Reprint, Millwood, NY, 1975.

Jones, Maldwyn Allen. *American Immigration*. Chicago, 1960; 2nd ed., Chicago, 1992.

_____. "Immigrants, Steamships and Governments: The Steerage Problem in Transatlantic Diplomacy." In Allen, Harry C. and Thompson, Roger (eds.). *Contrast and Connection: Bicentennial Essays in Anglo-American History*. London, 1976, pp. 178-204.

_____. "Aspects of North Atlantic Migration: Steerage Conditions and American Law, 1819-1909." In Friedland, Klaus (ed.). *Maritime Aspects of Migration*. Cologne, 1989, pp. 321-331.

Just, Michael. *Ost und südosteuropäische Amerikawanderung, 1881-1914*. Stuttgart, 1988.

Kahan, Arcadius. "Economic Opportunities and Some Pilgrims' Progress: Jewish Immigrants from Eastern Europe in the U.S., 1890-1914." *Journal of Economic History*, XXXVIII, No. 1 (1978), 235-251.

Kalvermark, Ann-Sofie. "Swedish Emigration Policy in an International Perspective, 1840-1925." In Runblom, Harald and Norman, Hans (eds.). *From Sweden to America: A History of the Migration*. Minneapolis, 1976, pp. 95-114.

Kamphoefner, Walter D.; Helbich, Wolfgang; and Sommer, Ulrike (eds.). *News from the Land of Freedom: German Immigrants Write Home*. Ithaca, NY, 1991.

Keeling, Drew. "Transatlantic Shipping Cartels and Migration between Europe and America, 1880-1914." *Essays in Economic and Business History*, XVII, No. 2 (1999), 195-213.

_____. "The Transport Revolution in Transatlantic Migration, 1850-1914." *Research in Economic History*, XIX, No. 1 (1999), 39-74.

_____. "Costs, Risks, and Migration Networks between Europe and the United States, 1900-1914." In Feys, Torsten, *et al.* (eds.). *Maritime Transport and Migration: The Connections between Maritime and Migration Networks*. St. John's, 2007, pp. 113-173.

_____. *The Business of Transatlantic Migration between Europe and the United States, 1900-1914*. Zurich, 2012.

Kennedy, Charles S. *The American Consul: A History of the United States Consular Service, 1776-1914*. Westport, CT, 1990.

King, Desmond. *Making Americans: Immigration, Race and the Origins of the Diverse Democracy*. Cambridge, MA, 2000.

King, Russell. "Generalizations from the History of Return Migration." In Ghosh, Bimal (ed.). *Return Migration: Journey of Hope or Despair*. Geneva, 2000, pp. 7-56.

Klebaner, Benjamin J. "State and the Local Immigration Regulation in the United States before 1882." *International Review of Social History*, III, No. 2 (1958), 269-295.

Kluger, Richard. *The Paper: The Life and Death of the New York Herald Tribune*. New York, 1986.

Kocka, Jürgen. "Comparison and Beyond." *History and Theory*, XLII, No. 1 (2003), 39-44.

Kohler, Max J. "Some Aspects of the Immigration Problem." *American Economic Review*, IV, No. 1 (1914), 93-108.

Kolko, Gabriel. *Railroads and Regulation, 1877-1916*. Princeton, 1965.

______. *The Triumph of Conservatism: A Reinterpretation of American History, 1900-1916*. Chicago, 1963. Reprint, Chicago, 1977.

Krabbendam, Hans. "Capital Diplomacy: Consular Activity in Amsterdam and New York, 1800-1940." In Harinck, George and Krabbendam, Hans (eds.). *Parallel Cities: Amsterdam and New York, 1653-2003*. Amsterdam, 2003, pp. 167-181. Reprinted in Swierenga, Robert P.; Sinnema, Don; and Krabbendam, Hans (eds.). *The Dutch in Urban America*. Holland, MI, 2004, pp. 59-75.

______. *Vrijheid in het verschiet: Nederlandse emigratie naar Amerika, 1840-1940*. Hilversum, 2006.

Kraut, Allan. "Bodies from Abroad: Immigration, Health and Disease." In Ueda, Reed (ed.). *A Companion to American Immigration*. Oxford, 2006, pp. 105-131.

Kurgan-van Hentenryk, Ginette. "Belgian Consular Reports." *Business History*, XXIII, No. 3 (1981), 268-270.

Lauck, W. Jett. "The Real Significance of Recent Immigration." *North American Review*, CXCV, No. 2 (1912), 201-211.

Laurent, Pierre-Henri. "Antwerp versus Bremen: Transatlantic Steamship Diplomacy and European Port Rivalry, 1839-1846." *Journal of World History*, IX, No. 4 (1966), 938-946.

Leblicq-de Champ, F. *Guide des sources de l'histoire des États-Unis et des relations belgo-américaine conservées en Belgique, 1776-1914*. Brussels, 1977.

Lee, Erika. "A Nation of Immigrants and a Gatekeeping Nation: American Immigration Law and Policy." In Ueda, Reed (ed.), *A Companion to American Immigration*. Oxford, 2006, pp. 3-35.

Leonard, Henry Beardsell. *The Open Gates: The Protest against the Movement to Restrict European Immigration, 1896-1924*. New York, 1980.

Leonard, Thomas. "American Progressivism and the Rise of the Economist as Expert." Unpublished working paper, Princeton University, 2006.

Lodge, Henry Cabot. "The Restriction of Immigration." *North American Review*, CLII, No. 1 (1891), 27-32.

_____. "Lynch Law and Unrestricted Immigration," *North American Review*, CLII, 5 (1891), 602-612.

Logan, Edward B. and Patten, Simon N. "Lobbying." *Annals of the American Academy of Political and Social Science*, CXLIV, No. 1 (1929), 1-91.

Lovoll, Odd S. "For the People Who Are Not in a Hurry: The Danish Thingvalla Line and the Transportation of Scandinavian Emigrants." *Journal of American Ethnic History*, XIII, No. 1 (1993), 48-67.

Loyen, Reginald, *et al.* (eds.). *Struggling for Leadership: Antwerp-Rotterdam Port Competition, 1870-2000*. Leuven, 2003.

Lucassen, Jan and Lucassen, Leo (eds.). *Migration, Migration; History, History: Old Paradigms and New Perspectives*. Bern, 1997. 3rd rev. ed., Bern, 2005.

Lucassen, Leo. "Eternal Vagrants? State Formation, Migration and Travelling Groups in Western Europe, 1350-1914." In Lucassen, Jan and Lucassen, Leo. *Migration, Migration; History, History: Old Paradigms and New Perspectives*. Bern, 1997, pp. 225-252.

_____. "The Great War and the Origins of Migration Control in Western Europe and the United States." In Böcker, Anita, *et al.* (eds.). *Regulation of Migration: International Experiences*. Amsterdam, 1998, pp. 45-72.

_____. "Revolutionaries into Beggars: Alien Policies in the Netherlands, 1814-1914." In Fahrmeir, Andreas; Faron, Olivier; and Weil, Patrick (eds.). *Migration Control in the North Atlantic World: The Evolution of State Practices in Europe and the United States from the French Revolution to the Inter-war Period*. New York, 2003, pp. 178-191.

Maesen, Linda. "De Regeringsbemoeiing in de organisatie van de emigratie via Antwerpen naar Latijns-Amerika (1843-1913)." Unpublished MA thesis, Ghent University, 1978.

Manitakis, Nicolas. "Transatlantic Emigration and Maritime Transport from Greece to the US, 1890-1912: A Major Area of European Steamship Company Competition for Migrant Traffic." In Feys, Torsten, *et al.* (eds.). *Maritime Transport and Migration: The Connections between Maritime and Migration Networks*. St. John's, 2007, pp. 63-74.

Martellini, Amoreno. "Il commercio dell' emigrazione: intermediari e agenti." In Bevilacqua, Piero, *et al.* (eds.). *Storia dell' emigrazione Italiana: La Partenza*. Rome, 2002, pp. 293-308.

Marx, Daniel. *International Shipping Cartels: A Study of Industrial Self-Regulation by Shipping Conferences*. Princeton, 1953. Reprint, Westport, CT, 1969.

Massey, Douglas. "Why Does Immigration Occur? A Theoretical Synthesis." In Hirschman, Charles; Kasinitz, Philip; and DeWind, Josh (eds.).

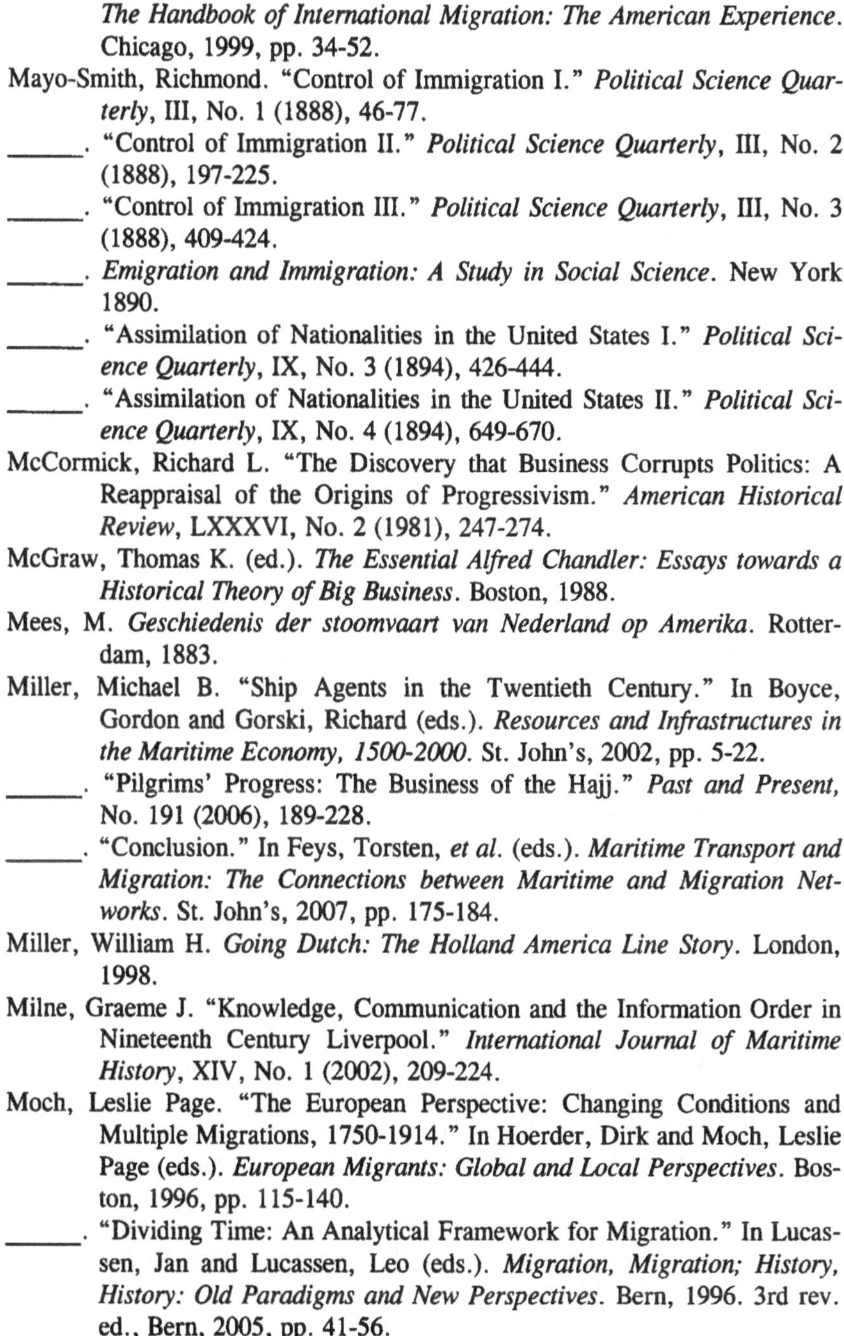

The Handbook of International Migration: The American Experience. Chicago, 1999, pp. 34-52.

Mayo-Smith, Richmond. "Control of Immigration I." *Political Science Quarterly*, III, No. 1 (1888), 46-77.

______. "Control of Immigration II." *Political Science Quarterly*, III, No. 2 (1888), 197-225.

______. "Control of Immigration III." *Political Science Quarterly*, III, No. 3 (1888), 409-424.

______. *Emigration and Immigration: A Study in Social Science*. New York 1890.

______. "Assimilation of Nationalities in the United States I." *Political Science Quarterly*, IX, No. 3 (1894), 426-444.

______. "Assimilation of Nationalities in the United States II." *Political Science Quarterly*, IX, No. 4 (1894), 649-670.

McCormick, Richard L. "The Discovery that Business Corrupts Politics: A Reappraisal of the Origins of Progressivism." *American Historical Review*, LXXXVI, No. 2 (1981), 247-274.

McGraw, Thomas K. (ed.). *The Essential Alfred Chandler: Essays towards a Historical Theory of Big Business*. Boston, 1988.

Mees, M. *Geschiedenis der stoomvaart van Nederland op Amerika*. Rotterdam, 1883.

Miller, Michael B. "Ship Agents in the Twentieth Century." In Boyce, Gordon and Gorski, Richard (eds.). *Resources and Infrastructures in the Maritime Economy, 1500-2000*. St. John's, 2002, pp. 5-22.

______. "Pilgrims' Progress: The Business of the Hajj." *Past and Present*, No. 191 (2006), 189-228.

______. "Conclusion." In Feys, Torsten, *et al.* (eds.). *Maritime Transport and Migration: The Connections between Maritime and Migration Networks*. St. John's, 2007, pp. 175-184.

Miller, William H. *Going Dutch: The Holland America Line Story*. London, 1998.

Milne, Graeme J. "Knowledge, Communication and the Information Order in Nineteenth Century Liverpool." *International Journal of Maritime History*, XIV, No. 1 (2002), 209-224.

Moch, Leslie Page. "The European Perspective: Changing Conditions and Multiple Migrations, 1750-1914." In Hoerder, Dirk and Moch, Leslie Page (eds.). *European Migrants: Global and Local Perspectives*. Boston, 1996, pp. 115-140.

______. "Dividing Time: An Analytical Framework for Migration." In Lucassen, Jan and Lucassen, Leo (eds.). *Migration, Migration; History, History: Old Paradigms and New Perspectives*. Bern, 1996. 3rd rev. ed., Bern, 2005, pp. 41-56.

Molinari, Augusta. "Porti, trasporti, compagnie." In Bevilacqua, Piero, *et al.* (eds.). *Storia dell' emigrazione Italiana: La Partenza*. Rome, 2002, pp. 237-256.

Moltmann, Günter. "Steamship Transport of Emigrants from Europe to the United States, 1850-1914: Social, Commercial and Legislative Aspects." In Friedland, Klaus (ed.). *Maritime Aspects of Migration*. Cologne, 1989, pp. 309-320.

Moore, K.A. *The Early History of Freight Conferences: Background and Main Developments until around 1900*. London, 1981.

Morawska, Ewa. *For Bread with Butter: The Life-Worlds of East Central Europeans in Johnstown, Pennsylvania, 1890-1940*. New York, 1986. Reprint, New York, 2004.

_____. "Return Migrations: Theoretical and Research Agenda." In Vecoli, Rudolph J. and Simke, Suzanne M. (eds.). *A Century of European Migrations, 1830-1930*. Urbana, IL, 1991, pp. 277-292.

_____. "Labour Migrations of Poles in the Atlantic World Economy, 1880-1914." *Comparative Studies in Society and History*, XXXI, No. 2 (1989), 237-272. Reprinted in Hoerder, Dirk and Moch, Leslie Page (eds.). *European Migrants: Global and Local Perspectives*. Boston, 1996, pp. 170-208.

Mörner, Magnus. "Divergent Perspectives." In Emmer, P.C. and Mörner, Magnus (eds.). *European Expansion and Migration: Essays on the Intercontinental Migration from Africa, Asia, and Europe*. New York, 1992, pp. 277-303.

Mullan, Berndan. "The Regulation of International Migration: The US and Western Europe in Historical Comparative Perspective." In Böcker, Anita, *et al.* (eds.). *Regulation of Migration: International Experiences*. Amsterdam, 1998, pp. 27-44.

Müller, Leos. "Swedish-American Trade and the Swedish Consular Service, 1780-1840." *International Journal of Maritime History*, XIV, No. 1 (2002), 173-188.

_____. *Consuls, Corsairs and Commerce: The Swedish Consular Service and Long Distance Shipping, 1720-1815*. Uppsala, 2004.

_____ and Ojala, Jari. "Consular Services of the Nordic Countries during the Eighteenth and Nineteenth Century: Did They Really Work?" In Boyce, Gordon and Gorski, Richard (eds.). *Resources and Infrastructures in the Maritime Economy, 1500-2000*. St. John's, 2002, pp. 23-41.

Murayama, Yuzo. "Information and Emigrants: Interprefectual Differences of Japanese Emigration to the Pacific Northwest, 1880-1915." *Journal of Economic History*, LI, No. 1 (1991), 125-147.

Murken, Erich. *Die grossen transatlantischen Linienreederei-Verbande, Pools und Interessengemeinschaften bis zum Ausbruch des Weltkrieges: Ihre Entstehung, Organitsation und Wirksamkeit*. Jena, 1922.

Nadell, Pamela S. "The Journey to America by Steam: The Jews of Eastern Europe in Transition." *American Jewish History*, LXXI, No. 2 (1981), 269-284.

Nathan, Kurt. *Die deutsches Schiffahrtskampf*. Kiel, 1935.

Navin, Thomas R. and Sears, Marian V. "A Study in Merger: Formation of the International Mercantile Marine Company." *Business History Review*, XXVIII, No. 4 (1954), 291-328.

Neuman, Gerald L. "Qualitative Migration Controls in the Antebellum United States." In Fahrmeir, Andreas; Faron, Olivier; and Weil, Patrick (eds.). *Migration Control in the North Atlantic World*. New York, 2003, pp. 106-119.

Neuman, W. Lawrence. "Negotiated Meanings and State Transformation: The Trust Issue in the Progressive Era." *Social Problems*, XLV, No. 3 (1998), 315-335.

Nieuwenhuys, Johan G.J.C.. *De haven Rotterdam in Verleden en Heden*. Rotterdam, 1952.

Noble, John Hawks. "The Present State of the Immigration Question." *Political Science Quarterly*, VII, No. 2 (1892), 232-243.

Noiriel, Gérard. *Le Creuset Français: Histoire de l'immigration (XIX et XX siècle)*. Paris, 1988.

North, Douglass C. "Ocean Freight Rates and Economic Development, 1740-1913." *Journal of Economic History*, XVIII, No. 4 (1958), 537-555.

Nothebohm, Friedrich. *Rapport sur la situation des ouvriers aux États-Unis*. Stockholm, 1905.

Nugent, Walter. *Crossings: The Great Transatlantic Migrations, 1870-1914*. Bloomington, IN, 1992.

Offrey, Charles. *Cette Grande Dame qui fut la Transat*. Paris, 1994.

Olegario, Rowena. "'That Mysterious People:' Jewish Merchants, Transparency, and Community in Mid-Nineteenth Century America." *Business History Review*, LXXIII, No. 2 (1999), 161-189.

Osborne, Dale K. "Cartel Problems." *American Economic Review*, LXVI, No. 5 (1976), 835-844.

Ottmüller-Wetzel, Birgit. "Auswanderung über Hamburg: Die HAPAG und die Auswanderung nach Nordamerika, 1870-1914." Unpublished MA thesis, Freie Universität Berlin, 1986.

Patterson, Thomas G. "American Businessmen and Consular Service Reform." *Business History Review*, XL, No. 1 (1966), 77-97.

Piore, Michael J. *Birds of Passage: Migrant Labour and Industrial Societies*. New York, 1979.

Pirrong, Stephen Craig. "An Application of Core Theory to the Analysis of Ocean Shipping Markets." *Journal of Law and Economics*, XXXV, No. 1 (1992), 89-131.

Pitkin, Thomas M. *Keepers of the Gate: A History of Ellis Island*. New York, 1975.

Plate, Antoine. "Onze Stoomvaart." *De Economist*, XVIII (1869), 558-571.

Platt, D.C.M. "The Role of British Consular Service in Overseas Trade, 1825-1914." *Economic History Review*, New ser., XV, No. 3 (1963), 494-512.

Portes, Alejandro. "Immigration Theory for a New Century: Some Problems and Opportunities." *International Migration Review*, XXXI, No. 4 (1997), 799-825. Reprinted in Hirschman, Charles; Kasinitz, Philip; and DeWind, Josh (eds.). *The Handbook of International Migration: The American Experience*. Chicago, 1999, pp. 21-33.

Powderly, Terence V. "A Menacing Irruption." *North American Review*, CXLVII, No. 2 (1888), 165-174.

______. "Immigration's Menace to National Health." *North American Review*, CLXXV, No. 1 (1902), 53-60.

Prüser, F. "Hamburg-Bremer Schiffahrtwettbewerb in der Zeit der grossen Segelschiffahrt und Dampfer." *Zeitschrift Des Vereins Fur Hamburgische Geschichte*, XLIX (1964), 147-189.

Reuchlin, Henri. *Zeil strijken, stoom op*. Rotterdam, 1975.

Rice, John G. and Ostergren, Robert C. "The Decision to Emigrate: A Study in Diffusion." *Geografiska Annaler*, LX, No. 1 (1978), 1-15.

Ripley, William Z. *The Races of Europe: A Sociological Study*. New York, 1898.

______. "Race Progress and Immigration." *Annals of the American Academy of Social and Political Science*, XXXIV, No. 1 (1909), 130-138.

Risch, Erna. "Joseph Crellius, Immigrant Broker." *New England Quarterly*, XII, No. 2 (1939), 241-267.

Roediger, David R. *Working towards Whiteness: How America's Immigrants became White*. New York, 2005.

Runblom, Harald and Norman, Hans (eds.). *From Sweden to America: A History of the Migration*. Minneapolis, 1976.

Safford, Jeffrey J. "The Decline of the American Merchant Marine, 1850-1914: An Historiographical Appraisal." In Fischer, Lewis R. and Panting, Gerald E. (eds.). *Change and Adaptation in Maritime History: The North Atlantic Fleets in the Nineteenth Century*. St. John's, 1985, pp. 51-85.

Salt, John and Stein, Jeremy. "Migration as a Business: The Case of Trafficking." *International Migration*, XXXV, No. 4 (1997), 467-494.

Sargent, Frank P. "Problems of Immigration." *Annals of the American Academy of Political and Social Science*, XXIV, No. 1 (1904), 153-155.

Reprinted in *Population and Development Review*, XXXV, No. 4 (2009), 817-822.

Schaap, Dick. *Brug naar de zeven zeeën: Holland Amerika Lijn 100 jaar*. Rotterdam, 1973.

Schepens, Luc. *Van vlaskutser tot Franschman: Bijdrage tot de geschiedenis van de Westvlaamse plattelandsbevolking in de 19e eeuw*. Bruges, 1973.

Schiller, Nina Glick. "Transmigrants and Nation States: Something Old and Something New in the US Immigrant Experience." In Hirschman, Charles; Kasinitz, Philip; and DeWind, Josh (eds.). *The Handbook of International Migration: The American Experience*. Chicago, 1999, pp. 94-119.

Scholl, Lars U. "German Maritime Historical Research since 1970: A Critical Survey." In Broeze, Frank (ed.). *Maritime History at the Crossroads: A Critical Review of Recent Historiography*. St. John's, 1995, pp. 113-133.

Schulteis, Herman J. *Report on European Immigration to the United States of America and the Causes which Incite the Same, with Recommendations for the Further Restriction of Undesirable Immigration and the Establishment of a National Quarantine*. Washington, DC, 1893.

Schuyler, Eugene. "Italian Immigration into the United States." *Political Science Quarterly*, IV, No. 3 (1889), 480-495.

Scott-Morton, Fiona. "Entry and Predation: British Shipping Cartels, 1879-1929." *Journal of Economics and Management Strategy*, VI, No. 4 (1997), 679-724.

Seager, Henry R. "The Recent Trust Decisions." *Political Science Quarterly*, XXVI, No. 4 (1911), 581-614.

Sebak, Per Kristian. "A Transatlantic Migratory Bypass: Scandinavian Shipping Companies and Transmigration, 1898-1929." Unpublished PhD thesis, University of Bergen, 2012.

Senner, Joseph H. "How We Restrict Immigration." *North American Review*, CLVIII, No. 4 (1894), 494-499.

______. "Immigration from Italy." *North American Review*, CLXII, No. 6 (1896), 649-657.

______. "The Immigration Question." *Annals of the American Academy of Political and Social Science*, X, No. 1 (1897), 1-19.

Shanks, Cheryl. *Immigration and the Politics of American Sovereignty, 1890-1990*. Ann Arbor, 2001.

Sickel, W.G. "Pooling Agreements." *Annals of the American Academy of Political and Social Science*, LV (1914), 144-154.

Sicotte, Richard A. "Competition and Cartels in Liner Shipping Industry: A Historical Perspective." In Olsson, Ulf (ed.). *Business and European*

Integration since 1800: Regional, National and International Perspectives. Gothenburg, 1997, pp. 141-161.

Sjostrom, William. "The Stability of Ocean Shipping Cartels." In Grossman, Peter Z. (ed.). *How Cartels Endure and How they Fail*. Cheltenham, 2004, pp. 82-110.

Sklar, Martin J. *The Corporate Reconstruction of American Capitalism, 1890-1916: The Market, the Law, and Politics*. New York, 1988.

______. *The United States as a Developing Country: Studies in U.S. History in the Progressive Era and the 1920s*. New York, 1992.

Sloan, Edward W. "Collins versus Cunard: The Realities of a North Atlantic Steamship Rivalry, 1850-1858." *International Journal of Maritime History*, IV, No. 1 (1992), 83-100.

______. "The First (and Very Secret) International Steamship Cartel, 1850-1856." In Starkey, David J. and Harlaftis, Gelina (eds.). *Global Markets: The Internationalization of the Sea Transport Industries since 1850*. St. John's, 1998, pp. 29-52.

Smith, J. Russell. "Ocean Freight Rates and Their Control through Combination." *Political Science Quarterly*, XXI, No. 2 (1906), 237-263.

Smith, Michael S. *The Emergence of Modern Business Enterprise in France, 1800-1930*. Cambridge, MA, 2006.

Spelkens, Eric. "Belgian Migration to the United States and Other Overseas Countries at the Beginning of the 20th Century." In Kurgan, Ginette and Spelkens, Eric. *Two Studies on Emigration through Antwerp to the New World*. Brussels, 1976, pp. 51-139.

Starkey, David J. and Harlaftis, Gelina (eds.). *Global Markets: The Internationalization of the Sea Transport Industries since 1850*. St. John's, 1998.

Steidl, Annemarie. "The 'Relatives and Friends Effect:' Migration Networks of Transatlantic Migrants from the Late Habsburg Monarchy." In Feys, Torsten, *et al.* (eds.). *Maritime Transport and Migration: The Connections between Maritime and Migration Networks*. St. John's, 2007, pp. 75-96.

Stevens, William H.S. "The Administration and Enforcement of Steamship Conferences and Agreements." *Annals of the American Academy of Political and Social Science*, LV (1914), 112-143.

Stigler, George J. "A Theory of Oligopoly." *Journal of Political Economy*, LXXII, No. 1 (1964), 44-61.

Stokvis, Pieter R.D. *De Nederlandse trek naar Amerika, 1846-1847*. Leiden, 1977.

Stols, Eddy. "Latijns-Amerikaanse vurigheid, utopieën en luchtspiegelingen." In Morelli, Anne. (ed.) *Belgische emigranten: oorlogsvluchtelingen, economische emigranten en politieke vluchtelingen uit onze streken van de 16de eeuw tot vandaag*. Berchem, 1999, pp. 229-247.

Strikwerda, Carl and Guerin-Gonzales, Camille. "Labor Migrations and Politics." In Guerin-Gonzales, Camille and Strikwerda, Carl (eds.). *The Politics of Immigrant Workers: Labor Activism and Migration in the World Economy since 1830*. New York, 1993. Rev. ed., New York, 1998, pp. 3-45.

______. "Tides of Migrations, Currents of History: The State, Economy, and the Transatlantic Movement of Labor in the Nineteenth and Twentieth Centuries." *International Review of Social History*, XLIV, No. 3 (1999), 367-394.

Supple, Barry E. "A Business Elite: German-Jewish Financers in Nineteenth-Century New York." *Business History Review*, XXXI, No. 2 (1957), 143-178.

Swierenga, Robert P. "The Journey Across: Dutch Transatlantic Emigrant Passage to the United States 1820-1880." In Hoefte, Rosemarijn and Kardux, Johanna C. (eds.). *Connecting Cultures: The Netherlands in Five Centuries of Transatlantic Exchange*. Amsterdam, 1994, pp. 101-134.

______. *Faith and Family: Dutch Immigration and Settlement in the United States, 1820-1920*. New York, 2001.

Tamse, C.A. "The Netherlands Consular Service and the Dutch Consular Reports of the 19th and 20th Century." *Business History*, XXIII, No. 3 (1981), 271-275.

Taylor, George Rogers. *The Distant Magnet: European Migration to the USA*. New York, 1972.

Thelen, David. "The Nation and Beyond: Transnational Perspectives on United States History." *Journal of American History*, LXXXVI, No. 3 (1999), 965-975.

Thielemans, Marie-Rose. "De Waalse emigratie naar Wisconsin." In Morelli, Anne (ed.). *Belgische emigranten: oorlogsvluchtelingen, economische emigranten en politieke vluchtelingen uit onze streken van de 16de eeuw tot vandaag*. Berchem, 1999, pp. 123-137.

Thistlethwaite, Frank. "Migration from Europe Overseas in the Nineteenth and Twentieth Century." In XI International Congress of Historical Sciences, *Rapport V: Histoire contemporaine*. Stockholm, 1960, pp. 32-61. Reprinted in Vecoli, Rudolph J. and Sinke, Suzanne M. (eds.). *A Century of European Migrations, 1830-1930*. Urbana, IL, 1991, pp. 17-49.

Thomas, Brinley. *Migration and Economic Growth: A Study of Great Britain and the Atlantic Economy*. Cambridge, 1954. 2nd ed., Cambridge, 1973.

Tichenor, Daniel J. *Dividing Lines: The Politics of Immigration Control in America*. Princeton, 2002.

Tilly, Charles. "Transplanted Networks." In Yans-McLaughlin, Virginia (ed.). *Immigration Reconsidered: History, Sociology, and Politics*. New York, 1990, pp. 79-95.

Torpey, John. *The Invention of the Passport: Surveillance, Citizenship and the State*. New York, 2000.

_____. "Passports and the Development of Immigration Controls in the North Atlantic World during the Long Nineteenth Century." In Fahrmeir, Andreas; Faron, Olivier; and Weil, Patrick (eds.). *Migration Control in the North Atlantic World*. New York, 2003, pp. 73-91.

Trenor, John J.D. "Proposals Affecting Immigration." *Annals of the American Academy of Political and Social Science*, XXIV (1904), 223-236.

Ueda, Reed. "An Immigration Country of Assimilative Pluralism: Immigrant Reception and Absorption in American History." In Münz, Rainer and Weiner, Myron (eds.). *Migrants, Refugees and Foreign Policy: U.S. and German Policies toward Countries of Origin*. New York, 1997, pp. 39-63. Reprinted in Bade, Klaus J. and Weiner, Myron (eds.). *Migration Past, Migration Future: Germany and the United States*. Providence, RI, 2000, pp. 39-63.

_____. (ed.) *A Companion to American Immigration*. Oxford, 2006.

Vale, Vivian. "Trusts and Tycoons: British Myth and American Reality." In In Allen, Harry C. and Thompson, Roger (eds.). *Contrast and Connection: Bicentennial Essays in Anglo-American History*. London, 1976, pp. 225-244.

_____. *The American Peril: Challenge to Britain on the North Atlantic, 1901-04*. Manchester, 1984.

Van den Bossche, Stefan. *Een kortstondige kolonie: Santo-Tomas de Guatemala (1843-1854): een literaire documentaire* Tielt, 1997.

Van der Valk, Leo A. "Landverhuizers via Rotterdam in de negentiende eeuw." *Economisch en Sociaal historisch jaarboek*. Amsterdam, 1976, pp. 149-171.

Van der Straeten-Ponthoz, Auguste-Gabriel. *Rapport sur un voyage d'exploration dans les États-Unis d'Amérique du Nord*. Brussels, 1846.

Vannoise-Pochulu, Marie-Françoise. "La politique de la Compagnie Générale Transatlantique et l'émigration vers les États-Unis à partir du Havre (1875-1914)." Unpublished MA thesis, University of Paris XII, 1993.

Van Stekelenburg, Henri. *Landverhuizing als regionaal verschijnsel van Noord-Brabant naar Noord-Amerika, 1820-1880*. Tillburg, 1991.

Vecoli, Rudolph J. and Sinke, Suzanne M. (eds.). *A Century of European Migrations, 1830-1930*. Urbana, IL, 1991.

Veraghtert, Karel. "De havenbewegingen te Antwerpen tijdens de negentiende eeuw: een kwantitatieve benadering." Unpublished PhD thesis, Catholic University of Leuven, 1977.

______. "The Slow Growth of Steam Navigation: The Case of Antwerp, 1816-1865." *Collectanea Maritima*, V (1991), 207-215.

______. "State Policy and Maritime Business in Belgium, 1850-1914." In Ertesvåg, Randi; Starkey, David J.; and Austbø, Anne Tove (eds.). *The North Sea: Maritime Industries and Public Intervention*. Stavanger, 2002, pp. 72-83.

Vervoort, Robert. *Red Star Line*. Antwerp, 1999.

Ville, Simon P. *Transport and the Development of the European Economy, 1750-1918*. London, 1990.

Von der Straten, Axel. *Die Rechtsordnung des Zweiten Kaiserreiches und die Deutsche Auswanderung nach Übersee, 1871-1914*. Berlin, 1997.

Wadhwani, Rohit Daniel. "Banking from the Bottom Up: The Case of Migrant Savers at the Philadelphia Saving Fund Society during the Late Nineteenth Century." *Financial History Review*, IX, No. 1 (2002), 41-63.

Walker, Mack. *Germany and the Emigration, 1816-1885*. Cambridge, MA, 1964.

Ward, Robert de C. "The Restriction of Immigration." *North American Review*, CLXXIX, No. 2 (1904), 226-237.

______. "Pending Immigration Bills." *North American Review*, CLXXXIII, No. 8 (1906), 1120-1133.

______. "The New Immigration Act." *North American Review*, CLXXXV, No. 4 (1907), 587-593.

______. "National Eugenics in Relation to Immigration." *North American Review*, CXCII, No. 1 (1910), 56-67.

Weber, John B. and Smith, Charles Stewart. "Our National Dumping-Ground: A Study of Immigration." *North American Review*, CLIV, No. 3 (1892), 424-438.

Wegge, Simone A. "Chain Migration and Information Networks: Evidence from Nineteenth-Century Hesse-Cassel." *Journal of Economic History*, LVIII, No. 4 (1998), 957-986.

Weil, Patrick. "Races at the Gate: Racial Distinctions in Immigration Policy: A Comparison between France and the United States." In Fahrmeir, Andreas; Faron, Olivier; and Weil, Patrick (eds.). *Migration Control in the North Atlantic World: The Evolution of State Practices in Europe and the United States from the French Revolution to the Inter-war Period*. New York, 2003, pp. 271-291.

Weinstein, James. *The Corporate Ideal in the Liberal State, 1900-1918*. Boston, 1968. Reprint, Westport, CT, 1981.

Wentholt, A.D. *Brug over den Oceaan: een eeuw geschiedenis van de Holland-Amerika Lijn*. Rotterdam, 1973.

Werner, Michael and Zimmerman, Bénédicte. "Penser l'histoire croisée: entre empire et réflexivité." *Annales: Histoire, Sciences Sociales*, LVIII, No. 1 (2003), 7-36.

Whelpley, James Davenport. "Control of Emigration in Europe." *North American Review*, CLXXX, No. 7 (1905), 856-867.

_____. *The Problem of the Immigrant: A Brief Discussion*. London, 1905.

"Who Was Who in America." In *Marquis Who's Who*. Chicago, 1966.

Wiborg, Susanne and Wiborg, Klaus. *Unser Feld ist die Welt, 1847-1997: 150 Jahre Hapag-Lloyd*. Hamburg, 1997.

Williams, David M. "Forum: Globalization and Sea Transport." *International Journal of Maritime History*, XI, No. 1 (1999), 201-220.

_____. "Recent Trends in Maritime and Port History." In Loyen, Reginald, *et al.* (eds.). *Struggling for Leadership: Antwerp-Rotterdam Port Competition, 1870-2000*. Leuven, 2003, pp. 11-26.

Williamson, Jeffrey G. and Hatton, Timothy J. "International Migration and the Labour Market: Integration in the Nineteenth and Twentieth Centuries." In Hatton, Timothy J. and Williamson, Jeffrey G. (eds.). *International Labour Market Integration and the Impact of Migration on the National Labour Markets since 1870*. Milan, 1994.

_____; _____; and O'Rourke, Kevin H. "Mass Migration, Commodity Market Integration and Real Wage Convergence: The Late Nineteenth Century Atlantic Economy." In Hatton, Timothy J. and Williamson, Jeffrey G. (eds.). *Migration and the International Labor Market*. London, 1994, pp. 203-220.

_____ and O'Rourke, Kevin H. *Globalization and History: The Evolution of a Nineteenth Century Atlantic Economy*. Boston, 1999.

Williamson, Samuel. "Six Ways to Compute the Relative Value of a U.S. Dollar Amount, 1790 to Present." Measuring Worth, 2009. http://www.measuringworth.com/uscompare.

Witthoft, Hans-Jürgen. *HAPAG: Hamburg-Amerika Linie*. Herford, 1973.

Wokeck, Marianne S. *Trade in Strangers: The Beginnings of Mass Migration to North America*. University Park, PA, 1998. Reprint, University Park, PA, 2003.

Wüstenbecker, Katja. "Hamburg and the Transit of East Europeans." In Fahrmeir, Andreas; Faron, Olivier; and Weil, Patrick (eds.). *Migration Control in the North Atlantic World*. New York, 2003, pp. 223-236.

Wyman, Mark. *Round Trip to America: The Immigrants Return to Europe, 1880-1930*. London, 1993.

Yans-McLaughlin, Virginia (ed.). *Immigration Reconsidered: History, Sociology, and Politics*. New York, 1990.

Zeidel, Robert F. *Immigrants, Progressives, and Exclusion Politics: The Dillingham Commission, 1900-1927*. Dekalb, IL, 2004.

Zevenbergen, Cees. *Toen zij uit Rotterdam vertrokken: emigratie via Rotterdam door de eeuwen heen*. Rotterdam, 1990.

Zolberg, Aristide R. "Reforming the Back Door: perspectives historiques sur la réforme de la politique américaine d'immigration." In Costa-

Lascoux, Jacqueline and Weil, Patrick (eds.). *Logiques d'États et Immigrations*. Paris, 1992.

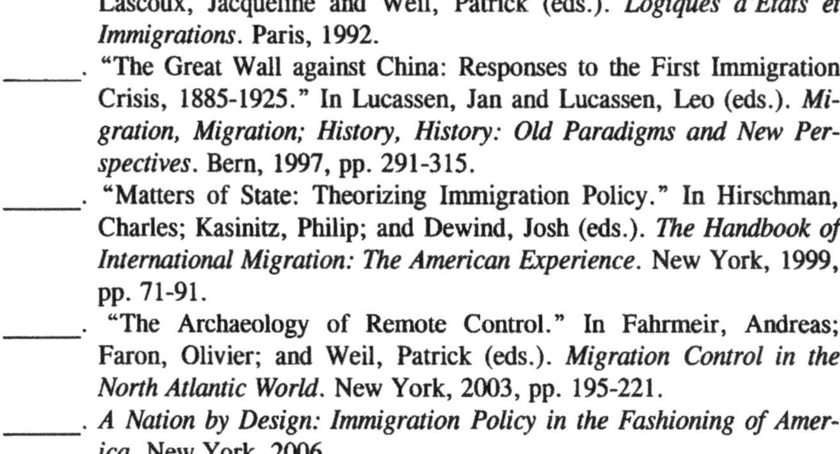

______. "The Great Wall against China: Responses to the First Immigration Crisis, 1885-1925." In Lucassen, Jan and Lucassen, Leo (eds.). *Migration, Migration; History, History: Old Paradigms and New Perspectives*. Bern, 1997, pp. 291-315.

______. "Matters of State: Theorizing Immigration Policy." In Hirschman, Charles; Kasinitz, Philip; and Dewind, Josh (eds.). *The Handbook of International Migration: The American Experience*. New York, 1999, pp. 71-91.

______. "The Archaeology of Remote Control." In Fahrmeir, Andreas; Faron, Olivier; and Weil, Patrick (eds.). *Migration Control in the North Atlantic World*. New York, 2003, pp. 195-221.

______. *A Nation by Design: Immigration Policy in the Fashioning of America*. New York, 2006.

Printed and bound by CPI Group (UK) Ltd, Croydon, CR0 4YY

16/04/2025

14658574-0004